STANLEY W. JACOB, M.D., F.A.C.S.

Associate Professor of Surgery
University of Oregon Health Sciences Center
First Kemper Foundation Research Scholar
American College of Surgeons
Markle Scholar in Medical Sciences

CLARICE ASHWORTH FRANCONE

Medical Illustrator
Formerly Head of the Department of Medical Illustrations
University of Oregon Health Sciences Center

WALTER J. LOSSOW, Ph.D.

Formerly Physiologist, Department of Physiology
and Donner Laboratory,
University of California, Berkeley
Formerly Lecturer in Human Anatomy and Physiology,
California State College at Hayward;
Merritt College, Oakland, California;
and Lassen College, Susanville, California
Formerly Member, Editorial Board,
Physiological Chemistry and Physics

STRUCTURE AND FUNCTION IN MAN

FOURTH EDITION

1978
W. B. SAUNDERS COMPANY
Philadelphia   London   Toronto

W. B. Saunders Company: West Washington Square
Philadelphia, PA   19105

1 St. Anne's Road
Eastbourne, East Sussex BN21 3UN, England

1 Goldthorne Avenue
Toronto, Ontario M8Z 5T9, Canada

Library of Congress Cataloging in Publication Data

Jacob, Stanley W.

Structure and function in man.

Bibliography: p.

Includes index.

1. Human physiology.   2. Anatomy, Human.
   I. Francone, Clarice Ashworth, joint author.
   II. Lossow, Walter J., joint author.   III. Title.

QP34.5.J3 1978   612   77–84673

ISBN 0–7216–5098–8

Listed here is the latest translated edition of this book together with the
language of the translation and the publisher.

Portuguese (3rd edition) Editora Interamericana Ltda.
              Rio de Janeiro, Brazil

Spanish (3rd edition) Editorial Interamericana S.A.
              Mexico 4 D.F., Mexico

Structure and Function in Man (4th edition)   ISBN   0-7216-5098-8

Last digit is the print number: 9   8   7   6   5   4   3   2   1

DEDICATION

To my wife, Gail, without whose help and understanding this would not have been possible.

STANLEY W. JACOB

To my son Don.

CLARICE ASHWORTH FRANCONE

To my students.

WALTER J. LOSSOW

Preface
to the Fourth Edition

Since the initial publication in 1965, *Structure and Function in Man* has received increasingly wider acceptance in both the United States and abroad. The First, Second and Third Editions were written by a clinical surgeon with teaching interests in anatomy and physiology at the medical school level in collaboration with a medical illustrator. For this Fourth Edition it was decided to enlist the help of a third author, a physiologist and teacher of anatomy and physiology at the college level, Dr. Walter J. Lossow. With Dr. Lossow's help, the Fourth Edition has been totally rewritten, not only making it an up-to-date text, but presenting additional current concepts in physiology including multiple teaching aids gleaned from over a decade of teaching experience.

During the period since the First Edition of *Structure and Function in Man* the physiological – in particular, the molecular physiological – approach has gained increasing emphasis in the health sciences, both for theoretical understanding of various structures and processes, previously conceived more generally, and for the practical treatment of disorders. Consequently, it is increasingly important that the student preparing for a career in the nursing or paramedical disciplines have a sound background in the basic foundations of this rapidly developing perspective. In this revision, the authors have markedly expanded the discussion of fundamental physiologic concepts.

The greater responsibility being given to nursing and paramedical personnel in the care of the patient requires a more extensive discussion in certain areas, even during introductory years. To this end, the following features have been added to the Fourth Edition:

1. Fifty-nine new illustrations to bring the total to 518.
2. Sixty-seven revised illustrations.
3. Nineteen new or revised Tables.
4. An Appendix of Basic Chemistry.
5. An expanded Glossary.
6. Prefix, Suffix and Combining Form Table.

Additionally, the Fourth Edition includes a more thorough discussion of the special senses, especially the process of vision; a revised section on the lymphatic system, with emphasis on newer concepts relating to immune responses; additional material in the chapter on the cell to better explain the citric acid cycle, DNA and RNA; additional data in the chapter on reproduction on the menstrual cycle, menopause and venereal disease, as well as an entirely new discussion of spermatogenesis, oogenesis, and the processes leading to ovulation; a more detailed section on the nervous system including additional basic cellular information; a revised section on the formation of urine to include current concepts of acid-base balance; a new section on the digestive system particularly at the biochemical level; an entirely new chapter on the muscular system with emphasis on the transmission of electrical impulses; total reorganization of the chapter on the skeletal system; simplification of the chapter on electrolyte therapy.

This volume should unfold broad vistas of stimulating experiences to both the student and the teacher in the field of anatomy and physiology.

STANLEY W. JACOB, M.D.
CLARICE A. FRANCONE
WALTER J. LOSSOW, PH.D.

Acknowledgments

If this text receives any measure of success many individuals will have made this possible.

We wish to express our appreciation to Barbara Weber, Terry Bristol, Beverly Methvin, Karen Clement, Anna Conley, Joel Cruz, Marilyn Jacob, Lois Locke, Blanche Palmer, Frances Kemper, Paula Burnett, Frank Weber, William Weaver, Ph.D., Helyn Galash, Robert Brooks, Ph.D., Marilyn Underdahl, Rebecca Meyer, and Bonnie Marble.

The authors wish to acknowledge the editorial and production assistance of the W. B. Saunders Company. A particular note of gratitude goes to Mr. Robert Wright and Ms. Helen Dietz, whose advice and encouragement contributed significantly to the completion of this manuscript.

Audiovisual Aids

To supplement the text and laboratory manual by Jacob, Francone, and Lossow, certain illustrations have been made into audiovisual teaching aids which can be purchased directly from the W. B. Saunders Co., West Washington Sq., Phila., Pa., 19105.

These aids consist of ten 35 mm. filmstrips in full color, based on illustrations from the text, and covering the structure and function of important body systems. Each filmstrip includes about 60 frames; each is accompanied by a narration on a tape cassette, and a printed script of the narration. Filmstrips can be projected in class with any standard filmstrip projector or slide projector with a filmstrip attachment. They can also be used for individual study in a desktop viewer. The narration is also available on long-playing records.

Preface
to the First Edition

Many centuries ago anatomy and physiology were taught in a single course—not so much for the benefit of the student, but because the two fields of knowledge were not really separate even in the minds of researchers and educators. At the time there was insufficient knowledge of either science to warrant separate treatment. As the years passed, intensive studies were completed by methodically curious scientists in both fields. These investigations were aided by the progressive development of the physical and chemical sciences and by advances in technology providing more refined methods for observation and experimentation.

Gradually, the accumulation of facts and the elucidation of general concepts made specialization necessary; so anatomy and physiology were taught as individual sciences. Recent years have witnessed a return to the older philosophy of treating them as one integrated subject in the hope that students would more readily understand life as the truly integrated process it is.

One cannot appreciate the subject matter of physiology without first learning the basic concepts of anatomy. One cannot realize the full significance of human structure without also understanding the complex functions associated with it. Thus, while specialization is still necessary for advanced students, beginning and reviewing students at every educational level benefit from an integrated presentation of anatomy and physiology.

Structure and Function in Man is designed for use by the beginning student. This book emphasizes physiology without neglecting anatomy, an accomplishment due to the incorporation of approximately 300 new half-tone drawings depicting the anatomy of the entire body. The text employs the Nomina Anatomica (N.A.) terminology, replacing such words as *eustachian* with *auditory* and *pituitary* with *hypophysis*. A brief survey of each organ system is presented; chapters are comprehensively summarized and study questions included. Complete lists of references have not been added; to do so in a field as wide as anatomy and physiology would have created a book of inordinate length. Clues to further reading are provided in a special section at the end of the text. This book is only a beginning.

"The hardest conviction to get into the mind of the beginner is that the education he is receiving in college is not a medical course but a life course for which the work of a few years under teachers is but a preparation."— Sir William Osler.

STANLEY W. JACOB
CLARICE A. FRANCONE

Portland, Oregon

Contents

UNIT 4

Reproduction

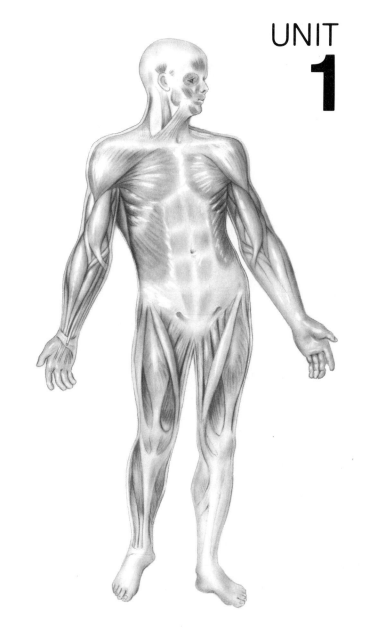

Introduction

UNIT

1

Introduction

The Body as a Whole

chapter 1

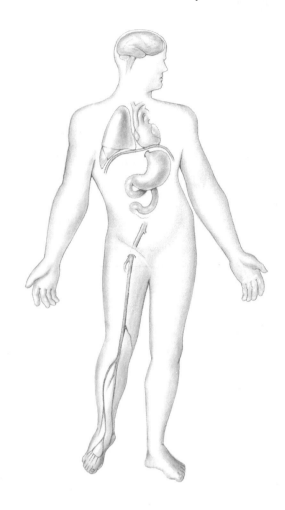

Objectives

The aim of this chapter is to enable the student to:

Distinguish between the study of anatomy and physiology.

Describe the basic mechanism for maintaining homeostasis.

Identify the major homeostatic organs and systems of the body.

Identify the two major types of communication mechanisms involved in the coordination of the body.

Construct a diagram of the body and label it with respect to anatomical directions, planes and cavities.

Define and relate the cell, tissue, organ and system as structural units.

List the ten major systems of the human body.

THE HUMAN BODY

The order and plan of creation have challenged man throughout history. His world is organized into a solar system, the solar system into a galaxy, and the galaxy into a universe. In the opposite direction, his world is divided into civilizations, civilizations into societies, societies into human individuals, and these human individuals into chemical elements. Man finds himself, like Huxley, overcome at the "wonderful unity of plan in the thousands and thousands of living constructions, and the modifications of similar apparatuses to serve diverse ends." Such is the human body.

The Complex Organism

Man as a living organism may be viewed as an assemblage of minute units called cells which are marvelously integrated both structurally and functionally. Cells eventually specialize or differentiate to a greater or lesser extent. An aggregate of similarly differentiated cells composes a tissue, such as the fat cells of adipose tissue. Tissues, in turn, form organs; organs form systems. Ultimately, systems combine in an intricate manner to create a thinking, acting human being. When viewing the human body in this fashion, one stands in awe at the complexity of the organization of the body and the fine balance and interdependence of the various parts. Anatomy and physiology describe this interdependence of structure and function.

Scientific Study

Anatomy Defined. *Human anatomy* is the science of the shape and structure of the body and its parts. *Gross anatomy* deals with the macroscopic structures uncovered by dissection and visible to the unaided eye. *Microscopic anatomy* employs the use of the light microscope. The most detailed studies involve the methods of *electron microscopy.*

Physiology Defined. *Human physiology* is the study of the functions of the body and its parts. *Cellular physiology* is the most prominent specialized branch and is concerned with the study of the activities of individual cells and their parts.

The division between *anatomy* and *physiology* is not always clear, and the use of these terms is best considered an indication of emphasis rather than a sharp division of subject matter. In many areas, the interplay between these two approaches of inquiry has become so close that scientists have tended to specialize in the study of particular *organs* and *organ systems,* the

definitions of which involve both structural and functional aspects. *Cardiology,* for example, is the study of the heart and related elements.

-ology: The Study of. On a more detailed level, the fields of *cytology,* study of the structure and function of the individual cells, and *histology,* study of tissue structure and function, have both become generally recognized disciplines.

Two other perspectives deserve special mention in a survey of the approaches to studying the structure and function of the human body. These are *pathology* and *embryology.* Pathology is the study of abnormal or disease states in the body, and is distinct from the more general inquiry into the normal structure and functioning of the organism. Embryology is the study of the development of the fertilized egg into the mature organism. The techniques of the anatomist, as well as those of the physiologist, are employed in both pathology and embryology.

Development of the Electron Microscope

Since the discovery and identification of atoms and molecules by Nineteenth Century physiologists, the single most impressive development in the study of biological structures has been the construction of the first electron microscope in the 1930's (Fig. 1). Electron microscopy is still a rapidly developing discipline, and it will perhaps be several decades before we have progressed sufficiently in our experimentation to reach the limits of its applicability. The impact of this instrument has been to multiply our potential source of data on evidence many times over. In fact, it is the slowness of the development of physiological techniques of analysis on the molecular level that most severely retards our ability to interpret meaningfully what the electron microscope reveals (Chapter 2).

The physiological side of analysis on the molecular level is termed *molecular biology,* and is based primarily on the use of sophisticated biochemical techniques. Further categorization or specialization on this level of detail does not occur, since there is a commonality in the object of study (molecules and molecular structures and mecha-

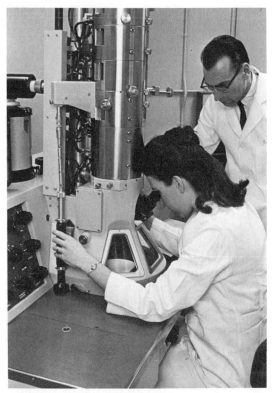

Figure 1. The electron microscope is now being employed to study structures at a magnification of 200,000×.

weight; *interstitial fluid,* 15 per cent; and *intracellular fluid,* 45 per cent. Hence, approximately 65 per cent of the body weight consists of water, two-thirds of which is found within the cells. The remaining 35 per cent of the body is composed of 15 per cent protein, 5 per cent mineral matter and 15 per cent fat. (See Chapter 16 and Table 1 for additional information.)

Homeostasis

To function properly, cells require a constant environment. The environment of the body cells, the interstitial fluid medium (derived from the blood stream) immediately surrounding each cell, is called the internal environment of the body. From the time the cell was identified as the basic structural and functional unit of life, physiologists have recognized the importance of maintaining a constant internal environment. Claude Bernard, the famous French physiologist who introduced the term "internal environment" (*milieu interieur*), is chiefly responsible for this basic concept. The American physiologist Walter Cannon extended the concept of a constant internal environment and coined the term *homeostasis* (G. *homoios,* like; G. *stasis,* position) for the "steady state" conditions (holding within normal ranges despite continuous change) that are maintained by coordinated physiological processes. Among the homeostatic control mechanisms now understood are those maintaining normal concentrations of blood constituents, body temperature, volume and pH of body fluids, blood pressure and heart rate.

All the homeostatic control mechanisms of the body operate by a process of *negative*

nisms) that is not apparent on more general levels of study.

Body Fluids

Body fluids are found within the cells (intracellular), or outside the cells in the *extracellular* space. The extracellular space is further divided into a *vascular,* or *plasma, compartment* and an *interstitial compartment* (between cells). In adults *plasma* accounts for about 5 per cent of the body

Table 1.   PERCENTAGE COMPOSITION OF REPRESENTATIVE MAMMALIAN TISSUES*

TISSUE	WATER	SOLIDS	PROTEINS	LIPIDS	CARBOHYDRATES
Striated muscle	72–78	22–28	18–20	3.0	0.6
Whole blood	79	21	19	1	0.1
Liver	60–80	20–40	15	3–20	1–15
Brain	78	22	8	12–15	0.1
Skin	66	34	25	7	present
Bone (marrow-free)	20–25	75–80	30	low	present

*Source: White, A., Handler, P., Smith, E., and Stetten, D.: *Principles of Biochemistry.* New York, McGraw-Hill, 1954.

feedback. The feedback is, in effect, an informational signal that tells the *driving mechanism* (or functional unit) how well it is doing at establishing or maintaining some variable at the desired level. For instance, if the oxygen concentration in the body fluids is too low, this information is fed back through nervous or hormonal stimulation to the mechanism for controlling oxygen, which automatically returns the oxygen to a higher level. The feedback is negative because it counterbalances, or negates, the change.

Coordination of the Body

It is perhaps apparent from the foregoing that the human body is not simply an aggregate or collection of substances or parts, but a highly organized and precisely coordinated unit that functions as an integrated whole. This structural and functional unity is achieved by means of structural organization and numerous interrelated control mechanisms. Each portion of the body — cell, tissue, organ, etc. — while retaining some degree of independence (autonomy) through self-control, is affected by and in turn affects other areas of the body. Similarly, the body as a whole is partly independent of environmental influence and yet is still affected by and affects its environment. For instance, such factors limit the performance of the long-distance runner; and it is important to note that training or conditioning can broaden this range of activity.

Several of the organs of the body can best be understood as homeostatic organs, since their primary function is directed toward maintenance of homeostasis; these organs include the heart, lungs, kidneys, liver, gastrointestinal tract, and skin. These organs have developed into distinct units precisely because a unitary structure has proved most advantageous for performance of the function involved; that is, the "fittest" structures have presumably best withstood the evolutionary tests of survival.

The coordination of bodily functions occurs through internal regulating mechanisms. These can be distinguished into two general types: the nervous and the hormonal. The central nervous system acts as a sort of hierarchical integrator, receiving messages from its network of sensory nerves and putting out messages through its motor nerves to compensate for any detected imbalance or disturbance.

The hormonal system is composed of eight major endocrine glands that secrete chemical substances called *hormones*. Hormones are transported in the extracellular fluids to all parts of the body to help regulate function. For instance, thyroid hormone increases the rate of almost all chemical reactions in all cells. In this way thyroid hormone helps to set the tempo of body activity.

Understanding Complex Behavior

It will be instructive to consider briefly a few of the diverse functions and control mechanisms which operate in the apparently simple behavior of eating. The activities implicated in ingesting food range at one end of the scale from mastication, swallowing, and salivation, which stimulate digestive processes, to the activities employed in the search for food, prey capture, begging, etc. at the other. Among the variables which regulate feeding behavior are the concentration of circulating nutrients, e.g., blood sugar, which in turn is under hormonal control; the body reserve and weight; sensations in the muscles of the stomach and other parts of the digestive tract; the odor, taste (flavor), and visual aspects of food; and many other less obvious factors.

Social, cultural, and personal influences in a person's life are by no means irrelevant to the physiological functioning of the body. The formation of habits, the impact of psychological conflict, and numerous other aspects of human experience have time and again been shown to have radical effects on the health of the body. Physicians estimate that between 40 and 70 per cent of all physiological disorders have psychosomatic features traceable to the patient's personal and social life.

ORGANIZATION OF THE BODY

Anatomic reference systems have been adopted to facilitate uniformity of description of the body. Four basic reference systems of organization are considered: direction, planes, cavities, and structural units.

Direction

The body in the anatomic position is erect, facing forward with the arms at the sides and the palms toward the front, as shown in Figure 2. All descriptions of location or position assume the body to be in this posture. The following directions are usually considered:

Superior—uppermost or above; for example, the head is superior to the neck.

Inferior—lowermost or below; the foot is inferior to the ankle.

Anterior—toward the front, ventral; the breast is on the anterior chest wall.

Posterior—toward the back, dorsal; the vertebral column is posterior to the digestive tract.

Cephalad—toward the head; the thoracic cavity lies cephalad (or superior) to the abdominal cavity.

Medial—nearest the midline of the body; the ulna is on the medial side of the forearm.

Lateral—toward the side; that is, away from the medial side; the radius is lateral to the ulna.

Proximal—nearest the point of attachment or origin; the elbow is proximal to the wrist.

Distal—away from the point of attachment or origin; the wrist is distal to the elbow.

Planes (Fig. 2)

The body is also discussed with respect to planes passing through it.

Midsagittal—the plane vertically dividing the body through the midline into right and left halves.

Sagittal—any plane parallel to the midsagittal line vertically dividing the body into right and left portions.

Horizontal (transverse)—any plane dividing the body into superior and inferior portions.

Frontal (coronal)—any plane dividing the body into anterior (or ventral) and posterior (or dorsal) portions at right angles to the sagittal plane.

Cavities

Cavity is a term used to describe the third organizational reference system. The body has two major cavities, each subdivided into two lesser cavities (Fig. 3A, 3B). The organs of a cavity are collectively referred to as viscera.

1. Ventral cavity
   A. Thoracic—pleural and pericardial cavities
   B. Abdominopelvic
2. Dorsal cavity
   A. Cranial
   B. Spinal

VENTRAL CAVITY. Organs of the ventral cavity are involved in maintaining a constant internal environment, or homeostasis.

The thoracic cavity is divided into the pericardial cavity, housing the heart, and the pleural cavities, surrounding each lung. The mediastinum is a space between the pleural cavities containing, in addition to the pericardial cavity and the heart, such structures as the esophagus, trachea, thymus, great blood vessels, lymph vessels and nerves.

The abdominopelvic cavity contains those organs inferior to the respiratory diaphragm but above the urogenital diaphragm, including the kidneys, stomach, large and small intestine, spleen, liver, gallbladder, ovaries, uterus, and pancreas.

DORSAL CAVITY. The dorsal cavity contains structures of the nervous system serving to coordinate the body's functions in a unified manner. It is divided into a cranial portion, containing the brain, and a spinal portion, containing the spinal cord.

The term *parietal* refers to the walls of a cavity; for example, the parietal peritoneum lines the abdominal wall. The term *visceral* refers to the covering of the organs; the visceral peritoneum covers the abdominal organs.

Structural Units

The fourth and final system of reference is the structural unit, subdivided into cells, tissues, organs, and systems.

Cells. All living matter is composed of

SUPERIOR

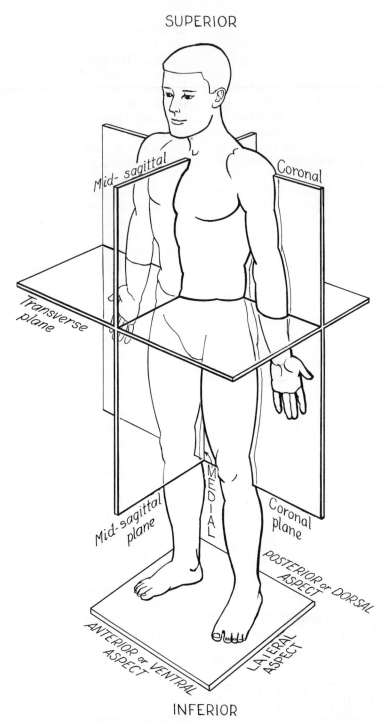

INFERIOR

Figure 2. Anatomic position of body (anterior view, palms forward) with reference systems.

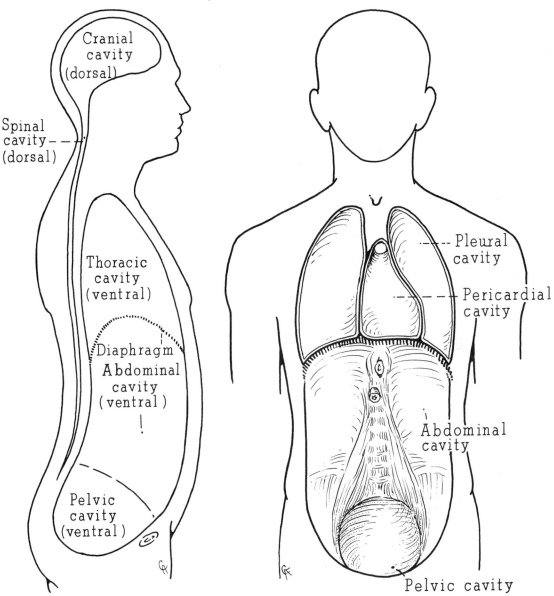

Figure 3. *A,* The body has two major cavities, dorsal and ventral, each subdivided into two lesser cavities. For convenience the abdominal and pelvic cavities pictured here are referred to simply as the abdominopelvic cavity. *B,* Frontal view of body cavities.

cells. The basic constituent of the cell is protoplasm, an aqueous colloidal solution of protein, lipid, carbohydrate, and inorganic salts surrounded by a limiting membrane. This "ground substance of life" performs all the activities necessary to maintain life, including metabolism, respiration, diges-tion, assimilation, excretion, and reproduc-tion. Each different kind of cell, taken as a group, constitutes a tissue (for example, muscle and bone). The tissues in turn compose the organs (such as the stomach and kidneys), each organ being fabricated of several different tissues. Finally, the organs themselves are grouped into organ systems (such as the digestive system or the nervous system), each system subserving some general function in the nutrition, responsiveness, or reproduction of the organism as a whole.

Tissues. Tissues are composed of cells and intercellular substance, or matrix. Generally, tissues contain cells similar in appearance, function, and embryonic origin.

All the diverse tissues of the body can be grouped under one of the following categories: epithelial, connective, muscle, or nervous tissue.

Epithelial tissue covers surfaces, forms glands, and lines most cavities of the body. It consists of one or more layers of cells with only little intracellular material. Muscle tissue is characterized by elongate cells, or fibers, which generate movement by shortening or contracting in a forcible manner. Nerve tissue is composed of nerve cells forming a coordinating system of fibers connecting the many sensory and motor structures of the body. Connective tissue binds together and supports other tissues and organs. It is made up of various kinds of fibrils contained in the matrix of intracellular material. The intracellular matrix is far more conspicuous than the cells by which this matrix is secreted. In fact, the character of the matrix mainly determines the properties of the particular kind of connective tissue in question (Chapter 3).

Organs. An organ is composed of cells integrated into tissues serving a common function. Examples of organs are the spleen, liver, heart, lungs, and skin.

Systems. Cells are grouped together to form tissues; tissues combine to form organs. A *system* is a group of organs. The system is the basis for the general structural plan of the body. Brief mention will be made of the various systems to give an idea of the general organization of the body shown in the figures of the human torso (Figs. 4 to 13).

The *skin* is made up of the epidermal and dermal layers and, as a system, includes the hair, nails, and sebaceous and sweat glands. Its primary functions are insulation of the body from various environmental hazards and temperature and water regulation.

The *skeletal system* is composed of bones and the cartilaginous and membranous structures associated with them. This system protects and supports the soft parts of the body and supplies levers for body movement. Connective tissue predominates in this area. Articulations (joints) will be described separately.

The *muscular system* is composed of muscles, fasciae, tendon sheaths, and bursae. The three types of muscles are: striated, moving the skeleton; smooth, found along the alimentary tract; and cardiac, found in the heart.

The *nervous system* consists of the brain, the spinal cord, cranial nerves, peripheral nerves, and sensory and motor terminals. It is the correlating and controlling system of the body, intimately connected with the other systems and with the outside world. Special senses include vision, hearing, taste, and smell.

The *circulatory system* comprises the heart, arteries, veins, lymph vessels, and capillaries. It pumps and distributes the blood carrying oxygen, nutrients, and wastes. The lymphatic system, which drains tissue spaces and carries absorbed fat into the blood, will be considered separately.

The *respiratory system* is composed of the air sinuses, pharynx, larynx, trachea, bronchi, and lungs. It is involved in bringing oxygen to and in eliminating carbon dioxide from the blood.

The *digestive system* includes the alimentary tract, with the associated glands, from the lips to the anus. It converts food into simpler substances that can be absorbed and utilized by the body.

The *urinary system* comprises the kidneys, ureters, urinary bladder, and urethra. Its chief functions are the formation and elimination of urine and the maintenance of homeostasis.

The *endocrine system* includes the hypophysis (pituitary), thyroid, parathyroids, suprarenals, pancreatic islets in the pancreas, ovaries, testes, pineal body, and placenta (during pregnancy). The endocrine glands are involved in the chemical regulation of body functions.

The *reproductive system* consists of the ovaries, uterine tubes, uterus, vagina, and vulva in the female, and the testes, seminal vesicles, penis, prostate, and urethra in the male. It functions in the perpetuation of the species.

Text continued on page 21

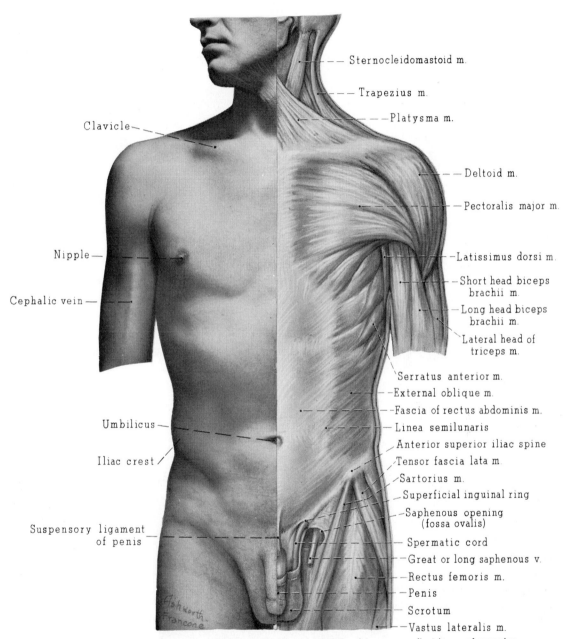

Clavicle

Nipple

Cephalic vein

Umbilicus

Iliac crest

Suspensory ligament
of penis

Sternocleidomastoid m.

Trapezius m.

Platysma m.

Deltoid m.

Pectoralis major m.

Latissimus dorsi m.

Short head biceps
brachii m.

Long head biceps
brachii m.

Lateral head of
triceps m.

Serratus anterior m.

External oblique m.

Fascia of rectus abdominis m.

Linea semilunaris

Anterior superior iliac spine

Tensor fascia lata m.

Sartorius m.

Superficial inguinal ring

Saphenous opening
(fossa ovalis)

Spermatic cord

Great or long saphenous v.

Rectus femoris m.

Penis

Scrotum

Vastus lateralis m.

Figure 4. Anterior surface of male, left half with skin removed to expose first layer of muscles.

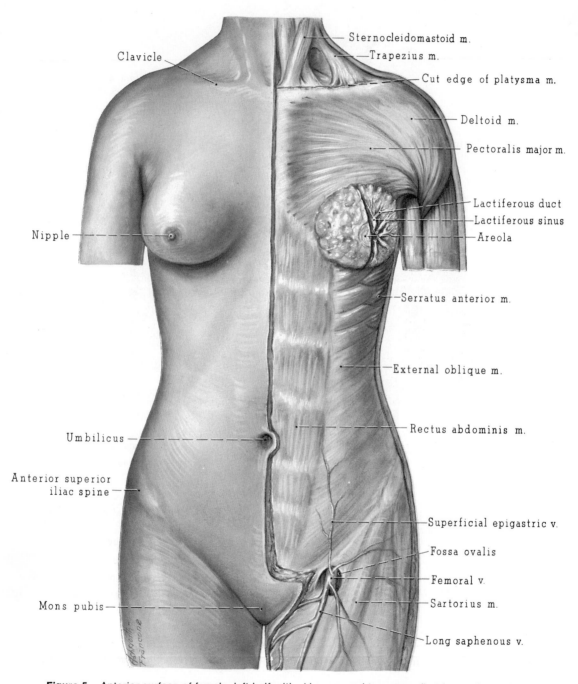

Figure 5. Anterior surface of female, left half with skin removed to expose first layer of muscles.

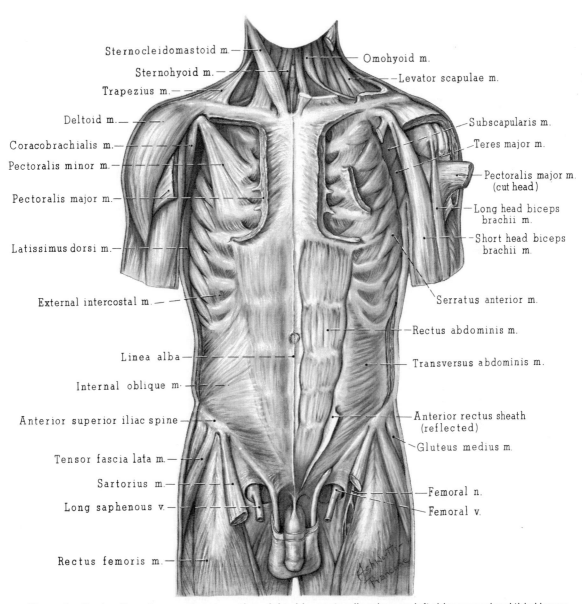

Figure 6. Pectoralis major muscle removed on right side, pectoralis minor on left side; second and third layers of abdominal muscles exposed.

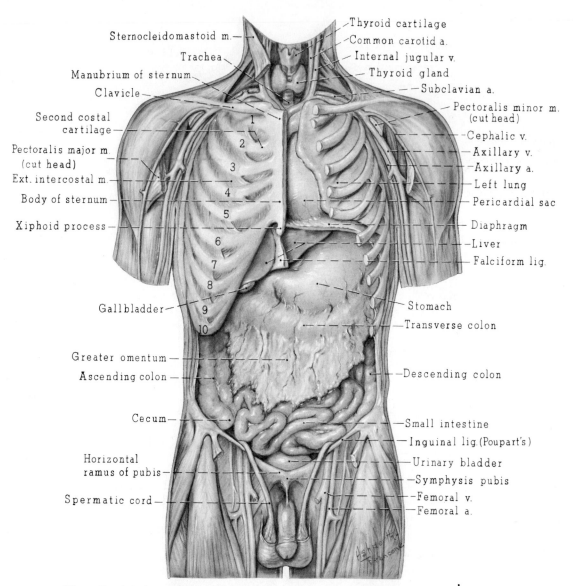

Sternocleidomastoid m.—
Trachea
Manubrium of sternum
Clavicle
Second costal cartilage—
Pectoralis major m (cut head)
Ext. intercostal m.—
Body of sternum—
Xiphoid process—
Gallbladder—
Greater omentum —
Ascending colon —
Cecum—
Horizontal ramus of pubis—
Spermatic cord—

Thyroid cartilage
Common carotid a.
Internal jugular v.
Thyroid gland
Subclavian a.
Pectoralis minor m. (cut head)
Cephalic v.
Axillary v.
Axillary a.
Left lung
Pericardial sac
Diaphragm
Liver
Falciform lig.
Stomach
Transverse colon
Descending colon
Small intestine
Inguinal lig.(Poupart's)
Urinary bladder
Symphysis pubis
Femoral v.
Femoral a.

Figure 7. Anterior muscles of chest and abdomen removed, showing underlying viscera.

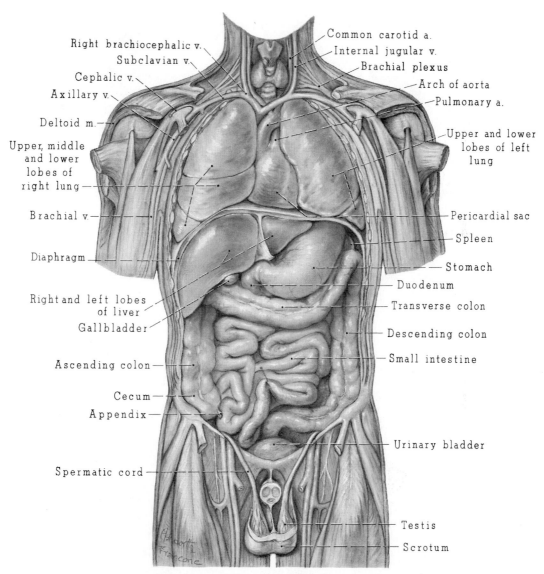

Figure 8. Rib cage and omentum removed, showing visceral relations.

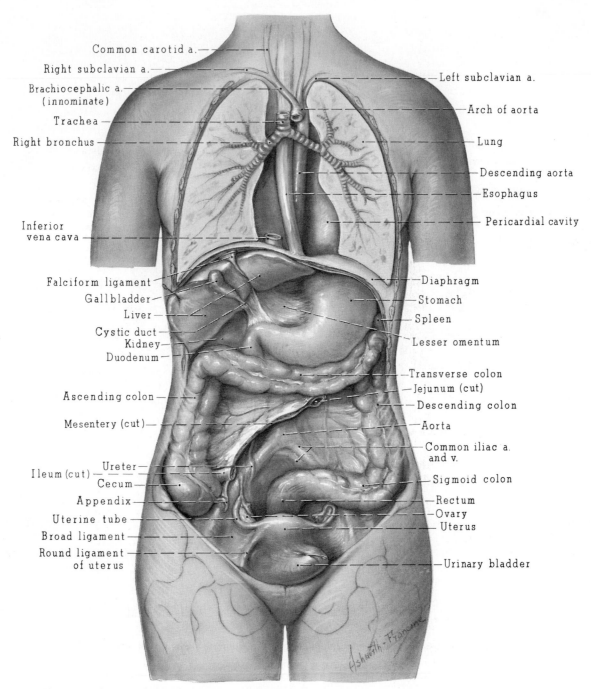

Figure 9.   Female, demonstrating visceral relations; lungs sectioned, heart and small bowel removed.

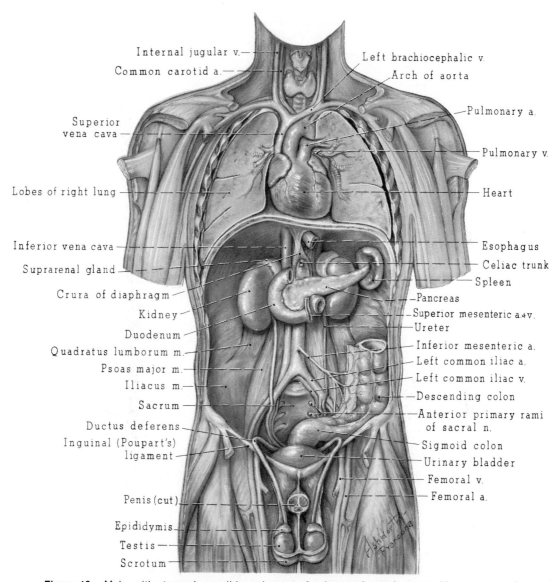

Figure 10.　Male, with stomach, small bowel, most of colon, and anterior part of lungs removed.

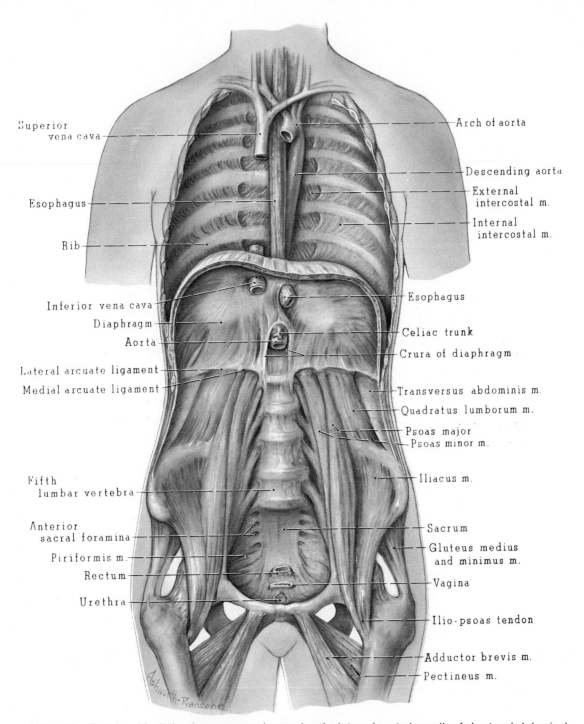

Superior
vena cava

Esophagus

Rib

Inferior vena cava
Diaphragm
Aorta

Lateral arcuate ligament
Medial arcuate ligament

Fifth
lumbar vertebra

Anterior
sacral foramina
Piriformis m.
Rectum
Urethra

Arch of aorta

Descending aorta
External
intercostal m.
Internal
intercostal m.

Esophagus

Celiac trunk
Crura of diaphragm

Transversus abdominis m.
Quadratus lumborum m.
Psoas major
Psoas minor m.

Iliacus m.

Sacrum
Gluteus medius
and minimus m.
Vagina

Ilio-psoas tendon

Adductor brevis m.
Pectineus m.

Figure 11. Female, with all the viscera removed, exposing the internal posterior walls of chest and abdominal and pelvic cavities.

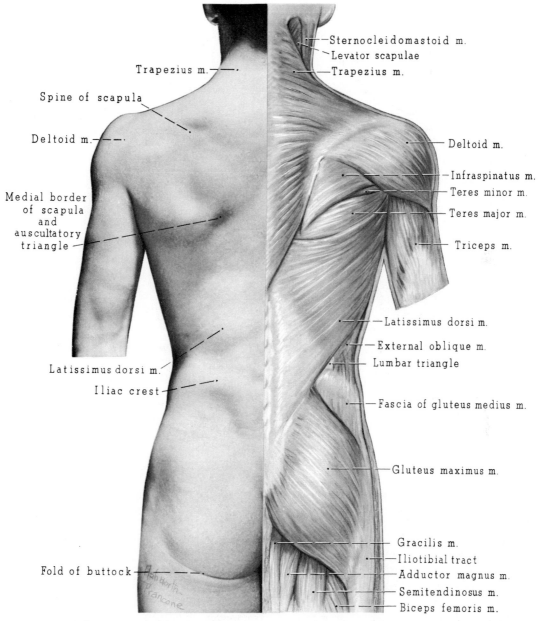

Sternocleidomastoid m.
Levator scapulae
Trapezius m.
Trapezius m.
Spine of scapula
Deltoid m.
Deltoid m.
Infraspinatus m.
Teres minor m.
Medial border
of scapula
and
auscultatory
triangle
Teres major m.
Triceps m.
Latissimus dorsi m.
External oblique m.
Lumbar triangle
Latissimus dorsi m.
Iliac crest
Fascia of gluteus medius m.
Gluteus maximus m.
Gracilis m.
Iliotibial tract
Fold of buttock
Adductor magnus m.
Semitendinosus m.
Biceps femoris m.

Figure 12. Posterior view of male, with skin removed on right side to expose first layer of muscles.

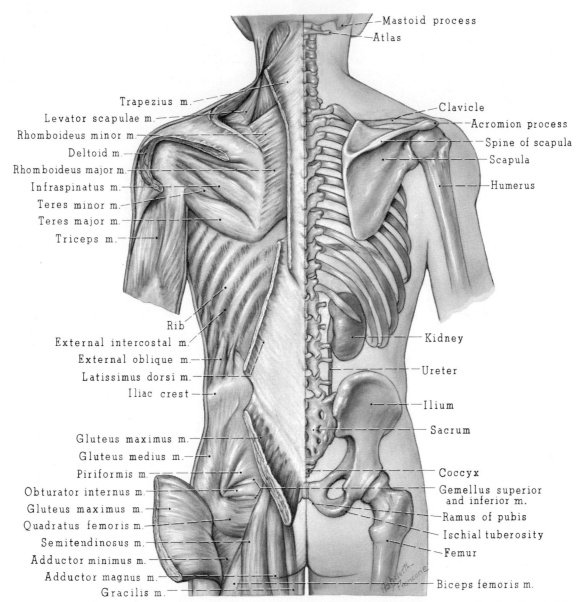

Figure 13. Most of the superficial muscles have been removed on the left side to expose the deep layers. All the muscles have been removed on the right side, exposing the skeletal framework.

SUMMARY

THE BODY AS A WHOLE

The Human Body

Specialized cells are structurally and functionally integrated to form an organism.

1. Anatomy: the study of the structure of the living organism.

2. Physiology: the study of the function of the living organism.

    a. Development of the electron microscope greatly enhanced the study of *molecular biology.*

    b. Water, the fluid medium of the body, accounts for about 65 per cent of the body weight. Two-thirds is within cells (intracellular fluid) and most of the remainder is between cells (interstitial fluid). The smallest proportion is in the circulatory system.

    c. Homeostasis involves control of internal environment of the body. The necessary constant environment for the cell is provided by homeostasis.

    d. Coordination of the body is primarily under nervous and hormonal control.

Organization of the Body

1. Four basic reference systems of organization are described:

    a. Direction: All descriptions of location or position assume the body to be erect and facing forward, with the arms at the side and the palms anterior. This is the so-called anatomic position. Directions include superior, inferior, anterior, posterior, cephalad, medial, lateral, proximal, and distal. Definitions of parietal and visceral are given.

    b. Planes: The body is discussed with respect to planes passing through it; these are the midsagittal, sagittal, horizontal, and frontal planes.

    c. Cavities

        (1) Ventral cavity, subdivided into the thoracic (further divided into the pleural and pericardial) and the abdominal cavities.

        (2) Dorsal cavity, divided into the cranial and spinal cavities; the dorsal cavity contains structures of the nervous system.

    d. Structural units

        (1) The cell: All living matter is composed of cells and cell products. The cell carries out all activities essential for maintaining life.

        (2) Tissue: Composed of cells and intercellular substance. Cells of a tissue are similar in appearance, function, and embryonic origin. The four types of tissues are epithelial, connective, muscle, and nervous.

        (3) Organs: A group of tissues serving a common function brought together to form a single structure, such as the heart or lungs.

        (4) System: Cells, tissues, and organs combine to form a system. The body contains the following major systems: skeletal, articular, muscular, nervous, circulatory, respiratory, digestive, urinary, endocrine, and reproductive.

chapter 2

The Cell

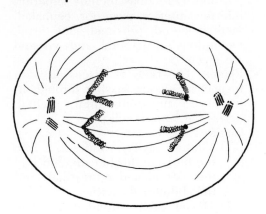

Objectives

The aim of this chapter is to enable the student to:

Explain the origin of the cell theory and the emergence of an understanding of how the genetic substance of the cell determines the nature of the cell.

Identify and describe some of the important functions of the major chemical constituents of cells and extracellular matter.

List the principal functions of each cellular organelle.

Identify the major mechanisms of movement of substances across the cell membrane and explain how they work.

Distinguish between the aerobic and anaerobic breakdown of glucose and describe how the aerobic process produces more ATP than does the anaerobic process.

Describe how the breakdown of fatty acids yields more energy than does the breakdown of glucose.

Explain what is meant by the cell cycle in populations of dividing cells.

Describe the four stages of mitosis and explain the difference between mitosis and meiosis.

Describe how the structure of DNA explains how an exact copy can be made prior to cell division and how it carries coded information for the synthesis of proteins.

Describe how proteins are synthesized from information coded in genes.

Explain how cancer cells differ from normal cells.

Describe how cellular differentiation takes place.

IMPORTANCE OF THE CELL

The human body is composed of cells, intercellular matrices, and body fluids. Of the three, only the cells are living, possessing the characteristics of growth, metabolism, irritability, and reproduction.

The cell is the structural, or morphologic, unit of the body, as well as its functional, or physiologic, unit. The human body develops from a single cell, the *fertilized ovum*. Repeated divisions of the ovum result in many types of cells differing from one another in composition and function; however, most of the basic structures of the cell are common to all cells.

The cell is regarded as a highly organized unit ceaselessly engaged in dynamic biochemical activities. Keeping the cell environment constant within a relatively narrow range is essential for optimum cell functioning.

All the organs, structures, and systems of the body can be viewed as designed to afford each individual cell its optimum environment. However, the nature of the living organism is more truly revealed when this is coupled with the recognition that, in the final analysis, it is the cells themselves which do the work to provide this optimum environment. This aspect of mutual internal reciprocity of every part of the body to every other is fundamental to understanding the relationship between physiology and anatomy.

HISTORY OF THE CELL

The word *cell* was introduced as a biological term in 1665 by Robert Hooke, an English scientist, to describe what reminded him of the cells of a honeycomb when he examined a section of cork with his 30-power microscope. Hooke came to the conclusion, after many years of study, that these boxlike compartments were fundamental to the structure of all living plants. However, a formal statement of what is known as the *cell theory* did not appear until the publication in 1838 and 1839 of monographs by M. J. Schleiden, a botanist, and Theodor Schwann, a zoologist. This generalization, a summary of their own findings and those of their contemporaries, described cells as the fundamental units of structure and function of all living things, capable of carrying out all of the processes of life as independent entities and, collectively, as complex systems. The origin of cells remained a matter of dispute until the writings of Rudolf Virchow in 1858 led to the general acceptance of the view that cells arise by division of preexisting ones. *"Omni cellula e cellula"* (all cells come from cells) is Virchow's widely quoted dictum. In 1882 Walther Flemming published remarkable drawings of cell division showing that discrete bodies, called *chromosomes*, which take form during cell division, appeared to be split lengthwise prior to cell division to form double strands. The strands separated and each daughter cell received a complete set of chromosomes. The inheritance of these bodies provides continuity from one cell generation to the next. A year later Edouard van Beneden observed that the sperm and egg cells of Ascaris, a parasitic worm, contained one-half as many chromosomes (haploid number) as nonsexual cells and that when a sperm cell fertilized an egg the sperm and egg nuclei fused to restore the full (diploid) number. Chromosomes, therefore, are the agents for continuity in sexual reproduction of the whole organism. At that time a number of leading biologists believed that a substance called nuclein (now known as nucleic acids), which had been isolated from the nucleus of human white blood cells by Friedrich Miescher, was responsible for the transmission of hereditary characteristics. But this idea was soon discarded, partly because of the prevailing belief that only nuclear protein was complex enough to carry genetic information. However, during the 1940's new observations proved that DNA, the nucleic acid component of chromosomes, rather than the protein component, is the hereditary substance. An intense search in laboratories all over the world culminated in the publication by James Watson and Francis Crick of the celebrated double helix model of DNA (described on page 50). This model explained how coded information could be built into DNA, and not many years after its publication the code itself was broken. The code and how it operates is described later in this chapter. For the present, all that needs to be said is that DNA resembles a tape subdivided into units (called *genes*) which contain instructions for the manufacture of proteins, including *enzymes*. Enzymes govern cellular processes by acting as biological catalysts, promoting chemical reactions but remaining intact at the end of the reaction. Without enzymes, cellular reactions could not occur and the constituents of the cell could be neither assembled nor broken down. Thus, the nature of a cell is determined ultimately by the genetic instructions for the synthesis of its enzymes.

The tissue culture studies begun in 1912 by Harrison have tested and confirmed the thesis that each (potentially or actually) independent cell, so long as it retains its capacity for growth and multiplication, must be considered an integral living unit.

The most dramatic advances in cytology (the study of cell structure) have occurred in the past 35 years, since the development of the electron microscope and increasingly sophisticated biochemical techniques and instruments. Although there has been some discussion recently about whether or not some substructures found within the cell should be considered independent living units and, further, whether some viruses are alive apart from a host cell, the general consensus seems to be that in the most obvious and relevant senses the cell is clearly the smallest living unit of which all definitely living things are composed (Fig. 14).

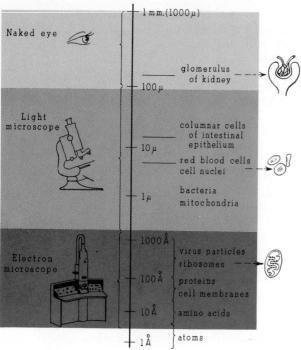

Figure 14. The limits of resolution of the electron microscope as contrasted to those of the eye and the light microscope. A millimeter, mm., is equal to $^1/_{1000}$ meter, or 0.03937 inch; a micrometer, μm, $^1/_{1000}$ millimeter; an angstrom, Å, $^1/_{10,000}$ micrometer.

BASIC CHARACTERISTICS OF A CELL

Chemical Constituents of Cells and Extracellular Matter

Protoplasm (G. *protos*, first; G. *plasma*, anything formed) is the name given collectively to the numerous substances which make up the living cell. To list all the substances that have been identified in the protoplasm of various types of cells, intercellular matrices, and body fluids would fill a volume in itself and is beyond the scope of this text. However, these substances can be characterized as belonging to two important and very general chemical groupings, organic and inorganic.

ORGANIC. The most common *organic* compounds are divided into four main classes: proteins, carbohydrates, lipids and nucleic acids. All these substances are made up principally of *carbon*, which rarely occurs in inorganic chemistry but is present in all organic compounds. In other words,

organic chemistry is the chemistry of carbon compounds.

Proteins. The most prevalent substance, next to water, in most cells is *protein*, constituting 10 to 20 per cent of the cell mass. Proteins are composed of **amino acids** linked together, forming long chains twisted into three-dimensional structures (Fig. 15). Since the bond formed between two amino acids is called a *peptide bond* (see Chemical Appendix), proteins, which generally contain 100 or more amino acids, are described as very large *polypeptides* (G. *polys*, many). Proteins serve a number of essential functions. First and foremost, all *enzymes* are proteins. Their action as biological catalysts makes possible chemical reactions that otherwise could not occur at body temperature. Proteins are also an important component of the intercellular fabric of connective tissues (such as tendons, bone and the dermis, the principal layer of the skin). *Collagen,* the major fibrous protein of the connective tissue matrix, constitutes 40 per cent of the body protein. In other roles proteins are 1) one of the major components of cell membranes, 2) the contractile elements of muscle, 3) hormones, 4) receptors on the cell surface and within the cell to which substances acting on cells, such as hormones, can become bound, 5) antibodies, 6) oxygen carriers, and 7) blood proteins (albumin, the most abundant one, is largely responsible for the osmotic pressure of blood plasma [see discussion of osmotic pressure on page 38]). A great many proteins have side chains of sugar and are therefore called *glycoproteins* (G. *glykys*, sweet).

Carbohydrates. The *carbohydrates* (simple and complex sugars) make up about 1 per cent of the cell mass. In addition, substances known as *protein-polysaccharides* (G. *sakchar*, sugar), also called mucopolysaccharides, consisting of carbohydrate combined with a small amount of protein, form the intercellular "ground substance" of connective tissues, in which the fibrous proteins are embedded. Carbohydrates are so named because the hydrogen and oxygen atoms attached to the carbon chain are present in the same ratio as in water and can be represented as C_x $(H_2O)_y$. Glycogen, a polysaccharide made up of many molecules of the simple 6-carbon sugar *glucose* (Fig. 16), is an important form of stored energy in

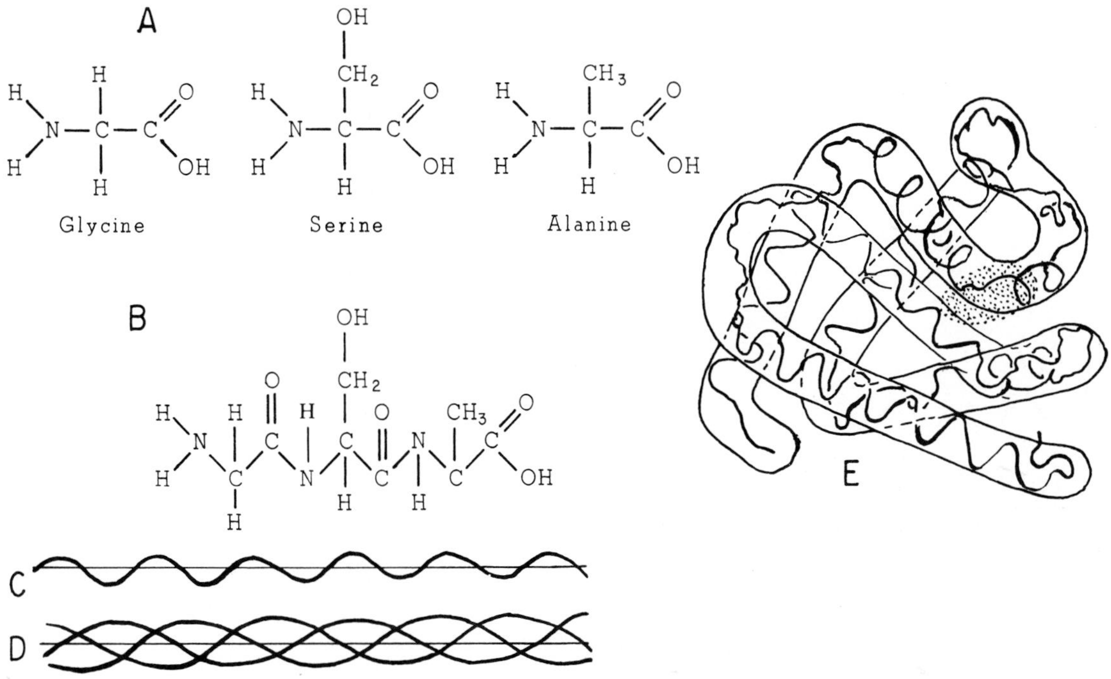

A

Glycine   Serine   Alanine

B

C

D

E

Figure 15. Protein constituents and structure. *A* shows three of 20 standard amino acids that constitute the building blocks of proteins. *B* shows these amino acids connected to form a fragment of a protein chain. *C* illustrates a coiled chain (helix configuration) forming part of collagen, a fibrous protein found chiefly in the intercellular matrix of connective tissues. *D* shows how three coiled chains, each containing about a thousand amino acids, wind around each other to form a triple helix, the basic collagen molecule from which collagen fibrils are assembled. The complex coiling and folding of a single chain in myoglobin, a globular protein, is illustrated in *E*. The lines drawn outside the chain as a tubular enclosure outline the course of the 153 amino acid chain. The disc embedded in the folds of the chain represents the nonprotein (heme) portion that binds oxygen. Myoglobin, found in muscle, serves as an oxygen store.

the body. During the absorption of a meal, glucose entering the blood stream furnishes almost all of the energy needs of the body. The excess is converted to glycogen or fat (discussed below).

Lipids. Lipid is the general term used to identify substances that are relatively insoluble in water but soluble in solvents such as

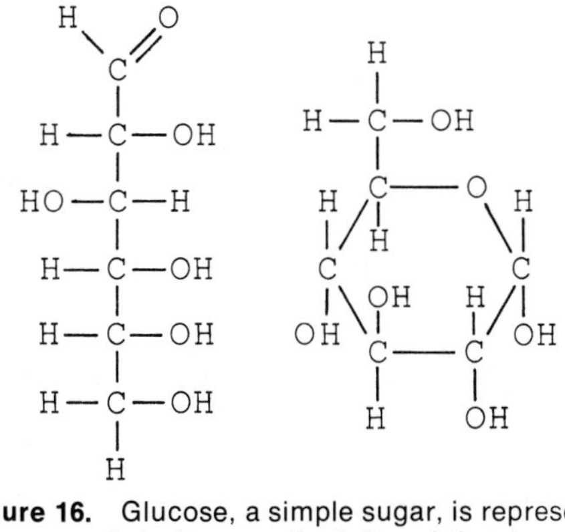

Figure 16. Glucose, a simple sugar, is represented in the open chain form on the left and the ring structure (the predominant form) on the right.

ether, chloroform or alcohol. Lipids of major importance are subclassified as *fats, phospholipids* and *steroids*.

Fats are a combination of three fatty acids and an alcohol called glycerol (Fig. 17). Fats, also called *triglycerides,* are the major reserve form of energy in the body and, in addition, in the skin form a layer of insulation and protective padding. Whereas the capacity to store carbohydrate as glycogen (chiefly in the liver) is limited, the capacity to store fat (in the skin, abdomen and other regions) is virtually unlimited. The bulk of any excess ingested calories is converted to fat, which supplies most of the energy needs of the cells of the body (except those of the brain, which, under normal conditions, uses glucose only) after a meal is completely absorbed.

Phospholipids resemble fat; the most common contain a phosphate group and a nitrogen-containing base in place of one of the fatty acids (Fig. 17). These groups are electrically charged and form the water-soluble "polar" heads of the molecule. The

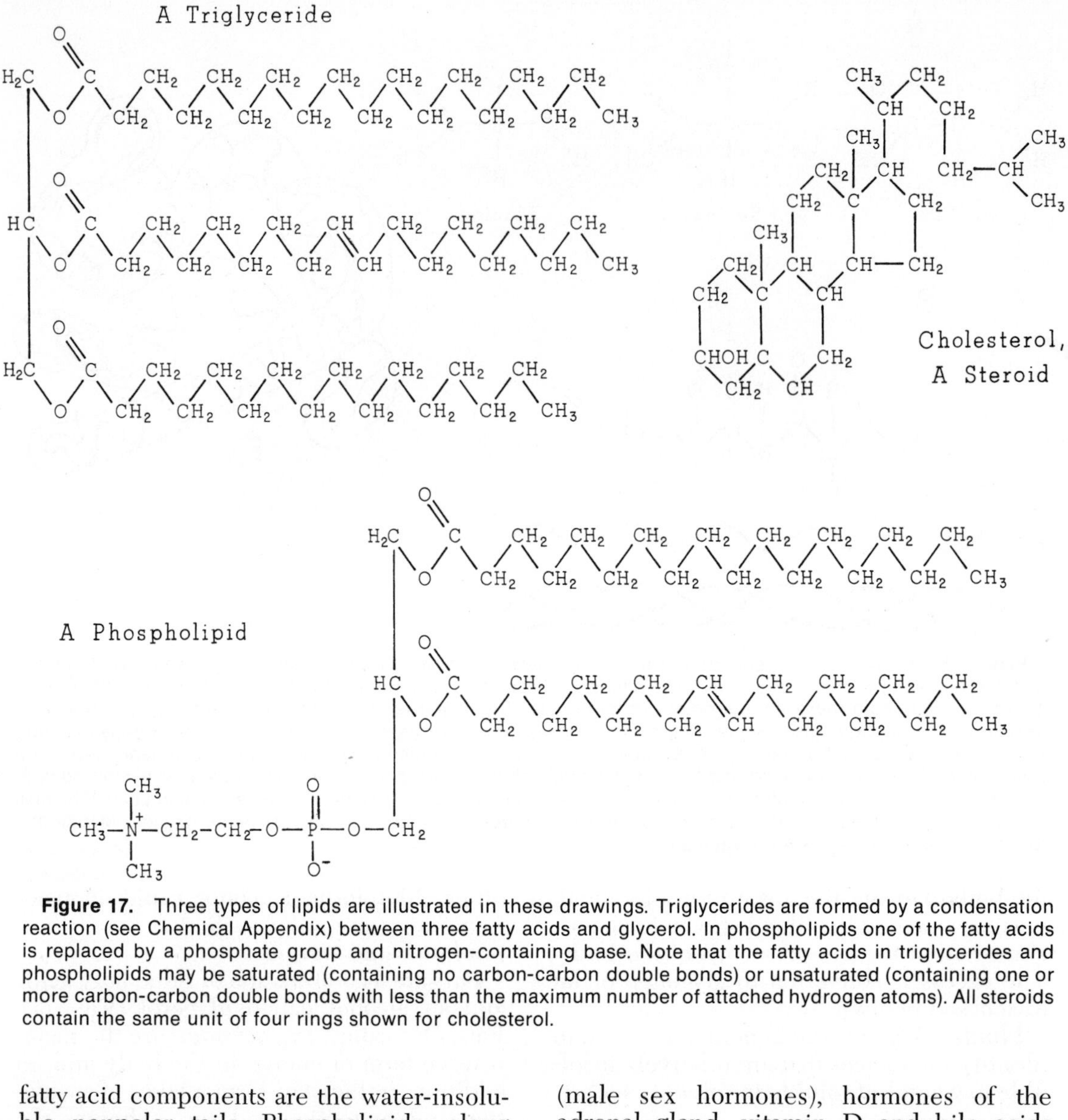

A Triglyceride

Cholesterol, A Steroid

A Phospholipid

Figure 17. Three types of lipids are illustrated in these drawings. Triglycerides are formed by a condensation reaction (see Chemical Appendix) between three fatty acids and glycerol. In phospholipids one of the fatty acids is replaced by a phosphate group and nitrogen-containing base. Note that the fatty acids in triglycerides and phospholipids may be saturated (containing no carbon-carbon double bonds) or unsaturated (containing one or more carbon-carbon double bonds with less than the maximum number of attached hydrogen atoms). All steroids contain the same unit of four rings shown for cholesterol.

fatty acid components are the water-insoluble nonpolar tails. Phospholipids, along with proteins, are the major constituents of cell membranes. They form the structural fabric of the membrane, and their solubility properties selectively limit passage of water-soluble substances.

Steroids contain a basic structural unit of four rings of carbon (Fig. 17). *Cholesterol,* the most common steroid in the body, is an important component of some cell membranes (membranes enclosing cells, especially red blood cells, contain more cholesterol than intracellular membranes). Cholesterol is also the precursor of a number of other essential steroids, such as estrogens (female sex hormones), androgens (male sex hormones), hormones of the adrenal gland, vitamin D and bile acids (substances secreted by the liver that aid lipid digestion and absorption). Lipids make up about 2 to 3 per cent of the cell by weight, except in adipose (fat) tissue, in which triglycerides occupy almost all of the interior of the fat cell.

Nucleic acids consist of long chains built up from **nucleotides.** A nucleotide is composed of a *5-carbon sugar,* a *phosphate group* and a *nitrogen-containing base.* DNA (deoxyribonucleic acid), the genetic matter of the cell, described later in the chapter, is an example of a nucleic acid. *ATP* (adenosine triphosphate), the direct source of energy for most chemical reactions in the

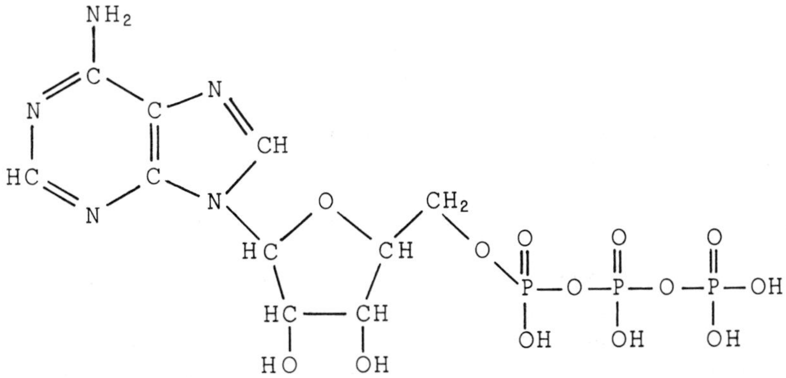

Figure 18. ATP (adenosine triphosphate) is a nucleotide (nitrogen-containing base, 5-carbon sugar and phosphate group) with two additional phosphate groups. (In ATP the base is adenine, the sugar ribose.) The terminal high-energy phosphate bond of ATP is the principal energy store of the cell.

cell, is a nucleotide with two additional phosphate groups (Fig. 18). The end phosphate forms what is called a high-energy bond. When it is cleaved, approximately 8000 calories of energy are made available to the cell (one *calorie* is the amount of heat required to raise the temperature of one gram of water 1° C).

INORGANIC. The *inorganic* grouping is the largest by volume and weight, primarily due to the high proportion of water. Also present are lesser amounts of mineral salts, both dissolved and attached to some organic compounds, and dissolved gases. The dissolved inorganic salts, acids, and bases are called electrolytes. The most important of these in the cell are potassium, magnesium, phosphate, sulfate, bicarbonate, and lesser quantities of sodium, chloride, hydrogen (H^+), and hydroxyl radicals (OH^-).

Water is the most prevalent substance in the body, the proportion in terms of weight being about 70 per cent. This water is by no means inert and unimportant. It is the chief *dispersion medium* of the body; that is, it is the liquid that dissolves, suspends, or otherwise disperses most of the various substances present in the cell and extracellular compartment of the body. Water is the most highly effective *solvent* of inorganic compounds and also dissolves numerous organic substances. The distribution of electrical charges of the water molecule is an important mechanism in its solvent power. In a water molecule each of the two hydrogen atoms shares a pair of negatively charged electrons with an oxygen atom (see Appendix for description of atomic structure). However, the electrons are more strongly attracted to the oxygen atom. This creates electrical polarity in the molecule

(Fig. 19), enabling water to effectively dissolve other polar substances. On the other hand, water is a poor solvent for nonpolar substances, such as fat.

Furthermore, water has an exceptionally high *heat capacity,* which serves to keep the temperature of the organism relatively stable when rapid changes in the temperature of the environment occur. The amount of heat required to increase the temperature of a substance is its *specific heat.* As defined above, a calorie is the amount of heat required to raise the temperature of a gram of water 1° C. Since approximately half a calorie will raise the temperature of alcohol 1° C, water has about twice the specific heat of alcohol. It has four times the specific heat of air. Coupled with this is its *heat conductivity,* which is high (for fluids) and facilitates temperature homeostasis, since even small changes in internal temperatures of one area are quickly dispersed

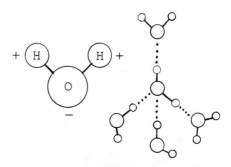

Figure 19. *Left,* Schematic drawing of a water molecule showing its electrical polarity. *Right,* Hydrogen bonding of a water molecule with four other water molecules in ice. The central water molecule and the one above and to the right of it are in the plane of the page. The bottom molecule is in front of this plane; the molecule on the left is behind this plane.

over large areas. Along the same line, water has a high *heat of vaporization.* It takes 500 calories to change one gram of liquid water to water vapor. This provides a cooling factor in organisms, generally through perspiration (vaporization) from body surfaces.

Many of the special properties of water, including its high specific heat and high heat of vaporization, are the result of a force of attraction between water molecules, known as the *hydrogen bond,* in which the electropositive hydrogen atom acts as a link between two very electronegative atoms (oxygen or nitrogen). Figure 19 illustrates how a water molecule can establish hydrogen bonds with four other water molecules. Hydrogen bonding accounts for the cohesive forces producing *surface tension* (the tendency of the surface to contract into a spherical shape, presenting the smallest possible surface) and *capillary action* (causing water to rise as a continuous column in a fine-bore tube) as well as the high heat input necessary to create the kinetic energy (energy of movement of molecules) reflected in a rise in temperature.

Protoplasm must be considered *particulate,* that is, made up of particles. The sizes of particles found in protoplasm vary a great deal. Particles visible in a compound light microscope or by means of the naked eye are termed *coarse.* Below this range, particles with diameters from 0.1 to 1 μ (see Appendix) are termed *colloidal* and are said

to form colloidal solutions or suspensions. Those particles with diameters smaller than 0.1 μ are in what is called the *crystalloidal* range, are dissolved in water, and are said to form *true solutions.*

STRUCTURE OF THE CELL

The cell may be defined structurally as an organized unit mass of protoplasm consisting of two complementary, mutually dependent parts: (1) the *nucleus,* a more or less central part; and (2) the *cytoplasm* (G. *kytos,* cell), a surrounding part. The nucleus is delineated from the surrounding cytoplasm by an exceedingly delicate *nuclear membrane;* the cytoplasm is bounded externally by a specialized layer, also very thin and delicate, which is called the *cell membrane* (Fig. 20).

Listed below are the structural functional parts of the cell:

1. Cell membranes
2. Nucleus
   a. Chromosomes
   b. Nucleoli
3. Cytoplasm
   a. Cytoplasmic organelles
      (1) Endoplasmic reticulum
      (2) Ribosomes
      (3) Golgi apparatus
      (4) Mitochondria
      (5) Lysosomes
      (6) Centrioles
   b. Cytoplasmic inclusions

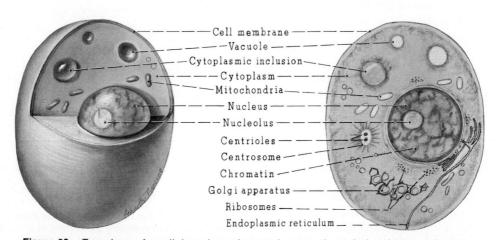

Cell membrane
Vacuole
Cytoplasmic inclusion
Cytoplasm
Mitochondria
Nucleus
Nucleolus
Centrioles
Centrosome
Chromatin
Golgi apparatus
Ribosomes
Endoplasmic reticulum

Figure 20.   Two views of a cell, based on what can be seen through the electron microscope.

Figure 21. *A,* Schematic drawing of a cell membrane. Phospholipids form a double layer with their water-repelling nonpolar tails facing inward, meeting at the center of the membrane, and their water-attracting polar heads facing away from the interior of the membrane. Membrane proteins are represented in various shapes partially or completely penetrating the phospholipid bilayer or not penetrating. Bending of some of the phospholipid tails is caused by the presence of unsaturated fatty acids and creates a more fluid condition in the membrane. *B,* Enlarged diagrammatic representations of phospholipids illustrate how a double bond of an unsaturated fatty acid, shown on the left, introduces a bend in the carbon chain.

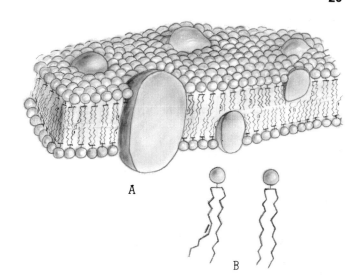

Cell Membranes

On all protoplasmic surfaces, a specialized layer or membrane is found that is denser than the rest of the protoplasm. In the cell, these membranes include the internal membranes enclosing the various organelles and the nucleus, as well as the external membrane, or *plasma membrane,* which forms the exterior layer.

The plasma membrane acts to regulate interchange between the cell and its environment and is a site for receiving signals from the immediate environment or from a distance that prompt adaptive changes essential for maintaining homeostasis of the cell and organism. Many hormones, for example, initiate their effects by becoming bound to specific receptors on the cell surface and activating enzymes in the cell membrane. Of equal importance is the action of internal membranes. The mitochondrial membrane (see page 33), for example, is the major site for the synthesis of ATP.

Phospholipids and proteins are the principal constituents of cell membranes. The former form the basic structure of the membrane; the latter are in large measure responsible for its functional properties. Analysis of x-ray data of membrane fragments indicates that the phospholipids form two parallel layers with their *hydrophilic* (water attracting; G. *hydōr,* water; G. *philein,* to love) polar heads facing away from

the center of the membrane and their *hydrophobic* (water repelling; G. *phobos,* fear) nonpolar tails facing the center of the membrane. The proteins are not arranged in an orderly pattern (Fig. 21). The technique known as freeze-etch electron microscopy has aided considerably in constructing the present picture of cell membranes. In this procedure a suspension of membranes in water is rapidly frozen (to liquid nitrogen temperature) and fractured with a sharp blade in a vacuum. The membrane is split in the plane between the two phospholipid layers. In the electron micrographs particles are revealed (presumed to be protein) along the inner surface of the bilayer 5 to 8.5 nanometers in diameter. In order for membrane proteins to function normally, the membrane must be in a fluid state (for example, see discussion of membrane transport on page 39). Fluidity is made possible by the presence of unsaturated fatty acids, which cause structural deformity of the phospholipid bilayer (Fig. 21).

The Nucleus

The nucleus is a specialized spherical mass of protoplasm, usually located in the center of the cell. It controls both the biochemical reactions that occur in the cell and reproduction of the cell. Each cell begins its existence with a nucleus which on occasion can be lost when the cell reaches its mature form as with the red blood cell, which extrudes its nucleus prior to entering the blood. A few cell types, such as the megakaryocyte (G. *megas,* large; G. *karyon,* nut or kernel) of bone marrow (which fragments to form platelets, essential factors in blood clotting), possess multiple nuclei.

The nuclear protoplasm, called the *karyoplasm,* and the surrounding cytoplasm are both typically colorless, transparent, and fluid and share a broadly comparable chemical constitution. Thus, staining by now-conventional techniques of cytology is necessary to examine the nucleus clearly. Certain dyes, especially hematoxylin, display a distinct affinity for the nuclear materials. When a cell is stained, there appears within the nucleus a densely stained network of relatively solid materials referred to as *chromatin.* This is easily distinguishable from the more fluid, colorless materials (Fig. 22). The chromatin consists of deoxyribonucleic acid (DNA), the genetic substance, and protein.

The chromatin network is composed of a specific number of very thin elongate threads looped and massed together in such a way as to give the appearance of a network. These threads are the **chromosomes.** Only during mitosis (cell division) do the chromosomes assume the often-pictured distinct rodlike structure.

Closely associated with the chromatin material can usually be found one to several larger masses, the *nucleoli.* At different times a nucleus may possess one, several, or no nucleoli. However, the number is usually fixed and definite for each type of cell. The nucleoli generally become enlarged during periods when a cell is actively synthesizing proteins. Unlike many other organelles, the nucleolus does not have a limiting membrane; rather, it is an aggregate of loosely bound granules composed mainly of ribonucleic acid (RNA). The nucleic acids were so named because they were first identified in the nucleus, although they were later found to exist in the cytoplasm as well.

In electron micrographs the nuclear membrane appears to be continuous at points with the endoplasmic reticulum (see below). During mitosis, the nuclear membrane disappears and a new one re-forms later in each daughter cell.

Cytoplasm

Protoplasm outside the nucleus is called *cytoplasm.* It makes up the general storage and working area of the cell. Under the light microscope, the main body of cytoplasm gives the appearance of an optically empty fluid in which a variety of visible bodies are suspended. Prior to the development of the electron microscope, this was termed the "clean cytoplasmic matrix." However, such an expression is misleading, for electron micrographs have since shown that this so-called "clean" cytoplasm possesses a complex, ultramicroscopic structure. The structures which are contained in or compose the cytoplasm are of two general types: *organelle* and *inclusion* (Fig. 23). Organelles are active, organized, living material, converting energy and usually possessing a surrounding membrane. Inclusions are passive, often very temporary materials such as pigment, secretory granules, and aggregates of stored protein, lipid or carbohydrate, which will be utilized by the cell in its life processes.

Cytoplasmic Organelles. ENDOPLASMIC RETICULUM. From a structural point of view, the most impressive organelle is the network of channels or tubules pervading the entire cytoplasm, called the *endoplasmic reticulum.* Two distinct varieties, *smooth* and *rough,* can be seen, each with different functions. The rough type derives its name from the numerous granular *ribosomes* (see following paragraph) scattered over its surface, giving it a rough appearance (Fig. 24). It functions in the synthesis of proteins that will be exported from the cell (such as digestive enzymes, hormones,

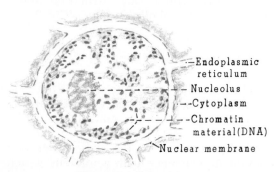

Endoplasmic
reticulum

Nucleolus

Cytoplasm

Chromatin
material(DNA)

Nuclear membrane

Figure 22.   Cell nucleus.

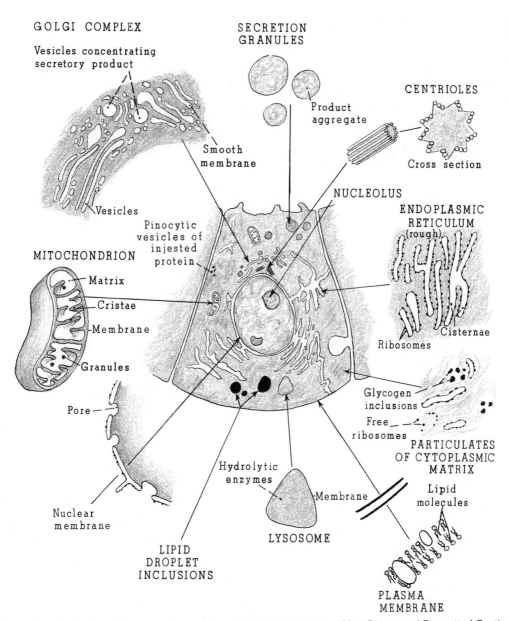

GOLGI COMPLEX

Vesicles concentrating
secretory product

SECRETION
GRANULES

Product
aggregate

CENTRIOLES

Cross section

Smooth
membrane

NUCLEOLUS

ENDOPLASMIC
RETICULUM
(rough)

Pinocytic
vesicles of
injested
protein

MITOCHONDRION

Matrix

Cristae

Membrane

Granules

Cisternae

Ribosomes

Glycogen
inclusions

Free
ribosomes

Pore

PARTICULATES
OF CYTOPLASMIC
MATRIX

Hydrolytic
enzymes

Membrane

Lipid
molecules

Nuclear
membrane

LYSOSOME

LIPID
DROPLET
INCLUSIONS

PLASMA
MEMBRANE

Figure 23. Parts of a cell as seen through the electron microscope. (After Bloom and Fawcett: *A Textbook of Histology,* eighth edition. Philadelphia, W. B. Saunders, 1962.)

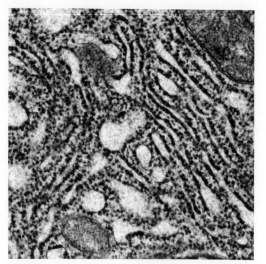

Figure 24. Electron micrograph of rough endoplasmic reticulum of a rabbit exocrine pancreatic cell (specialized for the synthesis of precursors of digestive enzymes). The attachment of numerous ribosomes (small, irregular, spheroidal bodies) to the external surface of the membranes of the endoplasmic reticulum (network of channels) gives rise to the term rough endoplasmic reticulum. Free ribosomes can also be seen in the cytoplasm between channels. (Magnification 41,000×.)

antibodies and collagen) or packaged by the cell as organelles known as *lysosomes* (described below), which contain digestive enzymes. The smooth endoplasmic reticulum, lacking attached ribosomes, is the site of various chemical transformations, including the synthesis of certain nonprotein substances, such as steroid hormones in cells of the adrenal gland and gonads, and detoxification of foreign substances in liver cells. In muscle cells the smooth endoplasmic reticulum, called the *sarcoplasmic reticulum* (G. *sarx*, flesh), sequesters and releases calcium ions, which act as the triggering agents for contraction.

RIBOSOMES. These are dense aggregations of RNA and protein. They are the site of protein synthesis and, as mentioned, when attached to the membrane of the rough endoplasmic reticulum, the proteins synthesized are packaged for export or as lysosomes. When packaging occurs, the proteins synthesized on the ribosomes are segregated from the cytoplasm of the cell in the cisternal space (cavity; L. *cisterna*, reservoir) of the rough endoplasmic reticulum and are transported to the *Golgi apparatus* (described in the following paragraph) for final processing. According to

George Palade and colleagues, pioneers in the study of secretory proteins, transport from the rough endoplasmic reticulum to the Golgi apparatus is probably accomplished by "shuttling vesicles" moving between the two organelles.

GOLGI APPARATUS. The *Golgi complex* or *apparatus* is named after the Italian microscopist, Camillo Golgi, who discovered these bodies in 1898 using a special silver stain of his own. The Spanish histologist Ramón y Cajal was the first person to suggest that these bodies take part in the production of a substance to be secreted from cells. He drew this conclusion in 1914 upon observing droplets of mucus in the region of the Golgi apparatus in cells of the small intestine called *goblet cells*, which secrete a mucus that forms a protective coating on the free surface of the intestine. As indicated in the foregoing paragraphs, the Golgi apparatus is involved in the last stages of the production of and in the packaging of proteins to be secreted or retained in lysosomes. All secretory proteins are glycoproteins. Side chains of sugars are added in the rough endoplasmic reticulum, but one of the specific functions of the Golgi apparatus is to add the terminal sugar units. Various other chemical transformations in the Golgi apparatus produce a finished product. When the secretory proteins are digestive enzymes or hormones, concentration of the product is carried out in the Golgi apparatus with the formation of what are known as *secretory granules*—dense bodies enclosed by a membrane derived from the Golgi apparatus. Enzymes stored in secretory granules are in an inactive form called *proenzymes*. Release of the contents of secretory granules to the exterior of the cell at the appropriate time occurs by a process called *exocytosis* (G. *exo*, outside). This involves fusion of the membrane of the secretory granule with the plasma membrane and discharge of the product from an open pocket in the membrane.

Much of our knowledge of the assembly line production and packaging of secretory proteins has been gained from studies that combine the techniques of electron microscopy and radioautography. In this procedure, sections of tissues are prepared at intervals after administering a radioactively labeled amino acid, sugar or other sub-

Figure 25. Schematic diagram of the synthesis, packaging, and secretion of precursors of digestive enzymes (proenzymes) by a pancreatic cell following the administration of a radioactively labeled amino acid. The solid red line follows the sequence of events. The amino acids pass into the cell from a blood vessel. Proteins manufactured on ribosomes move up inside the endoplasmic reticulum and are transported to the Golgi apparatus. The final stages of the synthesis take place here and the concentration of the secretory product begins. Concentration continues in condensing vacuoles, presumably derived from the Golgi apparatus. The concentration process ends with the formation of secretory granules (also called zymogen granules) in which the enzymes are temporarily stored. Release of the secretory product from the cell is brought about by fusion of the granule membrane with the cell membrane and discharge of the granule contents from an open pocket.

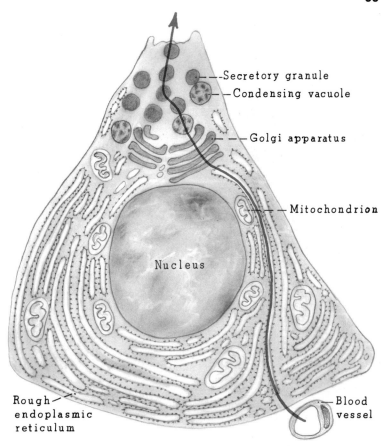

stance that will be incorporated into the new protein. Each section is coated with a photographic emulsion and stored in a light-tight box to allow the radioactivity to darken the film. Examination of the specimen in the electron microscope reveals the location of the newly synthesized protein in the cell. Figure 25 illustrates the course of events, as studied with this procedure, in the synthesis and secretion of digestive proenzymes by the pancreatic cell (which pass to the intestinal tract via the pancreatic duct).

MITOCHONDRIA. The "powerhouses" of the cell, *mitochondria*, contain the oxidative enzymes for the complete breakdown of fatty acids and for the terminal phase of the breakdown of glucose (described on page 40). In addition, they contain the enzyme system that accounts for the production of most of the ATP in the cell. In electron micrographs, mitochondria exhibit a double membrane arrangement, with the inner membrane lifted into folds called *cristae* (Fig. 26). The enzymes breaking down fatty acids and those participating in the *Krebs cycle,* which carry out the final phase of the oxidation of fatty acids and glucose (see page 41), are located in the interior soluble portion of mitochondria known as the *matrix space.* The inner membrane contains the system of enzymes called the *electron transfer chain* (described on page 41), which somehow couples energy built into the membrane system by electron transfer to the *phosphorylation* (adding a phosphate group) of ADP (adenosine diphosphate), thereby forming ATP, with its terminal high energy phosphate bond.

LYSOSOMES. The name of this organelle (G. *lysis,* a loosing; G. *soma,* body) suggests its nature — a body containing digestive enzymes. The enzymes present in these structures are described as hydrolytic (G. *hydor,* water) since they break down organic compounds by the addition of water. More than a dozen such enzymes, acting on

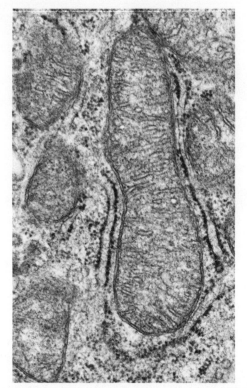

Figure 26. Electron micrograph of mitochondria from a human kidney tubule cell. Note the double membrane with invaginations of the inner one forming slender projections into the interior, called cristae. The interior portion of a mitochondrion is known as the matrix space. The space between the inner and outer membranes and between the cristal membranes is referred to as the intracristal space. (Magnification 41,000×.)

layering solutions of decreasing density from bottom to top in a centrifuge tube. During centrifugation the organelles of similar size come to rest in bands according to their densities (Fig. 27, *sequence B*).

Lysosomes are responsible for a number of cellular functions, including the following: 1) Digestion of bulky substances taken into the cell following *phagocytosis* (G. *phagein*, to eat), a process in which a section of the cell membrane forms a pocket enclosing the particle, which pinches free and then fuses with a lysosome (Fig. 28). The digested particle may be a source of nutrition, but more commonly is a potentially harmful agent. Lysosomes are especially prominent in certain types of white blood cells and in macrophages, large phagocytic cells located outside the blood stream (Fig. 29). 2) *Autolysis* (G. *autos*, self), the self-

virtually all classes of organic substances, have been identified in lysosomes.

Lysosomes were isolated in the early 1950's by Christian de Duve and associates. Their presence in the cell was suggested by the apparent leakage of a specific enzyme from a cell fraction containing mitochondria. De Duve and colleagues were using the newly developed procedure of centrifugal fractionation to isolate cell fractions. In this procedure the cells are disrupted in a homogenizer and centrifuged at successively higher speeds; each centrifugation yields a pellet containing a specific cell fraction (Fig. 27, *sequence A*). When de Duve *et al.* realized that the enzyme they were studying was not in mitochondria but in another organelle of similar density and size, they had to modify the final step of the fractionation by introducing a density gradient in order to separate the two organelle fractions. A density gradient is formed by

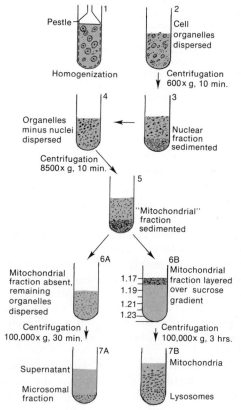

Figure 27. Isolation of cell organelles by centrifugation following disruption of the cell by homogenization is illustrated in these drawings. The sequence through 7A shows the recovery of nuclear, "mitochondrial" and microsomal (containing ribosomes) fractions. A modification of the procedure (6B and 7B), introduced by de Duve and colleagues, separates lysosomes from mitochondria in the "mitochondrial" fraction.

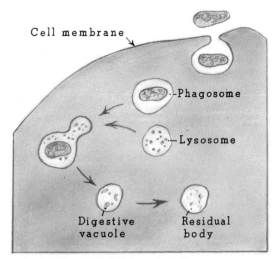

Figure 28. Digestion of a large particle by lysosomal enzymes following phagocytosis, showing fusion of a lysosome with the vesicle (phagosome) containing the particle to form a digestive vacuole.

destruction of cells after rupture of lysosomes. An example of this is the destruction of a structure formed during each menstrual cycle (the corpus luteum) that secretes

female sex hormones. 3) *Autophagy* (self-eating), the digestion of organelles or parts of organelles taken into lysosomes during starvation. 4) Destruction of extracellular matter by discharging lysosomal enzymes to the outside of cells. An example of this is the release by bone cells of enzymes that break down limited areas of bone matrix. This releases calcium from the bone and is one mechanism for maintaining normal levels of blood calcium (low blood calcium causes muscular irritability and, in extreme cases, convulsions). Release of lysosomal enzymes to the exterior of cells sometimes has harmful consequences. In arthritis, for example, the inflammation and tissue damage are caused by lysosomal enzymes. Aspirin and cortisone, drugs used to treat arthritis, stabilize lysosomal enzymes.

CENTRIOLES. These are a pair of small, hollow, cylindrical structures, usually oriented at right angles to one another, located just outside the nucleus. Two pairs are seen in dividing cells. At the onset of cell division the centriole pairs move apart and become the poles of the cell to which

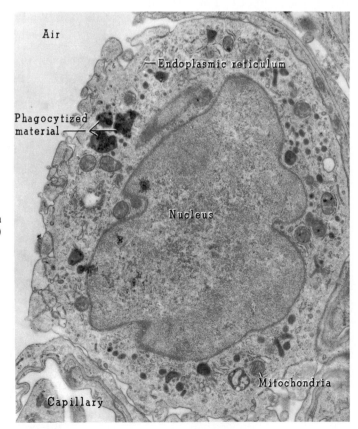

Figure 29. Electron micrograph of a lung macrophage (alveolar macrophage) magnified 18,000 ×.

each set of chromosomes migrates (for further details of cell division, see page 45).

Cytoplasmic Inclusions. These are various aggregations of material in the cell. They may be nutrients formed in the cell (such as glycogen granules, especially noticeable in liver and muscle cells, or fat droplets, which almost completely fill the fat cells of adipose tissue), pigments (such as melanin in cells of the skin), digestive vacuoles formed following phagocytosis, or the secretory granules described in the preceding paragraphs.

The Shape and Size of Cells. Different varieties of cells assume a wide spectrum of shapes. For example, nerve cells tend to be elongate and branched, while epithelial cells take the form of overlapping tiles, as in the skin, or of variously shaped bricks, as in the lining of the digestive tract. Generally speaking, the form of each cell bears a distinct relation to its particular function.

If a cell is removed from the restraining factors of its normal environment, it will tend strongly to a spherical shape as do all liquid particles because of the physics of the surface forces. For similar reasons, many cells are rounded and droplike when they first form by cell division and must expend energy to develop a desired shape. However, after a cell has assumed its final form, it may retain this shape in a variety of ways. It may secrete a rigid or semirigid nonliving coating that serves to hold the protoplasm in a definite mold; it may construct a delicate internal skeleton that supports the protoplasm; or it may, alternatively or in addition, stabilize its shape by a gelatinizing of the protoplasm or by pressure from surrounding cells.

As with shape, the size of the cell is related to its function. To support internal metabolism the cell must be able to obtain an adequate supply of oxygen and other nutrients and to give off carbon dioxide and other wastes. These necessary exchanges between the cell and the environment can occur only at the surface of the cell. Consequently, the surface of the cell must be adequately large in proportion to the protoplasmic volume. As the cell grows larger, the proportion of surface to volume steadily diminishes, with the surface area increasing as the square and the volume increasing as the cube of the diameter (Fig. 30).

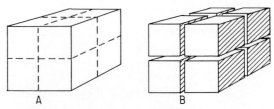

Figure 30. Illustrates increased surface area with fragmentation. *A* indicates lines of separation, *B* shows actual separation with increased surface area.

This upper limit on size varies according to each particular cell shape and according to the intensity of its metabolism. Generally speaking, human cells with basically symmetrical shapes range between 1 and 100 micrometers (0.001 and 0.1 mm). There are, of course, exceptions. The total length of a spinal sensory nerve fiber may reach from the toe to the medulla, but again the diameter is probably less than 10 micrometers, thus preserving a good surface-to-volume ratio.

The second physical limitation—the lower limit of size—seems to rest most critically on the physical properties of molecules and atoms. The specifics of this lower limit are still quite open to a variety of hypotheses because relevant data are scarce, primarily owing to the limitations, or lack, of instruments to probe at this level.

PHYSIOLOGY OF THE CELL

The human body is composed of about one hundred trillion cells which are arranged in tissues to carry out remarkably specialized functions, such as skeletal support, muscular contraction, and conduction of electrical impulses. Besides these specialized functions, most cells carry out vital general functions, three of which will be considered here. The three are movement of substances through the cell membranes, energy metabolism and enzymatic action.

Movement Across the Cell Membrane

In order to maintain life activities and perform a diversity of tasks cells must have rather precise control over their internal concentrations of various chemical substances. To regulate these concentrations, the cells must continually take in and expel

Table 2. CHEMICAL COMPOSITION OF BODY FLUIDS

	EXTRACELLULAR FLUID	INTRACELLULAR FLUID
Na^+	137 mEq/l	10 mEq/l
K^+	5 ''	141 ''
Ca^{++}	5 ''	0 ''
Mg^{++}	3 ''	62 ''
Cl^-	103 ''	4 ''
HCO_3^-	28 ''	10 ''
Phosphates	4 ''	75 ''
SO_4	1 ''	2 ''
Glucose	90 mgm%	0 to 20 mgm%
Amino acids	30 ''	200 ''
Cholesterol / Phospholipids / Neutral fat	0.5 gm%	2 to 95 gm%
PO_2	35 mmHg	20 mmHg ?
Pco_2	46 ''	50 '' ?
pH	7.4	7.1 ?

substances involved in cellular functioning. Table 2 lists the relative concentrations of a number of important substances found in the intracellular and extracellular fluids.

Cell physiologists have long considered an understanding of the exchange mechanisms between the cell and its environment to be fundamental to understanding the overall physiology of the cell and the integration of many cells to form higher organisms. Any exchange, of course, must occur at the surface of the cell, across the cell membrane. Mechanisms by which this exchange occurs include diffusion, osmosis, active transport, pinocytosis, and phagocytosis.

Physiochemical Basis of Diffusion. *Diffusion* may be described as a *net* transport of particles from a region in which they are more concentrated to a region in which they are less concentrated. This occurs because of the random motion of particles, which tends to bring about equal concentration of particles throughout a closed system. Characteristic of all matter is its kinetic or thermal (heat) motion; that is, the motion of atoms or molecules as units in relation to one another. At absolute zero ($-273°$ C)

movement ceases. It increases as the temperature increases. Solids are so tightly packed and strongly bound together that mixing or changing position of specific molecules in relation to one another does not occur. In this instance, thermal motion takes the form of a sort of rapid elastic oscillation (vibration), somewhat analogous to "running in place." When the heat content of a solid becomes great enough, the bonds are broken and mixing occurs; that is, the solid melts or becomes liquid. The temperature at which this occurs varies for different substances, e.g., $0°$ C for water, $2000°$ C for iron.

In liquids and gases, the intensity of the thermal agitation has overcome the strength of the cohesive bonds, with the result being a *continual dynamic* intermixing of the molecules (or ions).

If two salt solutions of different concentrations are placed in a closed container and separated by a membrane that does not present a barrier to the salt, the salt on both sides of the membrane will disperse throughout the chamber. In time, the concentration of salt on each side of the membrane will be equal, but a net movement of salt from the region of high to the region of low concentration will have occurred.

The equilibrium once achieved is not an idle one in which thermal motion and exchange of molecules between the two solutions ceases in any sense. Rather, it is dynamic, involving a continuous rearrangement of the relative positions of the molecules. Equilibrium is simply the point at which the exchanges are equivalent, producing no change in concentrations.

Diffusion Through the Cell Membrane. As mentioned earlier, the structural fabric of the cell membrane consists of a bilayer of phospholipids, with their hydrophilic heads facing the aqueous external and internal surfaces and their hydrophobic tails facing the center of the membrane. The incompatibility of the center of the membrane with water and small, water-soluble substances, such as metal ions, simple sugars and amino acids, creates a barrier through which they cannot freely diffuse (see Table 3). But the diffusion rates of these substances through biological membranes is greater than would be expected from the foregoing or from studies of their

Table 3. TABLE OF PERMEABILITIES (PASSIVE)

VERY RAPID	RAPID	SLOW	VERY SLOW	VIRTUALLY NO PENETRATION
Gases	Water	(Simple	Strong electrolytes	Complex (colloidal)
Carbon dioxide		organic	Inorganic salts	Compounds
Oxygen		substances)	Acids	Proteins
Nitrogen		Glucose	Bases	Polysaccharides
Fat solvents		Amino acids	Disaccharides	Phospholipids
Alcohol		Glycerol	Sucrose	
Ether		Fatty acids	Maltose	
Chloroform			Lactose	

From Marsland: *Principles of Modern Biology.* P. 116, Table 6–1.

passage through artificial phospholipid membranes (phospholipids spontaneously form bilayer films in water). This has led to the concept that membrane proteins provide channels and act as carriers to facilitate flow of these substances through cell membranes. Studies making use of compounds such as the antibiotic valomycin, which functions as a carrier for potassium, increasing its rate of diffusion through biological and artificial membranes, have provided experimental support for the carrier hypothesis. A carrier, it is assumed, binds a substance at one surface of the membrane, then migrates to the opposite surface and releases it. Carrier-aided transport is usually referred to as *facilitated diffusion* and is an important mechanism for controlling the permeability of membranes.

Osmosis is a special case of diffusion. It refers to the diffusion of water through membranes where a difference between concentration of solutes (dissolved substances) is maintained on opposite sides of the membrane by impermeability of the membrane to the solute or by active transport (discussed below) of the solute from one side to the other. Under this circumstance only the water molecules equilibrate. As a result there is a net transfer of water from the dilute solution (where the water molecules are more highly concentrated) to the concentrated solution. The force with which a solution draws water into it is called *osmotic pressure*. The higher the concentration of a solution, the greater is its osmotic pressure. Osmotic pressure can be conveniently measured in a *mercury osmometer* (Fig. 31). In it a semipermeable membrane (allowing only water to pass through it) separates distilled water from the solution to be tested. Water will flow

into the test solution until the pressure of the column of mercury balances the osmotic pressure of the test solution. The osmotic pressure of a solution is expressed as mm of mercury.

Cells in a *hypertonic* solution (one whose osmotic pressure is greater than that of the cell) will shrink. They will swell in a *hypotonic* solution (osmotic pressure lower

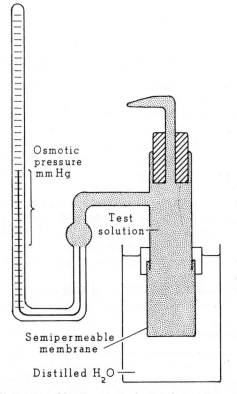

Figure 31. Measurement of osmotic pressure with a Pfeffer mercury osmometer. Distilled water passes through the semipermeable membrane into the test solution until the pressure of the column of mercury counterbalances the osmotic pressure of the test solution.

than the cell's). No change will occur in an *isotonic* solution (osmotic pressure the same as the cell's).

Active Transport. Diffusion and osmosis are referred to as passive transport processes because the driving force for transport is provided not by the membrane but by the *concentration gradient,* which causes the net movement of substances from regions of high concentration to regions of low. In active transport the cell uses energy to transport substances against a concentration gradient; that is, from a region of low concentration to one of high. For example, all cells maintain a high external concentration of sodium compared to the internal concentration; the reverse is true of potassium. If the production of ATP is blocked by metabolic poisons, the tendency of sodium and potassium to equilibrate will cause cell death. Active transport mechanisms exist for a number of other substances in addition to sodium and potassium. For example, the cells of the thyroid gland actively concentrate iodine (a component of the hormone thyroxine). In fact, practically all of the iodine in the body is inside these cells. Cells lining the intestines and kidney tubules transport various ions and certain sugars and amino acids against concentration gradients from their lumens (tubular interiors) to the blood stream. Active transport of glucose and certain other simple sugars appears to be coupled to the active transport of sodium. If active sodium transport (the so-called sodium pump) is blocked, active transport of these sugars will not occur.

Various models have been proposed to explain active transport. All assume that protein carriers which become mobile by changes in shape are involved. In one such model, illustrated in Figure 32, binding of the substance to be transported changes the shape of the carrier, enabling it to rotate. The carrier assumes an immobile form after releasing the substance on the opposite side of the membrane. Return to the mobile form requires the expenditure of metabolic energy.

Importance of Changes in the Permeability of Membranes. It should be emphasized that it is essential for the special functions of some cells for changes in permeability to occur in response to specific stimuli. In the membranes of nerve and

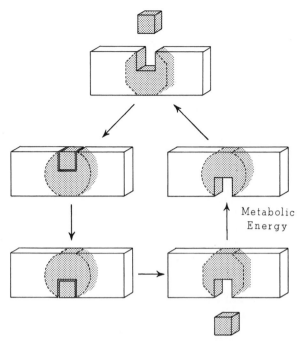

Figure 32. A suggested model for active transport. A protein carrier changes shape to a form that can rotate after binding a substance to be transported across the membrane. It returns to an immobile form after releasing the substance. To enable the carrier to return the binding site to its original position, energy input is required to change the shape of the protein to the mobile form. After rotating, it is again in an immobile form.

muscle fibers, for example, changes in the permeability to sodium and potassium following excitation are responsible for the initiation and propagation of the electrical impulse. Regulation of the volume of body fluids by the kidneys depends, in part, upon changes in the permeability of cells of the kidney tubules to water in response to ADH, the antidiuretic hormone.

Pinocytosis and Phagocytosis. Pinocytosis (G. *pinein,* to drink; G. *kytos,* cell) and phagocytosis (G. *phagein,* to eat) are energy dependent, active processes of ingestion by the cell of substances present in the extracellular fluid. The two processes are quite similar, each involving an incupping, or invagination, of the cell membrane and subsequent closure of the external opening to form a vesicle containing materials from the extracellular fluids. The term phagocytosis is applied to the ingestion of large particulate matter such as bacteria, coagulated organic matter, and some other cells, whereas pinocytosis is the ingestion of dissolved molecular substances. Phagocytic vesicles (phagosomes) are easily seen through the light microscope and were observed in white blood cells as long ago as the late 19th century by Elie Metchnikoff of the Pasteur Institute. However, pinocytic vesicles are considerably smaller and were first detected with time-lapse photography in tissue-culture cells in 1931 by the American physiologist Warren Lewis. Pinocytosis was largely ignored until it was widely observed with the electron microscope in the 1950's.

Phagocytosis, like pinocytosis, is an auxiliary means by which the cells may take in various substances needed for metabolic processes. Phagocytosis more commonly serves a further specialized function of great significance in the disease and infection treatment systems of the body. Certain types of white blood cells, generally known as phagocytes, are highly specialized to deal with foreign substances, including bacteria and small parasites, that enter the body and are potential causes of various harmful actions. Almost immediately after a vesicle moves toward the interior of the cell, it fuses with a lysosome to form a *digestive vacuole* (see Fig. 28, illustrating lysosome function). Indigestible matter remains in *residual bodies*, which are usually retained for a long time but may fuse with the cell membrane and excrete their contents. Phagocytic white blood cells die after accumulating excessive amounts of debris in this manner. The gradual accumulation of residues in other cells of the body is believed to contribute to their aging.

Energy Metabolism

Metabolism is a general term used to describe all the chemical reactions occurring in living matter. Energy metabolism refers to the chemical degradation of nutrients by the cell to produce the energy it needs to perform such functions as active transport, muscular contraction and biochemical synthesis. The energy released by the degradation of nutrient substances is not utilized directly by the cell for the performance of its work. Rather, the energy is used to synthesize ATP (adenosine triphosphate) and the energy stored in the terminal high-energy phosphate bond of ATP is the direct source of energy for work performed

by the cell. The terminal phosphate bond of ATP contains (and requires for formation) about 8000 calories of energy per mole of ATP. This is many times the energy stored in the average chemical bond, thus giving rise to the term "high energy." This high-energy bond is easily broken down with a splitting off of the phosphoric acid radical, leaving an ADP (adenosine diphosphate) molecule and releasing the energy stored in the bond.

Most of the ATP in the cell is produced during the breakdown of glucose and the fatty acid component of fat. The initial phase of the breakdown of glucose (to pyruvic or lactic acid) takes place in the cytoplasm of the cell. The remaining reactions occur in mitochondria. All of the enzymes involved in the degradation of fatty acid are located in mitochondria. The breakdown of fatty acids occurs under aerobic conditions only; that is, only in the presence of oxygen. The fatty acids are completely disrupted to carbon dioxide and water. Under most circumstances glucose, too, is aerobically degraded to carbon dioxide and water. But during strenuous exercise, when active muscles cannot be adequately supplied with oxygen, muscle cells can utilize glucose in the absence of oxygen. Under these (anaerobic) conditions the breakdown of glucose ends with the formation of lactic acid (a process called *glycolysis*). Much less ATP is produced by the anaerobic breakdown of glucose than by the aerobic breakdown. Maximum ATP production comes from the oxidative breakdown of fatty acids. Oxidation of a gram of fatty acid to carbon dioxide and water yields about two and one half times as much ATP as oxidation of a gram of glucose to carbon dioxide and water.

Figures 33 and 34 illustrate ATP formation during the breakdown of glucose and palmitic acid, a 16-carbon fatty acid, and include tabulations of ATP production. These illustrations are not meant to be an exercise in the study of biochemical pathways (subject matter for a course in biochemistry) but to show why the yield of ATP is maximal when fatty acids are oxidized to carbon dioxide and minimal when glucose is anaerobically degraded to lactic acid.

Let us follow first the **ATP yields from the anaerobic and aerobic breakdown of glu-**

cose. To begin with, it should be noted that ATP is synthesized by **two different kinds of reactions.** In one (shown in **steps 6 and 8**) the high-energy phosphate of chemical intermediates is directly transferred to ADP (adenosine diphosphate) to form ATP. (In prior steps, uptake of inorganic phosphate is associated with the formation of high-energy bonds.) The synthesis of ATP in this way is the only source of ATP under anaerobic conditions and a source as well during aerobic breakdown of glucose. Reaction 14 also involves the synthesis of ATP by phosphate transfer (from guanosine triphosphate, abbreviated GTP) but occurs only when the oxidative pathway is functioning. The other reaction sequence for the synthesis of ATP, which accounts for most of the ATP, occurs only under aerobic conditions and involves the *electron transport chain* of the mitochondrial membrane, mentioned earlier. In this pathway, pairs of electrons and hydrogen ions are removed from chemical intermediates (**steps 5, 9b, 12, 13, 15 and 17**) and are delivered to the electron transport chain (also called the respiratory chain). At three steps, shown in Figure 33, energy built into the chain as electrons pass through it is coupled to the synthesis of ATP from ADP and inorganic phosphate. Note that when NAD (nicotinamide adenine dinucleotide) is the electron carrier (called reduced NAD and written NADH + H when transporting electrons) the electrons enter the beginning of the chain and three ATP's are produced for each pair of electrons passing through it. When FAD (flavin adenine dinucleotide) is the electron carrier, two ATP's are produced for each pair of electrons, since the electrons enter the chain after the first ATP is produced. In the last step of the electron transport sequence, oxygen combines with the pair of electrons and two hydrogen ions to form water. If oxygen is absent, the electron transport scheme cannot function. What happens, then, when electrons cannot be delivered to the electron transport chain? The key is step 9a. Under anaerobic conditions electrons picked up in step 5 are given up in step 9a, with the conversion of pyruvic acid to lactic acid. The coupling of steps 5 and 9a is especially significant because it allows NAD to recycle to step 5 after releasing the pair of electrons in step 9a. Thus, the reaction sequence can continue to steps that result in a net gain of two ATP's in the absence of oxygen. The coupling of these two reactions also explains why lactic acid is the end product of the anaerobic pathway. When oxygen is present, the electrons picked up in step 5 are delivered to the electron transport chain, and lactic acid is **not** formed. Rather, pyruvic acid is converted to acetyl-CoA, which enters a cyclic pathway known as the Krebs, or citric acid, cycle, where its carbons are converted to carbon dioxide. The cycle is a rich source of electrons for the electron transport chain. In the aerobic pathway the net yield of ATP is 38. In the tabulation of the net ATP formation, the factor 2 is used because after step 4 two molecules of each intermediate are present for each initial glucose molecule.

ATP formation from the breakdown of the 16-carbon fatty acid, palmitic acid, can be considered in two stages: 1) disruption to eight acetyl-CoA units by a stepwise sequence which removes 2-carbon fragments one at a time, and 2) entry of the acetyl-CoA's into the Krebs cycle. The second stage, of course, is common to the oxidation of glucose and fatty acids. Since fatty acids contain more hydrogen atoms per carbon atom than glucose, more electrons and hydrogen ions can be removed from fatty acids than from glucose and delivered to the respiratory chain.

As illustrated in Figure 34, each time a 2-carbon fragment is split off palmitic acid to form acetyl-CoA, five ATP's are produced. The net yield from seven cleavages and the passage of eight acetyl-CoA fragments through the Krebs cycle is 130 ATP's per mole of palmitic acid. This is about $3\frac{1}{2}$ times the ATP yield per mole of glucose. Since the molecular weights of palmitic acid and glucose are 256 and 180, respectively, the *net yield of ATP per gram of palmitic acid comes to about $2\frac{1}{2}$ times the yield per gram of glucose.*

Fatty acids have more potential energy in their chemical bonds than does glucose and, as we have seen, oxidation of fatty acids makes more energy available to the cell as ATP than oxidation of glucose. The efficiency of the transfer of energy to ATP from these two fuels is about the same. A mole of glucose, for example, burned in a calorimeter generates about 686,000 calories. Thirty-eight moles of ATP yield

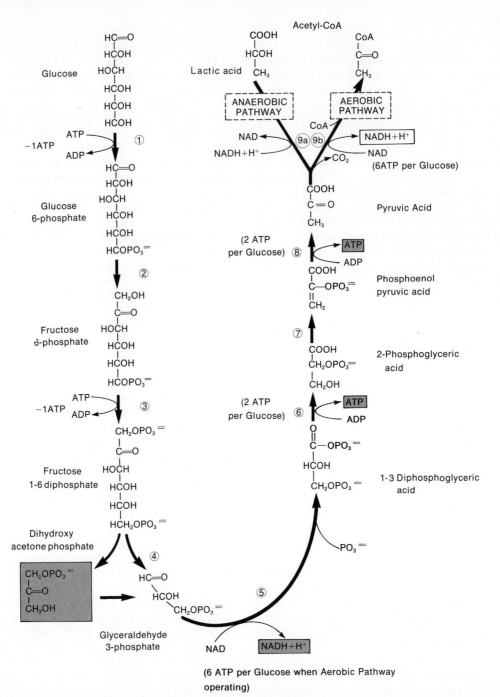

Figure 33. ATP production by the breakdown of glucose anaerobically (in the absence of oxygen) to lactic acid and aerobically (in the presence of oxygen) to carbon dioxide and water is depicted on these two pages. The anaerobic pathway yields a net of only two molecules of ATP; the aerobic pathway yields a net of 38 molecules of ATP. Most of the ATP produced aerobically is accounted for by the delivery of pairs of electrons (removed at reactions 5 and 9b in the steps leading to the formation of acetyl-CoA and reactions 12, 13, 15 and 17 in the Krebs cycle) to the electron transport (respiratory) chain. The electron carriers are abbreviated NAD (known as reduced NAD and written NADH+H$^+$ when carrying electrons) and FAD (reduced FAD, written FADH$_2$). ATP is produced at three sites in the chain when electrons are delivered by reduced NAD and at two sites when reduced FAD is the carrier. In the absence of oxygen, ATP is produced only at reactions 6 and 8 by the direct transfer of phosphate from chemical intermediates to ADP. Since the respiratory chain does not function in the absence of oxygen, electrons removed in reaction 5 under anaerobic conditions are given up in reaction 9a and the regenerated NAD is recycled to reaction 5. The letter Q in the electron transport chain represents coenzyme Q, or ubiquinone, a lipid-soluble, electron-transferring component. The letters b, c, a and a$_3$ designate the order of cytochromes, iron-containing, electron-transferring proteins.

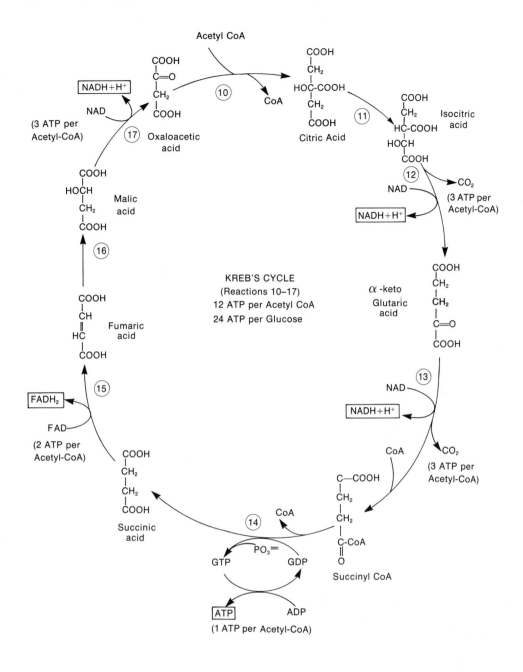

Acetyl CoA

NADH+H⁺

NAD

(3 ATP per Acetyl-CoA)

17 Oxaloacetic acid

10

CoA

Citric Acid

11

Isocitric acid

12

CO_2

NAD

(3 ATP per Acetyl-CoA)

NADH+H⁺

Malic acid

16

α-keto Glutaric acid

KREB'S CYCLE
(Reactions 10–17)
12 ATP per Acetyl CoA
24 ATP per Glucose

13

NAD

NADH+H⁺

Fumaric acid

15

FADH₂

FAD

(2 ATP per Acetyl-CoA)

CoA

CO_2

(3 ATP per Acetyl-CoA)

Succinic acid

14

CoA

Succinyl CoA

GTP PO_3⁼   GDP

ATP   ADP

(1 ATP per Acetyl-CoA)

ADP + PO_3⁼   ADP + PO_3⁼   ADP + PO_3⁼

NADH + H⁺   FAD   Fe⁺⁺ Fe⁺⁺⁺ Fe⁺⁺   Fe⁺⁺⁺ Fe⁺⁺   ½ O_2

Water formed from oxygen atoms 2 electrons and 2 hydrogen ions

Q   b   c   a   a₃

NAD   FADH₂ Fe⁺⁺⁺ Fe⁺⁺ Fe⁺⁺⁺ Fe⁺⁺ Fe⁺⁺⁺ H_2O

ATP   ATP   ·ATP

ELECTRON TRANSPORT CHAIN

ATP PRODUCTION DURING BREAKDOWN OF GLUCOSE

REACTION NUMBER		1	3	5	6	8	9b	10–17
ATP YIELD	AEROBIC 38 net	−1	−1	6	2	2	6	24
PER GLUCOSE	ANAEROBIC 2 net	−1	−1		2	2		

Figure 33 *Continued.*

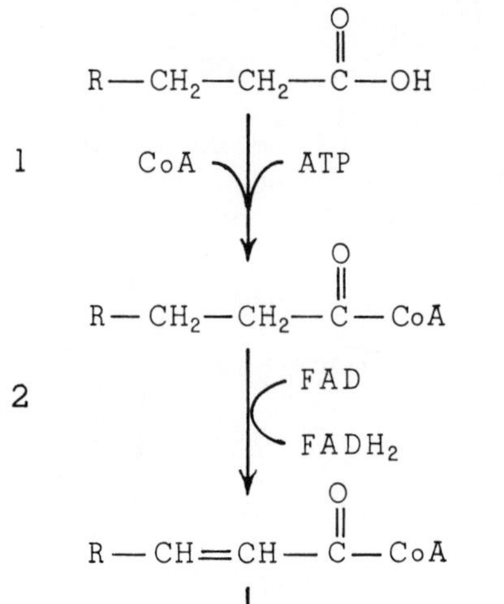

Figure 34. Sequence of reactions leading to the splitting off of the terminal two carbons of a fatty acid with the formation of acetyl-CoA. R represents the remainder of the fatty acid chain. Reactions 2 to 6 are repeated until the fatty acid is completely cleaved. In the case of palmitic acid, a 16-carbon fatty acid, cleavage occurs seven times, and eight molecules of acetyl-CoA are formed. Their passage through the Krebs cycle (Fig. 33) yields 8 × 12, or 96, molecules of ATP. Each sequence leading to the formation of a single molecule of acetyl-CoA yields five molecules of ATP—two resulting from the transport to the respiratory chain of electrons removed in step 2 and three from the transport to the respiratory chain of electrons removed in step 4 (see Fig. 33). Since palmitic acid is cleaved seven times, this produces 7 × 5, or 35, molecules of ATP. The complete oxidation of palmitic acid to carbon dioxide and water, therefore, yields 96 + 35, or 131, molecules of ATP. Subtracting one ATP used in the initial activation step, the net yield is 130 molecules of ATP.

38×8000, or 304,000, calories. Thus the efficiency of energy conversion is $\frac{304,000}{686,000} \times 100$, or approximately 44 per cent. The efficiency for fatty acids is about the same.

Enzymatic Action. As we have indicated, the cell is able to carry out chemical reactions under the limited physical and chemical conditions necessary for its existence (low temperature and pressure, and almost neutral pH) because of the presence of enzymes, the large protein molecules that act as catalysts to speed up the rates of chemical reactions. Without enzymes, reactions would proceed so slowly that life could not exist. Most enzymes are highly specific in their activity, each type being involved in only one reaction.

The word *enzyme* was coined from two Greek words meaning in yeast. Subsequent to Pasteur's discovery that the souring of milk and wine and fermentation of sugars depend upon the presence of contaminating yeast cells, it was found that yeast juice could also ferment sugars. Eventually, the study of these so-called cell-free extracts led to the discovery of enzymes, all of which were found to be proteins. The protein chains in enzymes are coiled and folded into various globular shapes. How enzymes function has been a subject of intense study by biochemists. For a long time it was believed that the *substrate* (substance acted upon by the enzyme) and the enzyme fitted together rigidly, as a key fits a lock, at a part of the enzyme called the active site. Interaction of substrate and enzyme at this site, it was thought, reduced the energy needed for chemical change. However, several lines of evidence, including x-ray analysis, which has revealed that parts of the enzyme molecule move with respect to one another when the substrate is bound to the active site, suggest that the lock and key model is incorrect. A more acceptable model, the "induced fit" model, formulated largely by Daniel Koshland and colleagues, proposes that the shape of the active site is not exactly complementary to that of the substrate, but is induced to take a complementary shape in the same way a glove takes the shape of a hand. This change causes distortions and other modifications of the substrate, leading to its rupture or activation. The "induced fit" model of enzyme action is consistent with the growing recognition that many actions of proteins, including, as already discussed, their action as carriers for active transport in cell membranes, involve changes in protein shape.

CELL REPRODUCTION

In the introductory history of the cell principle (page 23) it was pointed out that since the latter part of the 19th century biologists have agreed that new cells arise from preexisting parent cells. From their original formation, cells are continually growing and, eventually, reach a size (usually about double) at which they must either stop growing or divide. In the human body all populations of cells, except highly differentiated cells, such as nerve cells, are capable of undergoing cell division. In some regions of the body, such as in the skin, the lining of the intestines, and the blood cell forming system of the red bone marrow, cell division proceeds continuously under precise control so that the renewal rate exactly compensates for the death rate. Some parts of the body, such as the liver and kidneys, have been described as "discontinuous replicators." Cells in these organs divide at a low "wear and tear" replacement rate. Cells of the immunological defense system are an interesting special case. They multiply rapidly in response to contact with specific, harmful microorganisms or other foreign matter. Although the mechanism by which the rate of cell division is controlled is still not well understood, one widely discussed theory has received some experimental support. This theory proposes a negative feedback system in which the release of an inhibitor of cell division by mature cells of a given tissue controls cell proliferation of immature cells in that tissue. Substances that inhibit cell division, called **chalones** (a term derived from a Greek word meaning to slack off the main sheet of a sloop to slow it down), have been extracted from a variety of tissues. Chalones act only on the tissues from which they have been isolated. It is generally believed that the tissue specificity depends upon interaction between the chalones and the outer surface of the cell membrane. Loss of chalones, by wounds or surgical removal of large portions of an organ such as the liver, it is presumed,

stimulates cell division until repair or replacement is accomplished.

The Cell Cycle

In populations of dividing cells, the sequence of growth and cell division is generally referred to as the *cell cycle*. The period of cell division is called *mitosis;* the period of growth between divisions is known as *interphase*. During one phase of the latter period DNA replicates. This phase of the cell cycle (typically lasting about six hours) is designated the *S phase*, to signify that DNA synthesis is taking place. Periods of growth prior to and following the S phase are designated G_1 and G_2, respectively. G_1 usually lasts about eight hours, but in a long cell cycle lasts much longer. G_2 usually lasts about five hours. Mitosis, designated *M*, lasts about one hour.

Stages of Mitosis (Fig. 35)

PROPHASE. 1. Chromosome: The DNA protein complex (chromatin network of threads) becomes coiled, and chromosomes can easily be seen on stained sections. As the chromosomes become larger, they can be seen to be duplicated into two highly coiled strands (chromatids) which are attached to one another by a centromere.

2. Nucleolus: During the last part of prophase, the nucleolus disappears.

3. Nuclear membrane: The nuclear membrane disappears during the late prophase period.

4. Centrioles: Each pair of centrioles migrates to the opposite side of the cell and a figure called the *mitotic spindle* is formed which extends from one centriole pair to the other. The spindle is composed of thin fibrils, or *astral rays*.

METAPHASE. 1. Chromosomes: The chromosomes move toward the center of the cell and arrange themselves in a plane perpendicular to a line connecting the two centrioles. This plane is called the equatorial plate.

2. Nucleolus: Absent.

3. Nuclear membrane: Absent.

4. Centrioles and spindle: The thin fibrils

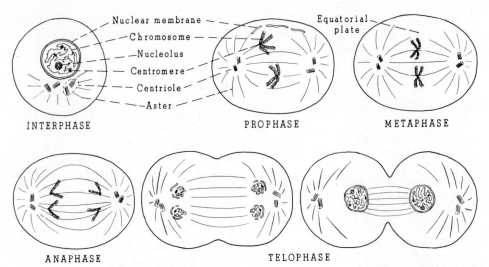

Figure 35. Mitosis, showing details of division. Shown are a pair of identical (homologous) chromosomes. Prior to the onset of mitosis, DNA replicates, giving rise to the double-stranded chromosomes that become apparent during mitosis. In prophase the two strands of each chromosome, attached to a common centromere, can be clearly seen. In metaphase the centromeres of the double-stranded chromosomes are lined up along the equatorial plate. The centromeres divide and, during anaphase, the single strands move toward the centrioles at opposite poles of the cell. The end results of mitosis are two daughter cells with the same genetic composition as the original parent cell.

from the centrioles appear to be attached to the chromosomes at the centromere.

ANAPHASE. 1. Chromosomes: The centromere divides, releasing the members of the chromatid pair from each other.

2. Nucleolus: Absent.

3. Nuclear membrane: Absent.

4. Centrioles and spindle: The astral ray fibrils give the appearance of pulling the chromatids toward the opposite centrioles by their attachments to the centromeres. When the chromatids have been separated from each other, they are again called chromosomes. The significant feature of this stage is that one chromatid from each chromosome finds its way into each daughter cell, giving each cell an identical complement of chromosomes.

TELOPHASE. 1. Chromosomes: The chromosomes reach the general location of the centrioles and begin to uncoil.

2. Nucleolus: A nucleolus appears in each cell.

3. Nuclear membrane: The nuclear membrane re-forms around each group of chromosomes.

4. Centrioles and spindle: As the chromosomes uncoil the spindle disappears.

5. Cell membrane: The cell membrane indents at the point of the equatorial plate, dividing the cytoplasm into two parts.

Mitosis permits perpetuation. There is a duplication of all cell parts with provision for transmitting a controlling mechanism into each of the cells produced. The details of the process are obscure, but the task is obviously performed with efficiency and accuracy, considering that it occurs more than a billion times during human development.

Chromosome Number

Number of Chromosomes in the Human Cell. There are 23 pairs, or 46 chromosomes, in human somatic, or body, cells and 23 in the gametes (sperm or ova). In Figure 36, illustrating the chromosomes of human body cells, note that the members of 22 of these pairs are exactly alike, that these identical pairs can be distinguished from one another by overall length and the position of the centromeres and that they are numbered from 1 to 22 in order of decreasing size. The 22 *homologous* (G. *homos,* one and the same) pairs, called *autosomes,* bear genes for the same traits. The 23rd pair, designated X and Y, are the sex chromosomes. Females have two X chromosomes, males one X and one Y. Genes present only on the larger X chro-

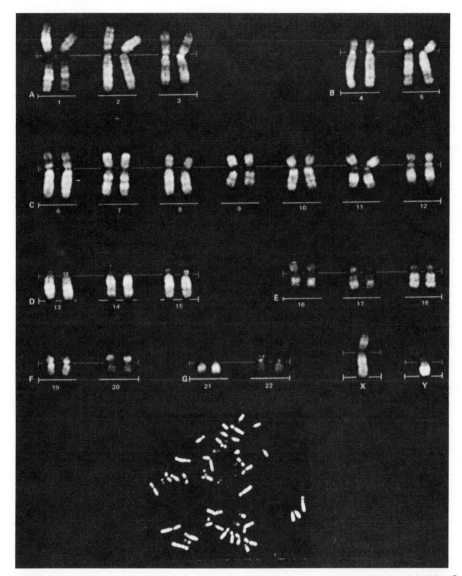

Figure 36. Normal human male karyotype, stained with quinacrine mustard dihydrochloride (Q-banded). The term karyotype refers to this standard arrangement, in which homologous chromosomes are identified by their length and the position of the centromere joining the separate strands of each chromosome and numbered in order of decreasing size. Chromosomes X and Y are the sex chromosomes. (Courtesy of Douglas Hepburn, Clinical Cytogenetics Laboratory, University of Oregon Health Sciences Center.)

mosome (the gene for color blindness, for example) are called sex-linked genes.

Meiosis. Body cells containing two of each type of chromosomes are described as diploid. Gametes, containing only one type of each, are called haploid cells. Meiosis is a special two-step sequence of cell division, occurring during the maturation of sex cells, in which the diploid number of chromosomes is reduced to the haploid number. The first division of the sequence is called the reduction division. At metaphase of the reduction division, double-stranded homologous chromosomes line up as pairs (synaptic pairs), rather than individually, in a row (Fig. 37). Each member of the pair is pulled to the opposite pole of the cell. Thus, reduction division gives rise to two cells containing one set of double-stranded chromosomes. The second division, mitotic division of the two daughter cells, will produce (if all cells formed survive) four

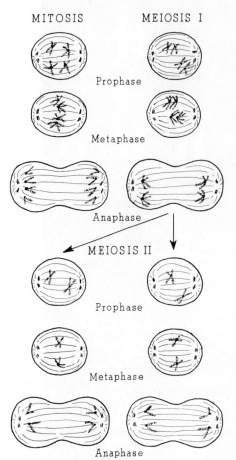

MITOSIS   MEIOSIS I

Prophase

Metaphase

Anaphase

MEIOSIS II

Prophase

Metaphase

Anaphase

Figure 37. Prophase, metaphase, and anaphase compared in mitosis and the two divisions of meiosis. Parent cells containing two pairs of chromosomes are shown to illustrate both processes. In prophase, each chromosome can be seen as a double strand (each strand called a chromatid). The four chromosomes lie apart in mitosis and as two paris (synaptic pairs) in meiosis I (the reduction division). During mitosis the four chromosomes are lined up in a single row along the equatorial plate in metaphase, and in anaphase the individual strands of each separate and are pulled to opposite poles. Completion of cell division results in two daughter cells, each containing two pairs of single-stranded chromosomes. In the reduction division, the synaptic pairs line up along the equatorial plate during metaphase, and in anaphase one member of each pair (still double-stranded) is pulled to the opposite pole. Reduction division gives rise to two cells, each containing one double-stranded member of each pair of chromosomes. When the second (mitotic) division of meiosis takes place and the double strands separate, each daughter cell receives one single-stranded member of each chromosome pair and thus contains half as many (haploid number) chromosomes as the parent cell. In humans, meiosis reduces the number of chromosomes from 46 in nonsexual cells to 23 in sperm and egg cells.

haploid gametes. In humans, four mature sperm cells but only one mature ovum (one cell surviving each division) are produced from each parent cell by the process of meiosis. The production of sex cells will be discussed in greater detail in Chapter 17.

CELLULAR GENETICS

The Gene

The science of genetics began over a hundred years ago when an Austrian monk, Gregor Mendel, watched successive generations of peas grow. Noting the specific gross characteristics of successive generations of plants, Mendel came to conceive the genetic information in terms of *units*, now called **genes** (from the Greek "to be born."). Thus, there is a gene for each characteristic — such as weight, color of flower, etc. — contributed to the fertilized seed by each parent. He also developed the ideas of dominant and recessive genes to explain the greater frequency of regular occurrence of one parent's trait over the other's. For instance, the gene determining a white flower was dominant and the gene for a red flower was recessive, so that the offspring of parents, each with a long ancestral history of only one of these genes, would tend to have more white flowers than red. Figure 38 illustrates this basic principle in the case of the inheritance of black (dominant) and white (recessive) coat colors in rabbits. Note that the recessive trait is visible *only* in the pure condition (both genes expressing white color).

Mendel published his findings in 1866, but they did not become known to the scientific world until about 1900. At that time they were "rediscovered," principally by the Dutch biologist Hugo De Vries, who was searching for a theoretical explanation for the phenomenon of *mutation*, a sudden change in the character of a species, now ascribed to a change in a gene. Mendel's principles are now, of course, an established part of the science of genetics. Experimental proof in the 1940's that DNA is the genetic matter of chromosomes marked the beginning of modern *molecular genetics*, the biochemical approach to understanding genic activity, distinct from the traditional Mendelian analysis using breeding experiments.

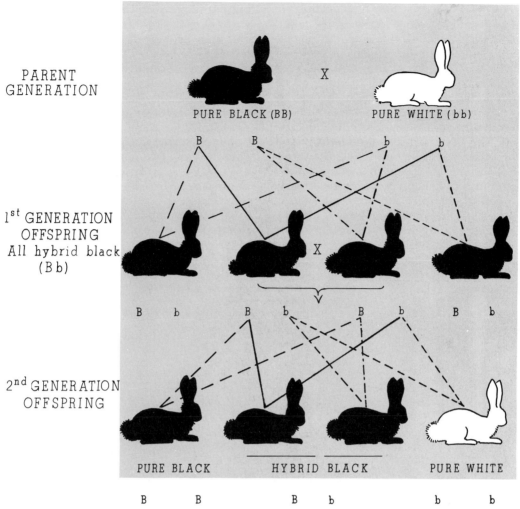

PARENT
GENERATION

PURE BLACK (BB) X PURE WHITE (bb)

B B b b

1st GENERATION
OFFSPRING
All hybrid black
(Bb)

X

B b B b B b B b

2nd GENERATION
OFFSPRING

PURE BLACK HYBRID BLACK PURE WHITE

B B B b b b

Figure 38. Simple Mendelian inheritance in coat color in rabbits, showing dominance of black coat color.

DNA and the Genetic Code

Proof that DNA is the genetic substance of chromosomes is generally credited to Oswald T. Avery and colleagues. In 1944 Avery, in collaboration with Colin M. MacLeod and Maclyn McCarty, reported that a mutant strain of pneumococcus that had lost the ability to manufacture a polysaccharide capsule which protected it against the body's defenses and was, therefore, unable to cause pneumonia (in mammals) could be transformed into a normal virulent type by adding to the culture of the mutant strain a "transforming principle" identified as DNA that had been extracted from the virulent strain. This work was not widely appreciated when it was published because it did not fit into the accepted body of knowledge

of the time. The chief stumbling block was the belief that DNA was a uniform structure composed of a single repeating unit (a tetranucleotide) and was, therefore, incapable of containing coded genetic information. By the late 1940's it was apparent from accumulated data that DNA was not a uniform structure. In the early 1950's it was reported that when a bacteriophage, a bacterial virus, infected a host bacterium most of the DNA of the virus entered the cell whereas most of its protein remained behind. These findings, among others, led to the general acceptance of the belief that DNA was, indeed, the genetic substance.

The publication by Watson and Crick in 1954 of the *double helix model* of DNA was certainly one of the most exciting events in the history of science. DNA, as we have already mentioned, is one type of nucleic acid (substances composed of units called nucleotides). In DNA the nucleotide components are a 5-carbon sugar called *deoxyribose*, a phosphate group, and one of 4 nitrogenous bases, namely, *adenine, guanine, thymine* or *cytosine* (Fig. 39). Thus, four different nucleotides, each containing a different nitrogenous base, are the constituent units of DNA. In the **double helix** model formulated by Watson and Crick, the molecule has the appearance of a chain ladder twisted into the shape of a spiral staircase. Two linear chains formed by alternating units of phosphate and sugar are linked by pairs of bases (attached to the sugar units) which form the rungs of the ladder (Figs. 40 and 41). The **base pairing** is quite specific: adenine is always linked to thymine, guanine always to cytosine. The specific base

pairing is an essential feature of the molecule. Thus, a sequence of bases attached to one strand, for example, one denoted by the letters G-A-A-C-T-G, is matched by a **complementary** sequence, C-T-T-G-A-C, on the other. The nucleotide units in the DNA polymer are held together by strong (covalent) bonds between the phosphate and sugar units in each chain. Weak hydrogen bonds (described on page 28) between base pairs link the two chains.

As Watson and Crick pointed out in their original description of the double helix, the model can explain how DNA functions, that is to say, the model can explain how DNA can be replicated (a necessary event before cell division to provide each daughter cell with copies of the genetic substance) and how coded information for the synthesis of enzymes and other proteins can be built

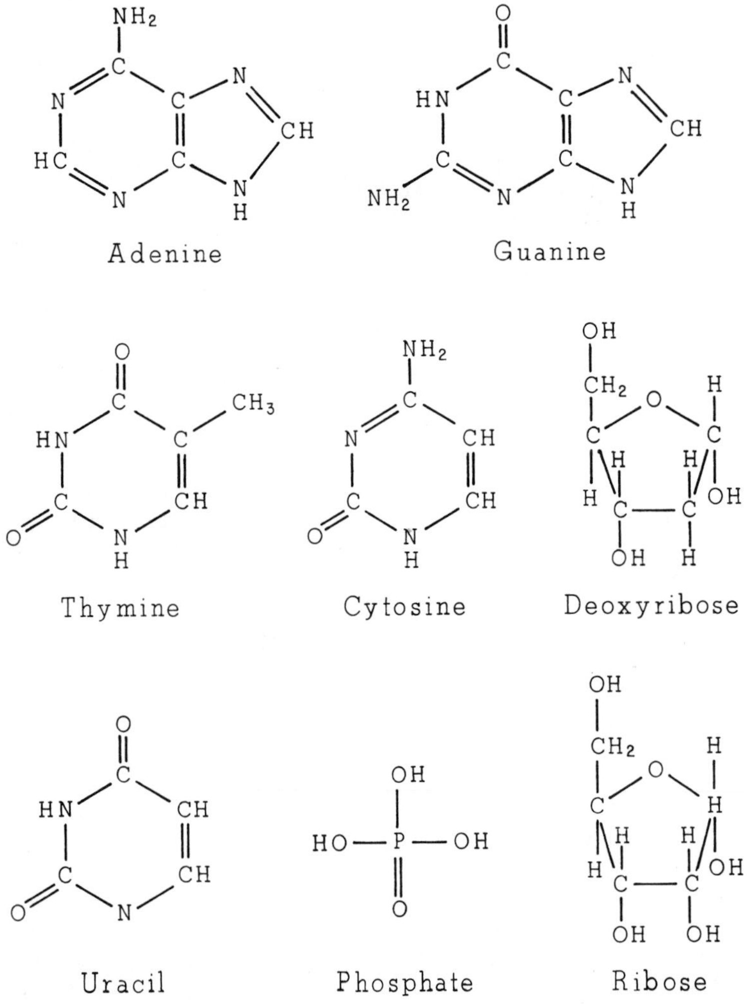

Figure 39. Components of DNA and RNA. DNA is constructed from basic units called nucleotides, each of which consists of one of four nitrogen-containing bases, adenine, guanine, thymine, or cytosine, the 5-carbon sugar deoxyribose, and a phosphate. In RNA, similarly built, ribose replaces deoxyribose and uracil replaces thymine. The bases adenine and guanine are called purines; thymine, cytosine, and uracil are called pyrimidines.

Figure 40. Chemical structure and diagrammatic representation of a segment of a DNA molecule and its components. (Courtesy of Richard Lyons, M.D.)

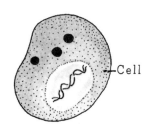

Cell

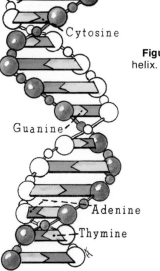

Figure 41. Diagrammatic representation of DNA helix.

into its structure (the very nature of a cell, remember, depends upon the kinds of enzymes it possesses).

Let us first consider **DNA replication.** Note that each half of double-stranded DNA is a complement of the other half. If the two chains are separated (by severing the weak hydrogen bonds joining base pairs), one half of the molecule can serve as a template for the synthesis of the other half. The specific pairing of bases during synthesis will ensure that the nucleotides are lined up in a sequence exactly complementary to that of the template. The newly synthesized complementary chains can then join to form an exact copy of the original double helix.

Now let us consider the process of **directing protein synthesis.** A protein, as mentioned earlier, consists of amino acids linked together in long chains that are coiled and twisted into various shapes. There are 20 different amino acids; the order in which they are joined is unique for each protein and determines its shape and function. If a section of the double strand of DNA is parted, a sequence of bases will be exposed on each chain. The first letter of the four bases on the exposed chain, A-G-C-T, can be thought of as a 4-letter alphabet from which words can be constructed, each word representing a specific amino acid. A *gene is now defined* as a DNA segment with a sufficient number of word sequences to code for the synthesis of a protein. Experiments conducted in the 1960's established that a specific sequence of three consecutive bases is a code word for a single amino acid.

As mentioned in the section describing cell organelles, proteins are synthesized on cytoplasmic bodies called ribosomes. To carry the base sequences specifying the order of amino acids in a protein to the site of protein synthesis, the code of a gene is copied into a type of nucleic acid called, appropriately enough, **messenger RNA,** which migrates to the ribosomes. In the copying process (known as **transcription**) the base sequence of the gene serves as a template for the synthesis of a complementary chain of messenger RNA. Messenger RNA is a single strand and, in distinction to DNA, contains the 5-carbon sugar *ribose* instead of deoxyribose (hence RNA) and the nitrogenous base *uracil* instead of thymine (Fig. 39). In the genetic code dictionary the word sequences, called **codons,** are given with the letters representing the bases in

Table 4.   AMINO ACIDS AND THEIR RNA CODE WORDS

AMINO ACIDS	RNA CODE WORDS					
Alanine (Ala)	GCU	GCC	GCA	GCG		
Arginine (Arg)	CGU	CGC	CGA	CGG	AGA	AGG
Asparagine (Asn)	AAU	AAC				
Aspartic acid (Asp)	GAU	GAC				
Cysteine (Cys)	UGU	UGC				
Glutamic acid (Glu)	GAA	GAG				
Glutamine (Gln)	CAA	CAG				
Glycine (Gly)	GGU	GGC	GGA	GGG		
Histidine (His)	CAU	CAC				
Isoleucine (Ileu)	AUU	AUC	AUA			
Leucine (Leu)	CUU	CUC	CUA	CUG	UUA	UUG
Lysine (Lys)	AAA	AAG				
Methionine (Met)	AUG					
Phenylalanine (Phe)	UUU	UUC				
Proline (Pro)	CCU	CCC	CCA	CCG		
Serine (Ser)	UCU	UCC	UCA	UCG	AGU	AGC
Threonine (Thr)	ACU	ACC	ACA	ACG		
Tryptophan (Tryp)	UGG					
Tyrosine (Tyr)	UAU	UAC				
Valine (Val)	GUU	GUC	GUA	GUG		

The above listing of codons accounts for 61 of 64 possible triplet combinations. The remaining three, UGA, UAA, and UAG, are signals for ending protein chains.

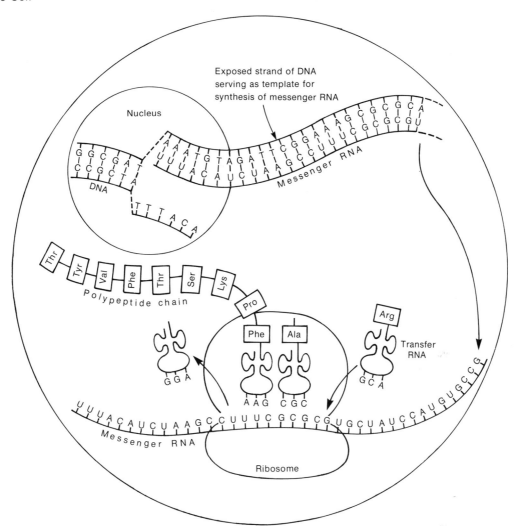

Figure 42. Schematic representation of the synthesis of a protein from instructions coded in a gene. The base sequence of a segment of one strand of DNA is transcribed in the nucleus into a complementary sequence in messenger RNA. Specific base triplets in messenger RNA, called codons, represent words for 20 amino acids, from which a protein is constructed. Messenger RNA passes from the nucleus to a ribosome in the cytoplasm. The code is "read" by transfer RNA's, each of which contains a triplet called an anticodon, complementary to a codon. A transfer RNA picks up a particular amino acid (each amino acid has one or more of its own transfer RNA's), carries it to the ribosome, and engages briefly in an anticodon-codon linkage. The illustration shows phenylalanine transfer RNA at the end of a short polypeptide chain connected to a complementary codon. Alanine transfer RNA is alongside it. When the ribosome moves to the right, alanine transfer RNA will displace phenylalanine transfer RNA, and alanine will be added to the growing chain.

messenger RNA. Since, in transcription, uracil rather than thymine is the complement of adenine, the letters of codons are U, C, A and G (Table 4).

As a protein is synthesized, the placement of amino acids in the sequence dictated by the triplet sequences in messenger RNA is made possible by the action of another type of RNA, called **transfer RNA**. Transfer RNA's combine with specific amino acids and bring them to the site of protein synthesis. There is a specific transfer RNA

for each of the 20 amino acids incorporated into proteins, and associated with each is an activating enzyme that promotes capture of the proper amino acid. Each transfer RNA has a triplet sequence, called an **anticodon,** appropriate for the amino acid it is transporting, that recognizes the relevant codon on messenger RNA. A temporary codon-anticodon linkage places the amino acids in the proper order as the protein is synthesized. Ribosomes apparently play a role as mechanical devices that hold in place both the growing polypeptide chain and each newly arrived transfer RNA with its bound amino acid (Fig. 42).

Genic Mutations

The mechanics of mutations are not well understood, but at this point, it seems they all result from one or more structural changes in the genic DNA. Such changes may involve (1) substitution in one or more of the base pairs, (2) subtraction of one or more base pairs, (3) addition of one or more base pairs, or (4) combinations of the foregoing. These changes are heritable, provided they are not lethal, because each segment of a DNA molecule (gene) is capable of duplicating itself.

Since the code for a specific protein starts at one end of the gene, if a single addition or subtraction occurs near the start of a genic series, the whole code is disrupted and the entire gene becomes inoperative. If, however, a subtraction occurs near the beginning and is *balanced* by an addition nearby, most of the gene triplets will be unchanged. The gene will then continue to function with slightly altered characteristics. Changes resulting in the alteration of one triplet, assuming it remains a triplet, might summon a single different amino acid into a protein change. This, indeed, appears to be the case in certain heritable diseases. For instance, in sickle cell anemia the hemoglobin molecule differs from the normal one by substitution of one amino acid, namely, valine for glutamic acid. From the genetic code dictionary on page 52 it can be seen that this substitution can be accounted for by a single base change, A to U in the middle position of either codon for glutamic acid.

Genetic Biology

What does genetic biology mean to medicine? Scientists are becoming increasingly aware that a number of clinical conditions may be the result of alterations in certain enzymes caused by a faulty or ineffective mechanism of the protein construction information stored in normal DNA. Many disorders arise because the structure of the ribosome on which enzymatic proteins are formed is defective. DNA controls the configuration of the ribosome through its coding of ribosomal RNA. Abnormal hemoglobin disorders, such as sickle cell anemia, are caused by substitution of only one out of approximately 300 amino acids forming the hemoglobin molecule. Some deformities are obvious, like Down's syndrome (Mongolism), which occurs once in every 600 births and is caused by the presence of an extra chromosome. Others, which have more subtle symptoms and are less easily spotted, result from the defective gene failing to order the synthesis of an essential enzyme needed to trigger or mediate various biochemical reactions.

Cystic fibrosis, characterized by abnormal secretion of certain glands and respiratory tract blockage that can lead to death by pneumonia, is the most common inborn error of metabolism. It is believed to be the product of a single defective gene. These are only a few in a list of many diseases that may be related to genetic factors. By 1972, scientists had succeeded in identifying more than 400 such defects and the list is still growing. To name a few: myopia, astigmatism, retinoblastoma (cancer of the retina), psoriasis, polydactyly (extra toes or fingers), muscular dystrophy, spastic paraplegia, diabetes and hemophilia.

Using the principles of Mendelian genetics, one can predict the mathematical odds by which two people will conceive a child with a genetic defect, *given* a good history of the conditions suffered by their ancestors and relations. For instance, if both parents carry the trait for sickle cell anemia, which is recessive, the odds are one in four that each of their children will have the disease. If only one parent carries the trait, he or she can pass the trait but not the disease itself to the offspring. If the gene involved is dominant (Fig. 38), the chances of passing it on are much greater. Huntington's chorea is a degenerative nerve disease that strikes its victims at around age 40 and is always fatal. If one parent carries the defective gene, there is a 50 per cent chance that each of his children will inherit it.

Amniocentesis. However, another technique recently devised gives doctors the ability to test for some genetic defects early in pregnancy, giving parents the option of therapeutic abortion if the results show definite deformity. The procedure, known as *amniocentesis*, involves inserting a long needle through the pregnant mother's abdomen and drawing off a small sample of amniotic fluid, the liquid in which the fetus floats. Fetal skin cells which slough off into the amniotic fluid during development are then placed in a nutrient bath, where they continue to grow. By examining these cells microscopically and analyzing them chemically, doctors can detect the presence of many genetic diseases.

Amniocentesis, performed between the 13th and 18th weeks of pregnancy is extremely accurate, but it is not without risk to both mother and child. As a consequence, until the procedure becomes less hazardous it will probably be used only when the family history or other factors strongly indicate presence of a genetic problem. Down's syndrome is one of the most easily detected defects by the new technique and, since it is known to be far more prevalent in pregnancies of older women than younger, it has been suggested that all pregnant women over the age of 40 be screened and offered therapeutic abortion when the test is positive. It is estimated that this policy could reduce the incidence of Down's syndrome by about 50 per cent. However, many genetic diseases (sickle cell anemia, for instance) are not detectable *in utero* by amniocentesis.

Eventually, it may be possible to *restore* the synthesis of a missing enzyme by providing the correct code for that enzyme in the form of RNA from normal cells.

It takes little imagination to foresee a future sequence of events. First, a particular coded gene in the formation of insulin could be located within the germ plasm of the parent. The defective gene could be removed by breaking the bonds holding it to the DNA strand. Finally, a normal gene from the donor could be installed in its place. Given power over heredity, who would exercise it and what would be its limits? This question may perplex man for generations.

In 1967 biochemists at Stanford University synthesized biologically active DNA. This step may lead toward the production of true life in the laboratory. Mendel foresaw the importance of heredity a hundred years ago, but he could not possibly have imagined the role that DNA and the control of the genetic code might play in solving the riddle of a long list of abnormalities, including cancer.

CANCER: ITS NATURE AND CAUSATION

Cancer is a disease of the cell that is recognized and measured by the extent to which the cell deviates from its normal behavior. The ultimate understanding of malignant disease will depend on an equal degree of understanding of the function of the normal cell. This is not yet adequate.

During recent years attention has been given to the growth patterns of cancer cells, for knowledge of cell growth could be the basis of effective treatment. Although development of cancer may require a certain preexisting set of conditions, such as failure of the normal immunologic defenses of the body, it is believed that the initial causative event is a change in a single cell. The cell presumably undergoes permanent changes in its genetic structure, and then in multiplying gives rise to billions of similarly altered cells.

Cancer cells differ from normal cells in a characteristic way. The cancer cell has escaped from the usual mechanisms by which the body controls cell multiplication. In normal, continuously renewing tissues, such as the intestines and the skin, only one of the two daughter cells arising from division of a parent cell will retain the capacity to divide. The other will differentiate, replace a lost cell, die and be shed. In cancer, on the other hand, differentiation apparently does not occur, and virtually all cells of the population grow and divide without restraint. We have mentioned the importance of chalones in regulating cell division in normal cell populations (see page 45). Control of cell division by chalones does not occur in cancer. A perhaps related phenomenon may be the absence of what is known as "contact inhibition" in cancer cell populations. It has been observed, for example, that normal skin cells cultured outside the body grow in a well-ordered monolayer and that cell division ceases when there is no longer a free surface. Tumor cells, in contrast, grow and move about randomly with no evidence of contact inhibition. Normal cells are confined to certain tissues in accordance with the general architecture of the body, whereas cancer cells may leave the original tissue, invade other tissues, and create new growths (metastases) in new body locations.

Interest in basic cancer research has been focused largely on changes in the genes within the cancer cell nucleus caused by viruses. Genes are composed of DNA, which has the ability to reproduce itself and direct the life processes of a cell. Through the intermediary action of RNA, DNA directs the formation of the proteins, the basic structural and functional materials of living organisms. Viruses are likewise composed of a nucleic acid genetic material, capable of reproducing itself, and a protein envelope surrounding the nucleic acid core. Cancer-inducing viruses contain either RNA or DNA as their genetic material, which may represent from a few to several hundred genes.

Studies on the fate of a DNA virus in a tumor cell suggest that a portion of the nucleic acid of the virus persists in the transformed (malignant) cell. Evidence rests in the discovery in such cells of new proteins whose production was specified by some of the genes of the DNA virus. These new proteins are called "virus-specific cellular antigens." A "transplantation antigen," present on the surface of transformed cells, has also been detected. Its presence on the surface of the cell suggests that it may be responsible for the altered relations of malignant cells with neighboring cells. So-called "T-antigens" are found in the nucleus of transformed cells.

Cancer is suspected as being a chance occurrence following a viral infection, which usually results in cell destruction and release of viruses into the blood stream, but which can occasionally result in the incorporation of part of the viral genes into the cell's *genome* (complete set of hereditary factors). The cell-destroying activity of the virus is suppressed, and the transformed cells evolve new functions involving unregulated growth.

Cell Differentiation

In the beginning of this chapter it was pointed out that an individual develops from a single cell, the fertilized ovum (zygote), and that, as cell division proceeds, a stage of development is reached at which cells become differentiated; that is, come to differ in structure and function. Specialized cell types become organized as tissues, each performing its unique functions. How cells differentiate is a question that has intrigued biologists for centuries. In the 1960's, nuclear transplant experiments carried out with frogs settled one aspect of this question—differentiation is not caused by a loss of genes. This had to be the case, since it was demonstrated that normal frogs could develop from an ovum from which the nucleus had been removed and replaced with one taken from a differentiated intestinal (epithelial) cell of a tadpole. Since the differentiated cell had to have a full complement of genes for this to happen, it became apparent that differentiation is accomplished by *switching genes off and on.* This switching continues in differentiated cells throughout the lifetime of an organism as the activities of cells undergo continuous change.

It has been clearly demonstrated that in bacteria, gene activity (that is, the transcription of its base sequence into a complementary sequence in messenger RNA) is regulated by the binding and release of proteins at specific sites on DNA. Some of these **regulatory proteins** have been isolated and identified. Although specific regulatory proteins have not been identified in higher forms of life, there is considerable evidence that such gene regulators do function in higher organisms.

SUMMARY

THE CELL

Importance of the Cell

1. The cell is the structural and functional unit of the body.

   a. The human body develops from a single cell, the fertilized ovum.

History of the Cell

1. Robert Hooke introduced the word *cell* as a biological term in 1665 to describe the boxlike compartments he recognized as basic structural units of plants.

2. In 1838 and 1839 M. J. Schleiden and Theodor Schwann formulated what is known as the cell theory.

    a. Described cells as the fundamental units of structure and function of all living things, capable of carrying out all the processes of life as independent entities and, collectively, as complex systems.

3. Before the end of the 19th century it became understood that

    a. Cells arise by division from preexisting ones

    b. Chromosomes, discrete bodies which take form during cell division, replicate prior to division and serve as the carriers of hereditary traits from one cell generation to the next.

4. In the 1940's DNA, the nucleic acid of chromosomes, was unequivocally identified as the hereditary substance.

    a. Not long afterward the publication of the double helix model of DNA explained how the genetic substance could carry a code in the form of instructions for the synthesis of enzymes and other proteins.

        (1) Since all cellular reactions depend upon the presence of specific enzymes and, in their absence, the constituents of the cell could be neither manufactured nor broken down, it became clear that the nature of a cell is determined by the genetic instructions for the synthesis of enzymes.

Chemical Constituents of Cells and Extracellular Matter

1. The most common organic constituents are classified as

    a. Proteins
    b. Carbohydrates
    c. Lipids
    d. Nucleic acids

2. Proteins: composed of amino acids linked together into long chains, twisted into various shapes.

    a. They serve, among other things, as enzymes, certain hormones, the contractile elements of muscles, a major component of cell membranes, and part of the intercellular framework of connective tissues.

3. Carbohydrates: hydrogen and oxygen atoms linked to carbon atoms in the same ratio as in water. The simple sugar glucose (a monosaccharide) is an important nutrient and supplies most of the energy needs during the absorption of a meal.

    a. Excess is converted to glycogen, a polysaccharide stored in the liver and muscles, and fat.

    b. Protein-polysaccharides (carbohydrates combined with a small amount of protein) form the intercellular ground substance of connective tissues, in which fibrous proteins, principally collagen, are embedded.

4. Lipids: substances that are relatively insoluble in water but soluble in ether and similar solvents. Major subclasses are fats, phospholipids, and steroids.

    a. Fats, or triglycerides: a combination of three fatty acids and glycerol. They are the principal energy stores of the body.

    b. Phospholipids: resemble fats, but one of the fatty acids is replaced by a "polar head"—a phosphate group and nitrogen-containing base. Phospholipids form the structural fabric of cell membranes.

    c. Steroids: constructed from a unit of four carbon rings.

        (1) Cholesterol, the major one, is a component of cell membranes and a precursor of vitamin D, bile acids and the sex and adrenal hormones.

5. Nucleic Acids: consist of nucleotides linked together as long chains. Each nucleotide is composed of a 5-carbon sugar, a phosphate group, and a nitrogen-containing base.

    a. DNA and RNA are examples of nucleic acids.

Structure of the Cell

The principal components of a cell are a **nucleus,** containing the genetic matter, enclosed by a nuclear membrane; **cytoplasm,** the substance outside the nucleus, containing various organelles; and a **cell membrane** enclosing the entire cell.

1. The cell membrane: composed principally of a phospholipid bilayer penetrated partially or completely by randomly distributed proteins.

   a. Regulates interchange between the cell and its environment.
   b. Serves as a receptive surface for substances initiating adaptive changes within the cell.

2. The *cytoplasmic organelles;* each enclosed by its own membrane, include the following:

   a. *Ribosomes:* dense aggregates of RNA and protein, serving as the site of protein synthesis.
   b. *Endoplasmic reticulum:* a network of tubules.
      (1) The rough type, with ribosomes scattered over the surface, functions in the synthesis of proteins that are packaged for secretion or incorporation into lysosomes.
      (2) The smooth type functions in the synthesis of nonprotein substances.
   c. The *Golgi apparatus:* saclike vesicles usually found in stacked piles. Completes the synthesis of and packages proteins to be secreted or retained in lysosomes.
   d. *Lysosomes:* bodies containing digestive enzymes, which function, among other things, in the destruction of harmful microorganisms following phagocytosis and the breakdown of extracellular matter, as in bone, to release stored calcium.
   e. *Mitochondria:* the so-called "powerhouses," where most of the cell's ATP is synthesized.
   f. *Centrioles:* paired structures that become the poles of the cell to which chromosomes migrate during cell division.

Physiology of the Cell

1. Movement of substances across cell membranes is accomplished by

   a. Diffusion
   b. Osmosis
   c. Active transport
   d. Pinocytosis
   e. Phagocytosis

2. *Metabolism*: a general term used to describe all of the chemical reactions occurring in living matter.

   a. Energy metabolism: the degradation of nutrients, principally glucose and fatty acids to produce energy, which is used in turn to synthesize ATP from ADP.
      (1) Splitting the terminal high-energy bond of ATP provides the direct source of energy for most of the work performed by the cell.
      (2) *Glucose* can be degraded either aerobically to carbon dioxide and water or anaerobically to lactic acid.
      (3) *Fatty acids* are degraded aerobically only. Maximum ATP yield is obtained by the breakdown of fatty acids, minimum by the anaerobic degradation of glucose.
   b. In the aerobic process most of the ATP is produced from energy released during the passage of electrons removed from chemical intermediates through the mitochondrial electron transport chain.
      (1) Since the electron transport chain cannot function in the absence of oxygen, ATP is produced during the anaerobic breakdown of glucose only in two steps in which phosphate is directly transferred from chemical intermediates to ADP.

3. Chemical reactions under the conditions of temperature, pressure and pH existing in cells can take place because of *enzyme action*.

   a. Enzymes act as biological catalysts, speeding the rates of reactions but remaining unchanged at the end of the reaction.

Cell Reproduction

1. *Cell cycle*: readily observed in populations of continuously dividing cells, such as the skin and the intestines. A period of growth (*interphase*) is followed by cell division (*mitosis*).

a. During an interval of interphase known as the S phase, DNA replicates.
   (1) Periods of growth occur prior to (called G_1) and following (called G_2) the S phase.
b. Mitosis, the shortest period, can be divided into four stages: prophase, metaphase, anaphase and telophase.
   (1) As a result of DNA synthesis during the S phase of interphase, each chromosome can be seen during prophase to be duplicated into two coiled strands.
   (2) The strands separate and, during anaphase, migrate to opposite sides of the cell so that each daughter cell receives the same number of chromosomes as the original parent cell.
c. *Meiosis* is the 2-stage sequence of cell divisions that produces haploid sex cells. There are 23 pairs of chromosomes in human body cells (diploid number) and half as many (haploid number) in sperm and egg cells.

Cellular Genetics

1. A *gene* can be described as a section of DNA containing coded information for the synthesis of a protein.

a. The concept that genetic traits are transmitted from parent to offspring by discrete units (genes), each parent contributing one for each trait, was introduced by Gregor Mendel over a century ago.

2. DNA consists of two long strands, formed by alternating units of phosphate and deoxyribose, linked by complementary pairs of bases (adenine joined to thymine, guanine to cytosine) spiraled to form the so-called double helix.

a. The order of bases in an individual DNA strand determines the sequence of *amino acids* in proteins. Sequences of three bases (triplets) code for each of the 20 amino acids constituting the building blocks of proteins.
b. The code is carried from DNA to a ribosome in the cytoplasm by "messenger RNA."
c. A code-reading vehicle, transfer RNA, binds and escorts specific amino acids to the ribosome so as to place each amino acid in the order dictated by the triplet sequence in messenger RNA.

Cancer

Cancer cells have escaped the usual mechanism for controlling cell division. Whereas in normal continuously renewing tissues only one of two daughter cells retains the capacity to divide (the other, after replacing a dead cell, in turn dies), in cancer populations all of the cells divide without restraint.

Cell Differentiation

1. During embryological development, cells come to differ in structure and function, and specialized types become organized into tissues.

a. Differentiation is accomplished by switching genes off and on as a result of the binding and release of regulatory proteins at specific sites on DNA.

chapter 3

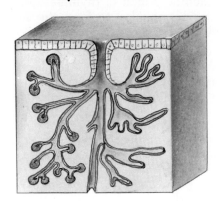

Tissues

Objectives

The aim of this chapter is to enable the student to:

Identify the four basic types of tissue and describe their functions.

Classify epithelial tissues according to shape, arrangement, and function.

List the various types of specialized connective tissue and distinguish their functions.

Define the four types of transplantation of tissue and give examples of each.

Evaluate the three general methods of tissue preservation with respect to longevity and potential future transplant.

Tissues compose all organs and, in turn, all organ systems. It is important to understand these components before individual organs are studied. Even prior to the discovery of the microscope, the integrated pattern of tissues could be seen.

The basic unit of the tissue is the cell. Cells are either tightly packed or separated by interstitial (L. *interstitium,* a place between) material. Tissues are subdivided into four major categories: *epithelial, connective, muscular,* and *nervous.*

EPITHELIAL TISSUE

Epithelial tissue functions in protection, absorption, secretion, and excretion. When serving a protective or absorbent function, epithelial tissue is found in sheets covering a surface, such as the skin. In its secretory function, the epithelial cells involute from the surface into the underlying tissues to form gland structures, specialized for secretion. Only a minimal amount of intercellular substance is found in epithelial tissue,

which is closely knit and not so readily penetrated as other tissues. Epithelial tissues are avascular (lack blood vessels). Nutrition and waste removal are provided by the network of blood vessels in underlying connective tissue. The epidermis and associated derivatives will be discussed in Chapter 4.

In general, epithelial cells are anchored to a specialized structure called the **basement membrane.** The basement membrane is important, since it serves as an anchor for the inner (attached) side of cells, affording protection to the underlying connective tissue. It is frequently used as a landmark delineating invasion of epithelial tumors. If the tumor has invaded the basement membrane, the outlook for the patient is poor. In the electron microscope the basement membrane can be seen to consist of two layers: (1) the *basal lamina* (the more conspicuous layer), composed largely of filamentous collagen fibrils which border (and are apparently secreted by) the epithelial cells, and (2) delicate, branching, reticular fibers (described below) embedded in a protein-polysaccharide ground substance, both products of fibroblasts, the connective tissue cells.

An epithelial tissue is named according to the outer (free) layer of cells, consisting of either one layer or several layers of different cell types. The free surface of an epithelial cell can be plain or can have definite structures, such as cilia (L. *cilium*, eyelash), motile hairlike processes which, by synchronized, wavelike movements (resembling a windblown field of grain), either move mucus or propel substances along a tract, and *microvilli,* cylindrical cell processes, which greatly increase membrane surface (especially of cells serving an absorptive function). Unique structures along the lateral surface of epithelial cells, known as *junctional complexes,* are responsible for the characteristic tendency of epithelial cells to maintain close contact with one another and form continuous sheets in some parts of the body. Furthermore, they play important functional roles. For one thing, "tight junctions" establish a relatively impenetrable barrier where epithelial tissue forms surface coverings. In addition, "gap junctions" permit free cell-to-cell passage of ions (first demonstrated by electrical coupling of adjacent cells) and other cellular substances. Presumably this intercellular communication enables epithelial cells to corrdinate their activities. An example of the physiological significance of junctional communication is the observation that regulation of cell division by contact inhibition (page 55) depends upon the integrity of such communication.

Classification

Cells composing epithelial tissues are classified according to their shape, arrangement of cell layers, or function.

Shape. Epithelial cells are classified as squamous, cuboidal, and columnar. **Squamous cells** (L. *squamosus*, scaly) are flat and often serve as a protective layer. Other epithelial cells can become squamous if subjected to repeated irritation. **Cuboidal cells,** resembling small cubes, are found in five regions of the body and include lining tissue for ducts, secretory glands, renal tubules, germinal coverings for the ovaries, and the pigmented layer of the retina of the

eye. **Columnar cells** are tall and often rectangular. They line ducts such as the urethra and are found in mucus-secreting tissues, including the mucosa of the stomach, bile ducts, villi (finger-like projections) of the intestines, uterine tubes, and upper respiratory tract.

Arrangement. Four of the most common arrangements of epithelial cells are simple, stratified, pseudostratified, and transitional epithelium (Fig. 43). The **simple** arrangement is one cell layer thick. The **stratified** arrangement is a layer several cells thick. The **pseudostratified** arrangement seems to consist of several layers, but is actually a single layer with all cells resting on the basement membrane. The basal, or supportive, cells, however, do not reach the free (outer) surface and vary so much in shape and in the position of their nuclei that they give the tissue a stratified appearance. **Transitional** epithelium consists of several layers of closely packed, soft, pliable, and easily stretched cells. When the surface is stretched, the cells are flat; but they appear sawtoothed when the epithelium is relaxed, as in a recently emptied bladder. The descriptive term for this type of epithelium arose from the belief that it was in transition between stratified squamous and columnar epithelium. The changing appearance, however, is merely a reflection of the distended and relaxed conditions. Transitional epithelium lines the pelvis of the kidney, the ureters, the urinary bladder, and the upper part of the urethra.

Function. In addition to the epidermal layer of the skin, epithelial tissue consists of four types: (1) the surface layer of mucous membranes, (2) glandular epithelium, (3) endothelium, and (4) mesothelium, the surface layer of serous membranes (Fig. 44).

MUCOUS MEMBRANE. Mucous membrane lines the digestive, respiratory, urinary, and reproductive tracts; it also lines the conjunctiva and the middle ear. These membranes consist of a surface layer of epithelial cells and an underlying layer of connective tissue. The digestive tract includes the buccal cavity, pharynx, esophagus, stomach, small intestine, large intestine, and anal canal. The buccal cavity, lower pharynx, and esophagus are lined with stratified squamous epithelium. Simple columnar epithelium is found in the

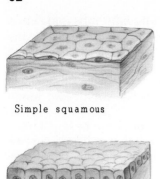

Simple squamous

Stratified squamous

Cuboidal

Pseudostratified ciliated columnar

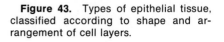

Figure 43. Types of epithelial tissue, classified according to shape and arrangement of cell layers.

Simple columnar

Pseudostratified columnar

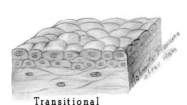

Transitional

remainder of the digestive tract from the stomach to the rectum. The anal canal is lined with stratified squamous epithelium.

In the respiratory tract the nasopharynx, trachea, large bronchi and parts of the larynx are lined with pseudostratified cili-

TYPES OF EPITHELIUM

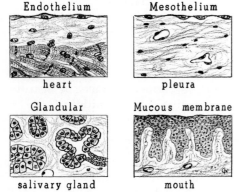

Endothelium — heart

Mesothelium — pleura

Glandular — salivary gland

Mucous membrane — mouth

Figure 44. Epithelial tissue types include endothelium, mesothelium (the surface layer of serous membranes), glandular tissue, and the surface layer of mucous membranes.

ated columnar epithelium. Smaller bronchi and bronchioles are lined with simple ciliated columnar epithelium. These cells change to cuboidal ciliated and nonciliated epithelium in the smallest bronchioles. Vocal cords are covered by patches of stratified squamous epithelium.

In the urinary system, Bowman's capsule and the descending loop of Henle are lined with thin squamous epithelium, and the remaining tubules with cuboidal epithelium. The cuboidal epithelium becomes columnar as it approaches the pelvis of the kidney, which is lined with transitional epithelium continuing into the ureters, bladder, and upper portion of the urethra.

In the reproductive tract, the epididymis and ductus deferens of the male are lined with pseudostratified columnar epithelium, in the female the uterine tube and the uterus itself with ciliated and nonciliated columnar epithelium. The entire mucosa of the uterus contains tubular glands extending down to and sometimes entering the muscular layer. A change to stratified squamous epithelium occurs at the point at which the cervix opens into the vagina.

Mucous membranes serve four general functions: protection, support for associated structures, absorption of nutrients into the body, and secretion of mucus, enzymes, and salts.

GLANDULAR EPITHELIUM. Glands arise as involutions of epithelial cells, specializing in synthesizing and secreting certain special compounds. The epithelial cells constitute the **parenchymal,** or functional, tissue in distinction to the supportive tissue of a gland. Glands can be divided into two types: exocrine (with excretory ducts) and endocrine (ductless). Exocrine glands have excretory ducts through which the secretory products pass to the surface and can be further divided into numerous gland types (Fig. 45). Simple or simple branched glands,. such as sweat glands, sebaceous glands and most glands of the alimentary tract, have single ducts or branches arising from a single duct. Compound glands have several component lobules and a complex system of branching ducts, and are found in the pancreas, mammary glands, and large salivary glands. The shape of the gland is either tubular or saccular (see Fig. 45), and glands may secrete either mucous or serous material.

ENDOTHELIUM. Endothelium is found in lymphatic vessels, blood vessels, and the lining of the heart (endocardium). The circulatory system is lined with a thin layer of endothelial cells, extending from the heart through the arteries into the capillaries and back again through the veins. The cells are a single layer of the squamous type.

MESOTHELIUM. The fourth general type of epithelial tissue is the mesothelium, the surface epithelial layer of **serous membranes** (the peritoneum, the pleura and the pericardium) that line the closed cavities of the body. Serous membranes have a simple squamous mesothelial cell layer overlying a thin sheet of connective tissue. These membranes include a parietal (L. *paries,* wall) portion lining the cavity wall and a visceral portion covering the organs. The *pleura* is the serous membrane lining the thoracic cavity and enveloping the lungs, the *pericardium* is the serous membrane covering the heart and lining the inner surface of the pericardial sac, and the *peritoneum* is the serous membrane lining the abdominal cavity and covering many

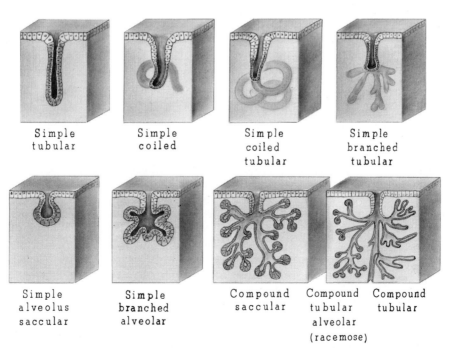

| Simple tubular | Simple coiled | Simple coiled tubular | Simple branched tubular |

| Simple alveolus saccular | Simple branched alveolar | Compound saccular | Compound tubular alveolar (racemose) | Compound tubular |

Figure 45. Exocrine glands. These glands may be tubular, coiled, saccular, or racemose (resembling a bunch of grapes on a stalk).

abdominal organs. Serous membranes perform functions such as protection and reduction of friction (the space between the visceral and parietal layers contains a lubricant secreted by the mesothelial cells).

CONNECTIVE TISSUE

The second major subdivision of tissue, connective tissue, which includes connective tissue proper and a number of specialized tissues (such as bone and cartilage), performs many functions, including support and nourishment for other tissues, packing material in the spaces between organs, and defense for the body by phagocytosis and antibody production. Tendons, which connect muscle to bone, allow movement to take place. In this tissue there is an abundance of intercellular material called **matrix,** which is variable in type and amount and is one of the main sources of difference between types of connective tissue. The vascularity of connective tissues varies considerably. Loose connective tissues (described below) have a rich supply of blood vessels; some dense connective tissues have few blood vessels. Cartilage is avascular. The connective tissue matrix consists of varying proportions of three types of glycoprotein **fibers,** collagenous, elastic and reticular, embedded in an amorphous protein-polysaccharide **ground substance.** Occasionally the fibers are not apparent (for example, in hyaline cartilage) but often they are quite obvious (tendon). *Collagenous fibers,* the most widespread, are highly inelastic and are responsible for the enormous tensile strength of tissues such as tendons. These fibers are composed of bundles of fibrils (Fig. 46) assembled from collagen molecules. The basic collagen molecule (called tropocollagen) consists of three helical polypeptide chains coiled into a triple helix (Fig. 15, page 25). Collagen is rich in hydroxylated lysine and proline, and the stability of the triple helix depends upon linkages involving these hydroxylated amino acids. A deficiency in hydroxylation during synthesis, one of the consequences of a dietary insufficiency of vitamin C, disrupts the normal assembly of collagen. This accounts for poor wound healing in scurvy. *Elastic fibers* give stretchability and resiliency to tissues. This is especially

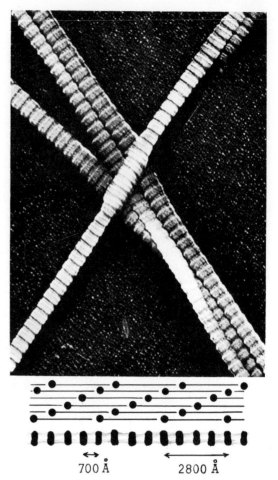

Figure 46. *Top,* Electron micrograph of collagen fibrils from human skin. *Bottom,* Diagrammatic representation of the overlapping of basic collagen (tropocollagen) molecules. The staggered alignment of the heads of many molecules is responsible for the crossbands along the length of the fibrils, about 700 Å apart. (From W. Bloom and D. W. Fawcett: A Textbook of Histology, 9th ed., Philadelphia, W. B. Saunders Co., 1968.)

important in structures that must expand and contract to function normally, such as the walls of large arteries. Elastic fibers are composed principally of an amorphous protein called elastin, shaped into a fibrous configuration by small amounts of surrounding microfibrils. *Reticular fibers* are composed of the same unit fibrils of collagen that form collagenous fibers. In reticular fibers, however, the fibrils form a loose, delicate network rather than coarse bundles. These fibers, as mentioned, form part of the basement membrane to which epithelial cells are anchored. They are present in abundance in loose connective tissues, especially the reticular tissues (see below). Reticular fibers are not seen in standard histological sections, but can be made visible by selective staining (silver impregnation).

Loose Connective Tissue

The fibers of loose connective tissue are not tightly woven. The tissue, filling spaces between and penetrating into the organs, is of three types: areolar, adipose, and reticular.

Areolar Tissue. The most widely distributed connective tissue is pliable and crossed by many delicate threads; yet, the tissue resists tearing and is somewhat elastic. Areolar tissue contains fibroblasts, histiocytes (macrophages), and mast and mesenchymal cells.

Fibroblasts are small, flattened, somewhat irregular cells with large nuclei and reduced cytoplasm. The term fibroblast refers to the ability of a cell to form fibrils. Fibroblasts are active in repair of injury. It is generally believed that suprarenal steroids inhibit and growth hormones stimulate fibroblastic activity. *Macrophages,* also called *histiocytes,* are phagocytic cells similar to leukocytes in blood; however, they perform phagocytic activity outside the vascular system. The histiocyte is irregular in shape and contains cytoplasmic granules. The cell is often stationary (or "fixed"), attached to fibers of the matrix. *Mast cells,* located adjacent to small blood vessels, are round or polygonal in shape and possess a cytoplasm filled with metachromatic granules. Mast cells function in the manufacture of heparin (an anticoagulant) and histamine (an inflammatory substance responsible for changes in allergic tissue). Depression in mast cell activity results from the administration of cortisol to patients. *Mesenchymal cells,* undifferentiated (embryonic) cells, resembling fibroblasts in appearance, but smaller, have also been identified in loose connective tissue. Present principally along the walls of blood vessels, they can develop into the mature cell types of loose connective tissue. Areolar tissue is the basic supporting substance around organs, muscles, blood vessels, and nerves, forming the delicate membranes around the brain and spinal cord and composing the superficial fascia, or sheet of connective tissue, found deep in the skin.

Adipose Tissue. Adipose (L. *adeps,* fat) tissue is specialized areolar tissue with fat-containing cells. The fat cell, like other cells, has a nucleus, endoplasmic reticulum, cell membrane, mitochondria, and, in addition, a large fat droplet. The cytoplasmic fat occupies most of the space, and the displacement of the nucleus to the edge of the cell gives the adipocyte the appearance of a signet ring. Adipose tissue acts as a firm yet resilient packing around and between organs, bundles of muscle fibers, nerves, and supporting blood vessels. Since fat is a poor conductor of heat, adipose tissue protects the body from excessive heat loss or excessive rises in temperature.

Reticular Tissue. Reticular fibers are widespread in the body, but the term *reticular tissue* is restricted to sites where these fibers are associated with so-called *primitive reticular cells,* which can apparently give rise to large phagocytic cells (macrophages), also abundant in most reticular tissue. Reticular tissue forms the framework of lymphoid tissue (see below), the liver and the bone marrow.

Dense Connective Tissue

Dense connective tissue is composed of closely arranged tough collagenous and elastic fibers with fewer cells than loose connective tissue. It can be classified according to the arrangement of the fibers and the proportion of elastin and collagen present. Examples of dense connective tissue having a regular arrangement of fibers are tendons, aponeuroses, fasciae and ligaments. Examples of dense connective tissue having an irregular arrangement of fibers are capsules, muscle sheaths, and the dermis, the principal layer of the skin. Where elastic fibers predominate, dense connective tissue is referred to as elastic tissue. The walls of hollow structures, such as the trachea and the bronchus, have large amounts of elastic tissue.

Specialized Connective Tissue

Cartilage. Cartilage has a firm matrix. Cells of cartilage, called *chondrocytes* (G. *chondros,* cartilage), are large and rounded with spherical nuclei and are clustered in small cavities called lacunae. Collagenous and elastic fibers are embedded in the matrix, increasing the elastic and resistive properties of this tissue. Cartilage is covered with a dense connective tissue called the *perichondrium* (G. *peri*, around), except where it is the articular surface of a bone at synovial (fluid) joints. Since, as mentioned, cartilage is avascular, chondrocytes are nourished by diffusion through the matrix of substances from perichondral blood vessels. Synovial fluid nourishes articular cartilage. The three types of cartilage are hyaline, fibrous and elastic.

In utero, hyaline (G. *hyalos*, glass) *cartilage* is the precursor of much of the skeletal system. It is translucent with a clear matrix caused by abundant collagenous fibers (not visible as such) and cells scattered throughout the matrix. Hyaline cartilage is gradually replaced by bone in many parts of the body through the process of ossification; however, some remains as a covering on the articular surfaces. The hyaline costal cartilages attach the anterior ends of the upper seven pairs of ribs to the sternum. The trachea is kept open by incomplete rings of surrounding hyaline cartilage. This type of cartilage is also found in the nose.

Fibrous cartilage contains dense masses of unbranching, collagenous fibers lying in the matrix. Cells of fibrous cartilage are present in rows between bundles of the matrix. Fibrocartilage is dense and resistant to stretching; it is less flexible and less resilient than hyaline cartilage. Fibrous cartilage, interposed between the vertebrae in the spinal column, is also present in the symphysis pubis, permitting a minimal range of movement.

Elastic cartilage, which is more resilient than either the hyaline or the fibrous type because of a predominance of elastic fibers impregnated in its ground substance, is found in the auricle of the external ear, the auditory tube, the epiglottis, and portions of the larynx.

Bone. Bone is a firm tissue formed by impregnation of the intercellular material with inorganic salts. It is living tissue supplied by blood vessels and nerves and is constantly being remodeled. The two common types are *compact*, forming the dense outer layer, and *cancellous*, forming the inner lighter tissue (Fig. 56, page 85).

Dentin. The dentin of teeth is closely related to bone. The crown of the tooth is covered by enamel, the hardest substance in the body. Enamel is secreted onto the dentin by the epithelial cells of the enamel organ before the teeth are extruded through the gums. Dentin resembles bone but is harder and denser (see Fig. 434, page 456).

Blood and Hematopoietic Tissue. Red bone marrow is the blood-forming (hematopoietic) tissue. The red blood cells (erythrocytes) and white blood cells (leukocytes) originate in the capillary sinusoids of bone marrow.

Blood is a fluid tissue circulating through the body, carrying nutrients to cells and removing waste products (see Fig. 323, page 333).

Lymphoid Tissue. Lymphoid tissue is found in the lymph nodes, thymus, spleen and tonsils. Reticular tissue forms its framework, and lymphocytes lie within the reticular tissue. A diffuse form of lymphoid tissue, not sharply delineated from the surrounding connective tissue, is found in mucous membranes, especially in the digestive and respiratory tracts. Lymphoid tissue plays a role in immunity.

Reticuloendothelial System. Connective tissue cells, carrying on the process of phagocytosis, are frequently referred to as the reticuloendothelial system or the macrophage system. The most frequently cited components of this system are the following: (1) macrophages distributed throughout loose connective tissues, which are especially numerous in mucous membranes of the digestive and respiratory tracts and in association with small blood vessels and lymphatics of subserous connective tissue of the pleura and peritoneum; (2) macrophages lining the alveoli (terminal air sacs) of the lungs; (3) monocytes in the blood stream; (4) macrophages lining the blood sinuses of the liver (Kupfer cells) and bone marrow; (5) macrophages lining the sinuses of lymph nodes and the spleen (in these locations also called large reticular cells); and (6) microglia of the central nervous system.

Synovial Membranes. Synovial membranes line the cavities of the freely moving joints and form tendon sheaths and bursae.

MUSCLE TISSUE

There are three types of muscle tissue: striated (voluntary), smooth (involuntary), and cardiac. *Striated* or voluntary muscle has cross-striations and can be controlled at will. *Involuntary* muscle is smooth, without striations, and is under the control of the autonomic nervous system. *Cardiac* muscle, although striated, is found exclusively in the heart and is not under voluntary control (see Fig. 114, page 146).

NERVOUS TISSUE

The fourth type of tissue is *nervous tissue*, divided into nervous tissue proper and interstitial tissue (neuroglia). Nervous tis-

Table 5. TISSUES

TISSUE	LOCATION
Epithelial tissue	
Simple squamous	Body cavities (mesothelium), cardiovascular and lymphatic vessels (endothelium), alveoli, Bowman's capsule and descending loop of Henle of kidney
Simple cuboidal	Many glands, pigmented epithelium of the retina, tubules of kidney
Simple columnar	Digestive tract from the esophagogastric junction to the anal canal, gallbladder
Simple ciliated columnar	Small bronchi, bronchioles, uterus, uterine tubules, efferent ductules of testes
Stratified squamous	Epidermis (skin), mouth and tongue, esophagus, anus, vagina, cornea
Pseudostratified columnar	Epididymis, ductus deferens, excretory duct of parotid gland
Pseudostratified ciliated columnar	Nasopharynx, trachea, large bronchi
Transitional epithelium	Urinary tract from renal pelvis to urethra
Connective tissue proper	
Loose connective tissue	
Areolar	Loosely arranged fibroelastic tissue between organs and muscles; supports blood vessels and nerves
Adipose	Subcutaneous fat, breast, yellow bone marrow
Reticular	Framework of liver, lymphoid tissues, bone marrow
Dense connective tissue	
Regular	Tendons, aponeuroses, ligaments
Irregular	Dermis, capsules, sheaths, septa
Specialized connective tissue	
Cartilage	
Hyaline	Articular surfaces of bones, costal cartilages, rings of trachea, tip of nose, larynx, fetal skeleton
Fibrous	Discs between vertebrae; symphysis pubis; knee and hip joints
Elastic	Auricle of external ear, auditory tube, epiglottis, cartilages of larynx
Bone	Skeleton
Dentin	Teeth
Hematopoietic	Red marrow of bones
Lymphoid	Lymph nodes, thymus, spleen, tonsils, mucous membranes of digestive and respiratory tracts (diffuse form)
Muscular tissue	
Striated skeletal (voluntary)	Skeletal muscles; muscles of the tongue, pharynx, larynx; extrinsic muscles of the eye
Smooth (involuntary)	Muscular walls of the digestive, respiratory and urinary tracts, blood vessels, iris; ciliary muscles; erector pili muscles
Cardiac	Heart
Nervous tissue	
Nervous tissue proper	Neurons and nerve fibers
Neuroglia	Supportive tissue in central nervous system

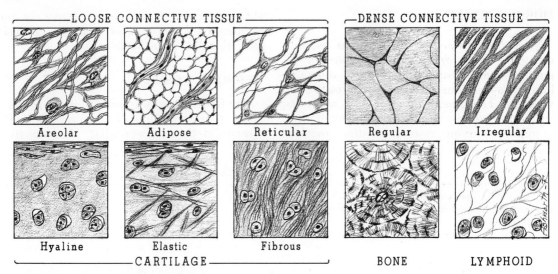

Figure 47. *Loose connective tissue:*
Areolar: loosely arranged fibroelastic connective tissue.
Adipose: regions of connective tissue dominated by aggregations of fat cells.
Reticular: makes delicate connecting and supporting frameworks, enters into the composition of basement membranes, produces macrophages, and plays important roles as scavenger and agent of defense against bacteria.
Dense connective tissue:
Regular: fibers that are oriented so as to withstand tension exerted in one direction.
Irregular: fibers that are arranged so as to withstand tensions exerted from different directions.
Cartilage:
Hyaline: the most fundamental kind of cartilage, consisting of a seemingly homogeneous matrix permeated with fine white fibers.
Elastic: specialized cartilage with elastic fibers in the matrix.
Fibrous: specialized cartilage emphasizing collagenous fibers in its matrix.
Bone: a tissue consisting of cells, fibers, and a ground substance, the distinguishing feature of which is the presence of a ground substance of inorganic salts.
Lymphoid tissue: a tissue consisting of two primary tissue elements—reticular tissue and cells, chiefly lymphocytes—intermingling in intimate association in the reticular interstices.

sue is the most highly organized tissue in the body, initiating, controlling, and coordinating the body's ability to adapt to its environment. In nervous tissue proper, the specialized conducting cells are *neurons*, linked together to form nerve pathways. The neuroglia (interstitial tissue) supports the neuron (see Fig. 227, page 226).

The various types of tissue are summarized in Table 5 and Figures 47 and 48.

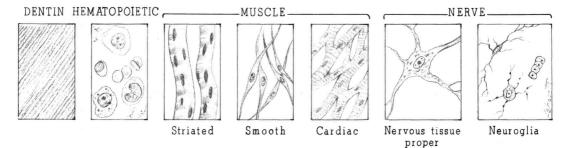

Figure 48. *Dentin,* like bone, consists of a collagenous mesh and calcified ground substance; unlike bone, it contains neither vessels nor total cells. *Hematopoietic tissue:* blood-forming tissues; i.e., red bone marrow. *Muscle tissue* has the properties of contractility and excitability (see Chapter 7). *Nervous tissue* has the properties of excitability and conductivity (see Chapter 8).

TISSUE TRANSPLANTATION

During the last two decades, an active interest has been taken in methods and mechanisms of tissue transplantation. The following should prove useful to the student embarking on a medical or paramedical career.

Definitions

Autotransplant. A transplant to the same individual from whom the tissue was removed. For example, a skin graft from the thigh to a burned surface of the hand of the same person.

Isotransplant. A transplant between individuals of the same genetic background (identical twins) or between animals of nearly the same genetic background (inbred strains).

Homotransplant. A transplant between two individuals of the same species with a different genetic background, as from one patient to another (not his identical twin).

Heterotransplant. A transplant between members of two different species, as from a rat to a dog.

It is currently accepted that when any tissue is grafted between two individuals who are not identical twins, the graft is rejected because of the development of "actively acquired immunity." When tissues are homotransplanted, the lipoprotein of the cell membrane leaves the transplanted cell as an antigen and enters the lymphatics of the recipient organism. The antigen then travels to the regional lymph nodes and initiates the production of T cell lymphocytes (see Chapter 11, page 416). These lymphocytes in turn reach the graft by way of the blood and bring about rejection of the homograft (Fig. 49).

Nature provides at least four exceptions to the concept that skin grafts between individuals are invariably destroyed: (1) Identical twins accept grafts. Inbred animal strains develop such a high degree of genetic similarity as to behave as identical twins and thus accept grafts. (2) Embryos accept grafts from each other. (3) Patients with certain disease states, such as thymic aplasia, will tolerate skin grafts (see Chapter 10). (4) Chimeras (organisms with two genetically different types of tissue) will accept skin grafts. The phenomenon of natural tolerance (chimerism) occurs in cattle twins and has been reported in nonidentical human twins. The possibility of tolerance to grafts between a mother and a child has been reported. Transplantation of kidneys is now a well-accepted routine in several medical centers.

In general, three approaches are being evaluated to prolong the life of homografts: (1) irradiation of the cells which have been

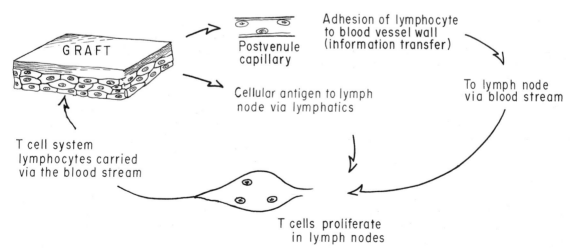

Figure 49. Skin graft showing rejection mechanism. Note that lymphatics, lymph nodes, and blood vessels are necessary in graft rejection.

sensitized by the antigens produced as a result of the graft; (2) transplanting the graft to a privileged site, such as the anterior chamber of the eye, in which not only the cornea will be accepted but other tissues as well; and (3) altering or lessening host response. Currently, drugs suppressing the cellular immune response are being employed; Imuran, cortisone and antilymphocytic serum have proved effective. The approach of altering host response offers the greatest promise.

Grafting of Specific Tissues

Blood Vessels. Homografts of arteries can be transplanted. This type of graft degenerates over a period of several years; however, the homologous arterial transplant functions as a so-called "homostatic" tissue. This means that viability is not necessary for successful transplantation, but the tissue acts as a foundation around which the individual's own cells can produce tissue. Today, plastics are used for replacement of arteries.

Bone. Osteocytes in autologous bone grafts survive as living entities. Osteocytes in homologous or heterologous grafts die after transfer. Homologous and heterologous bone form a foundation for bone cells from the host to grow inward and replace the grafted tissue.

Cartilage. Both autologous and homologous cartilage survive transplantation. Possible explanations for survival of homografts of cartilage include the lack of blood vessels in the graft itself and the fact that the protein-polysaccharide (mucopolysaccharide) matrix can act as a barrier against host cell infiltration.

Endocrine Tissues. An impressive group of studies indicates that homotransplants of certain endocrine tissues do not provoke the usual rejection reaction. Endocrine tissue may be less highly antigenic than other tissues.

Teeth. Dental reimplantation is the procedure of reinserting into the alveolar socket a tooth accidentally extracted or dislodged. Studies are underway in some institutions on homotransplantation of teeth.

PRESERVATION OF TISSUES

There are three general methods of tissue preservation: preservation in a nutrient medium at temperatures above freezing; preservation in a nonviable state by freeze-drying or chemical fixation (applicable to homologous grafts of blood vessels, since they do not have to remain alive to provide satisfactory function); and preservation by freezing, or depressing the freezing point with the tissue remaining viable. The best long-term method of preservation is probably freezing. Cells like spermatozoa and red blood cells will survive freezing with the use of protective agents such as glycerol. To date this has not been possible with an entire organ or whole animal.

SUMMARY

TISSUES

Types of Tissues

The four basic tissues of the body are
a. Epithelial
b. Connective
c. Muscular
d. Nervous

Epithelial Tissue

a. Classified according to shape
  (1) Squamous (flat)
  (2) Cuboidal
  (3) Columnar
b. Classified according to *arrangement*
  (1) Simple, one cell thick
  (2) Stratified, several layers
  (3) Pseudostratified, apparently several layers, but actually all cells attached to basement membrane
  (4) Transitional, several layers of closely packed cells, easily stretched
c. Named according to the layer on the free surface
  (1) Simple squamous (surface layer of serous membranes, endothelial lining of heart and blood vessels, and respiratory surface of lungs)
  (2) Simple cuboidal (many glands and ducts, kidney tubules, germi-

nal covering for ovaries, and pigmented layer of retina of eye)
  (3) Simple columnar (digestive tract)
  (4) Simple ciliated columnar (bronchioles)
  (5) Stratified squamous (epidermis)
  (6) Pseudostratified columnar (ductus deferens)
  (7) Pseudostratified ciliated columnar (nasopharynx, trachea, and large bronchi)
  (8) transitional (urinary tract)
  d. Classified according to *function*
  (1) Part of mucous membranes (surface layer of epithelium and underlying connective tissue) lining digestive, respiratory, urinary, and reproductive tracts
  (2) Glandular epithelium
  (3) Endothelium, lining heart, blood vessels, and lymphatics
  (4) Mesothelium, the surface layer of serous membranes (overlying a sheet of connective tissue) lining the great cavities of the body, peritoneum, pericardium, and pleura; they include a parietal portion (lining cavity wall) and visceral layer (covering organs). Epithelial tissues function in protections, absorption, secretion, and excretion

CONNECTIVE TISSUE

1. **Characterized by widely separated cells and abundance of intercellular material consisting of glycoprotein fibers and amorphous, protein-polysaccharide ground substance.**

  a. Supportive function, to provide nourishment for overlying epithelial tissues, link muscle and bone as tendons, allowing movement.
  b. Special functions in bone, teeth, and reticuloendothelial (macrophage) system.

2. **Loose connective tissue**

  a. Areolar tissue: the most widely dispersed connective tissue—fine, pliable, resistant, elastic; contains fibroblasts, macrophages, and mast cells. Areolar tissue is the basic supporting substance around organs, muscles, blood vessels, and nerves. It forms membranes around the brain and spinal cord; it composes superficial fascia.
  b. Adipose tissue: Specialized areolar tissue with many fat-containing cells; adipose tissue acts as a firm, resilient packing around and between organs and between bundles of muscle fibers. In its subcutaneous location, it protects the body from excessive heat loss or excessive increases in temperature.
  c. Reticular tissue: A framework of fine-branching fibrils, found in lymphoid organs, bone marrow, and the liver.

3. **Dense connective tissue**

  a. Contains closely packed collagenous and elastic fibers in regular array (tendons and ligaments) or irregular array (the dermis).
  b. Where elastic fibers predominate (as in the walls of large arteries, the trachea and bronchi), referred to as elastic tissue.

4. **Specialized connective tissue**

  a. Cartilage: Yields a firm matrix between cells; cells of cartilage are called chondrocytes. There are three types of cartilage.
  (1) Hyaline: The precursor of the skeletal system; during embryonic development much of it is gradually replaced by bone through the process of ossification. At termination of bone growth, it remains on articular surfaces. Also found in trachea, bronchi, larynx, costal cartilages and nose.
  (2) Fibrous: Contains dense masses of inbranching collagenous fibers lying in bundles. It is dense and resistant to stretching. The cells are located in rows between the bundles of matrix.
  (3) Elastic: The most resilient type of cartilage; found in the auricles of the ear, auditory tube, epiglottis, and larynx.
  b. Bone: Firm structure of living tissue

formed by impregnation of the inter-cellular material with inorganic salts. Bone is constantly being remodeled.

c. Dentin: Dentin of the teeth is similar to bone. It is covered by enamel.

d. Blood: A fluid tissue circulating through the body, carrying nutrients to cells and removing waste products.

e. Hematopoietic tissue: Red bone marrow is the blood-forming (hematopoietic) tissue.

f. Lymphoid tissue: Found in lymph nodes, thymus, spleen, tonsils, and adenoids; functions in immunity.

g. Reticuloendothelial system: Composed of connective tissue cells carrying on the process of phagocytosis. Strong line of defense against infection.

Muscle Tissue

1. Three types of muscle

a. Voluntary, or striated
b. Involuntary, or smooth
c. Cardiac

Nervous Tissue

1. Division of nervous tissue

a. Nervous tissue proper, consisting of neurons, the specialized conducting cells
b. Tissue composed of various supportive cells (neuroglia)

Tissue Transplantation

1. Types of transplants

a. Autotransplant
b. Isotransplant
c. Homotransplant
d. Heterotransplant

2. Transplanted tissues are usually rejected because of the development of "actively ac-quired immunity." This occurs when the lipoprotein of the transplanted cell leaves the cell as an antigen, travels to lymph nodes, and stimulates the production of T cell system lymphocytes, which then travel via the blood stream to destroy the graft.

3. Nature provides at least four exceptions to the concept that the skin grafts between individuals are invariably destroyed.

a. Identical twins accept grafts.
b. Grafts between embryos are accepted.
c. Patients with certain diseases accept grafts from each other.
d. Chimeras accept grafts.

4. Three approaches are being evaluated to prolong the life of homografts:

a. Irradiation on effector side
b. Transplanting the graft to a privileged site
c. Altering or lessening host resistance by immunosuppressive agents

5. Grafting of specific tissues

a. Homografts of arteries can be transplanted.
b. Osteocytes in autologous bone grafts survive transplantation.
c. Possibly certain endocrine tissues do not elicit rejection.
d. A tooth which has been accidentally extracted or dislodged can be reinserted into the alveolar socket.

Preservation of Tissue (Three General Methods)

1. In a nutrient medium at a temperature above freezing.

2. In a nonviable state by freeze-drying or chemical fixation.

3. By freezing or by depressing the freezing point with the tissue remaining viable.

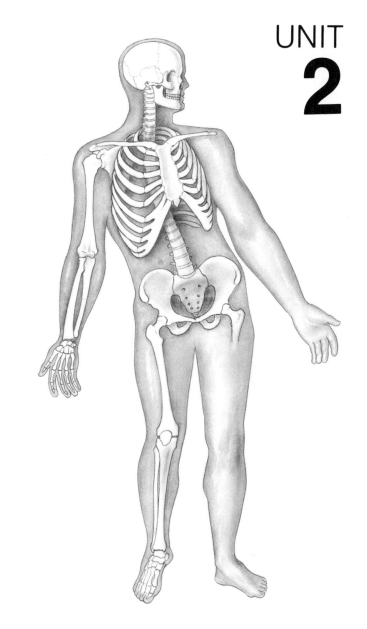

Framework of the Body

The Skin

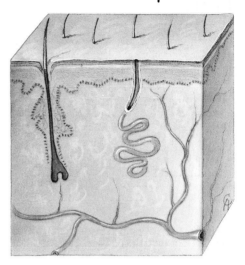

chapter 4

Objectives

The aim of this chapter is to enable the student to:

Distinguish between the epidermal and dermal layers of the skin.

Describe the important features of the layers of the epidermis.

Explain the functions of melanocytes of the epidermis.

Describe the appendages of the skin: hair, nails, sebaceous glands and sweat glands.

Describe hair growth.

List the functions of the skin.

Describe some of the common disorders of skin.

IMPORTANCE OF THE SKIN

The skin of an average adult covers over 3000 square inches of surface area, weighs approximately 6 pounds (nearly twice the weight of the liver or brain) and receives about one-third of all blood circulating through the body. It is elastic, rugged, and, under ordinary conditions, self-regenerating. The skin is almost entirely waterproof, providing an efficient, closely regulated thermal barrier and participating in the dissipation of water and in the temperature-regulatory functions of the body.

LAYERS OF THE SKIN

Epidermis

The outer, or epidermal (G. *epi,* upon; G. *derma,* skin), layer of the skin is composed of stratified squamous epithelial cells. The epidermis is thickest as it encloses the palms and soles and becomes thinner over the ventral surface of the trunk (Fig. 50).

The epidermis is composed of five layers, from superficial to deep (Fig. 51). They are the stratum corneum (horny layer), stratum lucidum (clear layer), stratum granulosum (granular layer), stratum spinosum (prickly layer), and stratum germinativum (regenerative layer).

The **stratum corneum** (L. *corneus,* horny) forms the outermost layer of the epidermis and consists of dead cells completely filled with a protein called keratin (G. *keras,* horn). They are commonly called keratinized cells and are continuously shed, requiring replacement. The stratum corneum consists of 20 per cent water, as compared to 70 per cent water in the stratum germinativum. The stratum corneum is composed of flattened cells resembling scales. It serves

75

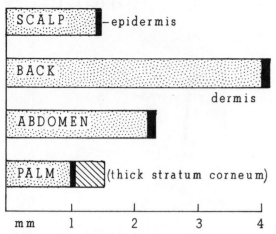

Figure 50. Graphic representation of skin thicknesses from various body sites.

as a physical barrier to light and heat waves, microorganisms, and most chemicals. The thickness of this layer is determined by the amount of stimulation of the surface by abrasion and weight bearing—hence thick palms and soles and the development of calluses.

The **stratum lucidum,** lying directly beneath the stratum corneum, is not seen in thinner skin. It is a layer of one to five cells thick, consisting of transparent, flattened, dead or dying cells, usually lacking nuclei.

The **stratum granulosum,** two to five layers of flattened cells, provides a transition into the subjacent layers. Granules accumulate in the cells, giving the layer its name; however, the granules do not contribute to skin color. The stratum granulosum is thought to be active in keratinization, a process in which cells manufacture

keratin and lose their nuclei, becoming more compact and brittle.

The **stratum spinosum** consists of several rows of "prickly" cells, polyhedral in shape. The cell outlines are spiny, hence the name, prickle cells. In some classifications this layer is included with the stratum germinativum as the malpighian layer.

The **stratum germinativum,** the deepest and most important layer of the skin contains cells capable of mitotic division. When new cells are formed, they undergo morphologic and nuclear changes as they move toward the most superficial layer. Simultaneously, these cells *give rise to all outer layers of the epidermis.* The epidermis will regenerate only so long as the stratum germinativum remains intact. The basal layer of these generative cells rests on a basement membrane which offers further protection from the environment.

Melanin, the principal pigment of the skin, is formed in the stratum germinativum by cells called **melanocytes** and is transferred from melanocyte processes to surrounding epithelial cells. The presence of carotene is in part responsible for the yellow color of skin. The darker color of the skin is due to melanin; the pink tint is caused by vessels in the dermis (there are no vessels in the epidermis). The strongest factor in increasing pigmentation is the sun's stimulating effect on melanocytes. Melanin is capable of crosslinking with protein to form a tough, resistant compound; hence, heavily pigmented skin is more resistant to external irritation.

A variation in melanin content is the principal factor responsible for color differences among races. Certain population groups have more active melanocytes in their skin. This causes black, yellow, brown, and white races. Darkly pigmented skin does not contain a greater number of melanocytes, but the melanocytes present are more active.

Dermis (Corium)

The dermis or corium, lying directly beneath the epidermis, is often called the true skin. It consists of connective tissue containing white collagenous and yellow elastic fibers. Blood vessels, nerves, lymph vessels, hair follicles, and sweat glands are

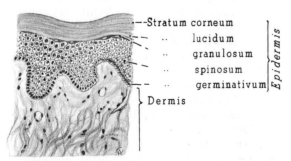

Figure 51. The epidermis (consisting of five distinct layers) and the dermis compose the protective covering of the body.

embedded in the dermis. The dermis is divided into the *papillary portion* adjacent to the epidermis and the *reticular portion* lying between the papillary layer and the subcutaneous (L. *sub*, under; L. *cutis*, skin) tissue.

Subcutaneous Tissue

A sheet of areolar tissue containing fat, known as subcutaneous adipose tissue or superficial fascia, attaches the dermis to the underlying structures.

APPENDAGES OF THE SKIN

The appendages associated with the skin include hair, nails, sebaceous glands, and sweat glands (Figs. 52 and Fig. 53).

Hair

Hair covers the entire body except the palms, soles, and portions of the genitalia; each unit of hair is composed of three parts—the cuticle, cortex, and medulla. The *cuticle*, the outermost portion, contains several layers of overlapping scalelike cells. The *cortex*, or principal portion of the hair, consists of elongated cells united to make

flattened fibers. In dark hair, the fibers contain pigment granules. The central axis of the hair, known as the *medulla*, is composed of many-sided cells frequently containing air spaces. The medulla is not present in very thin hair. The visible portion of the hair is the *shaft*. The cells at the base form the root, which develops into the shaft. Hair grows in a tubular invagination of the epidermis called the hair follicle, which is surrounded by dermal connective tissue (the dermal sheath). When the arrector pili muscles (bundles of smooth muscle fibers attached to the hair follicles) contract, the skin assumes a so-called "goose flesh" appearance where hair is sparse and results in a certain degree of "hair standing on its ends" where the hair is prominent.

Hair growth is similar to growth of the epidermis, with the deeper cell layers responsible for production of new cells. The epithelial matrix cells at the base of the hair follicle, which overlie the connective tissue papilla (Fig. 53), divide mitotically. Daughter cells move upward, keratinize, and form the horny layer of the shaft. When hair stops growing (resting phase), it forms a clublike base (club hair) that becomes firmly anchored to a shrunken follicle by fine filaments of keratin. New hair growth loosens the old hair, which is shed. Men, women and children have approximately the same number of hair follicles, but in women and

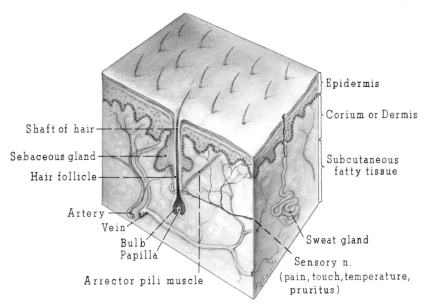

Figure 52. Three-dimensional view of the skin.

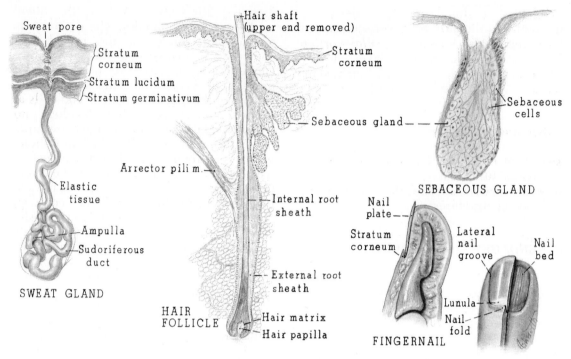

Figure 53.   The appendages associated with the skin.

children the hairs in many parts of the body are more rudimentary.

The keratin of the cortex is polymerized and crosslinked in a characteristic folded configuration (alpha keratin) rendering the fibers elastic. When stretched, the keratin chain is drawn out into a more linear form (beta keratin). Unless it is greatly distended or altered by chemical agents, it returns immediately to its normal configuration. When hair is wet, it can be elongated to one and one-half times its normal length. This is possible because keratin can be readily stretched in the direction of the long axis of the molecular chains of amino acids. Permanent wave sets act on this principle. After the hair has been stretched and molded into a desired wave, reducing agents rupture the disulfide bonds of the hair. Oxidizing agents are then applied, reestablishing the stabilizing crosslinks in a new position.

Hair Color.   Hair color is determined by complex genetic factors. Gray hair occurs when pigment is absent. White hair results from an absence of pigment plus the formation of air bubbles in the hair shaft. Heredity and other unknown factors determine the graying of hair. The hair of a black cat will turn gray from a diet deficient in pantothenic acid. Restoring this substance

to the diet causes the hair to return to its normal color. This fact is of interest but has not proved to be of importance in man.

Nails

The nails, a modification of the horny epidermal cells, are composed of hard keratin. Air mixed in the keratin matrix forms the white crescent, the *lunula*, at the proximal end of each nail. The nail plate arising from the proximal nail fold and attached to the nail bed grows approximately 1 mm. per week unless inhibited by disease. Regeneration of a lost fingernail occurs in 3½ to 5½ months; regeneration of a lost toenail occurs in 6 to 8 months.

Glands

Sebaceous Glands

Sebaceous glands generally arise from the walls of hair follicles and produce sebum, the oily substance primarily responsible for lubrication of the surface of the skin. Sebaceous secretion consists of entire cells containing sebum. When the cell disintegrates, sebum is secreted along the hair shaft onto the surface of the skin, providing a cosmetic gloss. In the few parts of the body where the glands are not associated with hair follicles, such as at the corners of the mouth, the glans penis and the labia minora, the ducts open directly upon the surface of the skin. Sebaceous glands are absent on the palms and soles.

Sebaceous secretion is under the control of the endocrine system, increasing at puberty and in late pregnancy and decreasing with advancing age. The pubertal increase contributes to the problem of acne in adolescents, and diminution is responsible for the relative dryness of the skin in later life.

The orifice of the sebaceous gland can become discolored as a result of oxidation of fatty material by the air, producing a "blackhead." Secretions retained in the gland provide a medium for growth of the pus-producing bacteria responsible for pimples and boils.

Sweat Glands. Sweat glands are simple tubular glands found in most parts of the skin except the lips and the glans penis, and most (*eccrine type*) are not associated with hair follicles. They are most numerous in the palms and soles. It has been estimated that there are 3000 sweat glands per square inch on the palm. Each consists of a secretory portion and an excretory duct. The secretory portion, located in the dermis tissue, is a blind tube twisted and coiled on itself. From the coiled secretory portion, the excretory duct spirals toward the surface. Each glandular tube is lined with secretory epithelium continuous with the epidermis. The secretory epithelium consists of two types of cells: (1) spindle-shaped, contractile, myoepithelial (G. *myo*, muscle) cells attached to the basement membrane, and (2) pyramidal cells that secrete sweat, resting on top of the myoepithelial cells.

Pure sweat contains the same inorganic constituents as blood but in lower concentration. The chief salt is sodium chloride. Organic constituents in sweat include urea, uric acid, amino acids, ammonia, sugar, lactic acid, and ascorbic acid. Sweat itself is practically odorless. The odor is produced by the action of bacteria on sweat. Ceruminous glands, which secrete wax, are found in the external meatus of the ear; ciliary glands, in the eyelids, secrete ocular fluid. Both are considered to be modified sweat glands.

Sweating leads to loss of heat in the body owing to the fact that heat is required to evaporate the water in the sweat; thus, sweating helps to lower the body temperature. Sweating is initiated by the effect of elevated blood temperature on cerebral centers. Denervated skin (without nerves) does not respond to temperature changes by sweating. Some individuals have congenital absence of sweat glands. Such persons can die of heat stroke if exposed to high temperatures even for brief periods. In some areas of the body, especially friction surfaces (palms and soles), sweat glands readily respond to stressful stimuli.

In contrast to the ordinary sweat glands (eccrine type) described above, sweat glands in certain regions of the body (known as the *apocrine type*), such as the armpits, anogenital area, navel and nipples, are connected to hair follicles and reach deeply into the subcutaneous layer of the skin. Beginning with puberty, these glands secrete a viscous, odorous fluid and respond to emotional, especially sexual, stimulation.

FUNCTIONS OF THE SKIN

The skin functions in *sensation, protection, thermoregulation,* and *secretion.* Located in the skin are specific receptors sensitive to the four basic sensations of pain, touch, temperature, and pressure. Upon stimulation of a receptor, a nerve impulse is sent to the cerebral cortex of the brain, where the impulse is interpreted. The brain must interpret among degrees of stimulation and among combinations of stimulations, the latter of which result in sensations such as burning, tickling, and itching.

The skin forms an elastic, resistant covering that protects man from his complex environment. It prevents the passage of harmful physical and chemical agents and inhibits excessive loss of water and electrolytes.

The acid mantle of skin helps protect its surface from irritants and bacteria. Some skin diseases destroy the acidity of certain areas, impairing the self-sterilizing ability of the skin. In this condition, the skin is prone to bacterial invasion.

Experimental evidence indicates that the normal intact human skin is usually impermeable to water, carbohydrate, fat, and protein. All true gases and many volatile substances will pass through the epidermis. For example, many deaths have resulted from absorption of large quantities of organic pesticide sprays through the skin. Sex hormones are readily absorbed when applied in a proper vehicle. Mercury, lead, and copper penetrate the skin under certain conditions. The numerous follicular orifices serve as channels for absorption. Substances passing through normal skin are soluble in fat and water.

Heat is lost from the body by conduction, convection, radiation, and evaporation. These processes are regulated by nervous and chemical activation of the sweat glands and by dilation and constriction of the cutaneous vessels (see page 487 in Chapter 13). As the body needs to dissipate heat, blood vessels of the skin dilate, allowing more blood to come to the surface, with a resulting heat loss.

The skin plays a part in the secretory functions of the body. Sebum secreted by sebaceous glands has antifungal and antibacterial properties and helps maintain the texture of the skin. Sweat is a secretion.

TRANSPLANTATION OF SKIN

The skin has a great capacity for regeneration and repair. If the epidermis is removed, the skin will regenerate, provided that isolated patches of the stratum germinativum remain. In a deeper wound, a new covering of epidermis is formed over the denuded area by active division of epidermal cells at the margin. In some cases, this natural process of repair is inadequate to secure an efficient return of function to the damaged tissue, as in third degree burns (Fig. 54), and transplantation of the skin offers a solution.

WOUND HEALING

Wound healing involves the reaction of the entire body to trauma, as well as local changes in the wound itself. The body responds *clinically* to injury by a temporary elevation of temperature and pulse rate. Chemically, loss of nitrogen and potassium is followed by nitrogen and potassium retention.

During wound healing, bleeding into the wound results in clot formation, and vasodilation permits circulating cells, oxygen, and nutrients to be carried to the wound area. Debris in the wound is removed by phagocytes, and endothelial capillary buds appear in the clot by the second day. The clot is composed of a network of threads of a protein substance called fibrin, which is enmeshed in bodies called platelets. In this network the blood corpuscles are entangled.

Fibroblasts multiply in the wound and migrate from the periphery to combine with endothelial tissue and young blood vessels. These constitute *granulation tissue*. Fibroblasts release precursors of collagen into the interstitial spaces which form collagen fibers in the wound itself.

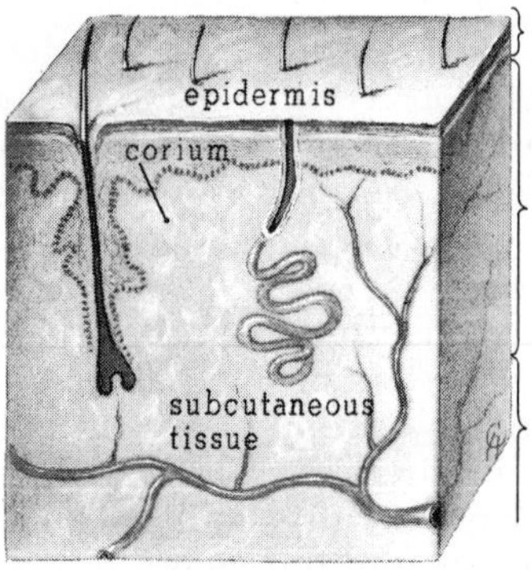

	Degree	Surface	Color	Pain
	1 st	dry no blisters	erythematous	painful hyperesthetic
	2 nd	moist blisters	mottled red	painful hyperesthetic
	3 rd	dry	pearly white or charred	little pain anesthetic

Figure 54. Extent of burn injury—first, second, and third degree. In a first degree burn only the epidermis is injured (as in sunburn); a second degree burn extends into the dermis; a third degree burn involves the full thickness of skin, epidermis, dermis, extending into subcutaneous tissue. (Courtesy of Parke, Davis.)

Figure 55. Terms used in connection with abnormalities of the skin. *Macule:* a discolored (especially reddened), unelevated spot, on the skin. *Papule:* a solid elevation of the skin. *Nodule:* a small node which is solid and irregular in form. *Wheal:* a flat edematous elevation of the skin, frequently accompanied by itching. *Polyp:* a pedunculated or sessile growth extending into the lumen of a body cavity or appearing on the skin. *Pustule:* an elevation filled with pus. *Ulcer:* a loss of substance on a cutaneous or mucous surface. *Cyst:* any sac, normal or otherwise, especially one which contains a liquid or semisolid substance without pus. *Fissure:* any cleft or groove.

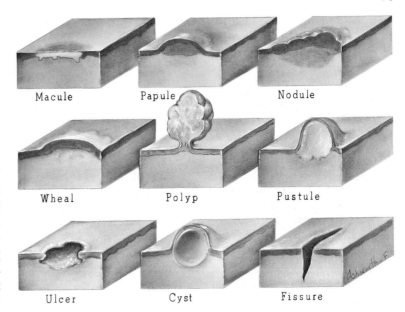

Macule Papule Nodule Wheal Polyp Pustule Ulcer Cyst Fissure

The *epidermis* is capable of rapid regeneration. Cell migration begins a few hours after an epidermal incision. A small defect will be covered completely after about 48 hours.

Factors interfering with wound healing. Many factors interfere with wound healing: inadequate nutrition; necrotic tissue (dead or dying tissue); foreign bodies; bacteria; interference with blood supply; blockage of lymphatics; systemic disease, such as diabetes mellitus; psychological factors.

Figure 55 illustrates various abnormalities of the skin.

Clinical Aspects

The appearance of the skin can be an important sign in diagnosis of various disorders. For instance, the skin may be red in hypertension (high blood pressure) and in other conditions in which the blood vessels of the skin are dilated. A pale skin suggests anemia (too few red corpuscles or too little hemoglobin). The color of the skin may be blue or purple (cyanosis) in severe heart disease and in such pulmonary diseases as pneumonia (in which the blood is not being adequately supplied with oxygen). A yellow skin (jaundice) indicates the presence of bile pigments in the blood in larger than normal amounts.

Acne (pimples) is caused by infection and subsequent inflammation of sebaceous glands.

Hives (urticaria) is a skin condition characterized by the sudden appearance of raised patches which are white in the center and itch severely. Hives occur when an individual takes medication or certain foods to which he is sensitive.

Psoriasis is a chronic inflammatory disease which is neither infectious nor contagious, characterized by dry whitish scales on reddish patches caused by excessive multiplication of epidermal cells. Although psoriasis has been considered incurable, a promising new treatment is available which combines high-intensity ultraviolet light with the ingestion of a photosensitizing drug (methoxalen).

Decubitus ulcers (bed sores) occur where there are areas of pressure on the body. Frequent turning and alcohol rubs help to prevent this distressing condition.

Sunburn is a condition in which the skin is swollen and red after excessive exposure to the sun, especially ultraviolet rays, and can occur even on a cloudy day. It is thought to be due to the production of a histamine-like substance that dilates the capillaries and leads to swelling or edema. Further damage may be caused by the release of hydrolytic enzymes from disrupted lysosomes. Other consequences of overexposure to sunlight include an increase in melanin formation, which darkens the skin, and an impairment in feedback control of cell division (see page 45), which results in thickening of the skin.

Boils (furuncles) are circumscribed inflammations of the corium and subcutaneous tissue due to bacteria which enter through the hair follicles.

SUMMARY

THE SKIN

1. The skin receives one-third of the blood circulating through the body. It is elastic, regenerates, and functions in sensation, protection, thermoregulation and secretion.
2. The skin consists of two layers.

a. The *epidermis:* composed of stratified squamous epithelium has the following layers (beginning with the outermost):
(1) Stratum corneum
(2) Stratum lucidum
(3) Stratum granulosum
(4) Stratum spinosum
(5) Stratum germinativum
The cells of the stratum germinativum divide and give rise to the upper layers. As the cells move upward, they undergo morphologic changes, become keratinized and gradually die. The flat, dead cells of the stratum corneum are continuously shed.
The principal pigment, melanin, is formed in the melanocytes of the stratum germinativum and injected into the surrounding epithelial cells. Melanocytes are more active in the darker races.

b. The *dermis:* a dense, vascular connective tissue divided into the papillary segment close to the epidermis and the reticular portion between the papillary layer and underlying subcutaneous tissue.

3. The subcutaneous tissue (superficial fascia), a loose connective tissue with variable amounts of fat, attaches the dermis to the underlying structures.

Appendages of the Skin

1. Hair

a. Consists of an outer, scalelike cuticle, central cortex (the principal portion) and inner medulla. The visible por-

tion is the shaft; the root is at the base.
b. Hair growth occurs by division of matrix cells at the base of the hair follicle (a tubular invagination of the epidermis). Daughter cells move upward and keratinize.
(1) When hair growth ceases, a clublike base becomes anchored to a shrunken follicle. The old hair is shed when loosened by new growth.
c. Contraction of arrector pili muscles (bundles of smooth muscle fibers attached to hair follicles) causes "goose flesh."

2. Nails

a. Composed of hard keratin; a modification of the horny epidermal cells.
b. Arise from the proximal nail fold.
c. Grow at the rate of approximately 1 mm per week.

3. Glands

a. *Sebaceous:* Most open into hair follicles.
(1) The secretion (sebum) consists of the oily substance and cellular debris of disintegrated cells. Secretion increases at puberty and late in pregnancy, declining with advanced age.
b. *Sweat glands:* Simple coiled tubular glands. The ducts of the most common (eccrine) type open directly onto the surface of the skin. The ducts of the less common (apocrine) type open into hair follicles; these glands are found in in the armpits, anogenital area, navel and nipples.
(1) The eccrine type secretes a watery fluid (containing the same inorganic constituents as in blood but in lower concentration) in response to elevated temperature. Eccrine glands on friction surfaces (palms and soles) also readily respond to emotional stimuli.
(2) Apocrine sweat glands secrete a viscous, odorous fluid at the onset of puberty and respond to emotional stimuli.
(3) Ceruminous glands in outer parts of the external auditory meatus and ciliary glands of the eyelids are modified sweat glands.

The Skeletal System

chapter 5

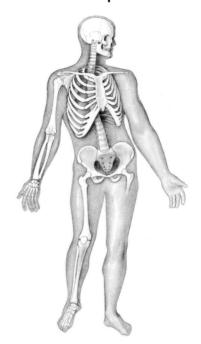

Objectives

The aim of this chapter is to enable the student to:

Describe the functions of bone.

Distinguish between the functions of osteoblasts, osteoclasts and osteocytes.

Describe the haversian system, the microscopic functional unit of bone.

Identify the types of bones.

Describe the formation and growth of bone.

List the vitamins and hormones that regulate bone formation and growth and describe how each functions.

Explain the roles of the parathyroid hormone and thyrocalcitonin in regulating the release of calcium from bone.

List and describe the various types of bone fractures and outline the stages of healing.

Identify the bones of the axial and appendicular skeletons.

FUNCTIONS

The supporting structure of the body is a joined framework of bones called the *skeleton.* It enables man to stand erect and to accomplish extraordinary feats of artistic grace, athletic endeavor, and physical endurance.

Contrary to appearance, the individual bones of the skeleton are indeed living tissues. Five general functions are ascribed to the skeleton as a whole.

1. It *supports* the surrounding tissues.

2. It *protects* vital organs and other soft tissues of the body.

3. It assists in *body movement,* giving attachment to the muscles and providing leverage.

4. It manufactures blood cells. This *hematopoietic* function occurs in the red bone marrow.

5. It provides a *storage* area for mineral salts, especially phosphorus and calcium, to supply body needs.

Leonardo da Vinci is credited with being the first anatomist to correctly illustrate the skeleton with its 206 bones. The Belgian physician Andreas Vesalius (1514–1564) reconstructed a human skeleton that is still in existence today as the oldest anatomic specimen. Current investigation centers on actual function of the cells of bone in health and disease.

COMPOSITION OF BONE

Bone is a form of connective tissue and, as such, consists of cells and a matrix of fibers and ground substance. The distinguishing feature of bone is that the ground substance is calcified and, therefore, rigid. The collagenous fibers of the matrix are responsible for its resilience when tension is applied, whereas the calcium salts deposited in the matrix (accounting for 65 per cent of the weight of bone) prevent crushing when pressure is applied. A substance closely resembling the structure of *hydroxyapatite* $[Ca_3(PO_4)_2]_3 \cdot Ca(OH)_2$ makes up the major portion of salts present in bone. Small amounts of calcium carbonate ($CaCO_3$) are also present.

Bone Cells

Three types of cells exist in bone: osteoblasts (active in bone formation), osteoclasts (associated with bone resorption), and osteocytes (the principal cells of mature bone). Although each type is readily identified, especially in growing bone, reversible transformation from one to the other apparently occurs.

Deposition of Bone by Osteoblasts. Bone develops from spindle-shaped cells called *osteoblasts* (G. *osteon,* bone; G. *blastos,* germ). This occurs not only when bone is initially formed, but also in the remodeling and repair of fully formed bone. The first function of the osteoblasts is to secrete the organic matrix components, namely the amorphous protein-polysaccharides and a precursor of the fibrous protein collagen, which, following chemical alteration, polymerizes into fibrils. A geometric array of collagenous fibers (which has been described as resembling the struts and girders of a bridge) embedded in the amorphous ground substance takes form to give the matrix a leather-like consistency. Calcium salts are then precipitated within the matrix, giving the bone its characteristic

quality of hardness. For these salts to be deposited it is necessary that calcium first combine with phosphate, producing calcium phosphate ($CaHPO_4$); this substance is slowly converted over a period of several weeks into a hydroxyapatite pattern.

REGULATION OF DEPOSITION. Deposition of bone is regulated partially by the amount of strain on the bone—the more strain the greater the deposition. Bones in casts, therefore, will waste away, whereas continued and excessive strain will cause the bone to grow thick and strong. In addition, a break in the bone will stimulate injured osteoblasts to proliferate, secreting large quantities of matrix for the deposition of new bone.

Resorption of Bone by Osteoclasts. Large cells called *osteoclasts* are present in almost all cavities of bone, and function to cause resorption (L. *resorbere,* to suck back) of bone. This is brought about by the release of enzymes from lysosomes that digest the protein portion of bone and split the salts. These phosphate and calcium salts are then absorbed into the surrounding extracellular fluid in the bone canaliculi (described under Histology).

The strength and, in some instances, the size of the skeletal bone will depend on the comparative activity of the bone. For example, it is obvious that during the growth period deposition is more active than resorption. The *osteoclasts* are associated with the removal of dead bone from the inner side during remodeling. As a result, the bone is prevented from becoming overly thick and heavy. Osteoblastic deposition continues to counteract the neverending process of resorption, even when the bones are no longer capable of growth.

It is possible for crooked bones to become straight due to this continual process. A broken bone that has healed crookedly in a child will straighten in a matter of a few years.

During the four-day flight of Gemini IV in 1965, one of the astronauts lost between 1 and 12 per cent of his bone mass, as measured by x-ray of his hands and feet. The flight of Gemini V, which lasted eight days, caused losses of more than 20 per cent. As a result of these findings, exercises in flight were prescribed which were found to reduce this loss.

Osteocytes

Osteocytes, which are osteoblasts that have become surrounded by bone matrix as bone is formed, are the principal cells of fully formed bone. Although the mature osteocyte no longer forms bone matrix at a rapid pace, it is presumed to be involved in the maintenance of the matrix. In addition, osteocytes apparently participate in bone resorption under the influence of the parathyroid hormone (see discussion on calcium homeostasis on page 90).

Types of Bone Tissue

There are two types of bone tissue, **compact** and **cancellous,** also called spongy (Fig. 56). Compact bone tissue is dense and strong. Cancellous bone tissue, on the other hand, has many open (marrow) spaces, giving the tissue a spongy appearance even without the aid of a microscope. The plates of bone forming the open network of cancellous bone are called *trabeculae* (Latin for little beams).

CLASSIFICATION OF BONES

Individual bones of the skeleton are divided according to shape into five types: long, short, flat, irregular and sesamoid.

1. **Long bones** (for example, humerus, radius, tibia and fibula) consist of a shaft, the diaphysis and two extremities, each called an epiphysis (Fig. 56). The shaft is formed primarily by compact tissue, which is thickest in the middle of the bone, where strain on it is the greatest. Strength of a long bone is further insured by a slight curvature of the shaft. The interior of the shaft is the *marrow cavity,* also called the *medullary canal.* The flared portions at each end of the diaphysis and each epiphysis are composed of a central core of cancellous bone surrounded by a thin layer of compact bone. In

Figure 56. *A,* Cross section of bone, showing relation of osteocytes to haversian system. *B,* This section has been magnified out of proportion to show haversian system and lamellae. (Note communication between periosteal vessels and haversian canal vessels by way of Volkmann's canals.) *C,* Diagram of the structure of a long bone. (After Lockhart.)

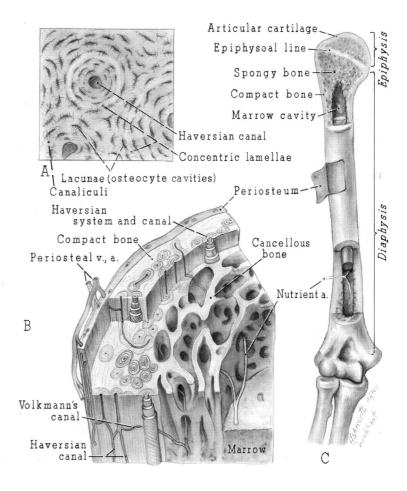

Articular cartilage
Epiphyseal line
Spongy bone
Compact bone
Marrow cavity
Epiphysis

Haversian canal
Concentric lamellae
Lacunae (osteocyte cavities)
Canaliculi
Haversian system and canal
Compact bone
Periosteal v., a.

Periosteum
Cancellous bone
Nutrient a.
Diaphysis

Volkmann's canal
Haversian canal
Marrow

growing bone the epiphysis and diaphysis are separated by the cartilaginous epiphyseal, or growth, plate, where longitudinal growth occurs. The extremities are generally broad and expanded, as compared to the shaft, to facilitate articulation with other bones and provide a larger surface for muscle attachment. The articular surfaces are covered with a layer of hyaline cartilage.

2. **Short bones,** exemplified by the *carpal* bones of the wrist and the *tarsal* bones of the ankle, have a somewhat irregular shape and are not merely shorter versions of a long bone type. Only a thin layer of compact tissue covers the cancellous tissue of a typical short bone.

3. **Flat bones** are found wherever there is a need for protection of soft body parts or for a provision for extensive muscle attachment. The *ribs,* the *scapula,* parts of the *pelvic girdle,* and the bones of the *skull* are all examples of flat bones. These bones consist of two flat plates of compact tissue enclosing a layer of spongy bone.

4. **Irregular bones** have the same basic structure as short and flat bones; however, this last group comprises bones of peculiar and differing shape, such as the vertebrae and the ossicles of the ear.

5. **Sesamoid bones** are generally considered a separate type, since they are small and rounded. Sesamoid bones are enclosed in tendon and fascial tissue and are found adjacent to joints. They appear to function in increasing the lever function of muscles. The patella, or kneecap, is included among the 206 bones of the skeleton. It is the largest and most definitive of the sesamoid bones.

Membranes of Bone

The **periosteum** (G. *peri,* around; G. *osteon,* bone) is the connective tissue sheath that covers the outer surface of bone except at the articular surfaces (which are layered with hyaline cartilage). The outer layer of the periosteum is relatively acellular, dense and vascular; the inner layer is loose and, during growth, contains osteoblasts. In the adult, the inner layer contains an abundance of spindle-shaped connective tissue cells which, when stimulated by normal mechanical stress or injury, assume the appearance and bone-forming activity of osteoblasts. The periosteum is anchored to bone by collagenous fibers (Sharpey's fibers) that penetrate the underlying matrix.

The **endosteum** (G. *endon,* within) is a thin, delicate membrane that lines all of the cavities of bone, including the marrow cavity of long bone (where it is most prominent), the marrow spaces of cancellous bone and the haversian canals (described below). It has both osteogenic and hematopoietic capabilities.

Marrow

The many spaces within cancellous bone of the ribs, vertebrae, sternum and pelvis are, in normal adults, filled with **red bone marrow.** This marrow, which is richly supplied with blood, consists mainly of blood cells and their precursors. Its primary function, referred to as hematopoiesis, is the formation of red and white blood cells and megakaryocytes, which fragment to form platelets (necessary for blood clotting). Therefore, cells in all stages of development are found within it. Red marrow is plentiful within the ends of the humerus and femur at birth but gradually decreases in amount throughout the years.

Yellow marrow is connective tissue that consists chiefly of fat cells, and is found primarily in the shafts of long bones, within the marrow cavity.

HISTOLOGY OF BONE

The **haversian system,** named for Clopton Havers, the English anatomist who first described it, is a prominent histologic feature of compact bone. This system permits effective metabolism of bone cells and has several components (Fig. 56). Running parallel to the surface of the bone are many small canals containing blood vessels (usually a single large capillary) that bring in oxygen and food and remove waste products. These canals, called **haversian canals,** are surrounded by concentric rings of bone, each layer of which is called a **lamella.** Between two lamellae of compact bone are several tiny cavities called **lacunae.** The lacunae are connected to each other and ultimately to the larger, central haversian canals by small canals, or **canaliculi.**

Each lacuna contains an osteocyte, or mature bone cell, suspended in tissue fluid. It is this fluid that circulates through compact bone via the haversian system. The haversian system functions to keep osteocytes alive and healthy.

In summary, the haversian system consists of lacunae and their contained osteocytes, the canaliculi, a central, haversian canal with blood vessels and the surrounding lamellae.

Blood vessels in the haversian canals interconnect by way of transverse and oblique canals and communicate through **Volkmann's canals** with the blood vessels of the surface periosteum and the endosteum lining the marrow cavity. The haversian systems of compact bone are closely arranged, with interstitial lamellae filling the spaces between haversian systems.

In the trabeculae of cancellous bone, the osteocytes also reside in lacunae between lamellae and are interconnected by canaliculi. But the haversian systems are not complete, since haversian blood vessels are absent. The osteocytes are nourished by direct communication between the network of canaliculi and the endosteum of the marrow spaces.

Bone Formation and Growth

Intramembranous Ossification. There are two types of ossification. The first of these, intramembranous ossification, is a process by which dense connective membranes are replaced by deposits of inorganic calcium salts, thus forming bone. The membrane itself becomes the *periosteum*, while immediately within the periosteum can be found compact bone with an inner core of *cancellous bone.*

Only the flat bones of the cranium form completely by this process.

Endochondral Ossification. Most bones form by the process of *endochondral ossification*, the replacement of a "scale model" of hyaline cartilage by bone. The cartilage skeleton is completely formed at the end of three months of pregnancy. During subsequent months of gestation, ossification and growth occur.

In long bones, endochondral bone formation starts at the center of the diaphysis of the cartilage model (Fig. 57). A number of events occur, more or less simultaneously, including the following: (1) Enlargement of cartilage cells and calcification of the matrix in the region of growth, which interferes with the nutrition of the hypertrophied cells. (2) Differentiation of cells in the perichondrium into osteoblasts (signaling the transformation of the perichondrium into periosteum), which deposit a collar of bone around the center of the shaft. (3) Invasion of the region of enlarged cartilage cells by osteoblasts and blood vessels through openings in the bone collar. (4) Replacement of dying cartilage cells by cancellous bone in what is known as the *primary center of ossification.* After the primary center of ossification is established, growth of the cartilage model, principally in length, occurs at each epiphysis. Cartilage cells multiply and enlarge, and toward the diaphyseal end of the region of growth calcification, death of cells and ossification take place. Expansion of the primary center of ossification in the diaphysis is accompanied by resorption of primary bone, its replacement by compact bone and continuous reconstruction. In addition, the shaft is hollowed to form the marrow cavity. At about the time of birth, secondary centers of ossification are established in each epiphysis, in which cancellous bone is formed. Gradually all of the cartilage in each epiphysis is replaced by bone except at the articular surfaces and between the epiphysis and diaphysis as a transverse disc known as the **epiphyseal,** or **growth, plate,** where subsequent lengthening of long bone occurs. When bone lengthens, proliferation of cartilage cells temporarily widens the plate, and cancellous bone replaces cartilage in essentially the same manner as during earlier periods of bone formation. As long bone increases in length, there is a proportional increase in diameter brought about by the deposition of compact bone beneath the periosteum (subperiosteal intramembranous ossification) and enlargement of the marrow cavity by resorption of bone. Bone resorption also elongates the marrow cavity as growth in length proceeds at the growth plate.

Longitudinal growth of bones continues in a definite sequence until approximately

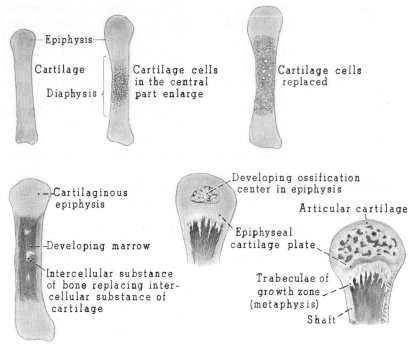

Figure 57. The bony deposit laid down around the diaphysis spreads toward the epiphysis, where ossification is also occurring. Gradual replacement of cartilage by bone occurs, and an increase in lengthwise direction of the bone accompanies this process. Growth in diameter of the bone occurs primarily with the deposit of bony tissue beneath the periosteum.

15 years of age in the female and 16 in the male. As the growing period comes to an end, proliferation of cartilage cells at the growth plate slows. When these sites are replaced by bone (an event called *closure of the epiphyses*), growth of bone ceases. A dense zone, called the **epiphyseal line**, is visible in adult bone at the site of union of the epiphysis and diaphysis. The relative contribution of the proximal and distal growth plate to bone elongation varies from bone to bone. The femur, for example, grows in length principally at the distal epiphysis. The tibia, on the other hand, lengthens principally at the proximal epiphysis.

The initial shape assumed by a bone during its formation is genetically determined. Extrinsic factors such as muscle strength, mechanical stress and biochemical environment assume a function in determining the shape of a bone. Wolff's law reflects the role of mechanical forces acting on bone and, briefly stated, suggests that every change in use of a bone leads to a change not only in the internal structure but also in its external form and function.

Regulation of Bone Formation and Growth by Vitamins and Hormones

Vitamin D. One disease resulting in physiologic changes in the bone is a manifestation of vitamin D deficiency. This clinical condition, in which the calcification of bone is inadequate because absorption of calcium from the small intestine is subnormal, is called **rickets** in children and **osteomalacia** in adults. The essential defect in rickets, failure of the bone to ossify, produces soft bones. When a baby with this condition begins to walk, the bones bend in response to mechanical stresses; various deformities, such as bowed legs, result.

Rickets was first described in England about 1650, when the use of soft coal had become prevalent. It was caused, it is now known, by a deficiency in the ultraviolet radiation of sunlight in factory towns, where coal smoke and dark alleys created a sunless environment. Ultraviolet radiation activates the conversion of a natural substance in the skin (7-dihydrocholesterol) to vitamin D_3. Vitamin D_3 must be further modified by chemical reactions (hydroxylations) in the liver and kidneys before it can carry out its essential function of increasing the absorption of calcium from the small intestine. The active substance (**1,25-dihydroxyvitamin D$_3$**), now called a hormone, is secreted by the kidneys in response to a need by bone for calcium. The intracellular action of dihydroxyvitamin D$_3$ in the small intestine is analogous to that of other steroid hormones (Chapter 15): after entering the intestinal cell it is bound by a receptor protein, which then can enter the nucleus and activate gene transcription. This results, in the case of dihydroxyvitamin D$_3$, in the synthesis of a calcium-binding protein that facilitates calcium transport. If a child is fed a balanced diet and exposed to sufficient sunlight, cod liver oil or other sources of vitamin D are not necessary. Cod liver oil is a good source of vitamin D$_3$ and therefore a useful antirachitic medicine because fish are able to synthesize the vitamin without benefit of ultraviolet light.

Growth Hormone. Growth hormone, also called somatotropic hormone or somatotropin, secreted by the hypophysis (pituitary gland), has a number of actions throughout the body. Its effect on bone is brought about by inducing the liver to release into the blood stream a substance called *somatomedin,* which stimulates the proliferation of cartilage cells at the growth plate. The consequence of a deficiency of growth hormone is inadequate lengthening of bone; excess of the hormone causes above-normal lengthening.

Vitamin C. Vitamin C is required for hydroxylation of the amino acid proline, an essential step in the synthesis of collagen (see Chapter 3, page 64). Defficiency during the period of bone formation and growth results in a weak bone matrix.

Thyroxine. One of the actions of thyroxine, a hormone secreted by the thyroid gland, is to increase the rate of replacement of cartilage by bone at the growth plate. A normal balance between growth hormone and thyroxine is important during the growth period. Administration of an excess of thyroxine to animals, for example, causes premature closure of the epiphyses. Thyroxine is also essential for the normal functioning of cells of the hypophysis that manufacture growth hormone. The stunted growth of severely hypothyroid children, called cretins, is in part the result of insufficient synthesis of growth hormone.

Estrogens and Androgens. The male and female sex hormones, among other things, promote the synthesis of bone matrix throughout life and ossification during growth. Since the resorption of bone matrix is a never-ending phenomenon, the drop in estrogen levels in elderly women can contribute to senile osteoporosis, a thinning and weakening of bone. Excessive lengthening of bone in eunuchs can be explained by a delay in epiphyseal closure.

Vitamin A. Vitamin A stimulates the release of enzymes from lysosomes that are responsible for bone resorption. Deficiency can hamper the hollowing and reshaping of bone. In an extreme case of vitamin A deficiency produced experimentally in growing dogs, the insufficient widening of openings in the skull through which cranial nerves pass caused degeneration of pinched nerves. An excess of vitamin A may weaken bone or erode epiphyseal cartilage and prematurely halt growth.

Role of Bone in Calcium Homeostasis

Ninety-nine per cent of the total calcium of the body exists in the bone. The small but important remainder is present in the blood plasma and in the interstitial fluid, where the ionized form of calcium participates in vital chemical reactions.

Calcium has several functions that are best understood by viewing the effects of a severe calcium deficiency. Lack of calcium results in the following: (1) Depolarization of nerve fiber membranes with transmission of uncontrolled impulses; under these conditions *tetany,* or spasm of the skeletal musculature, occurs. (2) Weakness of cardiac muscle with a consequent inadequate supply of blood to the total body circulation. (3) Interference with the process of blood coagulation (see Chapter 10).

Hormonal regulation of the release of calcium from the bone matrix is one of the important homeostatic regulatory mechanisms for maintaining normal blood calcium. (Two other control mechanisms involve governing the rate of calcium absorption from the small intestine and reabsorption from the kidneys.) Two hormones, one secreted by the *parathyroid gland,* the other *(thyrocalcitonin)* by the thyroid gland, regulate the release of calcium from bone. Below-normal concentration of blood calcium increases the release of the parathyroid hormone, which increases bone resorption, raising the concentration of blood calcium. Although an above-normal calcium concentration decreases the release of the parathyroid hormone, protection against the effects of high blood calcium (impairment of kidney function, for example) depends upon the release of thyrocalcitonin. Thyrocalcitonin lowers blood calcium by inhibiting bone resorption. Bone resorption initiated by the parathyroid gland apparently involves not only the activity of osteoclasts but also of osteocytes. Microradiographs of sheep bone, for example, have revealed that treatment with the parathyroid hormone causes the matrix to dissolve away around each osteocyte.

FRACTURES

The breaking of a bone or cartilage is known as a fracture. A fracture is usually accompanied by an injury in the surrounding soft tissue. The resultant injury can be comparatively minor—for example, torn skin or bruised muscles—however, it can be even more serious than the fracture itself, as when the broken bone divides an artery or punctures a lung. The various types of fractures are given proper descriptive terms. A fracture can be open (compound) if the broken bone protrudes through the skin, or closed (simple) if it does not. Because of the greater possibility of infection, a compound fracture is the more dangerous of the two.

Types of Fractures (Fig. 58). A fracture is either *complete* or *incomplete,* depending on whether or not the fracture line extends partially or entirely through the substance of the bone. Fractures are classified according to the location or direction of the fracture line in the bone, and are then named *transverse, oblique, longitudinal,* or *spiral.*

In addition to these general terms, one common specific type is the comminuted fracture, in which the bone is divided into more than two fragments by more than one fracture line.

Healing of Fracture

At the time of injury, bleeding occurs from damaged structures, and a blood clot forms between and around the bone fragments. The clot is invaded by fibroblasts and new capillaries. The mixture of fibroblasts and new capillaries, called *granulation tissue,* becomes transformed into a dense fibrous tissue, which in turn is transformed into the *temporary callus,* a fibrocartilaginous mass that knits the fracture. Osteoblasts, proliferating from the periosteum and endosteum, deposit the *bony callus,* a cancellous bone that gradually replaces the temporary callus. Healing is completed by reconstruction of the bony callus into compact bone.

Prompt medical attention is required in even the simplest of fractures to prevent serious complications. Optimal bone healing occurs when there is close and accurate approximation of the fracture ends. Provision for this by applying a splint or cast or by inserting a bone pin so that the structures are effectively immobilized and properly aligned is usually necessary for optimal repair.

BONE MARKINGS

The surface of a typical bone exhibits certain projections *(processes)* or depressions *(fossae).* These markings are functional in the sense that they help to join one bone to another or serve as a passageway for blood vessels and nerves. They also provide attachment for muscles. The following terms will often be encountered in any discussion of bone.

process—any marked, bony prominence

spine—any sharp, slender projection, such as spinous process

condyle—a rounded or knuckle-like prominence, usually found at the point of articulation with another bone.

tubercle—a small, rounded process

tuberosity—a large, rounded process

trochanter—a large process for attach-

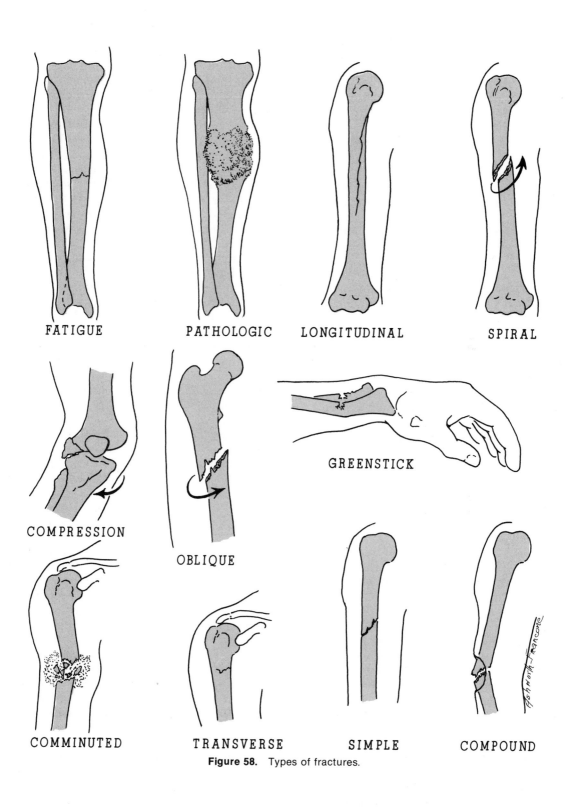

Figure 58. Types of fractures.

ment of muscle, such as the trochanter of the femur

    trochlea — a process shaped like a pulley

    crest — a narrow ridge of bone

    line — a less prominent ridge of bone than the crest

    head — a terminal enlargement

    fossa — a depression or cavity in or on a bone

    fissure — a narrow slit, often between two bones

    foramen — an orifice through which blood vessels, nerves, and ligaments pass

    meatus or *canal* — a long, tubelike passage

    sinus or *antrum* — a cavity within a bone

    sulcus — a furrow or groove

DIVISIONS OF THE SKELETON

There are 206 bones in the skeleton. The *axial part* consists of the *skull* (28 bones, including those of the face), the *hyoid bone,* the *vertebrae* (26 bones), the *ribs* (24 bones), and the *sternum.* The *appendicular part* of the skeleton consists of the *upper extremities* (64 bones, including the *shoulder girdle*), and the *lower extremities* (62 bones, including the *pelvic girdle*). Components of the axial skeleton will be discussed first.

THE AXIAL SKELETON

The Skull

Cranial Bones. The skull, in the proper use of the term, includes both the *facial* and *cranial* bones (Figs. 63–71 and Table 6, page 102). The bones of the cranium enclose and protect the brain and its associated structures, the special sense organs. The muscles of mastication as well as the muscles for head movements are attached to the cranium. At certain locations within the cranium, cavities, or *air sinuses,* are present (Fig. 72). These communicate with the nasal cavity.

The individual bones of the cranium are immovably united at *sutures,* or juncture lines. During infancy and early childhood, the articulation is formed by sheets of fibrocartilaginous tissue which gradually ossify. Union of the cranial bones continues as the bone itself grows by increments at its outside edges; thus, the bones grow toward each other, so to speak, and eventually meet at suture lines.

FRONTAL BONE. The frontal bone forms the forehead, roof of the nasal cavity, and orbits, the bony sockets which contain the eyes. It develops in two halves which fuse by the end of the second year of life. Paired cavities, the *frontal sinuses,* are present above the orbits near the midline. The notable markings of the frontal bone are the *orbital margin,* a definite ridge above each orbit, and the *supraorbital ridge,* a prominence overlying the frontal sinus. The two frontal sinuses act as sound chambers to provide resonance to the voice.

PARIETAL BONE. The two parietal bones form the sides and roof of the cranium and are joined at the *sagittal suture* in the midline. The line of articulation between the frontal bone and the two parietal bones is called the *coronal suture.* Like other parts of the cranium, the parietal bones exhibit a variety of grooves and depressions on their inner surfaces, lodging the venous sinuses and convolutions of the brain.

OCCIPITAL BONE. The occipital bone forms the back and base of the cranium and joins the parietal bones anteriorly at the *lambdoid suture.* The inferior portion of the bone has a large opening, the *foramen magnum* (literally, great opening), through which the spinal cord passes. It is at the level of the foramen magnum that the spinal cord joins the medulla oblongata of the brain. On each lower side of the occipital bone is a process called the *occipital condyle* for articulation with the first vertebra. Other obvious projections are the *external occipital crest* and the *external occipital protuberance.* These can be felt through the scalp at the base of the neck. Several ligaments and muscles are attached in this region.

TEMPORAL BONE. The paired temporal bones help to form the sides and base of the cranium. Each encloses an ear and bears a fossa for articulation with the lower jaw. The temporal bone is irregular in shape and consists of the *squamous, petrous, mastoid,* and *tympanic* parts. The *squamous* portion is the largest and most superior of the four. It is a thin, flat plate of bone forming the temple. Projecting for-

Text continued on page 104

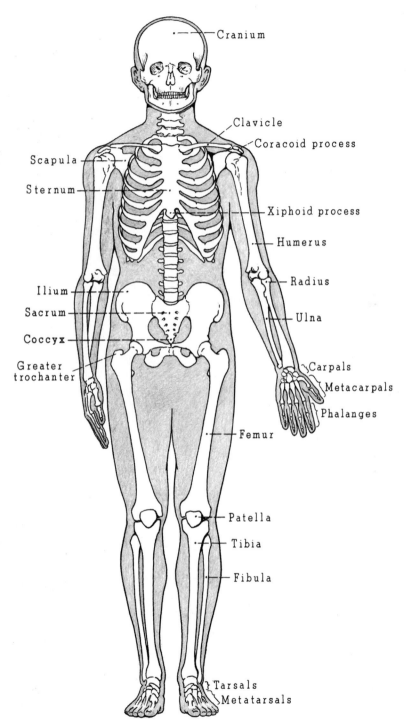

Figure 59. Anterior view of the skeleton.

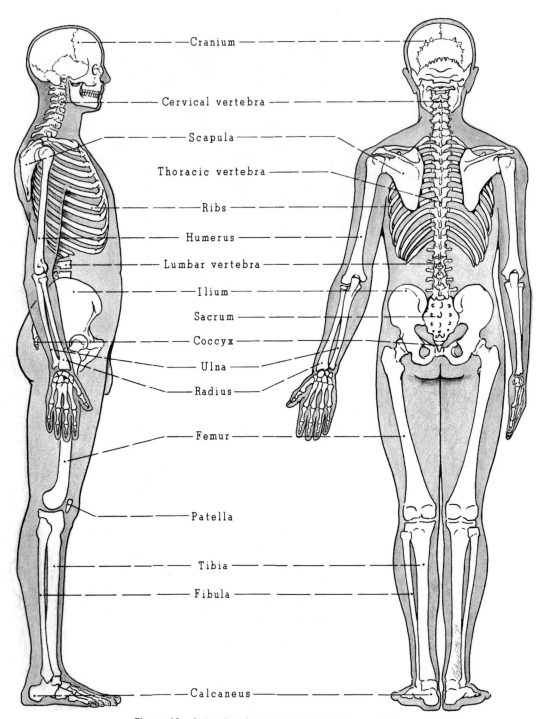

Cranium

Cervical vertebra

Scapula

Thoracic vertebra

Ribs

Humerus

Lumbar vertebra

Ilium

Sacrum

Coccyx

Ulna

Radius

Femur

Patella

Tibia

Fibula

Calcaneus

Figure 60.   Lateral and posterior views of the skeleton.

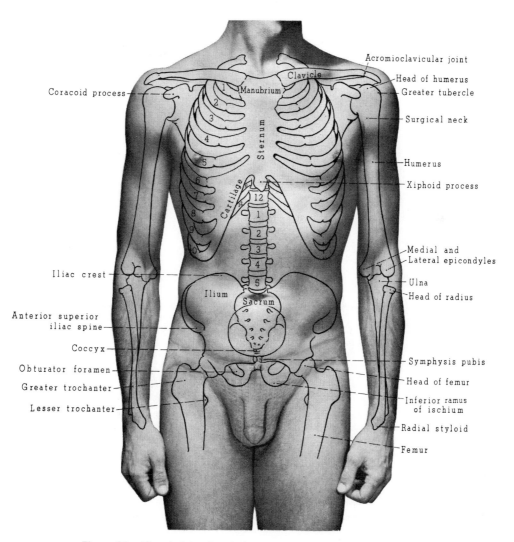

Figure 61. The skeleton in relation to surface markings, anterior view.

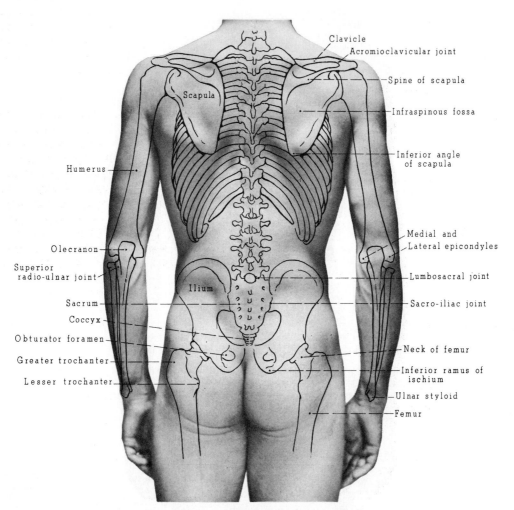

Figure 62. The skeleton in relation to surface markings, posterior view.

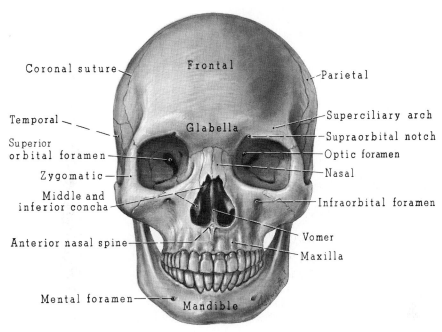

Figure 63. Frontal aspect of the skull.

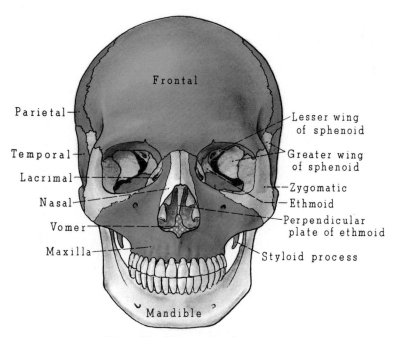

Figure 64. Bones of the face.

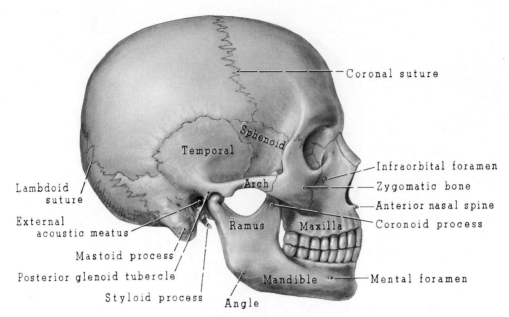

Figure 65. Right side of the skull.

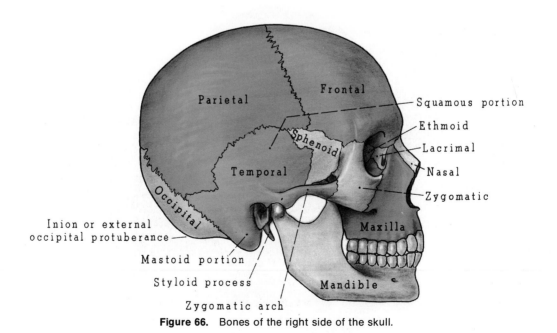

Figure 66. Bones of the right side of the skull.

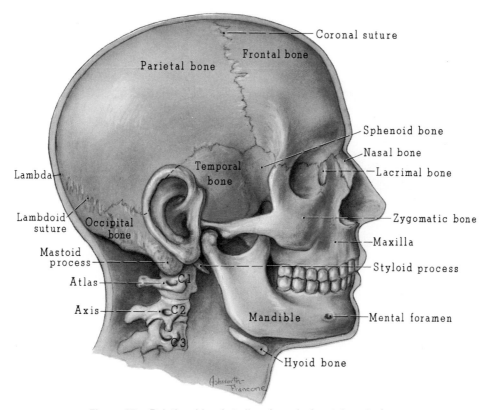

Figure 67. Relationship of skull and cervical vertebrae to face.

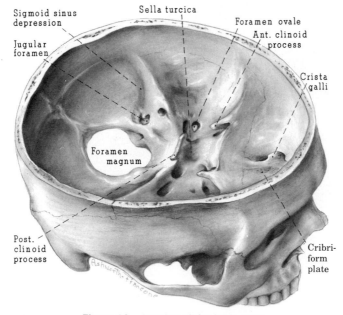

Figure 68. Interior of the brain case.

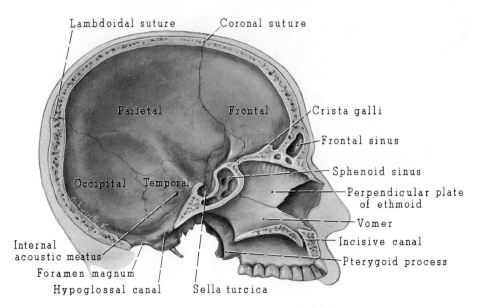

Figure 69. Sagittal section of skull.

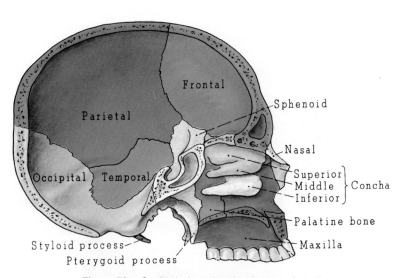

Figure 70. Sagittal view showing bones of skull.

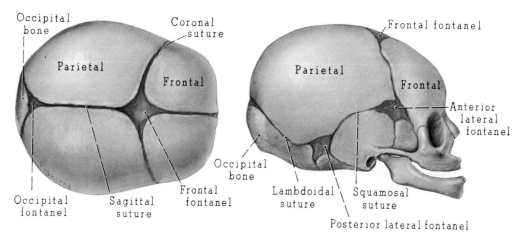

Figure 71. Fetal skull, demonstrating that ossification is not complete at birth. The frontal fontanel closes at about 18 months of age; the posterior fontanel closes about 6 to 8 weeks after birth.

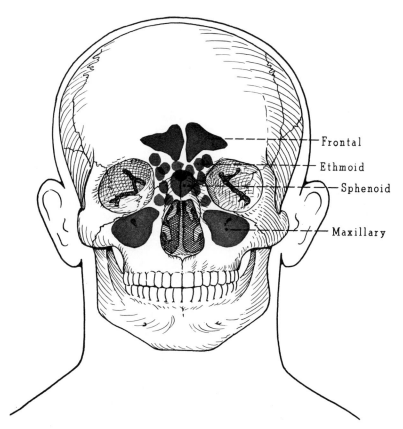

Figure 72. Sinuses of the skull.

Table 6. BONES

BONE	NUMBER	LOCATION
1. *Skull*	28 bones	
Cranium	8 bones	
Occipital	1	Posterior cranial floor and walls
Parietal	2	Forms the greater part of the superior lateral aspect and roof of the skull between frontal and occipital bones
Frontal	1	Forms forehead, most of orbital roof, and anterior cranial floor
Temporal	2	Inferior lateral aspect and base of the skull, housing middle and inner ear structures
Sphenoid	1	Mid-anterior base of the skull; forms part of floor and sides of orbit
Ethmoid	1	Between nasal bones and sphenoid, forming part of anterior cranial floor, medial wall of orbits, part of nasal septum, and roof
Face	14 bones	
Nasal	2	Upper bridge of nose
Maxillary	2	Upper jaw
Zygomatic (malar)	2	Prominence of cheeks and part of the lateral wall and floor of the orbits
Mandible	1	Lower jaw
Lacrimal	2	Anterior medial wall of the orbit
Palatine	2	Posterior nasal cavity between maxillae and the pterygoid processes of sphenoid
Vomer	1	Posterior nasal cavity, forming a portion of the nasal septum
Inferior nasal conchae (inferior turbinates)	2	Lateral wall of nasal cavity
Auditory Ossicles	6 bones	
Malleus (hammer)	2	Small bones in inner ear in temporal bone, connecting the tympanic membrane to the inner ear and functioning in sound transmission
Incus (anvil)	2	
Stapes (stirrup)	2	
Hyoid	1 bone	Horseshoe-shaped, suspended from styloid process of temporal bone
2. *Trunk*	51 bones	
Vertebrae	26 bones	
Cervical	7	Neck
Thoracic	12	Thorax
Lumbar	5	Between thorax and pelvis
Sacrum	1 (5 fused)	Pelvis—fixed, or false, vertebrae
Coccyx	1 (4 fused)	Terminal vertebrae in pelvis—fixed, or false, vertebrae

Table 6. **BONES** *Continued.*

BONE	NUMBER	LOCATION
Ribs	24	True ribs—upper seven pairs fastened to sternum by costal cartilages; false ribs—lower five pairs; eighth, ninth, and tenth pairs attached to the seventh rib by costal cartilages; last two pairs do not attach and are called floating ribs
Sternum	1	Flat, narrow bone situated in median line anteriorly in chest
3. *Upper Extremity*	64 bones	
Clavicle	2	Together, clavicles and scapulae form the shoulder girdle; the clavicle articulates with the sternum
Scapula	2	
Humerus	2	Long bone of upper arm
Ulna	2	The ulna is the longest bone of forearm, on medial side of radius
Radius	2	Lateral to ulna, shorter than ulna, but styloid process is larger
Carpals	16	Two rows of bones comprising the wrist
Scaphoid		
Lunate		
Triangular		
Pisiform		
Capitate		
Hamate		
Trapezium		
Trapezoid		
Metacarpals	10	Long bones of the palm of the hand
Phalanges	28	Three in each finger and two in each thumb
4. *Lower Extremity*	62 bones	
Pelvic	2	Fusion of ilium, ischium and pubis
Femur (thighbone)	2	Longest bone in body
Patella	2	Kneecap; located in quadriceps femoris tendon; a sesamoid bone
Tibia	2	Shinbone; antero-medial side of the leg
Fibula	2	Lateral to tibia
Tarsals	14	Form heel, ankle (with distal tibia and fibula), and proximal part of the foot
Calcaneus		
Talus		
Navicular		
Cuboid		
First cuneiform (medial)		
Second cuneiform (intermediate)		
Third cuneiform (lateral)		
Metatarsals	10	Long bones of the foot
Phalanges	28	Three in each lesser toe and two in each great toe

ward from the lower part of the squamous is the *zygomatic process,* forming the lateral part of the zygomatic arch, or cheek bone. The *petrous* part, shaped roughly like a three-sided pyramid with its apex directed medially, is located deep within the base of the skull between the sphenoid and occipital bones. The petrous contains the inner ear within its complexly fashioned cavities and also bounds a part of the middle ear. The *mastoid* portion is located behind and below the meatus, or opening, of the ear. In the adult, it contains a number of air spaces called *mastoid cells* or *sinuses,* separated from the brain only by thin, bony partitions. Inflammation of the cells of the mastoid (mastoiditis) is not uncommon and is a potentially dangerous source of infection which may invade the brain or its outer membranes.

The *mastoid process* is a rounded projection of the temporal bone easily found behind the external ear. Several muscles of the neck are attached to the mastoid process. The *tympanic plate* forms the floor and anterior wall of the *external auditory meatus* and lies below the squamous portion anterior to the mastoid process. The long, slender *styloid process* is seen extending from the under surface of the tympanic plate, but is attached for the most part to the petrous portion of the temporal bone.

SPHENOID BONE. The sphenoid bone forms the anterior portion of the base of the cranium. It is a single, wedge-shaped bone having a central body and two expanded wings that articulate with the temporal bones on either side. The sphenoid is joined anteriorly to both the ethmoid and frontal bones and posteriorly to the occipital bone. Thus, it serves as a kind of anchor, binding the cranial bones together. A septum, or partition, projects downward from the body of the sphenoid bone toward the nasal cavity and divides the two sphenoidal sinuses. Superiorly, there is a marked depression, the *sella turcica,* which is occupied by the *hypophysis* (pituitary gland). Medial and lateral plates extend from the base of the sphenoid to form a part of the walls of the orbit. These are perforated by several foramina, or passages, which transmit important nerves and blood vessels.

ETHMOID BONE. The ethmoid is the principal supporting structure of the nasal cavity and contributes to the formation of the orbits. It is the lightest of the cranial bones and consists predominantly of *cancellous tissue.* The *horizontal,* or *cribriform, plate* of the ethmoid forms the roof of the nasal cavity and unites the two lateral masses of air cells, the *ethmoidal labyrinths.* (The outer walls of these small air spaces are completed by various bones of the face.) Each labyrinth exhibits two or three bony plates, the nasal conchae, or *turbinate bones,* which project into the nasal cavity and allow for circulation and filtration of inhaled air before it passes to the lungs. The *perpendicular plate* of the ethmoid forms the upper part of the nasal septum.

AUDITORY OSSICLES. Three bones of the ear—the *malleus, incus,* and *stapes*—are highly specialized in both structure and function. They will be discussed in detail in Chapter 9.

WORMIAN BONES. The so-called *wormian bones* are located within the sutures of the cranium. These bones are inconstant in number. They are small and irregular in shape, and are not included in the total number of bones in the body. In summary, then, the cranial portion of the skull consists of the following bones:

1 frontal
2 parietal
1 occipital
2 temporal
1 sphenoid
1 ethmoid
6 auditory ossicles
wormian bones (variable number)

Facial Bones. Like those of the cranium, the bones of the face are immovably united by sutures, with a single exception—the mandible. The lower jaw is capable of movement in several directions and can be depressed or elevated, as in talking. It can also protrude or retract and move from side to side, as in chewing.

NASAL BONE. The paired nasal bones join to form the bridge of the nose. Superiorly, these flat bones articulate with the frontal bone and constitute a small portion of the *nasal septum.*

PALATINE BONE. The two palatine

bones form the posterior part of the roof of the mouth, or *hard palate*. This area is the same as the floor of the nose. Extensions of the palatine bones extend upward and help to form the outer wall of the nasal cavity. Each palatine bone is somewhat L-shaped with *perpendicular* and *horizontal plates*. The horizontal plate contributes to the palate and joins the maxillary bone anteriorly.

MAXILLARY BONE. The two maxillae constitute the upper jaw. Between the ages of 7 and 12, maxillary growth is responsible for vertical elongation of the face. Each maxillary bone consists of a *body*, a *zygomatic process*, a *frontal process*, a *palatine process*, and an *alveolar process*.

The massive *body* of the maxilla forms part of the floor and outer wall of the nasal cavity, the greater part of the floor of the orbit, and much of the anterior face below the temple. This part of the bone, covered by several facial muscles, also contains a large maxillary sinus located lateral to the nose.

The *zygomatic process* extends laterally to participate in the formation of the cheek. The *frontal process* extends superiorly to the forehead. The *palatine process* passes posteriorly in a horizontal plane to articulate with the palatine bone and to form the greater portion of the bony palate anteriorly.

The *alveolar process* bears the teeth of the upper jaw. Each tooth is embedded in a socket, or alveolus. In a preserved *edentulous* (without teeth) maxilla, vertical ridges may be seen on the more anterior (external) surface corresponding to the roots of the teeth.

The two maxillary bones are joined at the *intermaxillary suture* in the median plane. This fusion is normally completed before birth. When the two bones do not unite to form a continuous bone the resulting defect is known as a *cleft palate* and is usually associated with a *cleft lip*.

ZYGOMATIC BONE. The two bones forming the prominence of the cheek are also called *malar* bones and rest upon the maxillae, articulating with their zygomatic processes. The *orbital surface* of the zygomatic bone forms part of the lateral wall and floor of the orbit. The *malar surface* of each bone is broad and flat and is seen from both the lateral and anterior views of the face. The zygomatic bone has a *frontal process* extending upward to articulate with the frontal bone and a smaller *temporal process* articulating laterally with the temporal bone, thus forming the easily identified zygomatic arch.

LACRIMAL BONE. The paired lacrimal bones make up part of the orbit at the inner angle of the eye. These small, thin bones lie directly behind the frontal process of the maxilla. The lateral surface of the bone presents a *fossa* which lodges the *lacrimal sac* and provides a groove or canal for the passage of the *lacrimal duct*. One side of this groove is formed by a portion of the maxilla. Tears are directed from this point to the inferior meatus of the nasal cavity after cleansing the eye.

INFERIOR TURBINATE BONE. The two nasal conchae, or turbinate bones, are similar to those described with the ethmoid; the conchae of the ethmoid, however, occupy superior and middle portions. The inferior turbinate bones are larger, individual bones lying immediately below—one in each nostril on the lateral side. They are thin and fragile and consist of cancellous tissue covered by a thin layer of compact bone tissue in a scroll-like shape.

VOMER. The single, flat vomer constitutes the lower posterior portion of the nasal septum. The superior part of the bone has two lips, called *alae*, which articulate with the sphenoid superiorly. The word vomer is Latin for "ploughshare," to which the bone presumably bears a resemblance.

MANDIBLE (Fig. 73). Although the mandible (L. *mandibula*, jaw) develops in two parts, the intervening cartilage ossifies in early childhood and the bone becomes fused into a single continuous structure, the lower jaw. The mandible, also called the *inferior maxillary bone*, is the strongest and longest bone of the face. In the U-shaped *body* of the mandible are the alveoli containing the lower teeth. This alveolar portion is covered by the mucous membrane of the mouth. On either side of the body are the *rami* which extend perpendicularly upward. Each ramus presents a *condyle*, or condyloid process, for articulation with the mandibular fossa of the temporal bone. Also at the upper end of the ramus just anterior to the

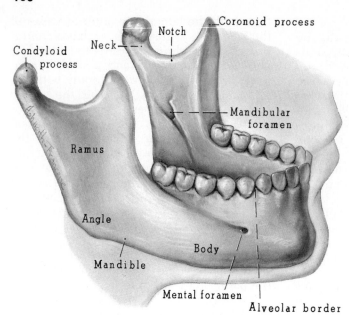

Condyloid process · Neck · Notch · Coronoid process · Mandibular foramen · Ramus · Angle · Mandible · Body · Mental foramen · Alveolar border

Figure 73. Mandible.

condyle is a *coronoid process* for attachment of the temporal muscle. The angle of the jaw is the area where the ramus meets the body of the mandible, rather than the region where the mandible articulates with the cranium.

The maxilla articulates with the cranium by way of the frontal bone and with the mandible by way of the temporal bone; thus, the upper and lower jaws are not connected to each other. In the elderly, the alveolar portion of the mandible ceases to grow. When the teeth are finally lost, the alveoli become absorbed by the body of the bone, and the chin develops an angle and appears more prominent.

In summary, then, the facial portion of the skull consists of the following bones:

1 mandible
1 vomer
2 maxillary
2 zygomatic
2 nasal
2 lacrimal
2 inferior nasal conchae
2 palatine

Orbits. The orbits are the two deep cavities in the upper portion of the face that serve to protect the eyes. To summarize, one orbit consists of the following bones (Fig. 74):

Area of Orbit	*Participating Bones*
roof	frontal (primary bone)
	lesser wing of sphenoid
floor	maxilla
	zygoma
lateral wall	zygoma
rear wall	greater wing of sphenoid
medial wall	maxilla
	lacrimal
	ethmoid
upper margin	frontal
lateral margin	zygoma
medial margin	maxilla

Nasal Cavities. The bony framework of the nose bounding the two nasal fossae is located in the middle of the face between the palate inferiorly and the frontal bone above. To summarize, the nose is formed by the following bones:

Area of Nose	*Participating Bones*
roof	ethmoid
	frontal bone
floor	maxilla
	palatine
lateral wall	maxilla
	palatine
septum or medial wall	ethmoid
	vomer (primary bone)
	nasal bone
bridge	nasal bone
conchae	ethmoid (superior and middle)
	inferior nasal conchae

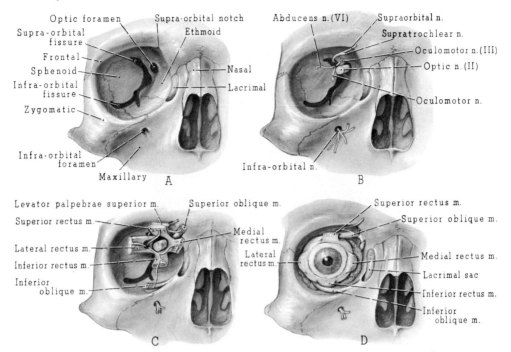

Figure 74. *A,* Skeletal structure of orbit. *B,* Innervation to eye muscles. *C,* Muscles of the eye with associated nerves. *D,* Attachment of muscles to eye.

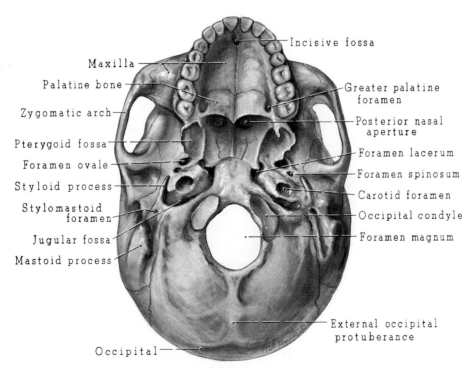

Figure 75. Inferior surface of the skull.

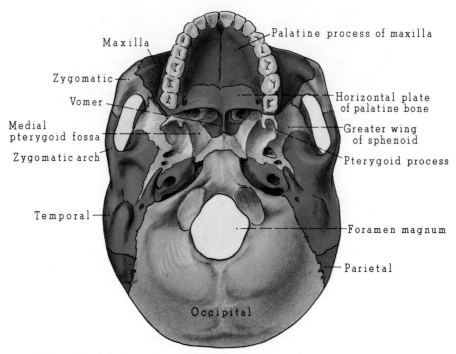

Figure 76. Inferior surface of skull, showing the various bones composing it.

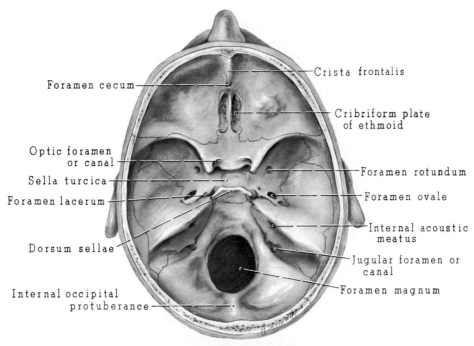

Figure 77. Floor of cranial cavity.

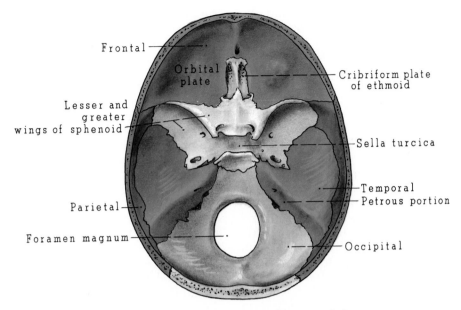

Figure 78. Floor of cranial cavity and its separate bones.

Foramina of the Skull. When viewing the floor of the cranial cavity from above, one observes the large foramen magnum and a number of considerably smaller foramina penetrating the individual bones. These openings are passageways for blood vessels and nerves (Figs. 75 to 78 and Table 7).

The Hyoid Bone

The single hyoid bone is the unique component of the axial skeleton since it has no articulations. Rather, it is suspended from the styloid process of the temporal bone by two *stylohyoid ligaments*. Externally, its position is noted in

Table 7

FORAMEN	LOCATION	TRANSMITTED STRUCTURE(S)
Carotid canal or carotid foramen	Petrous portion, temporal bone	Internal carotid artery
Infraorbital foramen	Maxillary bone at lower rim of orbit	Maxillary division of fifth cranial nerve
Jugular foramen	Suture between petrous portion of temporal and occipital bones	Ninth, tenth, and eleventh cranial nerves
Mandibular foramen of mandible	Inner ramus of mandible	Nerves and vessels to lower teeth
Mental foramen of mandible	Outer body of mandible	Terminal branches of nerves from mandibular foramen
Optic foramen	Lesser wing of sphenoid	Second cranial nerve (optic)
Foramen ovale	Greater wing of sphenoid	Mandibular division of fifth cranial nerve
Foramen rotundum	Greater wing of sphenoid	Maxillary division of fifth cranial nerve
Superior orbital fissure	Within sphenoid, opening into orbital cavity	Third, fourth, and part of fifth cranial nerve
Stylomastoid foramen	Between styloid and mastoid processes of temporal bone	Facial nerve (seventh cranial) leaves cranial cavity
Supraorbital foramen	Frontal bone at orbital margin	Supraorbital nerve and blood vessels

the neck, between the mandible and the larynx. It is shaped like a horseshoe, consisting of a *central body* with two lateral projections, the *greater* and *lesser cornua*. The hyoid bone functions as a primary support for the tongue and its numerous muscles.

The Torso or Trunk

The vertebrae, sternum, and ribs constitute the *trunk portion* of the axial skeleton. The *vertebral column* displays a remarkable combination of structural qualities, making it a highly versatile mechanism (Figs. 79 and 80). It is rigid enough to provide adequate support for the body, yet the discs between the vertebrae permit a high degree of flexibility. The vertebral column provides *protection* for the delicate and vital spinal cord contained within its articulated channel.

The spinal column is formed by a series of 26 vertebrae separated and cushioned by intervertebral discs, or cartilages. The inner (spinal) canal is formed by successive foramina of the individual vertebrae and by the ligaments and discs connecting them.

Vertebrae. All the vertebrae are constructed on the same basic plan, although they do exhibit characteristic specializations in the different anatomic regions. A typical vertebra is characterized by the following features:

1. A *body*—the thick, disc-shaped anterior portion. The upper and lower surfaces are roughened for attachment of intervening discs of fibrocartilage, and the anterior edge is pierced by small holes for vessels nurturing the bone.

2. The *arch* is formed by two posteriorly projecting *pedicles*, is completed by two *laminae* and encloses a space (the vertebral foramen) for passage of the spinal cord. The arch bears three processes for muscle attachment: a *spinous process,* directed backward from the junction of the two laminae, and two *transverse processes,* one on either side at the junction of a lamina and pedicle.

3. *Articular processes*—four in number (two superior and two inferior), arising on either side where a lamina and pedicle join with smooth, slightly curved surfaces

for articulation with the vertebrae immediately above and below.

4. The two pedicles are notched above and below, so that the articulated column has an opening, the *intervertebral foramen,* on each side. These foramina permit passage of nerves to and from the spinal cord. Frequently, several laminae, which form the posterior wall of the vertebral column, must be removed surgically after injuries to the vertebral column to relieve pressure on the spinal cord.

The vertebrae are named and numbered regionally from above downward. There are seven *cervical*, 12 *thoracic*, and five *lumbar vertebrae* (Fig. 80). These remain separate throughout life and are called movable vertebrae. In addition, there are five sacral vertebrae, which become fused in adult life to form the single sacrum, and four coccygeal vertebrae, which unite firmly into the single coccyx. These last two are called *fixed* vertebrae; consequently, the vertebrae are referred to as being 26 in number, rather than 33. (Since the sacrum and coccyx, along with the two pelvic bones, form the pelvis, or pelvic girdle, they are actually part of the appendicular as well as of the axial skeleton.) Regardless of the individual's body height, the adult vertebral column measures approximately 60 to 70 cm in length (24 to 28 inches).

CERVICAL VERTEBRAE. The cervical vertebrae are the smallest vertebrae, having somewhat oblong bodies and being broader from side to side than from front to back. The spinous processes of the third, fourth, and fifth cervical vertebrae are *bifid,* or forked, to cradle the strong ligaments supporting the head. The transverse process is pierced by a foramen to allow passage of the vertebral artery (Fig. 81).

The first two cervical vertebrae are unique (Fig. 82). The *atlas* supports the head by articulation with the condyles of the occipital bone. There is no typical body in the atlas, since it is a complete ring of bone having anterior and posterior arches and two lateral masses. The transverse processes, althrough present, are short and rounded, since they do not articulate with the ribs.

The *axis* (second vertebra) does have a body, from which the *odontoid process*

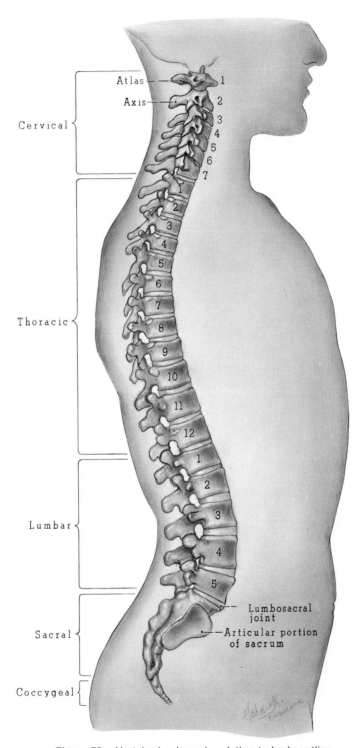

Figure 79.   Vertebral column in relation to body outline.

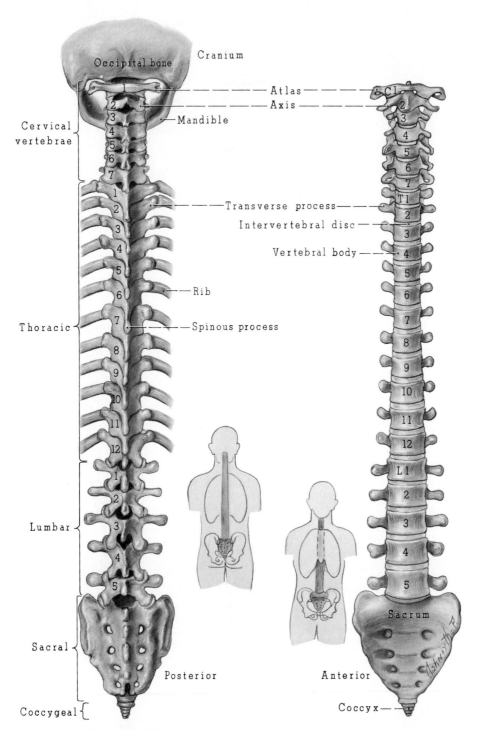

Figure 80. Posterior and anterior views of vertebral column.

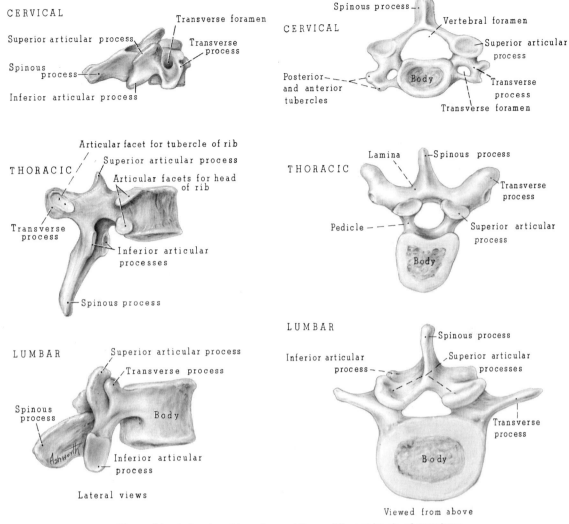

Figure 81.   Lateral and top views of three different levels of vertebrae.

projects up through the ring of the atlas to make a pivot on which the atlas and head rotate. There are flattened sides of the bone, *articular facets*, on each lateral mass of the axis for articulation with corresponding facets on the atlas.

Cervical vertebrae numbers 3, 4, 5, and

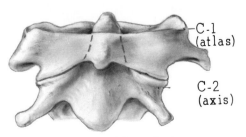

Figure 82.   Atlas and axis.

6 follow the typical patterns previously described. The seventh differs in that it has a long, undivided spinous process with a tubercle at its tip. The bone is called the *vertebra prominens*, since it can be seen and felt at the base of the neck.

THORACIC VERTEBRAE.   The bodies of the thoracic vertebrae are longer and more rounded than those of the cervical region. The thoracic vertebrae have two distinguishing characteristics—the long *spinous process*, pointed and directed downward, and *facets* on either side for articulation with the ribs (Figs. 81 and 83). The facets on either side of the bodies articulate with the heads of ribs. (The articulations for the heads of the second through ninth ribs are formed by facets on the superior and infe-

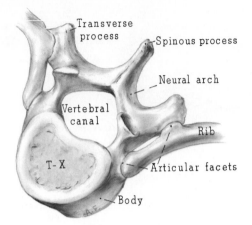

Figure 83. Vertebra showing articulation with rib.

COCCYX. The coccyx articulates with the tip, or apex, of the sacrum. Slight movement is possible at this joint, serving to increase the size of the birth canal during delivery.

Vertebral Column as a Whole. In the embryo, the vertebral column shows a single C-shaped curve with the convex surface of the curve directed posteriorly. After birth, raising of the head creates an anteriorly directed curve in the neck; at the age of about one year the assumption of an erect posture creates an anteriorly directed curve in the lumbar area.

The normal curves of the spine can become exaggerated as a result of injury, poor body posture, or disease. When the posterior curvature is accentuated in the thoracic area, the condition is called *kyphosis*, or more commonly, hunchback. When the anterior curvature in the lumbar region is accentuated, it is known as *lordosis*. A lateral curvature associated with rotation of the vertebrae is termed *scoliosis*.

rior edges of the bodies of adjacent vertebrae.) The transverse processes of all but the eleventh and twelfth vertebrae carry a facet for the tubercle of the rib.

LUMBAR VERTEBRAE. The lumbar vertebrae are the largest and strongest of the different types. Their various projections are short and thick, and the spinous processes are modified for attachment of the powerful back muscles.

Sacrum (Fig. 84). The sacrum is a triangular, slightly curved bone positioned at the base of the pelvic cavity between the two innominate bones. Its base articulates above with the fifth lumbar vertebra, and the anterior surface of this broad base forms the *sacral prominence*. The sacrum has a cavity which is a continuation of the spinal canal.

In addition to its functions of body support and movement, as well as protection of the spinal cord, the vertebral column is built to withstand forces of compression many times the weight of the body. The intervertebral discs of cartilage act as cushions, so that landing on the feet after a jump or fall will be less likely to fracture the vertebrae. The discs also act as shock absorbers to reduce a transmitted jarring or pressure on the brain. The very thick

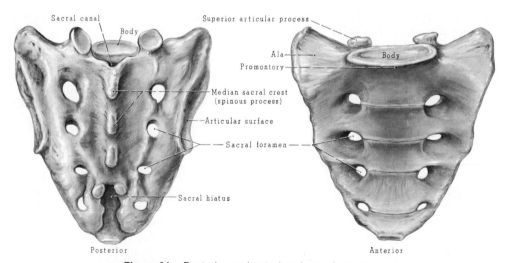

Figure 84. Posterior and anterior views of sacrum.

discs in the lumbar region are the most effective shock absorbers.

INJURIES TO THE SPINAL COLUMN. When the spinal column is subjected to violence, fractures or dislocations can result. The most frequent fracture is a crush injury to the vertebral body. Sometimes a combined flexion and hyperextension injury dislocates one vertebra over another, causing locking of the articular processes. This occurs most frequently in diving accidents.

HERNIATED INTERVERTEBRAL DISC. The intervertebral disc acts as a cushion between adjacent vertebral bodies. It is a fibrocartilaginous structure with a tough outer layer called the *annulus fibrosus* (L. *anulus,* ring) and a soft, resilient interior remnant of the notochord, the *nucleus pulposus.* If the annulus becomes injured, the pressure within the disc is decreased and the nucleus can protrude (Fig. 85). The herniated portion sometimes causes pressure on a spinal nerve, resulting in nerve root irritation, a frequent cause of leg pain. Disc pathology can result from injury but is most commonly (80 per cent of the instances) due to attrition caused by a lack of blood supply during adult life.

The Thorax (Figs. 86 and 87). That portion of the trunk consisting of the *sternum,* the *costal cartilages,* the *ribs,* and the bodies of the *thoracic vertebrae* is properly called the thorax. This bony cage encloses and protects the lungs and other structures of the chest cavity. The thorax also provides support for the bones of the shoulder girdle and upper extremities. In adult life, it is cone-shaped with a broad base.

STERNUM (Fig. 86). The "breastbone" (G. *sternon,* breast) develops in three parts—from above downward, the *manubrium,* the *gladiolus,* or body, and the *xiphoid process.* The parts are named for their resemblance to a sword (L. *manubrium,* a handle; L. *gladiolus,* small sword; L. *xiphoides,* sword-shaped). There are no ribs attached to the xiphoid, but the manubrium and gladiolus exhibit notches on either side for attachment of the first seven costal cartilages. At the upper and outer aspects, the manubrium of the sternum articulates with the clavicle. Between the two points of articulation is the *suprasternal,* or *jugular, notch,* easily felt through the skin. The diaphragm, linea alba and rectus abdominis muscle are attached to the xiphoid.

RIBS. The 12 pairs of ribs (costae) are named according to their anterior attachments. The upper seven pairs articulate directly with the sternum and are called *true ribs.* The lower five pairs join with

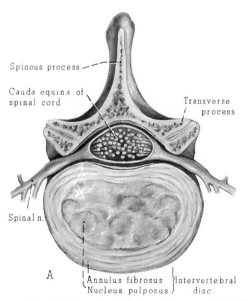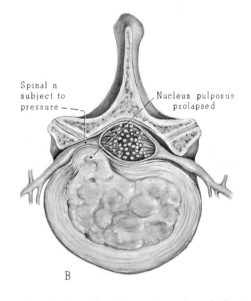

Figure 85. *A,* Normal relations of intervertebral disc to the spinal cord and nerve branches. *B,* Prolapsed pulposus of intervertebral disc impinging on the nerve. (After Netter.)

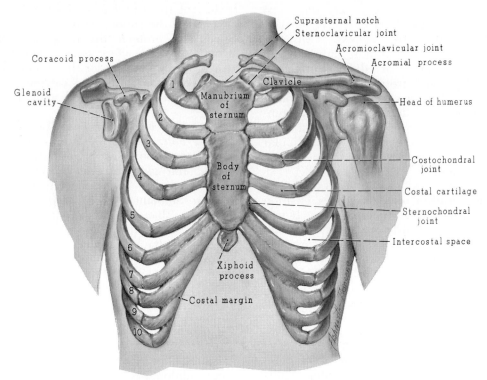

Figure 86. Anterior view of the rib cage.

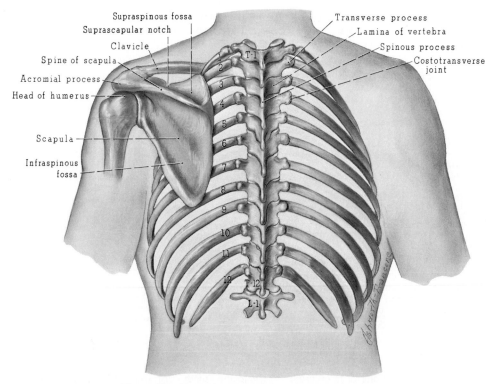

Figure 87. Posterior view of the rib cage and scapula.

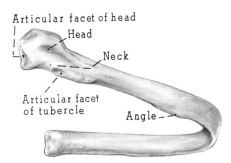

Figure 88. Detail of single rib.

the sternum only indirectly or not at all and are called *false ribs*. The *costal cartilages* of the eighth, ninth, and tenth rib pairs are attached to the cartilages of the rib above. The eleventh and twelfth "false" ribs have a second name, *floating ribs*, since their anterior ends are completely unattached. The posterior extremity of a typical rib presents a rounded *head* portion for attachment to facets on the body of the thoracic vertebrae. Ribs numbered 2 through 9 each articulate between the adjacent bodies of two vertebrae. The heads of ribs numbered 1, 10, 11, and 12 articulate with a single vertebral body (Fig. 83).

A lateral bulge, or tubercle, is located below the *head* and *neck*, except on the eleventh and twelfth ribs, which have neither a neck nor a tubercle. Each tubercle of ribs 1 to 10 rests on the facet of a single thoracic transverse process. From their posterior vertebral attachments, the curved ribs slope downward as well as outward, thus increasing the size of the thoracic cavity; however, the anterior margin of the cavity is considerably higher than the posterior margin, because the lower edge of the sternum is at the level of the tenth thoracic vertebra rather than the twelfth, and because the costal cartilages of the false ribs are necessarily directed upward toward the sternum (Fig. 86).

APPENDICULAR SKELETON

Bones of the Upper Extremities

Included are the bones of the shoulder girdle, arm, forearm, wrist, hand, and fingers.

The *clavicle* (collar bone) is a long, slim bone located at the root of the neck just below the skin and anterior to the first rib (Fig. 89). The medial two-thirds of the clavicle is bowed forward, while the lateral one-third is bowed backward. The medial end articulates with the *manubrium* of the sternum and the lateral end with the *acromial process* of the scapula. The joint between the clavicle and the sternum is the only bony articulation between the upper extremity and the thorax.

The *scapula* is a large, flat, triangular bone located on the dorsal portion of the thorax, covering the area from the second to the seventh rib (Fig. 90). The *coracoid process* of the scapula is a projection originating from the anterior surface of the superior border. It serves as the origin for some muscles that move the arm. The acromial process (acromion) is the point of the shoulder articulating with the lateral end of the clavicle.

The *humerus* is the long bone of the upper arm. Its head is rounded and joined to the rest of the body by the *anatomic neck*. The upper part of the bone has two prominences, the *greater* and *lesser tubercles*, serving as insertions for many of the muscles of the upper extremity. The *bicipital groove* is located between the tubercles and contains the tendons of part of the biceps muscle.

The surgical neck of the humerus—so called because it is the site of the most common fracture in the elderly—lies below the tubercles. Inferior to the neck on the shaft is the *deltoid tuberosity* on the lateral side.

The distal end of the bone becomes flattened and terminates in the *medial* and *lateral epicondyles*. The articular surface of the distal end of the humerus is formed by the *capitulum*, a smooth knob articulating with the radius, and the *trochlea*, a pulley-shaped area articulating with the ulna. The anterior surface of the distal end is the *coronoid fossa;* the posterior surface of the distal end is the *olecranon fossa*. Both fossae serve to receive the processes of the same name on the ulna.

The *ulna* (Latin for elbow) is the longer, medial bone of the forearm (Figs. 91 and 92). Its shaft is triangular and the lower (distal) end of the bone is known as the *head*. The head articulates with the ulnar

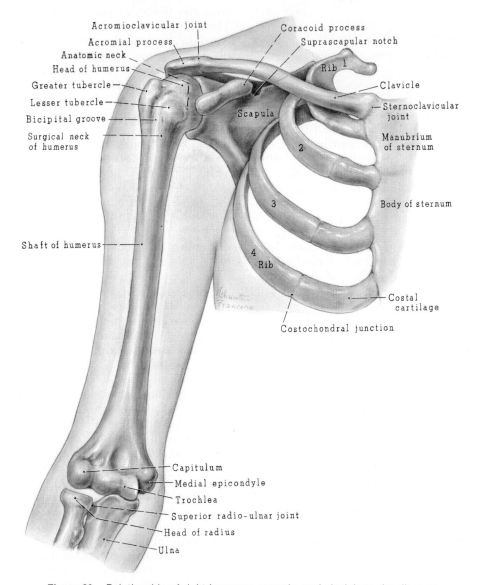

Figure 89.   Relationship of right humerus, scapula, and clavicle to the rib cage.

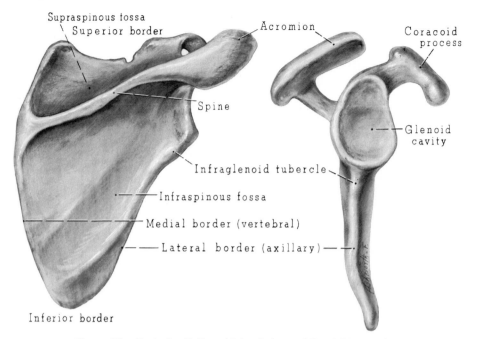

Figure 90. Posterior (*left*) and lateral views of the right scapula.

notch of the radius and a fibrocartilaginous disc that prevents the ulna from articulating with the wrist bones. Posterior to the head can be found the *styloid process.*

The *radius* joins with the ulna along its length by an interosseous membrane traversing the area between the shafts of the two bones. It is located lateral to the ulna. The radial head, at the proximal end, articulates with the capitulum of the humerus and the radial notch of the ulna. The shaft has a tuberosity on the medial side which serves for insertion of the biceps. The styloid process of the radius is larger than the styloid process of the ulna and articulates with the bones of the wrist.

The bones of the wrist are called *carpals,* and are situated in two rows of four each. In the proximal row from medial to lateral are the *pisiform, triquetrum, lunate,* and *scaphoid.* In the distal row from medial to lateral are the *hamate, capitate, trapezoid,* and *trapezium.*

The palm of the hand consists of five *metacarpal* bones, each with a base, shaft, and head. The metacarpals radiate from the wrist like spokes from a wheel, rather than being parallel, and articulate with the proximal phalanges of the fingers. Each finger (excluding the thumb) has three *phalanges*—a *proximal,* a *middle,* and a

terminal, or *distal, phalanx.* The thumb has only two phalanges.

Bones of the Lower Extremities

The pelvic girdle, formed by the two pelvic bones, the sacrum and the coccyx, supports the trunk and provides attachment for the legs. The paired os coxae (pelvic bone or "hipbone") originally consists of three separate bones, the *ilium, ischium,* and *pubis.* These names are retained as descriptive regions for areas of the fused adult pelvic bone.

The *femur* is the bone of the thigh (Fig. 93). It is the longest and heaviest bone in the body. The *patella,* or "kneecap," is the largest sesamoid bone. Forming the lower portion of the leg are the *tibia* ("shinbone") and *fibula* ("calfbone"). The ankle and foot are composed of the *tarsal* and *metatarsal* bones as well as the *phalanges.*

Pelvic Bone (Fig. 94). The two "hipbones" articulate with each other anteriorly at the pubic symphysis. Posteriorly, they articulate with the sacrum. The ring of bone thus formed and the coccyx compose the pelvic girdle, also known as the pelvis.

ILIUM. The uppermost and largest por-
Text continued on page 123

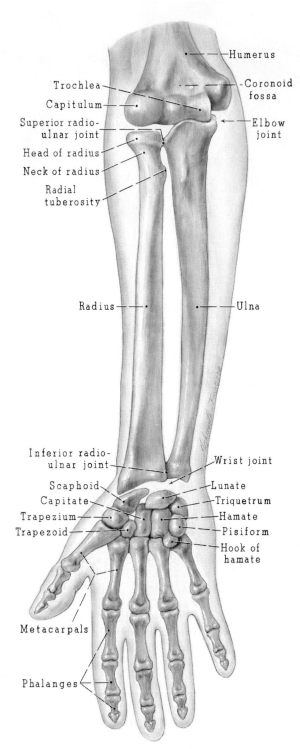

Figure 91.   Anterior view of bones of the right forearm and hand.

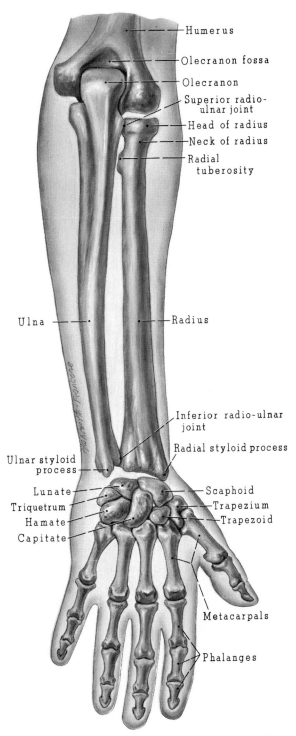

Humerus

Olecranon fossa

Olecranon

Superior radio-ulnar joint

Head of radius

Neck of radius

Radial tuberosity

Ulna

Radius

Inferior radio-ulnar joint

Radial styloid process

Ulnar styloid process

Lunate

Triquetrum

Hamate

Capitate

Scaphoid

Trapezium

Trapezoid

Metacarpals

Phalanges

Figure 92.   Posterior view of bones of the right forearm and hand.

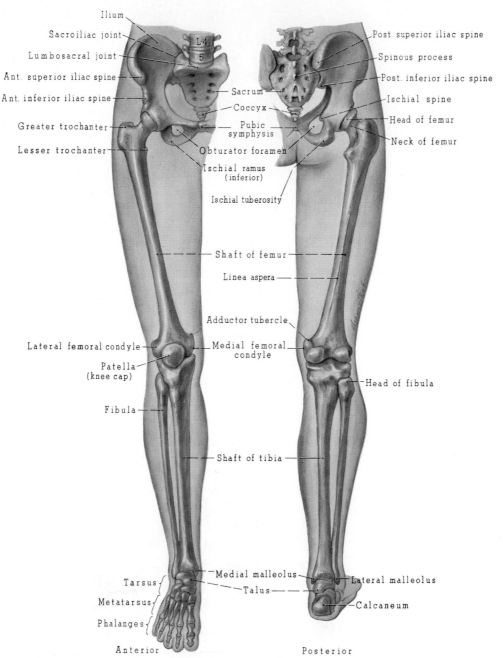

Ilium
Sacroiliac joint
Lumbosacral joint
Ant. superior iliac spine
Ant. inferior iliac spine
Greater trochanter
Lesser trochanter

L4
5

Sacrum
Coccyx
Pubic symphysis
Obturator foramen
Ischial ramus (inferior)
Ischial tuberosity

Post. superior iliac spine
Spinous process
Post. inferior iliac spine
Ischial spine
Head of femur
Neck of femur

Shaft of femur
Linea aspera

Adductor tubercle
Lateral femoral condyle
Medial femoral condyle
Patella (knee cap)

Head of fibula

Fibula

Shaft of tibia

Tarsus
Metatarsus
Phalanges

Medial malleolus
Talus

Lateral malleolus
Calcaneum

Anterior

Posterior

Figure 93. Anterior and posterior views of bones of the right leg and foot.

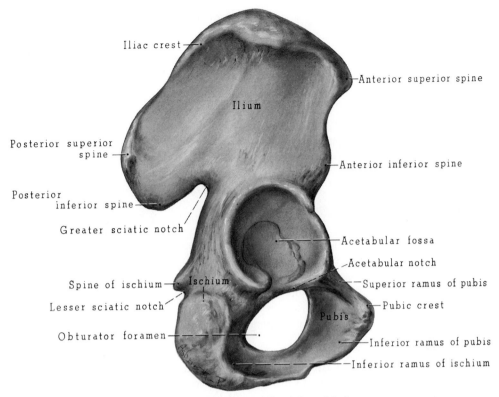

Iliac crest

Ilium

Anterior superior spine

Posterior superior spine

Anterior inferior spine

Posterior inferior spine

Greater sciatic notch

Acetabular fossa

Acetabular notch

Spine of ischium

Ischium

Superior ramus of pubis

Lesser sciatic notch

Pubic crest

Obturator foramen

Pubis

Inferior ramus of pubis

Inferior ramus of ischium

Figure 94. Lateral view of the right pelvic bone.

tion of the pelvic bone is the ilium, forming the expanded prominence of the upper hip. Its crest (where hands rest when on hips) is projected into the *anterior superior iliac spine*, below which is the *anterior inferior iliac spine*. The former is used as a convenient anatomic and surgical landmark, and both provide attachment to the muscles of the abdominal wall.

ISCHIUM. The strongest portion of the pelvic bone is the *ischium*, directed slightly posteriorly. Its curved edge is seen from the front as the lowermost margin of the pelvis. It bears the rounded ischial tuberosity, which takes the weight of the body in the sitting position.

PUBIS. The pubis is superior and slightly anterior to the ischium. Between the pubis and ischium is the large *obturator foramen*, the largest foramen in the body. It is filled with fibrous areolar tissue, nerves, and blood vessels, and is functional only in the sense that it lightens the weight of the "hipbone." The pubis consists of a *body*, a *ridge*, a *crest*, and two branches or *rami* (pubic rami). The infe-

rior rami join at the pubic symphysis to form what is known as the pubic arch, or angle, of the pelvis (Fig. 95).

ACETABULUM. On the lateral aspect of the "hipbone," just above the obturator foramen, is a deep socket called the acetabulum. All three portions of the pelvic bone meet and unite in this depression. The acetabulum receives the head of the femur to form the hip joint.

True and False Pelvis. As mentioned, the term pelvis (the Latin word for basin) is used to designate the bony ring formed by the two pelvic bones, the sacrum and the coccyx. The term also refers to the cavity bounded by the bony pelvis. This cavity consists of two parts, the true pelvis (below) and the false pelvis (above), separated by the *pelvic brim*, an aperture formed by the promontory of the sacrum and the *iliopectineal line* of each pelvic bone (a ridge on the ilium and pubis portions just below the iliac fossa extending to the pubic crest). (See Fig. 95.) The pelvic brim forms what is called the *inlet* of the true pelvis. The lower circumfer-

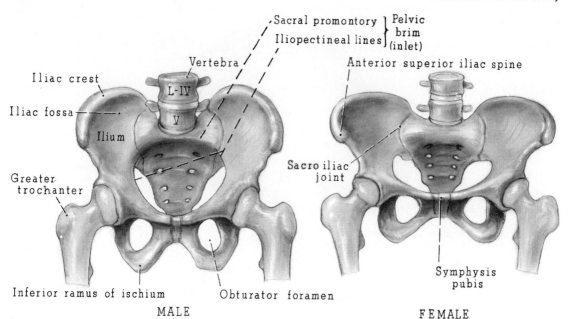

Figure 95. Comparison in proportions of the male and female pelves.

ence of the true pelvis, called the *outlet*, is bounded by the tip of the coccyx and the two ischial tuberosities. The true (or lesser) pelvis contains the rectum, bladder and, between these two organs in the female, the uterus and vagina. The false (or greater) pelvis provides support for the intestines. The pelvis of the female shows characteristic differences relating to adaptations for pregnancy and parturition. The male and female pelves are compared in Table 8 and Figure 95.

Femur. The Latin word for "thigh" is femur. This single large bone of the upper leg is *not* in a vertical line with the axis of the erect body. Rather, it is positioned at an angle, slanting downward and inward.

From the point of view of the skeleton, the two femurs appear as a "V." Because of the greater pelvic breadth, the angle of inclination of the femurs is greater in the female than in the male.

The *upper extremity* of the femur bears a rounded *head*, which projects medially upward to rest in the acetabulum, forming the hip joint. Below this is a constricted neck with greater and lesser trochanters. On the posterior aspect of the long shaft is a ridge called the *linea aspera*, the area of attachment for several muscles of the hip and leg.

The lower extremity of the femur is widened into a large *lateral* and even larger *medial condyle*, separated by the *intercon-*

Table 8. COMPARISON OF MALE AND FEMALE PELVES

	MALE (ANDROID)	FEMALE (GYNECOID)
Bone of pelvis	Heavy and rough	Small and slender
Sacrum	Narrow and curved	Broad, with a lesser curvature
False pelvis	Narrow	Wide
True pelvis	Deep but narrow, with less capacity	Shallow, wide, with greater capacity
Pelvic inlet	Heart-shaped	Oval, larger than in male
Greater sciatic notch	Narrow	Wide
Obturator foramen	Oval	Triangular
Pubic angle	Narrow, pointed	Wide, rounded
Direction	Tilted backward	Tilted forward

dyloid fossa. The femur articulates distally with the tibia. The knee joint thus formed approximates the line of gravity of the body.

Patella. The "kneecap" is a small, flat, somewhat triangular sesamoid bone lying in front of the knee joint and enveloped within the tendon of the quadriceps femoris muscle. The only articulation is with the femur. The patella is movable and serves to increase leverage of muscles that straighten the knee.

Tibia. The tibia is the larger of the two bones forming the lower leg. The upper end consists of two broad eminences, the *medial* and *lateral condyles.* Their concave surface articulates with the respective condyles of the femur. The lower extremity is smaller and prolonged as the *medial malleolus,* which forms the inner ankle bone. Slightly lateral to this projection is the surface for articulation with the talus, forming the ankle joint. The tibia also articulates with the fibula laterally at both upper and lower extremities.

Fibula. In proportion to its length, the fibula is the most slender bone in the body, lying parallel with and on the lateral side of the tibia. Its upper extremity does not reach the knee joint but articulates by means of an expanded head with the tibia. The lower extremity terminates in a pointed process, the *lateral malleolus,* or "outer ankle bone," to which are attached the outer ankle ligaments. The fibula articulates distally with both the tibia and the talus.

Bones of the Foot

TARSUS (Fig. 96). The bones of the tarsus consist of a group of seven short bones which resemble the carpal bones of the wrist but are larger. Tarsal bones are arranged in the *hindfoot* and *forefoot.* The hindfoot consists of the calcaneus and the talus, navicular, and cuboid bones. The calcaneus is the largest bone of the group and forms the prominence of the heel. The *talus,* or *astragalus,* lies above the calcaneus obliquely. Its head projects forward and medially in the general direction of the great toe. The head of the talus articulates with the *navicular joint,* or medial compartment of the midtarsal joint. The forefoot consists of the *medial cuneiform* (first), the *intermediate cuneiform* (second), the *lateral cuneiform* (third), the *metatarsals,* and the *phalanges.*

METATARSAL BONES. There are five metatarsal bones in the foot. Each is a long bone with a base, shaft, and head.

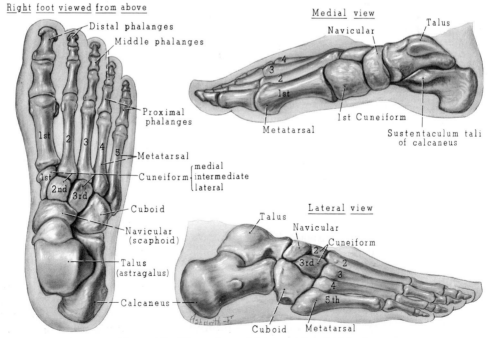

Figure 96. Three views of bones of the right foot.

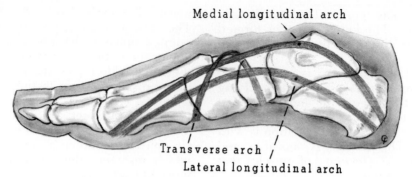

Medial longitudinal arch

Transverse arch

Lateral longitudinal arch

Figure 97. The three arches of the foot.

The *bases* of the first, second, and third metatarsals articulate with the three cuneiforms; the fourth and fifth metatarsals articulate with the cuboid. These joints are named the *tarsometatarsal* joints. The intrinsic muscles of the toes are attached to the shafts of the metatarsals. The heads articulate with the proximal row of the phalanges of the toe at the metatarsophalangeal joints. The first metatarsal is larger than the others, owing to its weight-bearing function.

PHALANGES OF THE TOES. Bones of the toes are classified as long bones in spite of their being short in length. Like the bones of the fingers, they are called phalanges. There are two phalanges in the great toe and three in each of the four lesser toes—a total of 14.

Arches of the Foot (Fig. 97). The bones of the foot form *two longitudinal arches* and a *transverse arch*, enabling the foot to bear *weight* and provide *leverage*.

The calcaneus, talus, navicular, cuneiforms, and first, second, and third metatarsals compose the *medial longitudinal arch*. This arch is supported by the calcaneus posteriorly and by the heads of the three metatarsals anteriorly. The "keystone" of the medial longitudinal arch is the talus.

The *lateral longitudinal arch* is shallower and consists of the calcaneus, cuboid, and fourth and fifth metatarsals. The "keystone" of the lateral longitudinal arch is the cuboid.

The second and third cuneiforms are considered to be the "keystone" of the *transverse arch*.

FLATFOOT. The term *pes planus*, or flatfoot, indicates a decreased height of longitudinal arches. This can be inherited or can result from muscle weakness in the foot. It is rarely a cause of pain.

SUMMARY

THE SKELETAL SYSTEM

Functions of the Skeletal System

a. Providing a support for the body
b. Protecting vital organs
c. Assisting in accomplishing body movement
d. Hematopoiesis
f. Providing a storage area for calcium

Organization of the Skeletal System

1. There are 206 bones in the skeleton.

a. The axial skeleton consists of the skull (facial and cranial bones), hyoid bone, vertebral column, ribs, and sternum
b. The appendicular skeleton consists of
(1) The shoulder girdle and the bones of the upper arm, forearm, wrist, and hands
(2) The pelvic girdle and the bones of the thighs, legs, ankles, and feet

Composition of Bone

Bone is a connective tissue consisting of cells and a matrix composed of collagenous fibers embedded in a ground substance of protein-polysaccharides and calcium salts (resembling the structure of hydroxyapatite).

Bone Cells

1. **Three types of cells are found in bone:**

   a. Osteoblasts, active in synthesizing the bone matrix
   b. Osteoclasts, functioning in bone resorption (breakdown of the matrix)
   c. Osteocytes, the principal cells of mature bone
      (1) Osteoblasts and osteoclasts are responsible for the formation and growth of bone, but remain active throughout life in remodeling and repairing fully formed bone.
      (2) Osteocytes are osteoblasts *that have become surrounded by matrix during bone formation.*
         (a) *Although osteocytes no longer rapidly synthesize matrix constituents, they are apparently involved in maintenance of the matrix.*
         (b) *Osteocytes also participate in bone resorption upon stimulation by the parathyroid hormone (part of the regulatory mechanism for maintaining normal blood calcium).*

Types of Bone

1. **Two types of bone are seen:**

   a. **Compact bone:** dense and strong.
   b. **Cancellous (spongy) bone:** consists of plates of bone, called trabeculae, which form open networks. The open (marrow) spaces give the tissue a spongy appearance without the aid of a microscope.

Classification of Bones

1. **Bones are identified as five types according to shape.**

   a. **Long bones** (such as the humerus and tibia) consist of a shaft (diaphysis) and two extremities, each called an *epiphysis:*
   (1) The interior of the shaft has a marrow cavity (medullary canal). The shaft is composed largely of compact bone.
   (2) The flared ends of the shaft and each epiphysis, as well as the other bone types, consist of a central core of cancellous bone surrounded by a thin layer of compact bone.
   b. **Short bones** (such as the carpals and tarsals): not only shorter, but also somewhat irregular in shape.
   c. **Flat bones** (such as the ribs, scapula, parietal bones, and pelvic bones).
   d. **Irregular bones** (such as the vertebrae).
   e. **Sesamoid bones** (such as the patella): small, rounded bones enclosed in tendon and fascial tissue, found adjacent to joints.

Membranes of Bone

1. **Periosteum, a fibrous connective tissue, covers the outer surface of bone except at articular surfaces (which are layered with hyaline cartilage).**

2. **Endosteum, a delicate connective tissue, lines all the cavities of bone, including the marrow spaces, marrow cavities, and haversian canals.**

3. **Both contain osteoblast precursor cells and therefore have osteogenic potential.**

Bone Marrow

1. **In adults, the marrow spaces of the ribs, vertebrae, sternum and pelvis contain *red bone marrow.***

   a. Functions in hematopoiesis—the formation of red and white blood cells and megakaryocytes (which disintegrate to form platelets).

2. **The marrow cavities (medullary canals) are filled with *yellow bone marrow* (essentially adipose tissue).**

Histology of Bone

1. **The microscopic, functional unit of compact bone is known as the *haversian system.***

   a. In each system a central haversian canal containing blood vessels is surrounded by concentric rings of bone matrix called *lamellae.*
   b. Osteocytes lie between the lamellae, each in a space called a *lacuna.*
   c. *Canaliculi* connect lacunae with each

other and with the central haversian canal.

    d. The haversian blood vessels are connected to the blood vessels of the periosteum and endosteum by *Volkmann's canals.*

2. The structure of cancellous bone is sometimes called an incomplete haversian system, since osteocytes in the bony plates reside in lacunae between lamellae and are interconnected by canaliculi.

    a. Haversian blood vessels are absent.

    b. The canaliculi communicate directly with blood vessels of the endosteum.

Bone Formation and Growth

1. There are two types of bone formation.

    a. **Intermembranous ossification:** bone forms directly in the embryonic connective tissue.

    b. **Endochondral ossification:** a "scale model" of hyaline cartilage is replaced by bone.

2. Most bones are formed by endochondral ossification. Only the cranial bones are formed completely by intermembranous ossification.

    a. In the endochondral process, the cartilage skeleton is formed in the embryo at the end of three months.

    b. During subsequent months ossification and growth occur.

    c. When endochondral bone formation is completed, growth in length occurs at the epiphyseal, or growth, plate (a transverse disc of cartilage remaining between the epiphysis and diaphysis).

    d. The plate is widened by multiplication of cartilage cells, and cancellous bone replaces dying cartilage cells.

    e. Growth in width occurs by the deposition of compact bone beneath the periosteum and enlargement of the marrow cavity by bone resorption.

    f. Bone growth ceases when the growth plate is replaced by bone (closure of the epiphysis).

Regulation of Bone Formation and Growth by Vitamins and Hormones

1. Vitamin D (now called a hormone) in- creases the rate of calcium absorption from the intestine.

    a. In the deficiency conditions, *rickets* in children and *osteomalacia* in adults, calcification of bone is inadequate.

    b. The active substance (1,25 dihydroxyvitamin D_3) is formed by the action of ultraviolet radiation on a precursor in the skin, followed by subsequent changes in the liver and kidney.

2. Growth hormone: secreted by the hypophysis.

    a. Induces the liver to release a substance which stimulates proliferation of cartilage cells at the epiphyseal disc.

3. Vitamin C is required for the synthesis of collagen.

4. *Thyroxine:* secreted by the thyroid gland.

    a. Increases the rate of replacement of bone at the growth plate.

    b. Also required for the synthesis of growth hormone.

5. Estrogens and androgens promote ossification and the synthesis of bone matrix throughout life.

6. Vitamin A stimulates the resorption of bone.

Calcium Release from Bone

1. Severe reductions in blood concentrations of calcium can cause

    a. Muscular spasms (tetany)

    b. Weakened cardiac muscle

    c. Deficiency in blood clotting

2. Two hormones, the parathyroid hormone and thyrocalcitonin (secreted by the thyroid gland), regulate the release of calcium from bone.

    a. Low blood calcium increases the release of parathyroid hormone, which increases bone resorption, thereby raising the concentration of blood calcium.

    b. High blood calcium stimulates the release of thyrocalcitonin. This hormone lowers blood calcium concentration by inhibiting bone resorption.

Fractures

1. A break in a bone or cartilage is termed a fracture.

2. A fracture can be compound or simple depending on whether or not the skin is broken.

3. It is described as complete or incomplete depending on whether or not the fracture line extends partially or entirely through the bone.

4. Classified according to direction, a fracture is transverse, oblique, longitudinal, or spiral.

5. In a comminuted fracture, the bone is divided into more than two fragments.

6. The stages of fracture healing include

    a. Clot formation.
    b. Formation of dense fibrous tissue, which is converted to a fibrocartilaginous mass (temporary callus).
    c. This in turn is converted to a bony callus.
    d. Reconstruction of the bony callus into compact bone.

Bone Markings

1. A projection is called a process and a depression is called a fossa. The following have been defined in the text:

process	trochlea	fossa
spine	crest	fissure
condyle	line	foramen
tubercle	head	meatus
tuberosity	sinus	canal
trochanter	sulcus	antrum

Vertebral Column Injuries

1. Exaggerations of the spinal curvature are termed

    a. *Kyphosis* when the posterior curvature is accentuated in the thoracic area.
    b. *Lordosis* when the anterior curvature is accentuated in the lumbar region.
    c. *Scoliosis* when there is a lateral curvature and rotation of the vertebrae.

2. The vertebral disc can become herniated when the outer covering (the annulus fibrosus) ruptures owing to trauma and the inner core (the nucleus pulposus) protrudes.

3. The table of bones lists the nature of each bone of the body.

chapter 6

The Articular System

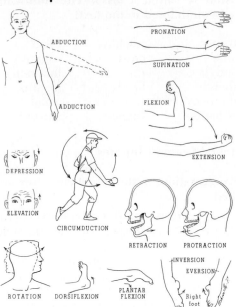

ABDUCTION

ADDUCTION

PRONATION

SUPINATION

FLEXION

EXTENSION

DEPRESSION

ELEVATION

CIRCUMDUCTION

RETRACTION   PROTRACTION

INVERSION

EVERSION

ROTATION   DORSIFLEXION   PLANTAR FLEXION   Right foot

Objectives

The aim of this chapter is to enable the student to:

Distinguish between the three major types of joints and give examples of each.

Identify the different types of diarthrodial joints and the actions of each.

Describe the anatomy of bursae and outline the characteristics of the common disorders.

Construct and label diagrams showing the gross anatomy of the knee joint.

List the major joints, classify them, and describe their action.

An articulation (L. *articulare,* to divide in joints) is a place of union between two or more bones—regardless of the degree of movement permitted by this junction. Thus, the sutures between the skull are considered as much a part of the articular system as the elbow or the knee joint. Following a general discussion of the anatomy and physiology of joints, special consideration will be given to the largest and most complex joint in the body, the knee joint.

CLASSIFICATION OF JOINTS

Joints are categorized into three groups according to the degree of movement they permit (Fig. 98). Subclasses associated with

each of the general categories are based on the structural components of individual joints.

Synarthroses

Synarthroses (G. *syn,* with, together; G. *arthrosis,* jointing) are joints which do not permit movement.

A *suture* (L. *sutura,* a sewing together) is an articulation in which the bones are united by a thin layer of fibrous tissue. Examples are the suture joints of the skull.

Synchondroses (G. *chondros,* cartilage) are joints in which two bony surfaces are connected by cartilage. This is a temporary joint, the cartilage being replaced by bone

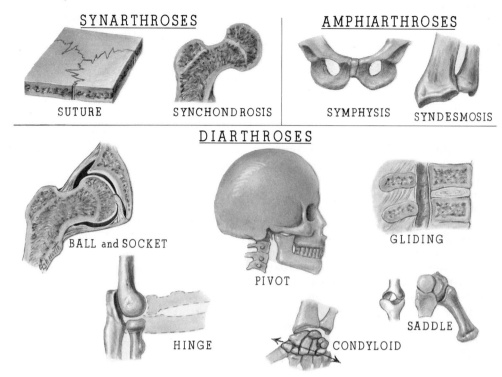

Figure 98. Joints are categorized into three groups, according to the degree of movement permitted. Each of these groups is in turn subdivided with respect to the structural components of individual joints.

in later life. An example is the joint between the epiphysis and diaphysis of a long bone.

Amphiarthroses

Amphiarthroses are slightly movable articulations.

Symphyses are joints in which the bones are connected by a disc of fibrocartilage. An example is the pubic symphysis.

Syndesmoses are joints in which the bones are connected by ligaments between the bones. An example is where the radius articulates with the ulna.

Diarthroses (Synovial Joints)

Anatomy. Diarthroses are freely movable articulations. These joints are characterized by a cavity enclosed by a capsule of fibrous articular cartilage, ligaments (L. *ligamentum,* band, tie) that reinforce the capsule, and cartilage that covers the ends

of the opposing bones (see Fig. 109, illustrating knee joint). The articular capsule is lined with synovial membrane, which produces synovial fluid.

Cartilage provides a smooth, gliding surface for opposing bone. This smooth gliding surface is made possible because of lubrication by the synovial fluid.

Articular cartilage receives its nourishment from the underlying bony surface via the synovial fluid and from a small number of subsynovial vessels primarily at the junction of the cartilage with the joint capsule. Synovial fluid, however, is the major source of nutrition for the cartilage, and in itself is able to sustain the viability of cartilage.

Articular discs are located between the articular cartilages of some synovial joints. The disc, composed of fibrocartilage, joins with the capsular ligament peripherally. It is thought that the articular disc functions as a buffer to minimize the impact of shock. Articular discs are supplied with nerve fibers providing sensory function and permitting the joints to respond more promptly and with precision to pressure changes within the joint cavity.

Collagenous fibers running directly from one bone to another compose the major element of the fibrous capsule enclosing a diarthrodial joint. Well-defined bands of fibers are usually differentiated as local thickenings of the capsule to form intrinsic, or capsular, *ligaments,* which further strengthen joints and play a part in restraining movements in certain directions (Fig. 99). Ligaments are usually arranged so that they remain taut while the joint is in the position of greatest stability.

The *capsule* of a hinge joint permits movements of flexion and extension. The range of joint motion is directly related to the laxity of the capsule. In the shoulder joint, for instance, which has the greatest range of motion in the body, the capsule is loose enough to permit the head of the humerus to be drawn away from the articular surface of the scapula. If one were actually to sever the muscles at the shoulder

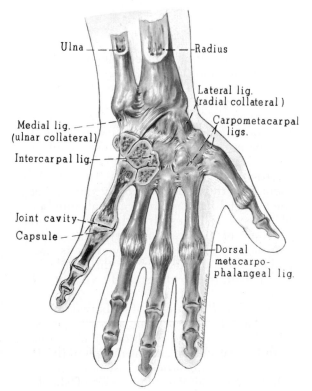

Figure 99. Ligaments of the hand with cross-sectional view of a synovial joint showing the joint cavity and capsule.

joint, while leaving the fibrous capsule still intact, the humerus would be drawn as much as 1 inch away from the scapula. On the other hand, in the hip joint, the range of motion is more limited in relation to the requirements of greater strength, and the capsule is thicker and shorter.

Muscles provide an important mechanism for maintaining the stability of joints. They possess many advantages over ligaments, particularly during relaxation and contraction in which the muscles maintain the articular surfaces in firm contact at every position of the joint. The importance of the musculature can be seen in paralysis, in which the related joints allow much greater range of motion than is normal.

In summary, joints serve the purposes of bearing weight and providing motion. They are so constructed as to afford stability. The joint capsule, ligaments, tendons, muscles, and articular discs provide stability. Viscous, synovial fluid functions in lubricating the joints and nourishing the cartilage.

Synovial Fluid. The vascular connective tissue lining the inner surface of the joint capsule is known as the synovial membrane. It consists of a dense connective tissue with fibers together with associated ground substance and irregularly distributed cells. This tissue functions to produce the lubrication of the joint.

Synovial fluid is usually slightly alkaline (pH 7.4), colorless to deep yellow, 95 per cent water and viscous. Its similarity in viscosity to egg white (G. *syn,* like; G. *ovum,* egg cell) accounts for the origin of the term.

The protein-polysaccharide of synovial fluid appears to be the chief lubricating factor. A single protein-polysaccharide, hyaluronic acid, containing 2 per cent protein, is responsible for imparting stickiness and viscosity to the fluid. This viscosity varies with temperature, a factor which may contribute to joint stiffness in cold weather.

Physiology of Synovial Joint. Synovial joint mechanisms of lubrication function to minimize friction on articular cartilages to such an extent that normally, during movement, less friction is created than ice sliding on ice.

Joint lubrication may be considered a type of hydrodynamic lubrication, with an incompressible fluid circulating through the joint during movement. No two joint sur-

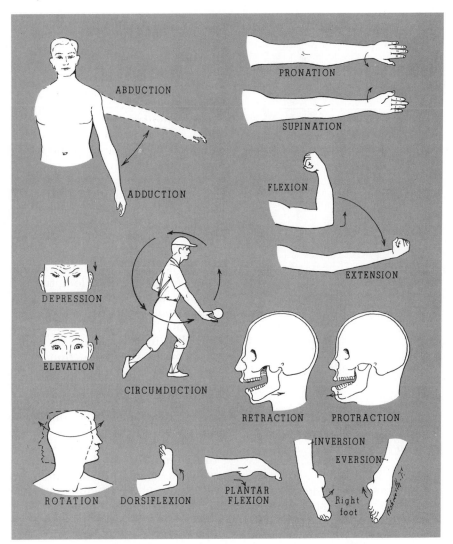

Figure 100. Types of movement permitted by diarthrodial joints.

faces fit together perfectly; therefore, a cushion effect must be provided. The synovial fluid maintains pressure at necessary points within the joint to keep the surfaces apart. This cushioning effect is complemented by a kind of weeping lubrication as synovial fluid oozes from articular cartilage under pressure. In this way, one might say that fluid is being pumped into the joint space under pressure to keep the moving surfaces separated. Elastic deformation of cartilage also aids in this function.

Movements. The following movements occur at synovial joints (Fig. 100).

1. *Flexion*—bending or decreasing the angle between two bones.

2. *Extension*—increasing the angle between two bones.

3. *Abduction*—moving the bone away from the midline.

4. *Adduction*—moving the bone toward the midline.

5. *Rotation*—moving the bone around a central axis; the plane of motion is perpendicular to the axis.

6. *Circumduction*—moving the bone so that the end of it describes a circle and the sides of it describe a cone.

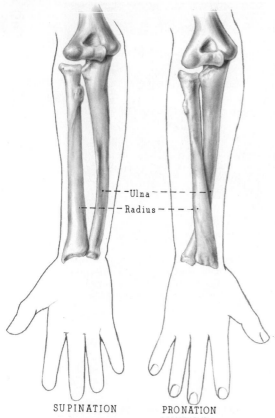

SUPINATION   PRONATION

Figure 101. Position of the radius and ulna in pronation and supination.

7. *Supination*—moving the bones of the forearm so that the radius and ulna are parallel; if the arm is at the side of the body the palm is moved from a posterior to an anterior position (Fig. 101).

8. *Pronation*—moving the bones of the forearm so that the radius and ulna are not parallel; if the arm is at the side of the body the palm is moved from an anterior to a posterior position (Fig. 101).

9. *Eversion*—moving the sole of the foot outward at the ankle joint.

10. *Inversion*—moving the sole of the foot inward at the ankle joint.

11. *Protraction*—moving a part of the body forward on a plane parallel to the ground.

12. *Retraction*—moving a part of the body backward on a plane parallel to the ground.

13. *Elevation*—raising a part of the body.

14. *Depression*—lowering a part of the body.

Types. Most joints in the body are of the diarthrodial type. These, in turn, are classified according to the shape of the articulating end of the involved bones. The shapes include the following:

1. *Ball and socket joint.* The ball-shaped head fits into a concave socket. This type of joint provides the widest range of motion, with movement in all planes in addition to rotation. An example of the ball and socket is the hip (Fig. 102).

2. *Hinge joint.* A convex surface fits into a concavity, and motion is limited to flexion and extension in a single plane. An example is the elbow joint.

3. *Pivot joint.* In the pivot joint, motion is limited to rotation; the joint is formed by a pivot-like process which rotates within a bony fossa around a longitudinal axis. Examples are the atlas and the axis.

4. *Condyloid.* An oval-shaped condyle fits into an elliptical cavity. Motion is possible in two planes at right angles to each other. Circumduction can be accomplished by combinations of flexion, abduction, extension and adduction. This type of joint does not permit radial rotation. An example is the wrist joint between the radius and carpal bones.

5. *Saddle joint.* This is a unique joint for the thumb. In it the articular surface is concave in one direction and convex in the other; the other articular surface is reciprocally convex-concave so that the two bones fit together. Movements are similar to those of a condyloid joint, but freer. Although this type of joint does not permit axial rotation, all movements, including some rotation, are possible.

6. *Gliding joint.* A gliding joint is formed by the opposing plane surfaces or slightly convex and concave surfaces, permitting only gliding movement. An example is the intervertebral joint (Fig. 103).

A tabulation of all types of joints appears on page 142.

BURSAE

Bursae are closed sacs with a synovial membrane lining similar to that of a true joint. A bursa can be found in the spaces of connective tissue between tendons, ligaments, and bones, or, generally, where friction would otherwise develop. Bursae facilitate the gliding of muscles or tendons

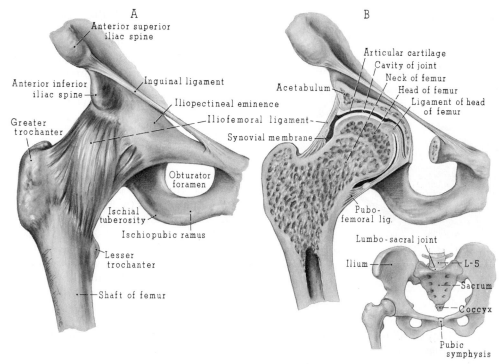

Figure 102. Hip joint, showing ligaments between femur and pelvic bone; intact (*A*) and sectioned (*B*) to show attachments.

over bony or ligamentous surfaces. *Subcutaneous bursae* are found between the skin and underlying bony processes, such as the olecranon in the elbow and the patella in the knee. *Subfascial bursae* are located beneath the deep fascia. *Subtendinous bursae* are found in locations where one tendon overlies another or overlies a bony projection. The walls of subtendinous bursae may be continuous with the synovial membrane

of a joint through an opening in the capsular wall (Fig. 104).

DISORDERS OF JOINTS

Bursitis

Bursitis is an inflammation of the synovial bursa which may result from excess stress or

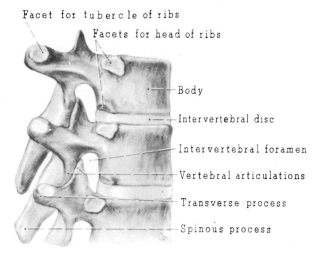

Figure 103. Relationship of vertebral bodies and intervertebral discs. Note articulations between vertebrae.

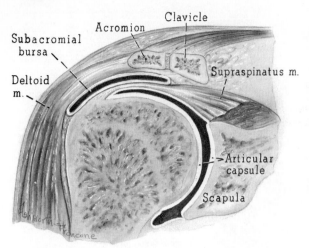

Figure 104. Subacromial bursa of the shoulder, cross sectioned to show attachments of muscles.

tension placed on the bursa, or from some local or systemic inflammatory process. It may occur in any of the periarticular bursae; the most frequent location is the subacromial bursa. The subacromial bursa lies close to the shoulder joint; consequently, in inflammation of this bursa, movement of the shoulder joint is limited and painful. Since the supraspinatus tendon, the major tendon involved in initiating the abduction of the humerus, forms the floor of the subacromial bursa, the patient with subacromial bursitis has limited abduction at the shoulder joint. Eventually, with inflammation, deposits of calcium occur in the supraspinatus tendon and further interfere with shoulder motion. If bursitis persists, the muscles eventually atrophy or degenerate. With chronic bursitis the shoulder can actually become stiff, even though the joint itself is not diseased. Inflammation of bursae located about the elbows, knees, ischial tuberosities, and attachment of the tendo calcaneus (Achilles tendon) causes similar changes.

Arthritis

Arthritis (G. *arthron,* joint; G. *-itis,* inflammation) is one of the most common and painful abnormalities of the articular system. Fifty varieties of arthritis are known. Three common types are rheumatoid arthritis, gouty arthritis, and degenerative joint disease.

Rheumatoid Arthritis. Rheumatoid arthritis is a systemic disease with widespread involvement of connective tissue. Its cause is unknown. The earliest stage in rheumatoid arthritis is an inflammation of the synovial membrane in which the tissue becomes thickened. This thickened synovial tissue (*pannus*) grows inward from the synovium along the surface of the articular cartilage. Growth of the pannus actually damages the cartilage. Next, the inflammatory tissue becomes invaded with tough fibrous material which is adherent and prevents motion of the joint. This stage is known as *fibrous ankylosis* (ankylosis means immobility of a joint). The fibrous tissue may ultimately become calcified and undergo changes to osseous tissue, resulting in a firm bony union, *bony ankylosis.* Rheumatoid arthritis, then, develops in four stages: inflammation of the synovium, formation of the pannus, fibrous ankylosis, and, finally, bony ankylosis. Alterations in the microcirculation of the joint give rise to characteristic clinical expressions of heat, redness, swelling, and pain. Although, as mentioned, the cause of rheumatoid arthritis is unknown, it is believed that the tissue damage is caused by lysosomal enzymes. The enzymes are apparently released because of the rupture of lysosomes in white blood cells (and possibly in synovial membrane cells as well) that have entered the joint and phagocytized complexes formed between antibodies and a normal blood protein that has been altered by an unknown initiating event, the "trigger" of the disease. Most drugs, such as aspirin, used to treat rheumatoid arthritis have the property of stabilizing lysosomal membranes.

Gouty Arthritis. Gout is a metabolic disorder, the major clinical manifestation of which is arthritis. It is a disturbance of purine metabolism usually associated with an elevated uric acid in the blood. In an attack of acute gout, the synovium is inflamed. With repeated attacks of gouty arthritis, urates deposit in and about the joint structures and together with inflammatory changes, cause severe damage to the articular cartilage.

Degenerative Joint Disease (Arthrosis). This disease is a non-inflammatory disorder of movable joints characterized by deterioration of articular cartilage and the formation of new bone at the joint surfaces. Joints are subject to a great deal or wear and tear. After years of use, degenerative changes are to be expected. Some evidence of degenerative joint disease is found in many individuals over the age of 45. The weight-bearing joints of the lower extremities and spine are particularly subject to wear and tear and often show early degenerative changes. There is initially a softening of the cartilage, followed by a separation of fibers and, later, by an actual disintegration of the cartilage, which soon thins out. As the cartilage wears thin, the bone beneath the cartilage becomes eburnated (converted into an ivory-like mass). It is the presence of these marginal bony growths that has given the disease its outdated name "hypertrophic arthritis." Hypertrophy means thickening or increasing size without an increase in the number of cells.

Rheumatic Fever

The musculoskeletal system may be involved in rheumatic fever, a disease characterized by inflammation of the synovial tissues, tendons, and other connective tissues about joints. Rheumatic fever begins abruptly with an intense inflammatory reaction of joints and then tends to subside after a brief period. No pannus occurs in rheumatic fever, so the cartilage and bone are not damaged. The functional disturbances of rheumatic fever can be attributed to active inflammation similar to changes noted in the early stages of rheumatoid arthritis. When the disease subsides, the patient usually does not show any residual functional damage of the articular system but frequently has permanent damage to the heart valves, which manifests itself in later life as rheumatic heart disease.

Primary Fibrositis

Primary fibrositis, sometimes called "rheumatism" by the layman, is an inflammation of fibrous connective tissue more than a disease of muscles. Fibrositis occurring in the low back is referred to in nonscientific circles as "lumbago." Chronic fibrositis either involves many structures simultaneously or migrates from one part of the body to another. The involved portions of the body are usually tender and stiff.

Since movement of the joints depends on function of periarticular and connective tissue and muscles, irritation of these structures leads to limitation of movement. Since the joints themselves are healthy, no permanent damage occurs. As soon as the connective changes are relieved, the locomotor system again functions normally.

Tenosynovitis

Tendon sheaths may become inflamed, interfering with the free passage of the enclosed tendon. Function of joints moved by these tendons will then be impaired. If the inflammation occurs along the sheaths of the flexor tendons of the fingers, the finger frequently cannot be extended by the flexor apparatus without assistance—a so-called "trigger finger." In many instances, inflammation of the flexor tendon sheath and palmar fascia may cause adhesions so strong that movement of the fingers is completely prevented. The fingers then become deformed and remain in positions of flexion. Dupuytren's contracture is an inflammation of the palmar fascia resulting in flexion deformities of the third, fourth, and fifth fingers.

THE KNEE JOINT

Anatomy (Figs. 105–110)

There are two *semilunar cartilages* (menisci) involved in the knee joint: the *medial semilunar cartilage* and the *lateral semilunar cartilage*. The *medial semilunar cartilage* attaches by short fibers to the tibia and is relatively fixed in position. It functions to deepen the socket for the medial femoral condyle. The *lateral semilunar cartilage* is semicircular and attached to the tibia, with its long fibers permitting gliding of the disc. It functions to insure smooth articulation.

Two sets of ligaments are involved in movement of the knee joint. These are the *anterior* and *posterior cruciate ligaments* and the *medial* and *lateral collateral ligaments*.

The anterior cruciate ligament limits extension and rotation. The posterior cruciate

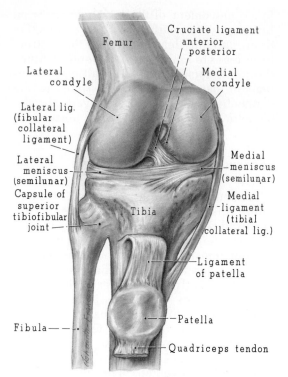

Figure 105. Anterior view of the right knee joint, slightly flexed. The patella has been severed from the quadriceps muscle and pulled down, exposing the ligaments between the femur and tibia.

essential during walking, as the joint flexes, to return the center of gravity toward the medial position.

The collateral ligaments prevent lateral dislocation of the knee. These extend from the lateral condyle of the femur to the head of the fibula (*lateral ligament*), and from the medial condyle of the femur to the capsule and medial surface of the tibia (*medial ligament*). The synovial membrane of the knee is attached to the articular cartilage of the femur and tibia. The synovial membrane does not merely line the fibrous capsule as it does in other joints, but actually excludes the cruciate ligaments from the interior portion of the joint. This membrane has many fat-filled folds which assist in reducing the open spaces in the joint cavity during movement. Several subcutaneous bursae are associated with the knee joint. These are found between the patella and the skin. Inflammation of these bursae may be the cause of so-called "housemaid's knee."

Internal Derangement of the Knee

The knee joint depends on strong ligaments and strong muscles of the thigh for its stability. The condyles of the femur and tibia are held in contact by these structures during flexion and extension. An *internal derangement* is a mechanical derangement of the function of the joint caused by some abnormality which eliminates the supporting strength of the major ligaments or

ligament prevents forward dislocation of the femur. The winding and unwinding of the cruciate ligaments are particularly important in stabilizing the knee joint during rotation. Although the principal movements are flexion and extension, some rotation is

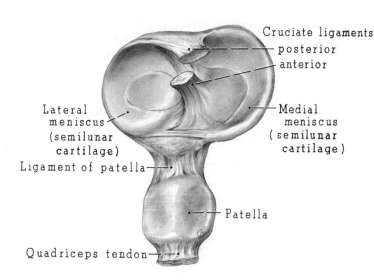

Figure 106. Articular surface of the right tibia.

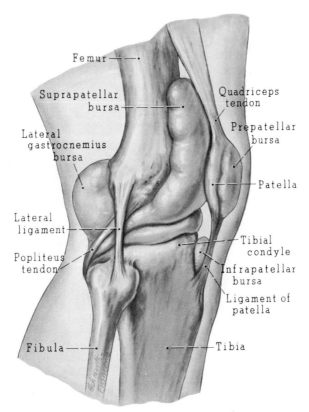

Figure 107. Lateral view of the right knee joint. The bursae have been expanded for clarity.

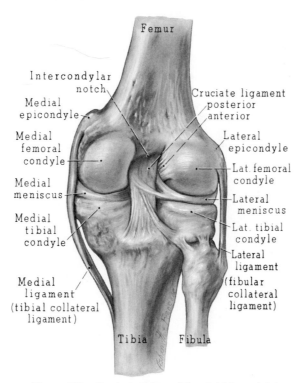

Figure 108. Posterior view of the right knee joint.

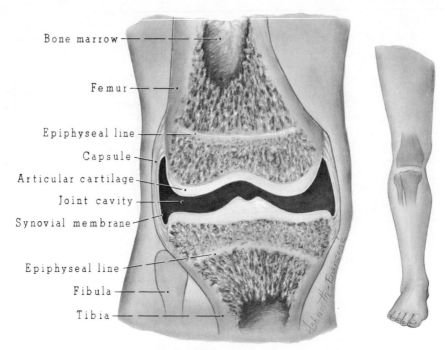

Bone marrow

Femur

Epiphyseal line

Capsule

Articular cartilage

Joint cavity

Synovial membrane

Epiphyseal line

Fibula

Tibia

Figure 109. Frontal section through the right knee joint.

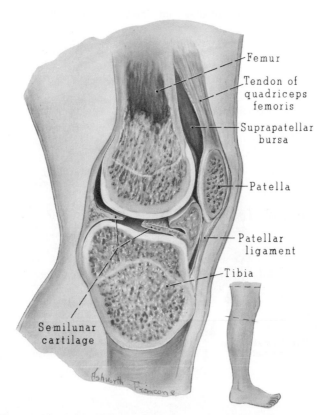

Femur

Tendon of quadriceps femoris

Suprapatellar bursa

Patella

Patellar ligament

Tibia

Semilunar cartilage

Figure 110. Lateral view of the right knee joint in sagittal section.

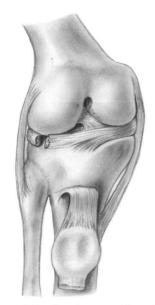

Figure 111. Semilunar cartilage tear.

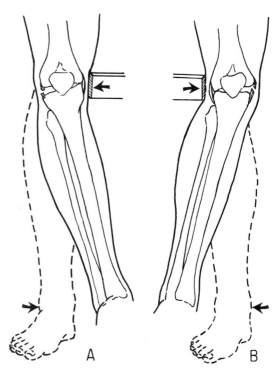

Figure 113. Collateral ligament tear. *A*, Fibular collateral ligament; *B*, tibial collateral ligament.

prevents the contact and smooth gliding of the condyles during flexion and extension of the knee. The most common derangement of the knee is a tear of the semilunar cartilage, which usually results from a twisting injury (Fig. 111). Normally, the cartilage buffers rotary grinding action of the condyles of the femur on the tibia. When the medial semilunar cartilage is torn, the patient presents a history of a twisting injury with a snapping sensation on the inner side of the knee. A patient with a torn lateral semilunar cartilage, on the other hand, also presents a history of a twisting injury, but with a snapping sensation on the outer side of the knee. The medial semilunar cartilage is more frequently damaged than the lateral one.

A patient with a torn semilunar cartilage experiences painful locking of the knee joint with tenderness at the site of injury. Usually a torn semilunar cartilage does not

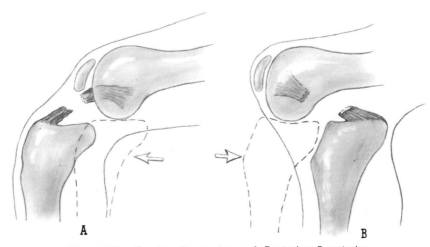

Figure 112. Cruciate ligament tear. *A*, Posterior; *B*, anterior.

Table 9. JOINTS

JOINT	TYPE	MOVEMENT
Vertebral	Diarthrodial Gliding	Flexion and extension of the spine by gliding
Atlanto-epistropheal	Diarthrodial Pivot	Rotation of the atlas upon the axis
Temporomandibular	Diarthrodial Hinge and gliding	Opening and closing of the jaws; protrusion of the mandible; lateral displacement of the mandible
Costovertebral	Diarthrodial Gliding	Gliding
Sternocostal	Amphiarthrodial, except for first rib, which is synarthrodial (immovable)	Slight
Sternoclavicular	Diarthrodial Gliding	Gliding
Acromioclavicular	Diarthrodial Gliding	Gliding of the clavicle on the acromion; rotation of the scapula upon the clavicle
Shoulder	Diarthrodial Ball and socket	Flexion, extension, abduction, adduction, rotation, circumduction
Elbow	Diarthrodial Hinge	Flexion, extension
Radioulnar	Diarthrodial Pivot	Pronation, supination (rotation)
Wrist (radiocarpal)	Diarthrodial Condyloid	All movements except rotation
Intercarpal	Diarthrodial Gliding	Flexion, extension
Carpometacarpal (first)	Diarthrodial Saddle	Flexion, extension, abduction, adduction, and some rotation
Metacarpophalangeal	Diarthrodial Condyloid	Flexion, extension, limited abduction, limited adduction, circumduction
Interphalangeal	Diarthrodial Hinge	Flexion, extension
Sacroiliac	(Diarthrodial in early life) Amphiarthrodial Symphysis	Limited
Symphysis pubis	Amphiarthrodial Symphysis	Slight
Hip	Diarthrodial Ball and socket	Flexion, extension, adduction, abduction, rotation, circumduction
Knee	Diarthrodial Hinge	Flexion, extension, some rotation
Tibiofibular	Diarthrodial Gliding	Gliding movement
Talocrural (ankle)	Diarthrodial Hinge	Dorsiflexion and plantar flexion
Intertarsal	Diarthrodial Gliding	Gliding—backward and forward from side to side
Tarsometatarsal	Diarthrodial Gliding	Slight gliding of the bones
Metatarsophalangeal	Diarthrodial Condyloid	Flexion, extension, adduction, abduction
Interphalangeal	Diarthrodial Hinge	Flexion, extension

heal, since cartilage has a poor blood supply. Surgical removal of the torn cartilage or torn portion of the cartilage is the only definitive treatment of this condition.

Major violence is necessary to completely rupture a ligament. More often than not there occurs only a partial tearing of the fibers of the ligament. The direction of force applied to the knee determines which ligament is most likely to be injured by the impact (Figs. 112 and 113).

SUMMARY

THE ARTICULAR SYSTEM

Classification of Joints

1. **There are three groups of joints.**

   a. Synarthroses: no movement.
      (1) Suture: fibrous tissue unites bones.
      (2) Synchondroses: cartilage unites bones.
   b. Amphiarthroses: slightly movable joints.
      (1) Symphyses: fibrocartilage disc unites bones.
      (2) Syndesmoses: interosseous ligament connects bones.
   c. Diarthroses: freely movable joints.
      (1) Anatomy of synovial joints
         (a) The synovial fluid is a viscous lubricant found in all synovial joint cartilages.
         (b) The articular cartilage acts as a cushion, providing a smooth gliding surface. Nourishment is obtained from the bony surfaces and synovial fluid.
         (c) Also present in synovial joints is the synovial membrane. This membrane surrounds the cavities and slips in and out of the openings caused by movement.
         (d) Articular discs consist of fibrocartilage and serve to buffer shock.
         (e) Ligaments help to maintain

the relationships between bones and limit motion.
(f) Articular muscles function to maintain the stability of joints by relaxation and contraction to insure firm contact throughout the articular surface.
   (2) Movements of synovial joints
      (a) Flexion—decreasing angle between two bones.
      (b) Extension—increasing angle between two bones.
      (c) Abduction—the bone moves away from the midline.
      (d) Adduction—bone moves toward the midline.
      (e) Rotation—the bone moves around the central axis.
      (f) Circumduction—bone describes the surface of a cone.
      (g) Supination—the palm is turned upward.
      (h) Pronation—the palm is turned downward.
      (i) Eversion—the sole of the foot is turned outward.
      (j) Inversion—the sole of the foot is turned inward.
      (k) Protraction—a part of the body is moved forward.
      (l) Retraction—a part of the body is moved backward.
      (m) Elevation—upward, non-angular gliding of one surface over another.
      (n) Depression—downward, non-angular gliding of one surface over another.
   (3) Types of synovial joints
      (a) Ball and socket
      (b) Hinge
      (c) Pivot
      (d) Condyloid
      (e) Saddle
      (f) Gliding

Bursae

1. **Bursae are found in close proximity to joints and are usually associated with spaces between connective tissue.**

2. **Bursae are closed sacs with a synovial membrane lining.**

Disorders of Joints

1. Bursitis is the inflammation of the synovial bursa; it may result from excess stress, local inflammation, or systemic disease.

2. Arthritis is the general term for inflammation of joints.

    a. Rheumatoid arthritis is a disease of unknown cause and is systemic in its effects. The stages of rheumatoid arthritis are inflammation of the synovium, formation of pannus, fibrous ankylosis, and bony ankylosis.

    b. Gouty arthritis is a metabolic disorder in purine metabolism which causes uric acid to be deposited in the blood.

3. Degenerative joint disease comes from wear and tear on joints in old age. The articular cartilage begins to wear thin and the surfaces adhere, causing pain and inflammation.

4. Rheumatic fever is a disease in which the synovial tissues become inflamed and then rapidly return to normal.

5. Primary fibrositis ("rheumatism" or "lumbago") in the lower back region is an inflammation of the fibrous connective tissue of joints.

6. Tenosynovitis: The tendon sheaths become inflamed and may deter movement of the involved joints.

The Knee Joint

1. Anatomy

    a. The knee joint is the largest and most complex joint in the body.

    b. Two semilunar cartilages are found in the knee joint.

    c. Two pairs of ligaments are found; the cruciate and collateral ligaments provide stability and necessary limitation of motion.

2. Internal derangement of the knee

    a. The most common internal derangement of the knee is a tear of the medial semilunar cartilage. The torn part or the entire cartilage should be removed, since cartilage has a poor blood supply and will not heal.

The Muscular System

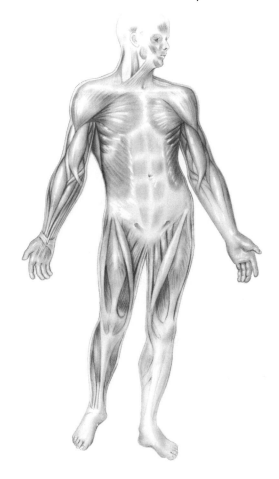

Objectives

The aim of this chapter is to enable the student to:

Describe the structure of a whole skeletal muscle, muscle fiber and myofibril.

Explain how the arrangement of thick and thin filaments in a myofibril gives rise to the striated appearance of the myofibril.

Describe the sliding filament model of muscular contraction and the associated structural changes seen in the electron microscope.

Explain how the release of calcium from the sarcoplasmic reticulum triggers the muscular contraction.

Describe how the nerve impulse is transmitted to the muscle fiber and how the impulse reaches the sarcoplasmic reticulum.

List the sources of energy for muscular contraction during moderate and strenuous exercise.

Identify the factors determining the strength of muscular contraction.

Define muscle tone.

Describe the differences between rapidly contracting and slowly contracting motor units.

Identify the distinguishing characteristics of smooth and cardiac muscle.

Describe how skeletal muscles are named according to action, shape and their origins and insertions.

Knowledge of the anatomy and physiology of the muscular system was uncertain and vague through the Renaissance. A few attempts to theorize the nature of muscular action were made by Hippocrates and Galen, but no real progress occurred until the seventeenth century, when Anton van Leeuwenhoek made the initial observations of muscle under the microscope. These observations laid the foundation for today's knowledge of the structure and function of muscle.

Muscles compose 40 to 50 per cent of the body's weight. When they contract, they effect movement of the body as a whole; of blood (circulation); of food through the digestive tract; of urine through the urinary tract; and of the chest, diaphragm, and abdomen during respiration. The two key words, then, are *contraction* and *movement*.

TYPES OF MUSCLE

The three types of muscle tissue are *skeletal, smooth,* and *cardiac* (Fig. 114).

Skeletal Muscle

Skeletal muscle is also called *striated* muscle because of the presence of alternating dark and light bands, and *voluntary* muscle because it is subject to voluntary control (although, of course, spontaneous contractions of unconscious origin do occur).

Mature skeletal muscle cells are long and slender, ranging from 1 to 50 millimeters in length and from 40 to 50 micrometers in diameter. Since their length is much greater than their width, these cells are called fibers. Each muscle cell is multinucleated and is surrounded by an electrically polarized membrane—the *sarcolemma* (G. *sarx,* flesh; G. *lemma,* husk). The nuclei are usually located just under the sarcolemma. The sarcolemma is bounded by delicate connective tissue called the **endomysium** (G. *endon,* within; G. *mys,* muscle).

The entire muscle consists of a number of skeletal muscle bundles known as *fasciculi* (Fig. 115). Fasciculi are bound by a sheath, the **perimysium** (G. *peri,* around), which is visible to the naked eye. The perimysium is continuous with the coarse, irregular connective tissue investing the muscle, the **epimysium** (G. *epi,* upon). The *fascia,* composed of areolar tissue, forms a covering over the entire muscle trunk. When viewed under the microscope, the skeletal muscle fiber is seen to have regular striations. These striations are due to transverse alternating dark and light bands on the **myofibrils,** which are parallel, threadlike structures in the *sarcoplasm* (muscle cytoplasm) of a muscle fiber (Fig. 116). Myofibrils, the smallest elements of the muscle fiber visible in the light microscope, are the contractile units of the fiber. With the electron microscope the striations on the myofibrils can be seen to arise from the arrangement of its subunits, **thick** and **thin filaments.** The former are composed of the protein *myosin,* the latter of three proteins, *actin* (the principal one), *tropomyosin* and *troponin.* The **dark,** or **A, band** of the myofibril corresponds to the thick filament, overlapped on either end with thin filaments; the **light,** or **I, band** corresponds to the nonoverlapping portion of the thin filaments (Fig. 117).

Two additional markings are of impor-

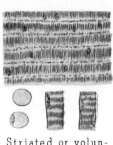

Striated or voluntary (skeletal m.)

Smooth muscle

Cardiac muscle

Figure 114. Types of muscle cells.

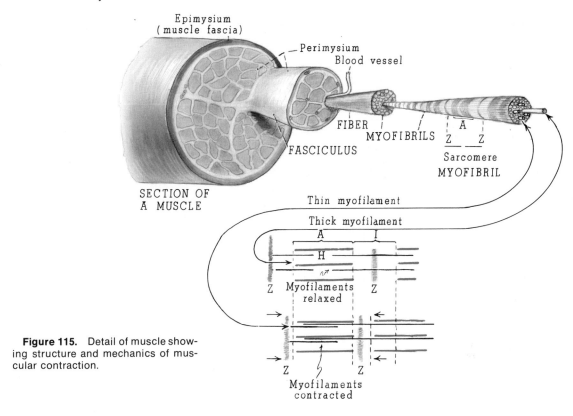

Figure 115. Detail of muscle showing structure and mechanics of muscular contraction.

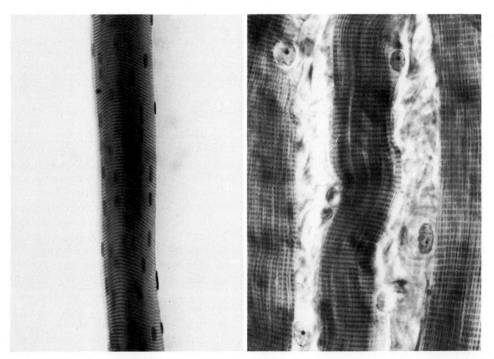

Figure 116. Photomicrographs of human skeletal muscle. *Left.* Portion of single intact fiber separated from the human gastrocnemius muscle. Note striations and numerous nuclei. (×275.) *Right.* Longitudinal section from lip showing portions of three fibers with connective tissue between them. In each fiber individual myofibrils with alternating dark and light bands can be seen. (×400.) (From Leeson, C. R., and Leeson, T. S.: Histology. 3rd ed., Philadelphia, W. B. Saunders Co., 1976.)

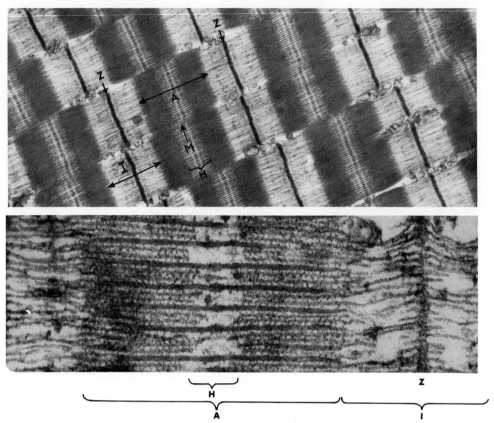

Figure 117.   Electron micrographs of skeletal muscle of the rabbit. *Top.* Each diagonal strip is a longitudinal section of a myofibril magnified 13,000 ×. *Bottom.* Very thin section of a myofibril magnified 74,000 ×. The A bands represent the thick filaments overlapped in the darker regions with thin filaments. The lighter, H, zones in the centers of the A bands are regions free of thin filaments. The I bands represent nonoverlapping segments of thin filaments attached to both sides of the Z lines. In the bottom micrograph two thin filaments can be seen between thick filaments extending into the A band as far as the H zone. Swellings in the center of the thick filament give rise to the dense M line seen in the top micrograph. (From Leeson, C. R., and Leeson, T. S.: Histology. 3rd ed., Philadelphia, W. B. Saunders Co., 1976.)

tance—the **Z line,** a narrow, dark-staining band in the central region of the I band representing a structure to which the thin filaments are attached on either side, and the **H zone,** a lighter region, located in the central portion of each A band, containing only the thick myosin filaments. The area between two adjacent Z lines is called a *sarcomere.*

Sarcotubular Systems.   Electron photomicrographs show muscle fibrils to be surrounded by structures made up of membrane in the form of vesicles and tubules. These structures form two systems (Fig. 118): One consists of what are called *T* (for transverse) *tubules,* which are actually invaginations of the membrane of the muscle fiber. The other, the principal system, called the *sarcoplasmic reticulum,* consists of tubules running parallel to the myofibrils. Each T tubule runs between a pair of

sacs formed by fusion of the sarcoplasmic reticulum. These three transverse structures make up what is known as a *triad.* The triad is important functionally because, although there is no open continuity between the sarcoplasmic reticulum and the T tubules at the triad, the close association of the two systems at this site enables the T tubules to function as a conduit for transmission of the electrical impulse, the normal muscle stimulus, to the sarcoplasmic reticulum. The arrival of the electrical impulse activates the release from the sarcoplasmic reticulum of calcium, the triggering agent for muscle contraction.

Physiology of Contraction

Motor Unit.   As a result of terminal branching, a single nerve fiber innervates, on the average, about 150 muscle fibers. All

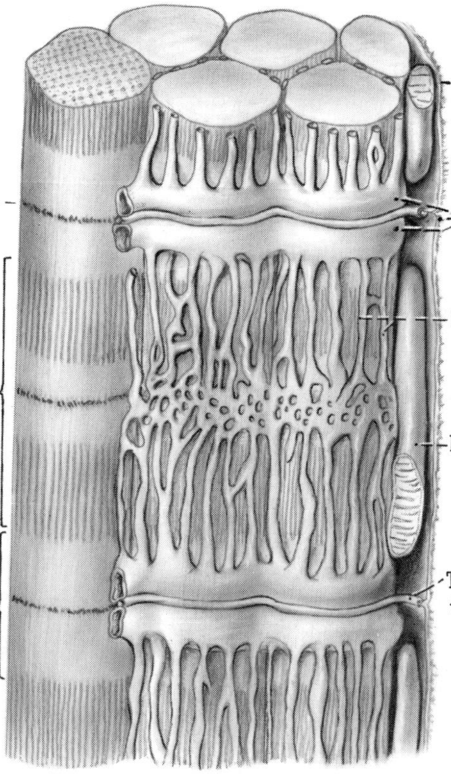

Figure 118. Diagrammatic representation of sarcoplasmic reticulum surrounding myofibrils of a fiber and of transverse tubules (invaginations of the sarcolemma). (Modified from Bloom and Fawcett: Textbook of Histology. 9th ed., Philadelphia, W. B. Saunders, 1968.)

of these fibers innervated by the same nerve fiber are called a *motor unit* because they are always excited simultaneously and contract in unison.

It is important to note that terminal divisions of a motor neuron are distributed throughout the muscle belly. Stimulation of a single motor unit, therefore, causes weak contraction in a broad area of muscle rather than a strong contraction at one specific point.

Muscles controlling fine movements are characterized by the presence of a few muscle fibers in each motor unit; that is, the ratio of nerve fibers to muscle fibers is high. For instance, each motor unit present in the ocular muscle contains only about 10 muscle fibers. On the other hand, gross movements may be governed by a motor unit containing 200 or more muscle fibers.

EXCITATION OF SKELETAL MUSCLE. Muscle fibers possess the property of being excitable. Any force affecting this excitability is called a stimulus, which, in muscle tissue, is usually conveyed by nerve fibers. The stimulus is an electrical impulse transmitted from a nerve fiber branch to muscle fiber at a junctional region

called the **neuromuscular junction.** At the junction a gap, the *synaptic cleft,* exists between a nerve branch terminal and a recess on the surface of the muscle fiber. A nerve impulse reaching the neuromuscular junction causes a sharp increase in the release of acetylcholine, a chemical mediator stored in vesicles of the nerve terminal. Acetylcholine crosses the gap and acts on the membrane of the muscle fiber, causing it to generate its own impulse, which travels along the muscle fiber in both directions at a rate of about 5 meters per second and, as mentioned, is conducted to the sarcoplasmic reticulum via the T system. (A discussion of the origin of the electrical impulse in nerve and muscle fibers and a more complete description of the neuromuscular junction appear on page 226 of Chapter 8, The Nervous System.)

MECHANISM OF CONTRACTION. The generally accepted conception of how muscle contracts, the "sliding filament" model, is based on elegant electron microscopy studies relating structural changes to functional events during contraction (shortening) of muscle. According to this model, the contraction is brought about by the *sliding of the thin filaments at each end of a sarcomere toward each other.* In sections of muscle, prepared at sequential stages of contraction, this shows up as a decrease in width of the I band of the myofibrils (the region with only thin filaments) as the thin filaments move toward the center of the sarcomere. The distance between Z lines decreases as the muscle contracts, but the A band, representing the length of the thick filaments, does not change in width (Fig. 115). The H zone of the A band, the lighter, central region containing no overlapping thin filaments in relaxed muscle, disappears as thin filaments come to completely overlap the thick filaments in the contracted state. When contraction is marked, a dense zone appears in the center of the A band as a result of overlap of thin filaments from opposite ends of a sarcomere. In cross section this overlap is identified as a doubling (over the relaxed condition) of the ratio of thin to thick filaments.

The movement of the thin filaments can be accounted for by crossbridges extending from thick to thin filaments, which are utilized as mechanical pulling devices. **Myosin molecules,** the constituents of thick filaments, consist of two subunits: (1) *head pieces,* largely globular, which have the property of combining with the actin component of thin filaments and contain ATP-splitting enzymes, and (2) linear *tail pieces,* with a self-combining property. Thick filaments are assembled by tail-to-tail aggrega-tion of myosin molecules, with the head pieces of each half, which form the cross-bridges, facing in opposite directions (Fig. 119). This built-in directionality explains how thin filaments at opposite ends of a sarcomere can be pulled inward toward the center of the thick filaments.

The sequence of events leading to the contraction of muscle may be summarized as follows: The electrical impulse traveling along the membrane of a muscle fiber reaches the sarcoplasmic reticulum via the T tubules. This causes the release of **calcium,** which combines with the troponin component of the thin filament. **Troponin** acts as a latch, blocking the formation of an active complex between a head of myosin in its charged state (combined with ATP) and *actin.* Calcium binding unlocks the blocked state, allowing ATP-charged myosin heads to interact with actin. When this occurs, ATP is split. This provides the energy for the propulsive force, probably a swiveling of myosin heads, for pulling the thin filaments toward the center of the sarcomere. Successive cycles (binding of ATP to myosin heads, detachment of myosin heads from actin and reattachment in a new position) result in the continued sliding of thin filaments. Contraction ends when calcium returns to the sarcoplasmic reticulum. The action of troponin appears to be mediated by the third component of the thin filament, *tropomyosin,* a protein forming a continuous strand around actin (Fig. 119). Calcium

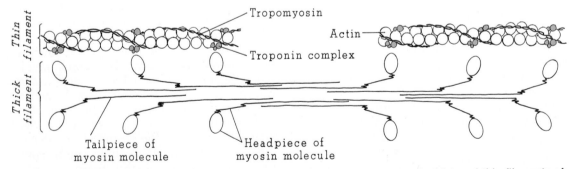

Figure 119. Schematic representation of the arrangement of the constituents in thick and thin filaments of skeletal muscle. Thick filaments are constructed from myosin molecules, which consist of linear tail pieces and globular head pieces with short tails. These filaments assemble by tail-to-tail aggregation of myosin molecules, so that the heads face opposite ends of the sarcomere. Actin, the principal component of thin filaments, consists of two strings of spheroidal molecules twisted into a double helix. A continuous strand of tropomyosin winds around actin, fitting into the grooves of the actin helix. Troponin complexes, each composed of three globular subunits, bind to tropomyosin and actin at regular intervals. When calcium, the triggering agent of contraction, is released from the sarcoplasmic reticulum, it is bound by the smallest subunit of troponin. This changes the configuration of troponin, causing it to release its hold on tropomyosin, which then moves more deeply into the actin groove, exposing a binding site on actin for ATP-charged myosin heads. Interaction of myosin and actin is followed by the splitting of ATP, providing energy for the propulsion of actin filaments from both ends of the sarcomere toward the center of the sarcomere, presumably by a swiveling motion of the heads of myosin molecules.

binding induces a structural change in troponin, which in turn causes a shift in the position of tropomyosin. This opens the site on actin to which myosin binds.

RIGOR COMPLEX. The detachment of the myosin crossbridge from actin after ATP is split can take place only after a new ATP binds to the headpiece of myosin. The low energy complex between actin and myosin without bound ATP is called a *rigor complex*. Rigor complexes, unlike active actin-myosin complexes, can form in either the absence or presence of calcium. The depletion of ATP after death results in the formation of rigor complexes and accounts for the development of *rigor mortis*.

ENERGY SOURCES. In the chapter on the cell we described the role of ATP as a direct source of energy for the variety of work, including muscular contraction, performed by cells. Described also was the synthesis of ATP during the aerobic (in the presence of oxygen) breakdown of glucose and the fatty acid component of fat to carbon dioxide and water, and during glycolysis, the anaerobic (in the absence of oxygen) breakdown of glucose (or glycogen) to lactic acid. ATP must be continuously resynthesized in muscle, since its reserves are meager. Muscle contains a small auxiliary source of high energy phosphate in the form of **creatine phosphate.** Creatine phosphate can be utilized during muscular contraction for the rapid resynthesis of ATP by phosphate transfer to ADP. When muscle is at rest, the reverse reaction, phosphate transfer from ATP to creatine, rebuilds the reserves of creatine phosphate. Muscle also has its own glycogen stores. Calculations based largely upon measurements of oxygen consumption and lactic acid production in human subjects suggest that during **moderate exercise** the energy is initially supplied by stored ATP and ATP resynthesized from creatine phosphate. Within a few seconds, the oxidation of fatty acids and glucose, taken up from the blood stream, provides an additional source of ATP. Oxygen consumption rises rapidly as increased amounts of fatty acids and glucose are oxidized. If any anaerobic breakdown of glycogen occurs under these conditions, it is too small to be detected. When the exercise is **strenuous,** a point is reached when the oxygen supply is insufficient to meet the energy needs of active muscle. When this occurs (estimated

as an energy expenditure of approximately 220 calories per minute per kilogram of body weight), glycolysis provides a sizable portion of the energy needs. As discussed in the chapter on the cell (page 40), far less ATP is produced by the anaerobic than by the aerobic processes. **Lactic acid** produced during strenuous exercise is released from the muscles into the blood stream to be subsequently taken up by the liver (where it is converted to glucose and glycogen). A reasonably accurate measure of the extent of glycolysis can be obtained by determining the concentration of lactic acid in a blood sample drawn two to three minutes after a strenuous exercise trial lasting up to a few minutes. Exercising to a state of exhaustion is associated with a steep and continuous rise in blood lactic acid. Reducing the effort or introducing rest intervals to the point where the exercise can be continued indefinitely is reflected in a leveling off of blood lactic acid concentrations.

OXYGEN DEBT. The depletion of energy stores during exercise represents a debt that is paid after exercise during a period when oxygen consumption returns gradually to normal. The oxygen debt is defined as the amount of oxygen consumed above the resting level during the postexercise period. If the exercise was moderate, the oxygen consumption returns to normal within a few minutes and the debt is small. Oxidation of fatty acids and glucose during this brief period replenishes the approximately half-depleted stores of ATP and creatine phosphate. Strenuous exercise results in a large oxygen debt, and the return to a resting oxygen consumption is slow (requiring an hour or more). The large debt is incurred because a portion of the glycogen stores as well as possibly all of the stores of ATP and creatine phosphate must be replaced. Furthermore, glycolysis continues during the recovery period in order to contribute to the replenishment of ATP and creatine phosphate. Since the glycogen used during this period must also be replaced, this adds to the debt.

ALL OR NONE LAW. The weakest stimulus that will initiate contraction of a single muscle fiber or all of the fibers of a motor unit is known as the *threshold, liminal,* or *minimal, stimulus.* To be effective the stimulus must also be applied for a minimum duration. A stimulus strong enough to elicit a response will produce maximal contraction. The contraction is either all or none. Increasing the strength of the stimulus will not increase the response. If the stimulus is of lesser intensity, it is called *subthreshold, subliminal,* or *subminimal.* The combination of two subminimal stimuli, when applied in rapid succession, may be equivalent to the minimal stimulus, causing contraction of the cell. This is known as *summation of stimuli.*

CONTRACTION OF ISOLATED SKELETAL MUSCLE. Contraction of a muscle can be recorded in the laboratory by attachment of a tendon to a moving lever. In common practice, the gastrocnemius muscle of the frog is used in such preparations. A single, brief contraction is called a *muscle twitch.* Analysis of such a contraction of skeletal muscle shows a brief period after stimulation before contraction occurs. This *latent period* is followed by a *period of contraction* and, finally, by a *period of relaxation* (Fig. 120).

The response depends on (1) the strength of a stimulus, (2) the speed of application of a stimulus, (3) the number of stimulations, (4) the initial length of the muscle, and (5) the temperature.

If a muscle is subjected to successive stimuli of increasing strength, motor units with higher thresholds will be excited and the force of the muscle twitch will increase progressively as increasing numbers of motor units contract.

It is also possible to increase the magnitude of the response by stimulating a muscle while a twitch is still in progress. This *summation of twitches* is believed to result in part from the release by the initial contraction of elastic elements (attributed, among other things, to connective tissue components of muscle and its tendinous attachments) which resist the shortening. A volley of stimuli at low frequency will produce a succession of rising peaks of contraction, a response known as *clonus,* or *incomplete tetanus* (Fig. 121). Stimulation at a high frequency will cause the fusion of summated twitches, resulting in a sustained contraction called *tetanus.*

It is perhaps apparent that the distinct muscle twitch is a laboratory phenomenon. In normal function smooth contractions are maintained by tetanization or, if the stimulation frequency is too low for tetanization, by asynchronous excitation of motor units by nerve impulses.

A curious phenomenon observed at the beginning of a series of complete muscle twitches is known as *treppe* (the German word for staircase). The magnitude of the first few twitches increases in a stepwise manner. Although this response is still not well understood, it has been suggested that a progressive buildup of calcium in the sarcoplasm by the successive stimuli could account for it. The calcium buildup would increase the propulsive energy by increasing the number of myosin-actin linkages.

The following phenomena are also observed if the stimulations are continued at a

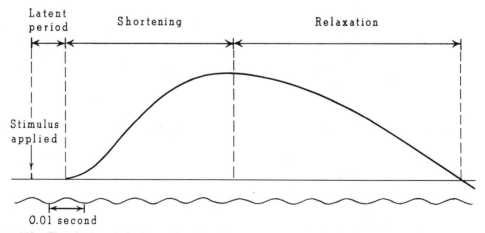

Figure 120. The single twitch. A muscle twitch occurs when the minimal stimulus is attained. All the muscle fibers associated with the stimulated nerve, after a period of latency, contract and then relax. The duration of this twitch is less than 0.1 second. Note that the period for relaxation is longer than the time needed for contraction. (After Carlson and Johnson.)

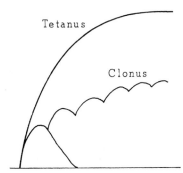

Figure 121. Clonus and tetanus in skeletal muscle. Tetanus occurs at stimulation rates between about 30 to 100 stimuli per second, depending upon the muscle.

constant rate: After treppe the magnitude of the contractions levels off. As the stimulations are continued, the contractions weaken. This state of *fatigue,* brought about by depletion of nutrients and oxygen and the accumulation of waste products (especially lactic acid), eventually leads to a complete absence of response. As the state of fatigue sets in, the muscle fails to relax completely after each contraction. This condition is known as *contracture.* The term contracture is also used clinically to describe a partially contracted state of muscle (see p. 155).

An important factor governing the force with which a muscle contracts is its initial length. Maximum force is obtained when a muscle is stretched to its approximate resting length in its normal attachments in the body. At this length there is a maximum overlap between thin filaments and the head pieces of myosin. This interrelationship makes possible maximum propulsive action. If weights are added to the muscle lever, stretching the muscle, the work performed when the muscle contracts (load × distance lifted) will increase to an optimum load, and decrease as more weights are added.

The optimum temperature at which muscles perform their best work is 37° C (98.6° F) in man. As the temperature rises above this level, excitability is lost, the muscle finally entering a state of heat rigor, or permanent shortening.

COMPARISON OF ISOMETRIC AND ISOTONIC CONTRACTION. In the foregoing descriptions of muscle contraction, the tension developed was utilized to perform work in moving a load some distance. This occurs normally when walking, climbing, lifting objects or turning the head. If a muscle does not shorten as it contracts, the tension may be utilized for such actions as holding an object in a fixed position or maintaining posture against the force of gravity. According to the classification introduced by Fick in the nineteenth century, the contraction is called *isotonic* when the muscle shortens against a constant load, exerting constant force, and *isometric* when it does not shorten, tension rising to a peak and then falling off. Maximum tension develops when a muscle contracts without shortening.

TONE. Tone is defined as that property of a muscle whereby a steady state of partial contraction is maintained, varying only in degree. This may be evidenced in maintenance of posture for long periods of time with little or no evidence of fatigue. This is accomplished as stimuli alternate among groups of motor units, allowing periods of rest. The asynchronous firing of motor units that makes this possible is dependent upon impulses arising from receptors in muscle (called muscle spindles) that are sensitive to stretch (a description of the muscle spindle appears in the chapter on the nervous system on page 284). Since all muscles, especially those subject to the force of gravity, are under some stretch, this discharge is continuous. Muscle tone is also modified by impulses from the brain.

CONTRACTION TIMES OF MUSCLES AND MOTOR UNITS. Muscles differ considerably in their contraction times. The durations of the contractions of the lateral rectus, gastrocnemius and soleus of the cat, for example, are, respectively, 7.5, 40 and 90 milliseconds. These contraction times correlate with normal functions: rapid eye movements (lateral rectus), moderately rapid movements in walking and running (gastrocnemius) and prolonged supportive action (soleus). In any given muscle the contraction times of individual motor units vary considerably. In the gastrocnemius muscle of cats it has been possible to correlate contraction times and other properties of motor units (determined in intact animals) with their histochemical profiles. Fibers of fast contracting units which also fatigue rapidly are of large diameter, have few capillaries and mitochondria, and contain an abundance of glycogen. Their apparent dependence upon anaerobic glycolysis could explain their rapid fatigue. Fibers of slowly contracting, fatigue-resistant units have small diameters, a rich capillary supply, many mitochondria and little glycogen. This profile suggests a high capacity for aerobic energy pathways. Another group of motor units described as fast contracting and fatigue resistant are of variable diameter and liberally supplied with capillaries. Their glycogen and mitochondrial content suggests utilization of both aerobic and anaerobic pathways. Small fibers are also known to contain large amounts of myoglobin, an oxygen-containing red pigment similar to hemoglobin. This feature and their vascularity account for the description of small fibers as "red," as distinguished from the large "white" fibers. Large, in contrast to small, fibers have a very extensive sarcoplasmic reticulum. This is consistent with their faster contraction.

Smooth Muscle

Smooth muscle is found in the digestive and respiratory tracts and other hollow structures, such as the urinary bladder and blood vessels. Other locations include the iris and ciliary muscles of the eye and the piloerector muscles of the skin. Since the contraction in smooth muscle is not induced at will, it is called *involuntary* muscle. Each smooth muscle cell contains a single large nucleus, and its fiber is more delicate than the fiber of striated muscle. The banding or cross-striation effect noted in skeletal muscle is absent in the smooth muscle fiber.

The smooth muscle of hollow structures such as the small intestine is grouped into an inner circular layer and an outer longitudinal layer. Simultaneous contraction of the two layers results in a reduction in both the circumference and length of the tubular structure.

Although the fiber arrangement and function of smooth muscle varies somewhat from organ to organ, two types are generally described. In the first, cells are found in rolled sheets, with the cell membranes of adjacent fibers in close contact. Relatively few nerve terminals are present. This pattern is found in most hollow organs of the body. This type of smooth muscle, known as *visceral*, or *unitary*, smooth muscle, exhibits the property of *automaticity*—it contracts in

the absence of nerve stimulation. The function of the nerve supply (by the autonomic nervous system) is to regulate the rate and degree of contraction. The electrical impulses, whether of external or internal origin, pass from one fiber to another via membrane junctions. Visceral smooth muscle produces a relatively slow contraction but permits greater extensibility. In the other arrangement, the smooth muscle pattern is less well organized but the fibers are separate and, by and large, independently innervated. This type, called *multiunit* smooth muscle, is found chiefly where finer gradations of contractions occur, such as in the iris and the ciliary muscles of the eye and the piloerector muscles of the skin. This type of smooth muscle is not characterized by automaticity.

Thick and thin filaments apparently are not so regularly arranged in smooth muscle as in striated muscle. Nevertheless, the contraction of smooth muscle is believed to occur in a similar way to contraction in skeletal muscle.

Cardiac Muscle

Cardiac muscle is involuntary muscle, possessing the striated appearance of voluntary muscle. The striations result from the same arrangement of thick and thin filaments as in skeletal muscle. The mechanism of contraction of the two types of muscle is essentially the same. Cardiac muscle fibers have a single, centrally placed nucleus and are branched at their ends (Fig. 122). Muscle fibers are functionally linked at their branched ends by junctional specializations, with interdigitations of cell membrane called *intercalated discs*. The resulting three-dimensional network, once thought to be a single, multinucleated mass of cytoplasm (a syncytium), is generally referred to as a *functional syncytium*. Two such functional syncytia are present in the heart. The walls and septum of the atria, the upper chambers of the heart, compose one and the walls and septum of the ventricles, the lower chambers of the heart, compose the other.

An important characteristic of cardiac muscle cells is the slow return of the membrane to a resting state following excitation by an electrical impulse. During the

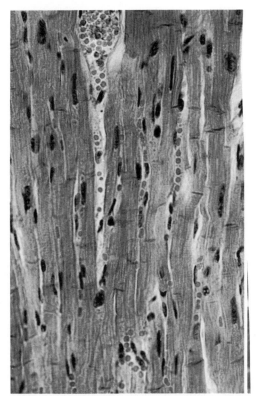

Figure 122. Photomicrograph of human cardiac muscle. Branching fibers with central nuclei are functionally linked by intercalated discs, which can be seen as dense transverse lines forming a steplike pattern. (From Leeson, C. R., and Leeson, T. S.: Histology. 3rd ed., Philadelphia, W. B. Saunders Co., 1976.)

recovery period it is insensitive, or *refractory,* to another impulse (this condition contrasts sharply with the very brief refractory period of skeletal muscle). The long refractory period of cardiac muscle prevents tetanization, which, of course, would interfere with its rhythmic pumping action.

The heart will continue to beat (although at a different rate) even when its nerve supply is cut. The intrinsic beat is generated by electrical impulses arising from the *"pacemaker,"* a concentration of specialized neuromuscular tissue in the right atrium. This neuromuscular tissue is also responsible for the rapid conduction of the impulse throughout the ventricles. (The properties of the neuromuscular tissue of the heart are discussed in more detail in the chapter on the circulation.) The functional syncytial arrangement of cardiac muscle and the presence of neuromuscular tissue make it possible for the upper and lower chambers to contract en masse. Regulation

of the heart rate is accomplished by the action of the autonomic nervous system on the pacemaker (see Ch. 10 for additional information).

DISORDERS OF MUSCLE

Disease of muscle originates in the nerve supply, the vascular supply or the connective tissue sheaths. The major symptoms of muscular disorders are paralysis, weakness, pain, atrophy, spasm, and cramps.

A condition in which a muscle shortens its length in the resting state is known as a *contracture.* Contractures occur when an individual remains in bed for prolonged periods and the muscles are not properly exercised. Eventually, the muscles readjust to the resting length of a flexed arm or leg. Contractures are treated by the painful and slow procedure of exercising and relengthening the muscle. Contractures can be prevented by keeping the body in correct alignment when resting and by periodically exercising the muscles. Muscular exercise can be either active (by the patient himself), or passive (by someone else).

Myalgia refers to muscular pain; *myositis* is the term used to describe inflammation of muscular tissue. *Fibrositis* is an inflammation of the connective tissue within a muscle, particularly near a joint. Usually a combination of fibrositis and myositis, *fibromyositis,* is present. Such a condition is commonly known as rheumatism, lumbago, or charley horse.

Two other entities affecting the muscle are *muscular dystrophy* and *myasthenia gravis.* Muscular dystrophy occurs most often in males and is a slowly progressive disorder ending in complete helplessness. In muscular dystrophy, the child begins to walk clumsily and tends to fall. Examination reveals pseudohypertrophy of some muscle groups and wasting of others. The term pseudohypertrophy is employed because the muscles feel large owing to the deposition of fat.

Myasthenia gravis is characterized by the weakness and easy fatigability of muscles. It is caused by an impairment of conduction of the normal impulse at the myoneural junction of striated muscle. This appears to be the result of a decrease in the number of receptors for acetylcholine on the muscle membrane at the junctions. This decrease is believed to be due to an autoimmune response (destruction of a natural substance by the body's immunological defense system). Neostigmine, a drug serving to interfere with cholinesterase (an enzyme that destroys acetylcholine) is given for therapy. Surgical removal of the thymus (if enlarged) has been beneficial, possibly because it reduces the autoimmune response.

In *atrophy* the muscle fibers degenerate because of disuse, as when limbs are placed in casts. Muscles can become a fraction of their normal size; within six months to two years the fibers are actually replaced by fibrous tissue (a form of connective tissue). Stimulation of nerves with an electric current keeps muscular tissue viable until full muscular activity returns. A reverse condition, *hypertrophy of use,* is a normal event and refers to the increase in size of exercised muscle due to an increase in the diameters of individual muscle fibers, with an increase in the number of their myofibrils.

Muscles act in an orderly fashion. The performance of even the slightest movement demands the cooperative effort of many muscles. This effort is called *coordination;* the cerebellum of the brain is devoted largely to the maintenance of this function. If a muscle becomes paralyzed, the sequence for coordination is disrupted and other muscles are unable to act in sequence; thus, coordination is destroyed and atrophy occurs.

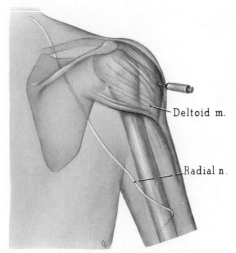

Figure 124. Intramuscular injection into the deltoid, two to three fingerbreadths below the acromion.

INTRAMUSCULAR INJECTION

The importance of a proper site for intramuscular injection is recognized by those who have experienced the pain resulting when a poor site is selected for injection. The ideal site is deep within the muscle, and away from major nerves and arteries. The best sites are the vastus lateralis, a thigh muscle, the deltoid, and the gluteal muscles.

The gluteal region has become the most common site for intramuscular injection. The area best suited is the upper and outer quadrant (Fig. 123). The student should

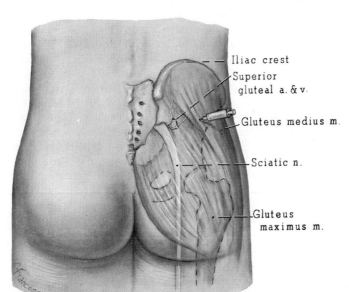

Figure 123. Intramuscular injection in the gluteal region should be in the upper outer quadrant.

remember that the gluteal region extends to the anterior superior iliac spine. This should be used as a landmark when defining the quadrants. When the upper outer quadrant is used, there is little danger of the needle piercing the sciatic nerve or the superior gluteal artery.

The deltoid muscle is thick and extends from the clavicle, acromion, and spine of the scapula to the deltoid tuberosity of the humerus (Fig. 124). Owing to the nonyielding tendinous septa in the upper and lower regions of this muscle, only a small area in the center provides a satisfactory site for injection. This site is found 2 cm. below the acromion. The gluteal region is preferred, since it has a greater muscle mass, permitting injection of larger volumes of fluid.

INTRODUCTION TO THE ANATOMY OF SKELETAL MUSCLES
(Figs. 125 and 127–222)

Tables 10 to 29 on pages 202 to 215 include most of the important muscles of the body. In addition to listing the muscles, the tables describe the origin and insertion of each muscle and its principal action and innervation. The more fixed attachment of a muscle that serves as a basis of action is called the **origin**. The movable attachment where the effects of movement are produced is the **insertion**. In some cases the action of a muscle can be altered by reversal of the origin and insertion. For example, the trapezius can either raise the shoulders or extend the head, depending upon whether

Text continued on page 167

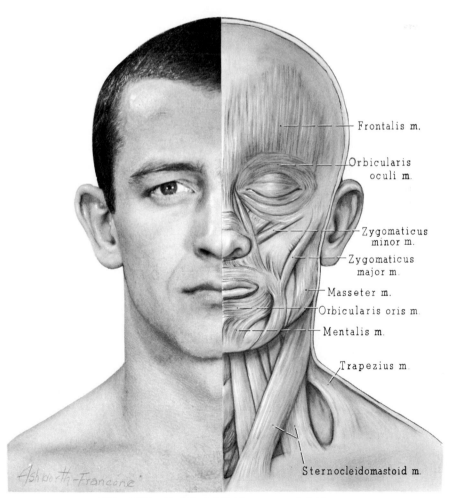

Frontalis m.

Orbicularis oculi m.

Zygomaticus minor m.

Zygomaticus major m.

Masseter m.

Orbicularis oris m.

Mentalis m.

Trapezius m.

Sternocleidomastoid m.

Figure 125.   Muscles of the face, superficial layer.

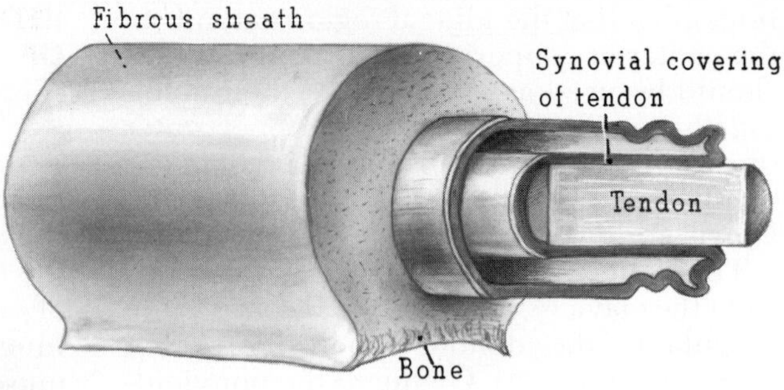

Fibrous sheath

Synovial covering
of tendon

Tendon

Bone

Figure 126. Synovial tendon sheath.
(From Crouch, J. E.: *Functional Human
Anatomy,* 2nd ed., Philadelphia, Lea and
Febiger, 1972.)

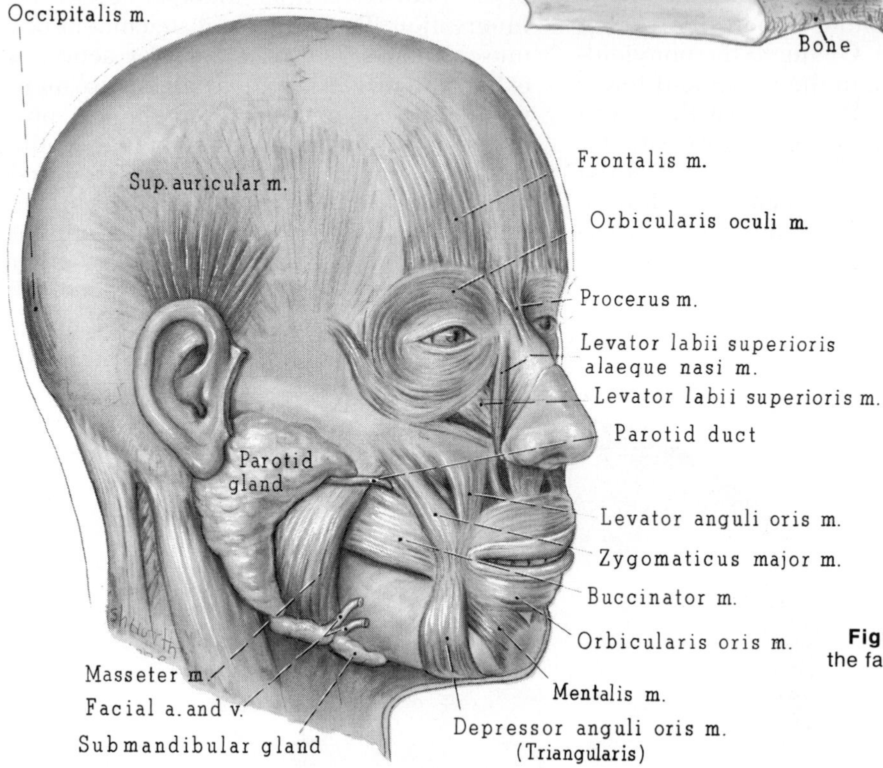

Occipitalis m.

Sup. auricular m.

Frontalis m.

Orbicularis oculi m.

Procerus m.

Levator labii superioris
alaeque nasi m.

Levator labii superioris m.

Parotid duct

Parotid
gland

Levator anguli oris m.

Zygomaticus major m.

Buccinator m.

Orbicularis oris m.

Masseter m.

Facial a. and v.

Submandibular gland

Mentalis m.

Depressor anguli oris m.
(Triangularis)

Figure 127. Muscles of
the face, deep layer.

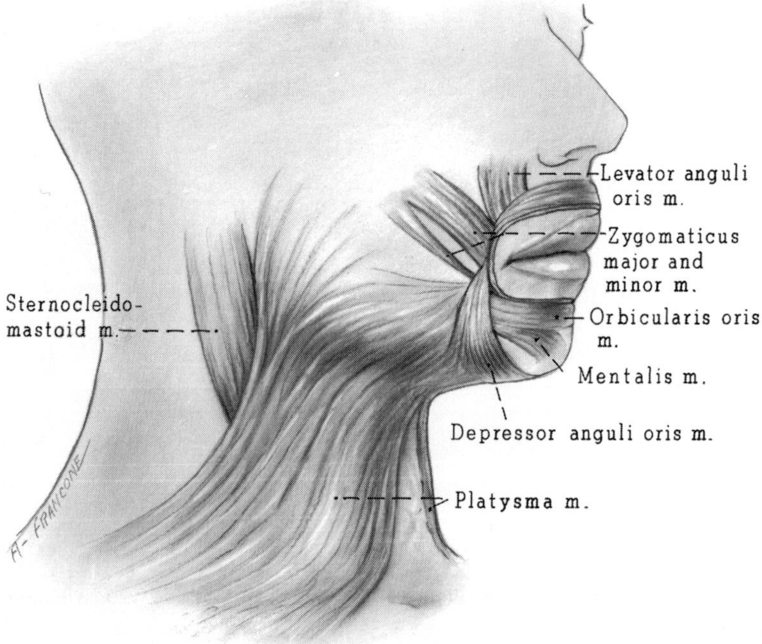

Figure 128. Superficial muscles of the neck and muscles
around the mouth.

Sternocleido-
mastoid m.

Levator anguli
oris m.

Zygomaticus
major and
minor m.

Orbicularis oris
m.

Mentalis m.

Depressor anguli oris m.

Platysma m.

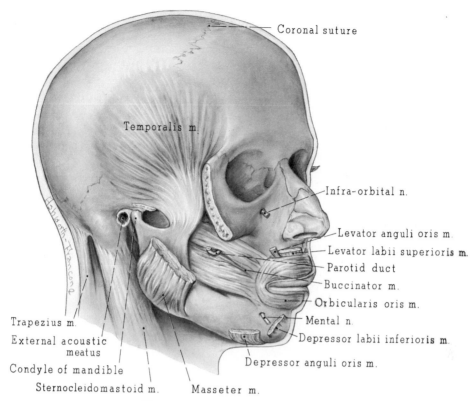

Figure 129. Muscles of mastication.

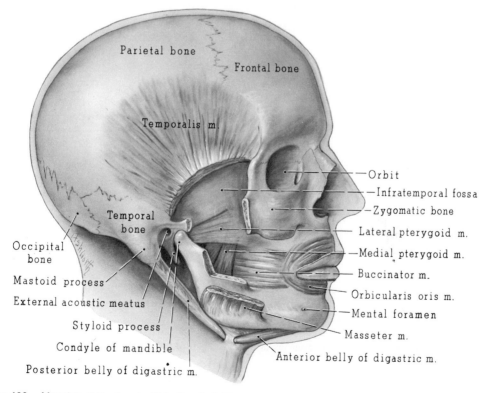

Figure 130. Muscles of the head within the skull. The temporalis, masseter, zygoma, and part of the mandible have been removed.

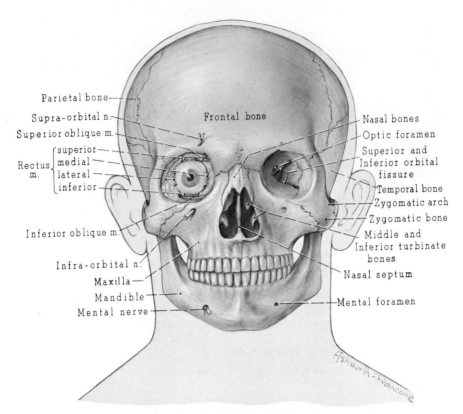

Parietal bone
Supra-orbital n.
Superior oblique m.
Rectus m. { superior
           medial
           lateral
           inferior
Frontal bone
Nasal bones
Optic foramen
Superior and Inferior orbital fissure
Temporal bone
Zygomatic arch
Zygomatic bone
Middle and Inferior turbinate bones
Inferior oblique m.
Infra-orbital n.
Maxilla
Mandible
Mental nerve
Nasal septum
Mental foramen

Figure 131.   Anterior view of the skull showing relation of eye muscles to the orbit.

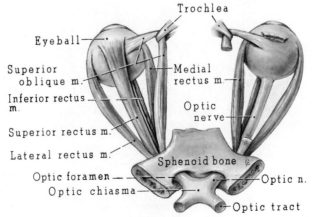

Trochlea
Eyeball
Superior oblique m.
Inferior rectus m.
Superior rectus m.
Lateral rectus m.
Optic foramen
Optic chiasma
Medial rectus m.
Optic nerve
Sphenoid bone
Optic n.
Optic tract

Figure 132.   Extrinsic muscles of the eye. (Inferior oblique m. not shown. See Fig. 74.)

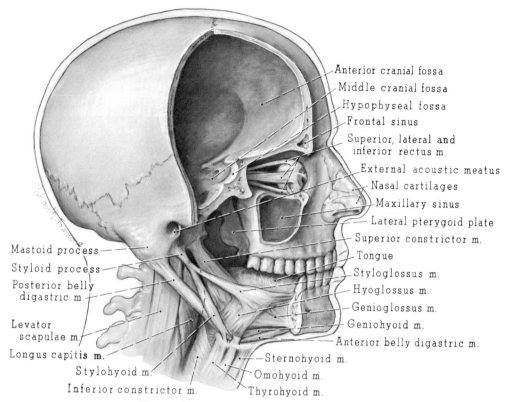

Anterior cranial fossa
Middle cranial fossa
Hypophyseal fossa
Frontal sinus
Superior, lateral and inferior rectus m.
External acoustic meatus
Nasal cartilages
Maxillary sinus
Lateral pterygoid plate
Superior constrictor m.
Tongue
Styloglossus m.
Hyoglossus m.
Genioglossus m.
Geniohyoid m.
Anterior belly digastric m.
Sternohyoid m.
Omohyoid m.
Thyrohyoid m.

Mastoid process
Styloid process
Posterior belly digastric m.
Levator scapulae m.
Longus capitis m.
Stylohyoid m.
Inferior constrictor m.

Figure 133. Muscles of the tongue and throat.

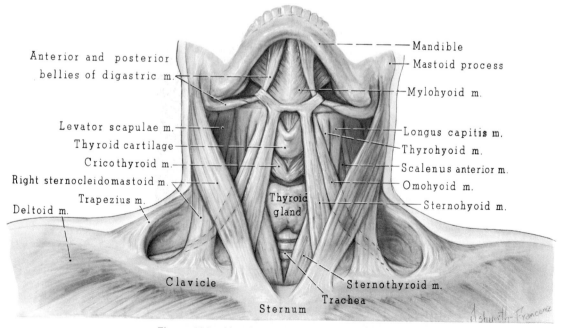

Mandible
Mastoid process
Mylohyoid m.
Longus capitis m.
Thyrohyoid m.
Scalenus anterior m.
Omohyoid m.
Sternohyoid m.
Sternothyroid m.

Anterior and posterior bellies of digastric m.
Levator scapulae m.
Thyroid cartilage
Cricothyroid m.
Right sternocleidomastoid m.
Trapezius m.
Deltoid m.
Thyroid gland
Clavicle
Sternum
Trachea

Figure 134. Muscles of the neck, superficial layer.

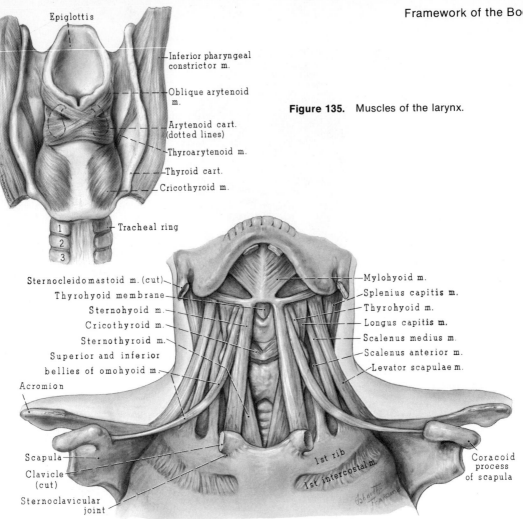

Epiglottis

Inferior pharyngeal constrictor m.

Oblique arytenoid m.

Arytenoid cart. (dotted lines)

Thyroarytenoid m.

Thyroid cart.

Cricothyroid m.

Tracheal ring

Figure 135. Muscles of the larynx.

Sternocleidomastoid m. (cut)
Thyrohyoid membrane
Sternohyoid m.
Cricothyroid m.
Sternothyroid m.
Superior and inferior bellies of omohyoid m.
Acromion

Mylohyoid m.
Splenius capitis m.
Thyrohyoid m.
Longus capitis m.
Scalenus medius m.
Scalenus anterior m.
Levator scapulae m.

Scapula
Clavicle (cut)
Sternoclavicular joint

1st rib
1st intercostal m.

Coracoid process of scapula

Figure 136. Second layer of muscles of the neck.

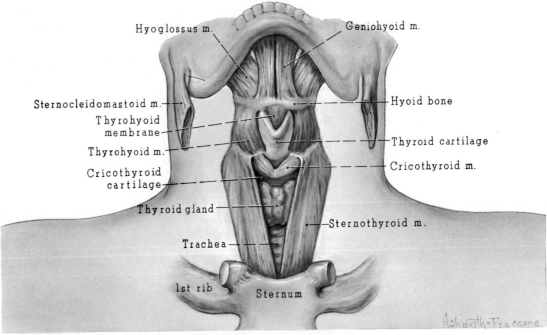

Hyoglossus m.
Geniohyoid m.

Sternocleidomastoid m.
Thyrohyoid membrane
Thyrohyoid m.
Cricothyroid cartilage
Thyroid gland
Trachea

Hyoid bone
Thyroid cartilage
Cricothyroid m.
Sternothyroid m.

1st rib
Sternum

Figure 137. Deep muscles of the neck.

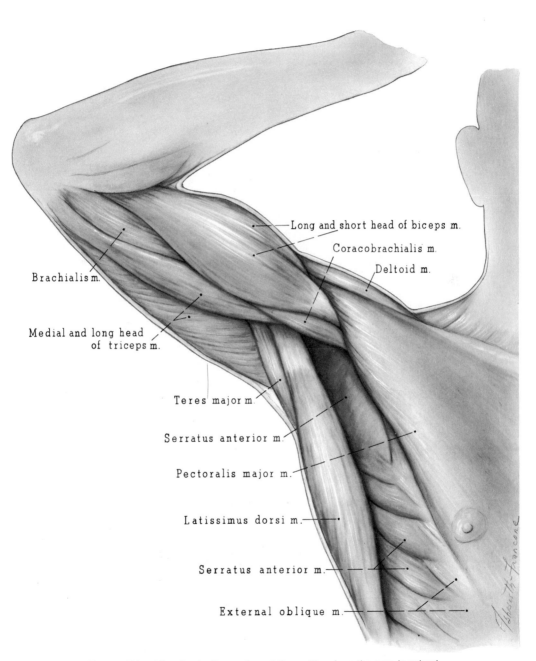

Long and short head of biceps m.

Coracobrachialis m.

Deltoid m.

Brachialis m.

Medial and long head
of triceps m.

Teres major m.

Serratus anterior m.

Pectoralis major m.

Latissimus dorsi m.

Serratus anterior m.

External oblique m.

Figure 138.   Muscles in the region of the axilla when the arm is raised.

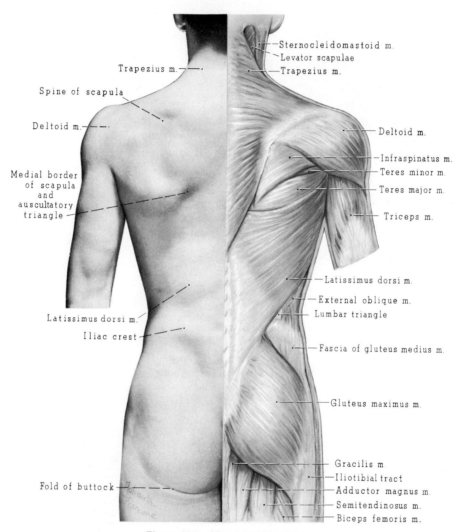

Trapezius m.

Spine of scapula

Deltoid m.

Medial border
of scapula
and
auscultatory
triangle

Latissimus dorsi m.

Iliac crest

Fold of buttock

Sternocleidomastoid m.
Levator scapulae
Trapezius m.

Deltoid m.

Infraspinatus m.
Teres minor m.
Teres major m.

Triceps m.

Latissimus dorsi m.

External oblique m.
Lumbar triangle

Fascia of gluteus medius m.

Gluteus maximus m.

Gracilis m
Iliotibial tract
Adductor magnus m.
Semitendinosus m.
Biceps femoris m.

Figure 139. Muscles of the back.

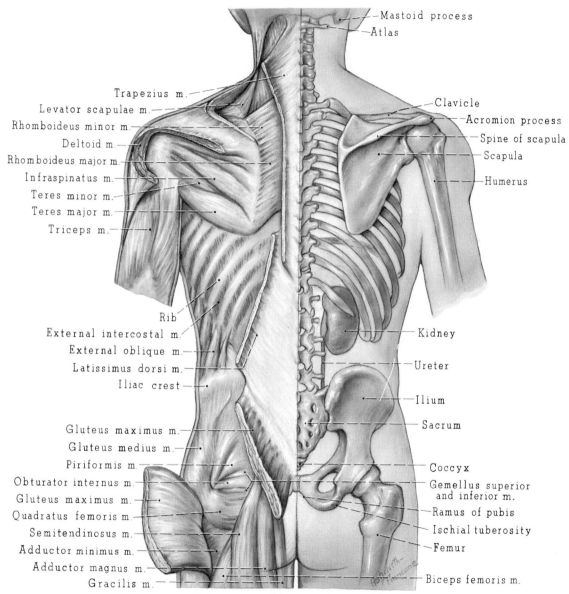

Figure 140. Deep muscles of the back.

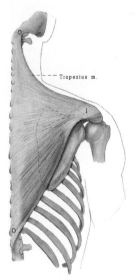

Figure 141

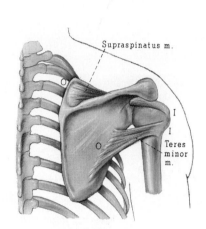

Figure 142A

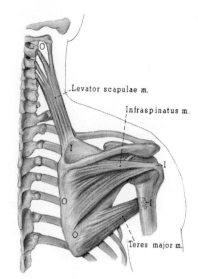

Figure 142B

KEY
O = origin
I = insertion

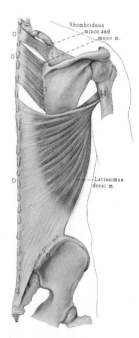

Figure 143

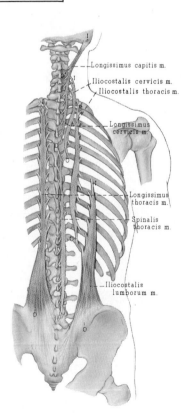

Figure 144

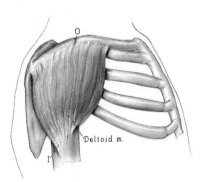

Figure 145

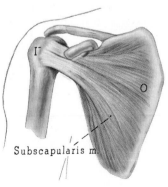

Figure 146

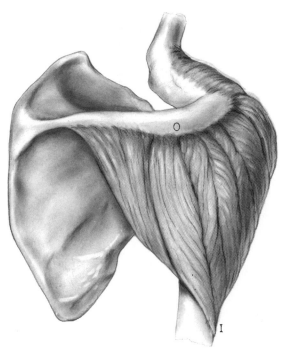

Figure 147. Posterior view of right deltoid.

the scapula and clavicle serve as part of the insertion or origin. The latissimus dorsi extends, adducts and rotates the arm (backstroke of the crawl in swimming) when the humerus is the insertion, and raises the trunk and pelvis (pulling the body up in rope climbing) when the humerus is the origin. The action of a muscle may also vary depending upon whether all or a part of the muscle contracts. Taking the trapezius again as an example, the extension of the head requires both sides of the muscle to contract. If it contracts on one side only, it will turn the head to one side. Another example is the deltoid muscle, which abducts, flexes or extends the arm, depending upon whether the whole muscle, the anterior fibers or the posterior fibers contract.

Most voluntary muscles are not inserted directly into bone but rather through the medium of a strong, tough, nonelastic fibrous cord called a *tendon* (Fig. 126). Tendons vary in length from a fraction of an inch to more than one foot. Muscles may have one of these connective tissue cords, consisting largely of closely packed bundles of white collagenous fibers, attached to each of the extremities. If the tendon is wide, thin and flat it is called an *aponeurosis*. Tendons and aponeuroses are continu-

ous with the epimysium of muscle and the periosteum of bone, an arrangement which firmly harnesses muscle to bone.

It should be remembered that muscles are named according to *action* (e.g., adductor and extensor); according to *shape* (quadratus); according to *origin* and *insertion* (sternocleidomastoid); according to number of *divisions* (triceps, with three heads, each adjacent to a separate origin, and digastric, with two bodies); according to *location* (tibialis and radialis); and according to *direction of fibers* (transversus).

Muscles are found in many sizes and shapes. The types include fusiform (spindle-shaped), quadrilateral (rhomboid), triangular and straplike. Muscles also vary in the arrangement of their fiber bundles. In most muscles the bundles are parallel and pass in a line of pull from the origin to the insertion. In others they obliquely join a central tendon in a feather-like arrangement (from both sides in the *bipennate* form, from one side in the *unipennate* form). In *multipennate* muscles the bundles converge on many tendons in a complex fashion. Pennate muscles contract with greater force but for shorter distances than muscles with a parallel arrangement of fibers. In another less common *radial* arrangement, bundles of fibers converge on a common tendon from a wide area.

Muscles which bend a limb at a joint are called *flexors*. Muscles which straighten a limb at a joint are called *extensors*. If the limb is moved away from the midline of the body, an *abductor* is at work; if the limb is brought toward the midline, *adductors* are responsible. There are also muscles *rotating* the involved limb. In movements of the ankle, muscles of *dorsiflexion* turn the foot upward, while muscles of *plantar flexion* bring the foot toward the ground. In movements of the hand, turning the forearm so that the palm of the hand faces upward is called *supination*, and turning it to bring the palm facing the ground is *pronation*. *Levators* raise a part of the body; *depressors* lower it.

In performing a given movement, such as bending the arm at the elbow, the muscles executing the actual movement are known as the *prime movers*, or *agonists*. Muscles straightening the elbow are *extensors*, also called *antagonists*. The agonist muscle, or flexor, must relax for the extensor muscle or

Text continued on page 215

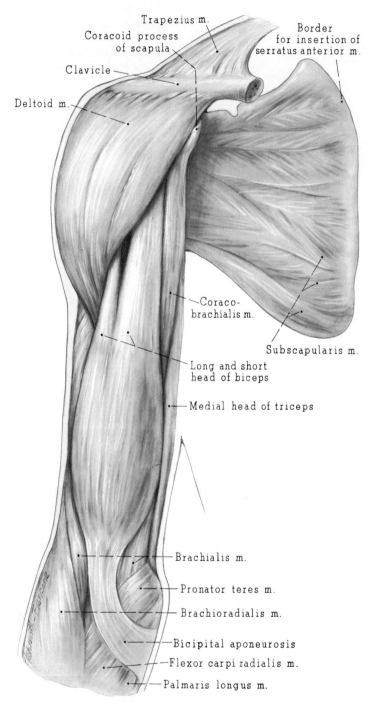

Figure 148.   Muscles of the shoulder and the upper right arm, anterior view.

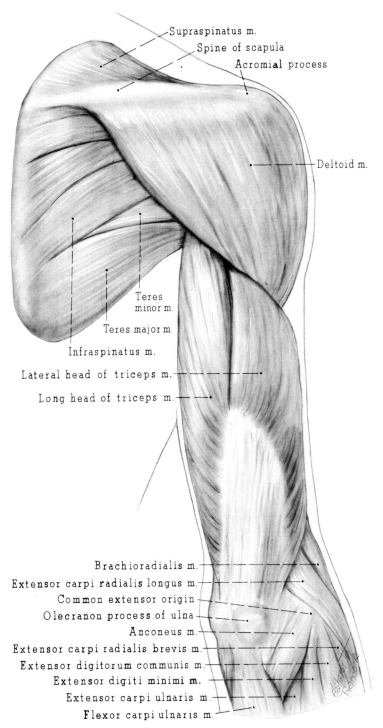

Supraspinatus m.

Spine of scapula

Acromial process

Deltoid m.

Teres
minor m.

Teres major m.

Infraspinatus m.

Lateral head of triceps m.

Long head of triceps m.

Brachioradialis m.

Extensor carpi radialis longus m.

Common extensor origin

Olecranon process of ulna

Anconeus m.

Extensor carpi radialis brevis m.

Extensor digitorum communis m.

Extensor digiti minimi m.

Extensor carpi ulnaris m.

Flexor carpi ulnaris m.

Figure 149. Muscles of the shoulder and upper arm, posterior view.

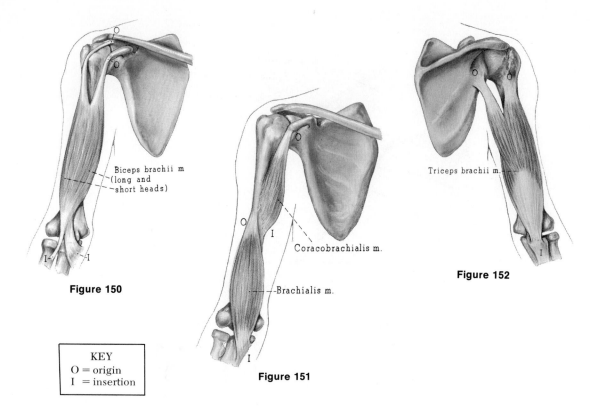

Biceps brachii m
(long and
short heads)

Figure 150

Coracobrachialis m.

Brachialis m.

Figure 151

Triceps brachii m.

Figure 152

KEY
O = origin
I = insertion

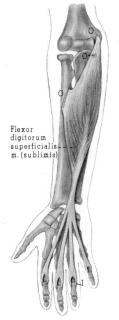

Flexor
digitorum
superficialis
m. (sublimis)

Figure 153

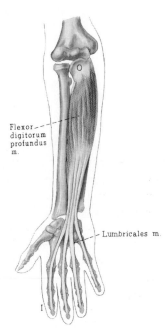

Flexor
digitorum
profundus
m.

Lumbricales m.

Figure 154

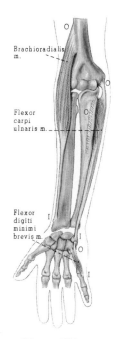

Brachioradialis
m.

Flexor
carpi
ulnaris m.

Flexor
digiti
minimi
brevis m.

Figure 155

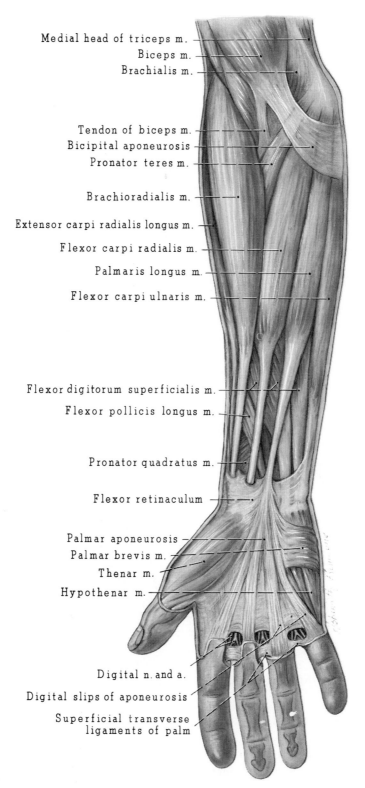

Medial head of triceps m.
Biceps m.
Brachialis m.

Tendon of biceps m.
Bicipital aponeurosis
Pronator teres m.

Brachioradialis m.

Extensor carpi radialis longus m.

Flexor carpi radialis m.

Palmaris longus m.

Flexor carpi ulnaris m.

Flexor digitorum superficialis m.

Flexor pollicis longus m.

Pronator quadratus m.

Flexor retinaculum

Palmar aponeurosis
Palmar brevis m.
Thenar m.
Hypothenar m.

Digital n. and a.

Digital slips of aponeurosis

Superficial transverse
ligaments of palm

Figure 156. Muscles of the palmar aspect of the right hand and forearm.

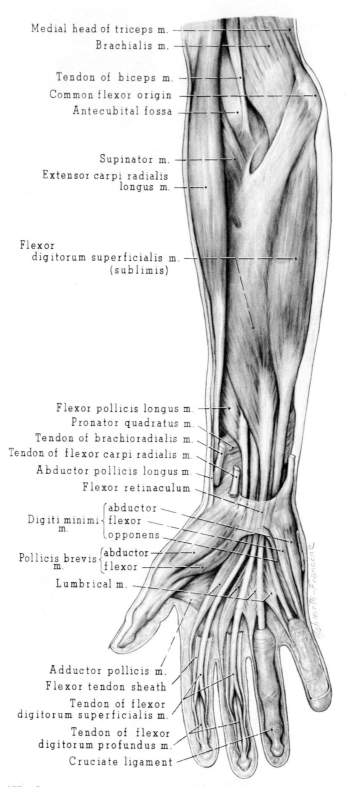

Medial head of triceps m.
Brachialis m.

Tendon of biceps m.
Common flexor origin
Antecubital fossa

Supinator m.
Extensor carpi radialis
longus m.

Flexor
digitorum superficialis m.
(sublimis)

Flexor pollicis longus m.
Pronator quadratus m.
Tendon of brachioradialis m.
Tendon of flexor carpi radialis m.
Abductor pollicis longus m.
Flexor retinaculum

Digiti minimi { abductor
              { flexor
        m.   { opponens

Pollicis brevis { abductor
          m.   { flexor

Lumbrical m.

Adductor pollicis m.
Flexor tendon sheath
Tendon of flexor
digitorum superficialis m.
Tendon of flexor
digitorum profundus m.
Cruciate ligament

Figure 157. Second layer of muscles of the right hand and forearm, palmar aspect.

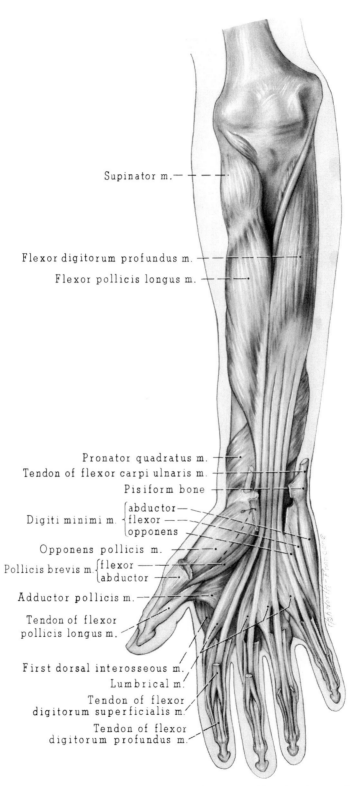

Supinator m.

Flexor digitorum profundus m.
Flexor pollicis longus m.

Pronator quadratus m.
Tendon of flexor carpi ulnaris m.
Pisiform bone

Digiti minimi m. { abductor
flexor
opponens

Opponens pollicis m.
Pollicis brevis m. { flexor
abductor

Adductor pollicis m.

Tendon of flexor
pollicis longus m.

First dorsal interosseous m.
Lumbrical m.
Tendon of flexor
digitorum superficialis m.
Tendon of flexor
digitorum profundus m.

Figure 158. Deep muscles of the right forearm and hand, palmar surface.

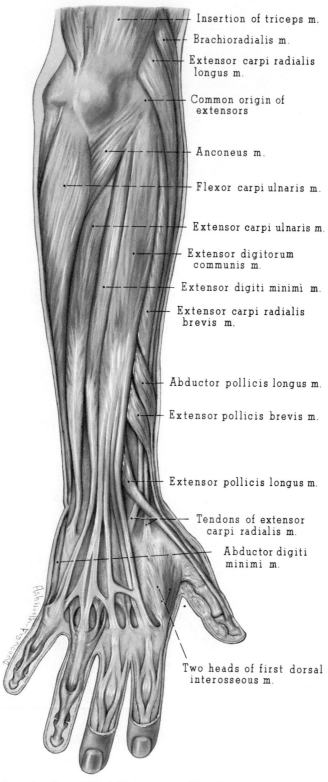

Insertion of triceps m.

Brachioradialis m.

Extensor carpi radialis
longus m.

Common origin of
extensors

Anconeus m.

Flexor carpi ulnaris m.

Extensor carpi ulnaris m.

Extensor digitorum
communis m.

Extensor digiti minimi m.

Extensor carpi radialis
brevis m.

Abductor pollicis longus m.

Extensor pollicis brevis m.

Extensor pollicis longus m.

Tendons of extensor
carpi radialis m.

Abductor digiti
minimi m.

Two heads of first dorsal
interosseous m.

Figure 159. Posterior view of the right forearm and hand, showing the superficial muscles.

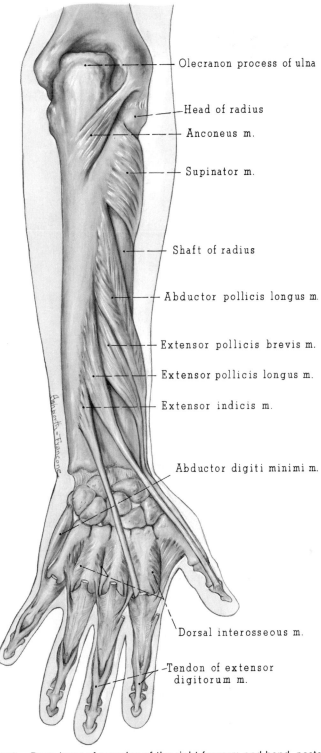

Olecranon process of ulna

Head of radius

Anconeus m.

Supinator m.

Shaft of radius

Abductor pollicis longus m.

Extensor pollicis brevis m.

Extensor pollicis longus m.

Extensor indicis m.

Abductor digiti minimi m.

Dorsal interosseous m.

Tendon of extensor
digitorum m.

Figure 160.   Deep layer of muscles of the right forearm and hand, posterior view.

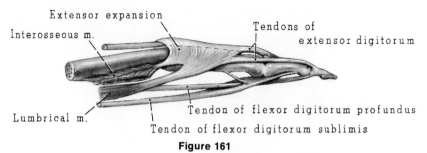

Extensor expansion

Interosseous m.

Tendons of
extensor digitorum

Lumbrical m.

Tendon of flexor digitorum profundus

Tendon of flexor digitorum sublimis

Figure 161

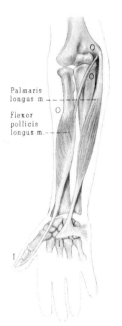

Palmaris
longus m.

Flexor
pollicis
longus m.

O

I

Figure 162

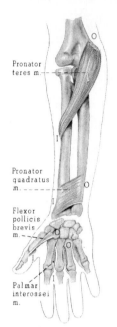

Pronator
teres m.

Pronator
quadratus
m.

Flexor
pollicis
brevis
m.

Palmar
interossei
m.

O

I

O

O

I

I

Figure 163

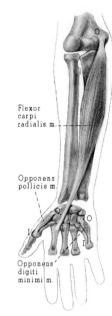

Flexor
carpi
radialis m.

Opponens
pollicis m.

Opponens
digiti
minimi m.

O

O

I

Figure 164

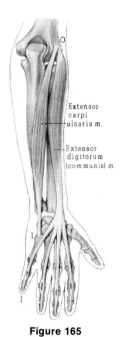

Extensor
carpi
ulnaris m.

Extensor
digitorum
(communis) m.

O

I

I

Figure 165

KEY
O = origin
I = insertion

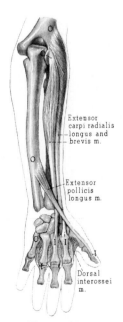

Extensor
carpi radialis
longus and
brevis m.

Extensor
pollicis
longus m.

Dorsal
interossei
m.

O

O

O

I

I

Figure 166

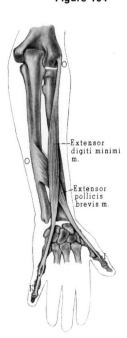

Extensor
digiti minimi
m.

Extensor
pollicis
brevis m.

O

O

I

Figure 167

KEY
O = origin
I = insertion

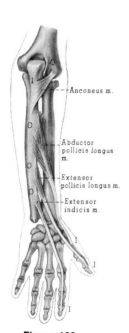

O
I
Anconeus m.
O
Abductor
pollicis longus
m.
O
Extensor
pollicis longus m.
O
Extensor
indicis m.
I
I
I

Figure 168

O
I
Supinator m.

Figure 169

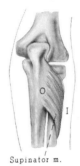

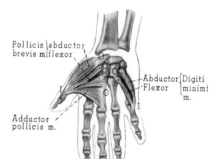

Pollicis
brevis m.
abductor
flexor
O
O
O
O
O
I
I
Abductor
Flexor
Digiti
minimi
m.
Adductor
pollicis m.

Figure 170

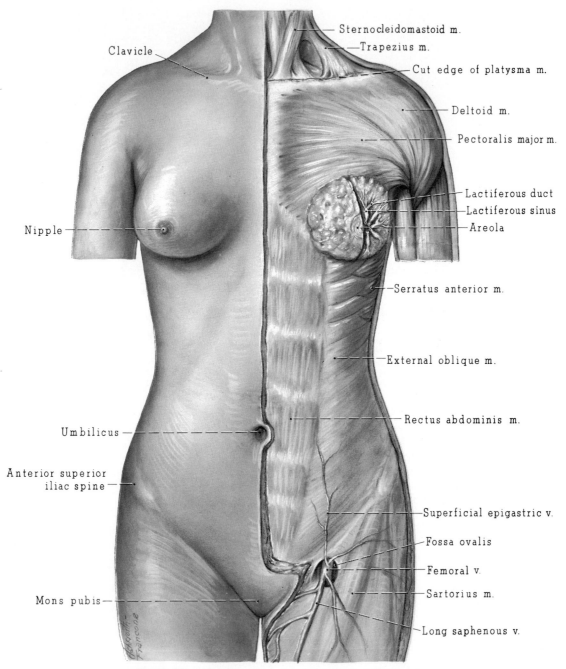

Clavicle

Sternocleidomastoid m.

Trapezius m.

Cut edge of platysma m.

Deltoid m.

Pectoralis major m.

Lactiferous duct

Lactiferous sinus

Nipple

Areola

Serratus anterior m.

External oblique m.

Rectus abdominis m.

Umbilicus

Superficial epigastric v.

Anterior superior
iliac spine

Fossa ovalis

Femoral v.

Sartorius m.

Mons pubis

Long saphenous v.

Figure 171.   Muscles of the anterior surface of the female.

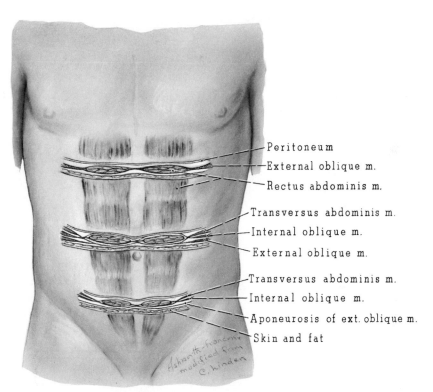

Peritoneum
External oblique m.
Rectus abdominis m.

Transversus abdominis m.
Internal oblique m.
External oblique m.

Transversus abdominis m.
Internal oblique m.
Aponeurosis of ext. oblique m.
Skin and fat

Figure 172.   Diagram of rectus muscles and sheaths of fascia enveloping them. The muscles have been cut to show the layers of fascia and peritoneum.

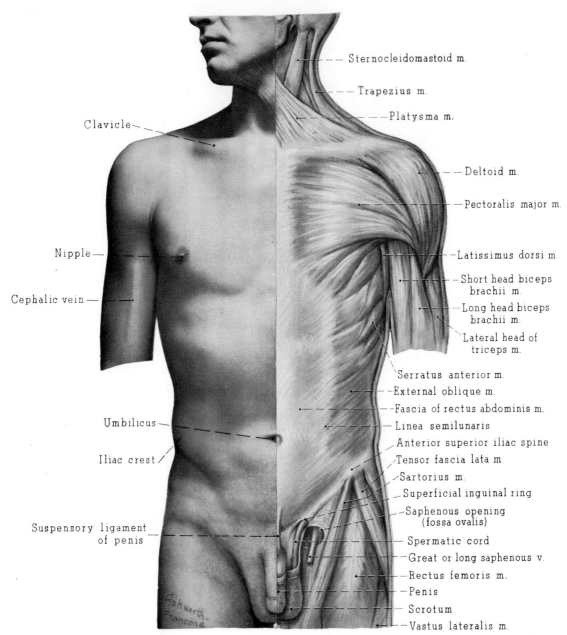

Sternocleidomastoid m.

Trapezius m.

Platysma m.

Clavicle

Deltoid m.

Pectoralis major m.

Nipple

Latissimus dorsi m.

Short head biceps
brachii m.

Cephalic vein

Long head biceps
brachii m.

Lateral head of
triceps m.

Serratus anterior m.

External oblique m.

Fascia of rectus abdominis m.

Umbilicus

Linea semilunaris

Anterior superior iliac spine

Iliac crest

Tensor fascia lata m.

Sartorius m.

Superficial inguinal ring

Saphenous opening
(fossa ovalis)

Suspensory ligament
of penis

Spermatic cord

Great or long saphenous v.

Rectus femoris m.

Penis

Scrotum

Vastus lateralis m.

Figure 173.   Muscles of the anterior surface of the male.

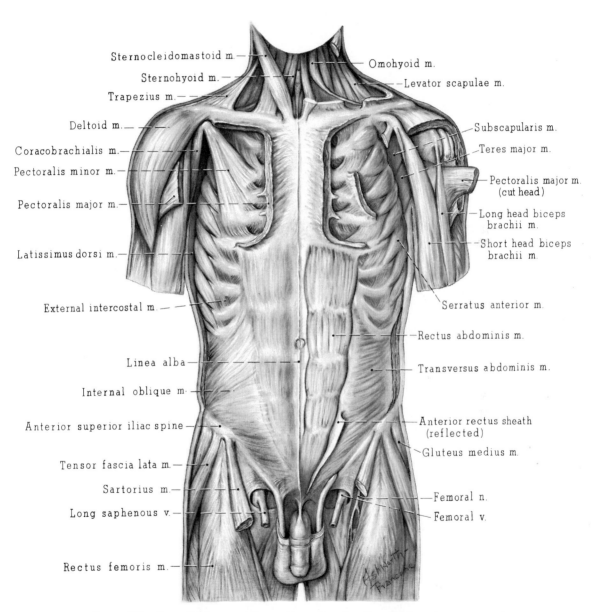

Sternocleidomastoid m.

Sternohyoid m.

Trapezius m.

Deltoid m.

Coracobrachialis m.

Pectoralis minor m.

Pectoralis major m.

Latissimus dorsi m.

External intercostal m.

Linea alba

Internal oblique m.

Anterior superior iliac spine

Tensor fascia lata m.

Sartorius m.

Long saphenous v.

Rectus femoris m.

Omohyoid m.

Levator scapulae m.

Subscapularis m.

Teres major m.

Pectoralis major m.
(cut head)

Long head biceps
brachii m.

Short head biceps
brachii m.

Serratus anterior m.

Rectus abdominis m.

Transversus abdominis m.

Anterior rectus sheath
(reflected)

Gluteus medius m.

Femoral n.

Femoral v.

Figure 174. Superficial musculature; skin and pectoralis major have been removed.

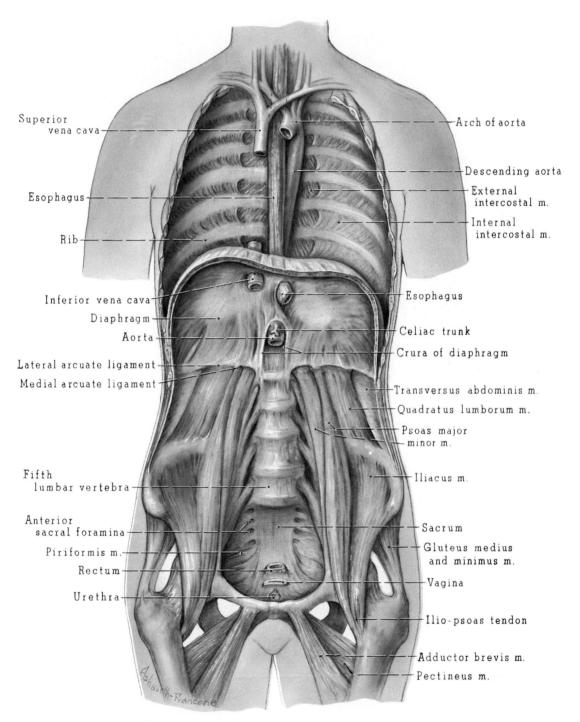

Superior
vena cava

Esophagus

Rib

Inferior vena cava

Diaphragm

Aorta

Lateral arcuate ligament

Medial arcuate ligament

Fifth
lumbar vertebra

Anterior
sacral foramina

Piriformis m.

Rectum

Urethra

Arch of aorta

Descending aorta

External
intercostal m.

Internal
intercostal m.

Esophagus

Celiac trunk

Crura of diaphragm

Transversus abdominis m.

Quadratus lumborum m.

Psoas major
minor m.

Iliacus m.

Sacrum

Gluteus medius
and minimus m.

Vagina

Ilio-psoas tendon

Adductor brevis m.

Pectineus m.

Figure 175.   Deep muscles of the thoracic, abdominal, and pelvic cavities.

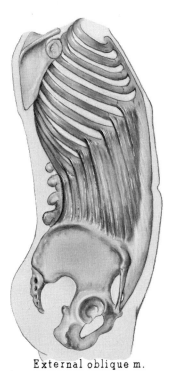

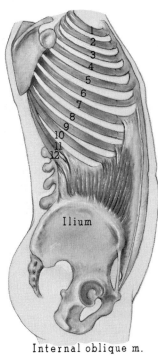

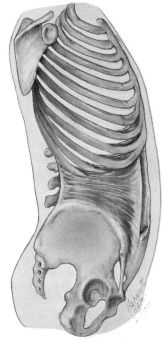

External oblique m.   Internal oblique m.   Transversus abdominis m.

Figure 176. Three layers of abdominal musculature.

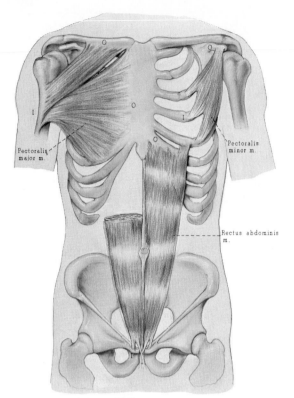

Pectoralis
major m.

Pectoralis
minor m.

Rectus abdominis
m.

Figure 177

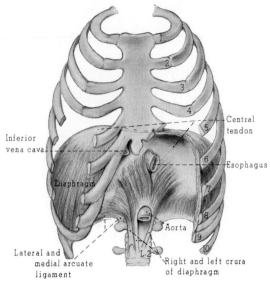

Inferior
vena cava

Diaphragm

Central
tendon

Esophagus

Aorta

Lateral and
medial arcuate
ligament

L-2

Right and left crura
of diaphragm

Figure 178

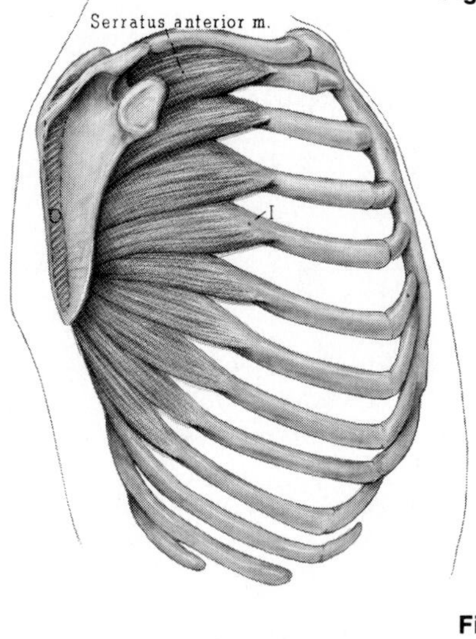

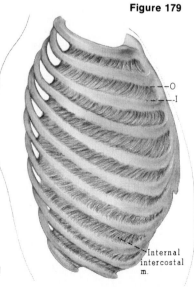

Serratus anterior m.

Figure 179

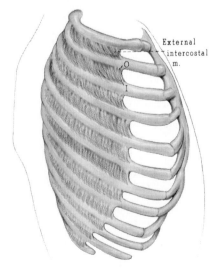

External
intercostal
m.

O

I

Figure 180

KEY
O = origin
I = insertion

O

I

Internal
intercostal
m.

Figure 181

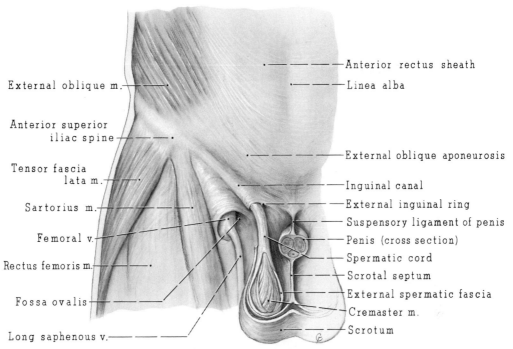

External oblique m.

Anterior superior
iliac spine

Tensor fascia
lata m.

Sartorius m.

Femoral v.

Rectus femoris m.

Fossa ovalis

Long saphenous v.

Anterior rectus sheath

Linea alba

External oblique aponeurosis

Inguinal canal

External inguinal ring

Suspensory ligament of penis

Penis (cross section)

Spermatic cord

Scrotal septum

External spermatic fascia

Cremaster m.

Scrotum

Figure 182.   Muscles of the inguinal region, superficial layer.

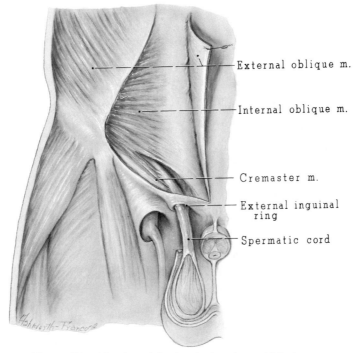

External oblique m.

Internal oblique m.

Cremaster m.

External inguinal
ring

Spermatic cord

Figure 183.   Muscles of the inguinal region, middle layer.

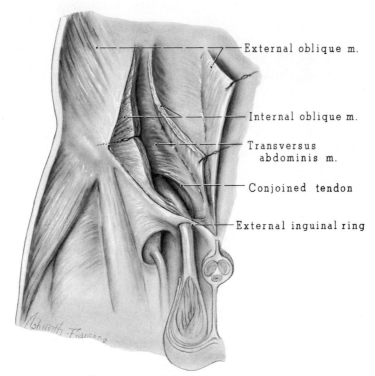

Figure 184. Muscles of the inguinal region, deep layer.

External oblique m.

Internal oblique m.

Transversus
abdominis m.

Conjoined tendon

External inguinal ring

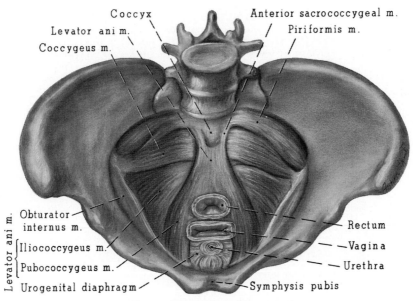

Coccyx   Anterior sacrococcygeal m.
Levator ani m.   Piriformis m.
Coccygeus m.

Obturator
internus m.   Rectum

Iliococcygeus m.   Vagina

Pubococcygeus m.   Urethra

Urogenital diaphragm   Symphysis pubis

Levator ani m.

Figure 185. Muscles of the pelvic floor.

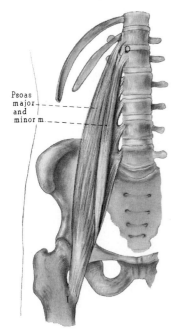

Psoas major and minor m.

Figure 186

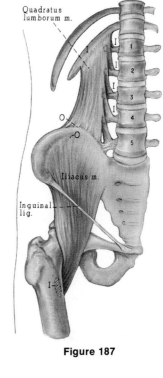

Quadratus lumborum m.

Iliacus m.

Inguinal lig.

Figure 187

KEY
O = origin
I = insertion

Gluteus maximus m.

Figure 188

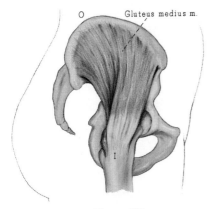

O Gluteus medius m.

Figure 189

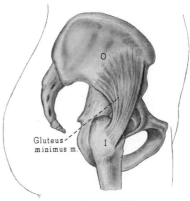

O

Gluteus minimus m.

Figure 190

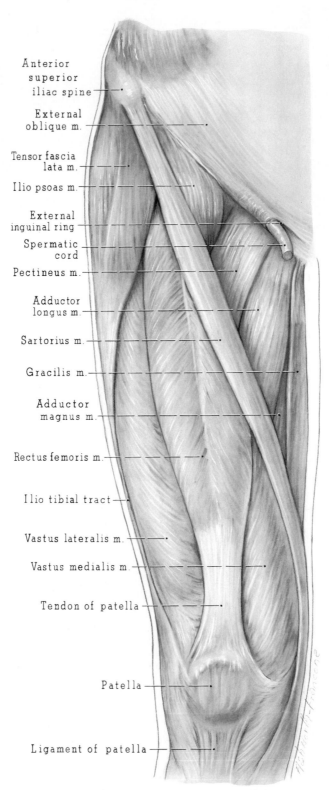

Anterior
superior
iliac spine

External
oblique m.

Tensor fascia
lata m.

Ilio psoas m.

External
inguinal ring

Spermatic
cord

Pectineus m.

Adductor
longus m.

Sartorius m.

Gracilis m.

Adductor
magnus m.

Rectus femoris m.

Ilio tibial tract

Vastus lateralis m.

Vastus medialis m.

Tendon of patella

Patella

Ligament of patella

Figure 191.   Superficial muscles of the right upper leg, anterior surface.

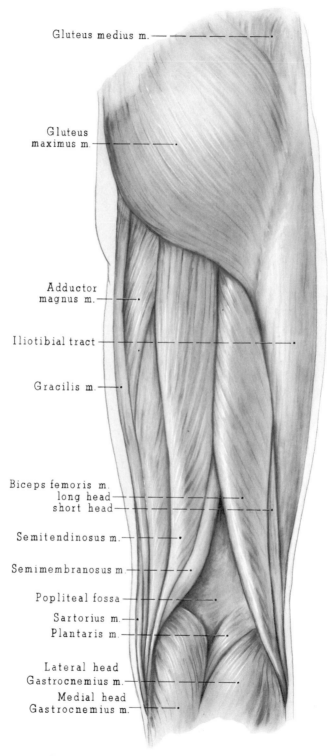

Gluteus medius m.

Gluteus
maximus m.

Adductor
magnus m.

Iliotibial tract

Gracilis m.

Biceps femoris m.
long head
short head

Semitendinosus m.

Semimembranosus m

Popliteal fossa

Sartorius m.

Plantaris m.

Lateral head
Gastrocnemius m.

Medial head
Gastrocnemius m.

Figure 192. Superficial muscles of the right upper leg, posterior surface.

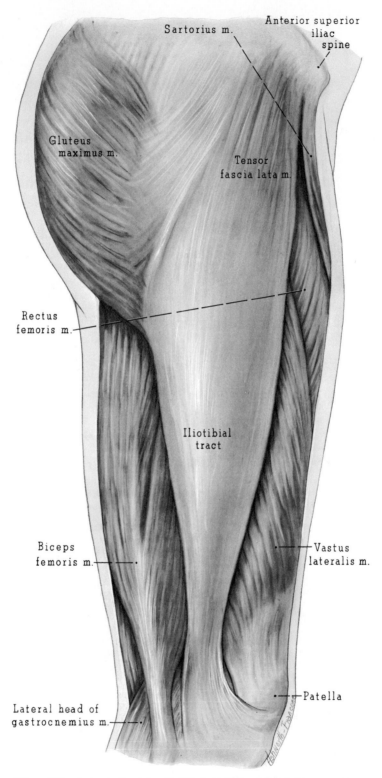

Figure 193. Lateral view of superficial muscles of the right upper leg.

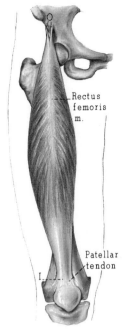

Rectus
femoris
m.

Patellar
tendon

I

O

Figure 194

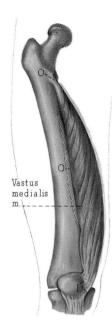

O

O

Vastus
medialis
m.

Figure 195

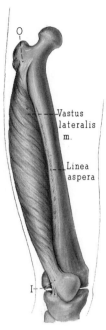

O

Vastus
lateralis
m.

Linea
aspera

I

Figure 196

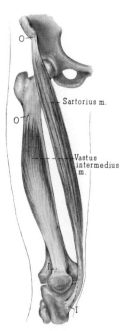

O

O

Sartorius m.

Vastus
intermedius
m.

I

I

Figure 197

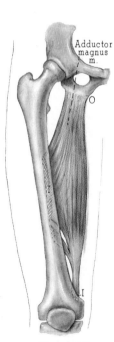

Adductor
magnus
m.

O

I

I

Figure 198

KEY
O = origin
I = insertion

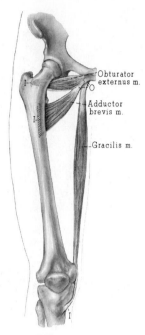

KEY
O = origin
I = insertion

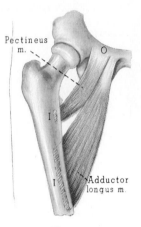

- Obturator externus m.
- Adductor brevis m.
- Gracilis m.

Figure 199

Pectineus m.

- Adductor longus m.

Figure 200

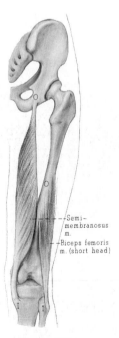

- Semimembranosus m.
- Biceps femoris m. (short head)

Figure 201

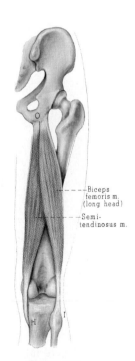

- Biceps femoris m. (long head)
- Semitendinosus m.

Figure 202

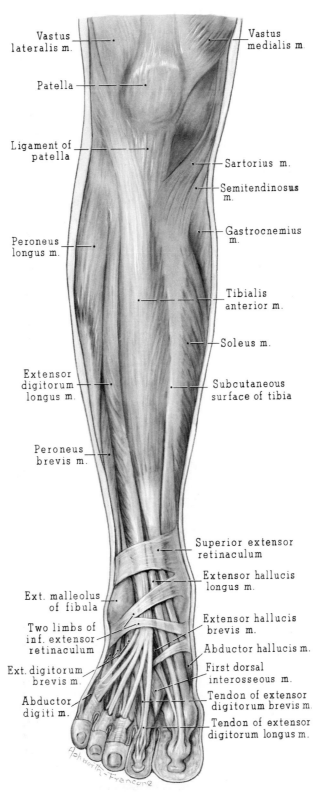

Figure 203. Superficial muscles of the right lower leg and foot, anterior surface.

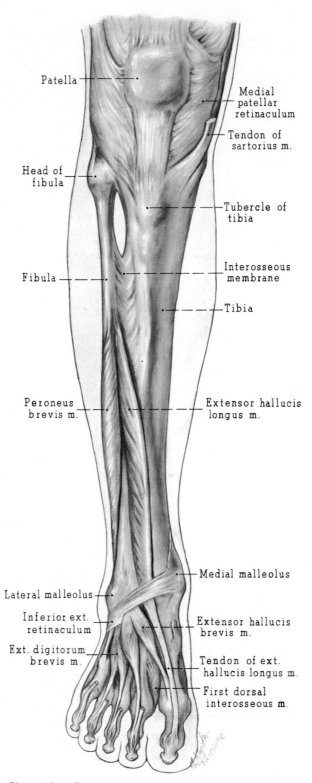

Patella

Medial
patellar
retinaculum

Tendon of
sartorius m.

Head of
fibula

Tubercle of
tibia

Interosseous
membrane

Fibula

Tibia

Peroneus
brevis m.

Extensor hallucis
longus m.

Medial malleolus

Lateral malleolus

Inferior ext.
retinaculum

Extensor hallucis
brevis m.

Ext. digitorum
brevis m.

Tendon of ext.
hallucis longus m.

First dorsal
interosseous m.

Figure 204.   Deep muscles of the right lower leg and foot.

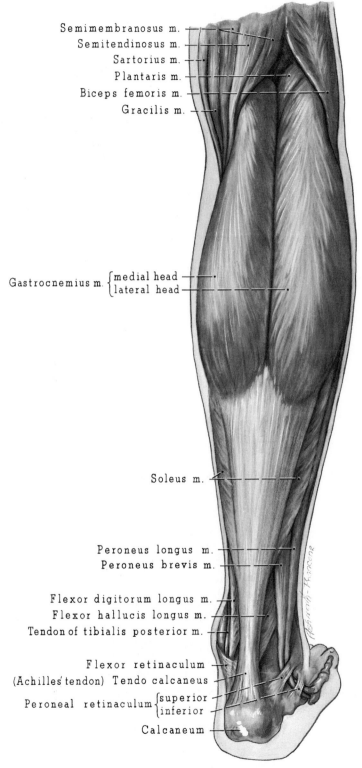

Semimembranosus m.
Semitendinosus m.
Sartorius m.
Plantaris m.
Biceps femoris m.
Gracilis m.

Gastrocnemius m. { medial head
                   lateral head

Soleus m.

Peroneus longus m.
Peroneus brevis m.

Flexor digitorum longus m.
Flexor hallucis longus m.
Tendon of tibialis posterior m.

Flexor retinaculum
(Achilles' tendon) Tendo calcaneus
Peroneal retinaculum { superior
                       inferior
Calcaneum

Figure 205.   Superficial muscles of the right lower leg, posterior view.

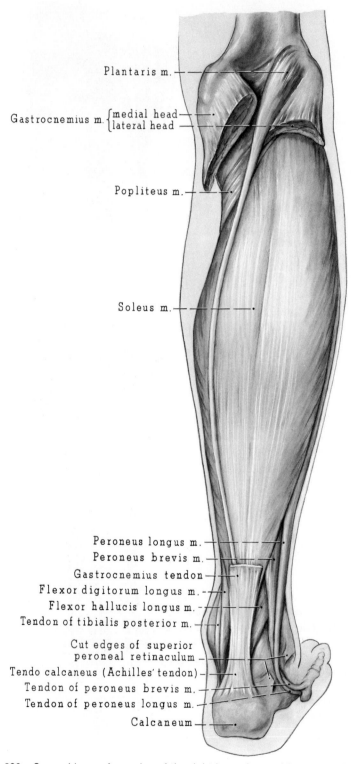

Plantaris m.

Gastrocnemius m. { medial head
                   lateral head

Popliteus m.

Soleus m.

Peroneus longus m.
Peroneus brevis m.
Gastrocnemius tendon
Flexor digitorum longus m.
Flexor hallucis longus m.
Tendon of tibialis posterior m.

Cut edges of superior
    peroneal retinaculum
Tendo calcaneus (Achilles' tendon)
Tendon of peroneus brevis m.
Tendon of peroneus longus m.
Calcaneum

Figure 206. Second layer of muscles of the right lower leg and foot, posterior view.

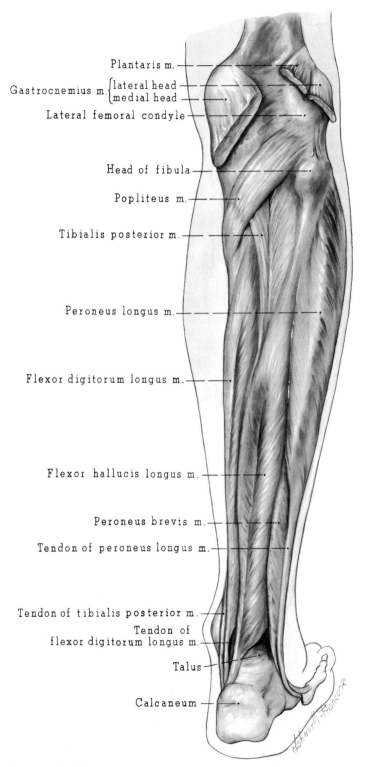

Plantaris m.

Gastrocnemius m. { lateral head
                  { medial head

Lateral femoral condyle

Head of fibula

Popliteus m.

Tibialis posterior m.

Peroneus longus m.

Flexor digitorum longus m.

Flexor hallucis longus m.

Peroneus brevis m.

Tendon of peroneus longus m.

Tendon of tibialis posterior m.

Tendon of
flexor digitorum longus m.

Talus

Calcaneum

Figure 207. Deep muscles of the right lower leg and foot, posterior view.

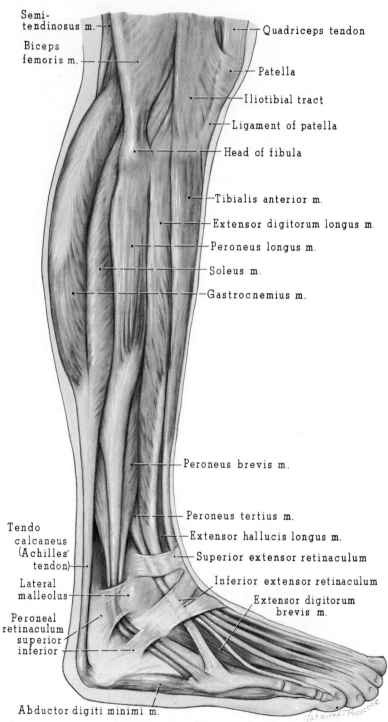

Semi-
tendinosus m.

Biceps
femoris m.

Quadriceps tendon

Patella

Iliotibial tract

Ligament of patella

Head of fibula

Tibialis anterior m.

Extensor digitorum longus m.

Peroneus longus m.

Soleus m.

Gastrocnemius m.

Peroneus brevis m.

Peroneus tertius m.

Extensor hallucis longus m.

Superior extensor retinaculum

Inferior extensor retinaculum

Extensor digitorum
brevis m.

Tendo
calcaneus
(Achilles'
tendon)

Lateral
malleolus

Peroneal
retinaculum
superior
inferior

Abductor digiti minimi m.

Figure 208.   Superficial muscles of the lower right leg and foot, lateral view.

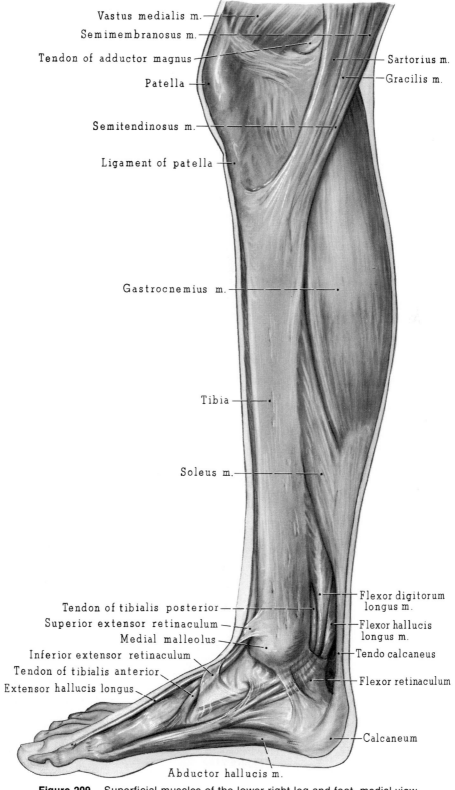

Figure 209.　Superficial muscles of the lower right leg and foot, medial view.

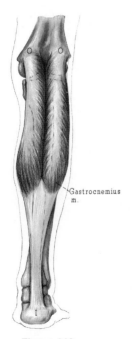

Tibialis
anterior m.

I

Figure 210

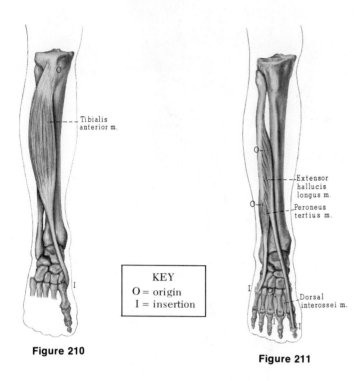

KEY
O = origin
I = insertion

Extensor
hallucis
longus m.

Peroneus
tertius m.

Dorsal
interossei m.

Figure 211

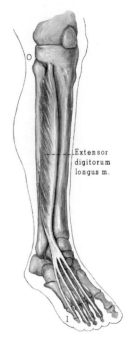

Extensor
digitorum
longus m.

I

Figure 212

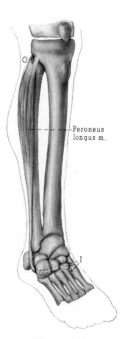

Gastrocnemius
m.

I

Figure 213

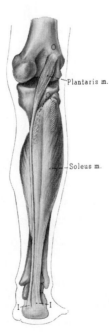

Plantaris m.

Soleus m.

I   I

Figure 214

Peroneus
longus m.

I

Figure 215

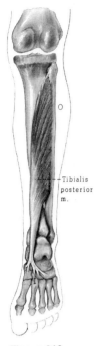

Figure 216

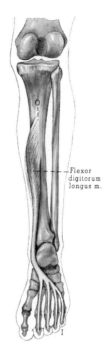

Figure 217

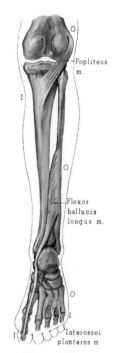

Figure 218

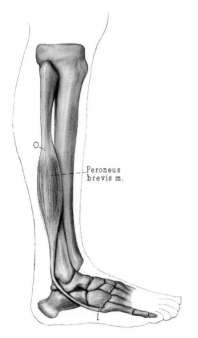

Figure 219

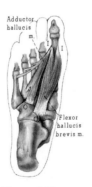

Figure 220

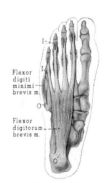

Figure 221

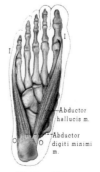

Figure 222

KEY
O = origin
I = insertion

Table 10.   MUSCLES OF FACIAL EXPRESSION*

MUSCLE	ORIGIN	INSERTION	FUNCTION	INNERVATION
Epicranial (occipitofrontalis)				
Occipitalis	Occipital bone and mastoid portion of temporal bone	Galea aponeurotica, epicranial muscle	Draws scalp backward	Facial
Frontalis	Galea aponeurotica	Frontal bone above supra-orbital line	Elevates eyebrows and wrinkles skin of forehead	Facial
Zygomaticus minor	Zygomatic bone	Greater alar cartilage and skin of nose, orbicularis oris	Draws upper lip upward and outward	Facial
Levator labii superioris	Inferior margin of orbit	Orbicularis oris	Elevates upper lip	Facial
Levator labii superioris alaeque nasi	Nasal process of maxilla	Cartilage of ala nasi and upper lip	Raises upper lip, dilates nostril	Facial
Buccinator	Alveolar processes of maxilla and mandible	Orbicularis oris at angle of mouth	Compresses cheek and retracts angle	Facial
Zygomaticus major	Zygomatic bone	Orbicularis oris	Pulls angle of mouth upward and backward when laughing	Facial
Mentalis	Incisive fossa of mandible	Skin of chin	Raises and protrudes lower lip, as in doubt or disdain	Facial
Orbicularis oris	Muscle fibers surrounding the opening of mouth	Angle of mouth	Closes lips	Facial

*Figures 125 to 128

Table 11. MUSCLES OF MASTICATION*

MUSCLE	ORIGIN	INSERTION	FUNCTION	INNERVATION
Masseter	Zygomatic bone and adjacent portions of maxilla	Angle and lateral surface of ramus of mandible	Closes jaw	Trigeminal
Temporalis	Temporal fossa of skull and from deep surface of temporal fascia	Coronoid process of mandible	Raises mandible and closes mouth; draws mandible backward	Trigeminal
Medial pterygoid	Pterygoid fossa of sphenoid; tuberosity of maxilla	Ramus of mandible	Raises mandible; closes mouth	Trigeminal
Lateral pterygoid (two-headed)	Upper head from zygomatic surface of sphenoid; lower head from lateral surface of pterygoid plate	Front of neck of mandible and capsule and disc of temporomandibular joint	Brings jaw forward	Trigeminal

*See also Figures 129 and 130.

Table 12. MUSCLES OF THE EYE*

MUSCLE	ORIGIN	INSERTION	FUNCTION	INNERVATION
Superior rectus	Apex of orbital cavity	Upper and central portion of eyeball	Rolls eyeball upward	Oculomotor
Inferior rectus	Apex of orbital cavity	Lower central portion of eyeball	Rolls eyeball downward	Oculomotor
Medial rectus	Apex of orbital cavity	Midway on medial side of eyeball	Rolls eyeball medially	Oculomotor
Lateral rectus	Apex of orbital cavity	Midway on lateral portion of eyeball	Rolls eyeball laterally	Abducens
Superior oblique	Apex of orbital cavity	Between superior and lateral recti of eyeball	Rotates eyeball on axis; directs cornea downward and laterally	Trochlear
Inferior oblique	Orbital plate of maxilla	Between superior and lateral recti of eyeball	Rotates eyeball on its axis; directs cornea upward and laterally	Oculomotor

*See also Figures 131 and 132.

Table 13. MUSCLES MOVING THE TONGUE*

MUSCLE	ORIGIN	INSERTION	FUNCTION	INNERVATION
Genioglossus	Internal surface of mandible near symphysis	Thin aponeurosis into hyoid bone	Depresses and thrusts tongue forward	Hypoglossal
Styloglossus	Styloid process of temporal bone	Entire length of and inferior surface of tongue	Draws tongue upward and backward	Hypoglossal
Stylohyoid	Styloid process	Body of hyoid	Draws hyoid and tongue upward	Facial
Digastric	Anterior body: mandible; posterior body; mastoid process of temporal bone	Hyoid	Raises hyoid or opens mouth	Mandibular and facial
Mylohyoid	Mandible	Body of hyoid	Elevates hyoid: supports mouth floor	Mandibular
Hyoglossus	Body of hyoid	Side of tongue	Depresses tongue	Hypoglossal
Geniohyoid	Internal surface of mandible near symphysis	Hyoid	Elevates, draws hyoid forward	First cervical

*Figures 133 to 137.

Table 14. MUSCLES MOVING THE THROAT*

MUSCLE	ORIGIN	INSERTION	FUNCTION	INNERVATION
Sternohyoid	Manubrium	Body of hyoid	Depresses hyoid and larynx	Cervical
Omohyoid	Superior border of scapula	Lateral border of hyoid	Depresses hyoid	Cervical
Sternothyroid	Manubrium	Thyroid cartilage	Depresses thyroid cartilage	Cervical
Thyrohyoid	Thyroid cartilage	Hyoid	Raises and changes form of larynx	Cervical

*Figures 133 to 137.

Table 15. MUSCLES MOVING THE HEAD*

MUSCLE	ORIGIN	INSERTION	FUNCTION	INNERVATION
Sternocleidomastoid	Two heads from sternum and clavicle	Tendon into mastoid portion of temporal bone	Rotates head to one side or the other; flexes neck and head	Spinal accessory

*Figures 133 to 137.

Table 16. MOVEMENT OF SHOULDER GIRDLE*

MUSCLE	ORIGIN	INSERTION	FUNCTION	INNERVATION
Levator scapulae	Upper four or five cervical vertebrae	Vertebral border of scapula	Elevates scapula	Dorsal scapular
Rhomboid major	Spines of second to fifth thoracic vertebrae	Vertebral border of scapula	Moves scapula backward and upward, producing slight rotation	Dorsal scapular
Rhomboid minor	Anterior spinous processes of last cervical and first thoracic vertebrae	Vertebral border of scapula at root of spine	Elevates and retracts scapula	Dorsal scapular
Pectoralis minor†	Upper margins and outer surface of third, fourth, and fifth ribs from aponeurosis covering intercostals	Medial border of coracoid process of scapula	Depresses shoulder and rotates scapula downward	Anterior thoracic
Trapezius	Occipital bone; ligamentum nuchae and spinous processes of seventh cervical to twelfth thoracic vertebrae	Acromial process and spine of scapula; lateral third of clavicle	Raises and pulls shoulders backward; rotates scapula; extends head; draws head to one side	Spinal accessory
Serratus anterior	Outer surfaces and superior borders of the upper eighth or ninth rib; from intercostals between ribs	Ventral surface of vertebral border of scapula	Moves scapula forward away from spine and downward and inward toward chest wall	Long thoracic

*See also Figures 138 to 146.
†See Figure 174 for pectoralis minor.

Table 17.   MUSCLES MOVING THE VERTEBRAL COLUMN*

MUSCLE	ORIGIN	INSERTION	FUNCTION	INNERVATION
Sacrospinalis (Erector spinae)				
Spinalis thoracis	Spinous processes upper lumbar and lower thoracic vertebrae	Spines of upper thoracic vertebrae	Extends vertebral column	Branches of spinal nerves
Longissimus thoracis	Transverse processes lumbar vertebrae and lumbosacral fascia	Transverse processes all thoracic and upper lumbar vertebrae; ninth and tenth lower ribs	Extends thoracic vertebrae	Lumbar and dorsal
Longissimus cervicis	Transverse processes fourth and fifth upper thoracic vertebrae	Transverse processes of second to sixth cervical vertebrae	Extends cervical vertebrae	Lower cervical and upper dorsal
Longissimus capitis	Transverse processes fourth and fifth upper thoracic vertebrae	Mastoid process of temporal bone	Draws head backward; rotates head	Branches of cervical nerves.
Iliocostalis lumborum	Iliac crest	Angles of lower sixth and seventh ribs	Extends lumbar spine	Branches of dorsal and lumbar
Iliocostalis thoracis	Upper border of angles of six lower ribs	Angles of six upper ribs	Keeps dorsal spine erect	Branches of dorsal
Iliocostalis cervicis	Angles of first six ribs	Transverse processes of fourth to sixth cervical vertebrae	Extends cervical spine	Branches of cervical
Quadratus lumborum	Iliac crest: iliolumbar ligament	Last rib and upper four lumbar vertebrae	Flexes trunk laterally	Branches of twelfth thoracic and first lumbar
Rectus abdominis	Crest of pubis and ligaments covering symphysis pubis	Cartilages of fifth to seventh ribs	Flexes vertebral column; assists in compressing abdominal wall	Branches of seventh to thirteenth intercostal
Psoas major	Transverse processes of lumbar vertebrae	Lesser trochanter of femur	Flexes, rotates thigh medially	Second and third lumbar
Psoas minor	Last thoracic and first lumbar vertebrae	Junction of ilium and pubis	Flexes trunk on pelvis	First lumbar

*Figures 138 to 146.

Table 18. MUSCLES MOVING THE HUMERUS*

MUSCLE	ORIGIN	INSERTION	FUNCTION	INNERVATION
Coracobrachialis	Coracoid process of scapula	Middle and medial surface of humerus	Flexes, adducts arm	Musculocutaneous
Pectoralis major	Anterior surface of sternal half of clavicle; sternum; aponeurosis of external oblique; six upper ribs	Crest and greater tubercle of humerus	Flexes, adducts, rotates arm medially	Anterior thoracic
Teres major	Posterior aspect of medial border of scapula	Medial border of bicipital groove of humerus	Adducts, extends, rotates arm medially	Lower subscapular
Teres minor	Dorsal surface of medial border of scapula	Greater tuberosity of humerus	Rotates arm laterally; adducts and draws humerus toward glenoid fossa	Branch of axillary
Deltoid	Clavicle; acromial process and posterior border of spine of scapula	Lateral surface of body of humerus	Abducts arm; flexes arm (anterior portion); extends arm (posterior portion)	Axillary
Supraspinatus	Fossa superior to spine of scapula	Greater tuberosity of humerus	Abducts arm	Suprascapular
Infraspinatus	Infraspinatus fossa on posterior aspect of scapula	Greater tubercle of humerus	Rotates humerus outward	Suprascapular
Latissimus dorsi	Broad aponeurosis attached to the spinous process of lower six thoracic vertebrae, spinous process of lumbar vertebrae, spine of sacrum; posterior part of crest of ilium; outer surface of lower four ribs	Bicipital groove of humerus	Extends, adducts, rotates arm medially; draws shoulder downward and backward; raises trunk and pelvis	Thoracodorsal

*See also Figures 138 to 146.

Table 19. MUSCLES MOVING THE ELBOW*

MUSCLE	ORIGIN	INSERTION	FUNCTION	INNERVATION
Brachialis	Lower half of anterior surface of humerus	Tuberosity of the ulna and coronoid processes	Flexes forearm	Musculocutaneous and branch of radial
Triceps brachii (three-headed) Long head	Axillary border of scapula	All heads insert into two aponeurotic laminae uniting above the elbow and in the olecranon of the ulna	Extends and adducts forearm (long head only); entire muscle extends forearm	Radial
Lateral head	Lateral and posterior surfaces of body of humerus			
Medial head†	Posterior surface of body of humerus below lateral head			
Biceps brachii (two-headed)			Flexes arm; flexes forearm, supinates hand; long head draws humerus toward glenoid fossa and strengthens shoulder joint	Musculocutaneous
Long head	Upper margin of the glenoid cavity	Tuberosity of radius		
Short head	Coracoid process by tendon	Tuberosity of radius		
Anconeus	Back of lateral epicondyle of humerus	Olecranon and dorsal surface of ulna	Extends forearm	Radial
Brachioradialis	External supracondyloid ridge of humerus	Lower end of radius	Flexes forearm	Radial

*Figures 148 to 155.
†Medial head of triceps not shown in figures.

Table 20. MUSCLES MOVING THE WRIST*

MUSCLE	ORIGIN	INSERTION	FUNCTION	INNERVATION
Flexor carpi radialis	Medial epicondyle of humerus	Base of second and third metacarpal	Flexes, abducts wrist	Median
Flexor carpi ulnaris	Medial epicondyle of humerus and upper two-thirds of dorsal border of ulna	Pisiform bone	Flexes, adducts wrist	Ulnar
Extensor carpi radialis brevis	External epicondyle of humerus	Base of third metacarpal bone	Extends and abducts wrist joint	Radial
Extensor carpi radialis longus	Lower third of external supracondylar ridge of humerus	Base of second metacarpal bone	Extends, abducts wrist	Radial
Extensor carpi ulnaris	External epicondyle of humerus	Prominent tubercle on ulnar side of the base of fifth metacarpal bone	Extends, adducts wrist	Radial
Palmaris longus	Medial epicondyle of humerus	Transverse carpal ligament; palmar aponeurosis	Flexes wrist joint	Median
Palmaris brevis	Palmar aponeurosis	Skin of medial border of hand	Tenses palm of hand	Ulnar
Extensor digitorum communis	External epicondyle of humerus	Common extensor tendon of each finger	Extends wrist joint	Posterior interosseus

*Figures 148 to 170.

Table 21. MUSCLES MOVING THE HAND*

MUSCLE	ORIGIN	INSERTION	FUNCTION	INNERVATION
Supinator	External epicondyle of humerus; ridge on ulna; radial ligament of elbow	Anterior and lateral surfaces of body of radius	Supinates hand	Posterior interosseus
Pronator teres	Medial epicondyle of humerus and coronoid process of ulna	Middle of lateral surface of body of radius	Pronates forearm	Median
Pronator quadratus	Lower 4th and anterior border of ulna	Volar surface of radius	Pronates forearm	Anterior interosseus

*See also Figures 156 to 170.

Table 22. MUSCLES MOVING THE THUMB*

MUSCLE	ORIGIN	INSERTION	FUNCTION	INNERVATION
Flexor pollicis longus	Volar surface of body of radius	Base of distal phalanx of thumb	Flexes second phalanx of thumb	Posterior interosseus
Flexor pollicis brevis	Transverse carpal ligament; tubercle of trapezium	Base of proximal phalanx of thumb	Flexes thumb	Median: ulnar
Extensor pollicis longus	Lateral side of dorsal surface of ulna	Base of second phalanx of thumb	Extends terminal phalanx of thumb	Radial
Extensor pollicis brevis	Dorsal surface of radius, interosseous membrane	Dorsal surface of proximal phalanx of thumb	Extends thumb	Posterior interosseus
Adductor pollicis	Trapezium, trapezoid, os magnum, shaft of third metacarpal	Ulnar side of base of first phalanx of thumb	Adducts thumb	Ulnar
Abductor pollicis longus	Posterior surfaces of radius and ulna	Radial side of base of 1st metacarpal bone	Abducts, extends thumb	Posterior interosseus
Abductor pollicis brevis	Navicular; anterior trapezium	Lateral surface, base of proximal phalanx of thumb	Abducts thumb	Median
Opponens pollicis	Anterior trapezium; transverse carpal ligament	Radial side of first metacarpal	Flexes and opposes thumb	Median

*Figures 156 to 170.

Table 23. MUSCLES MOVING THE FINGERS*

MUSCLE	ORIGIN	INSERTION	FUNCTION	INNERVATION
Flexor digitorum profundus	Anterior and medial surface of body of ulna; depression on medial side of coronoid process	Bases of terminal phalanges by four tendons	Flexes terminal phalanx of each finger	Ulnar and median
Flexor digiti minimi brevis	Hamate bone: transverse carpal ligament	Ulnar side base of proximal phalanx little finger	Flexes little finger	Ulnar
Interossei dorsales	Two heads from adjacent sides of metacarpal bones	Extensor tendons of second, third, fourth fingers	Abduct, flex proximal phalanges	Ulnar
Flexor digitorum superficialis	1, Two heads, medial epicondyle of humerus: coronoid process of ulna; 2, anterior border of radius	Middle phalanges of fingers	Flexes middle phalanges	Median
Extensor indicis	Dorsal surface of body of ulna: interosseous membrane	Common extensor tendon index finger	Extends index finger	Posterior interosseus
Interrosei palmaris	Sides of second, fourth, fifth metacarpal bones	Extensor tendons of second, fourth, fifth fingers	Adduct, flex proximal phalanges	Ulnar
Abductor digiti minimi	Pisiform bone: flexor carpi ulnaris tendon	Medial surface of base of proximal phalanx of little finger	Abducts little finger	Ulnar
Opponens digiti minimi	Hamate bone: transverse carpal ligament	Ulnar side fifth metacarpal bone	Rotates, abducts fifth metacarpal	Ulnar

*Figures 156 to 170.

Table 24. MUSCLES OF THE ABDOMINAL WALL*

MUSCLE	ORIGIN	INSERTION	FUNCTION	INNERVATION
External oblique	Lower eight ribs	Anterior half of outer lip of iliac crest; anterior rectus sheath	Compresses abdominal contents	Branches of eighth to twelfth intercostal; iliohypogastric, ilio-inguinal
Internal oblique	Inguinal ligament; iliac crest; lumbodorsal fascia	Costal cartilages of lower three or four ribs	Compresses abdominal contents	Branches of eighth to twelfth intercostal; iliohypogastric, ilio-inguinal
Transversus abdominis	Lateral third of inguinal ligament; anterior three-fourths of the inner lip of iliac crest; lumbodorsal fascia; inner surface of cartilages of lower six ribs	Xiphoid cartilage and linea alba	Constricts abdominal contents	Branches of seventh to twelfth intercostal; iliohypogastric, ilio-inguinal
Rectus abdominis	Crest of pubis and ligaments covering symphysis pubis	Cartilages of fifth, sixth, seventh ribs	Flexes vertebral column; assists in compressing abdominal wall	Branches of seventh to twelfth intercostal

*See also Figures 171 to 185.

Table 25. MUSCLES OF RESPIRATION*

MUSCLE	ORIGIN	INSERTION	FUNCTION	INNERVATION
Diaphragm	Xiphoid process; costal cartilages; lumbar vertebrae	Central tendon	Pulls central tendon downward to increase vertical diameter of thorax	Phrenic
External intercostals (11)	Lower border of rib	Upper border of rib below origin	Draws adjacent ribs together	Intercostal
Internal intercostals (11)	Ridge on inner surface of a rib	Upper border of rib below origin	Draws adjacent ribs together	Intercostal
Quadratus lumborum	Iliac crest; iliolumbar ligament	Last rib and upper four lumbar vertebrae	Flexes trunk laterally	Branches of twelfth thoracic and first lumbar

*See also Figures 174 to 181.

Table 26.   MUSCLES MOVING THE FEMUR*

MUSCLE	ORIGIN	INSERTION	FUNCTION	INNERVATION
Iliopsoas				
Psoas major	Transverse processes of lumbar vertebrae	Lesser trochanter of femur	Flexes, rotates thigh medially; flexes trunk	Second and third lumbar
Psoas minor	Last thoracic and first lumbar vertebrae	Junction of ilium and pubis	Flexes trunk	First lumbar
Iliacus	Margin of iliac fossa	Lateral side of tendon of psoas major	Flexes, rotates thigh medially; flexes trunk	Femoral
Gluteus maximus	Posterior gluteal line of ilium and posterior surface of sacrum and coccyx	Fascia lata, gluteal ridge	Extends, rotates thigh laterally; extends trunk; prevents jack-knifing of trunk during running or climbing	Inferior gluteal
Gluteus medius	Lateral surface of ilium	Strong tendon that runs into lateral surface	Abducts, rotates thigh medially; tilts pelvis (holding it over stance leg when opposite leg is lifted, as during walking)	Superior gluteal
Gluteus minimus	Outer surface of ilium	Anterior border of greater trochanter	Abducts, rotates thigh medially; tilts pelvis (see gluteus medius)	Superior gluteal
Tensor fascia lata†	Anterior part of iliac spine	Iliotibial band of fascia	Tenses fascia lata	Superior gluteal
Adductor brevis	Inferior ramus of pubis	Linea aspera of femur	Adducts, rotates, flexes thigh	Obturator
Adductor magnus	Ischial tuberosity, ischiopubic ramus	Linea aspera of femur, adductor tubercle of femur	Adducts, extends thigh	Sciatic and obturator
Obturator externus	Pubis, ischium, superficial surface of obturator membrane	Trochanteric fossa of femur	Rotates thigh laterally	Obturator
Pectineus	Junction of ilium and pubis. Spine of pubis	Femur distal to lesser trochanter	Flexes, adducts thigh	Obturator and femoral
Adductor longus	Crest and symphysis of pubis	Linea aspera of femur	Adducts, rotates, flexes thigh	Obturator

*Figures 186 to 200.
†Sometimes spelled fasciae latae.

Table 27.   MUSCLES MOVING THE KNEE JOINT*

MUSCLE	ORIGIN	INSERTION	FUNCTION	INNERVATION
Hamstrings				
Biceps femoris				
Long head	Tuberosity of ischium	Lateral side of head of the fibula and lateral condyle of tibia	Flexes leg; rotates laterally after flexed; extends thigh	Long head: tibial
Short head	Lateral lip of linea aspera of femur			Short head: peroneal
Semitendinosus	Tuberosity of ischium	Upper part of body of tibia	Flexes leg, extends thigh	Tibial
Semimembranosus	Tuberosity of ischium	Medial condyle of tibia	Flexes leg, extends thigh	Tibial
Popliteus	Lateral condyle of femur	Posterior surface of body of tibia	Flexes leg, rotates it medially	Tibial
Gracilis	Symphysis pubis and pubic arch	Medial surface of body of tibia	Adducts thigh, flexes leg	Obturator
Sartorius	Anterior superior spine of ilium	Medial border of tuberosity of tibia	Flexes thigh, rotates it laterally; adducts and flexes leg (crossing, tailor fashion)	Femoral
Quadriceps femoris (four heads)				
Rectus femoris	Two tendons: one from anterior inferior iliac spine; other from groove above the acetabulum	Insert into base of patella and condyles and tuberosity of tibia	Extend leg, flex thigh	Femoral
Vastus lateralis	Broad aponeurosis from greater trochanter and linea aspera of femur			
Vastus medialis	Medial lip of linea aspera; intertrochanteric line			
Vastus intermedius	Ventral and medial surfaces of body of femur			

*See Figures 191 to 202.

Table 28. MUSCLES MOVING THE FOOT*

MUSCLE	ORIGIN	INSERTION	FUNCTION	INNERVATION
Gastrocnemius	Two heads from lateral and medial condyles of femur; adjacent part of capsule of knee	Tendo calcaneus	Plantar flexes foot (points toes); flexes leg; supinates foot	Tibial
Soleus	Posterior aspect head of fibula and medial border of tibia	Tendo calcaneus	Plantar flexes foot	Tibial
Tibialis posterior	Interosseus membrane between tibia and fibula	Three cuneiform; cuboid navicular bone; second, third, fourth, metatarsals	Plantar flexes foot	Tibial
Tibialis anterior	Lateral condyle and upper portion of lateral surface of body of tibia	Undersurface of medial cuneiform and base of first metatarsal	Dorsally flexes foot	Deep peroneal
Peroneus tertius	Lower third of anterior surface of fibula and lateral tuberosity of tibia	Dorsal surface of base of fifth metatarsal bone	Dorsally flexes foot	Deep peroneal
Peroneus longus	Head and lateral surface of body of fibula	Lateral side of first metatarsal and medial cuneiform bone	Everts; plantar flexes foot	Peroneal
Peroneus brevis	Lower two-thirds of lateral surface of body of fibula	Tuberosity at base of fifth metatarsal	Everts foot	Peroneal
Plantaris	Lateral condyle of femur	Calcaneus	Plantar flexes foot	Tibial

*See also Figures 192 to 219.

Table 29. MUSCLES MOVING THE TOES*

MUSCLE	ORIGIN	INSERTION	FUNCTION	INNERVATION
Flexor hallucis brevis	Cuboid, third cuneiform	Base of proximal phalanx of great toe	Flexes great toe	Lateral and medial plantar
Flexor hallucis longus	Posterior surface of fibula	Base of distal phalanx of great toe	Flexes great toe	Posterior tibial
Extensor hallucis longus	Fibula and interosseous membrane	Dorsal surface base of distal phalanx of great toe	Dorsiflexes ankle, extend great toe	Deep peroneal
Interossei dorsales	Surfaces of adjacent metatarsal bones	Extensor tendons third, fourth toes	Abduct, flex toes	Lateral plantar
Flexor digitorum longus	Posterior surface of shaft of tibia	Distal phalanges of lateral toes	Flex toes, extend foot	Posterior tibial
Extensor digitorum longus	Anterior surface fibula, lateral condyle tibia, interosseous membrane	Common extensor tendon of four lateral toes	Extends toes	Deep peroneal
Flexor digitorum osseous brevis	Medial tuberosity of calcaneus, plantar fascia	Middle phalanges of four lateral toes	Flexes toes	Medial plantar
Abductor hallucis	Medial tuberosity of calcaneus, plantar fascia	Medial surface of base of proximal phalanx of great toe	Abducts, flexes great toe	Medial plantar
Abductor digiti minimi	Medial and lateral tubercles of calcaneus; plantar fascia	Lateral surface of base of proximal phalanx of little toe	Abducts little toe	Lateral plantar

*Figures 203 to 222.

antagonist to perform. *Synergists* are muscles assisting the agonist. They hold a joint crossed by the tendon of the prime mover in the best possible position for effective action.

Muscles acting only on joints between their respective origin and insertion produce movements only at these joints. For instance, the *brachialis,* the muscle attached to the ulna and humerus, produces movement only at the elbow. Ability to bend the elbow is at first limited, because most of the energy is expended in attempting to pull the ulna upward in a straight direction. As the elbow bends, the angle of pull increases and the muscle becomes increasingly efficient. The optimal angle of pull for any muscle is a right angle. The system of levers also has an influence on the efficiency of muscular contraction.

SUMMARY

THE MUSCULAR SYSTEM

The three types of muscle are skeletal, smooth, and cardiac.

Skeletal Muscle

1. **Structure and Nomenclature**

   a. Skeletal muscle is also called *striated muscle* because, when it is examined under the light microscope, alternating dark and light bands are seen, and *voluntary muscle* because it is subject to voluntary control.

   b. A muscle is composed of bundles (*fasciculi*) of muscle fibers, each a long, narrow, multinucleated cell bounded by a membrane called the *sacrolemma.*

   (1) Each muscle fiber is made up of *myofibrils,* composed of thick and thin filaments.
      (a). The thick filaments consist of the protein myosin.
      (b). The thin filaments contain three proteins: actin *(the principal one),* troponin, *and* tropomyosin. *The thin filaments are attached to a transverse structure (referred to as the Z line) and overlap the thick filaments.*

   (2) This arrangement of the filaments gives rise to the banded appearance of the myofibrils.
      (a). The thick filaments are the dark, or A, bands.

(b). The thin filaments, where they do not overlap the thick filaments, are the light, or I, bands.

c. Connective tissue called *endomysium, perimysium* and *epimysium* surrounds the fibers, fasciculi and whole muscle, respectively.

2. Mechanism of Contraction

a. When a muscle contracts, the thin filaments slide toward the centers of the thick filaments.
   (1) In the electron microscope this is seen as a shortening of the I band and a decrease in the distance between Z lines (the length of a sarcomere).
   (2) Rotation of the heads of myosin molecules (which face opposite ends of the thick filaments) apparently provides the propulsive force for the sliding of the thin filaments.
   (3) The contraction is triggered by the release of calcium from the sarcoplasmic reticulum.
b. Calcium combines with the troponin component of the thin filament, which functions as a latch, preventing the interaction of ATP-activated myosin heads and actin. Calcium binding releases the latch.
c. When myosin and actin interact, ATP is split (by an ATP-splitting enzyme in the heads of myosin), providing the energy for the swiveling of myosin heads.

3. Transmission of the Electrical Impulses to the Sarcoplasmic Reticulum

a. A single nerve fiber, as a result of terminal branching, innervates on the average about 150 muscle fibers, constituting a *motor unit.*
b. The transmission of an electrical impulse from a nerve fiber branch to a muscle fiber at the neuromuscular junction is mediated by *acetylcholine* released from the neuronal terminal.
c. The impulse traveling along the muscle fiber membrane reaches the sarcoplasmic reticulum via the T tubules, invaginations of the muscle fiber membrane.

d. The arrival of the impulse activates the release of calcium from the sarcoplasmic reticulum, thereby triggering contraction of the muscle fiber.

4. Energy Sources for Skeletal Muscle Contraction

a. During *moderate exercise* the sources of energy are stored ATP, ATP synthesized from creatine phosphate and ATP produced by the oxidation of fatty acids and glucose taken up from the blood. Oxygen consumption rises sharply.
b. During *strenuous exercise,* additional ATP is supplied by the anaerobic breakdown of muscle glycogen to lactic acid.
c. The *oxygen debt* (the amount of oxygen consumed above the resting level after exercise) is small following moderate exercise and represents replenishment of the approximately half-depleted stores of ATP and creatinine phosphate.
   (1) Following strenuous exercise, part of the glycogen and possibly all of the ATP and creatinine phosphate must be replaced, and the oxygen debt is large.

5. Principles of Muscular Contraction

a. The *all or none principle* states that a stimulus strong enough to elicit a response will produce maximum contraction of a motor unit. The weakest stimulus that will initiate contraction is known as the *threshold stimulus.*
   (1) Two subthreshold stimuli applied in rapid succession may be equivalent to a threshold stimulus (summation of stimuli).
b. Application of stimuli of increasing strength will excite motor units with higher thresholds and increase the force of contraction of a muscle.
c. Stimulating a muscle before it relaxes will increase the magnitude of the response.
   (1) A volley of stimuli at high frequency will cause a sustained contraction of increased magnitude (phenomenon known as *tetanus*).
   (2) Continued stimulation will re-

sult in weak contractions (*fatigue*) and incomplete relaxation (*contracture*).

d. Initial length of a muscle effects the force of contraction.
   (1) It is maximum when stretched to its approximate resting length in its normal attachments in the body.
e. When a muscle shortens against a constant load, exerting constant force, the contraction is called *isotonic*. It is called *isometric* when it does not shorten as tension rises.
f. Muscles are normally kept in a state of partial contraction in the body by a continuous asynchronous flow of stimuli from muscle spindles, receptors in muscle sensitive to stretch. This is called *muscle tone*.
   (1) This discharge is continuous because all muscles, especially those subject to the force of gravity, are under some stretch.
   (2) Impulses from the brain modify muscle tone.
g. *Red muscle fibers*—those with small diameters, a rich capillary supply, large amounts of myoglobin, many mitochondria and little glycogen—fatigue less readily and contract more slowly than *white muscle fibers*—those with large diameters, few capillaries and mitochondria, an abundance of glycogen and an extensive sarcoplasmic reticulum.

Smooth Muscle

1. Smooth muscle has no cross-striations and each cell has a single large nucleus.

   a. Since contraction is not induced at will, it is called *involuntary muscle*.

2. Smooth muscle is found in hollow structures, such as the digestive and urinary tracts and other locations, such as the iris and ciliary muscles of the eye.

3. Visceral, or unitary, smooth muscle, found in most hollow structures, contracts in the absence of nerve stimulation.

   a. Few nerve terminals are present.
   b. The fibers are in close contact.
   c. Electrical impulses pass from fiber to fiber via membrane junctions.

4. Multiunit smooth muscle, found where finer gradations of contractions occur, such as in the iris, does not contract in the absence of nerve stimulation.

   a. The fibers are by and large independently innervated.

5. Although thick and thin fialments are not so regularly arranged in smooth as in skeletal muscle, the contraction mechanism is believed to be similar.

Cardiac Muscle

1. Cardiac mucle, the muscle of the heart, has a striated appearance, resulting from the same arrangement of thick and thin filaments as in skeletal muscle.

2. Have a single nucleus and are functionally linked at their branched ends by junctional specializations called intercalated discs.

   a. This creates two **functional syncytia**—two atria forming one, two ventricles the other.

3. The heartbeat does not depend upon its nerve supply.

   a. Special neuromuscular tissue initiates the beat and is responsible for the rapid transmission of electrical impulses throughout the heart.

Intramuscular Injection

1. The proper site for intramuscular injection is one that avoids major nerves and blood vessels. The three areas best suited for intramuscular injection are

   a. The upper outer quadrant of the gluteal area
   b. The vastus lateralis
   c. The deltoid muscle, at least 2 cm below the acromion.

Introduction to Anatomy of Skeletal Muscles

1. Muscles are named according to action, shape, origin and insertion, number of divisions, location or direction of fibers.

2. Shapes of muscle: fusiform, quadrilateral, triangular, straplike or pennate.

3. The origin is the stationary attachment of the muscle to the skeleton. The insertion is the movable attachment of the muscle.

4. Muscle is usually attached to bone indirectly by means of tendons, consisting of strong nonelastic fibrous tissue.

5. Muscles act only on the joint between the origin and insertion.

6. Prime movers execute any action, while antagonists must relax for the action to occur.

7. Synergists assist the prime movers and act to reduce excess and unnecessary motion.

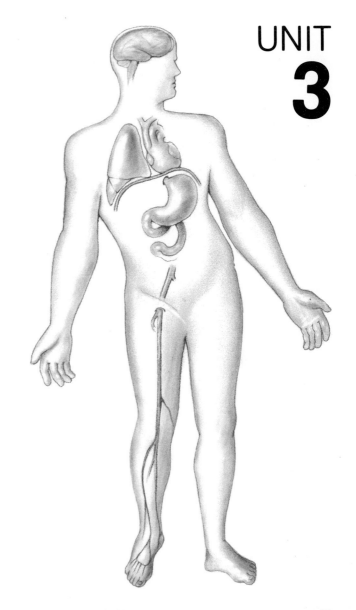

Integration and Metabolism

The Nervous System

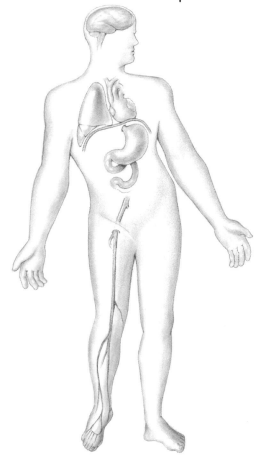

Objectives

The aim of this chapter is to enable the student to:

Describe the structure of neurons and distinguish between the different types.

Describe the changes in membrane permeability that give rise to a propagated nerve impulse.

Outline the succession of events in neuromuscular and synaptic transmission and identify the principal differences between the two types of transmission.

Explain how receptors function and how sensations are identified.

Identify the principal parts of the brain and the major functions of each.

Describe the meninges of the brain and spinal cord.

Describe the origin, function and circulation of cerebrospinal fluid.

Outline the principal features of the spinal cord.

Describe the anatomy and distribution of the spinal and cranial nerves.

Outline the anatomical characteristics and principal functions of the sympathetic and parasympathetic divisions of the autonomic nervous system.

Describe reflex action and enumerate the principal differences between stretch and withdrawal reflexes.

Outline the pathways for the perception of somesthetic sensations.

Discuss the different types of pain and the modulation of pain.

Describe the pathways for motor function and distinguish between the pyramidal and extrapyramidal systems, both structurally and functionally.

Explain the role of the limbic system in governing emotions.

Describe the functions of the language areas of the brain.

Throughout history the complexities of the human body have stimulated the imagination. Each mystery solved merely reveals the multiple avenues of complex organizational patterns intimately involved in the function of the living, thinking human being. Perhaps even more fascinating than molecular biology itself is the knowledge of man's ability to comprehend, learn, and act as an individual organism—not only to grasp the wonder of the world, but to question and study it. Man's awareness of his environment is made possible by the integrated functioning of the nervous system, a group of tissues composed of highly specialized cells possessing the characteristics of excitability and conductivity. The nervous system, in association with the endocrine system, not only creates an awareness of the environment but makes it possible for the human body to respond to environmental changes with the necessary precision.

DIVISIONS OF THE NERVOUS SYSTEM

For descriptive purposes, the nervous system can be divided into two parts: the central nervous system and the peripheral nervous system. The **central nervous system** includes the *brain* and *spinal cord,* enclosed in the cranium and the vertebral canal. The **peripheral nervous system** includes 12 pairs of *cranial nerves* and their branches and 31 pairs of *spinal nerves* and their branches. The peripheral nervous system provides input from *sensory receptors* to the central nervous system and output from it to *effectors* (muscles and glands). Communicating networks within the central nervous system and various brain centers which process incoming sensory information make possible the appropriate unconscious or conscious response to sensory input. For convenience, peripheral efferent nerve fibers distributed to smooth muscle, cardiac muscle and glands are referred to as the *autonomic nervous system.*

TYPES OF CELLS IN THE NERVOUS SYSTEM

The nervous system is composed of a special tissue containing two major types of cells: *neurons*, the active conducting elements, and *neuroglia* (G. *glia,* glue), the supporting elements.

Neurons

The basic unit of the nervous system is the neuron, or nerve cell, which conducts an electrical impulse from one part of the body to another. The neuron itself consists of a cell body (perikaryon), containing a single nucleus, and processes transmitting impulses to and from the cell body (Fig. 223).

Neurons have two types of processes: **axons** and **dendrites.** An axon is a single, elongate cytoplasmic extension carrying nerve impulses *away* from the cell body. The axon substance, or axoplasm, is jelly-like. The axon itself has a smooth outline, is of constant diameter, has surface sheaths and terminates in more minute branches,

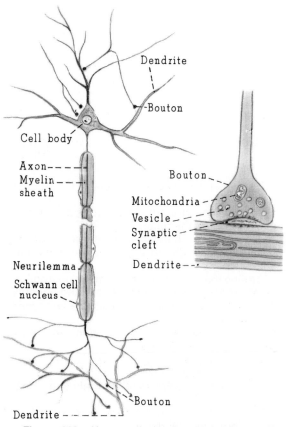

Figure 223. Nerve cell showing branching processes ending in boutons. Detail of synapse between bouton and dendrite on right.

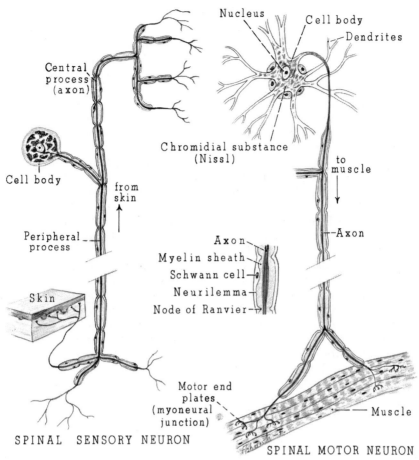

Figure 224. Motor and sensory neurons.

which form junctions with effectors and other neurons. There is only one axon per neuron, but side branches, called *collaterals,* may arise along the course of an axon.

The dendrites (G. *dendron,* tree) are processes that carry impulses *toward* the cell body. The word dendrite describes the manner in which the processes appear in true dendrites—numerous, short, branching and thickened at their point of origin. True dendrites are unsheathed and their surfaces have spinelike processes (dendrite spines) that are the principal sites of junctions between dendrites and axon terminals, where nerve impulses are transmitted from the latter to the former. Sensory neurons (those conducting sensory information to the central nervous system) have a single process that bifurcates a short distance from the cell body. One branch (the *peripheral process*) runs from a receptor to the cell body located just outside the central ner-

vous system. The other (the *central process,* or axon) runs from the cell body to the central nervous system (Fig. 224). The peripheral process has the smooth surface, is sheathed and is in other respects histologically similar to axons. *Sensory neurons, therefore, do not have true dendrites,* although the peripheral process is frequently called a dendrite because it conducts impulses to the cell body.

Cytoplasmic Organelles. Located in the cell body (except the axon hillock, the region from which the axon arises) and true dendrites are the *endoplasmic reticulum* and associated *ribosomes* (collectively called *Nissl bodies*) and the *Golgi apparatus.* These organelles serve the same function in neurons as in all cells, namely, the synthesis and packaging of proteins. Nissl bodies characteristically respond to injury of a nerve fiber by breaking up to a powder-like mass and dispersing in a reaction called chromatolysis. *Mitochondria* are found throughout the neuron, as are two other organelles, *microtubules* (250 Ångstroms in diameter) and *microfilaments* (40 to 60 Ångstroms in diameter). Microtubules and microfilaments may play a role in transporting neuronal substances. They also appear to be involved in nerve fiber growth. In tissue culture studies of axon growth, the tubules form a necessary supportive "skeleton" and the filaments seem to act as contractile "probes" at the growing tip. Drugs destroying these structures prevent growth.

The Nerve Fiber: The Elongate Neuron Process and Its Surface Coverings. The term *nerve fiber* refers to any single, elongate neuron process (such as axons and the peripheral processes of sensory neurons) and its surface sheaths. Almost all fibers of the peripheral nervous system have two sheaths, the *myelin sheath* and the *neurilemma*, overlying the cell membrane (the neurilemma is absent in fibers of the central nervous system). Figure 225 shows an axon and its sheaths, composing a typical nerve

fiber. The central core, or *axis cylinder,* is enclosed by the cell membrane of the axon (the *axolemma*), which in turn is surrounded by the myelin sheath and neurilemma. Bundles of fibers running together in the peripheral nervous system constitute a nerve. Surrounding each nerve fiber is a connective tissue covering, called the *endoneurium*, which binds together the fibers of a bundle, or *fascicle.* The connective tissue coverings of a bundle and a nerve are called, respectively, the *perineurium* and the *epineurium* (Fig. 225).

Both the myelin sheath and the neurilemma of peripheral nerve fibers are derived from accessory cells of the nervous system known as *Schwann cells*. The myelin sheath of peripheral nerve fibers is formed by repeated wrapping of the Schwann cell around the axon. The cytoplasm is expelled so that what remains is a tightly wound spiral of Schwann cell membrane. (As Schwann cells are not present in the central nervous system, this same function is thought to be performed by *oligodendroglia*.) The myelin encompasses the

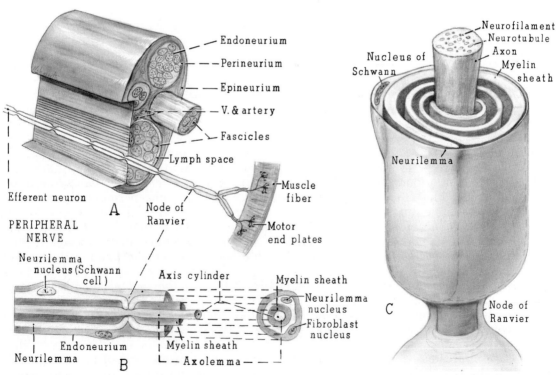

Figure 225. Diagrammatic representation of a peripheral nerve (*A*) and nerve fiber (*B*). (Modified from J. Z. Young.) *C,* Spiralling of a Schwann cell around the cell membrane of the axon (axolemma) to form the myelin sheath of a nerve fiber.

NERVE REGENERATION

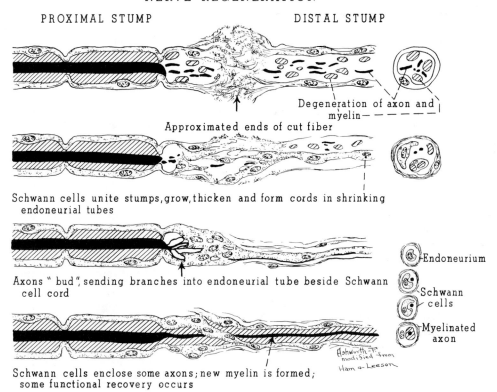

Figure 226.   Schematic drawing of nerve regeneration.

entire fiber, except at its termination and at periodic constrictions called *nodes of Ranvier.* Segments between nodes are called *internodes.*

Not all nerve fibers have a myelin sheath thick enough to be seen in the light microscope. It was formerly thought, in fact, that two groups of fibers existed: *myelinated,* those with myelin sheaths, and *nonmyelinated,* those without myelin sheaths. These terms are still used but now distinguish fibers with myelin sheaths thick enough to be seen with conventional light microscopy from those with insufficient myelin to be seen in this way. Myelin is an effective insulator and increases the speed at which electrical impulses are conducted (a property described below under Saltatory Conduction).

The neurilemma, also called the *sheath of Schwann,* consists of flattened, living Schwann cells (one per internode) and forms a thin, continuous membrane overlying the myelin sheath. The neurilemma plays an essential role in nerve fiber regen-

eration. When a nerve fiber is crushed, the part of the fiber connected to the cell body continues to transmit impulses, but the part distal to the injury (or the part that would be disconnected if the nerve fiber was severed) gradually disintegrates except for the neurilemma. If the nerve fiber is protected by a neurilemmal sheath, parts of the damaged portion can regenerate (Fig. 226). Damaged fibers of the optic and auditory nerves as well as fibers within the central nervous system cannot repair themselves by this method, since they lack the protection and guidance of a neurilemmal sheath.

Classification of Neurons. Neurons differ in size of cell body; length, size, and number of dendrites; length and size of axon and number of branches from the axon terminals. These differences are responsible for the differing reactions of neurons to stimuli and, therefore, for their varied functions.

NEURON TYPES ACCORDING TO STRUCTURE. Structurally, neurons fall into three groups: *unipolar, bipolar,* and *multi-*

polar. This classification depends on the number of processes extending from the cell body. A unipolar neuron has only one process. True unipolar neurons, those with a single axon, are rare, except in the embryo. Sensory neurons that have one process which divides in two a short distance after leaving the cell body are also classified as unipolar, although some authors describe them as *pseudounipolar,* since they develop from embryological bipolar cells and function as bipolar cells. Bipolar neurons have only two processes, one conducting impulses to the cell body (not a true dendrite, although often called one), the other an axon; such cells are found in the retina of the eye and in the olfactory epithelium. Multipolar neurons have many true dendrites and a single axon. The majority of neurons in the brain and spinal cord are multipolar.

NEURON TYPES ACCORDING TO FUNCTION. There are three types of neurons entering into the formation of nerve pathways. *Sensory,* or *afferent* (L. *afferre,* to carry to), neurons convey impulses from the skin or other sense organs to the spinal cord and brain. *Motor,* or *efferent* (L. *efferre,* to carry away), neurons carry impulses away from the brain and spinal cord to muscles and glands. *Interneurons,* or *internuncial neurons,* conduct impulses from one neuron to another, forming links in the neural pathways and lying entirely within the central nervous system.

Accessory Cells

The non-nervous elements consist of blood vessels, connective tissue and supporting cells known collectively as neuroglia. Schwann cells, which form the myelin sheath and neurilemma of fibers of the peripheral nervous system, have already been described. Mention has also been made of oligodendroglia, which form the myelin sheath of fibers of the central nervous system. Other accessory cells are *astrocytes, microglia* and *ependymal cells.*

Astrocytes (G. *astron,* star) are so named because their processes are star shaped (Fig. 227). Some of the processes have terminal expansions in contact with blood vessels. The capillaries of the central nervous system are relatively impermeable and constitute a so-called "blood brain barrier" (demonstrated by injecting certain dyes, such as trypan blue, which will stain all tissues but those of the central nervous system). Astrocytes, which occupy the space between capillaries and neurons, are believed to control the transport of substances between the blood stream and neurons.

Microglia, unlike all other cells of the nervous system, develop from the embryonic mesoderm (which gives rise, among other things, to connective tissue, muscles and the vascular system) rather than the ectoderm (from which the epidermis and neural tube develop). Microglia function as phagocytic cells.

Ependymal cells line the ventricles (cavities) of the brain and the central canal of the spinal cord. In the embryo these cells are columnar and ciliated, but in the adult are cuboidal in shape with few cilia.

The Nerve Impulse

Neurons function to conduct signals from one part of the body to another. When an impulse travels along a fiber, the characteristic transmission is *electrical;* when transmitted from one neuron to another across a junction, the transmission is typically *chemical.*

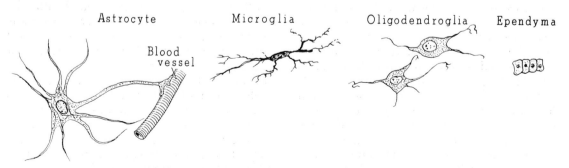

Figure 227.   Neuroglial cells of the central nervous system.

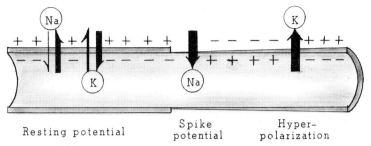

Resting potential   Spike   Hyper-
                        potential   polarization

Figure 228. Schematic representation of the resting membrane potential of a nerve fiber and of the nerve impulse. Sodium is actively pumped out of and potassium into the cell interior. More rapid diffusion of potassium outward creates the resting potential. A stimulus "opens the sodium gates," flooding the interior with sodium, giving rise to the spike potential. Halting the rapid outflow of sodium is followed by a rapid outflow of potassium. This returns the internal potential to negative and momentarily hyperpolarizes the membrane (interior more negative than the resting potential). This transitory disturbance, the nerve impulse, is propagated along the membrane.

The capacity for selective permeability to ions is a function of the cell membrane (see Chapter Two). It is this property of the nerve cell which is involved in the transmission of the nerve impulse. In the resting state the interior of a nerve fiber has a negative charge. This is the *resting membrane potential* of the nerve fiber (Fig. 228). It is brought about in the following manner: The active transport of positively charged sodium ions to the outside of the cell (the so-called sodium pump) with the reciprocal transfer of positively charged potassium ions to the inside maintains a high concentration of sodium outside and a high concentration of potassium inside the cell. Diffusion of sodium and potassium across the cell membrane in response to the concentration gradients created by the active transport mechanism results in the "leaking" of sodium back into and of potassium out of the cell. However, since the cell membrane is more permeable to potassium than to sodium, potassium diffuses to the outside faster than sodium diffuses to the inside. This creates a deficit of positive charges in the interior that is responsible for the resting membrane potential.

When a stimulus is applied to a nerve cell, an impulse, a transient reversal of the internal potential, is transmitted along the nerve fiber. This comes about as follows: The stimulus causes structural changes in the membrane that greatly increase its permeability to sodium ("opening the sodium gates"), causing a rapid inflow of sodium, which changes the internal potential locally from negative to positive (the

spike potential). This is followed by a halt of the rapid inflow of sodium and the onset of a rapid outflow of potassium, which returns the interior charge to negative. (For a brief period the membrane is "hyperpolarized"; that is, the interior charge is more negative than the resting potential.) These changes, the so-called *action potential*, can be recorded with an oscilloscope and are illustrated in Figure 229. The local disturbance stimulates the adjacent regions of the nerve fiber, and the action potential sweeps along the fiber. (In the body the stimulus is normally received at one end of the neuron and is propagated in one direction, but if a nerve fiber is artificially stimulated in the middle the action potential will be transmitted in both directions.)

Until the membrane returns to the resting state, the nerve fiber will not respond to a new stimulus. The interval of complete unresponsiveness is called the *absolute refractory period*. The absolute refractory period is followed by a *relative refractory period* (lasting about one-quarter as long as the absolute period), during which time a stronger than minimum effective impulse will lead to the transmission of a nerve impulse. For a large myelinated nerve fiber the absolute refractory period is about 1/2500th second, and from this one can calculate that such a fiber can carry a maximum of about 2500 impulses per second.

All-or-None Principle. The transmission of a nerve impulse by a nerve fiber is said to work on an all-or-none principle. This means that nerve fibers will not transmit an impulse unless the stimulus has a certain

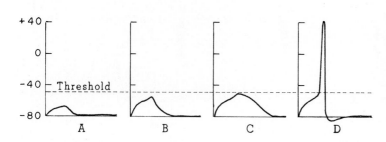

Figure 229. The potential changes in the interior of the nerve fiber of a squid, recorded on an oscilloscope, following subthreshold and threshold stimuli. Subthreshold stimuli of increasing strength causes successively greater, brief, non-propagated, upward deflections (A, B and C). A threshold stimulus gives rise to the so-called action potential (the propagated impulse), showing a sharp rising phase (spike potential) and rapid descent (D).

strength (the *threshold* of the nerve fiber). If the threshold is reached, the impulse is maximal. Each type of nerve fiber sends an impulse of only one strength—its characteristic impulse. A stronger stimulus does not lead to a larger impulse.

A stimulus just strong enough to lead to a propagated impulse is called a *threshold stimulus.* A *subthreshold stimulus* will cause the internal potential to become briefly less negative, deflecting the voltage upward (Fig. 229). Only when the threshold voltage of the nerve fiber is reached will the sodium influx be of sufficient magnitude to cause the sharp spike potential and propagated impulse.

Different nerve fibers have different thresholds—some will fire only with very strong stimulation, others with very weak stimulation, but all fibers work characteristically and on the all-or-none firing principle.

Chronaxie and Excitability of Nerve Fibers. To be effective, a stimulus must be of sufficient duration and intensity. The stronger the current, the shorter the time required to excite a fiber (Fig. 230). The time required for a current twice the minimum effective voltage (the rheobase) to excite a fiber is called *chronaxie* and is used as a convenient measure of the relative excitability of nerve fibers—the shorter the chronaxie, the greater the excitability.

Saltatory Conduction. Myelin is resistant to the flow of ions, and the thick myelin sheath of myelinated fibers prevents continuous passage of impulses along the length of the fiber. Ion flow at nodes of

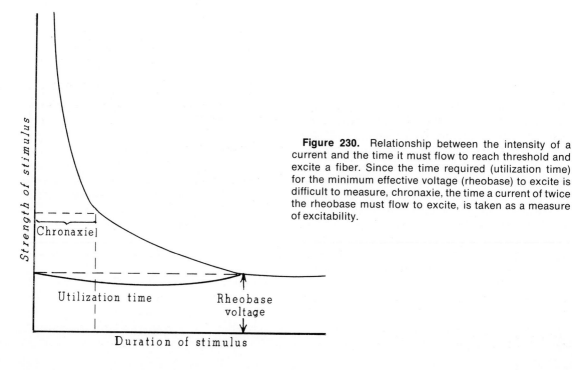

Figure 230. Relationship between the intensity of a current and the time it must flow to reach threshold and excite a fiber. Since the time required (utilization time) for the minimum effective voltage (rheobase) to excite is difficult to measure, chronaxie, the time a current of twice the rheobase must flow to excite, is taken as a measure of excitability.

Ranvier sets up potential differences between nodes, and the impulse jumps from one node to another. This process, called *saltatory conduction* (L. *saltatorius*, of dancing), greatly increases the transmission velocity of nerve impulses.

Transmission of the Impulse at the Neuromuscular Junction

Neurons usually enter the muscle at the equatorial plane and branch terminally. A single nerve fiber, therefore, innervates more than one muscle fiber. The junction at which a nerve fiber and a skeletal muscle fiber meet is called the *neuromuscular junction* (Fig. 231).

The terminal branching portion of the motor neuron is termed the *motor end plate*. *Sole feet* containing mitochondria and vesicles that store acetylcholine, a chemical mediator, project from the end plate and lie in invaginations of the muscle fiber membrane, called the *synaptic gutter*. Folds on the bottom of this synaptic gutter serve to increase the surface area of the fiber membrane for stimulation. The *synaptic cleft*, or

space between the sole foot and muscle fiber membrane, is filled with a gelatinous ground substance.

In the 1930's Sir Henry Dale and colleagues made the important discovery that the transmission of the electrical impulse from nerve to muscle required the intervention of a specific chemical mediator, *acetylcholine*. The arrival of a nerve impulse at the sole foot causes release of the contents of a few hundred vesicles within a millisecond into the synaptic cleft. It is theorized that this impulse causes calcium ions to move from extracellular fluid into the sole feet, in turn causing vesicles to fuse with the membrane of the sole feet and discharge acetylcholine. Acetylcholine diffuses across the synaptic cleft and is bound by a *receptor protein* in the membrane of the muscle fiber. Structural changes in the receptor protein alter the permeability of the membrane in the end plate region, leading to essentially the same sequence of events already described for the initiation of the nerve impulse. The influx of sodium ions causes a rise in membrane potential, the so-called *end plate potential*, which,

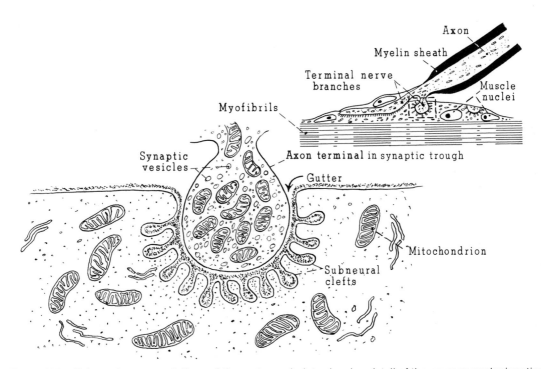

Figure 231. Schematic representations of the motor end plate showing detail of the neuromuscular junction. (From Bloom, W., and Fawcett, D. C.: *Textbook of Histology,* 9th ed., Philadelphia, W. B. Saunders Co., 1968.)

when it reaches the threshold voltage of the muscle fiber, generates a propagated action potential.

In order for the membrane to return to its original conformation and the membrane to its resting state of permeability, ready for a new stimulus, acetylcholine must be inactivated. This is accomplished by the enzyme *cholinesterase,* located around the top of the synaptic gutter. It functions to split acetylcholine into acetic acid and choline in about 1/500th second. The choline is used again for resynthesis of acetylcholine in the nerve terminal by the enzyme *choline acetyltransferase.*

Blockage of Transmission. Transmission at the neuromuscular junction can be blocked by injection of the drug *curare,* which has a greater affinity for the receptor protein than acetylcholine. This can cause death by asphyxia as a result of paralysis of the respiratory muscles. It has long been held that curare can act at junctions only. However, the observation that exposure of a single axon to curare blocks electrical activity at the nodes of Ranvier suggests otherwise. On the basis of this finding and the discovery that acetylcholine is present in the axolemma of nerve fibers, it has been suggested that acetylcholine plays the same role in the initiation of the nerve impulse as it does in transmission at junctions. According to this view, a stimulus releases acetylcholine from a bound site in the membrane. Uptake by a receptor protein leads to the same events as those described for the membrane of a muscle fiber at the end plate region. Supporting this view is the demonstration that inhibitors of cholinesterase (such as certain organophosphates widely used as insecticides) block activity of nerve fibers. Such inhibition would prevent the receptor protein from returning to its resting conformation. A new stimulus would, therefore, have no effect. Action of inhibitors of cholinesterase at neuromuscular junctions can cause muscular paralysis.

Transmission of the Impulse at the Synapse

A nerve fiber terminates in branches, each of which ends in a knoblike body closely associated with the dendrite or body of another cell. These junctions between the terminal endings of one neuron (the *presynaptic cell*) and the dendrites and bodies of another (the *postsynaptic cell*) are called *synapses.* The knoblike terminal endings, the *presynaptic knobs* (also called *presynaptic terminals, end feet,* or *boutons*), contain mitochondria and vesicles filled with a *transmitter substance* (Fig. 223). Each knob is separated from the dendrite or body of the postsynaptic neuron by a *synaptic cleft.* The vesicles of synaptic knobs, unlike those of the sole feet of neuromuscular junctions, which contain only the excitatory transmitter acetylcholine, may contain either an *excitatory* or *inhibitory* transmitter substance.

The arrival of the nerve impulse at the presynaptic terminal causes the discharge of the transmitter by the same process as at the neuromuscular junction. The changes induced by an excitatory neurotransmitter in the postsynaptic membrane are the same as in the membrane of the muscle fiber at the end plate region except that, whereas a single end plate potential will reach threshold voltage and lead to a propagated action potential, a single *excitatory postsynaptic potential* (EPSP) will not reach threshold voltage. *Convergence,* the innervation of a single neuron by the terminal branches of many neurons, makes it possible for a number of excitatory postsynaptic potentials, acting simultaneously, to generate an action potential. This phenomenon is called *spatial summation.* A succession of rapid impulses causes *temporal summation,* which can also generate an action potential. The term *facilitation* is used to describe an increase in neuronal response due to simultaneous or previous stimulation. Adding to the complexity of synaptic connections is *divergence,* the innervation of many neurons by the branches of a single neuron.

Inhibitory neurotransmitters acting on the postsynaptic neuron increase the outflow of potassium ions, thereby making the internal potential more negative ("hyperpolarized"), creating the so-called *inhibitory postsynaptic potential* (IPSP). Not uncommonly, whether or not threshold voltage is reached in a postsynaptic neuron will be determined by the algebraic sum of the excitatory and inhibitory postsynaptic potentials.

Synaptic inhibition can also be caused by a reduction in the release of an excitatory neurotransmitter from presynaptic terminals *(presynaptic inhibition).* Apparently, interneuron knobs overlying excitatory presynaptic terminals release a neurotransmitter that acts on these terminals.

Although a number of substances have been tentatively identified as neurotransmitters, only two, acetylcholine and norepinephrine, meet all of the criteria used by researchers for classification as such. These criteria are the presence of enzymes for its synthesis, a mechanism for termination of its action, reaction with a receptor site upon release and identification of a response. Among the substances that do not meet all of these criteria but are commonly accepted as neurotransmitters are dopamine, serotonin, gamma aminobutyric acid and glycine.

Any given neuron releases only one neurotransmitter and can be classified as either an excitatory or inhibitory neuron. Neurotransmitters are continuously synthesized in the cytoplasm of synaptic knobs. The enzymes required for their synthesis are manufactured in the neuronal cell body and transported down the fiber to the knobs. Excessive neuronal stimulation will eventually deplete the store of transmitter substance, thereby causing cessation of synaptic transmission. This *fatigue* serves as a protective device, as in limiting the duration of an epileptic seizure.

There is evidence that the number of presynaptic terminals may actually increase with prolonged repetitive stimulation. It has been postulated that these physical changes may in part form the basis of memory.

Acidosis and alkalosis affect synaptic transmission by decreasing or increasing excitability. A decrease in pH from the normal of 7.4 to 7.0 depresses neuronal activity, as in severe diabetic coma. An increase in pH from 7.4 to 7.8 often results in convulsions due to increased excitability.

Sensory Receptors

Input by sensory neurons to the central nervous system providing information about changes in the external and internal environment depends upon the existence of *receptors*. A receptor is a peripheral ending of a sensory neuron, or a structure or organ innervated by a sensory neuron, that is especially sensitive (but not exclusively) to a given kind of stimulus (called the *adequate stimulus*). Receptors vary in complexity from the free nerve endings sensitive chiefly to pain to the highly complicated organs for vision and hearing. Stimulation of a receptor causes physical or chemical changes that either directly induce a so-called *generator potential* in the peripheral endings of sensory neurons or evoke a potential in specialized cells of the receptor (such as the hair cells of the organ of hearing), which in turn stimulate sensory neurons.

Each sensory neuron transmits impulses to the central nervous system that will be identified as a specific kind of sensation, such as pain, touch and sound. Since each sensory neuron functions simply as a transmitter of nerve impulses, it is perhaps apparent that the identification of the sensation depends upon the connections made by the sensory pathways in the brain. From this it also follows that no matter how the sensory neuron is stimulated (by the adequate stimulus or otherwise) the sensation perceived will be the same. A greater than threshold stimulus to a receptor will not increase the magnitude of the propagated action potential (all-or-none law), but it will increase the frequency of the impulses. Increasing the intensity of the stimulus also excites more receptors (partly because of different receptor thresholds).

Receptors are difficult to classify, and several somewhat conflicting classification schemes have haphazardly arisen. The broadest classification distinguishes two principal types, receptors for the *general senses* distributed throughout the body and receptors for the *special senses* in the head region, namely, sight, hearing, taste, smell and equilibrium (receptors for the last-named sense are located in the inner ear). The general senses include pain, touch, pressure, cold, warmth and the kinesthetic sense (the perception of the position and movement of parts of the body made possible by receptors in tendons and tissues in and around joints). All of the foregoing receptors provide input that is consciously perceived. Other general receptors can detect bodily changes that are not consciously perceived but play vital roles in maintaining homeostasis. These include receptors for arterial pressure (in the aorta and the carotid sinus), arterial oxygen (in the aortic and carotid bodies), arterial carbon dioxide (in the medulla of the brain and the aortic and carotid bodies), blood temperature, osmotic pressure and glucose concentration (in the hypothalamus).

Among other terms frequently encountered in descriptions of sensory receptors are the following: *Proprioceptors* — receptors of vital importance for locomotor and postural responses, including kinesthetic receptors, the muscle spindle and equilibrium receptors in the inner ear. *Somesthetic receptors* (G. *soma,* the body; G. *aithetikos,* of perception) — frequently used to describe general body receptors for consciously perceived sensations. *Exteroceptors* — receptors responding to stimuli from the external environment, from a distance or on the body surface. *Interoceptors* — receptors responding to stimuli from the internal environment, excluding muscles, tendons and joints.

The simplest sensory receptors are *free nerve endings* — undifferentiated peripheral endings of sensory nerve fibers. All pain receptors are of this type. Although the largest proportion of free nerve endings are receptors for pain, functionally different free nerve endings apparently exist, not distinguishable anatomically, which are sensitive to crude touch, pressure, itch and temperature. *Meissner's corpuscles* (Fig. 232), receptors for discrete touch, are especially numerous in the upper dermis of the hands, feet, lips and nipples, and in the mucous membrane of the tip of the tongue. Other touch receptors include *Merkel's discs,* found in great numbers in the deepest epidermal layer of fingertips, and the end organs of hair (basket-like arrangements of nerve fibers around hair follicles). *Ruffini's end organs* and *Krause's end bulbs* have been described as warmth and cold receptors, respectively, but may also be receptors for touch and pressure. *Pacinian corpuscles* are very large receptors sensitive to deep pressure. They are widely distributed in such areas as the deep layers of the skin and under mucous and serous membranes. Ruffini's end organs located in joint capsules are the principal kinesthetic receptors. Other kinesthetic receptors are the *Golgi tendon receptors* and Pacinian corpuscles in tissues in and around joints.

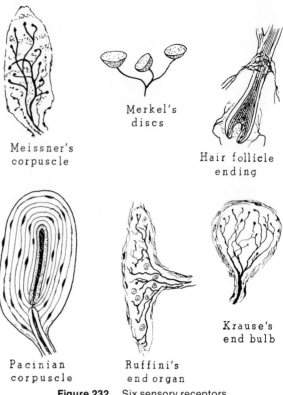

Merkel's discs

Meissner's corpuscle

Hair follicle ending

Krause's end bulb

Pacinian corpuscle

Ruffini's end organ

Figure 232.   Six sensory receptors.

A characteristic property of receptors is their *adaptation* to stimulation. This means that the frequency of impulses declines with the continued application of a stimulus of constant strength. Consequently, the sensation decreases in intensity and may disappear. In the case of *rapidly adapting receptors,* such as the Pacinian corpuscle and some of the touch receptors, namely, the hair receptors and Meissner's corpuscles, the impulses are extinguished within a second or less. Such receptors can provide information about changes in or movement of stimuli. Pacinian corpuscles, for example, which adapt to extinction within a few hundredths of a second, can detect high frequency vibrations. *Poorly adapting receptors* adapt slowly and not to extinction. Pain receptors are an example of poorly adapting receptors that continue to transmit impulses as long as they are stimulated. Other poorly adapting receptors are the muscle spindle, Ruffini's end organs, Merkel's discs and the receptors for blood pressure, oxygen and carbon dioxide.

Receptors and Nerve Fiber Types. Nerve fibers can be classified according to diameter (reflecting the degree of myelination) and velocity of conduction. Each kind of sensory receptor is served by a specific type of fiber. Type A fibers are myelinated and are subclassified (from the largest and fastest conductors to the smallest and slowest conductors) as A-α, A-β, A-γ and A-δ. Type B fibers are also myelinated but are slightly smaller than the A-δ fibers. Type C fibers are very small, nonmyelinated fibers with the slowest conduction rates. Impulses from muscle spindles are transmitted by A-α fibers (diameter, 13–20 μ; velocity, 70–120 meters/sec.). Receptors for discrete touch (Meissner's corpuscles and Merkel's discs), deep pressure and kinesthesia are innervated by A-β fibers (diameter, 8–13 μ; velocity, 10–40 meters/sec.). Pain is transmitted by two kinds of fibers: A-δ fibers (diameter, 1–4 μ; velocity, 5–15 meters/sec.), which transmit "fast" pain, and C fibers (diameter, 0.2–1 μ; velocity, 0.2–2 meters/sec.), which transmit "slow" pain. Pain is frequently sensed in two phases—an immediate, sharp, localized, painful sensation followed by a more diffuse burning sensation that may persist and become unbearable. The former is associated with A-δ fibers, the latter with C fibers. Aching pain, arising from deep structures and the viscera (often felt on the body surface), is also transmitted by C fibers.

CENTRAL NERVOUS SYSTEM

The *central nervous system,* as mentioned in the beginning of this chapter, includes the brain and spinal cord (Fig. 233).

The central nervous system is divided grossly into gray and white matter. **Gray matter** is so called because of its appearance and the preponderance of nerve cell bodies and true dendrites. **White matter,** on the other hand, is composed chiefly of myelinated nerve fibers—white in gross appearance—and few, if any, nerve cell bodies. In the spinal cord an H-shaped central region of gray matter is surrounded by white matter. In the brain the gray matter is broken into clumps or is present as a surface layer (cortex) of the cerebrum and cerebellum.

The term **nucleus,** when applied to the nervous system, designates a mass of gray

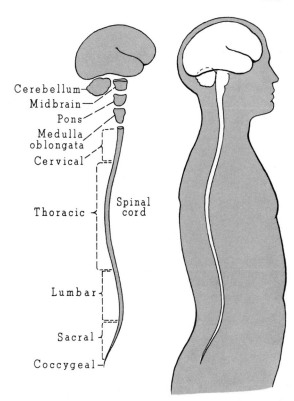

Figure 233. Diagram showing major anatomic divisions of the central nervous system.

matter in any part of the brain or spinal cord. **Ganglion** also means a cluster of nerve cell bodies and dendrites, but usually refers to those cells located outside the brain and spinal cord.

THE BRAIN

The first mention of the term *brain* is found in the Egyptian scrolls of papyrus. Historically, the Greeks did not have a word for the brain. Due to rhythmic movements which seemed closely related with what occurred in the mind, they placed its location in the midriff, since the rhythm of breathing is closely related to mental states.

The word brain actually refers to "that part of the central nervous system contained within the skull." It is the most complex and largest mass of nervous tissue in the body and contains literally billions of nerve cells. It has been estimated that an electron tube computer would have to be the size of a New York City skyscraper to contain the

FOREBRAIN $\begin{cases} \text{telencephalon} — \text{cerebrum} \\ \\ \text{diencephalon} \begin{cases} \text{thalamus} \\ \text{hypothalamus} \end{cases} \end{cases}$

MIDBRAIN —mesencephalon $\begin{cases} \text{corpora} \\ \quad \text{quadrigemina} \\ \\ \text{cerebral} \\ \quad \text{peduncles} \end{cases}$

HINDBRAIN $\begin{cases} \text{metencephalon} \begin{cases} \text{cerebellum} \\ \text{pons} \end{cases} \\ \\ \text{myelencephalon} — \begin{array}{l}\text{medulla} \\ \quad \text{oblongata}\end{array} \end{cases}$

Figure 234. Major subdivisions of the brain.

equipment in the 3 pounds or so of the human brain.

The weight of the brain is an indication of growth which, in early life, depends on enlargement of cells and their processes, an increase in the neuroglial constituents, and myelinization of the nerve fibers. The average weight of the human brain in the adult is approximately 1380 grams in the male and 1250 grams in the female. The brain grows rapidly up to the fifth year of life and stops growing after the age of 20. During old age, the weight of the brain decreases. When fully developed, the brain is a large organ filling the cranial cavity and applied closely to the inner wall of the skull. The brain is subdivided into three major areas (Fig. 234) which are, in turn, composed of subdivisions. These areas, arising during embryological development (Fig. 235), are the forebrain (prosencephalon), midbrain (mesencephalon) and hindbrain (rhombencephalon).

I. Forebrain
   A. Cerebrum (telencephalon)
      1. Gray matter (cerebral cortex, the covering)

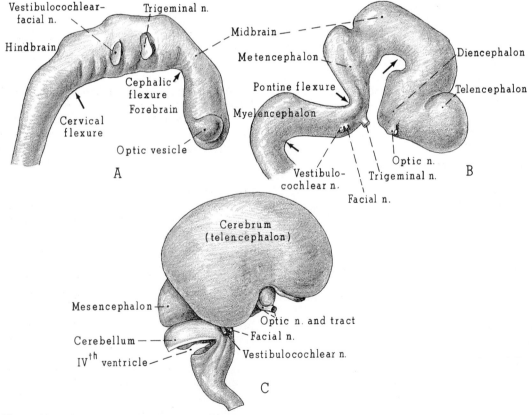

Figure 235. *Embryologic development of the brain.* Three primary brain vesicles can be recognized: the forebrain (prosencephalon), the midbrain (mesencephalon), and the hindbrain (rhombencephalon). *A* and *B* show development at about 3 weeks and 6 weeks, respectively. Ultimately the forebrain subdivides into the telencephalon and the diencephalon, the midbrain remains the mesencephalon, and the rhombencephalon becomes the metencephalon and myelencephalon. *C* shows the brain at approximately 11 weeks of development.

2. White matter (core)
   B. Diencephalon
      1. Thalamus
      2. Hypothalamus
II. Midbrain (mesencephalon)
III. Hindbrain (rhombencephalon)
   A. Pons
   B. Medulla
   C. Cerebellum

The term *brain stem* refers to those parts of the brain remaining after removal of the cerebrum and cerebellum.

Forebrain

Cerebrum. The cerebrum (Figs. 236 to 238) is the largest portion of the brain, representing approximately seven-eighths of its total weight. Nerve centers governing all sensory and motor activities, as well as poorly defined areas which determine reason, memory, and intelligence, are located in the cerebrum.

With the increase in brain size occurring during embryonic development, the area of cortical gray matter expands out of all proportion and volume to the white matter upon which it rests. As a result, the surface rolls and folds upon itself. Each bulge produced in this manner is called a **gyrus,** or convolution. These gyri do not occur haphazardly but are present in a distinguishable pattern. If the intervening furrow is shallow, it is called a **sulcus;** if it is deep, it is referred to as a **fissure.** The *longitudinal fissure* extends from the posterior aspect to the anterior border of the cerebrum, almost completely dividing it into two hemispheres.

The **cerebral hemispheres** with their coverings constitute the major part of the brain. These hemispheres are "mirror twins," each with a full set of centers for sensory and motor activities of the body, and each associated for the most part with one side of the body, i.e., the right side of the brain controls the left side of the body and the left side of the brain controls the right side of the body.

When one area of the cerebrum is damaged, the corresponding area of the other hemisphere can often develop control over the functions governed by the damaged region, illustrating great adaptability.

Fiber tracts connecting the two hemispheres are called **commissural fiber tracts.** The *corpus callosum* (the "great cerebral commissure") is the largest of the commissural tracts (Figs. 239 and 240). Its size and position suggest that its function is crucial to the proper performance of the cerebrum. If the corpus callosum is divided in two, an organism with two mental units is created, each with its own will competing for control over the whole. The corpus callosum allows the two hemispheres to share learning and memory.

Association fiber tracts connect parts of the same hemisphere. They may be short, connecting adjoining gyri, or long, connecting distant gyri. Connecting the cortex with other parts of the brain and the spinal cord are **projection fiber tracts.**

Each hemisphere possesses five sulci of significance. Each sulcus serves to locate its corresponding gyrus of known function (Figs. 241 and 242).

The *lateral sulcus* (fissure of Sylvius) sweeps backward above the temporal lobe and continues over the superolateral surface

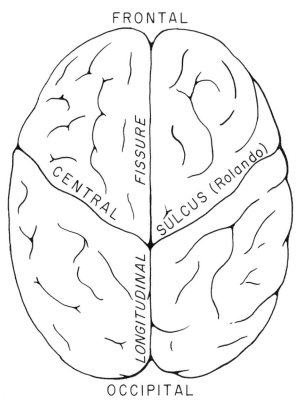

Figure 236. Major fissures of the brain, superior view.

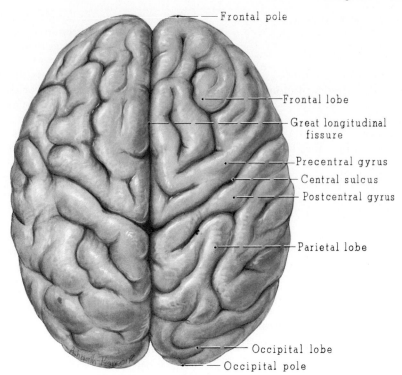

Frontal pole

Frontal lobe

Great longitudinal fissure

Precentral gyrus

Central sulcus

Postcentral gyrus

Parietal lobe

Occipital lobe

Occipital pole

Figure 237. Superior view of the brain.

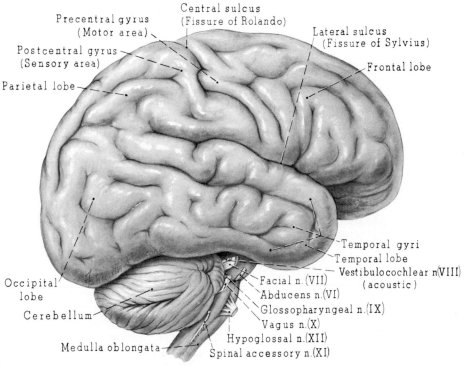

Precentral gyrus (Motor area)

Central sulcus (Fissure of Rolando)

Lateral sulcus (Fissure of Sylvius)

Postcentral gyrus (Sensory area)

Frontal lobe

Parietal lobe

Temporal gyri

Temporal lobe

Vestibulocochlear n(VIII) (acoustic)

Facial n. (VII)

Abducens n.(VI)

Occipital lobe

Glossopharyngeal n.(IX)

Cerebellum

Vagus n.(X)

Hypoglossal n.(XII)

Medulla oblongata

Spinal accessory n.(XI)

Figure 238. Right side of the brain showing cerebrum, cerebellum, and spinal cord. Several cranial nerves are seen.

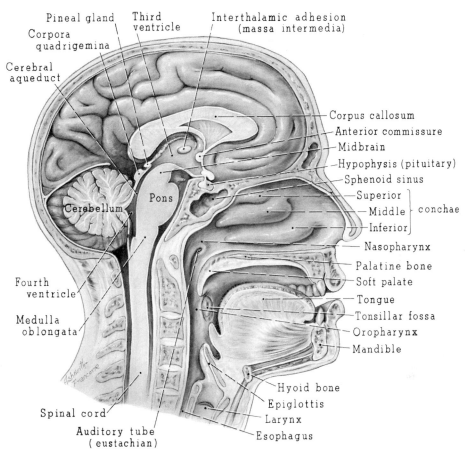

Figure 239. Sagittal section through the head showing relationship of cerebellum, cerebrum, and spinal cord to other parts of the head and neck.

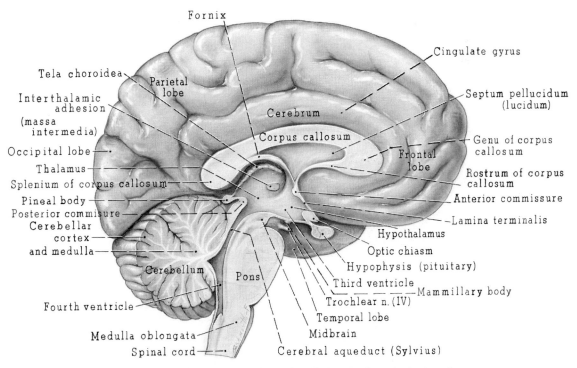

Figure 240. Sagittal view of the left half of the brain and spinal cord.

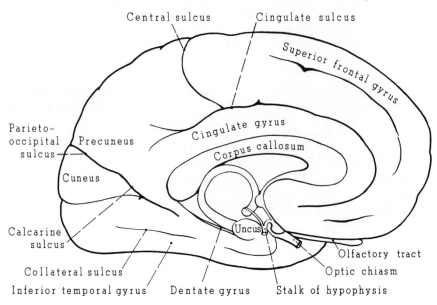

Figure 241.   Major landmarks of the medial portion of the left cerebral hemisphere.

almost horizontally backward. The lateral sulcus is associated with centers for speech and hearing.

The *central sulcus* (fissure of Rolando) commences at the midpoint of the superior border and extends inferiorly toward the lateral sulcus, separating the frontal and parietal lobes. The central sulcus is associated with centers for both motor and sensory function.

The *sulcus cinguli* is a prominent sulcus on the medial surface of the hemisphere, extending anteroposteriorly parallel to the corpus callosum. The cortex surrounding this sulcus functions in both olfactory and emotional responses.

The *calcarine sulcus* begins as the deep sulcus on the inferomedial surface above and adjacent to the corpus callosum. At the medial surface it divides into two smaller

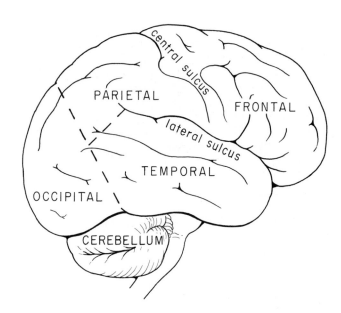

Figure 242.   Lobes of the cerebral cortex, lateral view, right side.

sulci, a lower horizontal one (postcalcarine) and an upper one (parieto-occipital). These sulci include the visual areas.

The *collateral sulcus* runs parallel to the medial border and is closely associated with the center of smell.

CEREBRAL CORTEX. The cerebral cortex is the gray outer layer of the cerebrum (Figs. 243 to 245). Even before knowledge of the microscopic anatomy of the cortex was available, feeble attempts were made to discern the function of the cerebral cortex. During the Renaissance, for instance, physicians speculated as to the nature of the "seat of intelligence." An understanding of brain physiology, however, was delayed until it became possible to stimulate and remove portions of the central nervous system in the living animal. In the nineteenth century, many studies on cerebral localization were undertaken, particularly in attempts to localize speech to a given region. It was Broca in 1861 who correlated

injury to the left frontal convolution with a loss of speech in a right-handed person; that is, a right-handed person will usually have a dominant left hemisphere. Recent studies have shown that most people have a dominant left hemisphere, whether or not they are right-handed. (Cerebral dominance is further discussed on page 300.)

Brodmann divided the human cortex into 52 areas and employed numbers to designate each. The Brodmann scheme will be utilized in subsequent discussions to describe association and projection areas of the brain.

Actual division of the cerebrum into lobes is a convenience, since these areas serve as reference points for discussion. These lobes bear the name of the overlying bones of the skull, and include the frontal parietal, temporal, and occipital lobes (Figs. 242 and 243).

Frontal Lobe. The frontal lobe includes all the cortex lying anterior to the central

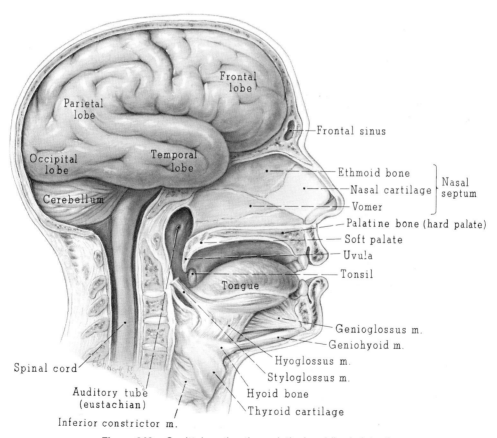

Figure 243. Sagittal section through the head (brain intact).

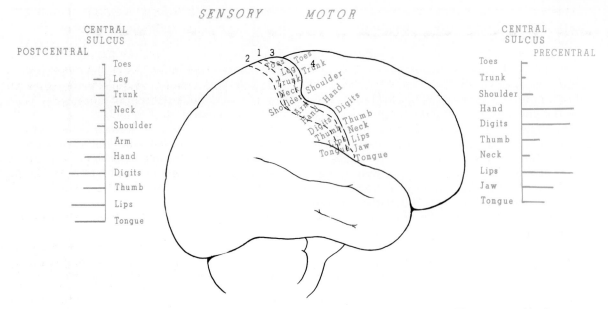

Figure 244. Lateral view of the brain showing somesthetic and primary motor areas. The amount of brain surface related to a specific part of the body is not proportionate to the size of the part but to the extent of its use, as illustrated diagrammatically.

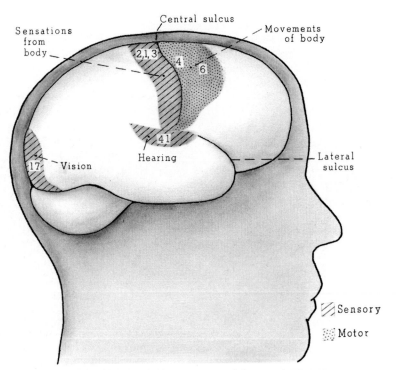

Figure 245. Major projection areas of the cerebral cortex.

sulcus and above the lateral sulcus. The precentral gyrus, or primary motor area, is area 4 of Brodmann. Immediately anterior to this is area 6, another important motor area.

Parietal Lobe. This lobe extends from the central sulcus about four-fifths of the way around the cortex and joins the occipital lobe at the posterior aspect of the brain. The parietal lobe includes sensory areas 1, 2 and 3 of Brodmann, which lie in the postcentral gyrus. The parietal cortex is the receptive area for fine sensory stimuli, and the highest integration and coordination of sensory information is carried on in this area.

Temporal Lobe. This lobe lies beneath the lateral sulcus. Area 41, the sensory receptive area for auditory impulses, and areas 41 and 42, the correlative centers for auditory impulses, are found in the temporal lobe.

Occipital Lobe. The occipital lobe occupies the posterior segment of the cerebral hemisphere. Actually no true separation exists between the occipital lobe and the parietal and temporal lobes, although the parieto-occipital sulcus is considered the anterior margin. Area 17, the primary visual area, and adjacent areas 18 and 19, the correlation centers for visual impulses, are found in the occipital lobe.

Projection Areas. Portions of the cortex that have become specialized for dispatch of motor directives (such as area 4) and for reception of sensory messages (such as areas 1, 2 and 3) are known as *projection areas* (Fig. 245).

Association Areas. The brain must possess memory to relate information of the moment with that of the past and to recognize its significance. This involves functional correction, repeated exchanges of data and synthesis of data. Such elaborate functions of the cortex are performed by the association areas. More than three-fourths of the cerebral cortex is occupied by association areas. Although these areas also receive projection fibers, their principal function is to integrate information received from various sources.

The Basal Ganglia (Figs. 246 and 247). The basal ganglia are four paired masses of gray matter embedded in the white matter of the cerebral hemispheres. The basal ganglia include the caudate nucleus (medial portion) and the putamen and globus pallidus (lateral portion), collectively called the lentiform nucleus. These nuclei, together with the white matter

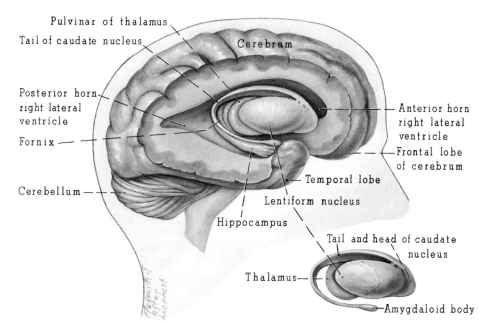

Figure 246. Schematic representation of basal ganglia.

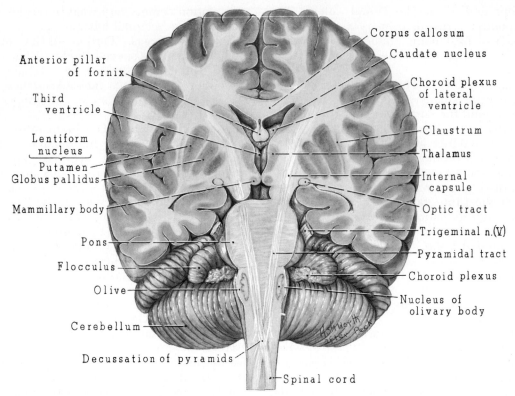

Figure 247. Frontal or coronal section through the brain showing basal ganglia and brainstem. Note discussation of the corticospinal (pyramidal) tract just prior to entering the spinal cord.

separating them, constitute the *corpus striatum* (Latin for striped body), so named for its banded appearance. The large mass of fibers constituting the white matter is called the *internal capsule.* It contains fibers leading to and from the cerebral cortex that connect the cortex to the rest of the brain and spinal cord. Fibers fanning out from the internal capsule to various parts of the cortex are known as the *corona radiata.* If a small blood vessel in the area ruptures (not uncommon in this region), an interference with the efferent tracts descending from the cortex can occur, with resultant paralysis. The basal ganglia play an important role in the control of motor function, and injury to them produces either unilateral or bilateral signs, including tremor, rigidity and uncontrolled, aimless movements. The functions of the basal ganglia are further discussed in the description of the extrapyramidal system on page 000.

Electroencephalograms – Electrical Activity of the Cerebral Cortex. Human brain cells generate electrical potentials that can be measured through the skull and are the basis of electroencephalography, a clinical diagnostic procedure used as an aid in diagnosis of epilepsy, brain tumor, hemorrhage and other disorders. The electroencephalogram is recorded by placing electrodes on the individual's head. EEG varies from the asynchronous, high frequency, low voltage response of the mentally active or excited state through the slow activity of the relaxed state (alpha rhythms) to the very slow activity of deep sleep. During epileptic seizures the EEG shows synchronous, very high voltage discharges.

The Diencephalon. The thalamus and hypothalamus constitute the diencephalon and are located in the forebrain along with the cerebrum.

THE THALAMUS. The *thalamus,* a paired structure, consists of large masses of gray matter located below the corpus callosum, joined in the midline by the *intermediate mass* (interthalamic adhesion). It is a relay center for all kinds of sensory impulses (except olfactory impulses) as they travel from the peripheral sensory receptors to the sensory areas of the cerebral cortex. The crude identification of stimuli as pain, variation of tempeature, or touch is the result of thalamic integrations. (For further details see description of sensory pathways to the brain on page 285.)

Besides its sensory activities, the thalamus is functionally interrelated with the major motor centers. It occupies a position between the cerebral motor cortex and the cerebellum, and also between the cerebral motor cortex and the basal ganglia, and relays efferent impulses from these centers to the motor cortex. Impulses passing from the hypothalamus to the prefrontal area of the cerebral cortex also are relayed in the thalamus and serve in the integration of emotional behavior. (Emotional behavior is further discussed on page 297.)

THE HYPOTHALAMUS (Fig. 240). The hypothalamus lies beneath the thalamus. Mainly through studies of laboratory animals, the hypothalamus has been found to be concerned with the regulation of peripheral autonomic nervous system discharges accompanying behavior and emotional expression. Among hypothalamic functions are the regulation of body water and electrolyte concentrations, temperature control, and regulation of feeding activities and the metabolism of fats and carbohydrates. It also manufactures hormones of the neurohypophysis (posterior pituitary gland) and controls secretion by both the posterior and the anterior pituitary, and thus has an important role in regulating endocrine functions and in maintaining normal sexual behavior and reproduction. The pituitary gland is attached to the hypothalamus by a narrow stalk, the *infundibulum.* The area of the hypothalamus adjacent to the infundibulum is called the *tuber cinereum.* In the posterior part of the hypothalamus is a pair of rounded *mammillary bodies.*

Mesencephalon (Midbrain)

The midbrain is found between the forebrain and the hindbrain. Several nuclear masses are located on its posterior surface, the tectum (Latin for roof) above the cerebral aqueduct (Fig. 239). Four of these nuclear masses are present as small elevations: the upper two, or *superior colliculi,*

are involved in visual reflexes, especially the coordination of tracking movements (described in Chapter 9, on page 314), and the lower two, or *inferior colliculi,* are associated with hearing. The four are known collectively as the *corpora quadrigemina.* Two large diverging stalks emerging ventrally from each half of the cerebrum form the anterior part of the midbrain. The stalks are called *cerebral peduncles;* they constitute the main motor connection between the forebrain and the hindbrain. The midportion of the mesencephalon, known as the *tegmentum,* contains important efferent and afferent pathways. The tegmentum also contains the *red nucleus,* which is connected with the cerebellum. This nucleus is involved in motor movement and postural reflex patterns.

Hindbrain

Cerebellum (Fig. 247). The cerebellum occupies the posterior cranial fossa. It is separated from the cerebral hemispheres by the *tentorium cerebelli* (see p. 245).

The cerebellum is oval in shape, with a central constriction and lateral expanded portions. The constricted central portion is called the *vermis* (Latin for worm) and the lateral expanded portions, the *hemispheres.* The cerebellum resembles the cerebrum in structure, with the gray matter forming a layer of cortex placed on the surface rather than centrally located, as in the spinal cord. Cross section of the cerebellum reveals its patterns of folds and fissures outlined by white matter, which led anatomists of the medieval period to give the cerebellar white matter the name *arbor vitae* (Latin for tree of life).

The cerebellum is divided into lobes by deep and distinct fissures. These lobes include the anterior, posterior and flocculonodular lobes. The *anterior* and *posterior lobes* are concerned with the function of movement; the *flocculonodular lobe* is concerned with the function of equilibrium. The cerebellum is connected by afferent and efferent pathways with all other parts of the central nervous system. In general, the cerebellum greatly aids the motor cortex of the cerebral hemispheres in the *integration* of voluntary movement. The role of the cerebellum is further discussed on page 295.

The Pons (Figs. 240 and 247). The pons lies anterior to the cerebellum and between the midbrain and medulla. On its ventral surface is a midline groove for the basilar artery. As the name implies, the pons is a bridgelike structure, consisting almost entirely of white matter linking the various parts of the brain and serving as a relay station from the medulla to the higher cortical centers. There are also several important nuclear groups for the cranial nerves.

Medulla Oblongata (Fig. 240). The medulla oblongata is continuous with the spinal cord on one end and with the pons on the other. It lies ventral to the cerebellum, and its posterior aspect forms the floor of the fourth ventricle (the ventricles of the brain are described on this page. On the ventral surface of the medulla are the *pyramids*, which, as the name implies, are pyramid-shaped tracts. These tracts are a posterior continuation of a portion of the tracts that constitute the cerebral peduncles of the midbrain (other tracts of the cerebral peduncles lead to the cerebellum via the pons). The pyramidal tracts are the pathways for initiating skillful movements of skeletal muscles (see discussion of the pyramidal system on page 293). Two prominent nuclei, the *nucleus gracilis* and *nucleus cuneatus*, are located on the posterior portion of the medulla. It is in these nuclei that fibers from the corresponding tracts in the cord (described on page 286) synapse. Externally, the medulla resembles the upper part of the spinal cord. Consequently, it is often called the spinal bulb; but the medulla is thicker than the cord and consists of central gray matter broken into more or less distinct nests of cell bodies, or nuclear masses, with columns of white matter interwoven among the nuclei. All the afferent and efferent tracts of the spinal cord are represented in the medulla, and many of these decussate, or cross, from one side to the other, whereas others terminate. The medulla functions primarily as a relay station for passage of impulses between the cord and the brain, and contains cardiac, vasoconstrictor and respiratory centers, as well as many mechanisms for controlling reflex activities.

Reticular Formation. Scattered throughout the area of the midbrain, pons, and medulla are numerous large and small neurons related to each other by small processes. These neurons and their fibers constitute the reticular formation. They are not often collected into distinct nuclei; but the lateral reticular and inferior olivary nuclei are exceptions, in that they are readily identified as nuclear groups. The reticular formation is capable of modifying the reflex activity of the spinal neurons. It is essential for cortical activities, such as initiating and maintaining wakefulness; hence, it is often called an activating system. Injury to this system can result in unconsciousness. (The functions of the reticular formation are further explained in connection with the description of sensory and motor pathways on pages 288 and 294.)

Ventricles of the Brain

At an early stage, the embryonic central nervous system is a hollow *neural tube.* The brain develops as an expansion of the superior end of this tube with the formation of cavities, called *ventricles,* continuous with the central canal of the spinal cord, the remnant of the embryonic neural tube. The ventricular system (Figs. 248 to 250) includes two lateral ventricles, the third ventricle, the cerebral aqueduct, and the fourth ventricle. The lateral ventricles are inside the cerebral hemispheres. Each possesses a posterior, anterior, and inferior portion (horn). The posterior horn extends into the occipital lobe, the anterior horn into the frontal lobe, and the inferior horn into the temporal lobe. The **lateral ventricles** are separated from each other by a thin, translucent partition, the *septum pellucidum* (Fig. 240). Each lateral ventricle communicates with the **third ventricle** by way of the **interventricular foramen** (foramen of Monro). The third ventricle is a small, slitlike cavity in the center of the diencephalon continuous with the **cerebral aqueduct of Sylvius,** a canal which passes lengthwise through the midbrain between the cerebral peduncles and the corpora quadrigemina to connect the third and fourth ventricles. The **fourth ventricle** lies between the cerebellum on the posterior side and the pons and medulla on the anterior side.

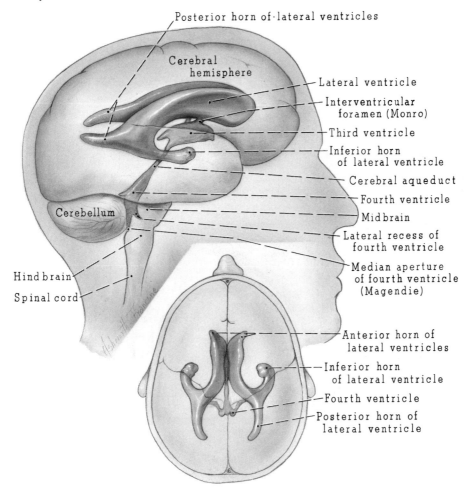

Posterior horn of·lateral ventricles

Cerebral hemisphere

Lateral ventricle

Interventricular foramen (Monro)

Third ventricle

Inferior horn of lateral ventricle

Cerebral aqueduct

Fourth ventricle

Midbrain

Lateral recess of fourth ventricle

Median aperture of fourth ventricle (Magendie)

Cerebellum

Hindbrain

Spinal cord

Anterior horn of lateral ventricles

Inferior horn of lateral ventricle

Fourth ventricle

Posterior horn of lateral ventricle

Figure 248. Ventricular system, lateral and superior views.

Meninges

Three membranes collectively known as the meninges (singular, meninx) provide protection to the brain and spinal cord (Fig. 251). From outside in, these are the dura mater, arachnoid, and pia mater.

Dura Mater. The dura mater (Latin for hard mother), the outer meninx, is made of dense fibrous tissue. There are two portions of the dura, cranial and spinal. The cranial dura is arranged in two layers, closely connected except where they separate to form sinuses for the passage of venous blood. The outer *endosteal layer* is adherent to the bones of the skull and forms the internal periosteum. This layer terminates at the foramen magnum, and its place is taken by the periosteal lining of the vertebral canal. The inner, or *meningeal*, layer

covers the brain and sends numerous prolongations inward for support and protection of the different lobes of the brain. The inner layer becomes continuous with the spinal dura mater.

Four extensions of the meningeal dura project into the cranial cavity: the falx cerebelli (between the two cerebellar hemispheres), the falx cerebri (in the longitudinal fissure separating the two cerebral hemispheres), the tentorium cerebelli (separating the cerebellum from the cerebrum) and the diaphragma sellae (overlying the pituitary gland). These projections also form the venous sinuses, situated between the endosteal and meningeal layers of the dura, which return blood from the brain to the blood stream (the veins of the brain open into the sinuses).

The Arachnoid. The arachnoid is a deli-

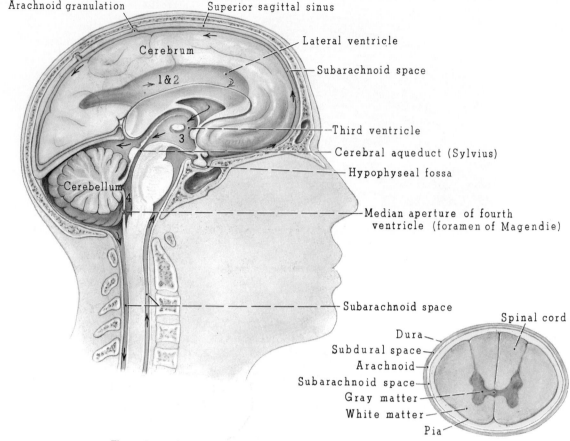

Figure 249.   Circulation of cerebrospinal fluid in brain and spinal cord.

cate serous membrane located between the dura and pia. As the name implies, it has the microscopic appearance of a spider web. The cranial portion invests the brain loosely and, with the exception of the longitudinal fissure, it passes over the various convolutions and sulci and does not dip down into them. The spinal portion is tubular and surrounds the cord loosely. The subarachnoid space between the arachnoid and the pia is occupied by thin, delicate connective tissue trabeculae, and intercommunicating channels in which cerebrospinal fluid is contained. Along the base of the brain, the pia and the arachnoid are separated to form the arachnoid cisternae.

The Pia Mater. The pia mater is a vascular membrane consisting of a plexus of fine blood vessels held together by areolar connective tissue. The cranial portion invests the surface of the brain and dips down between the convolutions; the spinal portion is thicker, less vascular, and closely

adherent to the entire surface of the spinal cord, sending processes into the ventral fissure.

The pia mater extends below the spinal cord (which ends in a conelike formation, the conus medullaris, at about the second lumbar vertebra) as a slender filament called the *filum terminale* (Fig. 252). The dura mater and underlying arachnoid also continue below the spinal cord, the dura forming a covering of the end of the filum terminale, called the *coccygeal ligament,* which blends with the periosteum of the coccyx. Cerebrospinal fluid (see below) can be conveniently obtained by tapping the subarachnoid space between the third and fourth lumbar vertebrae (Fig. 253).

Cerebrospinal Fluid

Cerebrospinal fluid (Fig. 249 *circulates within the ventricles, the central canal of*

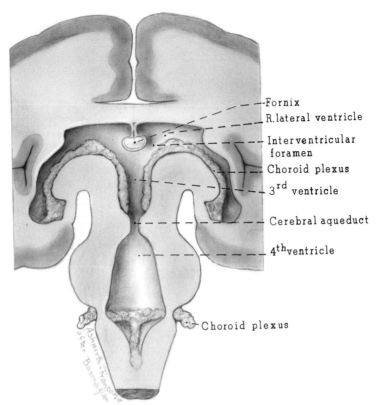

Figure 250.   Diagrammatic representation of the ventricles of the brain. (From Basmajian, J. V.: *Primary Anatomy,* Sixth Edition, Baltimore, The Williams & Wilkins Co., 1970.)

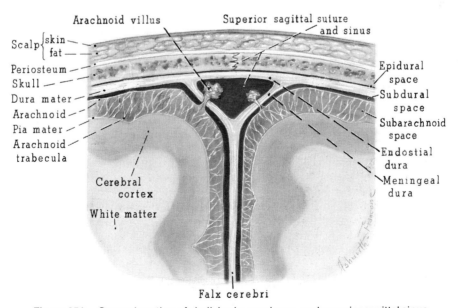

Figure 251.   Coronal section of skull, brain, meninges, and superior sagittal sinus.

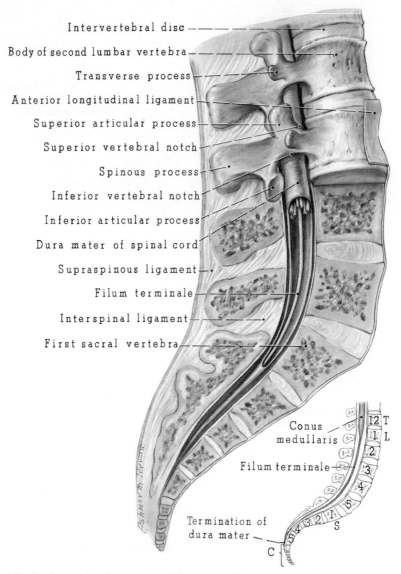

Figure 252. Vertebral column, showing structure of vertebrae, filum terminale, and termination of dura mater.

the spinal cord and also within meshes of the subarachnoid space. It is colorless, with a composition similar to that of lymph. It consists of water with traces of protein, glucose, lymphocytes and even some hormones.

The volume of cerebrospinal fluid ranges from 80 to 200 ml. Fifteen ml is found in the ventricular cavities, and the remainder is in the subarachnoid spaces. The fluid serves as a water jacket to guard the brain and spinal cord against injury. It also provides buoy-

ancy, reducing the effective weight of the brain about 30-fold.

Cerebrospinal fluid is continuously formed in all four ventricles by active secretion, principally from the capillaries of the **choroid plexuses** (pouchlike projections of the pia mater into the ventricles covered with the ependymal lining of the ventricles). The fluid circulates (Fig. 249) from each lateral ventricle through an interventricular foramen (Latin for opening) into the third ventricle and then passes through the

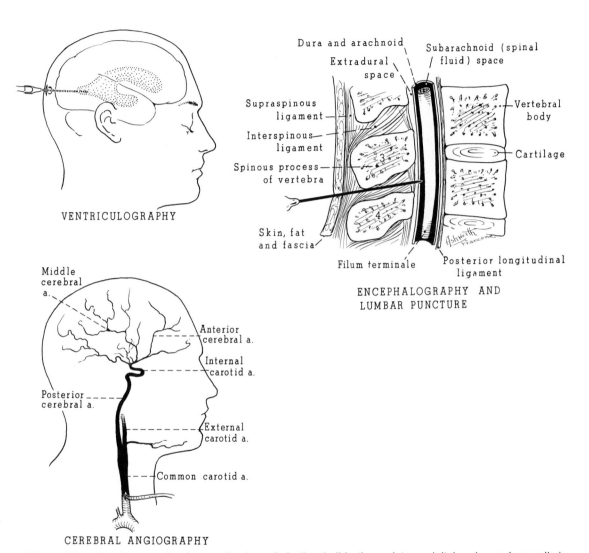

VENTRICULOGRAPHY

ENCEPHALOGRAPHY AND
LUMBAR PUNCTURE

CEREBRAL ANGIOGRAPHY

Figure 253. *Ventriculography:* An opening is made in the skull in the parieto-occipital region and a needle is introduced into the lateral ventricle. The cerebrospinal fluid is slowly withdrawn and replaced by air and x-ray examinations are made.

Encephalography: X-ray examination of the brain is made following replacement of cerebrospinal fluid by air via the lumbar puncture route.

Lumbar puncture: Tapping of the subarachnoid space in the lumbar region, usually between the third and fourth lumbar vertebrae.

Cerebral angiography: X-ray examination of the vascular system of the brain is made after the injection of radiopaque material into the common carotid artery.

cerebral aqueduct into the fourth ventricle and spinal canal. It flows into the subarachnoid space from the fourth ventricle via three foramina—one medial aperture (foramen of Magendie), and two lateral apertures (foramina of Luschka). Cerebrospinal fluid drains from the subarachnoid space into the sagittal venous sinus through projections of the arachnoid into the venous sinus called **arachnoid villi** (Fig. 251).

Hydrocephalus (Fig. 254). Hydrocephalus is a condition that occurs when blockage of circulation of cerebrospinal fluid increases pressure on the surface of the brain or cord. It is not common for an increased formation of fluid to be responsible for this condition except in a tumor of the choroid plexus. Congenital hydrocephalus is spoken of as either communicating or noncommunicating, depending on whether there is transmission of fluid between the ventricles and subarachnoid spaces. Obstruction of the flow of fluid is probably the commonest cause of hydrocephalus. If this obstruction occurs before the time the sutures of the skull ordinarily close, the increased intracranial pressure produces an expansion of the brain and its coverings, with the entire head increasing progressively in size. The soft bones of the infant's skull are pushed apart, and compression of the cortex results, until only a paper-thin ribbon of cerebral tissue remains. Despite marked depression of the cerebral cortex, the nerve cells frequently show a remarkable capacity for survival.

Following closure of the sutures, the brain can no longer yield to increasing hydrocephalus, and changes in brain tissue are then more destructive.

The signs and symptoms of hydrocephalus can be evident at the time of birth. The head enlarges, the anterior fontanelle bulges and the suture lines of the skull separate. The veins of the scalp dilate, becoming prominent.

Surgical treatment consists of shunting the cerebrospinal fluid from one compartment into another in the normal fluid pathways, or from the cerebrospinal fluid compartments to some other area of the body where it can be absorbed. One of the techniques is described in Figure 255.

Disorders Involving the Brain

Meningitis. Meningitis is an infection of the meninges. The diagnosis depends on a history of infection, the so-called meningeal

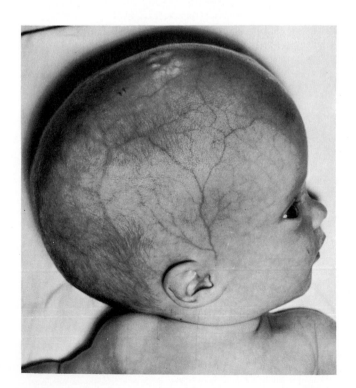

Figure 254. Child, age 4 months, with hydrocephalus.

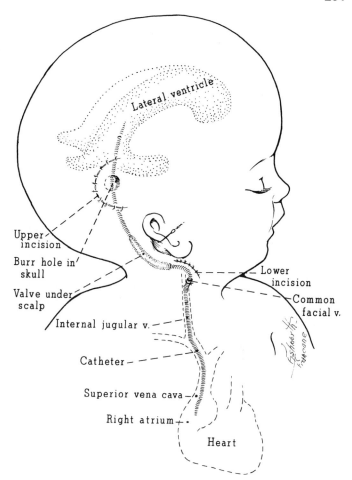

Figure 255. Operative procedure for hydrocephalus in which a catheter drains the ventricular system into the right atrium.

signs (such as stiffness of the neck), and abnormalities in the spinal fluid. In small infants, manifestations of mild meningitis are sometimes masked for several days, with the symptoms suggesting an upper respiratory infection.

Traumatic Head Injuries. A common injury is one in which a rapidly moving blunt object strikes the head or the head is flung against a hard surface. Such blunt head injuries almost always result in at least brief loss of consciousness, and even though the skull is not penetrated or bone fragments driven into the cavity, the brain may suffer gross damage, e.g., contusion, laceration, hemorrhage, swelling, herniation. Crushing injuries or injury from high-velocity missiles may produce severe and often fatal damage without immediate loss of consciousness.

Concussion is defined as a transient state of paralysis of nervous function, or loss of consciousness. Even when consciousness is

not lost, in a few days symptoms may arise, including headache, dizziness, loss of self-confidence, nervousness, fatigue, inability to sleep, and depression. No account has been given of the mechanism of these symptoms.

Other symptoms may occur that are an indication of some process in addition to concussion; symptoms include delayed traumatic collapse, epilepsy, monoplegia or paraplegia, coma or acute drowsiness, confusion, or headache. The bases of these symptoms can be several, ranging from contusion, laceration, and local or generalized edema to epidural or subdural hemorrhage and hematomas.

Interestingly, many patients who suffer actual skull fractures do not have serious or prolonged disorder of cerebral function. On the other hand, in fatal head injuries autopsy may reveal an intact skull in 20 to 30 per cent of cases.

Convulsive Seizures. Convulsive disorders are more commonly known as epilepsy. If the attack is characterized by an only momentary suspension of consciousness, it is called petit mal; if there is an immediate loss of consciousness and a violent, generalized convulsion, it is called grand mal.

SPINAL CORD

The spinal cord, lodged within the vertebral canal, is directly continuous superiorly with the medulla oblongata (see Fig. 239). It begins at the foramen magnum (at the point of the uppermost rootlet of the first cervical nerve). In its growth, the spinal cord lags behind the growth of the vertebral column after the third embryonic month. As a result, the cord in the adult *terminates at the junction of the first and second lumbar vertebrae.* The *conus medullaris* is the tapered lower end of the spinal cord lying opposite the first segment of the lumbar region (Fig. 252).

The spinal cord is flattened dorsoventrally and exhibits two swellings along its length—the cervical and lumbar enlargements. These enlargements are produced by the greater number of nerve fibers entering at these levels.

Cross Section of the Spinal Cord and General Function of Tracts (Figs. 256 to 259). In cross section, the spinal cord reveals an outer region of **white matter** and an inner region of **gray matter** arranged in the form of the letter *H*. There is a minute canal in the center of the cord—all that remains of the cavity of the neural tube. This opens into the fourth ventricle at its upper end and terminates blindly in the central canal of the filum terminale.

The transverse bar of the *H* is the *gray commissure* connecting the two lateral masses of gray matter. The portion of the gray substance dorsal to the central canal is called the *posterior gray commissure;* the *anterior gray commissure* is that part of the substance found ventral to the canal.

Several longitudinal furrows groove the cord and serve as borders to tracts of nerve fibers traversing it. These furrows include the deep median anterior fissure, the shallow median posterior fissure, the posterior lateral sulcus, and the anterior lateral sulcus. Each serves as a reference point locating tracts in the anterior, lateral, and posterior funiculi. The funiculi, in turn, consist of smaller segments, or fasciculi, which contain some ascending pathways to the brain from the cord and some descending pathways from the brain to the neurons in the spinal nerves (Fig. 259).

An **anterior,** or **ventral, horn** and a **posterior,** or **dorsal, horn** are found on each half of the gray matter. The anterior horn contains

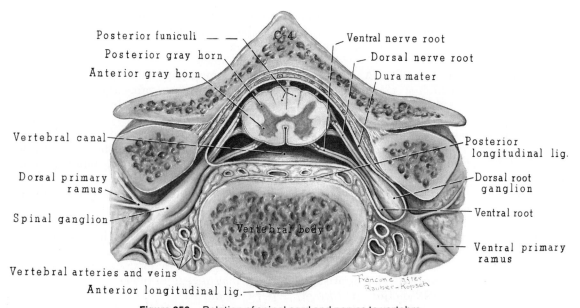

Figure 256. Relation of spinal cord and nerves to vertebra.

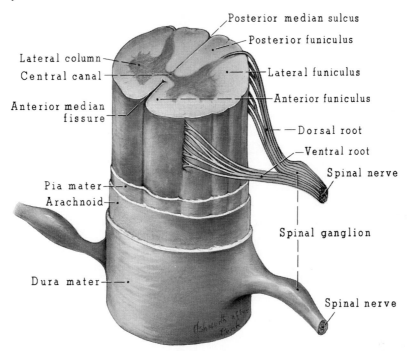

Figure 257. Section of spinal cord illustrating formation of spinal nerve and layers of meninges.

cell bodies from which motor efferent fibers of the spinal nerves arise. The posterior horn contains cell bodies from which afferent ascending fibers pass to the higher levels of the spinal cord into the brain after synapsing with sensory fibers from the spinal nerves. The gray matter also contains, among other things, a great number of neurons connecting impulses from one side of the cord to the other, and from one level of the cord to another.

The white matter of the spinal cord is in the form of three longitudinal segments, the axons of which extend the length of the cord. Each column, or funiculus, consists of several different bundles of fibers, or **tracts,**

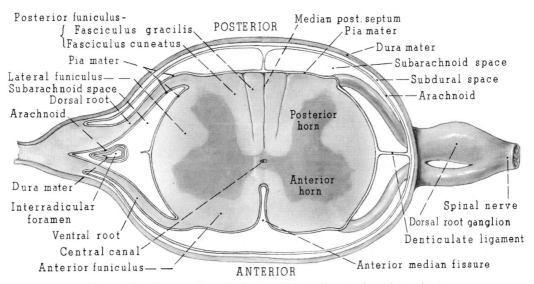

Figure 258. Cross section of spinal cord illustrating meningeal coverings.

POSTERIOR

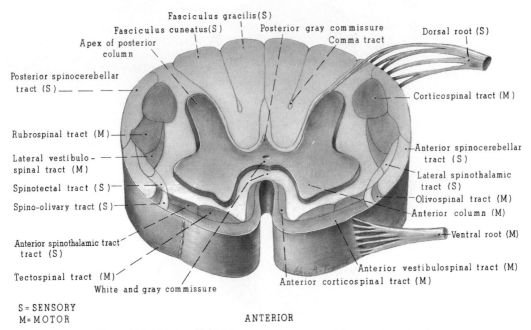

Fasciculus gracilis(S)

Fasciculus cuneatus(S)

Apex of posterior column

Posterior gray commissure

Comma tract

Dorsal root (S)

Posterior spinocerebellar tract (S)

Corticospinal tract (M)

Rubrospinal tract (M)

Lateral vestibulo-spinal tract (M)

Spinotectal tract (S)

Spino-olivary tract (S)

Anterior spinocerebellar tract (S)

Lateral spinothalamic tract (S)

Olivospinal tract (M)

Anterior column (M)

Anterior spinothalamic tract tract (S)

Tectospinal tract (M)

White and gray commissure

Ventral root (M)

Anterior vestibulospinal tract (M)

Anterior corticospinal tract (M)

S = SENSORY
M = MOTOR

ANTERIOR

Figure 259. Major ascending and descending tracts of the spinal cord.

functionally distinct from one another. Some tracts are ascending, or sensory, and serve as pathways to the brain for impulses entering the cord via the afferent fibers of spinal nerves. Others are descending, or motor, and transfer impulses from the brain to the motor neurons of the spinal column. Still other tracts consist of short ascending and descending fibers beginning in one region of the spinal cord and terminating in another.

The spinal cord functions to convey messages to and from the brain and its periphery. This function is made possible via the ascending and descending tracts. The name of each tract is usually sufficiently descriptive to indicate the funiculus in which it travels, the location of its cells of origin, and the level of location of its axon termination. For example, it can be concluded that in the lateral spinothalamic tract fibers travel in the lateral funiculus of the cord, the cells of origin lie within the cord, and the terminal processes of the axon connect with other neurons at a thalamic level.

Since the spinothalamic tract extends from the lower level of the cord to the thalamus at a higher level, it is an ascending, or afferent, tract. The axon fibers of the ventral corticospinal tract lie in the ventral funiculus; its cells of origin are in the cortex, and its terminal connections in the spinal cord. It could be concluded, therefore, that the ventral corticospinal tract is an efferent, or descending, pathway. The tracts of major functional significance are discussed in subsequent sections (pages 285 and 293).

Special Examinations of the Nervous System (Fig. 253)

Examination of the spinal fluid is often necessary. The fluid is obtained with the patient lying on his side. The tap, or *lumbar puncture,* is best performed between the third and fourth lumbar vertebrae. If the puncture has been performed without trauma, clear fluid is obtained.

Intracranial tumors can produce a distortion of the ventricles of the brain. The ventricles are outlined by removing a small area of bone and then injecting air through a needle inserted into the posterior horn of the lateral ventricle *(ventriculography)* or by injecting air into the lumbar subarachnoid space *(encephalography).*

In cerebral angiography, visualization of the intracranial blood vessels is accomplished by injecting radiopaque media into the carotid or vertebral arteries. With proper timing, both the arterial and venous phases of circulation can be outlined.

PERIPHERAL NERVOUS SYSTEM: SPINAL AND CRANIAL NERVES

SPINAL NERVES

A **nerve** is a bundle of nerve fibers outside the spinal cord or brain. Thirty-one pairs of nerves called spinal nerves (Fig. 260) arise from the spinal cord along almost its entire length and emerge from the vertebral canal through the intervertebral foramina. In a transverse section of a spinal nerve, large numbers of closely packed fibers, some myelinated and some nonmyelinated, can be seen by ordinary microscopy. These are grouped into small bundles called fascicles, each surrounded by a dense sheath, the *perineurium.* From the perineurium, strands of connective tissue called *endoneurium* extend into the spaces between the individual nerve fibers. The *epineurium* forms a protective covering for the entire nerve unit.

Attached to each segment of the spinal cord on either side is a **dorsal root** containing fibers of sensory neurons, and a **ventral root** containing fibers of motor neurons. Each dorsal root presents a *spinal ganglion* near or within the intervertebral foramen. Just distal to the ganglion, the dorsal root combines with the corresponding ventral root to form a spinal nerve. The cell bodies of sensory neurons lie in the spinal ganglia. The cell bodies of motor neurons lie in the ventral horns of the spinal cord.

The 31 pairs of spinal nerves are named for the region of the spinal column through which they exit. There are eight pairs of cervical spinal nerves, 12 thoracic, five lumbar, five sacral and one coccygeal. The first cervical spinal nerve, which often lacks dorsal roots, emerges between the atlas and the skull. The second to seventh cervical nerves leave the vertebral canal above the corresponding vertebrae; the eighth nerve leaves the vertebral canal below the seventh cervical vertebra. Thereafter, the nerves exit below their corresponding vertebrae. Because, as mentioned, the spinal cord is shorter than the vertebral column, the dorsal and ventral roots must descend progressively greater distances as they emerge further along the length of the cord in order to reach the appropriate intervertebral foramen before forming a spinal nerve. The roots arising from the terminal portion are drawn down to a collection called the **cauda equina** (Latin for horse's tail).

Many of the larger branches given off by the spinal nerves bear the same names as the artery they accompany or the part they supply. Thus, the radial nerve passes from the radial side of the forearm in company with the radial artery. The intercostal nerves pass between the ribs in company with the intercostal arteries. An exception to this rule is the large sciatic nerve, which divides into two branches supplying the leg and foot.

Soon after a spinal nerve leaves the cord, it branches in four directions. The *meningeal ramus* (Latin for branch) carries nerve fibers to and from the meninges of the spinal cord and the intervertebral ligaments. The *dorsal ramus* carries nerve fibers serving the muscles and skin of the back of the head, neck and trunk; the ventral and lateral parts of these structures as well as the upper and lower extremities are served by the usually larger and more important *ventral ramus.* The fourth branch belongs to the autonomic nervous system and has two portions, a *white ramus* and a *gray ramus.* (See section under Autonomic Nervous System.)

The **dorsal rami** extend backward through their transverse processes to reach muscular destinations. Nerves in this area are segmentally arranged and located from the back of the head to the coccyx, usually between the posterior angles of the ribs on both sides. C-1 supplies the muscles in the suboccipital region and is called the *suboccipital nerve.* C-2 helps form the suboccipital nerve, but deals mainly with the skin in the back of the head to the level of the vertex. This is called the *greater occipital nerve,* the major cutaneous nerve of the scalp over the occipital region.

The **ventral rami,** serving a more wide-

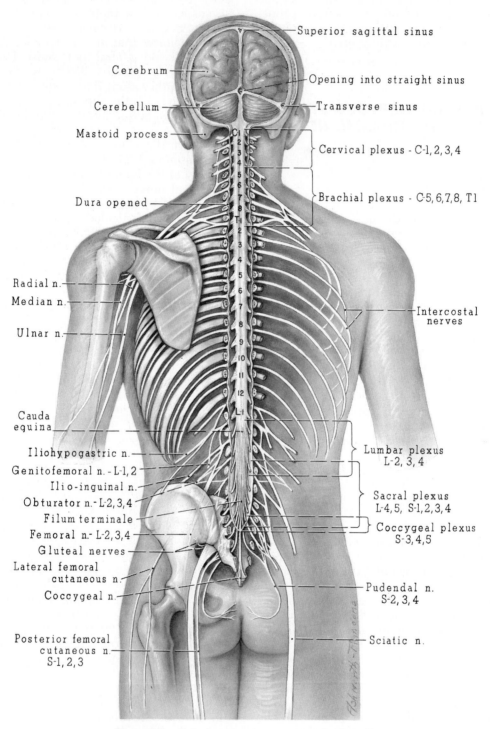

Figure 260.   Spinal cord and nerves emerging from it.

spread area of the body than the dorsal rami, are segmentally arranged in the thoracic region only. Here the ventral rami of thoracic nerves becomes the intercostal nerves serving the muscles and skin of the thorax and upper abdomen. In the cervical, lumbar and sacral regions *plexuses*, interlacing networks of nerves, arise from the ventral rami from which, in turn, *peripheral nerves* take their origin.

Plexuses (Figs. 260 and 261 and Tables 30 to 33)

Cervical Plexus. The first plexus formed is the *cervical plexus*, derived from the

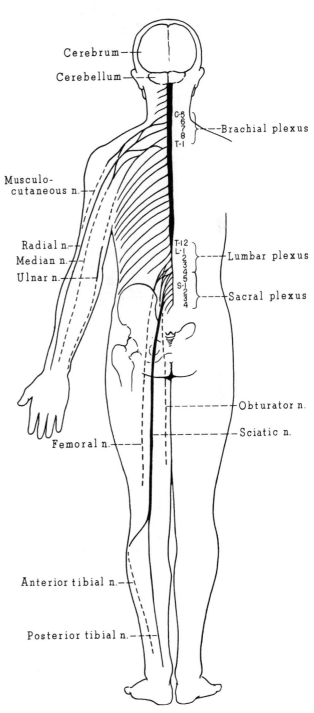

Figure 261. Branches of spinal cord as seen on left side of body only, posterior view.

Table 30. CERVICAL PLEXUS

NERVE	ORIGIN	INNERVATION
Lesser occipital	C–2, 3	Skin over lateral part of occipital region
Greater auricular	C–2, 3	Skin over angle of jaw, parotid gland, posteroinferior half of lateral and medial aspects of auricle, skin over mastoid region
Anterior cutaneous	C–2, 3	Supplies skin about the hyoid bone and the thyroid cartilage (ventral and lateral parts of the neck from chin to sternum)
Supraclavicular	C–3, 4	Skin of shoulder, most lateral regions of the neck, and upper part of breast
Phrenic	C–3, 4, 5	Diaphragm

Table 31. BRACHIAL PLEXUS

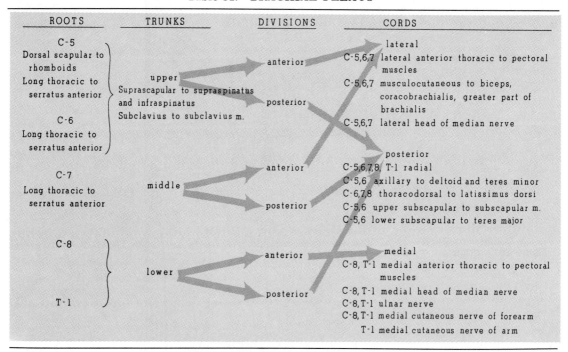

ROOTS	TRUNKS	DIVISIONS	CORDS

C-5
Dorsal scapular to rhomboids
Long thoracic to serratus anterior

C-6
Long thoracic to serratus anterior

C-7
Long thoracic to serratus anterior

C-8

T-1

upper
Suprascapular to supraspinatus and infraspinatus
Subclavius to subclavius m.

middle

lower

anterior

posterior

anterior

posterior

anterior

posterior

lateral
C-5,6,7 lateral anterior thoracic to pectoral muscles
C-5,6,7 musculocutaneous to biceps, coracobrachialis, greater part of brachialis
C-5,6,7 lateral head of median nerve

posterior
C-5,6,7,8 T-1 radial
C-5,6 axillary to deltoid and teres minor
C-6,7,8 thoracodorsal to latissimus dorsi
C-5,6 upper subscapular to subscapular m.
C-5,6 lower subscapular to teres major

medial
C-8, T-1 medial anterior thoracic to pectoral muscles
C-8, T-1 medial head of median nerve
C-8, T-1 ulnar nerve
C-8, T-1 medial cutaneous nerve of forearm
T-1 medial cutaneous nerve of arm

Table 32. LUMBAR PLEXUS

NERVE	ORIGIN	INNERVATION
Iliohypogastric	T–12, L–1	Skin over pubis and lateral gluteal region.
Ilioinguinal	L–1	Muscles of abdominal wall; skin of pubis, inguinal region, upper thigh, upper third of penis, and anterior scrotum (labium majus in female).
Genitofemoral	L–1, 2	Skin of scrotum and lateral half of thigh (dorsal and ventral) extending from lateral buttock to knee.
Lateral femoral cutaneous	L–2, 3	Skin of ventral and ventromedial surface of thigh, front of kneecap, medial side of leg and medial margin of foot.
Obturator	L–2, 3, 4	Supplies adductor muscles of thigh and gracilis. Cutaneous branch is distributed to the inner surface of the thigh.
Femoral	L–2, 3, 4	Motor branches to quadriceps femoris, sartorius and pectineus muscles. Cutaneous branches supply skin of hip region, anterior aspect of thigh and medial aspect of leg and foot.

Table 33. SACRAL PLEXUS

NERVE	ORIGIN	INNERVATION
Sciatic		
Tibial	L–4 to S–3	Muscles and skin of back of leg
Common peroneal	L–4 to S–2	Skin and muscles of anterior and lateral aspect of leg and dorsal surface of foot
Superior gluteal	L–4 to S–1	Gluteus medius and minimus and tensor fascia lata
Inferior gluteal	L–5 to S–2	Gluteus maximus
Posterior femoral cutaneous	S–1, 2, 3	Skin of lateral part of perineum, lower buttock and back of thigh and leg

ventral rami of C-1, 2, 3, and 4. A major nerve arising from this plexus is the *phrenic nerve,* which extends through the thorax to supply the large musculature of the diaphragm (Fig. 262). *Cutaneous nerves* arising from the cervical plexus include the lesser occipital, great auricular, anterior cutaneous and supraclavicular. These nerves supply the skin of the jaw, back of the ear, shoulder, lateral and anterior side of the neck and upper thorax. *Motor branches* of the cervical plexus form the *spinal portion of the spinal accessory nerve* (eleventh cranial nerve — see page 274) and supply the trapezius and sternocleidomastoid muscles.

Brachial Plexus. The *brachial plexus* extends downward and laterally to pass over the first rib and behind the middle third of the clavicle to enter the axilla (armpit). It is derived from the ventral rami of nerves C-5, 6, 7, and 8, as well as T-1, and provides the entire nerve supply for the upper extremities. A lateral and a medial cord are formed from the anterior divisions of the ventral rami; a posterior cord is formed from the posterior divisions (Fig. 263 and Table 31). Important nerves arising from the cords of the brachial plexus are the following (Figs. 263 and 264).

A. Lateral cord

1. The *musculocutaneous nerve* supplies the biceps brachii, coracobrachialis and brachialis. It is the sensory supply for the skin on the outer side of the forearm.

2. The *median nerve* (including a me-

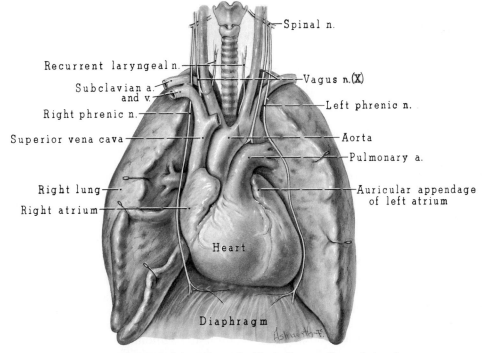

Figure 262. Contents of thoracic cavity, illustrating positions of phrenic nerve.

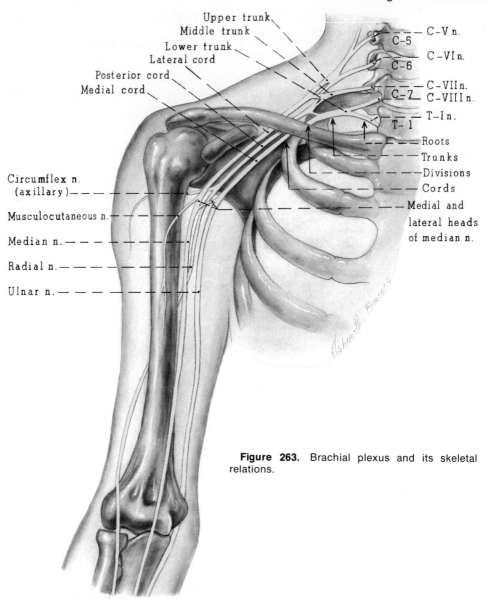

Upper trunk
Middle trunk
Lower trunk
Lateral cord
Posterior cord
Medial cord

C-5
C-6
C-7
T-1

C–V n.
C–VI n.
C–VII n.
C–VIII n.
T–I n.

Roots
Trunks
Divisions
Cords
Medial and
lateral heads
of median n.

Circumflex n.
(axillary)

Musculocutaneous n.

Median n.

Radial n.

Ulnar n.

Figure 263. Brachial plexus and its skeletal relations.

dial head from the medial cord), the great "flexor" nerve of the upper arm, supplies flexor muscles of the forearm, the three thenar muscles and the two lateral lumbricals.

B. Medial cord

The *ulnar nerve* innervates the flexor carpi ulnaris and the medial half of the flexor digitorum profundus in the forearm, as well as the muscles of the hand, except those supplied by the median nerve. If injured, it gives rise to a sensation of "pins and needles" in the area of its sensory distribution—the skin on the medial aspect of the elbow, wrist and hand.

C. Posterior cord

1. The *circumflex (axillary) nerve* supplies the branch to the teres minor, and terminates by innervating the deltoid and the skin over it.

2. The *radial nerve* spirals around the back of the humerus, supplying the triceps. It innervates all the muscles of the back of the forearm, and sensory branches serve the skin on the back of the forearm and hand. The radial nerve lies close to the humerus and can be seriously injured in fractures of the midshaft of the bone.

Lumbar Plexus. The ventral rami of the lumbar segments 1, 2, 3, and 4 form the *lumbar plexus*. The lumbar plexus is si-

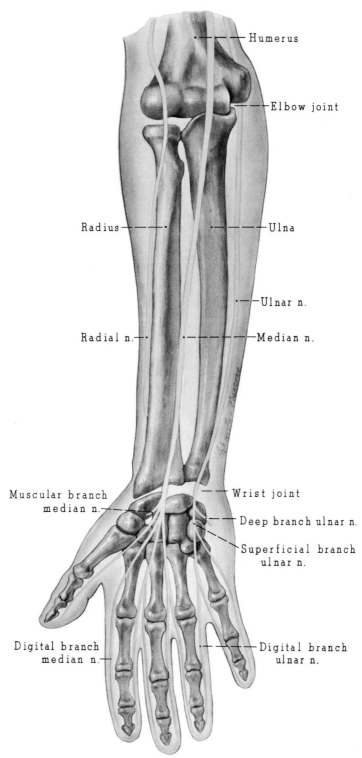

Figure 264.   Nerves of right forearm and hand (palmar view).

tuated on the inside of the posterior abdominal wall. There are three major nerves in this plexus (Fig. 265):

1. The *lateral femoral cutaneous nerve*

supplies the skin on the lateral half of the thigh.

2. The *femoral nerve* is the largest of the group, with the widest distribution. Motor

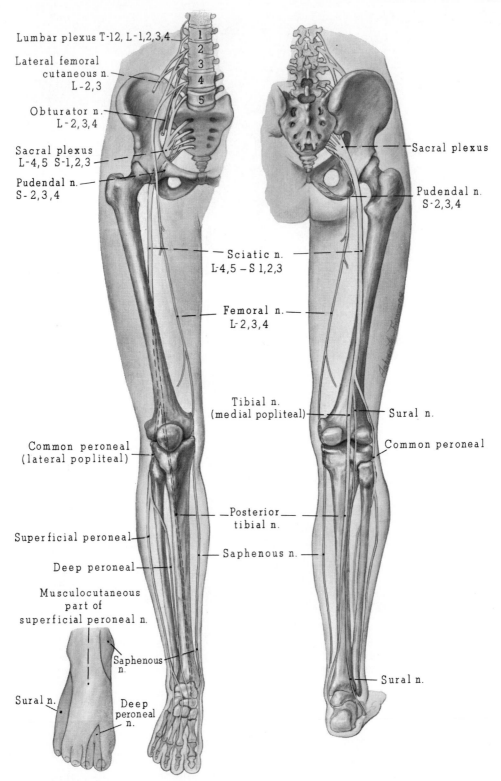

Figure 265. Anterior and posterior views of the right leg and foot, showing lumbar and sacral plexuses and the regions supplied. Inset shows areas of the foot supplied by the nerves.

branches supply muscles of the thigh (flexors) and leg; cutaneous branches supply the skin of the anterior thigh, the hip and the leg. The largest branch of the femoral nerve, the superficial *saphenous nerve,* extends into the foot, serving the skin on the medial aspect of the leg and foot.

3. The *genitofemoral nerve* supplies the scrotum and the skin of the thigh (not shown in Fig. 265).

Sacral Plexus. The *sacral plexus* is formed on the anterior aspect of the sacrum by the rami of L-4 and 5 and S-1, 2, 3, and 4. It gives rise to the largest nerve in the body, the sciatic nerve. The branches of the sacral plexus include the following (Fig. 265).

1. The *sciatic nerve,* formed from L-4 and 5 and S-1, 2, and 3, is located deep in the gluteus maximus muscle and travels down the posterior aspect of the thigh, dividing into two terminal branches—the *tibial* and *common peroneal nerves.* The common peroneal innervates the skin and muscles on the anterior and lateral surfaces of the leg and the dorsum of the foot. The tibial innervates the posterior muscles and the skin of the leg.

2. The *pudendal nerve* is formed by the rami of S-2, 3, and 4, and supplies the muscles of the external genitalia, the skin of the perineum, and the anal sphincter.

The fifth sacral nerve and coccygeal nerves are unimportant in man. In animals, these two spinal nerves supply the tail.

Dermatomes. The areas of the skin served by each pair of spinal nerves have been mapped. A strip of skin supplied by one pair of spinal nerves is called a *dermatome* (Fig. 266). Overlap between adjoining dermatomes minimizes damage to any one

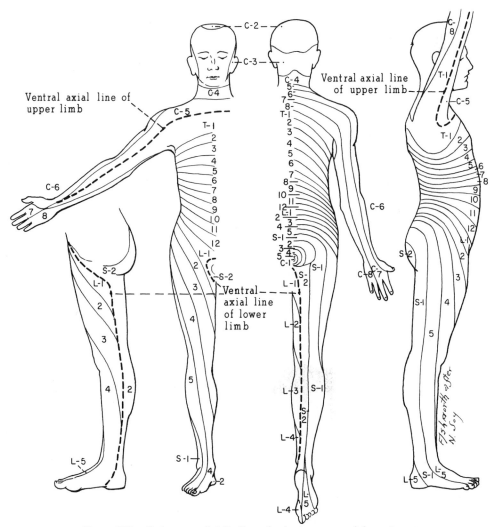

Figure 266. Cutaneous distribution of spinal nerves and dermatomes.

nerve. One of the procedures used to prepare these maps in humans entailed stimulation of the sensory roots of individuals in surgery and observing the resulting vasodilation. Data obtained from cases of herpes zoster, a painful condition caused by a viral infection, usually in a single dorsal root ganglion, have also been used to map dermatomes.

Degeneration and Regeneration of Peripheral Nerves (Fig. 226)

When a peripheral nerve is injured, there may be an anatomic or physiologic interruption of function. The nerve distal to the point of division undergoes changes originally described by Waller in 1852 and collectively known as *wallerian degeneration*. Within the first few days, the axons become granular at the site of injury. This granularity spreads distally throughout the whole axon; simultaneously, the myelin sheath disintegrates. Within 24 hours after injury, the axons of the proximal stump begin to regenerate, first forming buds, and then filaments which branch and grow at the rate of 1.5 mm. per day.

In the distal portion of the severed nerve, Schwann cells multiply and join the proximal and distal ends of the neurilemma. The fibers enter the tube in an orderly arrangement and follow this band of Schwann cells to reach their respective end organs. The nerve sheaths, bundles and trunks are replaced by growth of these structures from the proximal end of the nerve.

Sympathetic fibers of the autonomic nervous system (see page 277) regenerate most rapidly. A return of function in peripheral nerve injury can be recognized initially by an improvement in color of the skin. Sensory function returns next. This is shown initially by sensitivity of the paralyzed muscle to pressure or pinching, and is followed by a return of protopathic (perceiving only coarser stimuli) sensitivity to pain, pressure, heat, and cold. Epicritic sensibility (perceiving fine variations of touch and temperature) returns next, followed by sensitivity to joint movement and touch localization. The last function to return is motor. Finally, actual muscle contraction occurs.

Peripheral Nerve Injury. The most ac-curate motor tests for injury to the median and ulnar nerves at the wrist are those involving the actions of the small muscles of the hand. If a patient is asked to oppose the tip of the thumb to the tip of the little finger without flexion of the distal phalanx of the thumb or little finger, a perfectly adequate and accurate test for median nerve function will have been employed. Function of the ulnar nerve distal to damage at the wrist can be tested by having the patient abduct and adduct the extended fingers. If the patient is unable to extend the wrist when the hand lies flat upon the table, the radial nerve has been injured.

CRANIAL NERVES (Figs. 267 to 282)

The cranial nerves are 12 pairs of symmetrically arranged nerves attached to the brain. Each leaves the skull through a foramen at its base. The site where the fibers composing the nerve enter or leave the brain surface is usually termed the *superficial origin* of the nerve; the more deeply placed region from which the fibers arise or around which they terminate is called the *deep origin* of the nerves. The cell bodies of sensory neurons are located in ganglia just outside the brain; the cell bodies of motor neurons are located in nuclei within the brain.

The cranial nerves include the olfactory (I), optic (II), oculomotor (III), trochlear (IV), trigeminal (V), abducens (VI), facial (VII), vestibulocochlear (acoustic) (VIII), glossopharyngeal (IX), vagus (X), spinal accessory (XI), and hypoglossal (XII) (Table 34).

The greater number of cranial nerves are, like spinal nerves, mixed nerves, containing both motor and sensory fibers. Cranial nerves I (olfactory), II (optic) and VIII (vestibulocochlear), however, carry only sensory fibers (from the nose, eye and ear, respectively). Cranial nerves III (oculomotor), IV (trochlear) and VI (abducens), which supply the eye muscles, are largely motor nerves, containing no sensory fibers other than proprioceptive fibers from the innervated muscles. Cranial nerves XII (hypoglossal), which innervates the tongue, and XI (spinal accessory) have been described as purely motor nerves although, according to

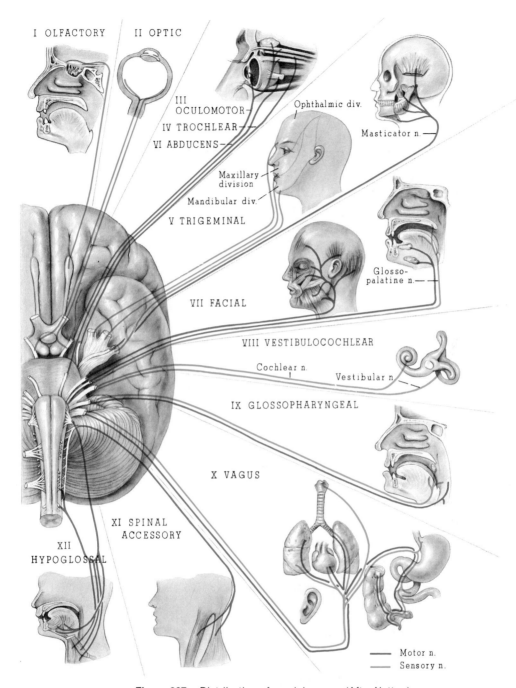

Figure 267.   Distribution of cranial nerves. (After Netter.)

some anatomists, they also contain fibers from muscle proprioceptors.

The **olfactory nerve** (I), serving the function of smell, is formed by 20 small bundles of afferent fibers (Fig. 270). These lead from each olfactory mucous membrane, where the cell bodies are located (the neurons are the olfactory receptors), and almost immediately enter the olfactory bulb. The olfactory tract runs backward from the bulb and

Text continued on page 268

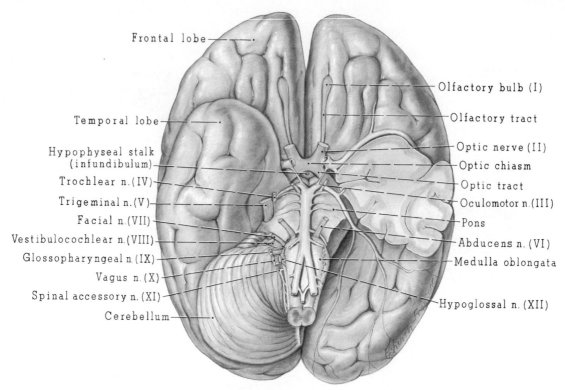

Frontal lobe

Olfactory bulb (I)

Temporal lobe

Olfactory tract

Optic nerve (II)

Hypophyseal stalk (infundibulum)

Optic chiasm

Trochlear n.(IV)

Optic tract

Trigeminal n.(V)

Oculomotor n.(III)

Facial n.(VII)

Pons

Vestibulocochlear n.(VIII)

Abducens n. (VI)

Glossopharyngeal n.(IX)

Medulla oblongata

Vagus n.(X)

Spinal accessory n.(XI)

Hypoglossal n. (XII)

Cerebellum

Figure 268.   Inferior surface of the brain showing sites of exit of the cranial nerves.

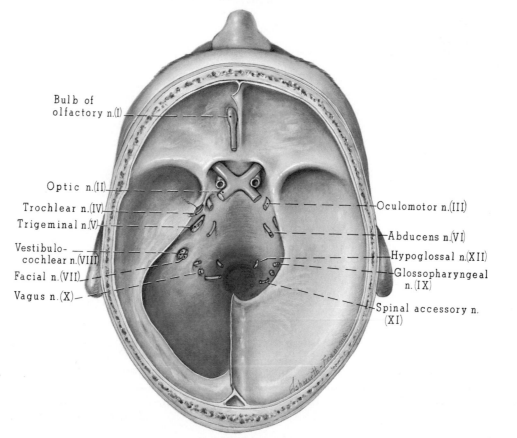

Bulb of olfactory n.(I)

Optic n.(II)

Oculomotor n.(III)

Trochlear n.(IV)

Trigeminal n.(V)

Abducens n.(VI)

Vestibulo-cochlear n.(VIII)

Hypoglossal n.(XII)

Glossopharyngeal n.(IX)

Facial n.(VII)

Vagus n.(X)

Spinal accessory n. (XI)

Figure 269.   Sites of exit of cranial nerves from the skull.

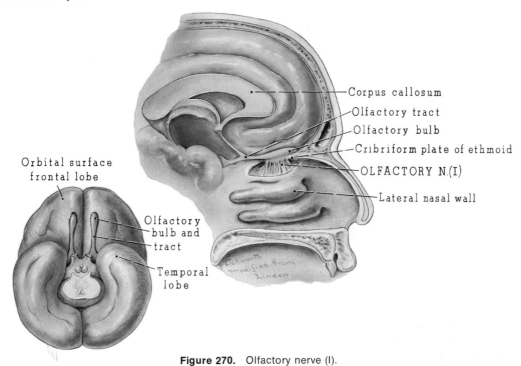

Corpus callosum
Olfactory tract
Olfactory bulb
Cribriform plate of ethmoid
OLFACTORY N.(I)
Lateral nasal wall

Orbital surface
frontal lobe

Olfactory
bulb and
tract

Temporal
lobe

Figure 270. Olfactory nerve (I).

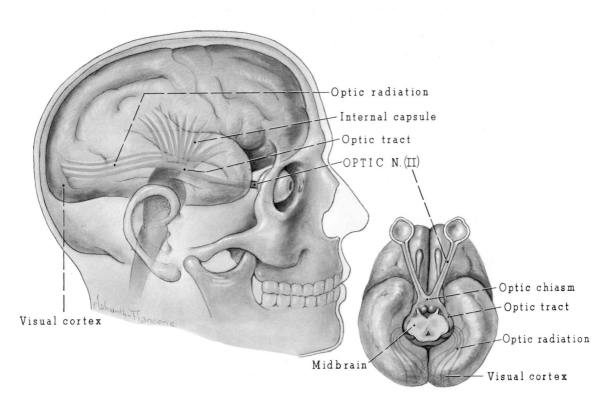

Optic radiation
Internal capsule
Optic tract
OPTIC N.(II)

Visual cortex

Optic chiasm
Optic tract
Optic radiation
Visual cortex

Midbrain

Figure 271. Optic nerve (II).

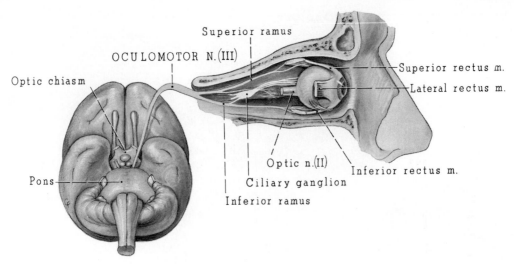

Figure 272. Oculomotor nerve (III).

extends to the lateral and medial olfactory gyri. In testing for smell, each naris should be separately examined for the presence of the sense of smell. A complete absence of this sense is called *anosmia*.

The **optic nerve** (II), conducting visual impulses, is composed of more than one million nerve fibers, or approximately 38 per cent of all the cranial nerve fibers (Fig. 271). Neither the olfactory nor the optic nerve is a cranial nerve in the usual sense

because the sensory fibers lead from rather than to neuronal cell bodies and can be regarded as extensions of the central nervous system.

Visual impulses are received through the rods and cones and are transmitted (via bipolar neurons) to the ganglionic cells. Fibers of the latter constitute the optic nerve for each eye. The two optic nerves unite after their entrance into the cranial cavity to form the optic chiasm. From this

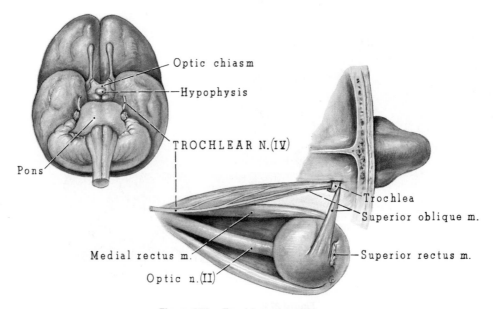

Figure 273. Trochlear nerve (IV).

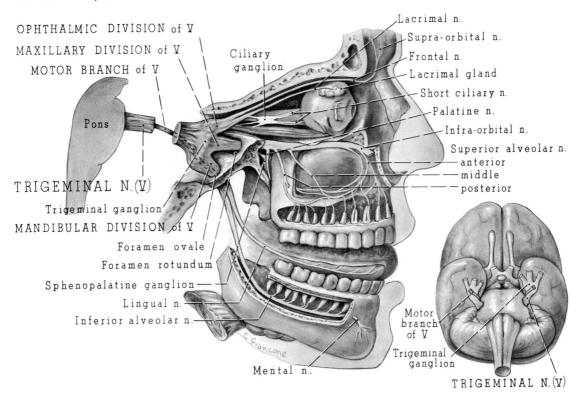

OPHTHALMIC DIVISION of V
MAXILLARY DIVISION of V
MOTOR BRANCH of V

Ciliary ganglion

Lacrimal n.
Supra-orbital n.
Frontal n.
Lacrimal gland
Short ciliary n.
Palatine n.
Infra-orbital n.
Superior alveolar n.
anterior
middle
posterior

Pons

TRIGEMINAL N.(V)

Trigeminal ganglion

MANDIBULAR DIVISION of V

Foramen ovale
Foramen rotundum
Sphenopalatine ganglion
Lingual n.
Inferior alveolar n.

C. Francone

Mental n.

Motor branch of V
Trigeminal ganglion

TRIGEMINAL N.(V)

Figure 274. Trigeminal nerve (V).

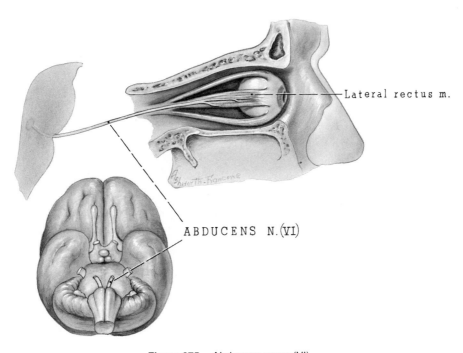

Lateral rectus m.

Gildorth-Francone

ABDUCENS N.(VI)

Figure 275. Abducens nerve (VI).

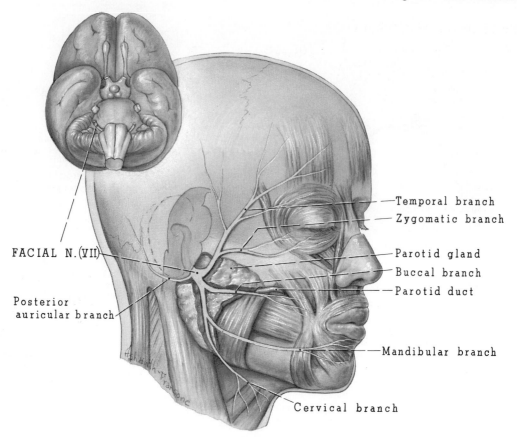

Temporal branch
Zygomatic branch
Parotid gland
Buccal branch
Parotid duct
FACIAL N.(VII)
Posterior
auricular branch
Mandibular branch
Cervical branch

Figure 276. Facial nerve (VII).

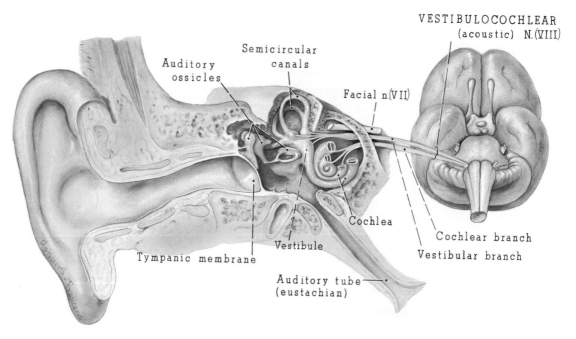

VESTIBULOCOCHLEAR
(acoustic) N.(VIII)
Semicircular
canals
Auditory
ossicles
Facial n(VII)
Cochlea
Vestibule
Tympanic membrane
Cochlear branch
Vestibular branch
Auditory tube
(eustachian)

Figure 277. Vestibulocochlear nerve (VIII).

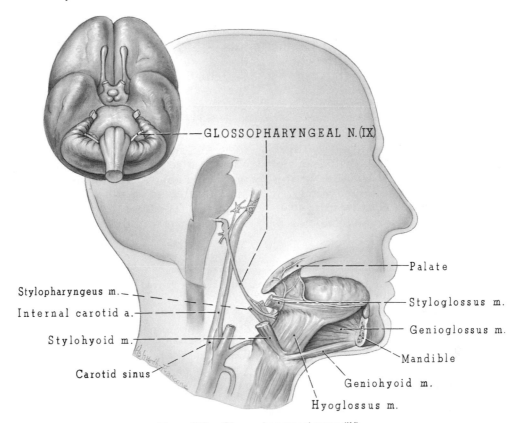

GLOSSOPHARYNGEAL N. (IX)

Palate

Stylopharyngeus m.

Internal carotid a.

Stylohyoid m.

Carotid sinus

Styloglossus m.

Genioglossus m.

Mandible

Geniohyoid m.

Hyoglossus m.

Figure 278. Glossopharyngeal nerve (IX).

point the nerves continue as the optic tracts.

The **oculomotor nerve** (III), predominantly motor, contains efferent nerves affecting four of the six external muscles that move the eye (Fig. 272). It also supplies fibers to the levator palpebrae superioris muscle, which raises the eyelid. The patient with third nerve damage complains of blurred vision or of seeing two objects instead of one (diplopia). Weakness of the extraocular muscles is determined by the patient's holding his head without moving it and following the examiner's fingertips with his eyes. The oculomotor nerve also contains efferent fibers belonging to the autonomic nervous system (page 278) that synapse with fibers leading to the smooth muscles of the eyes (iris and ciliary muscles).

The smallest of the cranial nerves, the **trochlear nerve** (IV, contains efferent fibers supplying the superior oblique muscle of the eye (Fig. 273). Its integrity is examined by checking movements of the eye.

The **trigeminal nerve** (V), the largest of the cranial nerves, is the general sensory nerve of the face, nose, mouth, forehead, and the top of the head, and motor nerve to the jaw muscles of mastication. It consists of three divisions: ophthalmic, maxillary, and mandibular (Fig. 274). The trigeminal nerve conducts efferent fibers to the muscles of mastication via the mandibular branch. It is also composed of afferent fibers located in the skin of the face and anterior scalp, mucous membrane of the mouth and nasal cavities, and meninges. Injury to the trigeminal nerve produces a loss of sensation to light touch and temperature on the corresponding half of the face. In addition to this loss of sensation, the cornea and the conjunctiva (a mucous membrane lining the exposed surface of the eyeball) are insensitive, as are the mucous membranes of the corresponding side of the nose, mouth and anterior two-thirds of the tongue. When the motor portion of the trigeminal nerve is affected, the masseter and other muscles of mastication are paralyzed and subsequently atrophy. The motor portion of the trigeminal nerve is tested by asking the patient to clench his teeth. The examiner feels the masseters to determine the strength of contraction. Examination of the sensory portion is conducted by evaluating the corneal (blink) reflex and sensation of the skin of the face.

Trigeminal neuralgia is perhaps the most agonizing of all benign afflictions of man. The maxillary and mandibular divisions of the fifth nerve are the usual sites of this disorder. The tic, or muscle twitch, of trigeminal neuralgia is characteristic. Pain is excruciatingly explosive and stabbing in quality and is present over the area of distribution of the involved division. It is usually so severe that the facial muscles on the affected side develop a spasm; hence the term **tic douloureux.** Initially the attacks are brief, lasting from a few seconds to two minutes. Invariably, the patient becomes aware of trigger zones which, if touched, set off pain. These are usually located in the region of the mouth or upper lip. Eventually, the attacks may become more frequent, producing almost continuous paroxysms of pain. The cause of trigeminal neuralgia is unknown. Treatment includes division of the sensory root of the fifth nerve.

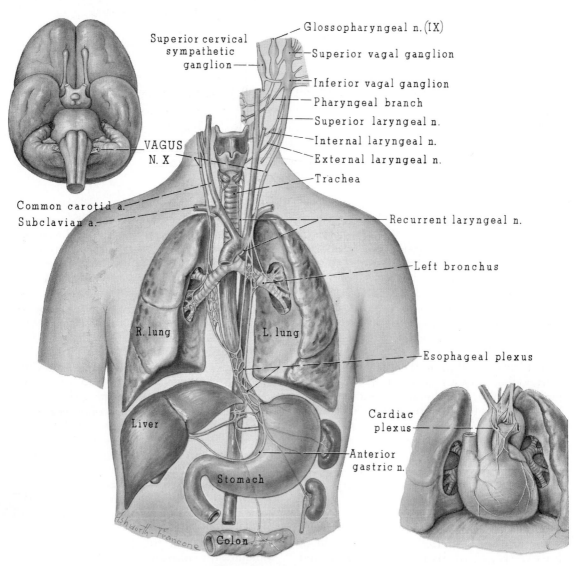

Figure 279.   Vagus nerve (X).

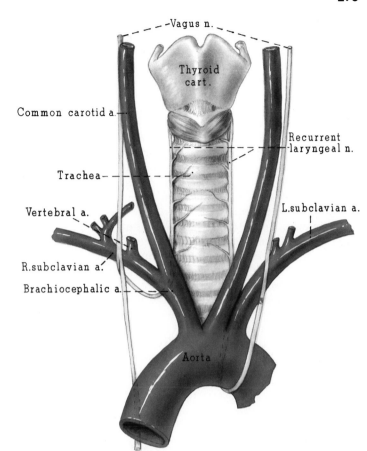

Figure 280. Course of recurrent laryngeal nerve. If, instead of the normal anatomy shown, an aortic aneurysm (dilatation) is present, the aorta could irritate the left recurrent laryngeal nerve innervating the vocal cords, causing hoarseness.

The **abducens nerve** (VI), composed of efferent fibers supplying the lateral rectus muscle of the eyeball, serves the function of lateral movement of the eye (Fig. 275).

The **facial nerve** (VII), principally a motor nerve, contains efferent fibers found in the muscles of the face and scalp (Fig. 276). The facial nerve serves the function of facial expression. It also contains efferent fibers of the autonomic nervous system which lead to activation of the lacrimal (tear), submandibular and sublingual (salivary) glands. It includes afferent fibers from the mucous membranes of the anterior two-thirds of the tongue, serving the function of taste.

When the seventh nerve is injured or diseased as it leaves the pons, the resulting paralysis gives the face a one-sided appearance, and the paralyzed side is flat and motionless. A loss of taste may occur in the anterior two-thirds of the tongue in the presence of damage to the facial nerve. In peripheral damage, such as occurs in **Bell's palsy** or injury to the facial nerve in the bony canal, all the muscles of facial expression are paralyzed. The patient cannot wrinkle his forehead or close his upper eyelid. In a central lesion, only the facial muscles below the eyelids are paralyzed.

The facial nerve is examined by asking the patient to wrinkle his forehead, to frown, to whistle, or to close his eyelids tightly. By these various simple maneuvers, muscles innervated by the facial nerve are tested and weakness or paralysis of the nerve is easily detected. The sensory function of the nerve is evaluated by asking the patient to protrude his tongue and by rubbing sugar, salt or quinine onto the tongue to check for taste.

The **vestibulocochlear (acoustic) nerve** (VIII) (Fig. 277) serves the functions of hearing and equilibrium. There are two portions—the auditory, or cochlear, portion concerned with hearing, and the vestibular portion, concerned with equilibrium. Injury to the vestibular portion of the acoustic nerve produces symptoms that include vertigo (a sensation of whirling movement) and nystagmus (involuntary rapid eye movements).

The **glossopharyngeal nerve** (IX) is

formed by five or six small fibrous bundles emerging from the medulla oblongata (Fig. 278). The ninth nerve serves the function of general sensation and taste for the posterior one-third of the tongue. It also contains sensory fibers from the mucous membrane of the pharynx, the carotid body and the carotid sinus. Motor fibers innervate the stylopharyngeus muscle, which aids in movement of the pharynx. The glosso-pharyngeal nerve also carries fibers of the autonomic nervous system leading to in-nervation of the parotid gland, a large salivary gland in front of the ear.

The **vagus nerve** (X) (Fig. 279) contains motor fibers innervating the pharyngeal and laryngeal muscles and sensory fibers from the pleura, aortic sinus and thoracic and abdominal viscera. The vagus nerve is also an important part of the autonomic nervous system, containing fibers that lead to inner-vation of the heart, pancreas, and smooth muscles of the lungs and digestive tract.

The vagus nerve is routinely tested by observing pharyngeal muscles, which is accomplished by asking the patient to phonate and say "ah." Under normal cir-cumstances, the soft palate and uvula will be pulled up in the midline. In the case of weakness of one side, the palate will be pulled to the healthy side upon phonation, while the diseased side droops.

The **recurrent laryngeal nerve** (Fig. 280), which takes its origin from the vagus nerve, is of particular importance in clinical medi-cine; when the thyroid gland is abnormal and removal indicated, damage to this nerve sometimes occurs. Damage to the recurrent laryngeal nerve results in hoarseness.

The **spinal accessory nerve** (XI) (Fig. 281) is divided into two parts: a cranial (bulbar) portion and a spinal portion. The cranial portion contains motor fibers leading to muscles of the pharynx and larynx. The spinal portion is composed of fibers arising from the upper five segments of the spinal cord, which join the cranial portion after passing up through the foramen magnum as a common trunk. Fibers of the spinal portion innervate the trapezius and ster-

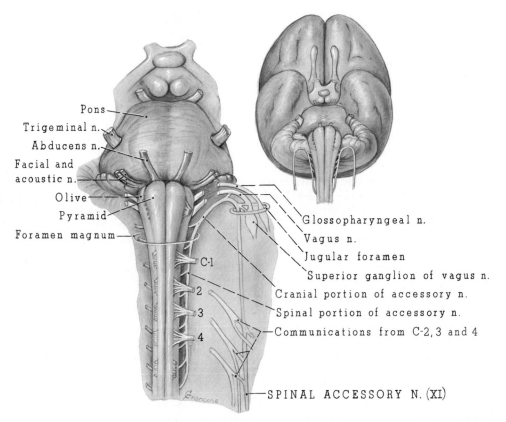

Figure 281. Accessory nerve (XI).

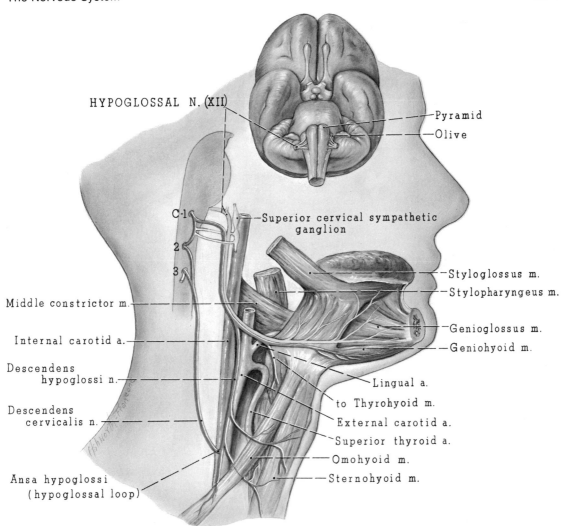

Figure 282. Hypoglossal nerve (XII).

nocleidomastoid muscles, which permit movement of the head and shoulders.

Weakness of the trapezius muscle is determined by having the patient raise his shoulders against resistance. Weakness of the sternocleidomastoid muscle is ascertained by asking the patient to turn his head to the right and left against resistance of the examiner's hand.

The **hypoglossal nerve** (XII) supplies muscles to the tongue, allowing movement of the tongue (Fig. 282). The function of the hypoglossal nerve can be determined by having the patient protrude his tongue. When there is injury to this nerve, the tongue will deviate toward the side of the injury.

AUTONOMIC NERVOUS SYSTEM

As mentioned in the beginning of this chapter, efferent peripheral nerve fibers distributed to smooth muscle, cardiac muscle and glands (exocrine and some endocrine) are generally described as belonging to the autonomic nervous system. Since autonomic nerves also carry sensory fibers from the viscera, some authors include these afferent pathways as part of the autonomic nervous system.

The autonomic nervous system, among other things, helps to control arterial pressure, gastrointestinal motility and secretion, urinary output, sweating, body temperature and various other functions. The overall

Table 34. CRANIAL NERVES

NUMBER	NAME	ORIGIN	EXIT FROM SKULL	FUNCTION
I	Olfactory	Cells of nasal mucosa	Cribriform plate of ethmoid	Sensory: olfactory (smell)
II	Optic	Ganglion cells in retina	Optic foramen	Sensory: vision
III	Oculomotor	Midbrain	Superior orbital fissure	Motor: external muscles of eyes except lateral rectus and superior oblique; levator palpebrae superioris Parasympathetic: sphincter of pupil and ciliary muscle of lens
IV	Trochlear	Roof of midbrain	Superior orbital fissure	Motor: superior oblique muscle
V	Trigeminal Ophthalmic branch	Lateral aspect of pons Semilunar ganglion	Superior orbital fissure	Sensory: cornea; nasal mucous membrane: skin of face
	Maxillary branch	Semilunar ganglion	Foramen rotundum	Sensory: skin of face; oral cavity; anterior two-thirds of tongue; teeth
	Mandibular branch	Semilunar ganglion	Foramen ovale	Motor: muscles of mastication Sensory: skin of face
VI	Abducens	Lower margin of pons	Superior orbital fissure	Motor: lateral rectus muscle
VII	Facial	Lower margin of pons	Stylomastoid foramen	Motor: muscles of facial expression Sensory: taste, anterior two-thirds of tongue Parasympathetic: lacrimal, submandibular, and sublingual glands
VIII	Vestibulocochlear Vestibular	Lower border of pons	Internal auditory meatus	Sensory: equilbrium
	Cochlear	Lower border of pons	Internal auditory meatus	Sensory: hearing
IX	Glossopharyngeal	Medulla oblongata	Jugular foramen	Motor: stylopharyngeus muscle Sensory: taste posterior one-third of tongue; pharynx; branch of the carotid sinus and carotid body Parasympathetic: parotid gland
X	Vagus	Medulla oblongata	Jugular foramen	Sensory: external meatus, pharynx, larynx, aortic sinus, and thoracic and abdominal viscera Motor: pharynx and larynx Parasympathetic: thoracic and abdominal viscera
XI	Accessory	Medulla oblongata	Jugular foramen	Motor: trapezius and sternocleidomastoid muscles; muscles of pharynx and larynx
XII	Hypoglossal	Anterior lateral sulcus between olive and pyramid	Hypoglossal canal	Motor: muscles of tongue

function of the autonomic nervous system seems to be to maintain homeostasis.

Anatomically, the efferent pathway of the autonomic nervous system is unique in the following way: Whereas a skeletal muscle is innervated by a neuron with its cell body in the central nervous system and its axon extending without interruption to the muscle, smooth muscle, the heart and glands are innervated by a 2-neuron chain—a *preganglionic neuron* with its cell body in the central nervous system and axon extending to a ganglion outside the central nervous system, and a *postganglionic neuron* with its cell body in a ganglion and axon extending to the muscle or gland. The ganglion, in effect, serves as a synaptic center between pre- and postganglionic neurons.

Autonomic Subdivisions

The autonomic nervous system may be divided, both functionally and structurally, into the sympathetic and parasympathetic nervous divisions.

The **sympathetic,** or **thoracolumbar, division** of the autonomic nervous system arises from all the thoracic and the first three lumbar segments of the spinal cord. The **parasympathetic,** or **craniosacral, division** of the autonomic nervous system arises from the third, seventh, ninth, and tenth cranial nerves, and from the second, third, and fourth sacral segments of the spinal cord. Under certain conditions it can be said that the sympathetic nervous system is involved in "fight" or "flight," while the parasympathetic system is involved in "repose" and "repair." The sympathetic system is the more primitive, sometimes exerting a mass action fortified by epinephrine from the medullary portion of the suprarenal gland. Among the general "fight or flight" responses are constriction of blood vessels in the skin and abdominal region and dilation of blood vessels in skeletal muscles (thereby shifting blood from the skin and abdominal organs to skeletal muscles); increase of the heart rate; dilation of the bronchioles (facilitating respiration); inhibition of the digestive tract and urinary bladder; accommodation for far vision; and an increase in the release of glucose into the blood stream from the liver (principally in response to epinephrine). The parasym-

pathetic system is more advanced structurally and functionally, and its actions are never as generalized as the sympathetic "fight or flight" response; its most important actions are on smooth muscles of the gut and digestive glands, increasing motility and secretion.

Pharmacologic Division. It has been found that the transmission of impulses by autonomic neurons and nerve fibers is associated with liberation of specific chemical substances at the ganglionic synapses and effector end organs.

Preganglionic stimulation of both sympathetic and parasympathetic nerves and postganglionic stimulation of parasympathetic nerves lead to liberation of acetylcholine in the corresponding ganglion or parasympathetic end organ. Stimulation of most postganglionic sympathetic nerves leads to liberation of norepinephrine at the effector end organ. Postganglion stimulation of some sympathetic fibers, however, leads to liberation of acetylcholine at the effector. On the basis of the substance liberated, autonomic fibers are called either *cholinergic* (forming acetylcholine) or *adrenergic* (forming norepinephrine, also called noradrenalin).

Adrenergic nerve fibers exert a different physiologic effect from the cholinergic ones; thus, stimulation of the sympathetic nerves to the heart, which are adrenergic, causes an increased heart rate, while excitation of the parasympathetic nerves, which are cholinergic, causes a decrease in heart rate. The actions of the autonomic nervous system are summarized in Table 35.

OUTFLOW OF THE SYMPATHETIC NERVOUS SYSTEM

The cell bodies of sympathetic preganglionic neurons are located in the lateral horn of the first thoracic to the third lumbar segments of the spinal cord. Each axon leaves the cord through a ventral root and passes into a **paravertebral ganglion** via a **white ramus communicans** (so called because preganglionic fibers are myelinated). The paravertebral ganglia are found on either side of the vertebral column, close to the bodies of the vertebrae. They form a series of 22 to 26 ganglia connected together in a chain or trunk extending from the base

Table 35. FUNCTIONS OF THE AUTONOMIC NERVOUS SYSTEM

ORGAN	SYMPATHETIC STIMULATION	PARASYMPATHETIC STIMULATION
Eye		
Iris	Stimulates radial fibers (dilates pupil)	Stimulates circular fibers (constricts pupil)
Ciliary	Inhibits (flattens lens)	Stimulates (bulges lens)
Salivary glands (parotid, sublingual, submaxillary)	Vasoconstriction may diminish secretion	Stimulates copious secretion high in enzyme content
Lacrimal glands		Stimulates secretion
Sweat glands	Copious sweating (cholinergic)	
Heart		
SA node	Increased rate	Decreased rate
Muscle	Increased force of contraction	
Lungs		
Bronchi	Dilation	Constriction
Stomach		
Wall	Decreased motility and tone	Increased motility and tone
Glands	Stimulates secretion of alkaline juice with low enzyme activity	Stimulates secretion of acid juice with high enzyme activity
Intestine		
Wall	Decreased motility and tone	Increased motility and tone
Anal sphincter	Contraction	Inhibition
Pancreas	Vasoconstriction may diminish secretion	Stimulates secretion of pancreatic enzymes
Suprarenal gland		
Medulla	Secretion of epinephrine	
Urinary bladder		
Wall	Inhibition	Excitation
Sphincter	Excitation	Inhibition
Penis	Ejaculation	Erection (vasodilation)
Arrector pili muscles of hair follicles	Contraction	
Arterioles		
Splanchnic region and skin	Constriction	
Skeletal muscles		
Baro- and chemoreceptor response	Constriction	
Responses to exercise and alarm	Dilation	

of the skull to the coccyx (Fig. 283). Some preganglionic fibers synapse in these ganglia; others continue to **prevertebral ganglia** and still others reach and supply cells in the suprarenal glands (Fig. 284). Prevertebral ganglia lie in the pelvis and abdomen, near the aorta and its branches. Three large prevertebral ganglia, named according to their positions near their respective arteries, are the celiac, superior mesenteric and inferior mesenteric. Preganglionic fibers leading to the prevertebral ganglia form the *splanchnic nerves.* The principal splanchnic nerves arising from the thoracic region are the greater, lesser and least splanchnic nerves (Fig. 285).

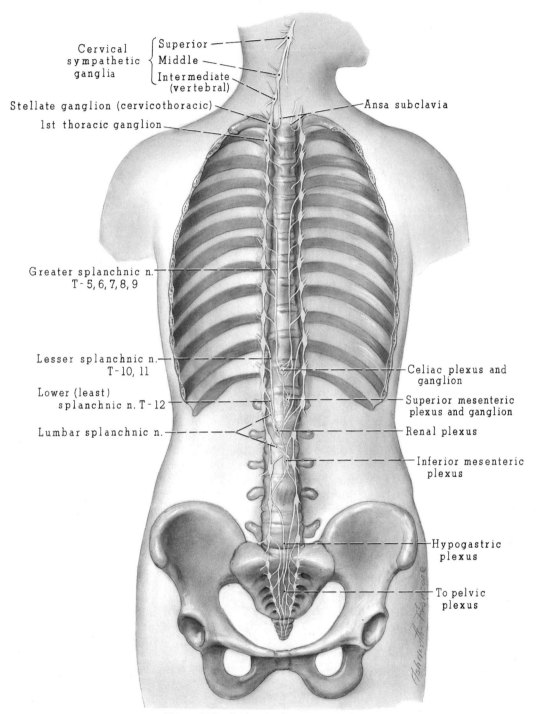

Cervical sympathetic ganglia
- Superior
- Middle
- Intermediate (vertebral)

Stellate ganglion (cervicothoracic)

1st thoracic ganglion

Ansa subclavia

Greater splanchnic n.
T- 5, 6, 7, 8, 9

Lesser splanchnic n.
T- 10, 11

Lower (least) splanchnic n. T- 12

Lumbar splanchnic n.

Celiac plexus and ganglion

Superior mesenteric plexus and ganglion

Renal plexus

Inferior mesenteric plexus

Hypogastric plexus

To pelvic plexus

Figure 283. Sympathetic nervous system.

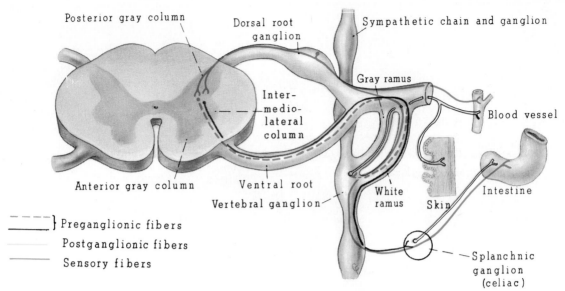

Figure 284.   Pathways for distribution of sympathetic fibers.

Some of the postganglionic sympathetic neurons that synapse with preganglionic neurons in paravertebral ganglia return to spinal nerves via the **gray ramus communicans** (so called because postganglionic fibers are nonmyelinated), and by traveling with these nerves supply, in the regions served by spinal nerves, smooth muscle of blood vessels in the skin and skeletal muscles, arrector pili muscles of hair follicles and sweat glands. Neurons whose postganglionic fibers are in gray rami communicating with spinal nerves in the cervical region (which serve, among other things, the upper extremities) and sacral region synapse with preganglionic fibers that have ascended the sympathetic chain from the thoracic region or descended from the lumbar region. Other postganglionic sympathetic neurons that synapse with preganglionic fibers in paravertebral ganglia do not return to spinal nerves and serve the head region generally and the thoracic viscera. The fibers of some of these postganglionic neurons travel with branches of cranial nerves to reach their destinations; others pass to individual organs. In the head region, the postganglionic fibers arise from cervical paravertebral ganglia and innervate the smooth muscles of the eye (the ciliary muscle, which controls the convexity of the lens,

and the iris, which controls the diameter of the pupil) and the pineal gland in addition to blood vessels of the skin and skeletal muscles, sweat glands and arrector pili muscles.

Since sympathetic innervation to the head, neck and upper extremities comes from preganglionic fibers in the white rami communicans of T-1, 2, 3, and 4, which must pass up to cervical paravertebral ganglia, it is obvious that division of the sympathetic trunk at a level between T-1 and C-8 results in an interruption of sympathetic supply to the head, neck and most of the upper extremities. This produces Horner's syndrome, which includes narrowing of the palpebral fissure, small pupil and absence of sweating over the involved area (head, neck and upper extremities).

Postganglionic neurons that synapse with preganglionic fibers in prevertebral ganglia serve the abdominal and pelvic viscera. These fibers form the great *plexuses* found in close relation to major arteries. The so-called "solar plexus," located in the abdomen alongside the celiac artery, is another name for the *celiac plexus*. This plexus contains postganglionic fibers derived from the celiac ganglia as well as some preganglionic parasympathetic fibers.

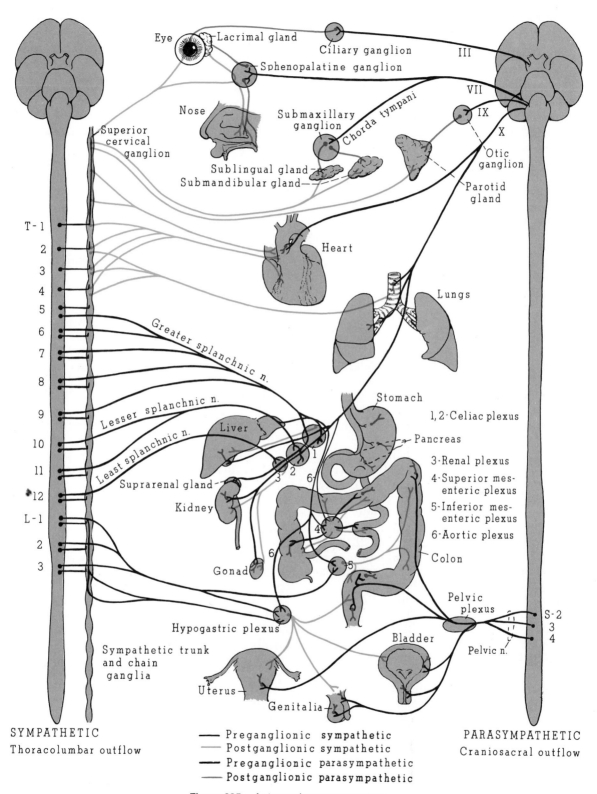

Eye — Lacrimal gland
Ciliary ganglion
III
Sphenopalatine ganglion
VII
Superior cervical ganglion
Nose
Submaxillary ganglion
Chorda tympani
IX
X
Otic ganglion
Sublingual gland
Submandibular gland
Parotid gland
T-1
2
3
4
Heart
5
6
7
8
Greater splanchnic n.
Lungs
9
Stomach
1,2·Celiac plexus
Lesser splanchnic n.
10
Liver
Pancreas
3·Renal plexus
11
Least splanchnic n.
1
4·Superior mesenteric plexus
12
Suprarenal gland
3 2 6
5·Inferior mesenteric plexus
L-1
Kidney
6·Aortic plexus
2
4
3
6
Colon
Gonad
5
Pelvic plexus
Hypogastric plexus
S-2
3
4
Sympathetic trunk and chain ganglia
Bladder
Pelvic n.
Uterus
Genitalia

SYMPATHETIC
Thoracolumbar outflow

—— Preganglionic **sympathetic**
—— Postganglionic sympathetic
—— Preganglionic **parasympathetic**
—— Postganglionic **parasympathetic**

PARASYMPATHETIC
Craniosacral outflow

Figure 285. Autonomic nervous system.

OUTFLOW OF THE PARASYMPATHETIC NERVOUS SYSTEM

The cell bodies of preganglionic parasympathetic neurons are located in the brain stem and in the second, third and fourth sacral segments of the spinal cord. Their axons are long and synapse with postganglionic fibers in four ganglia in the head (Fig. 285) or in *terminal ganglia* lying upon or within the walls of the innervated organs. **Cranial preganglionic fibers** exit via the third (oculomotor), seventh (facial), ninth (glossopharyngeal) and tenth (vagus) cranial nerves. They synapse with postganglionic fibers leading to innervation of the following organs: oculomotor, iris and ciliary muscles of the eyes; facial, salivary glands (submaxillaries and sublinguals) and lacrimal glands; glossopharyngeal, salivary glands (parotids); and vagus, thoracic, abdominal and pelvic viscera.

The **sacral preganglionic fibers** leave the spinal cord via the ventral roots, branching off to proceed peripherally as the *pelvic nerve,* which enters into the formation of the *pelvic plexus* (Fig. 285), from which branches lead to terminal ganglia. Sacral postganglionic fibers innervate the lower colon, rectum, bladder and reproductive organs.

The craniosacral, or parasympathetic, nervous system can be surgically altered in treatment of various disease states. The vagus nerves are divided for the treatment of duodenal ulcer. When the vagus nerves are divided, there is an important influence on hydrochloric acid secretion by the stomach. This results in the elimination of the cephalic phase of gastric secretion (see Chapter 13) with diminished production of hydrochloric acid by the parietal cells.

CONTROL OF THE AUTONOMIC NERVOUS SYSTEM

The hypothalamus is an important center for regulation and integration of both sympathetic and parasympathetic activity. It is connected with the cerebral cortex indirectly through the thalamus and also by direct afferent and efferent fibers with centers in the spinal cord. It joins with the peripheral and autonomic nervous systems, as well as with the hypophysis. Sympathetic control appears to reside in the posterior and lateral hypothalamic regions. Stimulation of these regions produces an increase in visceral and metabolic activities seen in the "fight-or-flight" response, including increase in heartbeat, dilation of the pupils, a rise in blood pressure and inhibition of the alimentary tract and urinary bladder.

Parasympathetic control apparently resides in the anterior and medial hypothalamus. If this region is stimulated, the cardiac rate is decreased and there is increased motility and tone of muscles of the alimentary tract and the urinary bladder.

ASPECTS OF THE FUNCTIONAL ORGANIZATION OF THE NERVOUS SYSTEM

To understand how the nervous system functions it is necessary to examine pathways for sensory input to specific parts of the central nervous system, interconnections between functional regions of the central nervous system and efferent pathways leading to specific actions. This section describes aspects of the functional organization of the nervous system from the simple to the complex, and includes discussions of reflexes, sensory perception, motor function, emotional behavior and language.

Reflex Action

A reflex action is an involuntary response to a sensory stimulus. A well-known example is the patellar reflex, or knee jerk. Many actions are partially voluntary and partially reflex. For example, a mixture of volition and reflex activity is involved in the act of swallowing. In general the numerous and diverse reflexes involved in a specific behavior pattern are so interrelated that the result is one continuous smooth and well-directed action, each reflex merging with the next in rapid sequence. Reflex actions are often thought of as machine-like, but they are also purposeful, in general serving to protect the body. For instance, the reflexive contraction of the pupil of the eye when illuminated by bright light serves to protect the retina.

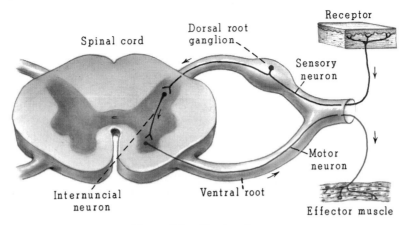

Figure 286.   Simple reflex arc.

The following elements are involved in a typical spinal cord reflex arc (Fig. 286):

1. A receptor.

2. A sensory neuron.

3. Synapse in the spinal cord between sensory and internuncial neurons (with the exception of the stretch reflexes, such as the knee jerk, described below).

4. Synapse between internuncial and motor neurons.

5. Junction between motor neuron and skeletal muscle.

It should be borne in mind that sensory neurons forming part of reflex arcs usually also make other synaptic connections including, if the sensation is consciously perceived, with neuronal pathways leading to the sensory cortex. In addition, internuncial neurons are usually not simply links in a single reflex arc, but have connections with other groups of internuncial neurons, thus making very complex reflex arcs possible.

Much of our knowledge of reflex action has come from studies of spinal cord reflexes in animals whose spinal cord has been transected. Two spinal cord reflexes that have been intensively studied are the stretch reflex, typified by the knee jerk, and the flexor reflex, also called the withdrawal reflex, in which withdrawal of a limb brought about by muscle flexion occurs in response to stimulation of pain, or *nociceptive* (L. *nocere*, to hurt; L. *capere*, to take), receptors (although almost any stimulus may elicit this response).

The **stretch reflex**, also called the *myo-*

tactic reflex (G. *mys*, muscle; G. *tasis*, a stretching), is a monosynaptic reflex and employs only two types of neurons—sensory and motor. A method used clinically to evaluate the state of the stretch reflexes is to check the knee jerk or other muscle jerks by striking, for instance, the patellar tendon with a reflex hammer. Striking the tendon produces a rapid stretching of the muscle that is picked up by the muscle spindle receptors. The signal then travels to the cord, and a motor neuron is triggered to stimulate the muscle.

The stretch reflex plays an essential role in maintaining normal posture and is most pronounced in the *antigravity muscles,* such as the elevators of the jaw and the extensors of the neck, back, knee and ankle. The reflex response to stretching the muscles by the force of gravity maintains, without conscious effort, an upright body and head and a closed jaw. Skeletal muscle tone, the steady state of partial contraction normally exhibited by all skeletal muscles, is dependent upon the integrity of the stretch reflex. Interrupting sensory input from muscle spindles to the spinal cord by cutting the dorsal roots will cause a muscle to become almost flaccid.

Muscle tone is also governed by excitatory and inhibitory impulses arising chiefly from the reticular formation that act on motor neurons and neurons that control the sensitivity of the muscle spindle called **gamma efferents.** This action makes possible continuous adjustments in muscle tone for maintaining balance and support. The

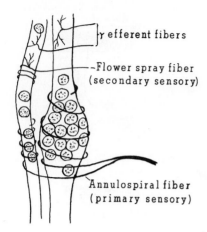

Figure 287.   Innervation of muscle spindle.

gamma efferents are so called because their fibers are Type A gamma (small diameter — see page 233) as distinguished from the Type A alpha fibers of the motor neurons, which stimulate muscle contraction, and of the primary sensory neurons of the muscle spindle. The spindle itself is composed of muscle fibers (called *intrafusal fibers*) of smaller diameter than the regular muscle fibers, surrounded by a capsule. The central, noncontractile portion of the muscle spindle fibers is innervated by sensory endings sensitive to stretch, the end portions by gamma efferents (Fig. 287). When a muscle is stretched, the entire lengths of the spindle fibers are stretched and the sensory endings are stimulated. Stimulation of muscle fibers by gamma efferents causes the ends to contract. This stretches the central region and thus has the same effect on the sensory endings as stretching the muscle. Decreased stimulation by gamma efferents has the opposite effect. The spindle fibers are innervated by two types of sensory neurons, namely, those forming **primary,** or **annulospiral, endings** and those forming secondary, or "flower spray," endings. The annulospiral endings respond very strongly to a change in length and adapt rapidly; the secondary endings respond less strongly to a change in length, and do not readily adapt.

Excessive stretching of a muscle, which could tear it, will inhibit the stretch reflex as a result of what is known as the *reverse myotactic reflex.* The receptors for this reflex (the *Golgi tendon organ*) respond to excessive stretch by triggering an inhibitory

reflex arc presumably formed by sensory fibers from the receptor leading to inhibitory internuncial neurons, which synapse with motor neurons.

The **flexor,** or **withdrawal, reflex** differs from the stretch reflex in a number of ways. The stretch reflex is, as mentioned, monosynaptic and its effect is circumscribed; that is, only the muscle that was stretched contracts. The withdrawal reflex, on the other hand, is diffuse, involving a complex network of synapses between sensory neurons and internuncial neurons, which in turn interconnect with other internuncial neurons in more than one segment of the cord both ipsilaterally (on the same side — L. *ipse,* self; L. *latus,* side) and contralaterally (on the opposite side — L. *contra,* against). Thus, stepping on a nail will normally cause withdrawal of the entire lower extremity with flexion of the knee and thigh. In addition, the opposite limb will be extended, giving rise to the *crossed extension reflex.* Furthermore, when the flexors causing the withdrawal are stimulated, the antagonists, the extensors, are inhibited and relax. Likewise, with the associated crossed extension reflex, stimulation of the extensors on the opposite side is accompanied by inhibition of the flexors. This phenomenon, inhibition of an antagonist when a prime mover contracts, is called *reciprocal innervation.* Another characteristic of withdrawal reflexes not displayed by stretch reflexes is a phenomenon called *after discharge,* the continuation of a response after the stimulation ends. The existence of alternate pathways in flexor responses (so-called parallel and reverberating circuits, illustrated in Fig. 288) can account for this.

Mention was made in the discussion of stretch reflexes of excitatory and inhibitory impulses from higher centers acting on spinal cord neurons. Normal reflex activity of the spinal cord depends upon these discharges, the net effect of which is normally excitatory. Their interruption by transection of the cord causes what is known as **spinal shock,** a condition in which, among other things, almost all spinal reflexes below the transection are completely abolished. In frogs, reflex activity returns to normal in minutes. Dogs and cats recover in days. Humans require months for recovery, and even then the reflex responses are generally abnormal and may be

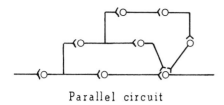

Parallel circuit

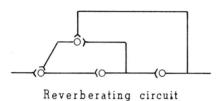

Reverberating circuit

Figure 288. Parallel and reverberating neuronal circuits.

weak, excessive or spasmodic. One of the responses seen in humans after accidental cord transection or damage to certain motor tracts (the pyramidal tracts usually—see page 293) is the *Babinski reflex,* an abnormal response to stimulation of the sole of the foot. The normal response to stimulation of the sole of the foot, called the *plantar reflex,* is plantar flexion of the toes. The sign of Babinski (observed in infants before they learn to walk as well as in cases of damage to the nervous system) is dorsiflexion of the big toe and fanning out of the others. Midbrain transection between the superior and inferior colliculi (decerebrate preparation) has a quite different effect from spinal transection. Extensor tone, especially of the antigravity muscles, is increased, producing a condition known as **decerebrate rigidity.** This occurs because inhibitory impulses acting on stretch reflexes are lost (because of interruption of input to the inhibitory area of the reticular formation principally from the cerebral cortex and basal ganglia) whereas facilitatory pathways arising from the intrinsically active vestibular nuclei of the medulla (which receive input from the equilibrium receptors of the inner ear, referred to as the vestibular apparatus) and the facilitatory area of the reticular formation are intact. The facilitatory area of the reticular formation is more than normally active in this condition because of the absence of inhibitory input signals from the cerebral cortex and basal ganglia.

In some reflexes involving sensory input and motor outflow in spinal nerves the coordinating centers are in the brain. One especially important group of reflexes of this type is the *tonic neck reflexes,* which bring about postural changes in the limbs in response to bending or rotation of the head that tend to provide support in the direction of the head movement. Turning or bending the head to the right, for example, will increase the tone of the extensors on the right side and of the flexors on the left.

Reflexes are sometimes distinguished as either superficial or deep. Superficial reflexes are those produced by stimulation on the surface of the body. The pupil contraction plantar and withdrawal reflexes previously mentioned are examples, as is the abdominal reflex, in which cutaneous stimulation of a quadrant of the abdomen results in contraction of the muscles of that quadrant. Deep reflexes involve stimulation of deep structures, such as the muscle spindle, tendon receptors or receptors in blood vessels.

While reflexes in themselves serve many important functions, such as avoiding injury, keeping the body and head upright, preventing excessive changes in blood pressure (by altering the diameter of arterioles and changing the rate and contractile force of the heart) and emptying the bladder, the question may be asked: Do they play roles other than those that can be clearly identified? It has been suggested that they do, or at least that sets of circuits involved in reflex responses constitute "prefabricated" units for building volitional movements, such as walking and performing athletic feats. It has been argued in support of this view that since, with minor exceptions, fibers descending from the motor cortex synapse only with internuncial neurons, it is at least in theory possible for this to occur.

Pathways for Conscious Sensory Perception

The pathways for sensations that are consciously perceived lead to the cerebral cortex. The sensory cortical projection areas are illustrated in Figure 244. Areas 1, 2 and 3, in the **postcentral gyrus** of the parietal lobe, are the receptive areas for touch, pressure, temperature, pain and kinesthesia (see page 231) from all parts of the body and head. Area 17, in the occipital lobe, is the sensory receptive area for vision; area 41, in the temporal lobe, is the cortical area for hearing. The area for equilibrium is believed to be closely associated with the area for hearing. The sensory projection area for taste is in the parietal lobe; for smell in the temporal lobe. All consciously perceived sensory impulses, except those for smell, are relayed through the **thalamus.** The thalamus is responsible for a primitive, or *protopathic,* sensibility—a crude awareness of the kind of sensation, whether the sensation is pleasant or unpleasant, and its general location. Discriminatory sensibility is dependent upon the cerebral cortex. The specific pathways for the special senses are described in Chapter 9. Described below are the pathways for touch, pressure, temperature, pain and kinesthesia. These sensations are often called the *somesthetic sensations,* and their cortical projection region in the postcentral gyrus is generally referred to as the *somesthetic cortex.*

The pathways for somesthetic sensations involve three neurons. The sensory neuron is the first-order neuron and leads from a receptor to the gray matter of the spinal cord or to nuclei in the brain. The second-order neuron passes to the thalamus and the third-order neuron to the somesthetic cortex.

Pathways for Pain, Temperature, Crude Touch and Pressure from the Body. The major pathways for pain, temperature and crude tactile sensations involve second-order neurons that ascend the spinal cord in the **spinothalamic tracts.** The sensory nerve fibers enter the cord through the dorsal roots and after ascending or, in some cases, descending a few spinal segments make synaptic connections with neurons that give rise to the lateral and ventral spinothalamic tracts, which decussate (cross) to the opposite side of the cord before ascending to the thalamus. The *lateral spinothalamic tracts* transmit principally pain and temperature sensations (Fig. 289). The *ventral spinothalamic tracts* transmit principally crude touch and pressure. The second-order neurons synapse in the thalamus with third-order neurons that convey impulses principally to the somesthetic cortex.

Pathways for Discriminatory Touch and Pressure and for Kinesthesia from the Body. The pathways for discriminatory tactile sensations and for kinesthesia from the body involve first-order neurons that ascend the spinal cord in the **dorsal columns.** The sensory neuron fibers forming the dorsal columns pass up the cord to nuclei in the medulla on the same side that they enter the cord in two tracts, the *fasciculus gracilis* and the *fasciculus cuneatus* (Fig. 290). In the medulla the first-order neurons synapse with neurons that cross to the opposite side and ascend to the thalamus in a broad band of fibers called the *medial lemniscus.* Third-order neurons project principally to the somesthetic cortex.

Although tactile sensations are transmitted by both the spinothalamic tracts and dorsal columns, only those transmitted via the dorsal columns provide precise localization, discrete two-point discrimination and an awareness of fine gradations of intensity and of vibratory sensations.

Somesthetic Sensory Input from the Head. Sensory fibers for touch, pressure, pain and temperature in the head are carried by the fifth (trigeminal) cranial nerve. Kinesthetic sensations are transmitted by those cranial nerves that contain motor fibers supplying the muscles of the head. These pathways also involve three neurons with fibers of the third-order neurons projecting from the thalamus to the somesthetic cortex.

Representation in the Somesthetic Cortex. Since all somesthetic sensations from the body are transmitted by tracts that decussate, either in the cord or the medulla, the postcentral gyrus of each cerebral hemisphere receives input from the opposite side of the body. The same is true for sensations from the head, except for pain and temperature. Each cerebral hemisphere receives pain and temperature input from both sides of the head.

The representation of the different parts of the body in the postcentral gyrus is illustrated in Figure 244. The size of the cortical area on this topographical map is proportional to the number of incoming fibers from a given part of the body. Thus the area for the fingers, which have a high concentration of receptors at their tips, is larger than the area for the entire trunk.

Determination of the shape, size, texture and weight of an object requires integration of sensory input in the somesthetic cortex. Further integration in the somesthetic asso-

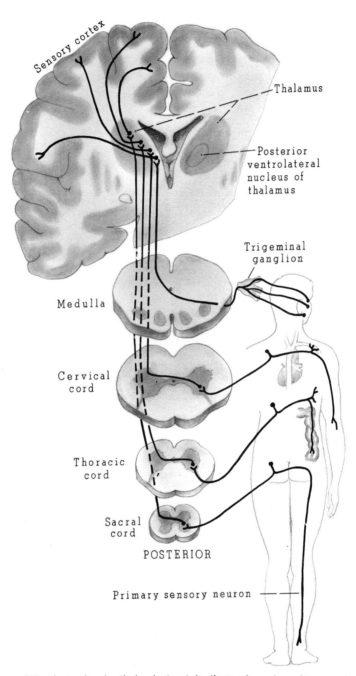

Figure 289. Lateral spinothalamic tract (pathway for pain and temperature).

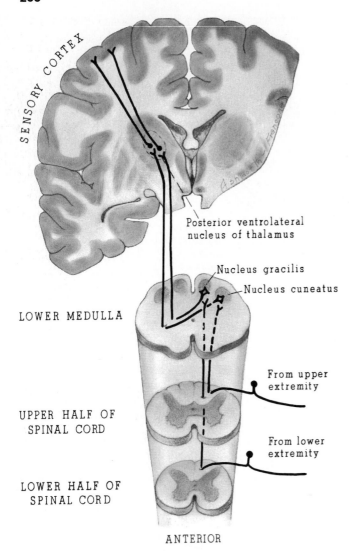

Posterior ventrolateral
nucleus of thalamus

Nucleus gracilis

Nucleus cuneatus

LOWER MEDULLA

From upper
extremity

UPPER HALF OF
SPINAL CORD

From lower
extremity

LOWER HALF OF
SPINAL CORD

ANTERIOR

Figure 290. Fasciculi gracilis and cuneatus of dorsal funiculus (pathway for kinesthesia and discrimenatory tactile sensations).

ciation areas adjacent to the postcentral gyrus makes it possible to identify a particular object; for example, a knife or a pencil. Synthesis of sensory data and the relation of information of the moment with that of the past in the association areas is necessary for the recognition of the nature and use of an object.

Role of the Reticular Activating System. In the late 1940's H. W. Magoun and Giuseppe Moruzzi discovered that electrical stimulation of parts of the reticular formation (see page 244) awakened a drowsing cat. Direction stimulation of the sensory cortex had been shown to have no such effect. Magoun and Moruzzi therefore concluded that the reticular formation,

among other things, functioned as an alarm to awaken the brain and so named it the *reticular activating system.* Since then it has been found that all sensory pathways leading to the cerebral cortex have branches passing to the reticular formation. With respect to the somesthetic sensory systems, fibers of second-order neurons leading to the thalamus give off collaterals that feed into the reticular formation. Just about any sensory input to the reticular activating system can initiate a general stimulation of the entire cerebral cortex and other parts of the brain. With experience, the reticular formation comes to be discriminating in its response to different stimuli, so that, for example, sounds of traffic will not cause a city dweller to be aroused but the smell of smoke may. The reticular activating system receives not only sensory input but also input from various parts of the cerebrum. This can account for the observation that activities such as whistling, conversation and movement can help maintain a wakeful state. Destruction of the reticular activating system will produce a permanent comatose state.

Degeneration of Areas of the Spinal Cord Affecting Sensory Pathways

Tabes Dorsalis. This is a disease caused by syphilis and characterized by progressive degeneration of the posterior columns. It results in ataxia (failure of muscular coordination). In addition, since individuals with this condition are unaware of the rate, force, direction and extent of movement of the limbs, they must watch their feet when walking to avoid staggering. Stereognosis, the ability to identify an object with the eyes closed, is also lost in tabes dorsalis.

Syringomyelia. Syringomyelia is a condition of the spinal cord in which there is excessive multiplication of the neuroglia in the central gray substance accompanied by formation of cysts. The fibers that cross in the white substance in this entity undergo degeneration, interrupting the pain and temperature pathways of the lateral spinothalamic tract. Sensations of touch, pressure and kinesthesia are not impaired. Tumors and hemorrhage within the spinal cord destroy parts of the cord with similar dissociation effects.

Multiple Sclerosis. Multiple sclerosis is a disease of the central nervous system characterized by a patchy demyelinization in multiple areas resulting in many symptoms involving both sensory and motor systems. These include virtually all the dysfunctions of the nervous system. There is no specific treatment. Multiple sclerosis is a chronic disease marked by periods of absence of symptoms sometimes lasting months or years. Recent findings suggest that it may be caused by a viral infection that provokes an autoimmune response in which the myelin sheath is attacked and changed by the body's own immune system.

Aspects of the Physiology of Pain

As described in the section on sensory receptors, painful stimuli are received at naked nerve endings and are carried through myelinated A-delta fibers (fast, sharp, localized pain) and nonmyelinated C fibers (slow, burning, diffuse pain).

Stimuli effective in arousing the sensation of pain vary to some degree for each tissue. The very existence of pain impulses arising from the viscera was debated until it was shown that adequate stimuli for pain originating in the heart or digestive tract, for example, were different from those producing pain in the skin. Skin is sensitive to cutting and burning, whereas this type of stimulation does not give rise to distress when applied to the stomach or intestine. Pain in the digestive tract is produced by distention or spasm of the smooth muscle, as well as by chemical irritation of an inflamed mucosa. Severe pain can occur in skeletal muscle when the blood supply is reduced — the basis of a condition known as intermittent claudication (pain in the calf associated with arterial disease of the lower extremities).

Ischemia (reduction in oxygen supply), the only proved cause of pain in the heart muscle, is responsible for angina pectoris (chest pain transmitted to the left shoulder and arm, usually caused by physical exertion or emotional stress in individuals with narrowed coronary arteries) and the pain of myocardial infarction (blockage of the coronary artery to the heart with death of heart muscle).

Most pain impulses from the viscera are carried by fibers running in sympathetic nerves. These fibers enter the cord through the dorsal roots by way of the white rami communicans (Fig. 284). A few visceral pain impulses are transmitted by sacral parasympathetic and cranial nerves.

Referred Pain (Fig. 291). When pain is aroused by stimulation of afferent endings in the viscera, it is usually referred to some other skin area, a fact of great diagnostic importance.

Afferent nerves from the viscera terminate in the spinal cord segment which supplies the particular viscus involved. Those areas to which pain from various organs is referred have been mapped out; they indicate

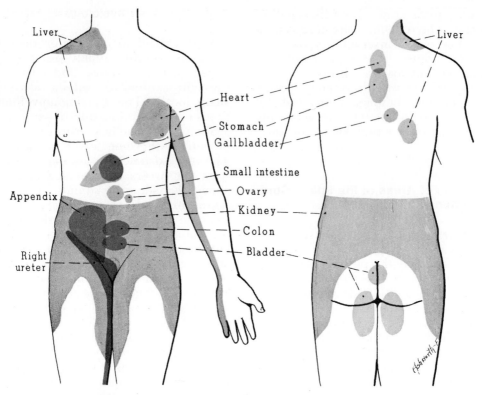

Figure 291.   Areas of referred pain, anterior and posterior views.

to the physician the internal source of irritation. For example, the sensory fibers from the heart terminate in the third cervical through the fifth thoracic cord segments, and pain arising in the heart as a result of ischemia is not localized specifically to the region of the heart, but to those superficial structures whose sensory nerves also terminate in these spinal segments. Therefore, the pain felt under the upper sternum usually radiates to the skin of the left shoulder and arm. It is believed that the pain is referred to the skin of the arm and shoulder because ascending second order neurons receiving impulses from the skin of the arm and shoulder also receive signals from the heart.

Parietal Pain.   Pain from the viscera may spread to the parietal layer of the peritoneum, pleura or pericardium, each of which is innervated by spinal nerves. Parietal pain is, in contrast to true visceral pain, sharp and localized directly over the painful organ.

Phantom Limb Pain.   Following an amputation, the patient can retain the amputated limb as a part of his body image. This

is a reflection of the association established between stimuli from the periphery and the cortical area of representation. Stimuli continue to arise from the severed sensory nerves and are interpreted centrally as arising, for example, from the hand. Yet the patient mistakenly feels that his pain is imaginary, since he knows his hand was amputated. Pain of this kind places additional psychological burdens on the patient who believes he is imagining things his reason tells him cannot exist. It is important to explain to this type of patient that the sensation of pain is real and not a figment of his imagination. The sensation can be defined clearly, and the patient will say that his arm is twisted or that his thumb is being pushed backward. The cortical image of the amputated extremity can remain fixed in the same position as when amputation occurred. This is particularly true in traumatic amputations.

The management of phantom limb pain is more effective if measures are taken to prevent it rather than treat it once the condition has been established. If pain is due to a surgical amputation, anesthetic infiltration of the nerve bundles at the site of amputation should be performed before surgery. In this way, the surgeon can probably minimize the locking or painful image in the patient's consciousness.

Distribution and Control of Pain. Not all second order neurons of pain pathways ascend directly to the thalamus in the spinothalamic tracts. Many fibers (probably all of the C type) synapse in the reticular formation. Here connections are made with neurons that send fibers to the hypothalamus as well as to the thalamus. The distribution of pain signals from the hypothalamus and thalamus is more widespread than for nonpain signals.

It is generally recognized that the reaction to pain can be influenced by such things as anxiety, thought processes, hypnosis and past experience, and by application of liniments, irritants or heat to the skin. These modifying effects can be explained by the degree of presynaptic inhibition (see p. 230) of nerve fibers conducting pain impulses in the cord or thalamus. Pain fibers, after entering the spinal cord, pass upward one or two segments and synapse with a group of interneurons that make up what is known as the *substantia gelatinosa*. Pain impulses are then transmitted through one or more interneurons, the last of which gives rise to the spinothalamic tracts. The substantia gelatinosa also receives input from interneurons that make synaptic contact with collaterals from nonpain sensory fibers. It is believed that modulation of pain signals in the substantia gelatinosa is brought about by presynaptic inhibition of pain fibers by these interneurons. This proposed action is generally referred to as the **"gate control" theory.** Control of pain by the cerebral cortex is brought about by descending pathways that have an inhibitory action in the substantia gelatinosa or thalamus.

Surgery for Control of Pain (Fig. 292)

Various methods have been employed to surgically relieve pain. In the majority of patients, however, medical measures are adequate. There remains, however, a group of people requiring surgical treatment.

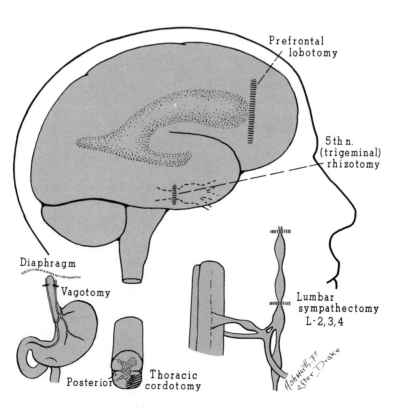

Figure 292. Surgery for control of pain.

From a physiologic point of view, interruption of pain impulses has been carried out at three points: (1) the autonomic nervous system; (2) pathways in the peripheral nerves, spinal roots, and spinal cord; and (3) interruption of pathways within the brain. The various procedures performed on the autonomic nervous system consist of some form of sympathectomy. The most frequently employed operation on the parasympathetic system is interruption of the vagus nerves.

Division of the peripheral nerves or spinal pathways is sometimes undertaken for pain not responsive to other means (intractable pain). The pathways within the spinal cord conveying pain impulses can be interrupted. The anterolateral, or spinothalamic, tracts are sectioned in an operation known as anterolateral *cordotomy*. A cordotomy can be performed as high as the second cervical segment if pain relief in the arm is required. However, the optimal site for division of the spinothalamic tract is the upper thoracic region. Posterior cordotomy occasionally gives good results in patients with phantom limb pain of the lower extremities. The trigeminal root ganglion can be interrupted for tic douloureux.

A distinction must be drawn between the sensations of pain and the response of the patient to the pain. By means of operations on the frontal cortex, it is possible to alter the patient's reaction, so that, while pain is felt, the reaction is completely changed. Operations on the frontal cortex are associated with personality changes (see Fig. 292 for location of this procedure).

Headache

Headache is one of the most common of all symptoms and can occur in the absence of definite pathology or as a manifestation of serious illness. Most headaches are transient, but a few are chronic, occurring over a period of months or years. A headache can result from stimulation of any pain-sensitive structure in the head.

Headaches that occur only occasionally are caused by fatigue, eyestrain, or perhaps dietary indiscretion. Headaches persisting for weeks or months without relief, except in intensity, are often associated with psy-chologic abnormalities. When headaches occur with emotional tension, the pain commonly starts in the occipital region and spreads over the entire head. Often the patient describes it as a pressure sensation arising within the head.

Migraine. Migraine is a disorder characterized by recurrent attacks of headaches with or without associated visual or gastrointestinal disturbances. It occurs in 5 to 10 per cent of the population, usually in women, and is most frequently noted in the second or third decade of life. Headache in patients with migraine can be preceded by a period of depression or restlessness. The pain is usually generalized, but is sometimes sharply localized to one side of the head. In any given case, the symptoms seem to follow a pattern. Nausea and vomiting are common during the first attack. A patient with a migraine headache has abnormal sensitivity to light.

Organic Sensations

Organic sensations include sensations such as hunger (appetite, hunger pangs, and hunger drive), thirst, urination and defecation urges, nausea, and sex sensation.

The nature of the internal conditions leading to the various components of hunger is still quite a mystery. *Appetite* is the longing for a preferred food substance, and is associated with conditioned reflexes such as salivation and secretion of stomach juices. Food preferences are determined by previous experience, genetic factors, and dietary deficiencies. Specific hungers often occur when the body needs certain substances. Human infants and primitive peoples usually prefer foods that are best for them. In one classic study, where babies were allowed to select their own foods, an infant with rickets at the beginning of the study cured himself by selecting large amounts of cod liver oil containing vitamin D. *Hunger pangs* can occur as the result of strong stomach contractions, although the hunger drive can clearly operate in the absence of these contractions, which may be only a by-product of the physiological state of the individual. Animals without stomachs exhibit a desire for food more often than do normal animals. Lowered blood sugar level apparently is an important factor in creating desire for food. This factor operates through centers in the hypothalamus, which contains more blood vessels than any other part of the nervous system and receives circulatory, chemical, sensory and neural stimuli. The hypothalamus plays an important role in the control of other drives such as thirst and sex. In the case of thirst, the intensity of the drive is related to the water deficit. Thus, a dehydrated individual will consume enough water to replace his water deficit within about 30 minutes. It is thought that concentration of salt and other chemical substances in the body fluids, as well as the total amount of fluid present in the body, helps to determine thirst.

Nausea is a disagreeable sensation in the epigastrium which may or may not be associated with vomiting, and which is carried by both the vagus nerve and by sympathetic nerves. There is a vomiting center in the reticular formation of the medulla which receives impulses from a *chemoreceptor trigger zone* located above the area postrema of the brainstem. This zone is the central site of action of the so-called *emetic* drugs, which cause vomiting.

The sensation of *air hunger* is a result of excess carbon dioxide accumulation in the lungs. Although oxygen is a constant requirement of the body, the body cannot respond directly to oxygen lack. However, as oxygen is used up, carbon dioxide collects in the lungs, causing great discomfort unless the reflex breathing mechanisms are able to again substitute oxygen for carbon dioxide. When oxygen starvation occurs in an atmosphere lacking excess carbon dioxide—for example at high altitudes—a kind of intoxication results. The individual may undergo memory impairment and paralysis or may shout or burst into tears. At the same time he feels confident of his abilities and does not realize the seriousness of his condition. There is evidence that partial oxygen starvation brings out emotional reactions which are normally held under voluntary control.

Consciousness of *fatigue* impels human beings to seek rest. Everybody is aware of how desperate the need for sleep can become. As a result of prolonged exercise, the chemistry of the blood is altered in several ways. An elevated concentration of lactic acid in muscles presumably stimulates the nervous system directly or activates certain receptors. In sleepiness, it may be that nerve and brain centers are directly stimulated by chemical conditions in the body. The story of fatigue is complicated by the fact that it sometimes seems to result not from physical exertion but from boredom, worry, or frustration.

Pathways for Motor Function

In humans the motor areas of the cerebral hemisphere are essential for movement. This is in distinction to lower animals, such as dogs and cats, in which reasonable locomotion is possible even after destruction of the motor cortex. *Area 4*, located in the frontal lobe in the precentral gyrus, is the **primary motor cortex.** Discrete movements involving a small number of individual muscles are initiated by activating specific loci in area 4. Figure 244 illustrates the topographical map of this area. The size of the cortical representation of a part of the body is proportional to the dexterity with which the movements are performed. Thus, the hand occupies the largest area. *Area 6*, located in the frontal lobe adjacent to area 4, is another important motor area. The parts of the body are not clearly represented in this area. Stimulation of certain loci in area 6 initiates coordinated movements involving groups of skeletal muscles rather than any individual muscle. Other smaller, supplementary motor areas are distributed throughout the cerebral cortex.

Distinction Between the Pyramidal and Extrapyramidal Systems

Two major motor pathways can be distinguished anatomically and functionally. They are (1) the **pyramidal system,** which initiates voluntary, skilled movements of skeletal muscles (especially of the fingers) via fibers that descend without interruption from the cortical motor areas to the spinal cord, and (2) the **extrapyramidal system,** which initiates some voluntary movement, regulates and coordinates the action of the pyramidal system to insure smoothness of movement, is responsible for various automatic movements, and controls breathing and various visceral functions, such as the heart rate and gastrointestinal motility and activities involving basic drives, such as eating, sleeping, and sex. The pathways of the extrapyramidal system, in contrast to those of the pyramidal system, do not lead from the motor cortex directly to the spinal cord, but rather compose an incompletely worked out network interconnecting various sites in the motor cortex and subcortical centers, including the thalamus, basal ganglia, cerebellum, and reticular formation. The major pathways to the spinal motor neurons arise in the reticular formation and are called the *reticulospinal tracts.*

The tracts of the pyramidal system are known as *pyramidal* or *corticospinal tracts.* The term *pyramidal* arises from the appearance of the tracts as pyramids in the medulla. These tracts arise principally from area 4. About 90 per cent of the fibers cross just below the pyramids; most of the remaining fibers cross at different levels of the cord just before terminating. With minor exceptions, fibers of the corticospinal tracts synapse with internuncial neurons that connect to motor neurons in the ventral horn. As a result of the crossing, the pyramidal system on one side of the brain initiates discrete movements, for the most part on the opposite side of the body. Tracts from the motor cortex to nuclei of cranial nerves that initiate discrete movements of facial muscles are called the *corticobulbar tracts.* The cortical areas for the face, in distinction to those for the body, generally exert bilateral control.

The voluntary movements initiated by the extrapyramidal system have been described as chiefly *axial,* such as bowing, walking, rolling, kneeling, sitting, and standing. Much of our understanding of extrapyramidal voluntary movements has come from the study of the **apraxias,** disorders in the execution of certain types of movements on command that can be explained by damage to fibers linking the language areas in the left cerebral hemisphere (see page 300) with cerebral motor areas. These disorders usually affect the left side of the body because of injury to the corpus callosum,

with the disruption of tracts connecting the left and right cerebral hemispheres. Such patients, upon command to "show me how you comb your hair," can usually carry out the command with the right arm only because the command cannot reach the motor areas in the right hemisphere which initiate voluntary movements via the pyramidal system on the left side of the body. However, commands to walk backwards, kneel, or bend the head down can be executed because the extrapyramidal system on one side of the brain controls axial muscles of the neck and body on both sides.

The extrapyramidal system controls the tone of postural muscles by inhibition or facilitation of the stretch reflexes. In animals such as the dog and cat the red nucleus and the rubrospinal tracts arising from it have important actions on muscle tone. In primates, these structures are small and of lesser importance.

The various types of automatic movements initiated by the extrapyramidal system include arm swinging while walking, gesticulating, and facial expressions such as smiling or frowning in response to emotional stimuli. A good illustration of the difference between facial movements executed deliberately by action of the pyramidal system and automatically by action of the extrapyramidal system in response to emotional stimuli is the difference between the artificial "pyramidal" smile produced when posing for a photograph and the natural "extrapyramidal" smile produced in response to an amusing remark.

Roles of the Basal Ganglia and the Cerebellum.   As mentioned, two important regulatory centers of the extrapyramidal system are the basal ganglia and the cerebellum. In exercising control over the pyramidal system, pathways to the motor cortex from these parts of the brain are relayed through the thalamus. Loss of such control as a result of lesions in the basal ganglia can cause tremor or aimless movements such as involuntary, rapid jerks (chorea as in St. Vitus' dance) or slow, involuntary, writhing movements (athetosis). Rigidity, due to reduction of inhibitory impulses acting on stretch reflexes, is often seen in damage to the basal ganglia. **Parkinson's disease,** a disorder affecting the elderly associated with degeneration of parts of the basal ganglia, is

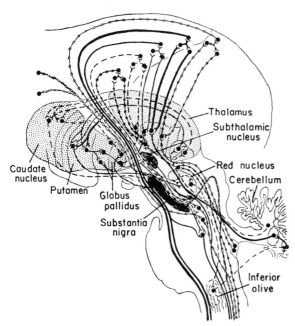

Figure 293. Pathways linking the basal ganglia with related structures of the brain stem, thalamus, and cerebral cortex. (From Jung and Hassler: Handbook of Physiology, Sec. I, Vol. II. The Williams & Wilkins Co., 1960.)

characterized by tremor of the extremities at rest (which disappears with activity), rigidity, hypokinesia (limited, slow movement), and a poverty of expressive, automatic movements. The common denominator of this condition appears to be a loss of neurons projecting from the substantia nigra (a midbrain structure regarded as a functional part of the basal ganglia system) to the caudate nucleus and putamen of the basal ganglia (see Fig. 293) that release the neurotransmitter dopamine (3,4 dihydroxyphenylethylamine). Since dopamine is unable to pass the blood-brain barrier, Parkinsonism is currently treated by administration of a precursor of dopamine that does pass the blood-brain barrier, namely, L-dopa (3,4 dihydroxyphenylalanine).

The cerebellum functions, in part, by comparing (unconsciously) sensory input (from proprioceptors providing information about the action of skeletal muscles, receptors in the internal ear detecting changes in the position and rates of rotation of the head, and receptors for touch, vision, and hearing) with input from the motor cortex and then sending inhibitory signals to the motor cortex that promote smooth, coordinated motor activity. The pathways leading from touch receptors in the skin and proprioceptors sensing muscular activity to the cerebellum are both indirect (collaterals from second order neurons of the dorsal column system ascending from the medulla to the thalamus) and direct (via the spinocerebellar tracts, Fig. 294). Sensory input to the cerebellum comes not only via the pathways from the aforementioned receptors but also from the somesthetic, visual, auditory, and equilibrium areas of the cerebral cortex.

A general term used to describe uncoordinated motor activity, such as is manifested in cerebellar disease, is **ataxia.** Specific disorders caused by cerebellar malfunction include (1) *disequilibrium*, with a drunkenlike gait; (2) *intention tremor*, such as increased shaking of the hand while eating as the fork approaches the mouth; (3) *adiadochokinesis* (G. *a*, absence; G. *diadochos*, succeeding; G. *kinesis*, motion), extreme difficulty with successive movements, such as alternating pronation and supination; (4) *dysmetria* (G. *dys*, abnormal; G. *metron*, a measure), the inability to judge the extent of movements, so that the individual cannot touch an examiner's fingertips without overshoot (hypermetria) or undershoot (hypometria) or carry out a simple act, such as lifting a glass of water, without reducing it to a number of independent, uncoordinated movements (decomposition of movement); and (5) *hypotonia*.

A new technique for controlling epileptic seizures currently under study, which was developed as a result of an understanding of cerebellar function, involves the use of electrodes implanted in the cerebellum. As mentioned, inhibitory signals from the cerebellum to the cerebral cortex prevent inappropriate movements. When an epileptic experiences warning signals of an approaching seizure, the cerebellum can be stimulated to block the seizure.

Paralysis

Paralysis is a complete loss of voluntary motor function. *Paresis* means incomplete paralysis. Types of paralysis include *monoplegia*, paralysis of a single extremity; *hemiplegia*, paralysis of half the body along with corresponding limbs, such as the right

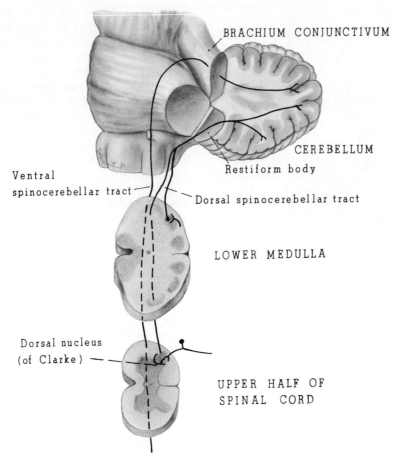

BRACHIUM CONJUNCTIVUM

CEREBELLUM

Restiform body

Ventral
spinocerebellar tract

Dorsal spinocerebellar tract

LOWER MEDULLA

Dorsal nucleus
(of Clarke)

UPPER HALF OF
SPINAL CORD

Figure 294.   Spinocerebellar tracts.

arm and right leg; *paraplegia,* paralysis of both lower extremities; *diplegia,* paralysis of either both upper or both lower extremities; and *quadriplegia,* paralysis of all four extremities.

Paralysis may be either spastic or flaccid. With flaccid paralysis there is a loss of muscle tone; with spastic paralysis there is increased muscle tone in the patient's limbs. Spastic paralysis follows damage to parts of the extrapyramidal system, removing the inhibitory controlling influences on the stretch reflex. Although voluntary movement is lost in spastic paralysis, reflex movement can be elicited. The deep reflexes are increased and the superficial reflexes are diminished or absent (see page 285). There is no muscle atrophy. If tested electrically, muscles react normally to stimulation. Flaccid paralysis usually results

from damage to lower motor neurons. (Lower motor neurons are those with cell bodies in the ventral horn and fibers extending directly to skeletal muscles, as distinguished from the so-called upper motor neurons, which descend from the brain to the spinal cord.) Destruction of the lower motor neurons causes a total loss of muscle tone and later a wasting of the innervated muscles. This is part of the condition referred to as lower motor lesion. Flaccid paralysis is also seen following damage to the pyramids.

Infantile Paralysis (Poliomyelitis). Poliomyelitis is caused by a virus that damages the anterior horn cells of the cord and the motor nuclei of the cranial nerves. It is characterized by flaccid paralysis of the lower motor neuron type without sensory disturbances.

Brain Centers and Pathways for Emotional Experiences and Behavior

One of the first physiologists to propose that specific parts of the brain are concerned with emotional experiences and responses was James W. Papez. In part on the basis of the observation that rabies, a disease causing severe emotional disturbances, seemed to damage parts of an area of the cerebral cortex referred to as the rhinencephalon (G. *rhis*, nose; G *enkephalos*, brain) because it apparently receives olfactory impulses, Papez suggested that centers for emotions were located in this region of the brain. The **hippocampus,** a curved elevation of modified cortex (containing three rather than six layers of neurons) on the floor of the inferior horn of the lateral ventricle, and the **para-hippocampal gyrus** form important parts of this region. Papez also drew upon the work of Bard, Cannon, and others, who demonstrated the roles of the thalamus and hypothalamus in autonomic responses accompanying emotional states in animals, and in 1937 proposed that interconnections among a group of structures forming part of what is

now called the **limbic system** play a key role in governing emotions. The term "limbic," derived from *limbus*, Latin for border, describes the ringlike border around the top of the brain stem formed by the cortical areas of this system, now well established as an important regulator of emotional experiences and behavior. Starting with the ventral surface of the frontal lobe beneath the septum pellucidum, the limbic cortex continues up and over the corpus callosum as the **cingulate gyrus,** and then posteriorly and ventrally as the parahippocampal gyrus (Fig. 295). This part of the cortex belongs to the oldest part of the cerebrum, the *paleocortex* (G. *palaios*, old, ancient). Among other subcortical structures of the limbic system, in addition to the **thalamus** and **hypothalamus,** is the **amygdala,** a group of nuclei adjacent to the hippocampus. The "Papez circuit" traces an important pathway of the limbic system. This circuit runs from the hippocampus to the mamillary body of the hypothalamus via tracts below the corpus callosum called the fornix. From there the circuit continues to the thalamus by way of the mamillothalamic tract and to

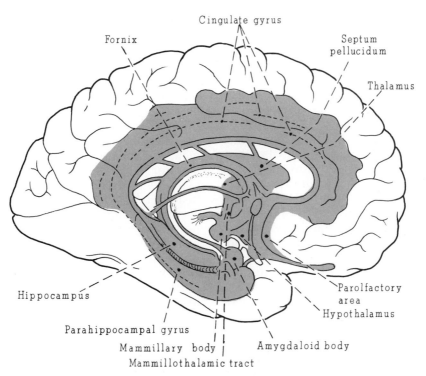

Figure 295. The limbic system, shown by the shaded areas of the diagram. (Modified from Warwick and Williams: Gray's Anatomy, 35th Brit. Ed., London, Longman Group Ltd., 1973.)

the cingulate gyrus via the internal capsule and corona radiata. A tract called the cingulum then runs from the cingulate gyrus back around to the hippocampus. Stimulation of various parts of the limbic system can arouse pleasant or unpleasant feelings or cause different kinds of emotionally directed responses. The hypothalamus, as mentioned earlier, contains centers for controlling the autonomic system and important parts of the endocrine system and for regulating such body functions as blood pressure, heart rate, body temperature, feeding behavior, body water, and digestive processes. Strategically situated in the center of the limbic system, it serves as an intermediary for bringing about emotional effects of the limbic system on these vegetative functions. In many instances these effects are initiated by sending signals to control centers in the medulla. Stimulation of the amygdala, which has reciprocal connections with all parts of the limbic system, especially the hypothalamus, induces many effects that can be initiated by stimulation of the hypothalamus, as well as various patterns of behavior, including those involving basic drives.

An important pathway concerned with the recognition of the quality of sensory input, especially those sensations that are pleasurable, and with governing emotionally inspired responses, especially those whose consummation satisfies basic needs and brings pleasure, is the *medial forebrain bundle*. This pathway is both ascending and descending and interconnects the reticular formation, hypothalamus, and the septal region of the cortex. Located along the course of the medial forebrain bundle, especially in the ventromedial nuclei of the hypothalamus, are the so-called *pleasure centers*, apparently concerned with the satisfaction of basic drives. These centers can be demonstrated by implanting electrodes in the brain of an animal and allowing it to self-stimulate these sites by pressing a lever. Lever pressing rates as high as 5000 times per hour have been recorded. If the particular center stimulated satisfies hunger, food deprivation will increase the rate of lever pressing, and giving the animal a choice between pressing a lever to receive food or an electrical stimulus will generally result in selection of the stimulus.

The neurotransmitter released at the nerve terminals of the medial forebrain bundle pathway is norepinephrine. There is some reason to believe that **schizophrenia** may be caused by a depletion of norepinephrine in these pathways as a result of the destructive effect of an abnormal metabolite formed during the synthesis of norepinephrine which, in consequence, leads to a reduction in the perception of pleasure and in behavior that would normally provide a pleasurable reward. The deficit in goal-oriented thinking and behavior is believed to account for the withdrawal from reality into fantasies of schizophrenic individuals.

Stimulation of the cortical regions of the limbic system can evoke autonomic responses similar to those observed upon stimulation of the hypothalamus or amygdala. But the underlying role of these cortical areas, it is believed, is to function as association areas, correlating immediate with past information of an emotional nature so as to give meaning to emotional experiences. Other areas of the cerebral cortex in addition to the limbic cortex apparently perform associative functions in connection with emotional sensations and responses. Much of the frontal lobe anterior to the motor association areas seems to be involved in emotional as well as certain kinds of mental functions. This area, which embraces parts of the limbic cortex, is referred to as the **prefrontal cortex.** It is also known as the *orbitofrontal cortex,* since it includes the orbital aspect of the frontal lobe. One of the most famous cases in the annals of medicine has to do with damage principally to this part of the brain. In 1848 Phineas Gage, a railroad construction foreman, had a tamping iron blown through the anterior pole of his brain, entering his left eye and emerging from the center of his head. He lived for 12 years after the accident but underwent severe changes in personality. According to the description by his physician, "He is fitful, irreverent, indulging at times in the grossest profanity (which was not previously his custom), manifesting but little deference to his fellows . . . at times pertinaciously obstinate yet capricious and vacillating, devising many plans for future operation which are no sooner arranged than they are abandoned. . . . His mind was radically changed, so that his friends and acquaintances said he was no longer Gage."

Among the prominent features of damage

to the anterior part of the frontal lobe are subtle disturbances in mental processes that interfere with the ability to concentrate, categorize information, and solve problems if the needed information is presented at intervals rather than simultaneously. A severe loss in the ability to retain information for short periods for future use, perhaps because of the inability to classify it for storage, makes it impossible to anticipate or plan for future events on the basis of past experience.

In the early 1930's it was discovered that ablation of the anterior frontal cortex (prefrontal lobectomy) or severing tracts connecting the anterior frontal cortex with the deeper portions of the brain (prefrontal lobotomy) alleviated the symptoms of experimental neurosis in monkeys. This led to the introduction of prefrontal lobotomy in 1935 by a Portuguese neurosurgeon, Egar Moniz, to treat humans, especially those with anxiety neurosis or manic-depressive psychosis. This operation became very popular (about 50,000 were performed), but unfortunately it created a large population of emotional vegetables. The introduction of tranquilizers called a halt to this form of surgery. The current approach to psychosurgery is to destroy selective areas of the limbic system. The most prevalent operation is *cingulotomy*, performed principally to relieve intractable pain and depression. Another is *amygdalotomy*, used to treat individuals subject to outbursts of uncontrollable violence. This new approach has aroused considerable controversy. Opponents argue that our present knowledge of brain function is inadequate to justify such surgical intervention and that any form of surgery could have a general blunting effect on emotions and thought processes.

Memory

Memory is the capacity to recall what one has learned or experienced. This function is performed by association areas throughout the brain. Memory traces apparently are not localized in any specific part of the brain, although at least one part seems to be especially important for deciding what is worth remembering (see below).

A distinction can be made between short-term and long-term memory. *Short-term memory*, useful for remembering limited pieces of information, such as a telephone number, for a brief interval, does not involve chemical or structural changes in the nervous system. *Long-term memory*, which makes possible recall days, months, or years later, apparently does involve such changes. Short-term memory is involved in all learning processes. It is utilized, for example, by a rat learning to run a maze with a minimum number of errors. If the animal can run the same maze weeks later with few errors, the learning has been consolidated for storage as long-term memory.

It has been found that injecting a substance into an animal that inhibits protein synthesis will prevent the establishment of long-term memory without affecting learning or short-term memory. Thus, a rat so treated before a series of maze-running trials will learn the task but will show no evidence of having learned it when tested weeks afterwards. The synthesis of protein, it is believed, signifies changes at synaptic terminals. Possibly alterations in membrane structure take place, or an increase in the size or number of terminals might accompany protein synthesis.

Claims have been made for the transfer of memory from one group of animals to another by injecting RNA extracted from animals that have learned a task into others that have not. The performance on initial trial after such treatment has been reported to be better than by animals injected with solutions containing no RNA. Such observations could be theoretically explained by RNA-directed protein synthesis at specific brain sites.

The hippocampus appears to play an essential role in the conversion of short-term to long-term memory (what some investigators call the "now print" mechanism, which decides what is important for long-term memory storage). An individual who has had the hippocampus removed bilaterally will retain memory stored prior to the operation and the ability to learn, but will not form new long-term memories. One such individual, whose hippocampus was removed for treatment of epilepsy, must now, it has been reported, be repeatedly reintroduced to people he has just met.

Language Areas of the Brain

Since language disorders are for the most part associated with damage to the left cerebral hemisphere, it is assumed that in most people the areas controlling language are located in the left side of the brain. This phenomenon, specialization of one side of the brain for a given function, is called **cerebral dominance.**

Most of our understanding of the functions of the parts of the brain concerned with language have come from careful study of language disorders in individuals suffering brain damage caused by occlusion of blood vessels, followed by postmortem examination of their brains.

The ability to speak requires the cooperation between two language areas. Lesions in either one can cause *aphasia* (G. *a*, not; G. *phasis*, speech), a general term for language disorders resulting from brain damage in which verbal output is linguistically incorrect. These areas are generally referred to as (1) **Broca's area** (area 44), located in the frontal lobe just anterior to the region in the primary motor cortex governing movement of the mouth, tongue, and vocal cords, and (2) **Wernicke's area,** situated in the temporal lobe adjacent to the primary auditory area (Fig. 296).

Paul Broca, writing in the 1860's, was the first person to relate speech disorders to specific brain lesions. Broca also established that the damage was almost always on the left side of the brain (in his cases in the area now referred to by his name). About 10 years later Carl Wernicke de-

scribed aphasias resulting from damage to the left temporal lobe. Wernicke established that there were differences between Broca's type of aphasia and those he described. Furthermore, Wernicke described a theoretical model, now generally accepted, to account for both kinds of aphasia.

An individual with lesions in Broca's area usually has normal language comprehension but speaks slowly, with great effort, in incomplete sentences with poor syntax. According to Wernicke's model, Broca's area is the center for programing the muscles responsible for speech production. Individuals with lesions in Wernicke's area may appear to speak normally, but their language comprehension is deficient (both written and spoken, since written language is learned in reference to spoken language) and their speech is lacking in meaningful content. Wernicke's area can be described as the locus for the comprehension of language. Tracts connect Wernicke's and Broca's areas, and when a person speaks an auditory pattern in Wernicke's area is relayed to Broca's area, where the muscles involved in speech are coordinated for articulation. If the tracts connecting Wernicke's area with Broca's area are interrupted, language comprehension is retained, but speech is abnormal.

In the 1890's another important language area was discovered, the **angular gyrus,** located between Wernicke's area and the visual areas in the occipital lobe. This area appears to contain programs that link Wernicke's area to the visual cortex. Lesions in

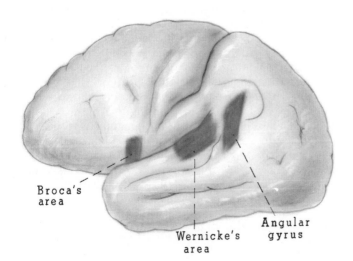

Figure 296. Language areas of the brain.

Broca's area

Wernicke's area

Angular gyrus

this area cause *alexia* (G. *lexis,* word), the inability to read with comprehension, and *agraphia* (G. *graphein,* to write), the inability to write with meaningful content. Damage to this area does not disturb speech or comprehension of the spoken language. Alexia occurs with this kind of brain damage because to read with understanding, the visual pattern in the visual association area must be converted by programs in the angular gyrus to an auditory pattern in Wernicke's area. Agraphia occurs because to write intelligibly, programs in the angular gyrus must convert the auditory pattern in Wernicke's area to a visual one in the visual association cortex.

When the brain receives visual sensations, everything in the left field of vision is transmitted to the right occipital lobe and everything in the right field is transmitted to the left lobe. (For details of the sensory pathways from the eyes to the brain, see page 313.) Therefore, damage to the corpus callosum, interrupting passage of visual information from the right occipital lobe to the angular gyrus and Wernicke's area in the left hemisphere, will make it impossible to comprehend reading matter in the left field of vision.

Special Functions of the Right Cerebral Hemisphere

The left cerebral hemisphere, as we have seen, plays the dominant role in language functions. It is also specialized for analytical and sequential processing of nonlinguistic information. The right hemisphere, on the other hand, seems to be specialized for processing information that can be visualized or perceived as a whole. Thus, identifying an object by feel is more dependent upon the right than the left hemisphere. A curious example of analytical processing by the left hemisphere and holistic processing by the right hemisphere is the observation that trained musicians identify melodies better with the right ear (which transmits more sound to the left hemisphere) than the left, whereas the reverse is true for nonmusicians. Musicians apparently identify a melody by analyzing its components; nonmusicians perceive the melody as a whole.

SUMMARY

THE NERVOUS SYSTEM

Divisions

The nervous system is divided for descriptive purposes into the **central nervous system** (the brain and spinal cord) and the **peripheral nervous system** (12 pairs of cranial nerves and their branches and 31 pairs of spinal nerves and their branches).

Types of Nerve Cells

1. **Neurons**
   a. Specialized for the conduction of nerve impulses, consisting of a cell body containing a nucleus and **processes** transmitting impulses to and from the cell body.
   b. The processes are of two types: dendrites and axons.
      (1) **Dendrites** are a group of short, unsheathed processes arranged like branches of a tree that transmit impulses to the cell body.
      (2) The **axon** is a single, elongate, sheathed process conducting impulses away from the cell body. Side branches arising along the course of an axon are called collaterals.

2. **Nerve Fibers and Nerves**
   a. Any single, elongate neuronal process (such as an axon or a peripheral process of a sensory neuron), together with its surface sheaths, is called a nerve fiber.
      (1) A central core (axis cylinder) enclosed by
      (2) the cell membrane
      (3) A myelin sheath (a tightly wound spiral of Schwann cell membrane)
      (4) A neurilemma (flattened, living Schwann cells overlying myelin sheath)
   b. In myelinated fibers (myelin thick enough to be seen in light microscope) impulses jump from one node of Ranvier (gaps in myelin sheath) to

another (saltatory conduction), greatly increasing transmission velocity.

c. The neurilemma is essential for regeneration of damaged nerve fibers; fibers of the central nervous system, which lack a neurilemma, cannot regenerate.

d. Nerves are bundles of nerve fibers running together in the peripheral nervous system.

    (1) Endoneurium surrounds each fiber

    (2) Perineurium surrounds each bundle

    (3) Epineurium surrounds the entire nerve

    (4) *A bundle of nerve fibers in the central nervous system is called a tract.*

3. The Nerve Impulse

a. In the resting state the interior of a nerve fiber has a negative charge (resting membrane potential) as a result of

    (1) Active transport of sodium ions to the exterior of the cell

    (2) Reciprocal transfer of potassium to the interior

    (3) More rapid "leaking" of potassium ions to the exterior

      (a) When membrane permeability is altered by a stimulus, a rapid inflow of sodium changes the interior charge locally from negative to positive; a halt to the inflow of sodium and rapid outflow of potassium returns the interior charge to negative. This "action potential" sweeps along the nerve fiber.

b. Transmission of the nerve impulse operates on the "all-or-none" principle:

    (1) If a stimulus is strong enough to excite a fiber (threshold stimulus), a maximal impulse is transmitted. Different nerve fibers have different thresholds.

4. Transmission of Impulses at the Neuromuscular Junction and Synapse

a. The junction between the terminal branching portions (motor end plates) of a motor neuron and the membrane of a muscle fiber is called the neuromuscular junction. The junction between the terminal endings (presynaptic knobs) of one neuron (the presynaptic cells) and the dendrites and body of another (the postsynaptic cell) is called the synapse. Both junctions are discontinuous—synaptic clefts separate a neuron and muscle fiber or two neurons.

b. Excitation of a muscle fiber by a motor neuron at the neuromuscular junction is brought about by an increase in the rate of release from vesicles in the motor neuron terminals of a chemical mediator, acetylcholine, which crosses the synaptic cleft and induces a propagated action potential in the muscle fiber.

c. At the synapse an excitatory or inhibitory transmitter substance is released by the presynaptic cell. The former, after diffusing across the synaptic cleft, induces an excitatory postsynaptic potential, the latter an inhibitory potential. Summation of a number of excitatory potentials is necessary for generation of an action potential in the postsynaptic cell; usually, whether an action potential is generated depends upon the algebraic sum of excitatory and inhibitory potentials.

5. Sensory Receptors

a. Receptors are sensory neuron endings or specialized structures or organs particularly sensitive (but not exclusively) to a specific stimulus.

    (1) Identification of the sensation takes place in the brain.

b. The simplest receptors are free nerve endings sensitive principally to pain. The most complex are the organs for vision and hearing.

c. General sensory receptors, in addition to free nerve endings, include Meissner's corpuscles (touch), Merkel's discs (touch), Pacinian corpuscles (pressure), Ruffini's end organs (warmth) and Krause's end bulbs (cold).

d. Receptors such as kinesthetic receptors in tendons and joints, the muscle spindle, and the equilibrium receptors of the middle ear, all of which play a vital role in locomotor and postural responses, are generally referred to as proprioceptors.

Central Nervous System

1. Brain

a. The three developmental divisions of the brain are the forebrain, which includes the cerebrum and the diencephalon (thalamus and hypothalamus); the midbrain; and the hindbrain, which includes the pons, medulla and cerebellum.

(1) **Cerebrum**

(a) *Represents seven-eighths of weight of brain; responsible for discriminatory identification of and integration of sensory information, memory, reasoning, use of language, emotional behavior and initiation of movement; surface layer of gray matter (cerebral cortex) greatly expanded by convolutions, or gyri.*

(b) *Longitudinal fissure divides cerebrum into two hemispheres, each divided for convenience into four major lobes bearing names of overlying bones of skull: frontal, parietal, temporal and occipital; frontal lobe contains areas for initiating movement, parietal lobe for perception of somesthetic sensations (tactile, temperature, pain, and kinesthesia), temporal lobe for the perception of sound, occipital lobe for the perception of visual sensations; association areas adjacent to sensory areas and spread throughout cortex correlate data and relate past and present data to give it significance.*

(c) *Commissural tracts connect two hemispheres (largest is corpus callosum); association tracts connect parts of same hemisphere; projection tracts connect cortex with other parts of brain and spinal cord.*

(d) *Imbedded in white matter of cerebrum are two pairs of nuclei (caudate and lentiform), collectively called basal ganglia, which play important role in controlling motor activity; between each nucleus is a large mass of white matter (internal capsule), which contains fibers leading to and from cerebral cortex that connect cortex to rest of brain and spinal cord.*

(2) **Thalamus**

(a) *Paired mass of gray matter situated below corpus callosum.*

(b) *Relay center for sensory impulses (except olfactory) from peripheral receptors to cerebral cortex; responsible for crude awareness of sensation (protopathic sensibility).*

(c) *Processes and relays coordinating motor impulses from the basal ganglia and cerebellum to the cerebral motor cortex.*

(d) *Relay and integration center for emotional behavior.*

(3) **Hypothalamus**

Involved in the regulation of body temperature, feeding activities, concentration and volume of extracellular fluid, autonomic nervous system responses, endocrine functions.

(4) **Midbrain**

(a) *Four rounded masses, superior and inferior colliculi (collectively called corpora quadrigemina), form roof (tectum) of posterior surface of midbrain; superior colliculi coordinate tracking movements of eyes in response to moving visual, auditory, or tactile stimuli; inferior colliculi involved in auditory reflexes.*

(b) *Two large bundles of fibers derived from internal capsule, called cerebral pedun-*

cles, form anterior part of midbrain; bundles contain major cerebral motor system (many fibers continuing posteriorly as corticospinal, or pyramidal, tracts); other fibers lead to pons, where connections are made to cerebellum.

(5) **Cerebellum**
  (a) *Like cerebrum, cerebellum has surface layer (cortex) of gray matter; outline of white matter surrounding deep folds and fissures of gray matter is known as arbor vitae.*
  (b) *Functions principally as integration center for promoting smooth, coordinated, voluntary movements; receives input from proprioceptors and receptors for touch, vision, and hearing as well as from motor cortex; then sends inhibitory signals to motor cortex that prevent inappropriate movements.*

(6) **Pons**
  (a) *Lies anterior to cerebellum between midbrain and medulla.*
  (b) *Bridgelike structure consisting almost entirely of white matter, linking various parts of brain.*

(7) **Medulla Oblongata**
  (a) *Continuous with spinal cord through foramen magnum.*
  (b) *Ventrally are pyradmids (corticospinal tracts).*
  (c) *Posteriorly are two prominent nuclei, gracilis and cuneatus, where corresponding tracts (pathway for discriminatory touch and kinesthesia) synapse.*
  (d) *Contains centers for regulating cardiovascular functions, maintaining and controlling breathing, and coordinating swallowing and vomiting reflexes.*

(8) **Reticular Formation**
  (a) *Diffusely scattered neurons throughout area of medulla, pons, and midbrain.*
  (b) *Receives input from all sensory pathways leading to cerebral cortex and is essential for arousal and maintaining wakefulness (in this respect known as reticular activating system).*
  (c) *Contains centers for facilitating or inhibiting stretch reflexes.*
  (d) *As part of extrapyramidal system, is site of origin of reticulospinal tracts leading to spinal motor neurons.*

b. **Ventricles of the brain**
  Four cavities, or ventricles, of the brain are continuous with the central canal of the spinal cord: two lateral ventricles, one in each hemisphere, one (third) in the diencephalon, and one (fourth) anterior to the cerebellum.

c. **Meninges of the brain**
  (1) **Dura mater** (outermost): Dense fibrous tissue consisting of two layers, an outer (endosteal dura), which forms the internal periosteum of the cranial bones, and an inner (meningeal dura). Extensions of the meningeal dura form four partitions: falx cerebelli, falx cerebri, tentorium cerebelli, and diaphragma sellae.
  (2) **Arachnoid** (middle meninx): A loose, delicate membrane with microscopic appearance of a spider web.
  (3) **Pia mater** (inner meninx): A vascular membrane.

d. **Cerebrospinal fluid**
  (1) Circulates within ventricles, central canal of spinal cord, and in subarachnoid space of brain and spinal cord (between arachnoid and pia mater), serving as protective jacket and providing buoyancy for brain.
  (2) Continously formed in ventricles, principally by choroid plexuses (pouchlike projections of pia mater into ventricles covered with ependyma). Circulates from lateral ventricles through foramina of Monro into third ventricle, passes through cerebral aqueduct into fourth ventricle (and spinal canal), then passes through three foramina into subarachnoid space. It drains into

sagittal venous sinus (a separation between endosteal and meningeal dura) through arachnoid villi (projections of arachnoid into sinus).

2. Spinal Cord

a. Extends from foramen magnum to second lumbar vertebra.
b. Central H-shaped core of gray matter surrounded by white matter.
c. Meningeal dura, arachnoid and pia mater of brain continuous with spinal meninges. Slender extension of pia mater below spinal cord is called filum terminale. Cerebrospinal fluid samples obtained by tapping the subarachnoid space below spinal cord between third and fourth lumbar vertebrae.

Peripheral Nervous System: Spinal and Cranial Nerves

1. Spinal Nerves

a. Thirty-one pairs: 8 cervical, 12 thoracic, 5 lumbar, 5 sacral and 1 coccygeal.
b. Formed by junction of a dorsal (sensory) root and a ventral (motor) root. Cell bodies of sensory neurons lie in spinal (dorsal root) ganglia. Cell bodies of motor neurons lie in ventral gray horn of spinal cord.
c. Dorsal and ventral roots descending from terminal end of spinal cord to reach appropriate intervertebral foramen are drawn into collection called cauda equina.
d. Shortly after a spinal nerve is formed from a dorsal and ventral root, it branches into
   (1) A meningeal ramus
   (2) A dorsal ramus, serving skin of the back of head, neck and trunk
   (3) A ventral ramus, serving ventral part of these structures as well as upper and lower extremities.
      (a) *Another branch with two divisions is part of sympathetic nervous system.*
e. In the cervical, lumbar and sacral regions the ventral rami give rise to interlacing nerve networks (plexuses), from which peripheral nerves arise.

2. Cranial Nerves

a. Twelve pairs. Names in order from I to XII: olfactory, optic, oculomotor, trochlear, trigeminal, abducens, facial, vestibulocochlear, glossopharyngeal, vagus, spinal accessory, and hypoglossal.
b. For distribution and function, see Table 34.

Autonomic Nervous System

1. Efferent nerve fibers distributed to smooth muscle, the heart and glands are, for convenience, referred to as the autonomic nervous system.

2. Distinctive anatomical feature. In this system a 2-neuron chain leads to an effector.

a. A preganglionic neuron with cell body in central nervous system and axon extending to ganglion outside central nervous system.
b. A postganglionic neuron with cell body in ganglion and axon extending to muscle or gland.

3. Divisions

a. **Sympathetic** (thoracolumbar): Preganglionic neuron cell bodies in lateral horn of first thoracic to the third lumbar segments of the spinal cord.
   (1) Axons pass (via white ramus) to paravertebral ganglia
   (2) Pass through to prevertebral ganglia in abdomen and pelvis
   (3) Synapse in paravertebral ganglia with the postganglionic neurons whose axons return to spinal nerves (via white ramus)
   (4) Synapse in paravertebral ganglia with the postganglionic neurons whose axons do not return to spinal nerves and serve the head region and thoracic viscera.
b. **Parasympathetic** (craniosacral): Cell bodies of preganglionic fibers in brain and second, third and fourth sacral segments of spinal cord.
   (1) Axons are long and synapse with postganglionic fibers in four ganglia in head or in terminal ganglia lying upon or within walls of innervated organs.
   (2) Cranial preganglionic axons travel with following nerves: oculomotor, facial, glossopharyngeal and vagus.

4. Distribution and Functions: See Figure 285 and Table 35.

Functional Organization of Nervous System

1. Reflexes

a. A reflex is an involuntary response to a stimulus such as withdrawal of a limb (by flexion) in response to an irritating stimulus, contraction of a muscle in response to the stretching of it, constriciton of the pupil in response to light, and dilation or constriction of arterioles in response to changes in blood pressure.

b. A simple spinal cord reflex arc includes
(1) A receptor
(2) A sensory neuron
(3) Synapse in spinal cord between sensory and internuncial neurons (with exception of stretch reflex)
(4) Synapse between internuncial and motor neurons
(5) Junction between motor neuron and skeletal muscle

2. Pathways for Conscious Perception of Somesthetic Sensations

a. Cortical projection: areas 1, 2 and 3 in postcentral gyrus of parietal lobe. On topographical map, size for each part of body is proportional to number of projected fibers.

b. Pain, temperature: lateral spinothalamic tracts; crude touch, pressure: ventral spinothalamic tracts. First-order neuron to spinal cord, second-order (after decussation) to thalamus, third-order to postcentral gyrus.

c. Discriminatory tactile and kinesthesia: dorsal columns (fasciculi gracilis and cuneatus). First-order neuron to medulla, second-order (after decussation) to thalamus, third-order to postcentral gyrus.

3. Pathways for Motor Function

a. Primary motor area: Precentral gyrus of frontal lobe (area 4). Initiates discrete movements. On topographical map, cortical representation of given part of body is proportional to dexterity of movements. Area 6, adjacent to area 4, is another important motor area.

b. Distinction between pyramidal and extrapyramidal systems
(1) Pyramidal system (corticospinal tracts): Tracts descend from cerebral motor cortex without interruption to spinal motor neurons and initiate skilled movements of skeletal muscles.
(2) Extrapyramidal system: Network interconnecting various parts of motor cortex and several subcortical centers (including thalamus, basal ganglia and cerebellum) with major pathways to spinal motor neurons arising from reticular formation. Functions include
(a) *Initiating some voluntary movement (chiefly axial, such as bowing and walking)*
(b) *Regulating action of pyramidal system to produce smooth, coordinated movements*
(c) *Bringing about automatic movements (smiling, gesticulating)*
(d) *Controlling visceral functions and activities involving basic drives.*

4. Brain Areas for Emotional Expression

a. Interconnected group of structures known as limbic system plays key role in governing emotions.

b. Among parts of brain included in system are hippocampus, parahippocampal gyrus, cingulate gyrus, amygdala, thalamus, and hypothalamus.

5. Language Areas of Brain

a. In most people the cortical language areas located in left cerebral hemisphere (cerebral dominance).

b. These areas are
(1) **Broca's area** in frontal lobe (center for programing muscles used in speech)
(2) **Wernicke's area** in temporal lobe (locus for language comprehension)
(3) **Angular gyrus,** which links Wernicke's area and the visual cortex.

Special Senses

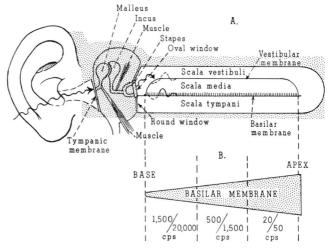

Objectives

The aim of this chapter is to enable the student to:

Describe the receptors for each of the special senses—vision, hearing, equilibrium, olfaction and taste—and explain how each functions.

Illustrate and interpret some of the common abnormalities of vision and hearing.

VISION

External Structures of the Eye

The external structures of the eye are the *orbital cavity,* the *extrinsic ocular muscles,* the *eyelids,* the *conjunctiva,* and the *lacrimal apparatus* (Fig. 297).

The Orbital Cavity. The orbital cavity contains the eyeball and is a bony, cone-shaped region in front of the skull lined with fatty tissue to cushion the eyeball. The bones forming the orbital cavity are fragile and thin. The bone at the rim of the orbit is thicker to protect the eye from injury (see Chapter 5).

Extrinsic Ocular Muscles. Six extrinsic, or external, muscles connect the eyeball to the orbital cavity and provide rotary movement and support. These muscles are four straight (rectus) muscles *(superior, inferior, lateral,* and *medial),* and two oblique muscles *(superior* and *inferior).* They are illustrated in Figure 132, page 160; Table 12, page 203, lists their functions.

The Eyelids. The eyelids, or *palpebrae,* are two movable "curtains" located anterior to the eyeball; they protect the eye from dust, intense light, and impact. The **palpebral fissure** is the interval between the eyelids. The *canthus* is the corner, or angle, at which the lids meet. The free margins of the eyelids are surmounted by eyelashes, which protect the eye from dust and perspiration.

A plate of condensed fibrous tissue, the *tarsus,* is located at the free edge of each eyelid, giving the lid substance and shape. The tarsal plate contains tarsal *(meibomian)* glands opening onto the lid margin. These glands, a modified form of sebaceous glands, secrete an oily substance onto the eyelids.

Conjunctival Membrane. The conjunctiva, a thin layer of mucous membrane, lines the inner surface of each eyelid and is reflected over the exposed surface of the eyeball as a protective cover. The apposed conjunctival membranes slide past each other when the eyelids open and close.

307

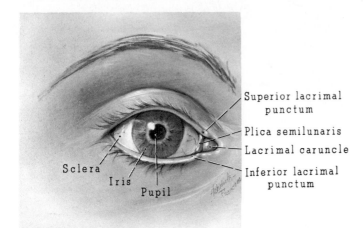

Superior lacrimal
punctum

Plica semilunaris

Lacrimal caruncle

Inferior lacrimal
punctum

Sclera

Iris

Pupil

Figure 297. External appearance of
the eye and surrounding structures.

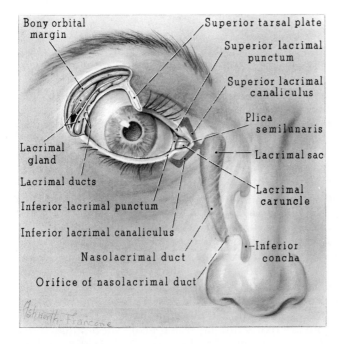

Bony orbital
margin

Lacrimal
gland

Lacrimal ducts

Inferior lacrimal punctum

Inferior lacrimal canaliculus

Nasolacrimal duct

Orifice of nasolacrimal duct

Superior tarsal plate

Superior lacrimal
punctum

Superior lacrimal
canaliculus

Plica
semilunaris

Lacrimal sac

Lacrimal
caruncle

Inferior
concha

Figure 298. Lacrimal apparatus in relation to the eye.

Lacrimal Apparatus. The eye is cleansed and lubricated by the lacrimal (L. *lacrima*, a tear) apparatus, which consists of four structures (Fig. 298):

1. The *lacrimal gland* is located in a depression of the frontal bone at the upper and outer angle of the orbit. Approximately 12 ducts lead from each gland to the surface of the conjunctiva of the upper lid, where they deposit lacrimal fluid (in excess, known as tears).

2. The *lacrimal canals (canaliculi)* are two ducts extending from the inner angle of the eyelid and emptying into the lacrimal sac. Two openings known as puncta, positioned at the inner canthus of the eye, open into these canals.

3. The *lacrimal sac* is located at the inner angle of the eyelids in a groove at the junction of the lacrimal bone with the frontal process of the maxilla. The lacrimal sac is an enlargement of the upper end of the nasolacrimal duct.

4. The *nasolacrimal duct* extends from the lacrimal sac to the inferior meatus of the nose, draining tears from the eye.

Fluid secreted by the lacrimal glands washes over the eyeball and is swept up by the blinking action of the eyelids. When the lids close, contraction of the pars lacrimalis muscle dilates the lacrimal sac, pulling fluid from the edges of the lids along the lacrimal canals into the lacrimal sac. When the lids open and the pars lacrimalis is relaxed, the lacrimal sac collapses, forcing fluid into the lacrimal duct. Gravitational force, in turn, moves the fluid down the nasolacrimal duct into the inferior meatus of the nose. Thus, the eyeball is continually irrigated by a gentle stream of fluid which prevents it from becoming dry and inflamed and has a bactericidal action because of the presence of an enzyme, lysozyme, which breaks down the cell walls of many bacteria.

Internal Structures of the Eye

Layers of the Eyeball. The wall of the eyeball is composed of three layers. The

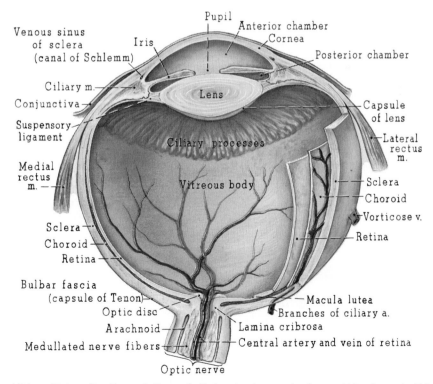

Figure 299. Mid-sagittal section through the eyeball showing layers of retina and blood supply. (After Lederle.)

outer consists of the **sclera,** a fibrous protective coat, and **cornea,** a transparent tissue serving as a refracting surface. The middle is composed of the **choroid,** a vascular, pigmented layer, **ciliary body,** and **iris.** The inner is the **retina,** a layer containing visual receptor cells (Fig. 299).

THE OUTER LAYER. The *sclera* (G. *skleros,* hard), or white of the eye, forms the fibrous external support of the eyeball. It covers the posterior three-fourths of the eyeball, joining with the transparent cornea covering the anterior portion of the eyeball.

The *cornea* extends anteriorly from the sclera. It is approximately 10 to 11 mm in diameter. The function of the cornea is similar to that of a photographic lens. It is the principal refracting medium of the eye, bending light rays to help focus them on the retina. When looking at a distant object, the cornea accounts for three-fourths of the eye's focusing capacity. Its focusing power, however, is fixed, and adjusting the focus to view objects at different distances is ac-

complished by changing the curvature of the lens (see below).

THE MIDDLE LAYER. The *choroid,* the membranous lining inside the sclera, is highly vascular and darkly pigmented. This pigmentation prevents the internal reflection of light.

The *ciliary body,* consisting of the ciliary processes and ciliary muscles, lies anterior to the choroid. It is located between the outer margin of the retina and the base of the iris.

The *iris* is a diaphragm located anterior to the lens and posterior to the cornea. It has a circular opening in its center (the pupil) regulating the amount of light admitted to the interior of the eyeball. Circular and radiating muscle fibers are present in the iris. The circular fibers contract the pupil in strong light and near vision; the radiating fibers dilate the pupil in dim light and far vision.

THE INNER LAYER. The *retina* is the photoreceptive layer of the eye. It translates light waves into neural impulses. It has no

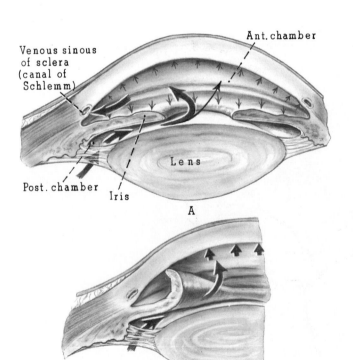

Figure 300. *A,* Normal movement of aqueous humor through posterior chamber, anterior chamber and out the canal of Schlemm. *B,* Blockage of fluid flow causing fluid retention, resulting in acute glaucoma.

anterior portion, extending forward only as far as the posterior part of the ciliary body.

Eye Humors

The **aqueous humor** fills the **anterior cavity** of the eye (that portion of the eye in front of the lens), which is subdivided into an *anterior chamber* (in front of both the lens and iris) and a *posterior chamber* (between the lens and iris). Aqueous humor is secreted by the ciliary processes and is drained into the venous system by a ring-shaped sinus, the sinus venosus sclerae **(canal of Schlemm),** located within the sclera (Fig. 300). Defective outflow of fluid increases the internal pressure, a condition called glaucoma. Severe glaucoma may cause blindness. One of the consequences of an elevated intraocular pressure that leads to blindness is compression of the arteries leading to the optic nerve (disc), reducing the necessary blood supply. The aqueous humor nourishes the lens and cornea, which do not possess a blood supply of their own. The aqueous humor and the vitreous humor (described below) also act as refracting media.

The **vitreous humor,** a soft, jellylike material, fills the posterior cavity of the eye (the portion behind the lens) and maintains the spherical shape of the eyeball.

The Lens

The **lens,** lying immediately posterior to the iris, is a biconvex, crystalline body enclosed in a transparent *capsule.* From this capsule, suspensory ligaments extend in medially to the edge of the choroid. Adjusting the tension of the *suspensory ligaments* changes the shape of the lens to keep the object continually focused on the retina. For distant vision, the lens thins; for near vision, the lens thickens. When the ciliary muscles of the eye are relaxed, the suspensory ligaments are tensed by their attachments, and tension transmitted to the lens capsule flattens the lens. Accommodation for near vision is brought about by contraction of the ciliary muscles. This draws the ring of insertions of the suspensory ligaments in the choroid forward and inward. The tension on the suspensory ligaments and lens capsule is eased, and the intrinsic elasticity of the lens causes the lens (principally its anterior surface) to become more convex. Accommodation for near vision can increase the refractive power (and thus the ability to bend diverging rays from close objects to focus them on the retina) of the lens in infants from 15–29 diopters. The diopter is the unit used for measuring the strength of a lens. A lens that focuses parallel rays (those entering from a

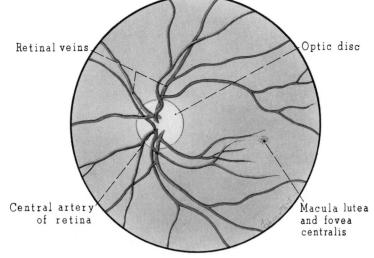

Figure 301. Retina of the normal eye as seen through the ophthalmoscope.

Retinal veins

Optic disc

Central artery of retina

Macula lutea and fovea centralis

distance greater than 20 feet) at a point 100 cm from its center (focal distance of 100 cm) has a strength of one diopter. Increasing the convexity shortens the focal distance, increasing the diopters.

Physiology of Vision

For conscious reception of a visual image, the image must be formed on the retina and transformed into nerve impulses, which are relayed to the sensory projection areas in the occipital lobes.

The focusing of the image on the retina by the lens is called *accommodation*. Regulation of the amount of light admitted through the action of the iris and alignment of the visual axes of the two eyes are reflexes associated with this act. Thus, when the eyes are accommodating for near vision the lens becomes more convex, the eyes converge (keeping the image in the same place on each retina), and the pupils constrict (increasing the depth of focus).

Function of the Retina. When the image is formed on the retina, the photosensitive cells of the retina (the **rods and cones**) translate the light energy into nervous impulses. Each eye contains approximately 6 million cones and 120 million rods. The majority of cones are massed together in a small area called the *macula lutea*, within which is a small region called the **fovea centralis** containing only cone cells. The concentration of cones diminishes away from the macula, whereas the concentration of rods reaches a maximum about 4 mm from the fovea. The fovea is the central focusing point for the optic system of the eye. Since rods are absent in the fovea centralis, it is considered a "blind spot" in dim light (Fig. 301).

Rods are sensitive to dim light, and function in night vision. They contain a photosensitive chemical called **rhodopsin** (visual purple), a combination between *retinene* (visual yellow, an aldehyde of vitamin A—also called retinal) and a protein, *scotopsin*. When light is absorbed by rhodopsin, retinene changes shape from a bent chain (*cis* form), possessing the property of forming a stable combination with scotopsin, to a straight chain (*trans* form),

which does not possess this property. This initiates a chain reaction resulting in the formation of a number of unstable intermediates and ending with the separation of retinene from scotopsin. Rhodopsin is then re-formed from retinene and scotopsin (Fig. 302). If a shortage of retinene exists, caused by a deficiency in its precursor, vitamin A, rhodopsin cannot be formed and a condition known as *night blindness* results. It is currently believed that during the breakdown cycle of rhodopsin, ionized segments of scotopsin are exposed which attack the nerve cell membrane and produce a nerve impulse.

Rods are slender cells consisting of an outer segment composed of stacked, rhodopsin-containing discs and an inner segment (facing the interior of the eyeball) containing the organelles that synthesize the constituents of rhodopsin. The outer segment is continually renewed by the assembly of discs at the base of the outer segment which migrate to the tip, where they are shed. Epithelial cells adjacent to the rods phagocytize the shed discs.

The photochemistry of color vision (daylight vision) involves cones. Three types of cones have been identified, each containing a different pigment maximally sensitive to red, blue, or green light (Fig. 303). Color vision depends upon the combination of these colors in the sensory cortex. In the most common forms of *color blindness* the individual cannot distinguish between red and green because of a lack of either the red-sensitive or green-sensitive pigment. Since the gene for color blindness is recessive and sex-linked (carried only on the X

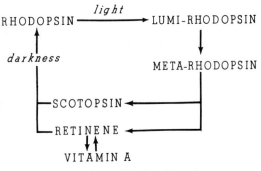

Figure 302. Rhodopsin cycle.

chromosome), this condition is much more rare in females than males.

Nervous Pathways for Vision (Figs. 304 and 305). Impulses generated by the rods and cones are relayed to **bipolar cells,** which in turn make synaptic connections with **ganglion cells,** whose fibers form the optic nerve. In the fovea, the region of maximum visual acuity, there is little overlap in the synaptic connections between receptor and bipolar cells and between bipolar and ganglion cells. In the periphery, on the other hand, the overlap is considerable and a single ganglion cell receives input from several cone cells and as many as hundreds of rod cells. The intensity of the ganglion cells' response can be modified by two types of neurons, namely, **horizontal cells** and **amacrine cells,** both of which carry signals across the retina (Fig. 304). The principal function of horizontal cells apparently is to mediate communication between bipolar cells and a surrounding group of receptor cells. Input from horizontal cells reduces the magnitude of the bipolar cells' response. This has the effect of heightening the contrast between concentric regions of ganglion cell fields. Amacrine cells, which connect to bipolar and ganglion cells and to each other, also have an inhibitory effect in the outer ring of the field of a given ganglion cell. However, whereas horizontal cells respond to sus-

tained illumination, amacrine cells respond to changes in illumination—"turning on" or "turning off"—and have their effect on change detecting ganglion cells. Ganglion cells of this type are activated by changes in illumination in the center of their fields; changes in the region surrounding the center activate the amacrine system, which reduces the intensity of the ganglion cells' response. Processing of visual data in this way in the retina enables ganglion cells to transmit to the brain with greater acuity information about the amount of light-dark contrast in the visual field.

The axons of ganglion cells form the optic nerve by perforating the sclera at the optic disc, creating a sievelike structure, the *lamina cribrosa.* An absence of the visual end organs at this point accounts for the *blind spot* in the field of vision. The optic nerve extends from the disc to the **optic chiasm,** where the fibers undergo partial decussation—fibers arising from the nasal half of each retina cross; those from the temporal half do not. From the chiasm, the fibers (now called the *optic tracts*) continue to the lateral geniculate bodies of the **thalamus.** From the lateral geniculate bodies, fibers arise, passing through the posterior limbs of the *internal capsule* and into the visual cortical areas of the **occipital lobes.**

As illustrated in Figure 305, when the

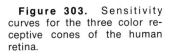

Figure 303. Sensitivity curves for the three color receptive cones of the human retina.

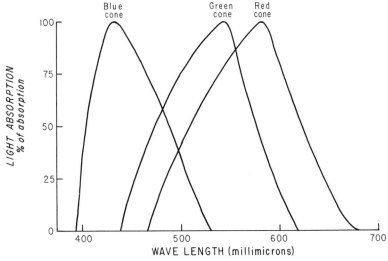

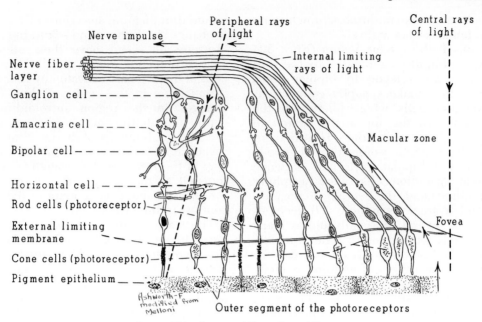

Figure 304.   Layers of the retina of the eye.

eyes are fixed on a point in the field of vision, objects to the left of this point form an image to the right of the fovea on each retina. This is the temporal half of the right retina and the nasal half of the left retina. Since nerve fibers arising from the nasal half of the retina cross in the optic chiasm, *stimuli in the left field of vision of both eyes excite the right visual cortex.* The reverse is true for the right field of vision of both eyes.

Not all optic tract fibers lead to the thalamus. Those forming part of the pathway for the *light reflex* (constriction of the pupil in response to light) pass to the **pretectal region** (between the corpora quadrigemina and the thalamus). Synaptic connections are made here with neurons whose axons lead to nuclei of the oculomotor nerve, which carries parasympathetic fibers leading to the smooth muscles of the eye. Other optic tract fibers terminate in the **superior colliculus,** which also receives input from the visual cortex and the auditory and somesthetic systems (from both the periphery and cerebral cortex). The principal role of the superior colliculus is to coordinate tracking movements of the eyes—eye movements in response to mov-

ing visual, auditory, or tactile stimuli. Damage to the superior colliculus impairs the efficiency of these movements. The superior colliculus also relays visual impulses to the cerebellum. Additional visual input to the cerebellum comes from the visual cortex, relayed through the pons (see page 295 for the functions of the cerebellum).

Binocular Vision. Man's eyes are arranged so that the visual fields of the two eyes overlap to a considerable extent (Fig. 305), with each eye receiving a slightly different view. The difference between the two views, called *binocular parallax,* leads to a disparity between the retinal images of the third dimension of an object, which makes possible the perception of depth. Points on each retina forming identical images equidistant from the fovea are called *corresponding points.* Figure 306 illustrates how the images of the flat surface of an object lie on corresponding points, whereas the images of the third dimension do not—they lie on what are called *disparate retinal points.* The disparity is responsible for three-dimensional vision. Binocularly activated neurons in the visual cortex of each hemisphere synthesize the two views into a three-dimensional picture.

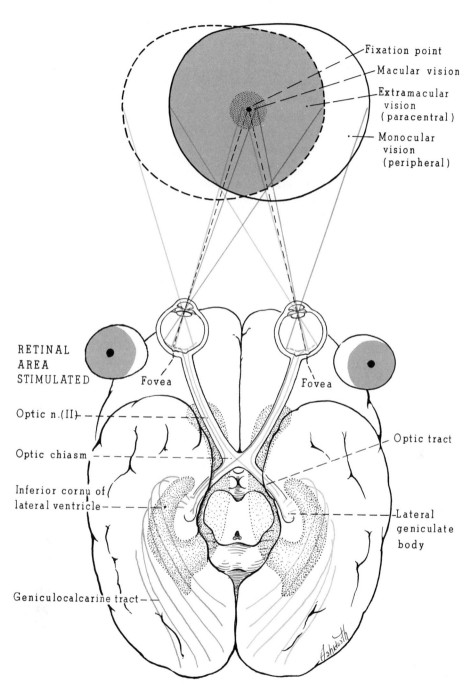

Fixation point

Macular vision

Extramacular
vision
(paracentral)

Monocular
vision
(peripheral)

RETINAL
AREA
STIMULATED

Fovea

Fovea

Optic n.(II)

Optic chiasm

Inferior cornu of
lateral ventricle

Geniculocalcarine tract

Optic tract

Lateral
geniculate
body

Figure 305. Nervous pathways for vision.

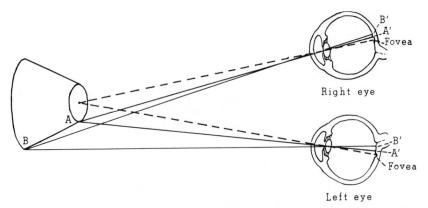

Figure 306. Disparity between the two retinal images of the third dimension of an object, which gives rise to binocular depth perception, is illustrated in this drawing. The images of the bottom of the bucket lie on corresponding retinal points; that is, the two circles are equidistant from the fovea (the distance from the fovea to A, representing point A on the left side of the bottom of the bucket, is the same on both retinas). The images of the top of the bucket lie on disparate retinal points (the distance from the fovea to B, representing point B on the left side of the top of the bucket, is not the same on each retina).

Binocular vision is maintained through nervous and muscular coordination of eye movements. If the muscles are not coordinated, *strabismus* results. In strabismus, the visual axes of the eyes are not parallel. The brain cannot cope with the excessive disparity, and double vision (diplopia) results.

Abnormalities of the Eye

The focusing properties of the eye are often imperfect, causing nearsightedness (myopia), farsightedness (hyperopia), old-sightedness (presbyopia), and uneven focusing in different planes (astigmatism). Other abnormalities of the eye include cataracts, opacities of the cornea, inflammations of the conjunctiva (conjunctivitis), and sty.

Myopia results from an abnormally long distance between the cornea and lens or lens and retina or too powerful a lens, and is a condition in which the image of a distant object (beyond 20 feet, at which distance light rays entering the eye are almost parallel) focuses in front of the retina. Myopic individuals cannot see distant objects clearly without the aid of glasses. By use of a concave lens of proper power, the position of the image is moved farther back to focus on the retina (Fig. 307). **Hyperopia**

(farsightedness) is the opposite condition, resulting from an abnormally short distance between the cornea and lens or a weakened lens; in hyperopia the image of a distant object focuses behind the retina. In the normal condition, the ciliary muscle is relaxed when the image of a distant object is focused on the retina. In the farsighted condition, however, near vision accommodation must be carried out to focus distant objects on the retina. Furthermore, the near point (i.e., the nearest point at which objects are seen distinctly) is farther away from the eyes in hyperopic than in normal or myopic individuals. Hyperopia is corrected by use of a convex lens of proper power to move the image forward and focus it on the retina (Fig. 308) **Presbyopia** (G. *presbys*, old man; G. *ops*, eye) occurs with increasing age. In presbyopia, the lens gradually loses its elasticity, interfering with correct accommodation, so that the near point is a yard or more away from the eye; consequently, older individuals need a convex lens to clearly see objects less than a yard away.

Astigmatism (G. *a-*, not; G. *stigma*, a point) is a visual defect resulting from distortion of the curvature of the cornea or lens of the eye. It is corrected by a cylindrical lens placed in the proper axial position (Fig. 309).

Senile cataract is an aging process in the lens in which vision is obscured by an

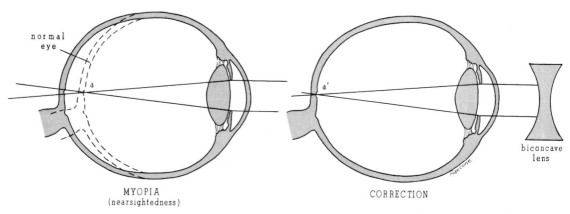

MYOPIA
(nearsightedness)   CORRECTION

Figure 307. Myopia, or nearsightedness; note how the image focuses in front of the retina. A biconcave lens is used as a corrective device for this condition. *a* indicates incorrect point of focus; *a'* indicates focus after correction.

opacity—a region in which light scattering occurs (Fig. 310). The light scattering is a consequence of a sudden change in the concentration of the protein fibers that form the lens, a condition arising because of alterations in protein structure. When this happens in the core of the lens, the cataract is called nuclear; when it happens in the outer layers, it is called cortical. Cataract formation may be accelerated or initiated, among other things, by specific diseases, inherited metabolic disorders, or exposure to x-rays and other forms of radiation. The primary symptom of cataract is a progressive, painless loss of vision. The degree of this loss depends on the location and the extent of the opacity. Nearsightedness develops in the early stages of nuclear cataract so that some elderly patients may discover that they can read without glasses (second sight). Pain is absent unless the cataract swells.

Well advanced cataracts appear as gray opacities in the lens. Gradual loss of vision in middle aged or older patients is characteristic of both cataract and glaucoma. The vision lost through cataract can be restored by operation to remove the lens.

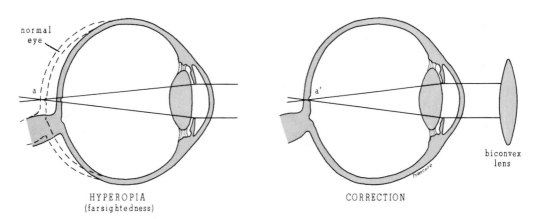

HYPEROPIA
(farsightedness)   CORRECTION

Figure 308. Hyperopia, or farsightedness; note how the image focuses behind the retina. A biconvex lens is used as a corrective device for this condition. *a* indicates incorrect point of focus; *a'* indicates focus after correction.

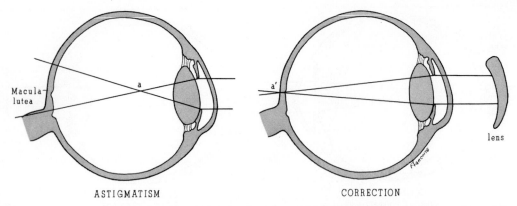

ASTIGMATISM   CORRECTION

Figure 309. Astigmatism: uneven focusing of the image resulting from distortion of the curvature of the lens or cornea. *a* indicates incorrect point of focus; *a'* indicates focus after correction.

Frequent eye examinations and change of eye glass prescriptions will help maintain useful vision during development of a cataract. Removal of the lens is necessary when useful vision is lost. After a cataract lens is surgically removed (Fig. 311), strong glasses must be worn to correct the very farsighted condition of a lensless (aphakic) eye. Corrective glasses for a single eye cause the image on the retina of the lensless eye to be more than 10 per cent larger than the image in the normal eye. Since the brain cannot fuse two such images, surgery is ordinarily not performed until both cataract lenses must be removed. If only one lens is removed, contact lenses that avoid excessive magnification are used.

Injuries or infections of the cornea can lead to *corneal opacity*, causing blindness. A corneal transplant is a method of treatment. In a successful transplant, the transparency of the graft will persist. Homotransplants of the cornea are tolerated, since the cornea of the eye lacks blood and lymph vessels. Blood and lymph vessels are necessary for graft rejection. If corneal tissue is transplanted to another area, such as under the skin, it will be destroyed. If skin is transplanted to the anterior chamber of the eye, it will survive.

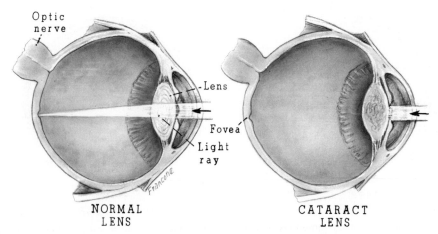

NORMAL LENS   CATARACT LENS

Figure 310. The transmission of light through a normal lens to stimulate the retinal fovea, and the blockage of light to that area by the opacity of the lens in the condition known as cataract.

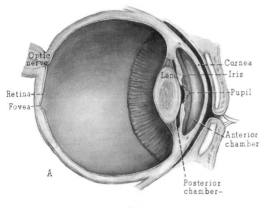

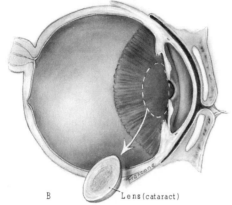

Figure 311. *A,* Cataractous changes of the lens in relation to other structures of the eye. *B,* Removal of the lens from surrounding structures as in cataract surgery. After surgery, glasses or contact lenses must be worn.

Conjunctivitis (inflammation of the conjunctiva) is the most common infection of the eye. It can be caused by any irritation from dust, pollen, bacteria, or viruses, and is characterized by inflammation and an increased flow of tears. The conjunctival membrane takes on a pink or fiery red color. Mild cases will clear spontaneously if further irritation of the eye is prevented.

Sty is an inflammation of one or more of the sebaceous glands of the eyelid.

AUDITORY AND EQUILIBRIUM SENSES

When sound is produced, the atmosphere is disturbed by sound waves (compressions and rarefactions of air created by a vibrating object) radiating from the source. Sound waves impinge on the eardrum (tympanic membrane), and the membrane vibrates at the same frequency as the source creating the sound. Sound vibrations are carried from the tympanic membrane to the inner ear to be transformed into nerve impulses.

Structures of the Ear

The ear consists of three portions: an external, middle, and inner ear (Figs. 312 to 314).

External Ear. The auricle (ear flap) of the external ear collects sound waves and transmits them through the *external acoustic meatus,* or *auditory canal,* to the **tympanic membrane.** The external auditory canal is an S-shaped structure about 2½ cm in length, lined with numerous glands secreting a yellow, waxy substance, *cerumen.* Cerumen lubricates and protects the ear.

Middle Ear. The middle ear (tympanic cavity) is a tiny cavity in the temporal bone. Within it are the three auditory ossicles: the **malleus** (hammer), **incus** (anvil), and **stapes** (stirrup). Two small muscles, the *stapedius* and *tensor tympani,* are also found in the middle ear. The stapedius muscle is attached to the stapes, and the tensor tympani muscle to the handle of the malleus.

The middle ear has five openings—the opening covered by the tympanic membrane; the opening of the *auditory,* or eustachian, *tube,* which connects the middle ear with the nasopharynx and through which outside air can enter; the opening into the mastoid cavity; and the openings into the inner ear (round and oval windows). Three functions have been ascribed to the middle ear. The first function is to transmit energy from sound vibrations in the air column of the external auditory meatus across the middle ear into the fluid contained within the *cochlea* (the central hearing apparatus). The bones of the middle ear pick up the vibrations from the tympanic membrane and transmit them across the middle ear to the *oval window* (the opening to the inner ear). The second function of the middle ear is protective; it reduces the amplitude of vibrations accompanying intense sounds of low frequency. Contraction of the tensor tympani and the stapedius

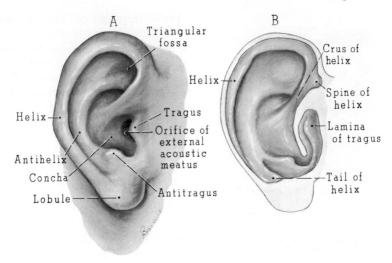

Figure 312. *A*, External ear. *B*, Cartilage portion of ear.

restricts the motion of the chain of ossicles and minimizes shock to the inner ear. The third function of the middle ear is to equalize air pressure on both sides of the membrane via the auditory tube to prevent the tympanum from rupturing.

The Inner Ear. The inner ear consists of bony and membranous labyrinths. The bony labyrinth, composed of a series of canals hollowed out of the temporal bone, is filled with perilymph. The membranous labyrinth, lying entirely within the bony

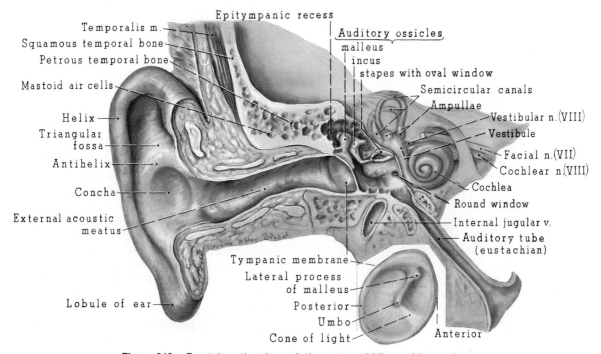

Figure 313. Frontal section through the outer, middle, and internal ear.

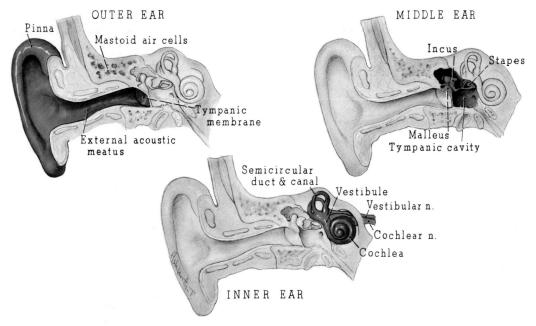

OUTER EAR

Pinna

Mastoid air cells

Tympanic
membrane

External acoustic
meatus

MIDDLE EAR

Incus

Stapes

Malleus
Tympanic cavity

Semicircular
duct & canal

Vestibule

Vestibular n.

Cochlear n.

Cochlea

INNER EAR

Figure 314.   Three divisions of the ear.

labyrinth, is filled with endolymph. The **bony labyrinth** consists of the *cochlea,* containing the organ of hearing, and the *vestibule* and *semicircular canals,* containing the organs of equilibrium (Fig. 315). The **membranous labyrinth** consists of the *cochlear duct* within the cochlea, the utricle and saccule within the vestibule, and the *semicircular ducts* within the semicircular canals. Those portions of the inner ear concerned with equilibrium are collectively called the *vestibular apparatus.*

Physiology of Equilibrium

The utricle and saccule contain within their walls a structure called the macula, containing *hair cells* oriented in different directions. The cilia, or hairs, of these cells are embedded in a gelatinous membrane containing crystals of calcium carbonate called *otoliths* (G. *ous,* ear; G. *lithos,* stone) which make contact with the hairs. The pull of gravity exerted on the otoliths bends the hairs, and the orientation of the head determines which hairs will be bent. Max-

imum effect is obtained with slight changes from an upright position. The bending of the hairs sets up impulses in sensory neuron fibers innervating the hair cells, thereby apprising the brain of the relationship of the head with respect to the pull of gravity and helping maintain *static equilibrium.* The utricle and saccule, in addition to helping maintain static equilibrium, also assist in maintaining equilibrium during *linear acceleration and deceleration.* Thus, a sudden movement forward has the effect of a backward pull on the otoliths, and the resulting sensation is one of falling backward, which leads to a compensatory leaning forward.

There are three semicircular canals in each ear at right angles to each other, each containing a membranous, semicircular duct. When the head is bent forward 30 degrees, the lateral canal (Fig. 315) is in a horizontal plane and the superior and posterior canals are in vertical planes, one projecting forward 45 degrees, the other backward 45 degrees. Within the dilated portion *(ampulla)* at the base of each semicircular duct (near the junction with

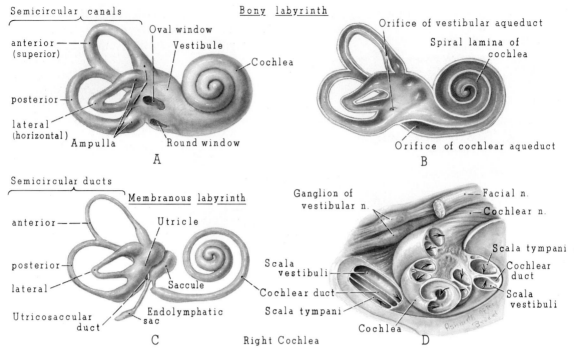

Figure 315. Bony (*A, B*) and membranous (*C, D*) labyrinths of the inner ear.

the utricle) is a structure called the crista, which contains *hair cells* embedded in a gelatinous dome (the *cupola*) and is sensitive to angular acceleration or deceleration. As the head begins to rotate, inertia of the *endolymph* in the semicircular ducts is equivalent to movement of the endolymph in the direction opposite to the rotation. As a result, the cupola "moves," bending the embedded hairs in the direction opposite to the rotation. At the cessation of rotation, fluid inertia causes bending of the hairs in the same direction as the ceased rotation. Bending of the hairs in a specific direction (toward the utricle in the case of the horizontally oriented lateral ducts, away from the utricle in the case of the vertically oriented superior and posterior ducts) sets up nerve impulses essential for maintaining *dynamic equilibrium.*

Nervous Pathways for Equilibrium. Sensory neuron fibers innervating the hair cells of the organs of equilibrium travel with the *vestibular branch of the eighth cranial nerve,* and most of them terminate in the vestibular nuclei of the medulla. The connections made from this point are widespread and include fibers to the spinal cord (medial vestibulospinal

tracts to the cervical region and lateral vestibulospinal tracts to all other regions), cerebellum, reticular formation, nuclei of the third, fourth, and sixth cranial nerves and to the sensory projection area for equilibrium in the temporal lobe (relayed through the thalamus). Branches of the eighth cranial nerves also pass directly to the cerebellum.

Signals transmitted by the vestibulospinal tracts are important for maintaining the tone of antigravity muscles. The interconnections between the vestibular nuclei, reticular formation, and cerebellum play a vital role in making reflexive adjustments in muscle tone (via impulses sent through the reticulospinal and vestibulospinal tracts) to maintain equilibrium as the body falls to one side, forward or backward. Nerve impulses passing from the vestibular nuclei to the reticular formation also form part of the activating input of the reticular formation (see page 288).

The arrival of equilibrium impulses in the cerebral cortex makes possible conscious awareness of equilibrium sensations. This input becomes essential for conscious orientation of the head in the absence of visual or tactile clues. Thus, individuals with congenital defects of the vestibular apparatus may drown in deep water since the defect prevents orientation by labyrinth receptors, and orientation by sight or touch is not possible.

Eye reflexes are mediated by cranial nerves III, IV, and VI. Readily observable are reflexive eye movements in response to angular acceleration. As the head begins to turn, the eyes turn slowly in the opposite direction to maintain the gaze at a fixed point; but, as the head continues to turn, they swing quickly to fix the gaze on a new point. These alternating movements, quick phase followed by a slow deviation, are called *nystagmus* (G. *nystagmos*, drowsiness). The quick phase designates the direction of the rotation. The nystagmus disappears when the rotation continues for a while at a constant rate. For a brief period following rotation, nystagmus in the direction opposite to the rotation can be observed.

Physiology of Hearing

The cochlea is coiled two and one-half times in the shape of a snail shell about a central axis of bone (Figs. 315 to 317). Three compartments compose the hollow cochlea. The upper passage, or *scala vestibuli*, ends at the oval window; the lower passage, or *scala tympani*, ends at the round window. These two passages connect at the apex of the spiral; both contain perilymph. A third passage, the *cochlear duct*, filled with endolymph, lies between the scala vestibuli and the scala tympani.

The cochlear duct is bounded above by the *vestibular membrane* and below by the basilar membrane. The **basilar membrane** has tightly stretched fibers; the shorter fibers are located at the base, and the longer ones at the apex. The **organ of Corti**, the organ of hearing, lies on the basilar membrane; it contains numerous receptor hair cells.

Auditory Responses. Sound is a sensation produced when vibrations initiated in the external environment strike the tympanic membrane. The waves travel at a speed of 344 m/sec (775 mph) at 20° C at sea level. The speed at which sound waves travel increases with increased temperature and altitude. Other media also conduct sound waves, but at different velocities. For

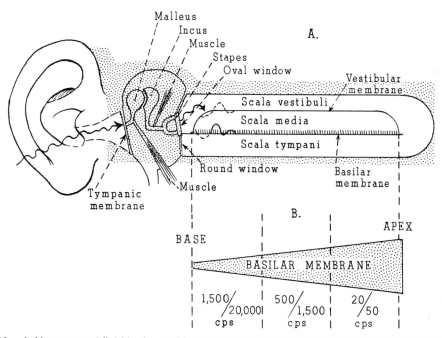

Figure 316. *A*, Movement of fluid in the cochlea set up by sound waves reaching the tympanic membrane. *B*, High frequency; vibration causes basilar fibers close to the oval window to vibrate; fibers toward the apex are some 12 times longer and are influenced by sounds producing fewer waves or cycles per second (CPS). (From McNaught, A. B., and Callander, R.: *Illustrated Physiology.* Edinburgh, Churchill Livingstone, 1970.)

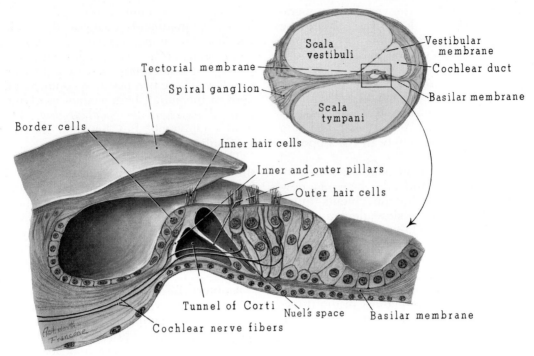

Figure 317. Spiral organ of Corti. Insert of cross section of cochlea shows location of organ of Corti.

example, sound waves travel at a speed of 1428 m/sec (3215 mph) in water.

The amplitude of a wave determines loudness, whereas pitch is correlated with the frequency or number of waves per unit of time. The greater the amplitude, the louder the sound; the greater the frequency, the higher the pitch.

The unit used for measuring the loudness of sound is known as a *bel*, a measure of air pressure changes. For convenience, 1/10 of a bel, or decibel, is normally used in describing noise levels associated with hearing. The threshold of hearing for humans is designated 0 decibels. Since the bel scale is logarithmic (and a given number of bels represents an exponent to the base 10), two bels (20 decibels) is 10^2 (100) times louder than threshold and six bels (60 decibels) is 10^6 (one million) times louder than threshold. Normal conversation measures around 65 decibels.

Sound frequencies audible to the human ear range from 20 to 20,000 cycles/sec. The threshold of hearing varies with the pitch of the sound, greatest sensitivity occurring between 1000 and 3000 cycles/sec.

Sound waves entering the acoustic meatus create vibrations in the tympanic membrane. The ossicles of the middle ear, in turn, carry these vibrations to the oval window. Vibrations in the oval window set up sound waves in the perilymph which travel through the thin vestibular membrane to the endolymph of the cochlear duct. The waves pass through the basilar membrane to the perilymph of the scala tympani and are dissipated against the membrane of the round window. The sound waves, depending on the frequency of sound, set up sympathetic sound waves in various portions of the basilar membrane. Movement of the basilar membrane bends the hair cells of the organ of Corti to initiate electrical impulses in the hair cells, which in turn stimulate terminal endings of sensory neurons (Fig. 317).

High frequency sounds cause maximum displacement of the basilar membrane at the base of the cochlear duct (near the stapes, where the fibers are shorter and stiffer); low frequency sound waves cause maximum displacement near the apex. Increased intensity of sound causes increased frequency of nerve impulses.

Tympanic Reflex. Excessive stimulation of the auditory receptors by strong sound waves is guarded against by the tympanic reflex. Such stimulation causes contraction of the tensor tympani muscle of the middle ear. Originating in the cartilaginous portion of the auditory canal and inserting on the malleus, contraction of this muscle increases the tension on the tympanic membrane, thus guarding against injury.

Nervous Pathway for Hearing. Neurons initiating the nerve impulses for sound have their endings scattered among the hair cells of the organ of Corti. The axons of these neurons, located in the *cochlear division of the auditory (eighth) cranial nerve,* travel to the dorsal and ventral cochlear nuclei in the medulla, where they synapse. From here the pathway continues through a number of stations to the auditory cortical area in the upper part of the **temporal lobe.** The intermediate points include the superior olivary nucleus, the nucleus of the lateral lemniscus, the inferior colliculus, and the medial geniculate body of the thalamus. All fibers synapse in the medial geniculate body; most also synapse in the superior olivary nucleus and the inferior colliculus. In addition, some synaptic connections are made in the nucleus of the lateral lemniscus. As a result of partial decussation at several points, the auditory cortex receives bilateral input. Each ear, however, has greater representation at all levels on the opposite side of the brain. The reticular activating system (see page 288), the superior colliculus (see page 314) and the cerebellum (see page 295) also receive input from the auditory system.

Sound Localization. Determining the direction from which sound is coming requires sound reception by both ears and depends, for the most part, upon differences in the intensity and time of arrival of sound at the two ears. The ear on the side of the sound receives a more intense and earlier stimulus. Sound localization does not involve conscious judgment on the part of the listener. In studies with cats, intensity and time cues have been related to neural responses. Presenting a sound to one ear only will excite more neural activity in the brain on the opposite side. The same observation is made when a more intense sound is presented to one ear than to the other. When a sound is delivered to one ear just before it is delivered to the other, a greater response is recorded in the brain on the side opposite the ear receiving the earlier signal. The principle of sound localization by a difference in intensity has

been used to identify malingerers claiming to be deaf in one ear. For example, if a tone is presented simultaneously to both ears through earphones, but more intensely to the left ear, a normal person will say the sound is coming from the left. An individual deaf in the left ear will hear the sound in the right ear. A person feigning deafness in the left ear will say he does not hear any sound. This test clearly shows that sound localization does not require a comparison of separate sensations aroused in two ears. A single localized sound is heard.

Abnormalities of the Ear

Deafness. Any portion of the auditory apparatus can be affected by disease or injury, leading to partial or total deafness. The extent of hearing loss at various frequencies can be determined with the aid of an **audiogram.** An audiogram is the record of a test performed with an audiometer, an instrument through which pure tones are delivered through earphones, starting with the intensity at each frequency that is barely audible to a normal person. The number of decibels each tone must be raised before a subject can hear it is a measure of the hearing loss for that frequency. The audiogram in Figure 318 shows three types of hearing loss.

CONDUCTIVE, OR TRANSMISSION, DEAFNESS. This condition is caused by interference in the transmission of sound vibrations through the external or middle ear. Vibrations may be blocked by wax or foreign bodies in the external or middle ear, or by adhesions of the bones of the middle ear. Transmission deafness is not characterized by damage to end organs or nerves; therefore, a person suffering from transmission deafness can hear with a hearing aid. Ossification around the footplate of the stapes, or otosclerosis, is an example of transmission deafness.

PERCEPTIVE DEAFNESS. Perceptive deafness results from disease of the organ of Corti or of the auditory nerve. Hearing aids are not useful in this type of deafness.

Tinnitus. Tinnitus, ringing in the ear, can be caused by cerumen (wax in the ear), perforations of the tympanic membrane, fluid in the middle ear, or any disturbance of the auditory nerve, brainstem, or cortex.

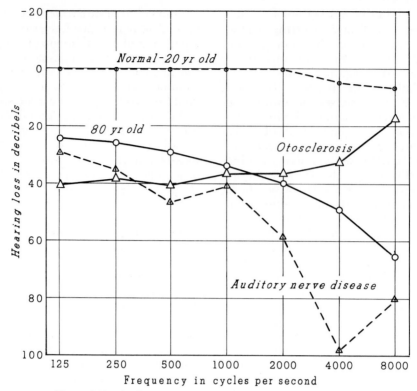

Figure 318. Audiogram showing three types of abnormalities.

Tinnitus sometimes follows administration of drugs. Two of the most common offenders are aspirin and streptomycin. If the administration of streptomycin is discontinued when the tinnitus initially appears, ringing will cease. If streptomycin administration is maintained, tinnitus can be permanent.

Perforation of the Tympanic Membrane. Perforation of the tympanic membrane can impair hearing. The degree of hearing loss depends upon the size and location of the perforation. A patient with almost complete loss of the tympanic membrane can still hear slightly, since the vibrations bypass the tympanum and travel to the inner ear by way of the bones of the skull.

OLFACTORY SENSE (SENSE OF SMELL)

Receptor Cells

Less is known about the sense of smell than about the more complex senses. Re-

ceptors for smell are located in the *olfactory* (L. *olfacere,* to smell) *epithelium,* an area about 2.5 cm square in each nostril, located in the roof of the nasal cavity (Fig. 319). The olfactory epithelium contains supporting cells and actual olfactory cells.

Olfactory cells are bipolar neurons with their cell bodies in the mucosal epithelial layer. At the mucosal surface they divide into many fine hairlike processes, or cilia, which lie uncovered except for a thin layer

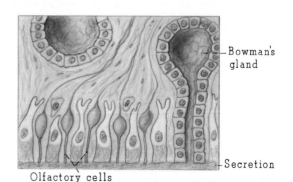

Figure 319. Olfactory epithelium showing supporting cells and olfactory cells.

of mucus; nowhere else in the body are nerve endings so exposed. The axons of the olfactory cell bodies pass through the *cribriform plate* of the *ethmoid bone* as fibers of the *olfactory nerve* to the *olfactory bulb* above each nasal cavity (Fig. 270, page 267). Here synaptic connections are made with neurons (mitral cells) whose axons form the *olfactory tract.* The exact route these axons follow is uncertain. They are believed to terminate largely in the parahippocampal gyrus.

Physiology of Olfaction

In order for a substance to arouse the sensation of smell it must first of all be volatile so that it can be carried by eddy currents to the olfactory epithelium. A relatively high water and lipid solubility are characteristic of substances with strong odors. Water solubility is necessary for the substance to dissolve in the layer of mucus covering the olfactory cells. Lipid solubility presumably aids penetration of the membranes of the receptor cells.

A number of theories have been presented attempting to explain the mechanism of smell. An underlying assumption of many of these theories is that some kind of interaction occurs between odoriferous molecules and the membranes of the olfactory cells, possibly with specific receptors, which alters permeability of the membranes and induces a nerve impulse.

Although olfactory receptors are sensitive to exceedingly low concentrations of odor-producing substances, the differential sensitivity of olfaction is considered to be poor. According to most reports, the concentration of an odor-producing substance must be changed by about 30 per cent before a difference can be detected. In a recent study, however, in which fluctuations in the concentrations of stimulants were reduced to a minimum, changes in concentration, in some cases as low as 5 per cent, could be detected. Comparable visual discrimination threshold is a 1 per cent change in light intensity. Maximum odor intensity is achieved with a 50-fold increase above the threshold concentration. This is a small range compared to most sensory systems.

Humans can distinguish between 2000 and 4000 different odors. Evidence indicates that the direction from which the odor comes can be detected by the slight difference in the time of arrival of odoriferous molecules in the two nostrils.

Sniffing. That portion of the nasal cavity containing the olfactory receptors is poorly ventilated. The amount of air reaching this region is greatly increased by sniffing, thereby increasing the intensity of the odor.

Receptors for smell adapt quickly at first—about 50 per cent in the first second—and slowly thereafter. Nevertheless, after a minute or more of continuous stimulation by a specific odor, the ability to recognize the odor is lost. Central mechanisms are believed to be involved in this phenomenon. If another odor is immediately smelled, adaptation to the first in no way seems to impair the sensing of the second.

Many attempts have been made to classify odors, but none helps to explain the physiology of smell. Each substance causes its own particular sensation. A multitude of distinct odors can be recognized, and individual odors in a mixed smell can be distinguished.

GUSTATORY SENSE (SENSE OF TASTE)

Receptor Cells

Like the sense of smell, the sense of taste provides a chemical sensitivity for an organism, enabling it to decide if particles should be ingested or rejected. The specialized structures for the reception of taste are the **taste buds.** Approximately 9000 of these structures are found on the tongue. Taste buds are onion-shaped receptors containing a tiny pore opening onto the surface of the tongue. They measure 50 to 70 micrometers in diameter and consist of supporting cells and five to 18 *hair cells,* or gustatory (L. *gustare,* to taste) receptors. These hairs project into the taste pore. The buds are found in numerous small projections *(papillae)* on the tongue. The large papillae forming a V-line on the posterior portion of the tongue are *vallate papillae.* The *fungiform papillae,* more numerous and smaller, are located chiefly on the tip and sides of the tongue (Fig. 320).

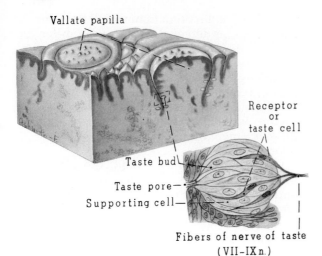

Figure 320. Taste bud and section from tongue showing where it is found.

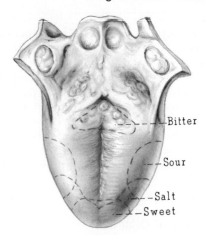

Figure 321. Taste areas of the tongue.

Physiology of Taste

Only when a substance is in solution can it stimulate the gustatory hairs. Substances arousing taste sensations are believed to in some way alter the ionic permeability of the hair membranes and thereby evoke a change in electrical potential. Receptor potentials of the taste cells then generate impulses in the endings of the sensory neurons innervating taste cells.

Taste studies in animals and humans have demonstrated the existence of functionally distinct types of taste receptor cells (with no corresponding histological difference). Taste buds show sensitivity to combinations of four primary taste sensations—*sweet, salty, sour,* and *bitter.* Their distribution on the tongue gives rise to maximum sensitivity to sweet taste at the tip, sourness at the sides, bitterness at the back, and salty taste at the tip and sides (Fig. 321).

Intensity of discrimination is relatively crude; a 30 per cent change in concentration is necessary for discrimination to occur.

Acids taste sour, the sourness being generally proportional to the hydrogen ion concentration. A salty taste is produced principally by the cation of salts. Sweet substances are usually organic and include sugars, alcohols, and aldehydes. Bitter-tasting substances are frequently organic also, and include chemicals classified as alkaloids, such as quinine, caffeine, and nicotine. Flavor is accomplished when a variety of tastes is synthesized from the four basic taste components. Many substances are identified by combinations of gustatory and olfactory sensations, aided also by touch, pressure, temperature, and pain sensations.

The sense of taste has been found to be an important factor in nutrition. Animals deprived of the sense of taste suffer from malnutrition even when an adequate diet is available to them.

Most special senses are supplied by a single nerve extending from the receptor to the brain; however, taste is made possible by multiple nerves. It is served by the *chorda tympani* nerve (VII) for the front of the tongue, the *glossopharyngeal* nerve (IX) for the back of the tongue, and the *vagus* nerve (X) for the deeper recesses of the throat and pharynx. Axons of these nerves lead to taste nuclei in the medulla. From here second order neurons pass to the thalamus, where synaptic connections are made with neurons whose fibers lead to the projection area for taste in the parietal lobe (the lower end of the somesthetic area of the postcentral gyrus). Taste fibers also pass to the reticular formation and to nuclei in the medulla serving salivatory reflexes.

SUMMARY

SPECIAL SENSES

Vision

1. External Structures of the Eye

   a. Orbital cavity (contains eyeball)

b. Extrinsic ocular muscles (provide support for and control movement of eyeball)
c. Eyelids (give protection)
d. Conjunctiva (line each eyelid and exposed surface of eyeball)
e. Lacrimal apparatus (lubricates eye)

2. **Internal Structures of the Eye**

a. Layers of the eyeball
   (1) Outer layer (consists of sclera posteriorly, cornea anteriorly)
   (2) Middle layer (consists of choroid posteriorly, ciliary body [ciliary processes and ciliary muscles] and iris anteriorly)
   (3) Inner layer (consists of retina)
b. Fluid media of the eye
   (1) Aqueous humor (fills anterior and posterior chambers of anterior cavity of eyeball, nourishes lens and cornea)
   (2) Vitreous humor (fills posterior cavity, maintains spherical shape of eye)

3. **Accommodation**

a. Cornea is principal refracting medium of eye, accounting for two-thirds of focusing power when viewing distant objects.
b. Focusing on objects closer than 20 feet from eyes involves increasing convexity of lens. This is accomplished by contracting ciliary muscles, which draw choroid and ciliary processes forward, easing tension on suspensory ligament and lens capsule.
c. Accommodation for near vision includes, in addition to focusing image on retina, contraction of circular fibers of iris (constricting pupil) and aligning visual axes of eyes.
d. Accommodation for far vision involves relaxation of ciliary muscles, contraction of radial fibers of iris (dilating pupil) and aligning visual axes.

4. **Physiology of Vision**

a. Retina changes image focused on it into nerve impulses.
b. Retina contains rods sensitive to dim light and cones sensitive to bright light. Cones function in color vision.

c. Rods and cones are receptor cells having photosensitive chemicals that undergo changes to initiate nerve impulse.
d. After initiation, nerve impulses are relayed via bipolar cells to ganglion cells, axons of which form optic nerve.
e. Horizontal and amacrine cells transmit inhibitory signals across retina to heighten contrast in visual field.
f. Stimuli in left field of vision of both eyes excite right visual cortex in occipital lobe, and vice versa.

5. **Binocular Vision**

Disparity between left and right retinal images of third dimension of an object, resulting from different views seen by each eye (binocular parallax), is synthesized by brain into three-dimensional picture.

6. **Abnormalities of the Eye**

a. Problems of focus include nearsightedness (myopia), farsightedness (hyperopia), oldsightedness (presbyopia), and uneven focusing in different planes (astigmatism).
b. Other abnormalities include cataract, an alteration in concentration of protein fibers of lens, causing light scattering; corneal opacity; and conjunctivitis, an inflammation of the conjunctiva.

Auditory Sense

1. **Sound vibrations in air cause eardrum (tympanic membrane) to vibrate; vibrations in turn are conveyed to inner ear and transformed into nerve impulses.**

2. **Structure of the Ear**

a. **External ear:** Auricle collects sound waves and directs them through external acoustic meatus to tympanic membrane.
b. **Middle ear** includes malleus, incus, and stapes. These three bones transmit sound vibrations from tympanic membrane to inner ear and reduce amplitude of large vibrations. Pressure on both sides of tympanic mem-

brane is equalized by way of auditory, or eustachian, tube.

c. **Inner ear** has bony labyrinth consisting of cochlea, containing organ of Corti, end organ of hearing, and semicircular canals and vestibule, containing organs for balance of body. Within cochlea is membranous cochlear duct. Organ of Corti rests on floor of cochlear duct, formed by the basilar membrane.

3. **Physiology of Hearing**

a. Sound waves cause tympanic membrane to vibrate.
b. Bones of middle ear transmit these vibrations to oval window of inner ear, which in turn transmits vibrations to perilymph of passageway (scala vestibuli) above cochlear duct.
c. As vibrations pass through endolymph of cochlear duct to perilymph in passageway (scala tympani) below cochlear duct, vibrations are set up in basilar membrane — high frequency sounds causing maximum displacement of basilar membrane at base of cochlea, low frequency at apex.
d. Vibrations of basilar membrane bend hairs of hair cells of organ of Corti, initiating electrical impulses, which in turn stimulate sensory neurons whose fibers travel to medulla in cochlear branch of eighth cranial nerve.
e. As result of partial decussation of fibers at several stations in pathway from medulla to cerebrum, auditory cortex receives bilateral input, but each ear has greater representation on opposite side.

Equilibrium

1. The utricle and saccule (portions of the membranous labyrinth located in the vestibule) contain receptors for static equilibrium and linear acceleration and deceleration that consist of hair cells embedded in a gelatinous membrane containing calcium carbonate crystals (otoliths). Gravitational pull on the otoliths, determined by head orientation, bends the hairs, setting up impulses in sensory neurons.

2. In the ampulla, at the base of each of three semicircular ducts (inside each semicircular canal), are receptors for dynamic equilibrium. Angular acceleration or deceleration stimulates hair cells, initiating nerve impulses.

Olfactory Sense

Olfactory receptor cells are bipolar neurons with their cell bodies in the olfactory epithelium. Their axons become the olfactory nerve.

Gustatory Sense

1. Approximately 9000 taste buds, the receptors for taste, are found on the human tongue in the fungiform and vallate papillae. Hairs of taste cells project from a taste bud through a pore to the surface of a papilla.

2. Taste buds are sensitive to combinations of four primary tastes — sweet, salty, sour, and bitter — and their distribution results in maximum sensitivity to sweet taste at the tip of the tongue, sourness at the sides, bitterness at the back, and salty taste at the tip and sides.

chapter 10

The Circulatory System

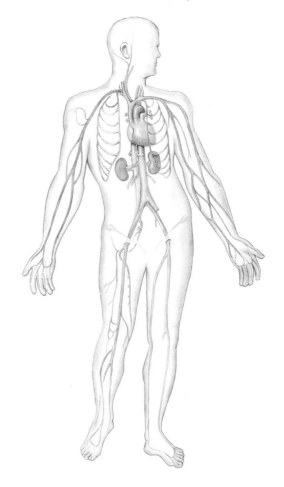

Objectives

The aim of this chapter is to enable the student to:

Describe the major components of blood and distinguish between the functions of the different types of blood cells.

List, in sequence, the basic steps in blood clotting.

Describe the basic organization of the circulatory system.

Enumerate the steps of the cardiac cycle.

Explain the origin of the heartbeat.

Describe an ECG.

Name and describe the difference in structure and function of the different types of blood vessels.

List the major factors governing arterial blood pressure and explain the role of the medullary vasomotor and cardiac centers in regulating blood pressure.

Name the major vessels of the circulatory system.

Explain the unique features of the circulation through the liver.

Describe coronary heart disease and some of the congenital defects of the cardiovascular system.

In 1628, after 9 years of careful observation, William Harvey published the first scientific treatise demonstrating the continuous circulation of blood. Since that time, a great deal of physiologic and biochemical data on the circulatory system has accumulated. Recent advances, such as the replacement of diseased valves in the heart, have stirred the imagination. Several patients with three artificial heart valves are now alive. Surgeons are now capable of transplanting an entire heart.

The circulatory system nourishes every part of the body. The fluid bathing the body tissues is derived from the blood; the pump circulating the blood is the heart; the tubes through which the blood flows are the blood vessels.

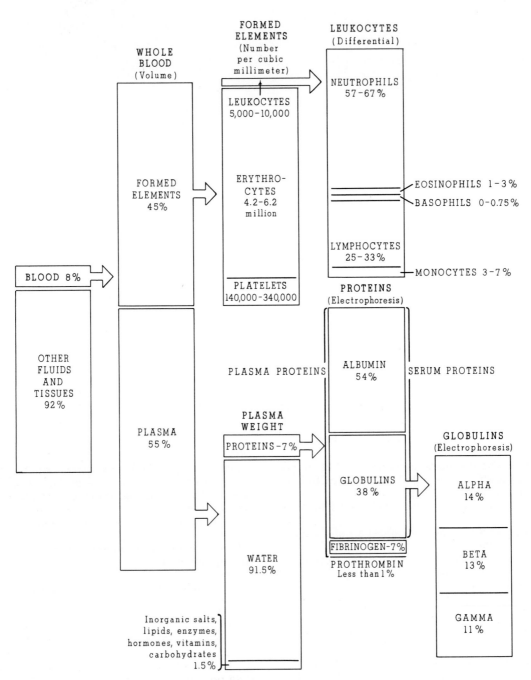

Figure 322.   Composition of blood.

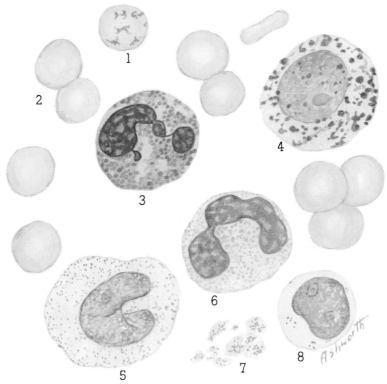

Figure 323. Blood cells: 1, reticulocyte; 2, erythrocyte; 3, eosinophil; 4, basophil; 5, monocyte; 6, neutrophil; 7, platelets; and 8, lymphocyte. Numbers correspond to those in Figure 324, illustrating the stages of blood cell formation.

BLOOD

The Nature of Blood

Although blood appears homogeneous, if a thin layer is placed under a microscope, its heterogeneous character becomes obvious. If blood is centrifuged or allowed to stand, it separates into two distinct fractions. Less than half the blood consists of "formed" elements—**red blood cells, white blood cells,** and **platelets** (Figs. 322 and 323). These normally constitute 38 to 52 per cent of the total blood volume. The remainder is the straw-colored fluid, the **plasma.** The *hematocrit* (G. *haimo,* blood; G. *krinein,* to separate) is the percentage of "formed" elements by volume. Thus, if the percentage of "formed" elements is 45, the hematocrit is 45.

Blood Plasma

Blood plasma is a straw-colored liquid composed of a solution of water (91 per cent) and chemical compounds (9 per cent), mainly protein. The total plasma volume and ratio of plasma to formed elements are held constant by the homeostatic mechanisms of the body. *Serum* differs from plasma in that it is the fluid remaining after formation of a blood clot and, therefore, does not contain a number of the clotting factors present in plasma. Plasma can only be maintained if an anticoagulant is added to keep clotting from occurring. (See Table 36 for constituents of blood plasma and Table 37 for characteristics of blood.)

The four major plasma proteins are *albumin, globulin, fibrinogen,* and *prothrombin.* Albumin is important in maintaining the osmotic equilibrium of the blood. Since albumin cannot readily pass through the capillary wall, it remains in the blood stream and exerts an osmotic pressure, attracting water from the tissue spaces back into the blood stream. If plasma protein, particularly serum albumin, leaks from the capillaries as a result of injury, such as a severe burn, water cannot be retained and the blood volume drops. If the loss is

Table 36. BLOOD CONSTITUENTS IN NORMAL AND ABNORMAL STATES

CONSTITUENT	NORMAL LEVEL	ALTERATIONS IN DISEASE STATES
Total bilirubin	Less than 1 mg./100 ml.	Increased in hemolytic anemia and in obstruction to biliary flow, such as a stone in the common bile duct
Calcium	4.5–5.5 mEq./l.	Increased in hyperparathyroidism; decreased in hypoparathyroidism
Total cholesterol	140–250 mg./100 ml.	Increased in hypothyroidism; decreased in hyperthyroidism and starvation
Fibrinogen	0.2–0.4 gm./100 ml.	Increased in severe infections; decreased in primary liver disease and malnutrition
Glucose	70–110 mg./100 ml.	Increased after meals and in diabetes mellitus; decreased in Addison's disease
Non-protein nitrogen (NPN)	20–35 mg./100 ml.	Includes urea, uric acid, creatinine, ammonia, and amino acids; increased in disease of the kidneys
Protein-bound iodine (PBI)	3–7 mg./100 ml.	Increased in hyperthyroidism; decreased in hypothyroidism
Phosphate	3–4.5 mg./100 ml.	Increased in renal disease and hypoparathyroidism, as well as in Addison's disease; decreased in vitamin D deficiency and hyperparathyroidism
Potassium	3.5–5.0 mEq./l.	Increased in Addison's disease and diseases of the kidney; decreased after diarrhea, and with administration of adrenocortical hormones
Total protein Albumin Globulin	6–7.8 gm./100 ml. 3.2–4.5 gm./100 ml. 2.3–3.5 gm./100 ml.	Decreased in diseases of the kidney and liver, and in malnutrition; globulin is elevated in chronic infection
Sodium	140–148 mEq./l.	Increased in diseases of the kidney; decreased in Addison's disease
Uric acid	2.6–7 mg./100 ml.	Increased in kidney disease and gout

severe, shock results. Treatment necessary to counteract this state includes the intravenous injection of serum albumin.

Globulin is important, since it contains antibodies involved in the body's immune mechanism. If globulin is examined by *electrophoresis*, it can be separated into three groups: alpha, beta, and gamma. The gamma globulin is the antibody fraction.

The electrophoretic method used in separating the plasma proteins involves placing the serum or plasma in an electric field, causing the negatively charged protein molecules existing as ions in plasma to

Table 37. CHARACTERISTICS OF BLOOD

CHARACTERISTIC	NORMAL VALUE
Specific gravity	Males, 1.057 Females, 1.053
Average blood volume	69 ml./kg. of body weight
Viscosity (relative to water)	Whole, 3.5–5.4 Plasma, 1.9–2.3
pH	Arterial, 7.39 Venous, 7.35
Arterial oxygen content	Total, 20.3 ml. oxygen/100 ml. of blood In plasma, 0.3 Combined with hemoglobin, 20.0

migrate toward the positive electrode. The protein molecules move at different speeds, depending on size, shape, and charge, and eventually become separated from each other.

Fibrinogen and prothrombin are important in the process of coagulation and will be discussed subsequently.

Blood Cell Formation

All blood cells originate from undifferentiated **stem cells** called hemocytoblasts. Primitive cells of each family have similar morphologic characteristics. As primitive cells change to the more mature cell forms, they undergo alterations in nuclear and cytoplasmic characteristics; cells decrease in size; the relative and absolute size of the nucleus decreases (in the erythrocytic series, the nucleus actually disappears); and the intensity of the stain taken up by the cytoplasm diminishes (Fig. 324).

The first recognizable blood cells in the human embryo forming in islands within the *mesenchyme* of the yolk sac originate from hemocytoblasts. During the second month of intra-uterine life, the liver assumes a major role in the formation of blood cells. During the fifth month, the spleen is the dominant producer, but this activity rapidly subsides. At birth, some *hematopoietic* (formation of blood) activity may remain in the liver but none is occurring in the spleen.

Development of blood cells within the bones commences during the fifth month of fetal life. Blood-forming elements appear initially in the centers of bone marrow cavities; the blood-forming centers later expand to occupy the entire marrow space. This widely dispersed blood cell formation continues until puberty, when the marrow in all the ends of the long bones becomes less cellular and more fatty, giving rise to yellow bone marrow, in which most of the hematopoietic tissue has been replaced by fat. In the adult, only the **red bone marrow,** located principally in the skull, vertebrae, ribs, sternum, and pelvis, retains hematopoietic activity. The total productive bone marrow in the adult is about 1400 gm. In elderly individuals, areas of bone marrow, once occupied by active cell production, become fat laden. This helps explain the difficulty elderly individuals experience in regenerating lost blood.

Types of Blood Cells

Erythrocytes

Red blood cells, or *erythrocytes* (G. *erythros,* red; G. *kytos,* cell), transport oxygen (principally bound to hemoglobin) from the lungs to other tissues and carbon dioxide from the tissues to the lungs. Just before a red cell reaches maturity, the nucleus is extruded. The mature red blood cell has the shape of a **biconcave disc,** resembling a doughnut with a thin central portion instead of a hole. This shape provides a large absorptive surface, the total surface area of erythrocytes representing approximately 3200 square meters, or 1500 times the surface of the human body. The diameter of red blood cells is approximately 7 micrometers. They are elastic and increase in size as the pH of the blood diminishes. Thus the erythrocyte is larger in venous blood than in arterial.

The number of red cells per cubic millimeter of blood can be determined by counting a limited number of cells spread on a ruled microscopic slide, the hemocytometer. The red cell count is approximately 5,400,000 cells per cubic millimeter in males and 4,700,000 per cubic millimeter in females. Muscular exercise and emotional states are associated with a temporary increase in the number of red cells. The increase occurs from the expulsion of stores of blood in the spleen and liver.

Regulation of Red Blood Cell Production. Red blood cell production, or *erythropoiesis* (G. *poiesis,* production), is regulated by **erythropoietin,** also called erythropoietic stimulating factor (ESF). Erythropoietin is responsible for the increase in the rate of production of red blood cells by any condition that reduces the oxygen supply to the tissues *(hypoxia).* Hypoxia causes the concentration of erythropoietin to rise to detectable levels in the blood. After a person ascends to a high altitude, for example, the concentration of erythropoietin in the blood rises daily and the rate of erythrocyte formation rises sharply after two days to a maximum in five days. Erythropoietin also controls the rate of red blood cell production under normal conditions. The best evidence for this is the observation that the injection of antibodies to erythropoietin into mice essentially abolishes erythropoiesis. Erythropoietin is formed in the blood by the action of an enzyme released principally from the kidneys called renal erythropoietin factor (REF). REF cleaves a portion of a plasma protein to produce the active substance. For many years it was believed that erythropoietin acted by stimulating the stem cell. Recent findings, however, indicate that it acts rather on an erythropoietin-sensitive progeny of the stem cell. To cite one example, in studies with mice injected with a known number of stem cells after destruction of their bone marrow by irradiation, the effect of erythropoietin on the rate of red blood cell production could be accounted for only if it acted not on the stem cell but on a greater number of proliferating progeny.

HEMOGLOBIN. Hemoglobin, contained in the red cells, plays an essential role in oxygen transport. It is formed during the manufacture of the red blood cells in the bone marrow. Each red blood cell contains approximately 280 million hemoglobin molecules. The hemoglobin molecule consists of four protein chains (two called *alpha*, two called *beta*), each of which enfolds an oxygen-carrying nonprotein group called *heme*. Heme is a complex of iron and protoporphyrin (a ring structure with a framework of four groups called pyrols, each containing four carbons and a nitrogen). Each iron atom can take up one molecule of oxygen. Hemoglobin carries over 98 per cent of the oxygen transported by the blood; less than 2 per cent is carried in simple solution in the plasma. The normal levels for hemoglobin are 15 gm per 100 ml in males and 13 to 14 gm per 100 ml in females.

Destruction of Erythrocytes. The life span of erythrocytes is approximately 80 to 120 days. When their usefulness is impaired by age, the red cells are destroyed by the macrophages of the *reticuloendothelial system*, especially of the spleen. Two to ten million red cells are destroyed each second, yet, because of replacement, the number of circulating cells remains remarkably constant. When red cells are destroyed, hemoglobin is set free and broken down into its components, heme and the protein globin. The heme decomposes into its constituents, protoporphyrin and iron. The iron is utilized to form new erythrocytes or, if an excess of iron exists in the body, it is brought to the bone marrow, spleen, and liver for storage. Protoporphyrin is converted to *bilirubin*, which is carried to the liver and excreted with the bile. It is the bilirubin that gives bile its golden-yellow color.

HEMOLYSIS AND CRENATION OF RED BLOOD CELLS. *Hemolysis in vitro* (in a vessel outside the body) is the rupture of red cell membranes and resultant liberation of hemoglobin from the red corpuscles. It may result from osmotic forces such as would result from the injection of distilled water, or by mechanical stress as in heating or freezing. Hemolysis is characterized by a red tinge to the serum or plasma from which the red blood cells have been separated.

Crenation is a shriveling of the cell, noted when the cells are placed in a salt solution of high concentration. The fluid within the cell passes into the surrounding medium. Crenation does not alter the integrity of the cell wall and hemoglobin does not escape, thus differentiating it from hemolysis.

Anemias. Anemia is a condition characterized by a deficiency in the amount of oxygen carried by red blood cells to the tissues. It is most commonly caused by a decrease in the rate of formation of red blood cells, an increase in their rate of destruction, or a reduction in hemoglobin synthesis. When red blood cell production is reduced as a result of damage to the red bone marrow, the condition is called hypoplastic, or, in severe cases, **aplastic, anemia.** Bone marrow can be destroyed, among other things, by radiation, infections, and drugs, especially some used in cancer chemotherapy. In **pernicious anemia** there is a reduction in the formation of red blood cells because of a deficiency in vitamin B_{12}, known as the maturation factor. The underlying cause of this condition is a failure of the stomach to produce enough "intrinsic factor," a glycoprotein that facilitates the absorption of vitamin B_{12} from the small intestine into the blood stream. The red blood cell count is very low in pernicious anemia and the cells produced are large (*macrocytic*), oddly shaped, and fragile.

Hemolysis *in vivo* (in the body) refers to a

shortened life span of red blood cells, whatever the cause may be, and whether or not rupture (by agents such as cobra venom, for example) occurs intravascularly. Anemias brought about by a reduced life span of erythrocytes, therefore, are called **hemolytic anemias.** A number of hereditary diseases exist in which structural abnormalities in the red blood cells lead to their premature removal from the circulation, principally by the spleen. One such, *thalassemia,* is common in Greece and the Mediterranean coastal region and is characterized by fragile cell membranes. Another is **sickle cell anemia,** an unusual condition caused by an abnormality in the structure of the protein portion of hemoglobin (substitution of valine for glutamic acid in the sixth position of the beta chains). In this disease, when the oxygen concentration in the blood is lowered following the release of oxygen from the red blood cells, the abnormal hemoglobin molecules aggregate and distort the cells into various bizarre shapes, including the originally described crescent, or sickle, shape. Because the sickle cell is rigid, it causes clogging of the capillaries (an event associated with severe bouts of pain), which leads to the early destruction of the cells. The sickle cell gene is apparently linked to a gene that protects against malaria. As a consequence, a high frequency of the gene is maintained in populations throughout the world where malaria is prevalent.

Insufficient hemoglobin synthesis occurs in **iron deficiency anemia.** In this type of anemia the number of red blood cells is usually normal, but the individual cells are much smaller and pale *(microcytic, hypochromic),* owing to a lack of sufficient hemoglobin. Iron deficiency anemia usually follows chronic blood loss. When the supply of iron becomes depleted because of increased red blood cell formation to compensate for the blood loss, hemoglobin production is diminished and anemia results. This deficiency may also occur when the demand for iron is unusually great, as during infancy, adolescence, or pregnancy.

Leukocytes (Table 38)

Three general types of white blood cells, or *leukocytes* (G. *leuco,* white), are found in blood: **granulocytes** (cells with numerous granules) and the nongranular forms, namely, **lymphocytes** and **monocytes.** *Neutrophils,* the most numerous of the granulocytes, are phagocytic, functioning in the destruction of pathogenic microorganisms and other foreign matter. The granules, it was established in the 1960's, are actually lysosomes, organelles containing digestive enzymes (see Chapter 2, pages 33 and 39). At wound or infected sites the number of invading neutrophils rises to a peak in 24 hours. Neutrophils and two other subtypes of granulocytes (Fig. 323) are classified on the basis of the staining properties of their granules. *Basophils* are readily stained with the basic dye methylene blue, *eosinophils* with the red acid dye eosin, and neutrophils

Table 38. WHITE BLOOD CELLS (LEUKOCYTES)

TYPE	NUMBER/MM^3	FUNCTION	INCREASED COUNT	DECREASED COUNT
Neutrophil	3000–6000 (57–67%)	Phagocytosis	Pyrogenic infections; leukemia	Toxic reactions such as occur with the administration of certain drugs
Eosinophil	150–300 (1–3%)	Phagocytosis of antigen-antibody complexes	Allergy; parasitic infections; leukemia	Administration of adreno-cortical hormones
Basophil	0–100 (0.5–1%)	Exact function unknown	Leukemia	Unknown
Lymphocyte	1500–3000 (25–33%)	Production of antibodies; nonphagocytic	Infectious mononucleosis; chronic infections; viral infections; leukemia	Adrenocortical hormones
Monocyte	100–600 (3–7%)	As a macrophage	Tuberculosis; protozoal infection; leukemia	No known cause

only weakly with both types of dye. Eosinophils apparently phagocytize antigen-antibody complexes (see Chapter 11). The function of basophils is still uncertain.

Lymphocytes are a somewhat heterogeneous group of cells important in the process of immunity, producing antibodies and other agents involved in the immune process; all have essentially the same staining characteristics. Monocytes possess a relatively large amount of cytoplasm and a round or kidney-shaped nucleus. They function as phagocytes, becoming transformed into macrophages after invading infected sites, where their numbers reach a peak in 48 hours.

DISEASES INVOLVING ABNORMALITIES OF THE WHITE CELL SERIES. Many diseases are characterized by a change in the number of circulating leukocytes. An increase in the white cell count, generally indicating an acute infection, is called **leukocytosis. Leu-**

kopenia, a reduction in the number of white cells, occurs occasionally in viral diseases.

The total white cell count ranges from 5000 to 10,000 per cubic millimeter; however, it may be as high as 500,000 per cubic millimeter in *leukemia.* Leukemia is characterized by a rapid and abnormal growth of leukocytes and by the presence of immature leukocytes in the peripheral blood. The type of leukocyte involved differentiates the varieties of leukemia—granulocytic, lymphocytic, and monocytic.

Infectious mononucleosis is a benign disease associated with an increase in mononuclear leukocytes. It usually occurs in children and young adults, and is believed to be caused by a virus. The patient with infectious mononucleosis evidences a slightly elevated temperature, enlarged lymph nodes, fatigue, and a sore throat.

Platelets. Platelets, or thrombocytes (G. *thrombos,* lump), are cytoplasmic fragments

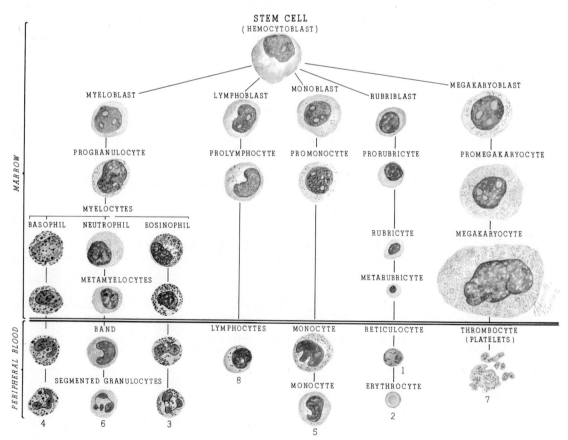

Figure 324. Stages in the formation of the peripheral blood cells. Numbered cells correspond to cell types in Figure 323.

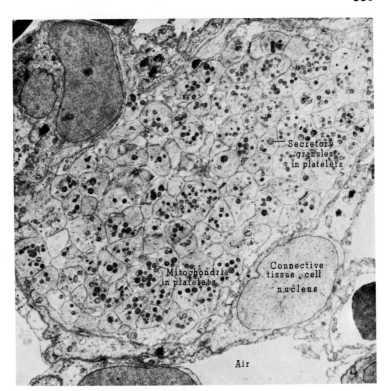

Figure 325. A lung capillary containing numerous blood platelets. (Magnified 12,000 ×.)

of giant, multinucleated red bone marrow cells called *megakaryocytes* (Fig. 324) and play a role in hemostasis (G. *statikos*, causing to stand), the process of checking bleeding. They are about half the size of erythrocytes, number from 140,000 to 340,000 per cubic millimeter of blood, are irregular in shape, and are capable of ameboid movement. Although the platelet is a fragment of cell, it is rich in ATP and contains many of the organelles normally present in cells (Fig. 325). Platelets clump together to form a plug in the initial phase of controlling bleeding. This process is accelerated by thrombin, an enzyme involved in blood clotting. Clumping is followed by the retraction of platelet pseudopods with enmeshed fibrin and blood cells to produce a hard clot (for details, see below). A deficiency in platelets causes a tendency to bleed. One such condition is known as *idiopathic thrombocytopenic purpura* (ITP). Idiopathic means cause unknown; thrombocytopenia means low platelet count; purpura (Latin for purple) is a condition in which hemorrhages (G. *rhegnynai*, to burst) occur in the skin and mucous and serous membranes, most commonly of pinhead size (petechia). Some individuals

with this disease apparently have a substance in their blood that destroys platelets.

Hemostasis

Three separate mechanisms are involved in hemostasis: platelet clumping, or agglutination (L. *agglutinare*, to glue), contraction of blood vessels, and formation of a fibrin clot. When a vessel larger than a capillary is cut or damaged, platelets rapidly accumulate at the site of injury and adhere to the vascular endothelium. The aggregate of platelets forms a temporary plug capable of arresting the bleeding in small arteries and veins. Simultaneously with platelet agglutination, vasoconstriction of muscle-containing vessels occurs. Shortly after the appearance of the initial aggregate, platelets fuse into a dense, structureless mass. The mass forms a temporary solid seal at the site of injury. When a platelet agglutination occurs, a second type of vasoconstriction takes place affecting the injured vessel and many neighboring vessels. This is the result of the release of serotonin from platelets. Only after the sequence of platelet change

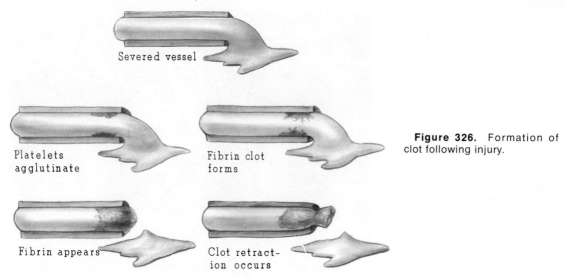

Severed vessel

Platelets
agglutinate

Fibrin clot
forms

Fibrin appears

Clot retract-
ion occurs

Figure 326. Formation of clot following injury.

does actual coagulation, or clotting, occur, completing the process of hemostasis.

Mechanism of Coagulation. The formation of the **fibrin clot,** generally referred to as blood coagulation, is the most complex of the hemostatic mechanisms. Formation of insoluble fibrin from the soluble protein *fibrinogen* is brought about by the action of **thrombin.** Thrombin is a proteolytic enzyme—it removes two pairs of low molecular weight peptides from each molecule of fibrinogen to form molecules of fibrin monomer. Many monomers polymerize to produce fibrin threads. The enzymatic action of fibrin stabilizing factor (further binding the monomers covalently) strengthens the threads.

The clot is now a meshwork of randomly distributed fibrin threads that will trap blood cells, platelets, and plasma.

A few minutes after the clot has formed, it begins to contract, apparently as a result of the contraction of platelet pseudopods that adhere to the fibrin meshwork. Most of the plasma is thus expelled from the clot within 30 to 60 minutes. As the clot retracts, the edges of the broken blood vessel are pulled together, thus contributing to the ultimate state of hemostasis.

Thrombin, the enzyme responsible for the formation of fibrin, is not present in the blood stream. It is formed from an inactive precursor, *prothrombin,* by the action of *prothrombin activator,* also called prothrombin-converting principle. The production of prothrombin activator is initiated in two ways, via (1) a pathway designated

extrinsic, triggered by the release of a lipoprotein *(thromboplastin)* from injured tissue, and (2) a pathway designated **intrinsic,** which does not require contact with injured tissue. The intrinsic pathway can be triggered by surface contact with glass, which contains an agent that activates a blood protein known as clotting factor 12, or the *Hageman factor.* In the body the intrinsic pathway is thought to be initiated by the adhesion of platelets to the broken surfaces of blood vessels. Figure 327 illustrates the intrinsic and extrinsic pathways leading to a formation of prothrombin activator. Because of the stepladder sequence of the intrinsic pathway, it has been described as a waterfall or cascade. Deficiencies in the intrinsic pathway are associated with a number of hereditary bleeding diseases.

Calcium ions appear necessary for the operation of both the intrinsic and extrinsic processes. However, these ions do not actually enter into any of the reactions. They simply act as cofactors, causing reactions to take place. Factor 3 of the intrinsic pathway, released from platelets, is a phospholipid. Factors 5 through 12 are plasma proteins. Prothrombin and factors 7, 9 and 10, proteins similar to prothrombin, require vitamin K for their synthesis, which takes place in the liver.

A malfunction or absence of any of the clotting factors causes some degree of bleeding tendency. The most frequently implicated factor is 8, the antihemophilic factor. Individuals with **hemophilia** synthesize an abnormal, functionally defective

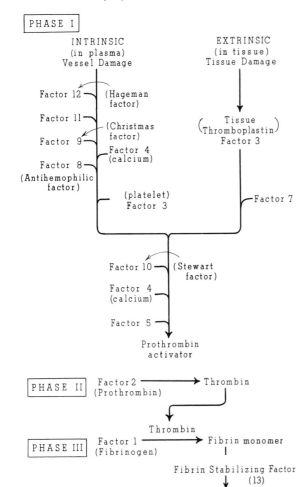

PHASE I

INTRINSIC
(in plasma)
Vessel Damage

EXTRINSIC
(in tissue)
Tissue Damage

Factor 12 (Hageman factor)

Factor 11

(Christmas factor)

Factor 9

Factor 4 (calcium)

Factor 8
(Antihemophilic factor)

(platelet)
Factor 3

Tissue
Thromboplastin
Factor 3

Factor 7

Factor 10 (Stewart factor)

Factor 4
(calcium)

Factor 5

Prothrombin activator

PHASE II   Factor 2 ⟶ Thrombin
(Prothrombin)

Thrombin

PHASE III   Factor 1 ⟶ Fibrin monomer
(Fibrinogen)

Fibrin Stabilizing Factor
(13)
Fibrin polymer

Figure 327. Phases of fibrin formation. Two pathways, intrinsic and extrinsic, lead to the activation of Stuart factor, which interacts with other clotting factors to form what is known as prothrombin activator, an enzyme that converts prothrombin to thrombin by splitting prothrombin into two fragments, one of which is active thrombin. Thrombin, a proteolytic enzyme, removes two pairs of peptides from fibrinogen to form the so-called fibrin monomer. Many monomers polymerize to produce insoluble fibrin threads. The threads are strengthened by the enzymatic action of fibrin stabilizing factor.

form of the clotting factor. Since this condition is transmitted as a sex-linked recessive trait, it is only rarely seen in females.

Thrombosis is clotting in blood vessels. A clot, or *thrombus*, forming in the blood vessels of the leg or arm may be associated with local damage; if it should block the blood supply to the heart or brain, it can be fatal. A *thromboembolus* is a clot that has become dislodged from its place of origin and has lodged elsewhere in the body.

Anticlotting Factors. *Heparin* occurs naturally in the body tissues, although it has rarely been demonstrated in blood. It reduces the ability of blood to clot by blocking the change of prothrombin to thrombin. Heparin is produced by *mast cells*, found in most organs of the body, and is employed clinically to prevent the enlargement of thrombi in patients.

The fibrinolytic system involves the digestion of fibrin clots into a number of soluble fragments. Fibrinolysis is mediated by an enzyme called *plasmin*, or *fibrinolysin*, present in the body in the form of the active precursor, *plasminogen*. Plasminogen, a widely distributed globulin, is converted enzymatically to plasmin, a *proteolytic* enzyme capable of digesting the fibrin.

Dicumarol is a drug clinically employed as an anticoagulant. It inhibits the manufacture of clotting factors 2 (prothrombin), 7, 9, and 10 by its inhibitory action on vitamin K, which is necessary for their synthesis.

Hemostasis in Capillaries. The control of capillary bleeding is made possible by a different mechanism. Capillary constriction does not play a significant role, since capillaries do not contain contractile tissue. Also, platelet plugs have not been shown to develop in severed capillaries. It has been suggested that capillary bleeding may be arrested by adhesion of the endothelial walls of the capillary, aided by torn connective tissue fibers and pressure of tissue fluids.

Blood Grouping

The safe administration of blood from donor to recipient requires typing and cross-matching. These procedures are necessary, since a patient receiving blood incompatible with his own can experience a serious or fatal reaction. The systems of classification are based on the presence of specific *antigens (agglutinogens)* in the red cell. An antigen is a substance or a part of a cell, normally foreign to the body, possessing a chemical group that induces an immune response on the part of immunologically active lymphocytes that includes, among other things, the production of *antibodies*. Antibodies combine with the of-

Table 39. BLOOD GROUPING

TYPE	PERCENTAGE OF POPULATION	RED CELL ANTIGENS OR AGGLUTINOGENS	PLASMA ANTIBODIES OR AGGLUTININS
ABO			
A	41%	A	Anti-B
B	10%	B	Anti-A
AB	4%	A, B	
O	45%	°	Anti-A, anti-B
Rh (D)			
Positive	85%	Rh	
Negative	15%		†

° Type O blood is sometimes called the "universal donor," since it does not contain agglutinogens A and B.
† Anti-Rh does not occur naturally in blood, but will result if an Rh negative individual is given Rh positive blood.

fending antigens as the first step in inactivating them (for further details, see Chapter 11). The primary classification systems are the ABO and Rh (Table 39).

ABO Grouping. Blood groups are named for the antigens (mainly protein) contained in the red cells. In each case the blood contains antibodies (also called agglutinins) to antigens *not* present in the blood as well as immunological cells that can produce more of these antibodies. Thus, type A blood has anti-B agglutinins; type B, anti-A agglutinins; type O, both agglutinins; and type AB, neither. The reason for the presence of these antibodies is uncertain. But since few, if any, are present at birth, it has been suggested that their production is caused by the entry into the body of A and B antigens in food or in other ways. Blood typing is based upon the clumping, or agglutination, of a given type of red blood cells in a blood specimen brought about by the agglutinins in a sample of antiserum.

It is perhaps apparent that, when giving a blood transfusion, blood cannot be donated that contains antigens not present in the recipient's blood. Such blood is alien to the recipient, whose blood contains antibodies that will cause agglutination and hemolysis of the donor's red blood cells. Thus, individuals with type A blood cannot accept a transfusion of blood types B or AB; type B individuals cannot accept A or AB blood; and type O individuals cannot accept A, B or AB blood. Individuals with AB blood, whose blood contains both A and B antigens, are universal recipients. Type O individuals, whose blood contains neither antigen, are universal donors.

Rh Factor. The Rh factor, so named because it was first found in the blood of the rhesus monkey, is a system consisting of 12 antigens. Of these, "D" is the most antigenic; the term Rh positive, as it is generally employed, refers to the presence of antigen "D." The Rh negative individual does not possess the "D" antigen, and consequently forms anti-D antibodies when injected with "D" positive cells. Anti-D agglutinin does not occur naturally in the blood.

The initial transfusion of Rh positive blood into an Rh negative individual may merely sensitize the recipient and cause the development of agglutinins without the occurrence of severe symptoms; however, once sensitized, the recipient will probably experience a severe reaction to subsequent infusions of Rh positive blood.

The same reaction may occur when an Rh negative mother has an Rh positive baby. If at the time of delivery some of the infant's blood enters the mother's blood stream, she may become sensitized. This could cause a problem with a subsequent Rh positive fetus. Antibodies produced as a result of the initial sensitization could enter the circulation of the fetus and cause agglutination and hemolysis. The infant with this condition, called **erythroblastosis fetalis,** might be born dead or with hemolytic anemia. During the 1960's it was discovered that this could be avoided by giving the mother a shot of Rh antibodies shortly after giving birth to an Rh positive child. This treatment prevented the development of antibodies by the mother's immune system.

BASIC DIVISIONS OF THE CIRCULATORY SYSTEM

The basic divisions of the circulatory system are (1) the **heart,** a muscular pump consisting of two receiving chambers (atria) and two pumping chambers (ventricles) and (2) two closed circuits (Fig. 328), the **pulmonary circuit,** carrying oxygen-poor blood from the heart (right ventricle) to the respiratory (alveolar) surfaces of the lungs and oxygenated blood back to the heart (left atrium), and the **systemic circuit,** carrying oxygen-rich blood from the heart (left ventricle) to all parts of the body except the respiratory surfaces of the lungs and oxygen-poor blood back to the heart (right atrium). When the ventricles contract, blood is propelled simultaneously into both circuits (these circuits are considered in more detail in a later section). The *arteries,* which receive this blood at high pressure and velocity, and conduct it throughout the body, are thickly walled with elastic fibrous tissue and a wrapping of muscle cells. The arterial tree terminates in short, narrow, muscular vessels called *arterioles,* from which blood enters simple endothelial tubes known as *capillaries.* These microscopically thin capillaries are permeable to oxygen, carbon dioxide, vital cellular nutrients, hormones, and waste products, and serve as the site for the exchange of substances between the blood stream and the interstitial fluid surrounding the body cells.

From the capillaries, the blood, moving more slowly and under low pressure, enters small vessels called *venules,* which converge to form *veins,* ultimately guiding the blood back to the heart.

THE HEART (Fig. 329)

The heart is a four-chambered, hollow, muscular organ lying between the lungs in the middle mediastinum. Approximately two-thirds of its mass is to the left of the midline. It is about the size of a man's fist, and in the normal male weighs approximately 300 gm. The heart is shaped like an

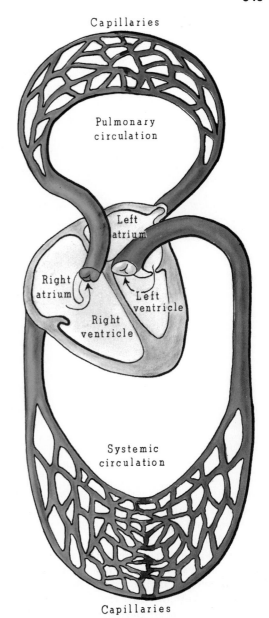

Figure 328. Schematic drawing showing relationship between systemic and pulmonary circulatory circuits. Observe that in this drawing of the pulmonary circuit the veins are colored red and the arteries blue to denote the higher level of oxygenation of the blood in the pulmonary veins.

inverted cone, with its apex pointed downward (Figs. 330 and 331).

Structure

The structures of the heart include the *pericardium,* the sac enclosing the

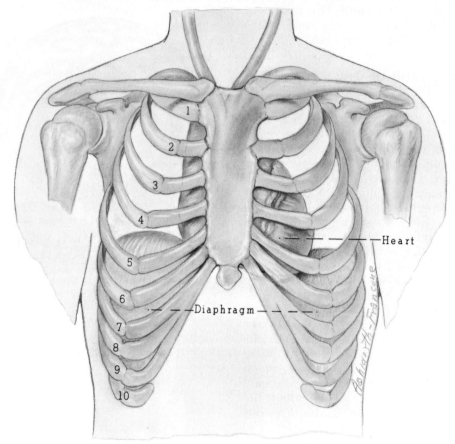

Figure 329. Relationship of the heart and diaphragm to rib cage.

chambers; *valves;* and *arteries,* which supply blood to the heart muscle.

Pericardium. The pericardium (Figs. 332 and 333) is an invaginated sac consisting of an **external fibrous coat** and an **internal serous membrane.** The outer, or parietal, layer of the serous membrane (called the *parietal pericardium*) lines the fibrous coat. The inner, or visceral, layer of the serous membrane (the *visceral pericardium*) adheres to the heart and becomes the outermost layer of the heart, the *epicardium.*

Ten to 15 ml of pericardial fluid is normally found between the parietal pericardium and the visceral pericardium. With every heartbeat this serous fluid lubricates the two membranes as their surfaces glide over each other. Pericarditis is an inflammation of the pericardium and may result from viral or bacterial infection or cancerous growth.

Wall of the Heart. The wall of the heart consists of three distinct layers—the **epicardium** (external layer, the visceral pericardium), the **myocardium** (middle muscular layer), and the **endocardium** (inner layer of endothelium). Coronary vessels supplying arterial blood to the heart traverse the epicardium before entering the myocardium, the layer responsible for the ability of the heart to contract. The myocardium consists of interlacing bundles of cardiac muscle fibers (for a description of cardiac muscle, see Chapter 7, page 154). Cardiac muscle has a high concentration of mitochondria (also called sarcosomes) and, like red skeletal muscle, depends primarily on aerobic metabolism. Its principal fuel is fatty acids derived from the blood stream. The bundles of muscle fibers are so arranged as to result in a wringing type of movement, efficiently squeezing blood from the heart with each beat (Fig. 334). The thickness of the myocardium varies according to pressure generated to move blood to

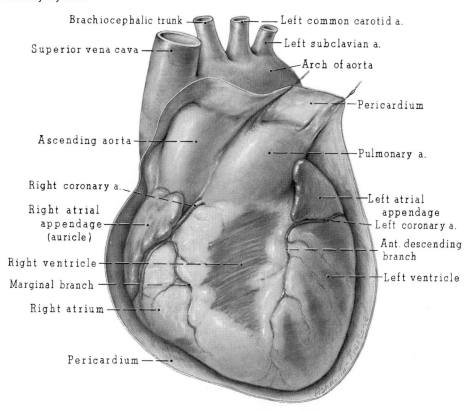

Brachiocephalic trunk

Superior vena cava

Left common carotid a.

Left subclavian a.

Arch of aorta

Pericardium

Ascending aorta

Pulmonary a.

Right coronary a.

Right atrial
appendage
(auricle)

Left atrial
appendage

Left coronary a.

Ant. descending
branch

Right ventricle

Marginal branch

Left ventricle

Right atrium

Pericardium

Figure 330.   Anterior view of the heart.

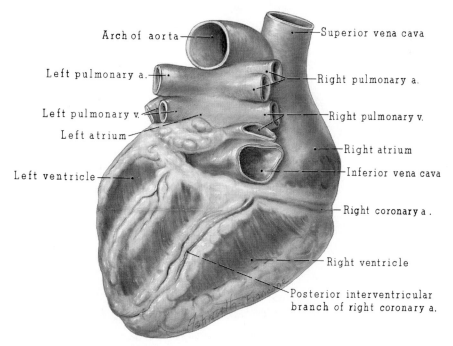

Arch of aorta

Superior vena cava

Left pulmonary a.

Right pulmonary a.

Left pulmonary v.

Left atrium

Right pulmonary v.

Left ventricle

Right atrium

Inferior vena cava

Right coronary a.

Right ventricle

Posterior interventricular
branch of right coronary a.

Figure 331.   Posterior view of the heart.

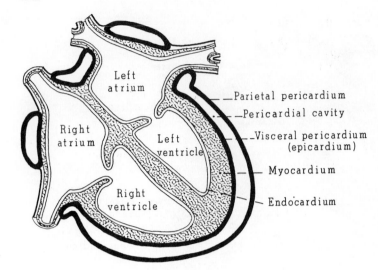

Figure 332. Heart wall and pericardium. (Note the thickened left ventricular wall.)

its destination. The myocardium of the left ventricle is, therefore, thickest; the myocardium of the right ventricle is moderately thickened, while the atrial walls are relatively thin.

Forming the inner surface of the myocardial wall is a thin layer of endothelial tissue which forms the endocardium. This layer lines the cavities of the heart, covers the valves and small muscles associated with opening and closing the valves, and is continuous with the lining membrane of the large blood vessels. Inflammation of the endocardium is called *endocarditis.*

Chambers of the Heart. The heart is divided into right and left halves, with each half subdivided into two chambers. The upper chambers, the *atria,* are separated by the *interatrial septum;* the lower chambers, the *ventricles,* are separated by the *interventricular septum.* The atria serve as receiving chambers for blood from the

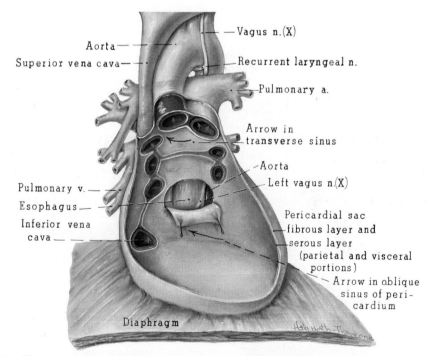

Figure 333. The heart has been removed from the pericardial sac to show the relations of the blood vessels, esophagus, and vagus nerve.

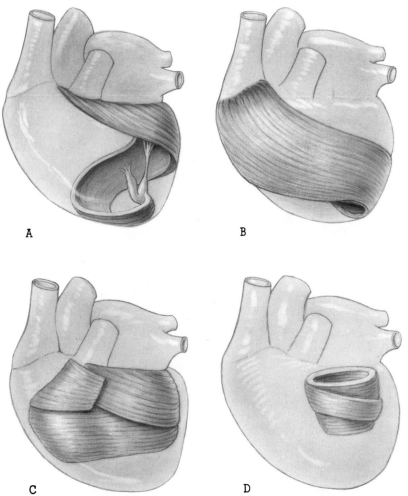

Figure 334. *A* and *B* illustrate the superficial muscle layer of the heart winding around both ventricles. *C* shows the middle myocardial layer winding around only the upper 3/4 of both ventricles, whereas the inner layer is present only around the left ventricle (*D*).

various parts of the body, the ventricles as pumping chambers.

The **right atrium** constitutes the right superior portion of the heart. It is a thin-walled chamber receiving blood from all tissues except the lungs. Three veins empty into the right atrium: the superior and inferior venae cavae, bringing blood from the upper and lower portions of the body; and the coronary sinus, draining blood from the heart itself. Blood flows from the atrium to the right ventricle.

The **right ventricle** constitutes the right inferior portion of the heart's apex. The pulmonary artery carrying blood to the lungs leaves from the superior surface of the right ventricle.

The **left atrium** constitutes the left superior portion of the heart. It is slightly smaller than the right atrium, with a thicker wall. The left atrium receives the four pulmonary veins draining oxygenated blood from the lungs. Blood flows from the left atrium into the left ventricle.

The **left ventricle** constitutes the left inferior portion of the apex of the heart. The walls of this chamber are three times as thick as those of the right ventricle. Blood is forced through the aorta to all parts of the body except the lungs.

Valves of the Heart.   There are two types of valves located in the heart: the **atrioventricular valves,** located between the atria and ventricles (*tricuspid* on the right side;

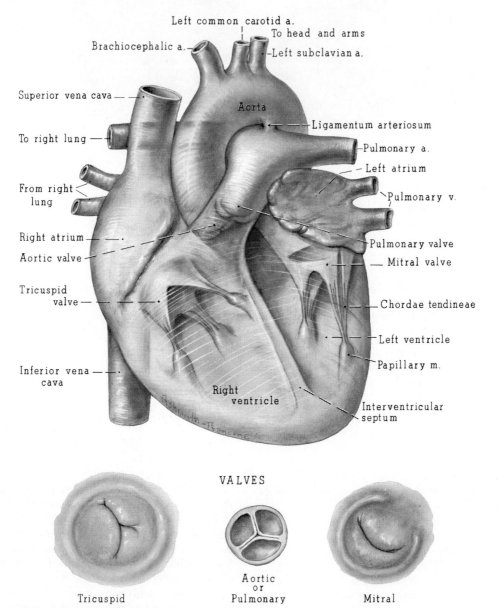

Left common carotid a.

To head and arms

Brachiocephalic a.

Left subclavian a.

Superior vena cava

Aorta

Ligamentum arteriosum

To right lung

Pulmonary a.

Left atrium

From right lung

Pulmonary v.

Right atrium

Pulmonary valve

Aortic valve

Mitral valve

Tricuspid valve

Chordae tendineae

Left ventricle

Papillary m.

Inferior vena cava

Right ventricle

Interventricular septum

VALVES

Tricuspid

Aortic or Pulmonary

Mitral

Figure 335. Schematic "transparent" drawing of the heart showing the relations of the various heart valves.

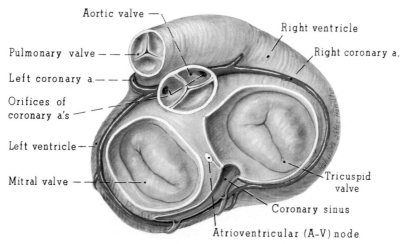

Figure 336. A view of the heart from above, showing the valves, coronary arteries, and sinus.

biscuspid, or *mitral,* on the left), and the **semilunar valves** (*pulmonary* and *aortic*), located between the ventricles and the pulmonary artery (right side) and aorta (left side) (Figs. 335 to 338).

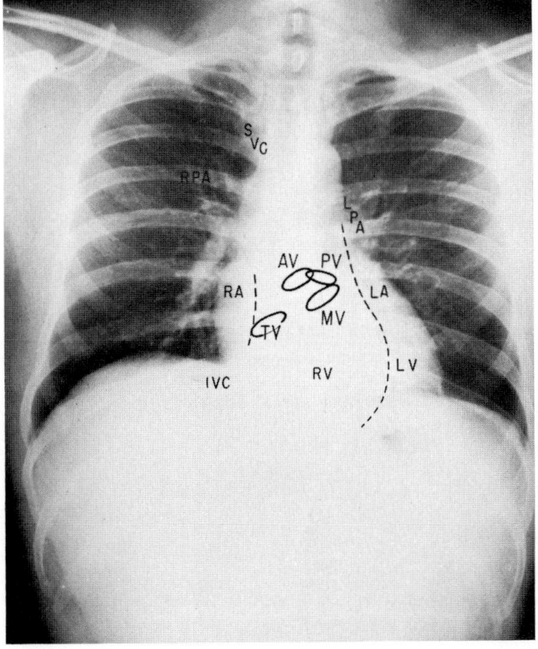

William Harvey, in his treatise *De Motu Cordis* (Concerning the Motion of the Heart), published in 1628, in which he described for the first time the continuous circulation of the blood, made particular note of how the arrangement of the heart's valves allowed blood to flow through the heart in one direction only. In so far as the

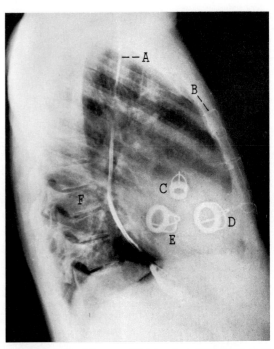

Figure 337. X-ray of anterior aspect of thoracic region.

SVC—superior vena cava
RPA—right pulmonary artery
RA —right atrium
IVC —inferior vena cava
LPA—left pulmonary artery
LA —left atrium

LV —left ventricle
RV —right ventricle
AV —aortic valve
PV —pulmonary valve
MV—mitral valve
TV —tricuspid valve

Figure 338. Three artificial valves implanted in a patient's heart by Dr. A. Starr of the University of Oregon Medical School. *A,* esophagus; *B,* wire sutures in sternum; *C,* aortic valve; *D,* tricuspid valve; *E,* mitral valve; and *F,* vertebral column.

heart performs as a pump to drive blood through the blood vessels, the atrioventricular valves are **inlet valves.** They open into the ventricles, allowing blood to enter these pumping chambers when their muscular walls relax. The semilunar valves are **outlet valves.** When the ventricles contract, they open into the pulmonary artery and aorta, and blood is propelled into these vessels.

The atrioventricular valves are thin, leaf-like structures. The tricuspid valve, guarding the right atrioventricular opening, is so called because it consists of three irregularly shaped flaps (or cusps) formed mainly of fibrous tissue and covered by endocardium (Figs. 335 and 336). These flaps are continuous with each other at their bases, creating a ring-shaped membrane surrounding the margin of the atrial opening. Their pointed ends project into the ventricle and are attached by cords called the *chordae tendineae* to small muscular pillars, the *papillary muscles,* within the interior of the ventricles. The bicuspid, or mitral, valve, guarding the left atrioventricular opening, is so named because it consists of two flaps and resembles a bishop's miter.

The mitral valve is attached in the same manner as the tricuspid, but it is stronger and thicker since the left ventricle is a more powerful pump.

When the ventricle contracts, blood is forced backward, passing between the flaps and walls of the ventricles. The flaps are thus pushed upward until they meet and unite, forming a complete partition between the atria and ventricles. The expanded flaps of the valves resist any pressure of the blood which might force them to open into the atria, since they are restrained by the chordae tendineae and papillary muscles.

Each semilunar valve consists of three pockets of tissue attached at the point at which the pulmonary artery and aorta leave the ventricles (Figs. 335 and 336). Their closure prevents backflow of blood into the ventricles.

Blood Supply to the Heart. Owing to the presence of the watertight lining of the heart (the endocardium) and the thickness of its muscle walls, it is necessary for the heart to possess a vascular system of its own. Two arteries, the **left** and **right coronary arteries,** branch from the aorta as it leaves

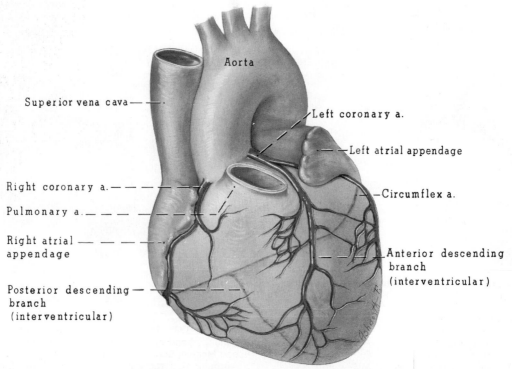

Figure 339. Coronary arteries supplying the heart.

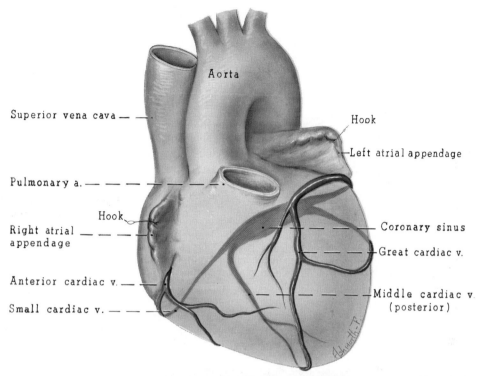

Aorta

Superior vena cava

Hook

Left atrial appendage

Pulmonary a.

Hook

Right atrial appendage

Coronary sinus

Great cardiac v.

Anterior cardiac v.

Middle cardiac v. (posterior)

Small cardiac v.

Figure 340.   Venous drainage of the heart.

the heart and curl back across the chambers of the heart, sending twigs through the muscular walls (Fig. 339).

These vessels are the first branches of the aorta and are so named because they form a crown around the base of the heart. The left coronary artery branches immediately. The anterior descending branch supplies blood to the anterior part of the left ventricle and a small part of the anterior and posterior portions of the right ventricle. The circumflex branch supplies blood to the left atrium and upper front and rear of the left ventricle. The branches of the right coronary artery supply blood to the right atrium and ventricle and portions of the left ventricle.

Blood is drained from the heart principally into the right atrium by way of the **coronary sinus,** which collects blood from the coronary veins (Fig. 340). About 25 per cent of the blood drains directly into the ventricles via deep channels, the arterioluminal, the arteriosinusoidal and the Thebesian vessels.

Cardiac Cycle

The heart exhibits a definite rhythmic cycle of contraction (**systole**) and relaxation (**diastole**). Figure 341 shows the pressure alterations in the left heart and aorta during the cycle.

The spread of electrical excitatory impulses through the ventricle is followed by contraction of the ventricle. This results in a rise in the ventricular pressure. When ventricular pressure exceeds atrial pressure, the atrioventricular valves close. The pressure in the ventricles, contracting as a closed chamber, rises steeply and, when the ventricular pressure exceeds aortic pressure, the aortic valve opens and blood flows from the ventricle into the aorta, rapidly at first (rapid ejection phase) and then more slowly (reduced ejection phase). During this period, the ventricle and aorta become a common chamber.

Ventricular pressure exceeds aortic pressure for about a third of the ejection phase. When it drops below the aortic pressure,

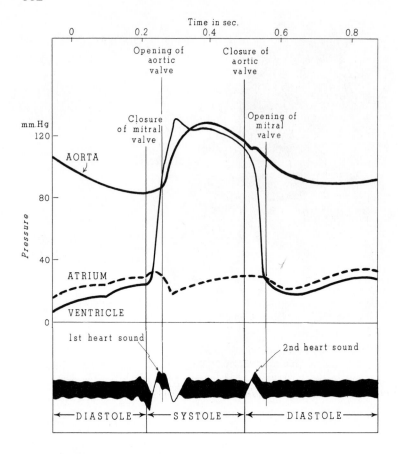

Figure 341. Blood pressure and heart sounds during cardiac cycle.

aortic blood flow slows, comes to a halt, then momentarily reverses itself. The reversal of blood flow closes the aortic valve. As the blood bounces off the valves, a transient rise in aortic pressure is seen on the aortic pressure curve as a notch known as the **incisura**. Contraction of the ventricle ceases just before closure of the aortic valve. Immediately after the aortic valve closes, the pressure in the ventricle, relaxing as a closed chamber, falls abruptly. When the ventricular pressure falls below the atrial pressure, the atrioventricular valve opens and ventricular filling commences, the filling occurring rapidly at first, then more slowly. During this period of ventricular filling the atrium and ventricle are essentially a common chamber in which the pressure rises as blood enters from the great veins. Atrial contraction produces a slight increase of pressure in two chambers; however, the majority of ventricular filling occurs early in diastole, when the pressure difference between the two chambers is at a maximum. If ventricular filling is incomplete because of a narrowed atrioventricular

valve opening, pumping of blood through the narrowed opening by atrial contraction provides a margin of safety.

The entire cardiac cycle lasts about 0.8 second. Ventricular systole normally occupies about 30 per cent of the cycle. The principal effect of increasing the heart rate on the cycle is to decrease the length of ventricular diastole.

Heart Sounds. Closure of the heart valves is associated with an audible sound. The first sound occurs when the mitral and tricuspid valves close, marking the approximate beginning of systole, the second with the closing of the pulmonic and aortic semilunar valves following the end of systole (Fig. 341). These characteristic heart sounds appear to be caused principally by the vibration of the valves and walls of the heart and major vessels around the heart. The first sound, "lub," is soft, low pitched, and relatively long. The second sound, "dup," is shorter, sharper, and higher pitched than the first and coincides with the incisura of the aortic pressure curve.

The first heart sound is followed after a

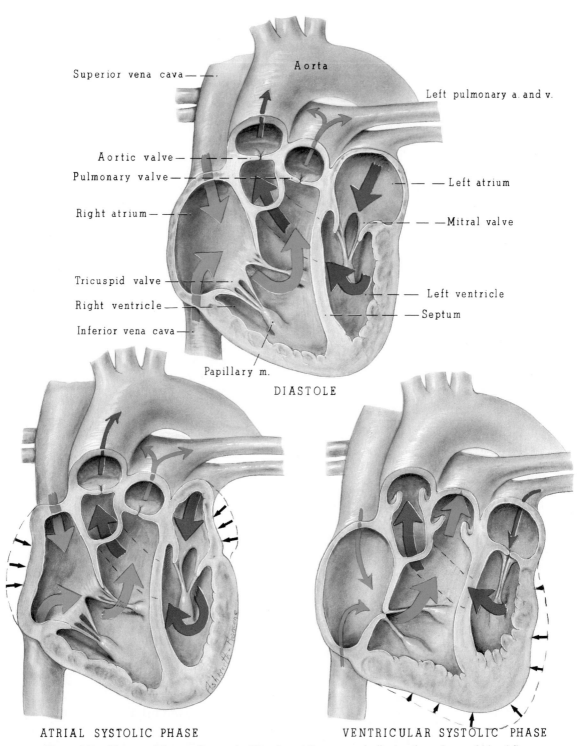

Superior vena cava

Aorta

Left pulmonary a. and v.

Aortic valve

Pulmonary valve

Right atrium

Left atrium

Mitral valve

Tricuspid valve

Right ventricle

Inferior vena cava

Left ventricle

Septum

Papillary m.

DIASTOLE

ATRIAL SYSTOLIC PHASE

VENTRICULAR SYSTOLIC PHASE

Figure 342. Phases of the cardiac cycle. The size of the arrows indicates the volume of blood flow.

short pause by the second. A pause about twice as long comes between the second sound and the beginning of the next cycle. The clinician takes the interval between the first and second sound as an approximate measure of the length of systole.

Narrowing of the openings (stenosis) by calcification of the valves, for example, or incomplete closure of the valves (insufficiency) can create abnormal sounds called **murmurs.** Murmurs caused by narrowed openings can be explained by the increase in velocity of blood flow through the constricted openings and the resulting turbulence. Collision of blood moving in opposite directions contributes to murmurs caused by incomplete closure of AV valves.

Cardiac Output

The volume of blood ejected per beat is known as the *stroke volume.* Stroke volume times the number of beats per minute is called the *minute volume,* or *cardiac output.* Under resting conditions, cardiac output approximates 5 liters per minute—an amazing fact considering that the total blood volume of an average man is only 5 to 6 liters. The average volume of blood ejected by the heart per beat is 60 to 70 ml. The output of the heart depends on venous return, cardiac rate, and the force of cardiac contraction.

VENOUS RETURN. Cardiac output increases with an increase in venous return. Venous return is influenced by the following factors: contraction of skeletal muscles squeezing the veins, forcing the blood to move; increased negative pressure in the pleural cavity with inspiration; and higher pressure in the capillaries than in the veins, forcing the blood toward the heart. Gravity aids the venous return from areas that are above the level of the heart. With a decreased blood volume, as in hemorrhage, venous return is lowered. Dilatation of the vessels, particularly the veins, allows for pooling of blood and a consequent drop in venous return.

HEART RATE. In the resting individual with a constant venous return, the normal frequency of the heart provides sufficient diastolic time for both venous filling and recovery of the cardiac muscle. When the

venous return is increased (with no increase in heart rate), a two- or threefold increase in stroke volume and cardiac output results. Increasing the heart rate without a concurrent increase in venous return has only a limited effect upon cardiac output because, as mentioned, as the heart rate increases, the duration of ventricular diastole and, therefore, filling of the ventricles decreases. A moderate increase in rate will cause some increase in output, since the largest volume of blood enters the ventricles during the initial rapid inflow period of diastole. Increasing the heart rate from 70 to 90 beats per minute can increase the cardiac output by about 20 per cent. Further increases in rate will not significantly increase cardiac output. Very high rates (above about 140 beats per minute), in fact, will decrease cardiac output because of a pronounced decrease in ventricular filling and stroke volume.

FORCE OF CARDIAC CONTRACTION. The force of the heart contraction depends on the initial length of the fibers, the length of the diastolic pause, the oxygen supply, and the integrity and mass of the myocardium.

Starling's Law of the Heart states that "the energy of contraction is proportional to the initial length of the cardiac muscle fiber"; that is, the greater the initial length of the muscle fibers in the heart, the more forceful the contraction. When venous return is relatively great, this tends to expand the heart and, consequently, to stretch the muscle fibers prior to each beat. As Starling's Law states, the muscle fibers actually have the property that the more they are stretched (within reasonable physiological limits) prior to contraction, the more forceful will be that contraction. Since increased venous return necessitates that the heart do more work in pumping this added amount of blood, the "increased stretch–increased contraction strength" property of the muscle fibers serves as an automatic regulator so that the heart can keep up naturally with its work load, which is supplied in this case by the venous return. This interesting property of a muscle fiber to contract more strongly when it is stretched prior to contraction is a property of all striated muscle and not simply of cardiac muscle. There are limits to this stretch response, however, and if venous return is excessive and the fibers overstretched, a weakened contraction will result, with diminished cardiac output; consequently, the heart will not empty adequately. The force of the heart is also diminished if the diastolic phase is too short and there is inadequate filling.

The Heartbeat

The heart is inherently rhythmic. This was apparently recognized by the Greek anatomist Erasistratus in the third century B.C. In 1890 Newell Martin of Johns Hopkins University demonstrated that the heart of a mammal will continue to beat (although at a different rate) when cut off completely from its nerve supply. The function of the nerve supply is to regulate the beat and make possible homeostatic control of the heart rate.

The heartbeat is generated by specialized neuromuscular tissue of the heart. It has been shown by cell culture techniques that cardiac tissue is actually composed of two functionally different types of cells, corresponding in the intact heart to muscle cells specialized for contraction and neuromuscular cells specialized for initiating and conducting the electrical impulses that cause the heart to contract. Individual cells of the latter type beat rhythmically in culture. The neuromuscular tissue of the heart consists of (a) the **sino-atrial (SA) node,** called the pacemaker because the heartbeat is generated by electrical impulses arising spontaneously from it; (b) the **atrioventricular (AV) node;** and (c) the **Purkinje system,** which includes the left and right branches of the AV bundle (bundle of His) and the peripheral Purkinje network (see Fig. 343).

The *sino-atrial node* is a small strip of tissue, about 3 × 5 cm in length, located in the posterior wall of the right atrium,

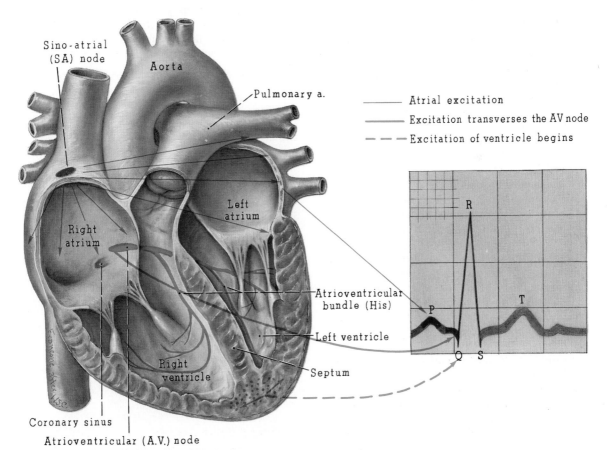

Figure 343. Conducting system of the heart showing source of electrical impulses produced on electrocardiogram.

immediately beneath and medial to the point of entry of the superior vena cava. As an impulse is generated in the SA node, it immediately spreads through the atrial muscle in a ripple pattern similar to that of waves generated when a stone is thrown into a pool of water and initiates its contraction. Impulses from the SA to the AV node are preferentially conducted by pathways (called internodal tracts) consisting apparently of a mixture of fibers similar to Purkinje fibers and ordinary muscle fibers. The AV node is located beneath the endocardium of the right atrium at the base of the interatrial septum. To permit sufficient time for complete atrial contraction before subsequent simultaneous contraction of the ventricles, the impulse is delayed slightly in its passge through the AV node. The fibers which leave this node constitute the *Purkinje system.* These fibers pass into the interventricular septum, where right and left bundle branches project downward beneath the endocardium on either side of the septum. They then curve around the tip of the ventricular chambers and back toward the atria along the lateral walls. These fibers terminate in the ventricular muscle, and excitation in the muscle fibers is initiated.

The average normal heart rate is about 70 beats per minute. Rates from 60 to 100 are considered normal. A too rapid rate is called *tachycardia* (G. *tachys,* swift); a too slow rate is called *bradycardia* (G. *bradys,* slow).

The spontaneous origin of electrical impulses at the SA node can be explained by the unstable resting membrane potential of nodal cells due to a leakage of sodium into these cells (see Chapter 8, page 226, for a description of the nerve impulse). In recordings of electrical potential at the SA node this is seen as a gradual upward deflection in voltage, called the **prepotential.** Each time threshold voltage is reached, an impulse is initiated.

If the SA node is destroyed, the spontaneous initiation of impulses at the AV node will generate a heart rate of about 40 to 50 beats per minute, with the atria and ventricles contracting simultaneously. Yet patients have been known to survive 20 to 30 years with the AV node acting as pacemaker.

Nervous Control of the Heart

Adjustments in the heart rate to maintain homeostasis and meet the demands of changing conditions is made possible by innervation of the SA node by the *sympathetic* and *parasympathetic* divisions of the autonomic nervous system. Increased stimulation of sympathetic nerves increases the release of *norepinephrine* by the nerve endings and increases the impulse rate of the SA node. Increased stimulation of the vagus (parasympathetic) nerve increases the release of *acetylcholine* by nerve endings and decreases the impulse rate at the SA node. The vagus nerve exerts a strong, continuous restraining action on the heart. In dogs, this can be demonstrated by blocking the action of the vagus nerve with atropine. The result is about a 2½-fold increase in heart rate. Massive vagal stimulation can stop the heart for several seconds. Stimulation of the vagus nerve also delays conduction through the AV node; sympathetic stimulation has the reverse effect. The atria are supplied by both sympathetic and parasympathetic nerves, the ventricles largely by sympathetic nerves (Fig. 344).

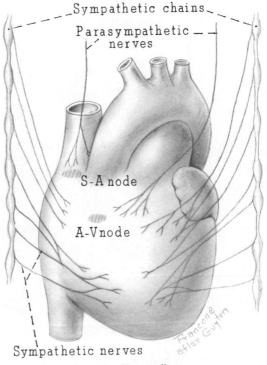

Figure 344.   The cardiac nerves.

Consequently, control over the force of the contraction of the heart is exercised primarily by the sympathetic system. Sympathetic stimulation can bring about up to a threefold increase in heart rate and force of ventricular contraction. This action is especially important during exercise.

Effect of Ions on Heart Function. Potassium and calcium have a marked influence on impulse transmission within cardiac muscle. In addition, calcium ion concentration is important in the contractile process. The concentration of ions in extracellular fluids also affects cardiac function.

Excess potassium ions in extracellular fluid, in addition to slowing the heart rate, cause the heart to dilate and become flaccid. There is general weakness of cardiac muscle. This weakening of the strength of contraction is caused by a decreased resting membrane potential.

Calcium ions in excess produce just the opposite effect; the heart goes into spastic contraction. This is believed to be caused as the excess calcium ions excite the process of cardiac contraction. Conversely, a deficiency causes cardiac weakness. There is, however, little danger of excess calcium ions within the extracellular fluid in cardiac muscle since excess calcium is precipitated as salts in bone before a dangerous level is reached in the heart.

Presumably due to an increased permeability of muscle membrane to ions, temperature may also affect heart function. Heart rate increases as temperature increases and, conversely, decreases as temperature decreases.

The Electrocardiogram (Figs. 345 and 346). As an impulse travels along the cardiac muscle fibers, an electric current is generated by the flowing ions. This current spreads into the fluids around the heart and a minute portion actually flows to the surface of the body. An *electrocardiogram* is a record of this electrical activity as measured by a *galvanometer*. Leads are placed on the surface of the body at various points, depending on the type of information desired. An electrocardiogram thus has the prime function of assessing the ability of the heart to transmit the cardiac impulse. Each portion of the cardiac cycle produces a different electrical impulse, causing the characteristic deflections of an ECG recording needle. The deflections, or *waves*, on the recording apparatus are, in order, the *P wave*, the *QRS complex*, and the *T wave*. As a wave of depolarization (reversal of electrical charges across the cell membranes) passes over the atria, the impulse is recorded as the P wave. As it continues on through the ventricles, it is registered as the QRS complex. The T wave is caused by currents generated as the ventricles return to the resting, polarized state. This recovery process is completed in the muscle of the ventricles about 0.25 second after depolarization. There are, therefore, both depolarization and repolarization waves represented in the ECG.

The atria repolarize at the same time that the ventricles depolarize. The atrial repolarization wave is, therefore, obscured by the larger QRS wave.

ATRIOVENTRICULAR BLOCK (HEART BLOCK). Atrioventricular block is an impairment in the conduction of impulses from the atrium to the ventricle. The disturbance is located in the atrioventricular node and usually indicates myocardial disease. In the first degree block, a delay in atrioventricular conduction occurs. The delay cannot be clinically recognized, but is indicated by a prolonged PR interval in the electrocardiogram. Second degree atrioventricular block is recognized by the "dropped beat;" that is, ventricular contraction is completely missed at regular intervals. Thus, in second degree heart block with a 2:1 atrioventricular response, a ventricular rate one-half that of the atrial rate will be recorded on the ECG. Complete atrioventricular block (third degree block) represents a total dissociation of the atrial and ventricular rhythms. The ventricle sets its own rhythm in the atrioventricular node or in the bundle of His at a rate of 30 to 45 beats per minute. At times, the rate is higher.

ATRIAL FLUTTER. In this cardiac disturbance, regular atrial rhythm is 240 to 360 beats per minute. Atrial flutter is usually indicative of severe damage to the heart muscle. It is encountered occasionally in normal hearts, but occurs mostly in patients with heart disease. Since the atrioventricular node cannot respond to each impulse, a 2:1, 3:1, or 4:1 rhythm develops. This means that the atrioventricular node and ventricle respond to only one out of two,

ELECTROCARDIOGRAM

The wave of excitation spreading through the heart wall is accompanied
by electrical changes.

The record of these changes is an ELECTROCARDIOGRAM (ECG)

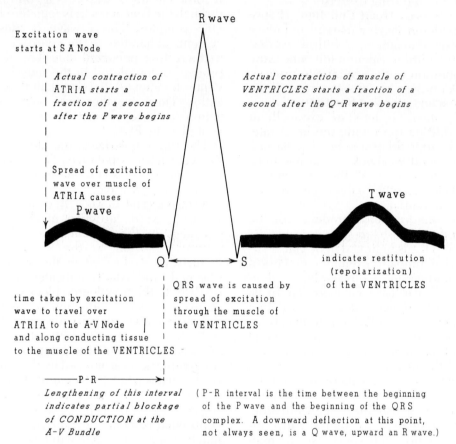

R wave

Excitation wave
starts at S A Node

*Actual contraction of
ATRIA starts a
fraction of a second
after the P wave begins*

*Actual contraction of muscle of
VENTRICLES starts a fraction of a
second after the Q-R wave begins*

Spread of excitation
wave over muscle of
ATRIA causes

P wave

T wave

Q   S

indicates restitution
(repolarization)
of the VENTRICLES

time taken by excitation
wave to travel over
ATRIA to the A-V Node
and along conducting tissue
to the muscle of the VENTRICLES

QRS wave is caused by
spread of excitation
through the muscle of
the VENTRICLES

——————P-R——————→

*Lengthening of this interval
indicates partial blockage
of CONDUCTION at the
A-V Bundle*

(P-R interval is the time between the beginning
of the P wave and the beginning of the QRS
complex. A downward deflection at this point,
not always seen, is a Q wave, upward an R wave.)

Figure 345. Electrocardiogram.

three, or four atrial impulses. Thus, the
electrocardiogram can show an atrial rate of
240 and a ventricular rate of 120.

ATRIAL FIBRILLATION. In atrial fibrillation, the excitation wave passes through the
atrial musculature more rapidly and irregularly than in atrial flutter. The atrioventric-

ular node is bombarded by numerous
impulses. Atrial fibrillation is characterized
by an irregularity of the rhythm and
strength of the ventricular beat. Some beats
are too weak to be felt as a pulsation in the
peripheral arteries because too little blood
is ejected from the ventricles owing to

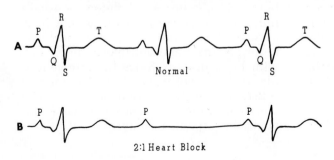

A   P   R   T   P   R   T

        Q   S   Normal   Q   S

B   P   P   P

        2:1 Heart Block

Figure 346. An electrocardiogram. *A,*
Normal. *B,* Heart block (there is only one
ventricular contraction for every two atrial
contractions).

inadequate ventricular filling from short diastole. Thus, the observer can count a rate of 140 beats per minute at the cardiac apex with a stethoscope and palpate only 110 beats per minute at the wrist—a pulse deficit of 30. This pulse deficit represents the ventricular contractions which are too weak to transmit the pulse wave peripherally. Blood pressure determination in such cases is inaccurate, since it varies with the strength of the beat. Weak beats are not caused by myocardial weakness. They are caused by an inadequate diastolic filling period and, thus, by a reduced stroke volume.

OTHER ABNORMALITIES OF CARDIAC RHYTHM. Spasmodic atrial tachycardia is the commonest *arrhythmia* (any variation in the normal heart beat). It usually occurs in young adults but can occur at any age and often is not associated with severe heart disease. The heart rate is between 100 and 200 with a regular rhythm.

In *ventricular fibrillation*, the rapid, tremulous contractions lack propulsive force, and blood circulation ceases; death generally follows within minutes. Ventricular fibrillation can occur immediately after a severe heart attack, as damage to heart muscle causes disturbances in excitation.

Since the QRS wave represents the passage of a depolarization process through the

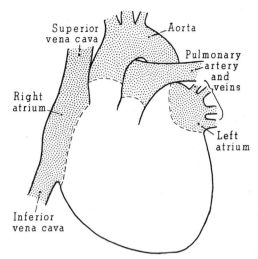

Figure 347. Diagrammatic representation showing anastomoses in heart transplant. (Shaded areas are recipient.)

ventricle, any pathology causing abnormal impulse transmission will alter the shape, voltage, or duration of the QRS complex.

Closed Cardiac Massage

When the heart stops, the procedure of choice for maintaining circulation is closed cardiac massage. Closed cardiac massage must be started as soon as possible after the heart stops. If as long as 4 minutes is

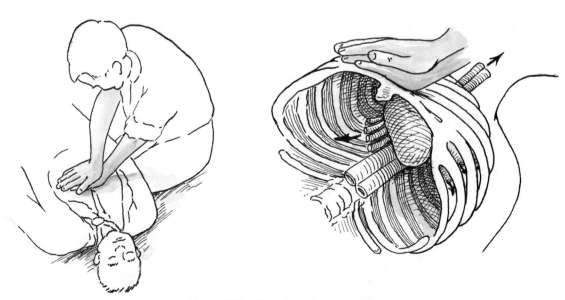

Figure 348. Closed cardiac massage.

allowed to elapse, there can be irreversible damage to the brain.

In performing closed cardiac massage, the patient should be placed on a firm surface. Cardiac massage should not be undertaken with the patient lying on a soft bed. The individual performing the massage stands at right angles to the trunk of the patient, with one hand on top of the other, and places the heel of the hand over the patient's sternum, applying pressure vertically about once every second. The sternum should move approximately 2 inches toward the vertebral column. At the completion of each maneuver, the hands are completely relaxed to permit full chest expansion. Throughout external cardiac massage, an assistant should maintain mouth-to-mouth or mouth-to-nose ventilation (Fig. 348).

BLOOD VESSELS

The blood vessels consist of a closed system of tubes functioning to transport blood to all parts of the body and back to the heart. As in any biological system, structure and function of the vessels are so closely related one cannot be discussed without bringing into account the other. It should be noted that the inner surface of the entire circulatory system consists of endothelium (the descriptive term for a single layer of squamous epithelium in the heart and blood and lymphatic vessels). Additional layers are specializations.

Arteries. Arteries transport blood to the various body tissues under high pressure exerted by the pumping action of the heart. The heart forces blood into these elastic tubes, which recoil, sending blood on in pulsating waves. It is, therefore, imperative that they possess strong, elastic walls to insure fast, efficient blood flow to the tissues.

The wall of an artery consists of three layers (Fig. 349 and Table 40), the innermost consisting of an inner surface of smooth endothelium limited externally by elastic fibers; the two form the *tunica intima*. The tunica intima also contains a small number of smooth muscle cells surrounded by extracellular components of connective tissue. The *tunica media*, or middle coat, consists of smooth muscle cells having a circular arrangement intermingled with elastic fibers and small amounts of noncellular connective tissue elements. In larger vessels, the tuncia media is thicker and composed primarily of elastic fibers. As arteries become smaller, the number of elastic fibers decreases and the number of smooth muscle fibers increases. The outer limiting layer is the *tunica adventitia,* which is the strongest of the three and is a connective tissue with collagenous and elastic fibers. It provides a limiting barrier, protecting the vessel from overexpansion. Also characteristic of this layer is the presence of small blood vessels, the *vasa vasorum,* which supply the walls of larger arteries and veins; the inner and middle layers are nourished by diffusion from the blood being transported. The tunica media

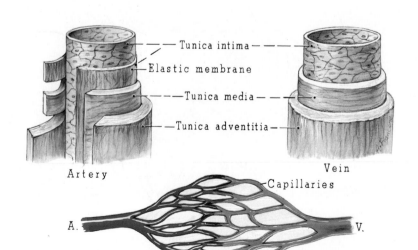

Tunica intima

Elastic membrane

Tunica media

Tunica adventitia

Artery

Vein

Capillaries

A.

V.

Figure 349. Component parts of arteries and veins.

Table 40. STRUCTURE OF BLOOD VESSELS

VESSEL	OUTER LAYER: TUNICA ADVENTITIA	MIDDLE LAYER: TUNICA MEDIA	INNER LAYER: TUNICA INTIMA
Large arteries (elastic)	Thick layer, consisting of connective tissue	Layer consists largely of elastic fibers with some muscle	Thin endothelial cells resting on elastic lamina
Muscular arteries (medium)	Thick layer, consisting of connective tissue	Fewer elastic fibers, more smooth muscle	Thin endothelial cells resting on elastic lamina
Small arteries (arterioles)	Thin	Consists of muscular tissue	Layer composed almost entirely of endothelium
Capillaries	Absent	Absent	Endothelial layer one cell thick
Veins	Thin layer	Thinner; little muscle or elastic tissue	Endothelial lining with scant connective tissue

and adventitia are separated by elastic fibers, the external elastic lamina.

Arterioles. The transition from artery to *arteriole* is gradual, marked by a progressive thinning of the vessel wall and a decrease in the size of the lumen, or passageway. The tunica intima is still present as an endothelial lining and internal elastic lamina. One or more layers of circular or spiral smooth muscle fibers now comprise the tunica media, while the tunica adventitia is very thin.

Being the last small branches of the arterial system, arterioles must act as control valves through which blood is released into the capillaries. The muscular wall of arterioles is capable of completely closing the passageway or dilating to several times its normal size, thereby vastly altering blood flow to the capillaries. Blood flow is, therefore, directed to tissues which require it most.

As the arterioles become smaller in size, the three coats become less and less definite. The smallest consists of little more than endothelium surrounded by a single layer of smooth muscle.

Metacapillaries. *Metacapillaries* (G. *meta*, between), called *metarterioles* by some authors, are intermediate in structure between the smallest arterioles and the capillaries. They consist of endothelium, spiraling smooth muscle cells scattered at intervals along their lengths, and a thin connective tissue coat that blends with the surrounding connective tissue. Metacapillaries are sometimes called "thoroughfare channels" because major capillary networks arise from them. The flow of blood from metacapillaries into capillary networks is regulated by precapillary sphincters, each a ring of smooth muscle surrounding a capillary where it branches from a metacapillary (Fig. 350). Opening and closing of these sphincters alternately irrigates different capillary networks.

Capillaries (Fig. 350). The focal point of the entire cardiovascular system is the network of some 10 billion microscopic capillaries functioning to provide a method whereby fluids, nutrients, oxygen, carbon dioxide and wastes are exchanged between the blood and interstitial spaces. Capillaries are simply thin endothelial tubes with a surrounding *basement membrane* serving to maintain the integrity of the vessel. They have an average diameter of from 7 to 9 micrometers (similar to that of a red blood cell).

A single capillary unit consists of a branching and anastomosing network of vessels, each averaging 0.5 to 1 mm in length. The number of capillaries in active tissue, such as muscle, liver, kidney, and lungs, is greater than the number in less metabolically active tissues, such as tendons and ligaments.

The endothelium of capillaries may be (a) *continuous*, as in skeletal muscle, the skin and the lungs, with no interruptions in the endothelial layer; (b) *fenestrated* (L. *fenestra*, window), as in the intestine, the pancreas, and the glomerulus of the kidney, containing a continuous layer of endothelial cells but with pores (which may be covered by a thin diaphragm) penetrating the cells; and (c) *discontinuous*, as in the liver, with gaps between cells. The discontinuous type

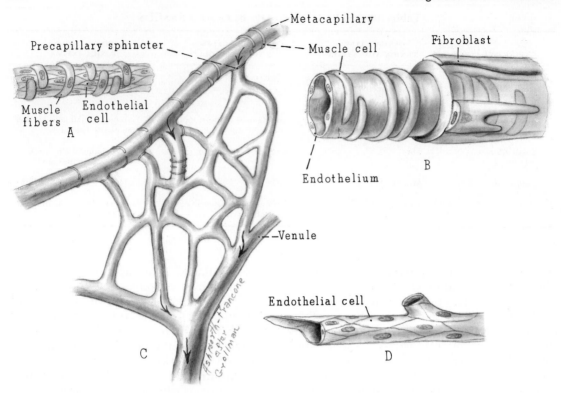

Figure 350. Diagrammatic representation of a capillary bed showing (A) a portion of a metacapillary, (B) arteriole, (C) capillary bed, and (D) true capillary.

are called *sinusoids*. Their walls are, in part, formed by *phagocytes*. In the continuous and fenestrated types the walls are completely surrounded by basement membrane.

The permeability of capillaries varies from one region to another in the body. How substances are transported across capillary walls is still under intensive study. It is generally believed that exchange can occur both between and through endothelial cells. In continuous capillaries, *pinocytotic vesicles* apparently play a transport role, taking up substances on one side of the cell and discharging them on the other (see Chapter 2, page 39, for a description of pinocytosis). It also seems likely that in fenestrated capillaries the pores are sites of transfer.

The distribution of fluid between the blood stream and the interstitial space is governed largely by the balance between the *hydrostatic pressure* (compression pressure) of the blood, which forces fluid out of the capillaries, and the *osmotic pressure*

(see Chapter 2, page 38 of blood, created principally by the concentration of plasma proteins (albumin, chiefly), which draws fluid into the capillaries. The osmotic pressure of blood is approximately 25 mm of mercury. The hydrostatic pressure exceeds the osmotic pressure on the arterial side of capillaries and is lower on the venous side. Thus, the balance of flow is outward at the arterial end, inward at the venous end. A severe loss of fluid from the blood stream can occur as a result of a reduction in osmotic pressure (as in starvation, which leads to a reduction in blood protein synthesis in the liver) or an increase in capillary hydrostatic pressure (as when the return of venous blood to the heart is impaired). When the increase in volume of interstitial fluid can be recognized by a clinician, the condition is called **edema**.

Venules. These vessels collect blood from the capillary beds. A venule consists of an endothelial tube supported by a small amount of collagenous tissue and, in a larger venule, by a few smooth muscle fibers as well. As venules continue to increase in size they begin to show the characteristic wall structure of arteries but are much thinner.

Veins. Veins function to conduct blood from the peripheral tissues to the heart. An endothelial lining similar to that in the venule is surrounded by the tunica media, which contains less muscle and elastic tissue than found in the arterial wall. The tunica adventitia is composed chiefly of connective tissue. Blood pressure in these vessels is extremely low compared to that in the arterial system, and blood must exit at an even lower pressure, creating a need for a special mechanism whereby blood will be kept moving on its return to the heart rather than being allowed to pool and create more resistance to capillary flow. To achieve this, veins possess a unique system of **valves,** formed by paired semilunar folds in the tunica intima which open toward the heart. They serve to direct the flow of blood to the heart, particularly in an upward direction, preventing backflow when closed (Fig. 351). Movement of blood in veins toward the heart is brought about largely by the massaging action of contracting skeletal muscles and by the pressure gradient created by breathing when, during inspiration, the pressure in the thoracic cavity decreases and the pressure in the abdominal cavity increases. Insufficiency of the valves can cause veins to become **varicose,** that is, swollen with accumulated blood,

knotted, and tortuous. The veins lose their elasticity as a result of the continuous distention. Varicosity commonly occurs in the superficial veins of the lower extremities, which are subject to strain when the individual stands for long periods of time. It is thought that there is a genetic predisposition to the development of varicose veins. Pregnancy and obesity hasten their development.

Veins tend to follow a course parallel to that of arteries but are present in greater number. Their lumina are larger than those of arteries and the walls subsequently thinner.

BLOOD PRESSURE

Basic Principles

Blood pressure is pressure exerted by the blood against the walls of the vessels. The term applies to arterial, capillary, and venous pressure. Usually it indicates pressure existing in the large arteries—commonly measured at the brachial artery just above the elbow. The blood pressure is highest in the brachial artery at the time of contraction of the ventricles (ventricular systole). This level is known as the **systolic pressure.** Pressure during ventricular diastole (relaxation of the ventricles) is called **diastolic pressure** and is principally the result of force exerted by the elastic rebound of the arterial wall. Blood pressure is usually expressed as a fraction—for example, as 120/80, in which 120 in mm of mercury represents systolic pressure and 80, diastolic pressure. The difference between the systolic and diastolic pressure is the **pulse pressure.**

Blood pressure is subject to fluctuations. In general, the healthy individual has a systolic pressure of 100 to 120 mm of mercury and a diastolic pressure of 60 to 80 mm of mercury. The upper limits of normal blood pressure are usually defined as 165 mm of mercury systolic and 95 mm diastolic. Pressures above this level (hypertension) shorten life expectancy.

A simple model of the cardiovascular system may help to visualize the major factors governing arterial blood pressure. If, as is illustrated in Figure 352, the large arteries are regarded as a blood chamber

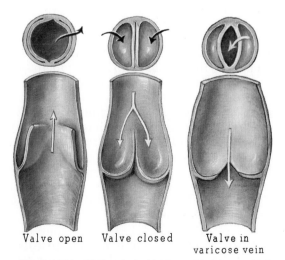

Valve open   Valve closed   Valve in varicose vein

Figure 351. Veins contain bicuspid valves which open in the direction of blood flow, but prevent regurgitation of flow when pockets become filled and distended.

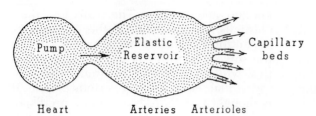

Figure 352. Schematic representation of arteries as an elastic reservoir with inflow from the heart and drainage through arterioles into capillary beds. Inflow and outflow rates determine the average pressure in the reservoir.

acting as an elastic reservoir, pressure builds up as it overfills. Increasing the inflow (cardiac output) into the reservoir and/or decreasing the outflow (drainage through the arterioles into the capillary beds) from the reservoir will raise the average arterial pressure. Decreasing the cardiac output and/or arterial drainage will lower the average arterial pressure. Arteriolar drainage is altered largely by decreasing (constricting) or increasing (dilating) the diameter of arterioles. These relationships are generally expressed as follows: $BP = CO \times R$, where BP is the arterial pressure, CO the cardiac output and R the *peripheral resistance* — the resistance of blood flow through the arterioles. The elasticity of the arterial walls has a considerable influence on arterial pressure. Expansion of the arteries reduces the build up of systolic pressure. Elastic recoil prevents the diastolic pressure from falling to too low a value. If the elasticity of the large arteries is diminished, the systolic pressure will be abnormally high and the diastolic pressure abnormally low.

The magnitude of systolic pressure largely depends upon the amount of blood ejected from the ventricle, the level of pre-existing diastolic pressure, and the elasticity of the aorta. The diastolic pressure is influenced chiefly by the duration of diastole and the peripheral resistance. The longer the duration of diastole, the lower the diastolic pressure.

It should be apparent that by constricting or dilating arterioles in specific areas of the body, such as skeletal muscles, the skin, and the abdominal region, it is possible not only to regulate the blood pressure but also to alter the distribution of blood in various parts of the body. It is perhaps also apparent that the number of capillary beds open at any one time also affects arteriolar drainage — closing most of them down would obviously reduce drainage. The low pressure

in the pulmonary circuit (about one-sixth the pressure in the systemic circuit) is, in part, accounted for by the large number of open capillary beds in the respiratory surfaces of the lungs. In addition, pulmonary arterioles have thinner muscular coats and larger diameters than arterioles of the systemic circuit.

Figure 353 illustrates the blood pressure, blood velocity, and cross-sectional area in each segment of the vascular tree. Note that the greatest fall in blood pressure, about 50 mm of mercury, occurs during the passage of blood through the arterioles. In this portion of the circulation, blood is flowing through a vast number of minute vessels, representing a larger total cross-sectional area than the arteries. The energy loss from friction as the blood passes through numerous vessels of small diameter is considerable. This dissipation of energy accounts for the drop in pressure. The pressure continues to fall progressively as blood flows through the capillary networks and the veins. It can also be seen from the curves for blood velocity and the vascular cross-sectional area in Figure 353 that velocity declines in the arterioles and capillaries as the cross-sectional area increases in these regions. Velocity increases in the veins as the cross-secitonal area decreases in this portion of the vascular tree. This phenomenon is identical to the common observation that a river runs slowly where it is wide and rapidly where it is narrow.

Regulation of Arterial Blood Pressure and the Distribution of Blood

Arterial blood pressure and the distribution of blood in the circulatory system are principally controlled by the activity of the **vasomotor** (L. *vas*, a vessel) and **cardiac centers**, located in the medulla. The

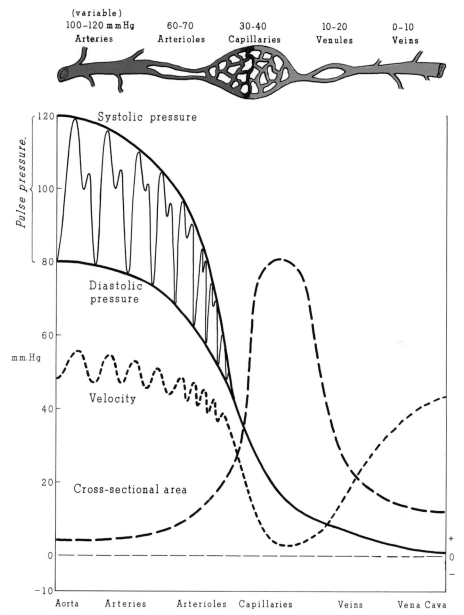

Figure 353. Blood pressure, blood velocity, and cross-sectional area of the vascular tree in various segments of the circulatory system. (Modified from Zoethout and Tuttle: *Textbook of Physiology,* twelfth edition. St. Louis, The C. V. Mosby Co., 1955.)

vasomotor center functions largely as a regulator of the tone of smooth muscles of arterioles by acting through the sympathetic division of the autonomic nervous system. An increase or decrease in tone is brought about by an increase or decrease in the release of norepinephrine at sympathetic nerve endings. Spontaneous activity of the vasomotor center maintains arteriolar tone, which can be increased or decreased by input to the center from peripheral receptors, other brain centers, or substances in the blood stream. By stimulating specific areas of the vasomotor center, excitatory (pressor) or inhibitory (dilator) portions can be identified. The cardiac center governs the heart rate via sympathetic and parasympathetic (vagus nerve) innervation of the SA node. Increased sympathetic stimulation (which increases the release of norepinephrine) and decreased parasympathetic stimulation (which decreases the release of acetylcholine) increase the rate; the reverse actions slow it. An increase or decrease in the force of ventricular contraction is brought about largely by increasing or decreasing sympathetic stimulation of cardiac muscle. The best known and most important regulatory mechanism mediated by these medullary centers is the *baroreceptor reflex*, adaptive changes in blood pressure initiated by arterial pressoreceptors. Changes in blood pressure and distribution by excitation or inhibition of the control centers in the medulla can also be brought about by, among other things, changes in the oxygen and carbon dioxide concentrations in the blood, emotional or physical stress, and changes in body temperature.

The Baroreceptor Reflex. *Baroreceptors*, receptors responding to changes in blood pressure and providing input to the vasomotor and cardiac centers, are located in the aortic arch and internal carotid arteries. A drop in arterial pressure reduces the rate of impulses from these receptors to the medullary centers. The principal effect is constriction of arterioles in skeletal muscles and, if the pressure drop is pronounced, in the skin and splanchnic region (spleen, liver, intestines, pancreas, and stomach). Constriction of small venules, which promotes the return of blood to the heart, also occurs with large pressure drops. In addition, the heart rate may increase. The restoration of blood pressure to normal by these changes, and the reduction in blood flow through the regions where the arterioles are constricted, maintains an adequate flow of blood to the brain and heart. A deficiency in baroreceptor response can cause unconsciousness when, upon the assumption of an upright from a supine posture, blood pools in the lower extremities. Responses to a rise in pressure are the reverse of those to a fall in pressure.

Responses to Changes in Oxygen and Carbon Dioxide Concentrations in the Blood. Changes in oxygen concentration have their effect on blood pressure principally by acting on *chemoreceptors* in the aortic arch and internal carotid arteries. Changes in carbon dioxide concentration, on the other hand, act principally directly on the vasomotor center. The response to a low oxygen concentration or a high carbon dioxide concentration, or both, in the blood is similar to the baroreceptor response to low arterial blood pressure—vasoconstriction in the skeletal muscles, splanchnic region, and the skin. Since carbon dioxide accumulates in oxygen-deficiency states, this response can be viewed as a means of maintaining an adequate supply of oxygen to the brain.

Cardiovascular Changes in the Alarm Response. The most distinctive reaction to emotional stimuli is to danger—the so-called "fight or flight," or alarm, response. Input to the vasomotor and cardiac centers is mediated by the hypothalamus, and the cardiovascular changes include constriction of arterioles in the splanchnic region and the skin and an increase in the heart rate and its force of contraction. The release of norepinephrine and epinephrine by the adrenal medulla, as a part of the generalized sympathetic discharge (Chapter 8, page 277), supports these circulatory adjustments.

Cardiovascular Changes in Anticipation of and During Exercise. The circulatory responses occurring in anticipation of and during exercise are basically the same as the alarm response except that overheating in the course of heavy exercise causes dilation of the arterioles in the skin (see below). Since the prospect of the demands of physical stress initiates adaptive changes, presumably the hypothalamus is the mediator of the responses as it is in the alarm response. It has also been suggested that at the onset of exercise the medullary centers are profoundly influenced by input from the motor cortex. During strenuous exercise mass sympathetic discharge, with the release of norepinephrine and epinephrine, plays the same supportive role as in the alarm response. One of the important circulatory adjustments made at the onset of exercise as well as in the alarm response, namely, dilation of the arterioles in skeletal muscle, is not mediated by the medullary centers. It is brought about, rather, by pathways leading directly from the hypothalamus to the spinal cord that activate sympathetic vasodilator fibers (according to some studies, by acting on beta, or vasodilator, receptors). The greatly increased blood supply to active muscles during exercise is maintained by a local response—relaxation of precapillary sphincters.

Circulatory Responses to Temperature Changes. The regulation of body temperature calls forth a number of homeostatic adjustments, such as sweating and shivering, all mediated by a center in the hypothalamus which is sensitive to temperature changes in the blood and receives input from peripheral receptors. The circulatory response alters the blood flow through the skin. The effect of a rise in temperature is dilation of arterioles in the skin. This increases heat loss from the surface of the body. A fall in temperature has the opposite effect.

Blood Pressure Measurement. Blood pressure is measured with a *sphygmomanometer* (G. *sphygmos*, pulse; G. *manos*, thin; G. *metron*, to measure). The pressure of blood within the artery is balanced by an external pressure exerted by air contained in a cuff applied externally around the arm. Actually, what is measured is the pressure within the cuff. The steps employed in determining blood pressure with a sphygmomanometer are the following:

1. The cuff is wrapped securely around the arm above the elbow.

2. Air is pumped into the cuff with a rubber bulb until pressure in it is sufficient to stop the flow of blood in the brachial artery. At this point, the brachial pulse disappears. Pressure within the cuff is shown on the scale of the sphygmomanometer.

3. The observer places a stethoscope over the brachial artery just below the elbow and gradually releases the air from within the cuff. The decreased air pressure permits the blood to flow, filling the artery below the cuff. Faint tapping sounds corresponding to the heartbeat are heard. When the sound is first noted, the air pressure from within the cuff is recorded on the scale. This pressure is equal to the systolic blood pressure.

4. As the air in the cuff is further released, the sounds become progressively louder. Then the sounds change in quality from loud to soft and finally disappear. At the point where the sounds change from loud to soft, the manometer reading corresponds to the diastolic pressure.

The American Heart Association recommends that when a wide difference exists between the point at which the sound becomes dull and muffled and the point at which the sound completely disappears, the level at which the sound completely disappears should also be recorded as diastolic blood pressure. If the two levels are identical, only one level would be recorded.

Pulse

An impulse can be felt over an artery lying near the surface of the skin. The impulse is secondary to alternate expansion and contraction of the arterial wall resulting from the beating heart. When the heart ejects blood into the aorta, its impact on the elastic walls creates a pressure wave continuing along the arteries. This impact is the pulse. All arteries have a pulse, but it is most easily felt where the vessel approaches the suface of the body. The pulse is readily distinguished at the following locations (Fig. 354).

1. Radial artery: on radial side of wrist.

2. External maxillary (facial) artery: at the point of crossing the mandible.

3. Temporal artery: at the temple above and to the outer side of the eye.

4. Carotid artery: on the side of the neck.

5. Brachial artery: on the inner side of the biceps.

6. Femoral artery: in the groin.

7. Popliteal artery: behind the knee.

8. Dorsalis pedis artery: anterosuperior aspect of the foot.

The radial artery is most commonly used to check the pulse. Several fingers should be placed on the artery just proximal to the wrist joint. More than one fingertip is preferable because of the large, sensitive surface available to palpate the pulse wave. During palpation of the pulse, certain data should be recorded, including the number of pulses per minute, the force and strength of the pulse, and the tension offered by the artery to the finger. Normally, the interval between pulses is of equal length. Irregularity occurs when there is abnormal cardiac

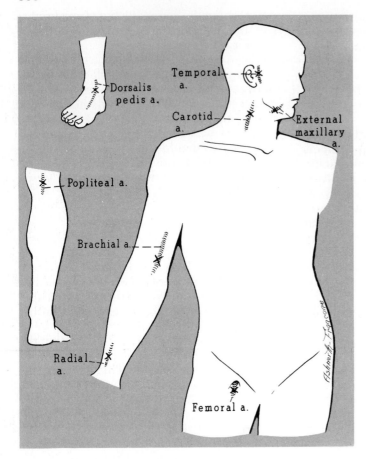

Figure 354. The pulse is readily distinguished at any of the above pressure points.

rhythm, such as in atrial fibrillation. In this condition, as previously noted, there is a pulse deficit, with the rate counted at the apex being greater than that counted at the radial artery of the wrist.

Coronary Heart Disease

Coronary heart disease, the major cause of death in the United States, occurs when the coronary arteries become so narrowed by *atherosclerosis* (localized areas of thickened tunica intima associated with the accumulation of smooth muscle cells and lipids) that they are unable to deliver sufficient blood to the heart muscle to meet its demands for oxygen. A primary sign of this condition is *angina pectoris,* periodic severe pain in the chest generally radiating to the left shoulder and down the inner side of the arm, usually precipitated by physical exertion or emotional stress. In a heart attack the pain is caused by *myocardial infarction,* death of a part of the heart muscle due to total blockage of one of the coronary arteries or its branches. Whether or not the victim survives depends largely upon the amount of heart muscle destroyed. The occlusion, it is generally believed, is caused by the formation of a blood clot (thrombus) over the atherosclerotic lesion, or plaque, but there is reason to believe that in some cases the plaque itself may cause complete blockage.

Atherosclerotic plaques (see Fig. 355) develop most commonly in the aorta and in the coronary, cerebral, iliac, and femoral arteries, especially at junctions. One view that has widespread support is that injury to the endothelial cells, possibly induced by mechanical forces or chemicals, is the initiating event of the disease. The damage to the endothelium allows one or more substances that stimulate the proliferation of smooth muscle cells to penetrate the wall. Smooth muscle cells are only occasionally seen in the intima of children's arteries, but they accumulate slowly with

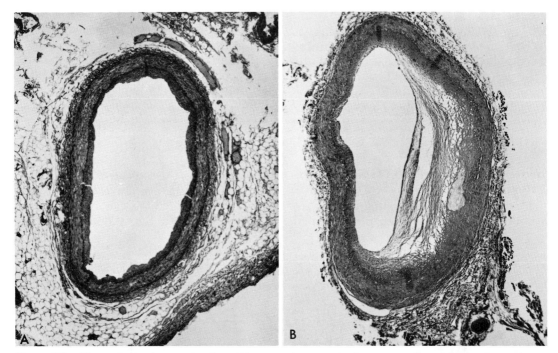

Figure 355. These photomicrographs show (*A*) a normal artery seen in cross section and (*B*) a diseased artery in which the channel is partially occluded by atherosclerosis. (By permission: David M. Spain, M.D., previously published: Scientific American, August, 1966.)

age, even in "normal" arteries. Once the development of a lesion is initiated, the number of smooth muscle cells increases rapidly as they migrate from the tunica media through the internal elastic lamina into the intima and multiply. Platelets accumulating at the site of injury appear to be the source of a smooth muscle cell growth promoting factor. The cholesterol-bearing plasma low-density lipoproteins (see Chapter 13, page 485) also promote the multiplication of smooth muscle cells because, it is believed, they supply nutrients for new membrane synthesis. As the lesion progresses, smooth muscle cells become filled with lipids (called foam cells when this happens). In the initial phase, raised areas of intima, called fatty streaks, appear. Following this, thick fibrous plaques take form, consisting of deposits of extracellular lipid and cell debris encapsulated by foam cells, collagen and elastic fibers, and other connective tissue matrix components (all synthesized by smooth muscle cells). In the advanced, or complicated, lesion the plaques become calcified.

Hypertension (usually defined as blood pressure exceeding 165/95), elevated levels of low-density lipoproteins, and cigarette smoking are the three major coronary risk factors. Hypertension may mechanically damage arterial endothelial cells. Furthermore, a high arterial pressure increases the oxygen requirements of the heart by increasing its work load. Low-density lipoproteins in high concentration appear in some way to inflict damage on arterial endothelium and, as mentioned, they promote the multiplication of smooth muscle cells. Cigarette smoke contains toxic substances that damage the lungs and impair their function. It also contains carbon monoxide, which combines with hemoglobin more readily than oxygen, thereby reducing the oxygen-carrying capacity of red blood cells. The heart of a cigarette smoker, therefore, receives less oxygen than that of a nonsmoker. Furthermore, the reduced oxygen concentration of the blood and possibly toxic substances inhaled in cigarette smoke seem to accelerate plaque formation.

Aneurysm

An aneurysm (G. *aneurysma,* dilatation) is a dilatation of the wall of an artery, forming a blood-filled sac. It occurs most frequently in the descending aorta, and eventually may rupture, causing hemorrhage and death. A congenital defect in the cerebral artery known as berry aneurysm is the most common cause of subarachnoid hemorrhage.

Congenital Defects of the Cardiovascular System

The most common congenital defects are patent ductus arteriosus, ventricular septal defects, atrial septal defects, the so-called tetralogy of Fallot, and coarctation of the aorta (Fig. 356).

Patent ductus arteriosus is a condition characterized by the presence of a channel joining the left pulmonary artery to the aorta. This occurs normally in the fetus, and usually the patent ductus closes within a few weeks after birth. If it does not close, it must be closed surgically.

Septal defects are small holes within the septum between the atria or ventricles. Small openings usually cause little difficulty; large openings can result in death shortly after birth. Septal defects are closed

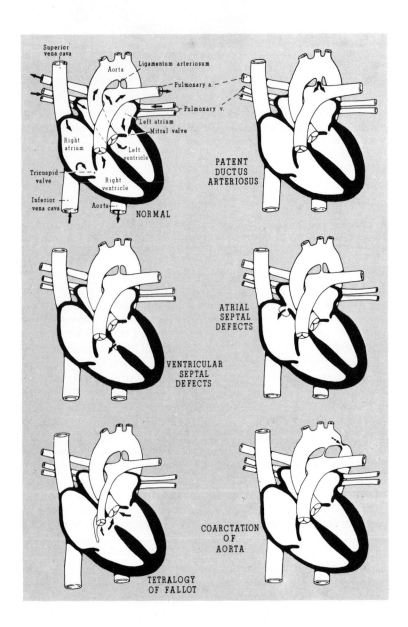

Figure 356. Congenital defects of the heart.

directly, while maintaining general circulation by means of a heart-lung machine.

Tetralogy of Fallot is a bizarre combination of defects including pulmonary stenosis (valvular or subvalvular narrowing), ventricular septal defect, enlargement of the right ventricle, and apparent displacement of the aorta to the right. The result of this combination of defects is that much of the blood does not flow through the pulmonary system. The most characteristic feature is severe cyanosis, or a bluish appearance of the skin, because of a lack of oxygenated blood. A common procedure for increasing pulmonary blood flow is to shunt the blood from the systemic circulation to the pulmonary circulation; this is accomplished by joining the subclavian artery or aorta to the pulmonary artery. Currently, tetralogy of Fallot is frequently treated by a direct attack, using the heart-lung machine and correcting the abnormalities.

Coarctation of the aorta is a congenital defect involving a drastic narrowing of the aorta. It causes an increased work load on the left ventricle. If severe, collateral circulation develops. A pressure 10 to 15 mm of mercury higher in the right than the left brachial artery might indicate coarctation between the right and left subclavian arteries. The condition is corrected either by removing the constricted portion and joining the two open ends of the aorta or by substituting a plastic portion for the removed part of the aorta.

Techniques Employed to Evaluate the Heart and Vascular System

Right Heart Catheterization. Right heart catheterization is performed by inserting a catheter (a long tube) into the antecubital vein (at the elbow), the saphenous vein, or the femoral vein. The catheter, which is opaque to x-ray, is advanced into the right atrium, right ventricle, and pulmonary artery under fluoroscopy. This procedure, by measuring pressure and oxygen saturation in the right heart chamber, is used to diagnose valvular abnormalities of the right side of the heart (Fig. 357).

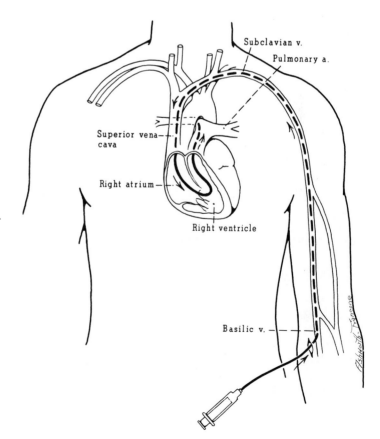

Figure 357. Right heart catheterization.

Subclavian v.

Pulmonary a.

Superior vena-cava

Right atrium

Right ventricle

Basilic v.

Left Heart Catheterization. Left heart catheterization is accomplished by introducing a catheter into the brachial or femoral artery and advancing it through the aorta across the aortic valve and into the left ventricle. Mitral and aortic valvular defects and myocardial disease can be evaluated by this technique.

Circulation Time. The circulation time between two points in the cardiovascular system is measured by injecting an indicator substance into one area of the circulation and recording its arrival time at another. Arm to lung circulation time is measured by timing the appearance of ether in the lung after its injection into a peripheral vein. Arm to tongue circulation is measured by injecting a substance such as calcium gluconate or Decholin into the antecubital vein and recording the time until the patient tastes this material. Circulation time depends on the velocity of blood flow and the

dimensions of the circulatory pathway involved. A high cardiac output is generally associated with a reduced circulation time. A low cardiac output accompanying venous congestion usually has a prolonged circulation time.

Angiocardiography. (See Figs. 358–361.) X-ray outlines of the cardiac chambers and great vessels are provided by rapidly injecting x-ray opaque material through an arm vein or through a catheter threaded into the right or left side of the heart. This procedure is followed by a series of rapid exposures to x-ray or to x-ray movies called cineangiography. Angiocardiography permits direct visualization of the cardiac chambers and great vessels. By outlining abnormal circulatory pathways it provides one of the best methods of detecting the site and extent of congenital abnormalities of the heart. It can also be used to study arteries and veins.

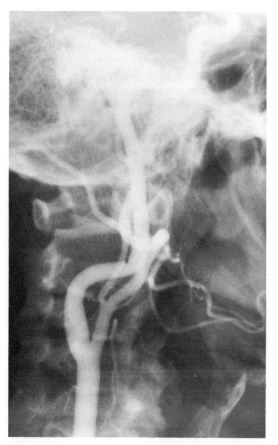
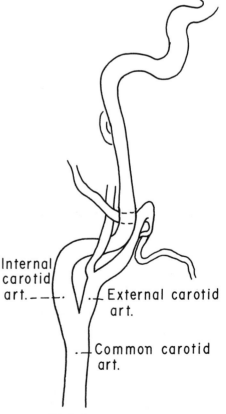

Internal carotid art.

External carotid art.

Common carotid art.

Figure 358. Angiograph for common carotid study.

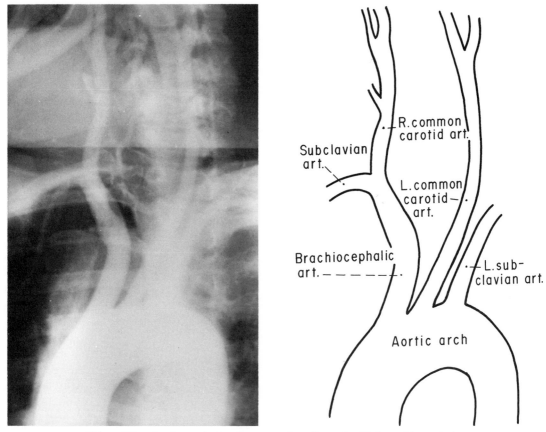

Figure 359. Angiograph showing normal aortic arch with branching arteries.

Vein to Artery Graft. The accurate diagnosis of peripheral and coronary arterial disease or damage, coupled with the development of new surgical techniques, has led to more frequent use of vein grafts in the repair of damaged arteries. These grafts can be obtained from various parts of the vascular system and are used to replace the damaged or diseased portion of the artery. This procedure is being utilized more and more as treatment of circulatory occlusions of the heart caused by conditions such as atherosclerosis.

Central Venous Catheterization. In order to alleviate vein irritation and discomfort caused by long term venous therapy the relatively sophisticated technique of central venous catheterization has been recently developed. The procedure involves positioning a large-gauge needle in the subclavian, internal jugular, or external jugular vein and passing a catheter through the needle into the vein and, subsequently, into the superior vena cava. In this way a rapid and convenient method is provided to monitor central venous pressure and provide a route for parenteral alimentation, long term intravenous therapy with anticoagulant solutions, and rapid infusion of large volumes of fluid. It provides an immediate route for emergency treatment of conditions such as cardiac arrest, for temporary placement of a pacemaker, or for obtaining pulmonary arteriographs.

Blood Volume

The normal adult has a blood volume of approximately 5 liters. Normal blood volume may be reduced by a loss of whole blood in hemorrhage, a deficiency of red cells (anemia), or a loss of plasma. Dilation of the arterioles, venules, and capillaries traps blood in the periphery of the vascular system, thus causing a diminished available blood volume without actual blood loss. An increase in blood volume occurs in certain

Text continued on page 376

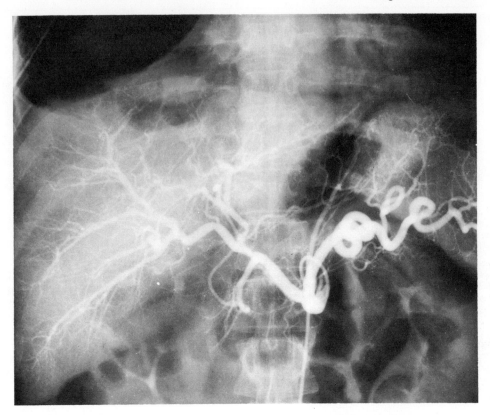

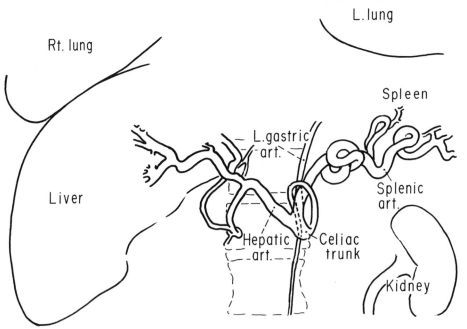

Figure 360. Normal celiac angiograph with normal hepatic, left gastric, and splenic branches. The liver, kidneys, and spleen are all well seen in their relationship to one another. In this particular angiograph the patient was noted to have right lung collapse with mass. Lung cancer was diagnosed with no evidence of liver metastases.

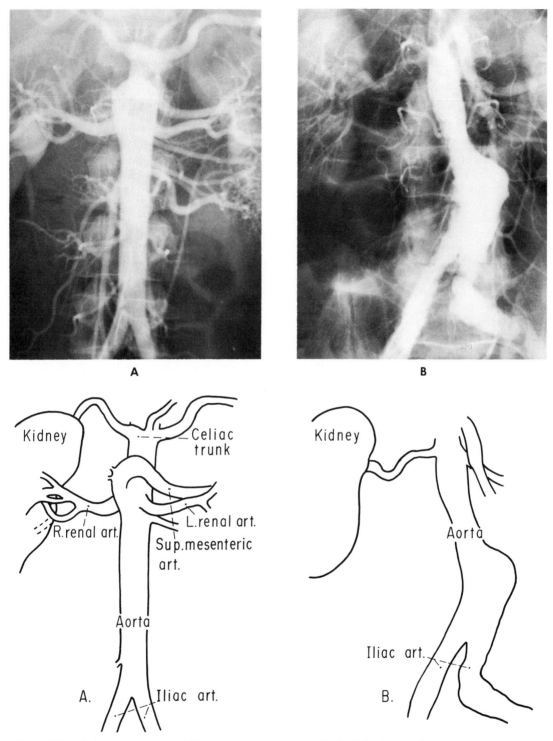

Figure 361. *A,* An aortogram and iliac study on a young patient. *B,* For comparison, an aortogram from a 69-year-old male with severe arteriosclerosis is shown. The aorta and iliacs are dilated and irregular.

diseases but is usually less marked than blood loss.

The integrity of the endothelial membrane of the capillaries is a vital factor in maintaining normal blood volume. Many factors alter the permeability of the capillaries. When the endothelium is injured, its permeability to plasma proteins is increased, leading to a loss of fluid into the interstitial spaces. Damage to the endothelium can occur from many factors, including toxins, hypoxia and low oxygen content.

Shock. Shock is produced either by a reduction of the blood volume or by a vasodilation which greatly increases vascular capacity (volume) with constant blood volume. Both mechanisms lead to a decrease in venous pressure and venous return, and a consequent decrease in cardiac output or in arterial blood pressure, or both. The consequent reductions in circulatory activity tend to produce a vicious deterioration cycle by progressively damaging vascular and tissue tone and functional integrity, which in turn leads (through a variety of mechanical or chemical imbalances) to either a further decrease in cardiac output or in blood pressure, which again leads to further deterioration of tissues. Unless this trend is reversed, death soon results. The initial stages of progressive shock are characterized by apprehension, cold skin, cyanosis of the fingertips, reduced blood pressure (most often), shallow respiratory activity, sweating, and rapid pulse.

Any mechanical, chemical, neurological, or psychological trauma can potentially lead to shock, the initial effect being either a reduction of blood volume or an increased vascular capacity (vasodilation), which then produces a reduction of cardiac output and/or a decrease in blood pressure. Hemorrhage is a frequent cause of shock when 10 to 15 per cent (sometimes less) of the blood volume is lost. This leads to decreased venous return, which produces a decrease in cardiac output and usually a decrease in blood pressure—the net result being a reduction of circulatory activity and efficiency. The reduction of circulatory efficiency in turn can cause, in a matter of minutes to hours, tissue damage which, in turn, produces imbalances that further affect the vasomotor tone to decrease efficiency.

A loss of over 40 per cent of the blood volume causes vascular collapse (collapse of the arteries). This condition frequently does not respond to blood transfusions and is known as "irreversible shock." More generally, the "irreversible" stage of shock occurs whenever the circulatory system is unable to sustain even the temporary recovery of blood pressure and cardiac output produced by transfusion or any other therapy. This state is typically caused by actual damage to the heart or by tissue oxygen debt which is excessive beyond reversal. Sudden losses of small quantities of blood can occasionally produce consequences more serious than slow losses of large volumes. Massive heart injury leading to an inadequate cardiac output is also an important initiating cause of shock.

In the absence of hemorrhage or actual damage to the heart, the reason for loss of effective circulating blood volume is not clearly understood. Three widely held views which attempt to explain such blood loss are increased capillary permeability; actual plasma loss (as in burns or dehydration); and generalized dilation or loss of vasomotor muscle tone. In this last view, dilation greatly increases vascular capacity so that even the normal amount of blood becomes incapable of adequately filling the circulatory system, and pooling of venous blood occurs in the peripheral capillary bed. As venous return decreases, following Starling's Law, cardiac output decreases and again leads to overall deterioration of physiologic tone, since circulatory activity and efficiency are inadequate. Among the common causes of vasodilation (neurogenic) shock are deep general anesthesia, high spinal anesthesias, brain damage, and fainting. In fainting, the venous pooling and consequent shock often can be avoided if the patient is placed in a head-down position.

Chemical shock, septic shock (blood poisoning or widespread infection), and various traumatic shocks generally produce the same effects of decreased cardiac output, loss of blood pressure, and either initial or consequent vasodilation and loss of vasomotor tone.

PHYSIOLOGIC RESPONSES TO SHOCK FOLLOWING HEMORRHAGE. In shock following hemorrhage, the reduced blood volume diminishes venous pressure. This

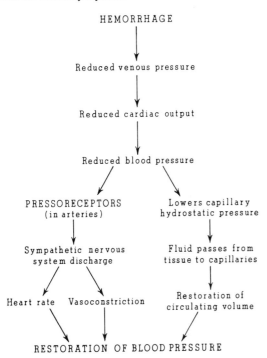

HEMORRHAGE

Reduced venous pressure

Reduced cardiac output

Reduced blood pressure

PRESSORECEPTORS (in arteries)

Lowers capillary hydrostatic pressure

Sympathetic nervous system discharge

Fluid passes from tissue to capillaries

Heart rate   Vasoconstriction

Restoration of circulating volume

RESTORATION OF BLOOD PRESSURE

Figure 362. Factors in restoration of blood pressure after hemorrhage has occurred.

lowers the cardiac output, and blood pressure drops. With the drop in blood pressure, the baroreceptors decrease their rate of impulse transmission to the vasomotor center, which is followed by a sympathetic nervous system discharge producing vasoconstriction and raising the heart rate, thereby restoring blood pressure. It should also be noted that, with the initial decrease in venous pressure, there is a lowering of capillary hydrostatic pressure on the venous end, with a resultant increase in the flow of fluids from the tissues into the capillaries, which leads to an increase in vascular fluid volume; the amount and significance depend on the length of time and severity as well as other factors. This aids in restoration of normal venous return and restoration of blood pressure (Fig. 362).

PULMONARY AND SYSTEMIC CIRCUITS

As mentioned in the beginning of the chapter, blood is pumped from the heart into two circuits: pulmonary and systemic. These are described in more detail in this section (see Figs. 363–383). Special consideration is also given to the circulation

through the liver and brain and to the fetal circulation.

Pulmonary Circulation

The pulmonary system carries blood from the right ventricle to the respiratory surfaces of the lungs and back to the left atrium. The pulmonary trunk, originating from the superior surface of the right ventricle, passes diagonally upward to the left across the route of the aorta. Between the fifth and sixth thoracic vertebrae, the trunk divides into two branches—the right and left pulmonary arteries—which enter the lungs. After entering the lungs, the branches subdivide, finally emerging as capillaries. Capillaries surround air sacs (alveoli) and pick up oxygen and release carbon dioxide. Gradually, the capillaries unite, assuming the characteristics of veins. Veins join to form pulmonary veins, which carry oxygenated blood from the lungs to the left atrium.

A pulmonary embolus is a clot lodged in the pulmonary artery (Fig. 384). It can result from blood, air, fat, a tumor, or clumps of bacteria. An embolus can obstruct the main pulmonary artery or one of its large branches. This condition often results in death. Frequently, the patient will recover if the main pulmonary artery is not involved. If the major pulmonary artery is obstructed, cardiac output falls suddenly, the skin becomes pale because of intense vasoconstriction, the blood pressure drops, and the patient manifests evidences of shock. There is usually an increased heart rate.

Systemic Circulation

The systemic circulation carries oxygen, nutrients, and wastes for the entire body, including the bronchial tree (nonrespiratory portion) of the lungs. All systemic arteries spring from the aorta. The aorta emerges from the superior surface of the left ventricle, passes upward underneath the pulmonary artery as the *ascending aorta,* and then turns to the left as the *aortic arch,* passing downward as the *descending aorta.* The descending aorta, lying close to the vertebral bodies, passes through the diaphragm

Text continued on page 398

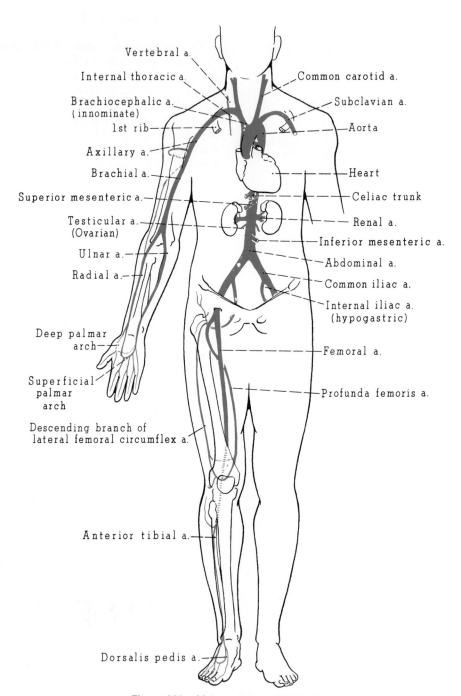

Vertebral a.

Internal thoracic a.

Brachiocephalic a.
(innominate)

1st rib

Axillary a.

Brachial a.

Superior mesenteric a.

Testicular a.
(Ovarian)

Ulnar a.

Radial a.

Deep palmar
arch

Superficial
palmar
arch

Descending branch of
lateral femoral circumflex a.

Anterior tibial a.

Dorsalis pedis a.

Common carotid a.

Subclavian a.

Aorta

Heart

Celiac trunk

Renal a.

Inferior mesenteric a.

Abdominal a.

Common iliac a.

Internal iliac a.
(hypogastric)

Femoral a.

Profunda femoris a.

Figure 363. Major arteries of the body.

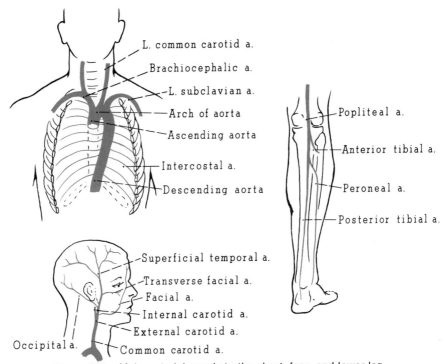

Figure 364. Major arterial supply to the chest, face, and lower leg.

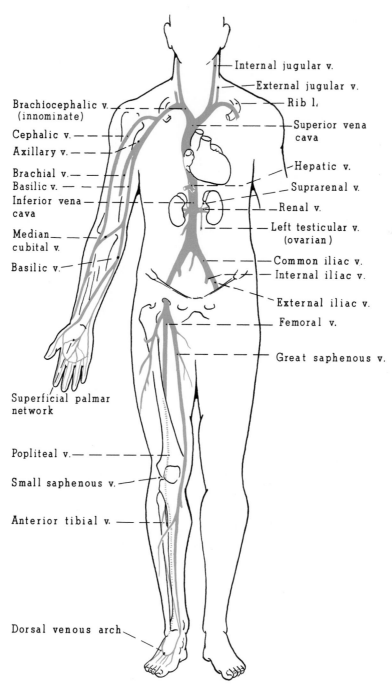

Brachiocephalic v.
(innominate)

Cephalic v.

Axillary v.

Brachial v.

Basilic v.

Inferior vena
cava

Median
cubital v.

Basilic v.

Superficial palmar
network

Popliteal v.

Small saphenous v.

Anterior tibial v.

Dorsal venous arch

Internal jugular v.

External jugular v.

Rib l.

Superior vena
cava

Hepatic v.

Suprarenal v.

Renal v.

Left testicular v.
(ovarian)

Common iliac v.

Internal iliac v.

External iliac v.

Femoral v.

Great saphenous v.

Figure 365.   Major veins of the body.

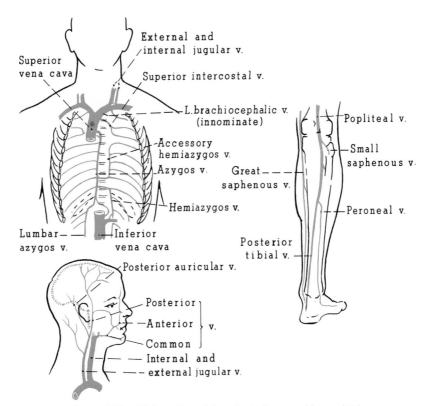

Figure 366.   Major veins of the chest, face, and lower leg.

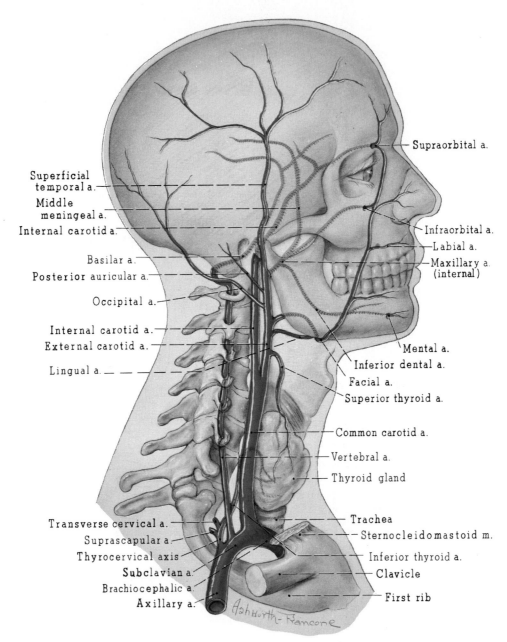

Figure 367.   Arterial supply to the head and neck.

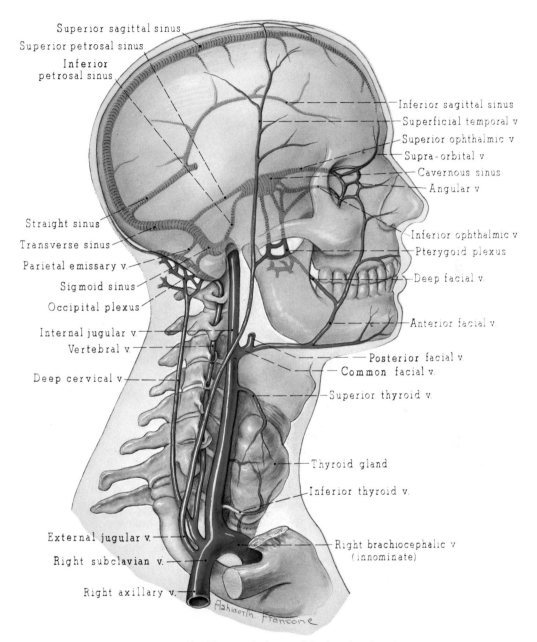

Figure 368. Venous drainage of the head and neck.

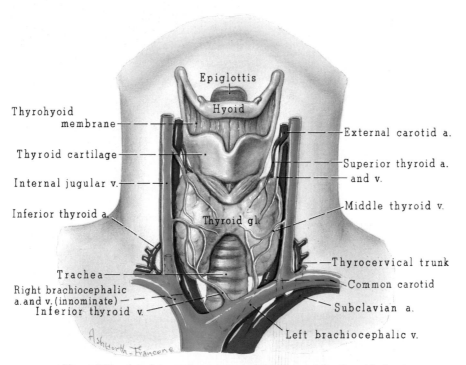

Figure 369.   Arterial supply and venous drainage of the thyroid gland.

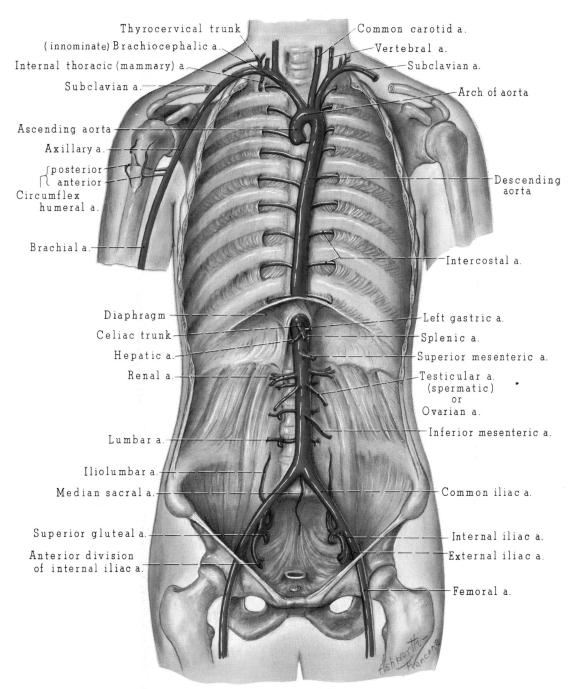

Figure 370.   The aorta and its major branches.

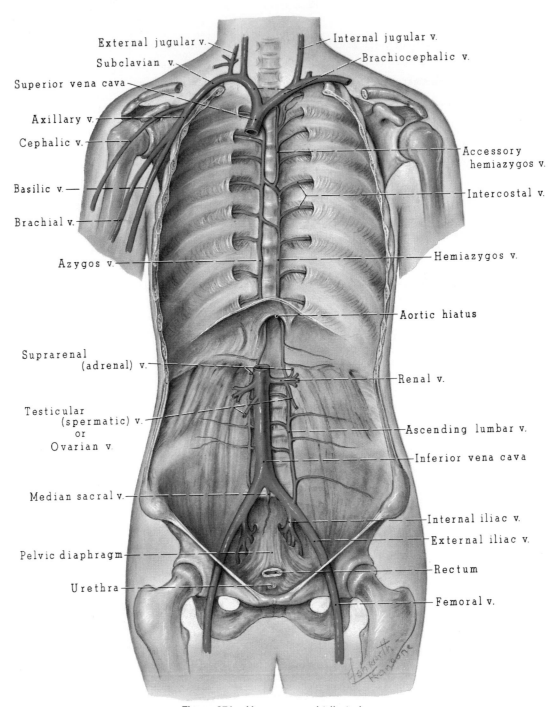

Figure 371. Vena cava and tributaries.

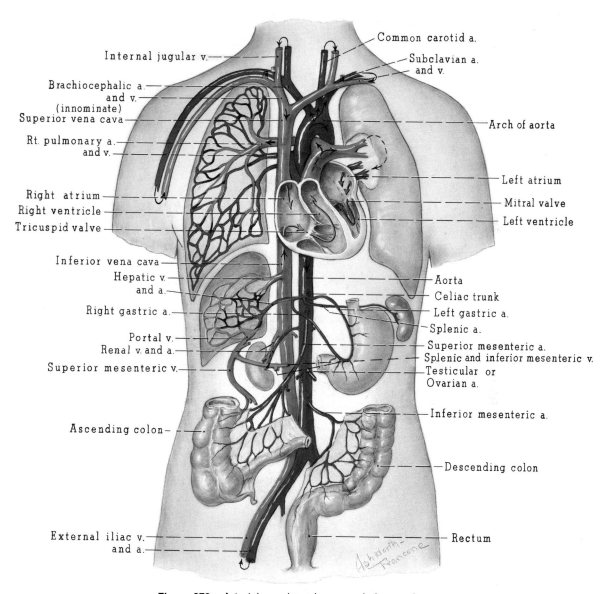

Figure 372. Arterial supply and venous drainage of organs.

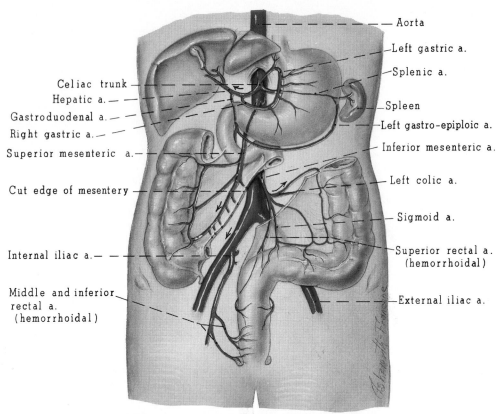

Aorta

Left gastric a.

Splenic a.

Celiac trunk

Hepatic a.

Gastroduodenal a.

Right gastric a.

Superior mesenteric a.

Cut edge of mesentery

Internal iliac a.

Middle and inferior rectal a. (hemorrhoidal)

Spleen

Left gastro-epiploic a.

Inferior mesenteric a.

Left colic a.

Sigmoid a.

Superior rectal a. (hemorrhoidal)

External iliac a.

Figure 373. Arterial supply to the abdominal viscera.

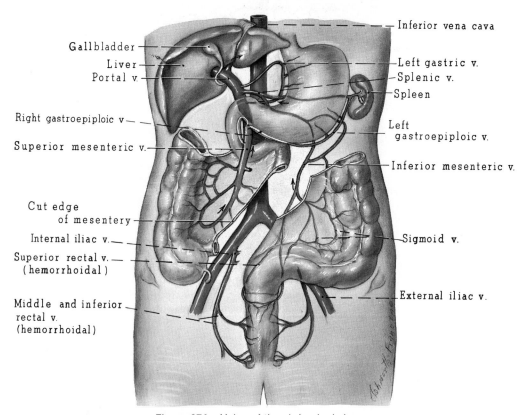

Inferior vena cava

Gallbladder

Liver

Portal v.

Right gastroepiploic v

Superior mesenteric v.

Cut edge of mesentery

Internal iliac v.

Superior rectal v. (hemorrhoidal)

Middle and inferior rectal v. (hemorrhoidal)

Left gastric v.

Splenic v.

Spleen

Left gastroepiploic v.

Inferior mesenteric v.

Sigmoid v.

External iliac v.

Figure 374. Veins of the abdominal viscera.

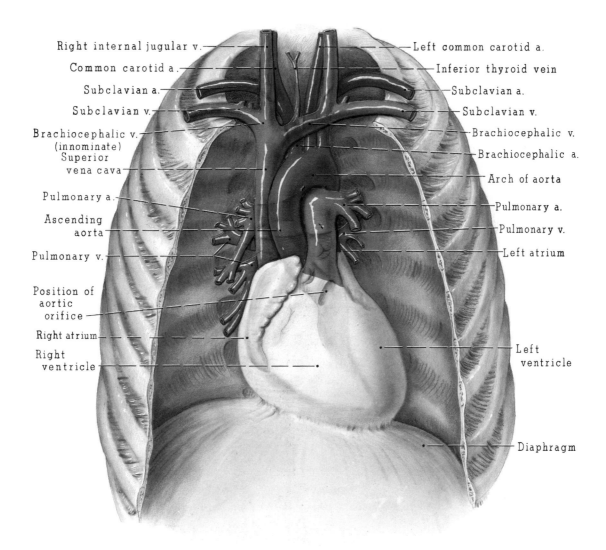

Right internal jugular v.

Common carotid a.

Subclavian a.

Subclavian v.

Brachiocephalic v.
(innominate)
Superior
vena cava

Pulmonary a.

Ascending
aorta

Pulmonary v.

Position of
aortic
orifice

Right atrium

Right
ventricle

Left common carotid a.

Inferior thyroid vein

Subclavian a.

Subclavian v.

Brachiocephalic v.

Brachiocephalic a.

Arch of aorta

Pulmonary a.

Pulmonary v.

Left atrium

Left
ventricle

Diaphragm

Figure 375. The heart in situ, showing its relation to the chest cavity and diaphragm with the major arteries and veins of the chest.

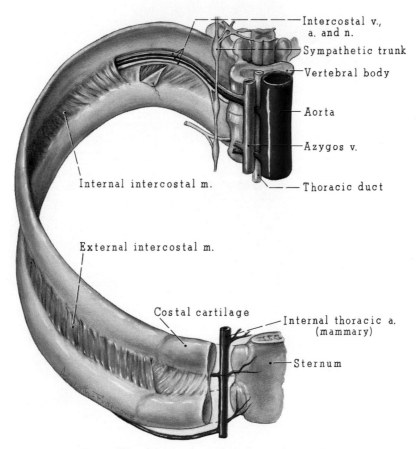

Figure 376.   Artery, vein, and nerve supply to a rib.

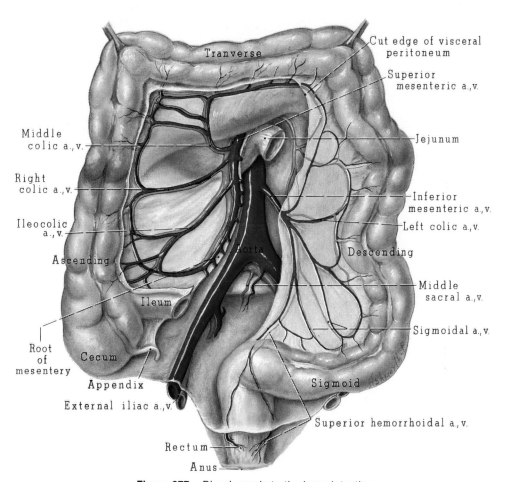

Figure 377. Blood supply to the large intestine.

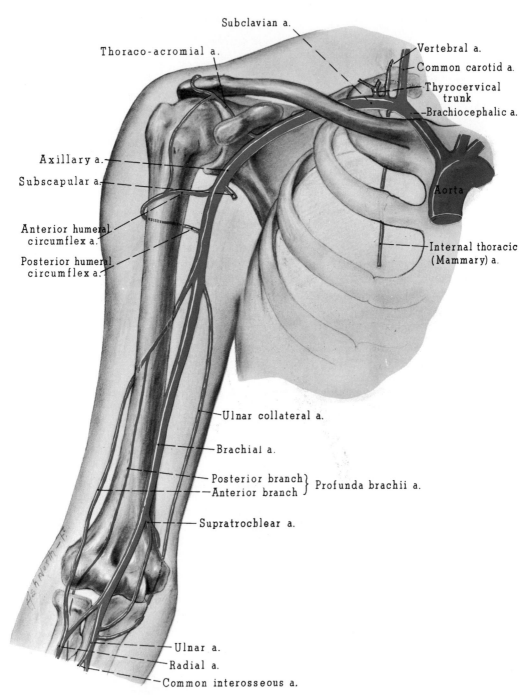

Figure 378. Arteries of the right shoulder and upper arm.

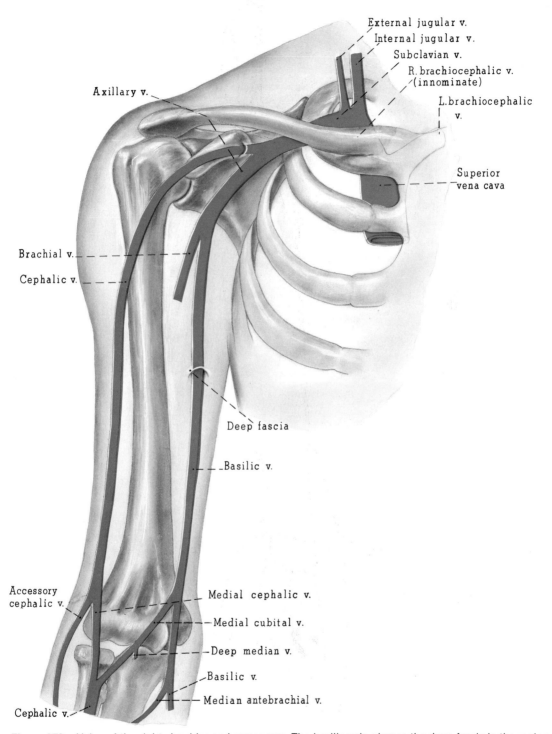

External jugular v.

Internal jugular v.

Subclavian v.

R. brachiocephalic v.
(innominate)

L. brachiocephalic
v.

Axillary v.

Superior
vena cava

Brachial v.

Cephalic v.

Deep fascia

Basilic v.

Accessory
cephalic v.

Medial cephalic v.

Medial cubital v.

Deep median v.

Basilic v.

Median antebrachial v.

Cephalic v.

Figure 379. Veins of the right shoulder and upper arm. The basilic vein pierces the deep fascia in the region of the middle of the arm.

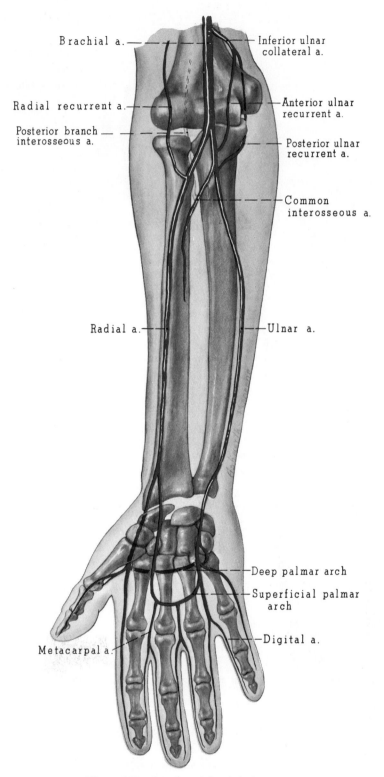

Figure 380. Arteries of the right lower arm.

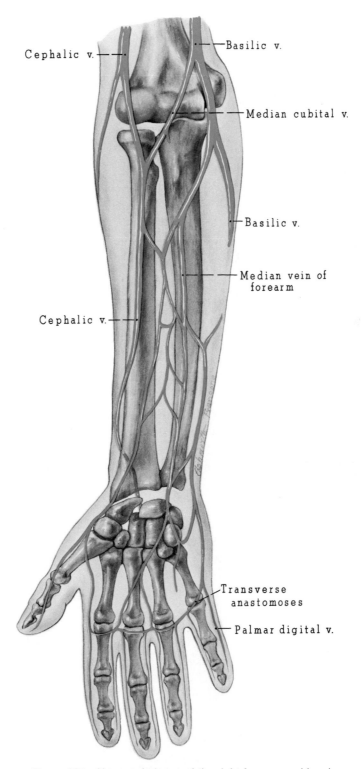

Cephalic v.

Basilic v.

Median cubital v.

Basilic v.

Median vein of forearm

Cephalic v.

Transverse anastomoses

Palmar digital v.

Figure 381. Venous drainage of the right forearm and hand.

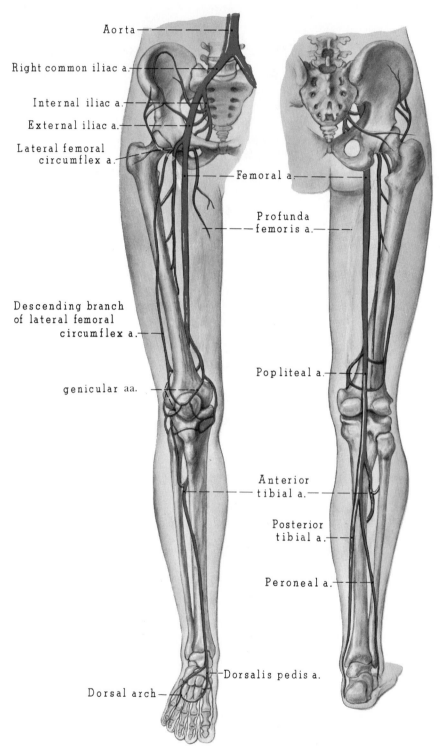

Figure 382. Arteries of the right pelvis and leg.

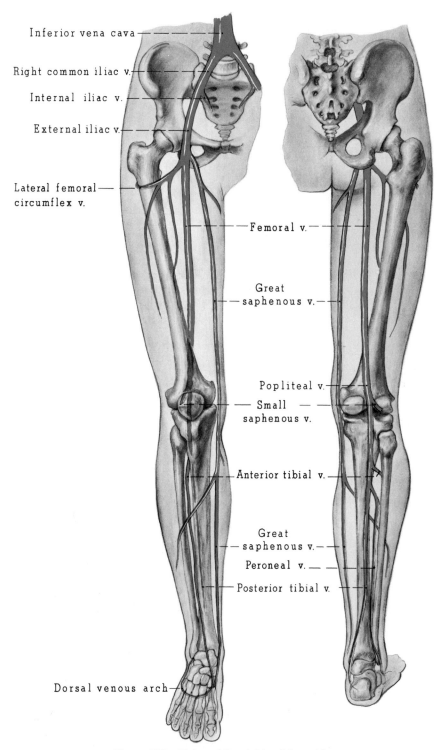

Inferior vena cava

Right common iliac v.

Internal iliac v.

External iliac v.

Lateral femoral
circumflex v.

Femoral v.

Great
saphenous v.

Popliteal v.

Small
saphenous v.

Anterior tibial v.

Great
saphenous v.

Peroneal v.

Posterior tibial v.

Dorsal venous arch

Figure 383. Veins of the right pelvis and leg.

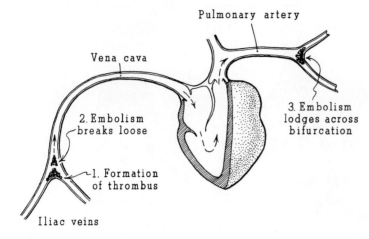

Figure 384. Formation of thrombus with secondary pulmonary embolus. (From D'Amour: *Basic Physiology.* Chicago, University of Chicago Press, 1961.)

to the level of the fourth lumbar vertebra. It terminates by dividing into the two common iliac arteries. The descending aorta is divided into the thoracic segment (above the diaphragm) and the abdominal segment (below the diaphragm). Major arteries of the body spring from the aorta. They are described in Figures 385 to 388.

The veins emerge from the capillaries. All veins of the systemic circulation flow into either the inferior or superior vena cava, which in turn empties into the right atrium.

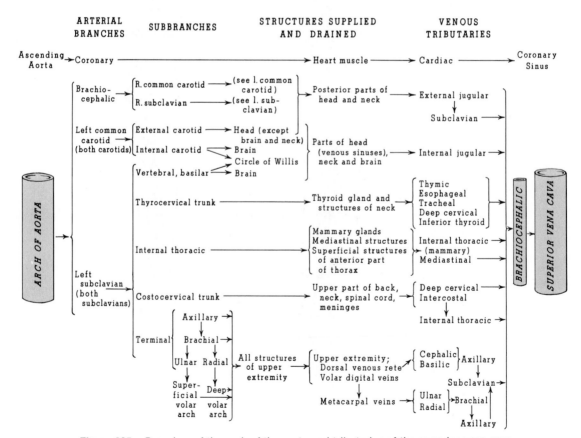

Figure 385. Branches of the arch of the aorta and tributaries of the superior vena cava.

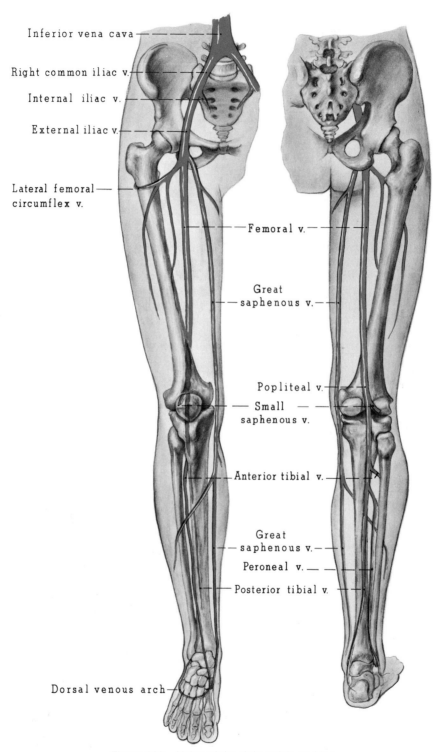

Figure 383. Veins of the right pelvis and leg.

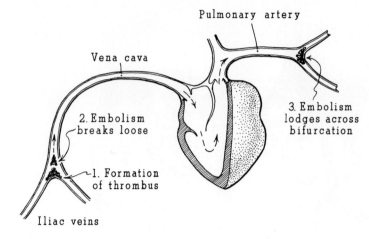

Pulmonary artery

Vena cava

2. Embolism
breaks loose

3. Embolism
lodges across
bifurcation

1. Formation
of thrombus

Iliac veins

Figure 384. Formation of thrombus with secondary pulmonary embolus. (From D'Amour: *Basic Physiology.* Chicago, University of Chicago Press, 1961.)

to the level of the fourth lumbar vertebra. It terminates by dividing into the two common iliac arteries. The descending aorta is divided into the thoracic segment (above the diaphragm) and the abdominal segment (below the diaphragm). Major arteries of the body spring from the aorta. They are described in Figures 385 to 388.

The veins emerge from the capillaries. All veins of the systemic circulation flow into either the inferior or superior vena cava, which in turn empties into the right atrium.

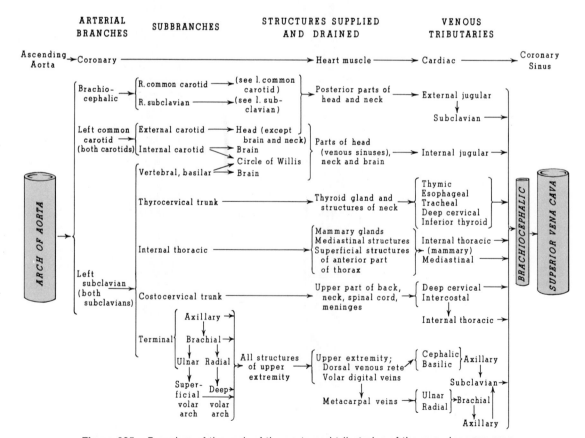

Figure 385. Branches of the arch of the aorta and tributaries of the superior vena cava.

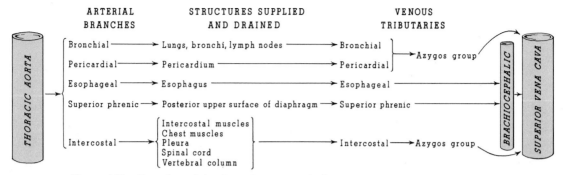

Figure 386. Branches of the thoracic aorta and tributaries of the superior vena cava.

The major veins of the body are described in Figures 385 to 388.

Circulation Through the Liver

Blood flowing to the liver comes from the hepatic artery (20 per cent) and the hepatic portal vein (80 per cent); blood leaving the liver flows through the hepatic vein, which empties into the inferior vena cava. The hepatic arterial blood supplies oxygen requirements for the liver. The hepatic portal circuit is unique in that blood from the intestines, stomach, spleen, and pancreas first passes through the liver before entering the vena cava and going to the heart. This type of circulation, in which blood from one or more organs circulates through another before returning to the heart, is referred to

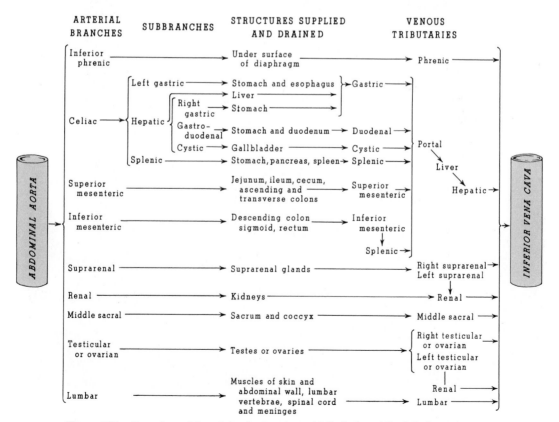

Figure 387. Branches of the abdominal aorta and tributaries of the inferior vena cava.

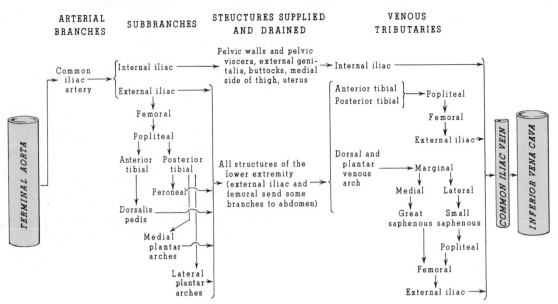

| ARTERIAL BRANCHES | SUBBRANCHES | STRUCTURES SUPPLIED AND DRAINED | VENOUS TRIBUTARIES |

Figure 388. Branches of the terminal aorta and tributaries of the inferior vena cava.

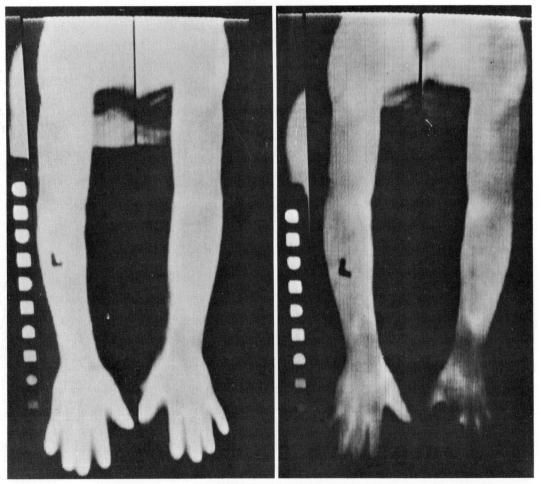

Figure 389. Effect of nicotine on the circulation is seen in thermograms of a man's arms before he smoked (*left*) and 15 minutes after he smoked a cigarette (*right*). Nicotine has constricted blood vessels, reducing the amount of blood in the arms and lowering their temperature. (By permission: J. Gershon-Cohen, M.D. Previously published Scientific American, February 1967.)

400

in a general way as a *portal system*. Another example of this is the flow of venous blood from the hypothalamus to the neurohypophysis, or posterior pituitary gland (described in Chapter 15). Substances in the hepatic portal blood are processed by the liver; agents such as fibrinogen and prothrombin are added to the blood in the liver.

Vascular Supply to the Brain (Figs. 390 to 392)

The intracranial contents receive arterial blood from the internal carotid and vertebral arteries. Venous drainage is via the cerebral veins and dural venous sinuses. The diploic and emissary veins are communications between the intracranial and extracranial venous channels.

Importance of Oxygen Supply to the Brain. It is not possible to overemphasize the importance of a constant oxygen supply to the body and especially to the brain. The nervous system actually consumes oxygen at a very slow rate. However, this consumption goes on at all times, and neural damage can occur after a few minutes of severe oxygen lack (hypoxia). In fact, temporary asphyxia at birth often causes serious damage to the brain, resulting in mental retardation and other abnormalities, such as epileptic seizures and paralysis. In a recent study of 40,000 births, feeblemindedness was found to be many times more common among children who suffered any anoxia at birth than among their siblings who had normal births.

Arterial Supply. The *internal carotid arteries* arise from the common carotid arteries, which bifurcate at the level of the thyroid cartilage, enter the carotid canal in the skull, pass along the anterior border of the tympanic cavity, and turn medially to pierce the dural lining on the side of the sphenoid bone. The internal carotid artery gives origin to the ophthalmic artery, the anterior and middle cerebral arteries, and the anterior communicating arteries.

The *vertebral artery* arises from the subclavian, passes through the foramina in cervical vertebrae, perforates the dura mater between the atlas and occipital bone,

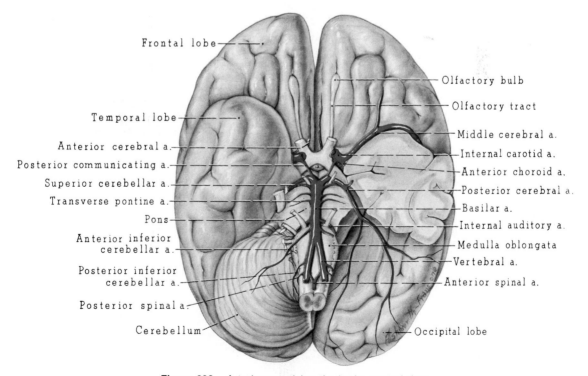

Figure 390. Arteries supplying the brain, ventral view.

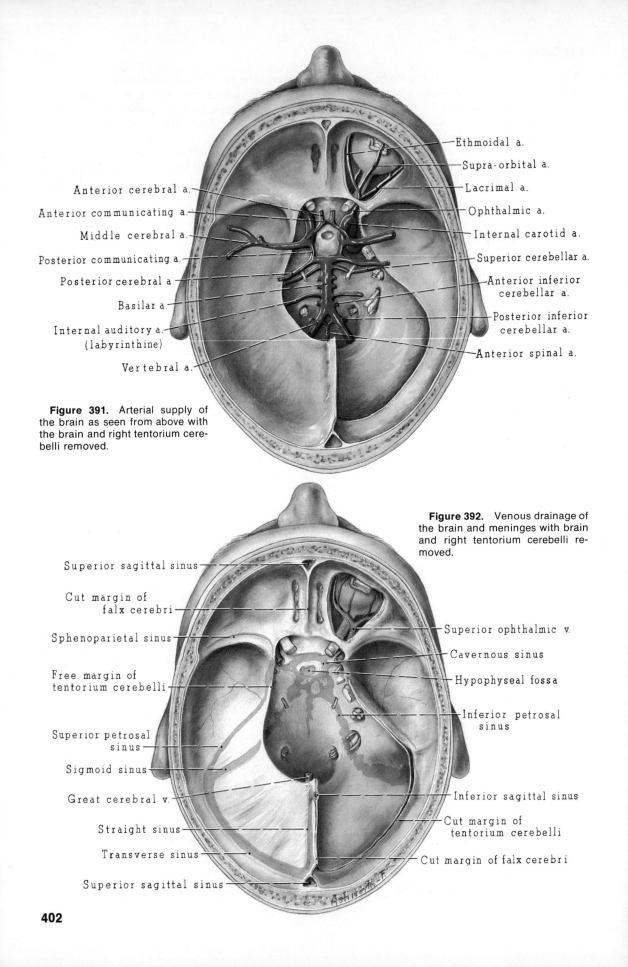

Ethmoidal a.

Supra-orbital a.

Lacrimal a.

Ophthalmic a.

Internal carotid a.

Superior cerebellar a.

Anterior inferior
cerebellar a.

Posterior inferior
cerebellar a.

Anterior spinal a.

Anterior cerebral a.

Anterior communicating a.

Middle cerebral a.

Posterior communicating a.

Posterior cerebral a.

Basilar a.

Internal auditory a.
(labyrinthine)

Vertebral a.

Figure 391. Arterial supply of
the brain as seen from above with
the brain and right tentorium cerebelli removed.

Figure 392. Venous drainage of
the brain and meninges with brain
and right tentorium cerebelli removed.

Superior sagittal sinus

Cut margin of
falx cerebri

Sphenoparietal sinus

Free margin of
tentorium cerebelli

Superior petrosal
sinus

Sigmoid sinus

Great cerebral v.

Straight sinus

Transverse sinus

Superior sagittal sinus

Superior ophthalmic v.

Cavernous sinus

Hypophyseal fossa

Inferior petrosal
sinus

Inferior sagittal sinus

Cut margin of
tentorium cerebelli

Cut margin of falx cerebri

402

and bends upward and medially in front of the medulla. Before uniting anteriorly at the lower margin of the pons to form the basilar artery, the vertebral arteries give rise to the posterior inferior cerebellar arteries. The anterior inferior cerebellar and superior cerebellar arteries arise from the basilar artery.

The *basilar artery,* in turn, bifurcates to form two posterior cerebral arteries. This system is connected to the internal carotids by the posterior communicating arteries, while the anterior communicating artery serves to join the anterior cerebral arteries. Thus, the circle of Willis, a site of aneurysms, is formed by the two posterior cerebral arteries, the two anterior cerebrals, the two internal carotid arteries, and the posterior and anterior communicating arteries.

Cerebral hemorrhage and *thrombosis* usually occur after the age of 45. Both are more common in men than in women and are generally secondary to atherosclerosis. The commonest site for thrombosis is the middle cerebral artery. An attack can occur without warning, or there may be some premonitory symptoms such as dizziness or disturbance in speech.

Fetal Circulation

The circulatory system of the fetus differs from that of the adult in that the lungs and alimentary canal of the fetus are nonfunctional and, therefore, receive only a minimal blood supply from the fetal heart. Another basic difference stems from the fact that the fetal heart must pump relatively large amounts of deoxygenated blood back to the placenta, from which it originally receives oxygenated blood. The primary features distinguishing fetal from adult circulation can be seen in Table 41 and Figures 393 and 394.

The oxygenated blood from the placenta enters the fetus by way of the umbilical vein. It then passes through the ductus venosus into the inferior vena cava, mainly bypassing the liver. From the inferior vena cava, the blood enters the right atrium of the beating fetal heart. At this point about two-thirds of this oxygenated (placental) blood is deflected directly into the left atrium, passing through the foramen ovale. This portion of the oxygenated blood, which has been deflected directly to the left side of the heart, bypassing the right side, moves then from the left atrium into the left ventricle, is pumped out the aorta, and is channeled primarily to the head and upper extremities.

The remaining original oxygenated blood in the right atrium is mixed with the deoxygenated blood returning through the superior vena cava from the head and upper extremities. This mixture is primarily deflected into the right ventricle. From the right ventricle this blood is pumped out into the large pulmonary artery. A small portion of the blood circulates through the lungs. The largest portion, however, flows through the ductus arteriosus into the aorta. It enters the aorta distal to the point at which the blood to the head leaves. This basically independent stream of blood from the right ventricle then moves down the descending branch of the aorta. Some of the blood supplies the lower areas of the body. The

Table 41.   DIFFERENCES IN ADULT AND FETAL CIRCULATION

STRUCTURE	FUNCTION IN FETUS	FUNCTION IN ADULT
Umbilical artery	Joins fetus to placenta	Atrophies to become the lateral umbilical ligament
Umbilical vein	Joins fetus to placenta	Becomes the round ligament of the liver (ligamentum teres)
Ductus venosus	Vessel connecting the umbilical vein to the inferior vena cava	Becomes a fibrous cord (ligamentum venosum) embedded in the wall of the liver
Foramen ovale	An opening between the two atria	Closes shortly after birth
Ductus arteriosus	Blood vessel connecting the pulmonary artery with the aorta	Closes and atrophies after birth, becoming the ligamentum arteriosum

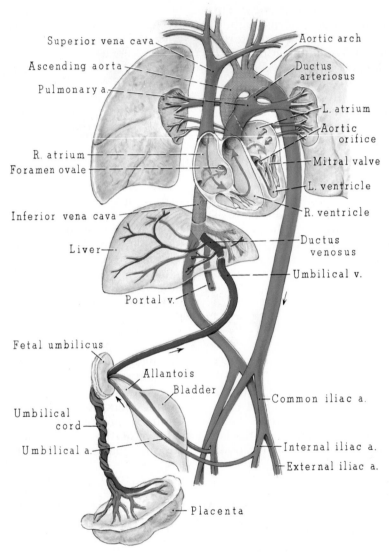

Figure 393.   Circulatory system of the fetus. (For comparison with adult circulation, see Figure 367.)

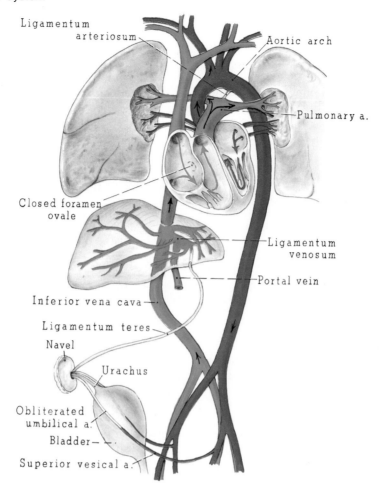

Figure 394. Adult circulation.

remainder returns to the placenta via the umbilical arteries.

At birth, changes are the result of inflation of the lungs, permitting routing of the blood through the pulmonary system instead of the umbilical vessels. The changes are described in Table 41.

SUMMARY

THE CIRCULATORY SYSTEM

Blood

1. Composed of plasma and cells — red blood cells, white blood cells and platelets.

2. Blood cell formation (hematopoiesis) in the adult occurs in the red bone marrow, located principally in the skull, vertebrae, ribs, sternum and pelvis. All blood cells originate from undifferentiated cells called stem cells.

3. Red Blood Cells

a. Function in the transport of respiratory gases (oxygen and carbon dioxide). Almost all of the oxygen in the blood is carried by hemoglobin.

b. Production is under the control of erythropoietin, a substance formed in the blood by the action of an enzyme released principally by the kidney called renal erythropoietin factor.

c. Life span is about 80 to 120 days. Aged cells are destroyed principally in the spleen. Their destruction gives rise to the bile pigment bilirubin.

d. Deficiency in the amount of oxygen transported by red blood cells results

in anemia. It is most commonly caused by
   (1) A decrease in the rate of formation of red blood cells (as in pernicious anemia)
   (2) Insufficient hemoglobin synthesis (as in iron deficiency anemia)
   (3) Increased rate of destruction of red blood cells (as in sickle cell anemia)

4. White Blood Cells (Leukocytes)

a. Three general types: granulocytes, lymphocytes and monocytes.
b. Neutrophils, the most numerous granulocytes, are phagocytic; the granules are lysosomes.
c. Lymphocytes function in the immune response.
d. Monocytes become transformed into macrophages at sites of infection.

5. Platelets (Thrombocytes)

Cytoplasmic fragments of megakaryocytes; essential for normal blood clotting.

6. Blood Coagulation (Clotting)

a. In the initial phase, platelets clump and fuse to form a temporary seal at the site of injury.
b. Retraction of platelet pseudopods with enmeshed fibrin produces a hard clot.
c. Thrombin promotes clumping of platelets and functions as an enzyme, converting fibrinogen, a soluble protein, into thrombin monomers, which assemble into insoluble fibrin threads.
d. Active thrombin is formed from an inactive precursor, prothrombin, by the action of prothrombin activator.
e. Two pathways, extrinsic and intrinsic, lead to the formation of prothrombin activator.

7. Blood Grouping

a. **ABO series**
   (1) Blood types A, B, AB, and O are named for the antigens contained in the red blood cells.
   (2) Type O individuals have no antigens and are, therefore, universal blood donors.
   (3) Type AB individuals, with antigens A and B, are universal blood recipients.
b. **Rh factor:** Problem arises if offspring of an Rh positive father and Rh negative mother is Rh positive and, at the time of delivery, infant's blood enters the blood stream of the mother. Antibodies produced by mother could cause hemolytic anemia in subsequent Rh positive fetus.

Divisions of the Circulatory System

The circulatory system consists of (1) the heart, a muscular pump with two receiving and two pumping chambers, and (2) two closed circuits, the pulmonary circulation, carrying blood from the right ventricle to the respiratory surfaces of the lungs and back to the left atrium, and the systemic circulation, carrying blood from the left ventricle to the remaining parts of the body and back to the right atrium.

Structure of the Heart

1. Pericardium

Fibroserous sac enclosing heart. Pericardial fluid between parietal pericardium (lining fibrous pericardial coat) and visceral pericardium (lining heart) lubricates membranes.

2. Wall

a. Epicardium (external), the visceral pericardium
b. Myocardium (middle), the cardiac muscle
c. Endocardium (inner), the endothelium

3. Chambers

a. Right and left atria (receiving chambers)
b. Right and left ventricles (pumping chambers)

4. Valves

a. Atrioventricular (bicuspid, left; tricuspid, right) open from atria into ventricles
b. Semilunar (pulmonary and aortic) open from ventricles into pulmonary artery and aorta

5. Blood Supply

a. Right and left coronary arteries (first branches of aorta)

b. Drained principally by coronary sinus into right atrium.

Cardiac Cycle

1. Rhythmic cycle of contraction (systole) and relaxation (diastole).

2. During systole, when ventricular pressure rises above aortic and pulmonary pressure, blood is ejected from ventricles; during diastole, when ventricular pressure falls below atrial pressure, blood flows into the ventricles.

3. The interval between the first and second heart sounds is an approximate measure of length of systole (ordinarily half as long as diastole).

a. First sound (low pitch) associated with closure of atrioventricular valves

b. Second (higher pitch) associated with closure of semilunar valves.

Cardiac Output

1. Stroke volume (volume ejected per beat) times beats per minute is called cardiac output. Under resting conditions it is approximately 5 liters per minute.

2. As venous return increases, stretched cardiac muscle fibers contract more forcefully, enabling the heart to effectively eject a larger volume of blood.

3. Increasing the heart rate with no increase in venous return has limited effect on cardiac output because shortened diastole reduces filling of ventricles.

The Heartbeat

1. The heart is intrinsically rhythmic—it beats when isolated from its nerve supply.

2. The generation and spread of electrical impulses responsible for the heartbeat is the function of specialized neuromuscular tissue: the SA node, AV node and Purkinje system.

a. The beat arises in the SA node (pacemaker).

b. The impulse spreads through the atria, initiating their contraction, to the AV node.

c. The Purkinje system, arising from the AV node, distributes the impulse to all parts of the ventricles, initiating ventricular muscle excitation and contraction.

3. **The electrocardiogram is a record of the spread of electrical activity through the muscle of the heart.**

a. The P wave registers excitation of the atria, the QRS complex, the spread of activity through the ventricles.

b. The T wave records the recovery in the ventricles.

4. **Innervation of the SA node by the autonomic nervous system makes possible homeostatic regulation of the heart rate. Parasympathetic (vagus nerve) stimulation decreases, sympathetic stimulation increases, the heart rate.**

Blood Vessels

1. **The inner surface of the entire circulatory system is lined with endothelium.**

2. **Arteries contain two distinct additional layers:**

a. Tunica media (middle coat)—smooth muscle intermingled with noncellular connective tissue elements, especially elastic fibers

b. Tunica adventitia—fibroelastic connective tissue

3. **Arterioles contain little or no tunica adventitia; smallest consist of endothelium surrounded by a single, spiraling layer of smooth muscle.**

4. **Capillaries are simply thin endothelial tubes.**

5. **Venules contain small amounts of collagenous tissue surrounding the endothelium.**

6. **Veins have three coats similar to those of arteries, but much thinner, and valves which open toward the heart and prevent backflow when closed.**

7. **Arteries and arterioles conduct blood from the heart to capillaries, where nutrients pass to the tissues and wastes to**

the blood; venules and veins carry blood from the capillaries to the heart.

Blood Pressure

1. Usually expressed as the ratio of systolic pressure in mm Hg to diastolic pressure in mm Hg. Average normal ratio is 120/80. Hypertension usually defined as ratio exceeding 165/95.

2. Increasing cardiac output and/or peripheral resistance (resistance of blood flow through the arterioles) increases average arterial pressure and vice versa. Peripheral resistance is altered by constriction or dilation of arterioles.

3. Expansion of elastic walls of arteries reduces buildup of systolic pressure; elastic recoil of arteries prevents excessive fall in diastolic pressure.

4. The major centers for regulating peripheral resistance and the rate and force of contraction of the heart are the vasomotor and cardiac centers of the medulla. The most important regulatory mechanism mediated by these centers is the baroreceptor reflex, involving receptors in the aortic arch and carotid arteries sensitive to changes in arterial blood pressure. A fall in pressure reduces the rate of impulses from the baroreceptors to the medullary centers. The major effect is constriction of arterioles in skeletal muscle, skin, and splanchnic region as a result of an increase in sympathetic nerve stimulation of arteriolar smooth muscle. The heart rate may also increase. A rise in blood pressure has the reverse effect. Contraction of the heart with greater force, as occurs during exercise, is brought about by increased sympathetic stimulation of the ventricles.

The Lymphatic System

chapter 11

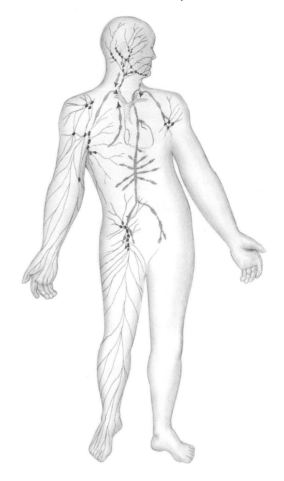

Objectives

The aim of this chapter is to enable the student to:

List the components of the lymphatic system.

Follow the course of lymph from the intercellular space to the blood stream.

Explain the functions of the lymphatic system.

Describe the organs related to the lymphatic system.

Distinguish between the B cell and T cell immune systems.

COMPONENTS OF THE LYMPHATIC SYSTEM

Originating in the tissue spaces of the body is an entirely separate vessel system serving as an accessory system for the flow of fluid from tissue spaces into the circulation. This is called the *lymphatic system*.

The lymphatic system consists of lymph capillaries, lymphatic vessels, lymphatic ducts, and lymph nodes. Lymph capillaries originate as microscopic blind ends and converge to form larger and larger vessels, which drain into two main trunks, the *thoracic duct*, which empties into the left subclavian vein at its junction with the

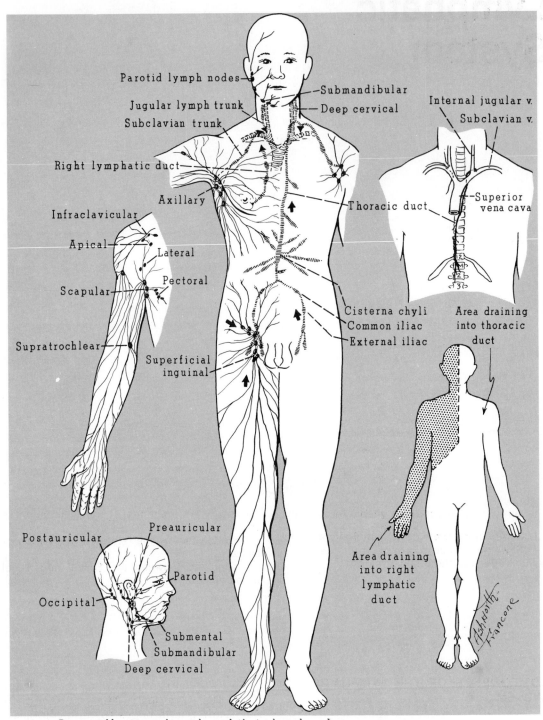

Deep collecting channels and their lymph nodes

Superficial collecting channels and their lymph nodes

Figure 395.   The lymphatic system and drainage.

internal jugular vein, and the *right lymphatic duct,* which empties into the right subclavian vein at its junction with the right internal jugular vein (Fig. 395). Lymph nodes, situated at intervals in the course of the lymphatic vessels, are especially numerous along the main tributaries that empty into the thoracic duct or right lymphatic duct.

Tissue fluid in the lymphatic vessels is called **lymph** (L. *lympha,* water). Its composition is similar to that of plasma, except for the low concentration of proteins. Lymph contains large numbers of white cells, particularly lymphocytes. It is generally a clear liquid, but lymph from the intestines becomes milky after a meal. The milky appearance results from the presence of minute, protein-coated lipid globules (chylomicrons) collected from the alimentary tract. Such lipid-laden lymph is called *chyle.*

FUNCTIONS OF THE LYMPHATIC SYSTEM

The lymphatic system has three main functions:

1. *Conservation of plasma proteins and fluid.* The lymph circulation returns to the blood stream vital substances, chiefly proteins, that have leaked out of the capillaries along with accumulated interstitial fluid.

2. *Defense against disease.* The lymphatic system protects the body against disease-producing microorganisms and other invading foreign substances in two ways:

    a. By *phagocytosis.* Macrophages lining the channels of lymph nodes phagocytize and digest foreign matter.

    b. By the *immune response.* Two types of lymphocytes in lymph nodes proliferate in response to contact with foreign substances, giving rise to specialized cells that manufacture antibodies or to cells that inactivate the invading agent by other means (see page 416 for a description of the immune response).

3. *Lipid absorption.* Intestinal lymphatics are the pathways for the absorption of digested lipids from the alimentary canal.

LYMPHATICS

Lymph Capillaries. Lymph capillaries, the smallest conducting vessels of the lymphatic system, are thin-walled tubes composed of a single layer of overlapping endothelial cells attached by anchoring filaments to the surrounding connective tissue. The interior overlapping edges of the cells seem to act as valves, forming openings into the capillaries through which fluid can enter and, when closed by back-flow, preventing outflow.

Lymph Vessels. Lymph vessels, into which the lymph capillaries drain, have three-layered walls similar to the walls of veins, and valves, more numerous than in veins, which permit lymph to flow in only one direction. These valves give lymph vessels a characteristic beaded appearance.

Lymph is propelled along lymph vessels by the massaging action of skeletal muscles on the vessels, pressure changes secondary to breathing (decreasing in the thorax and increasing in the abdomen during inspiration), and the contraction of stretched smooth muscle of the vessel walls, providing an intrinsic pumping mechanism. Each segment of a vessel between valves functions as an independent pump as it stretches upon filling and contracts to force lymph forward into the next section, which in turn contracts. Other factors contributing to the flow of lymph include the continuous formation of new lymph pushing old lymph forward and the pulsations of arteries.

Thoracic Duct. The thoracic duct, the largest lymph vessel in the body, originates in the abdomen at the upper end of the *cisterna chyli,* an elongated sac located in the right lumbar region of the abdominal cavity under the diaphragm. The cisterna is a receiving area for lymph from the three major lymph vessels—the right lumbar, left lumbar, and intestinal trunks. The right and left lumbar trunks convey lymph from the lower extremities, the pelvis, the kidneys, the suprarenal glands, and the deep lymphatics of the abdominal walls. The intestinal trunk carries lymph from the stomach, the spleen, a major portion of the liver, and the small intestine. The thoracic duct ascends to the right side of the lower

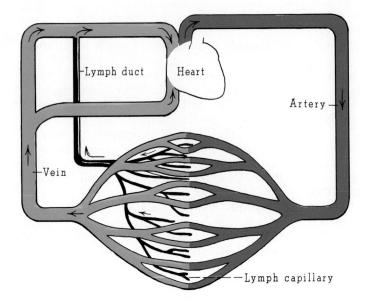

Figure 396. Diagrammatic representation of lymphatic system, showing its
relationship to the circulatory system.

thoracic vertebral bodies. It is located
between the thoracic aorta and the azygos
vein. At the level of the aortic arch, the
thoracic duct crosses obliquely to the left
and continues superiorly, lying to the left
side of the esophagus. The thoracic duct
arches laterally behind the left carotid
sheath at the root of the neck and enters the
left subclavian vein at its junction with the
left internal jugular vein.

Right Lymphatic Duct. The right lymphatic duct is a vessel one-half inch in
length lying on the scalenus anterior muscle. It joins the right subclavian vein at its
junction with the right internal jugular vein.
The right lymphatic duct returns lymph
from the upper surface of the right lobe of
the liver, the right lung and pleura, the right
side of the heart, the right arm, and the right
side of the head and neck.

IMPORTANCE OF LYMPH FLOW

It has been estimated from studies in dogs
with radioactively labeled plasma proteins
that in one day 50 per cent or more of the
total plasma protein is lost from the capillaries and returned to the blood stream by
the lymphatic circulation. Furthermore, the
amount of fluid filtered from the capillaries
is greater than the amount reabsorbed.
Inadequate lymph drainage can lead to an
excessive accumulation of fluid in the interstitial space, a condition called edema.

Some **lymphedemas** (edemas resulting from
deficient lymph drainage) can cause gross
disfiguring. An example is *elephantiasis,* a
specific lymphedema resulting from blockage of lymph vessels. In a form of elephantiasis common in the tropics, the blockage
follows invasion by a parasitic roundworm
(filaria).

LYMPH NODES

Lymph nodes are small oval bodies found
at intervals in the course of the lymphatic
vessels. Each node consists of lymphatic
tissue enclosed in a fibrous connective
tissue capsule (Fig. 397).

Lymph passes through several groups of
nodes before entering the blood. It enters
the nodes through several afferent channels
(sinuses) and leaves through one or two
efferent channels. As mentioned, the sinuses, lined with macrophages, act as filter-
ing beds for removing potentially harmful
matter before it can enter the blood stream.
Functioning in this way, the lymph nodes
are part of the **reticuloendothelial system**
(see Chapter 3, page 66).

Lymph nodes usually appear in groups,
among which are the following: superficial
nodes, including the cervical (neck), axillary (axilla), and inguinal (groin) nodes;
deep nodes, including the iliac (in the iliac
fossa), lumbar (adjacent to the lumbar vertebrae), thoracic (root of the lungs), mesen-

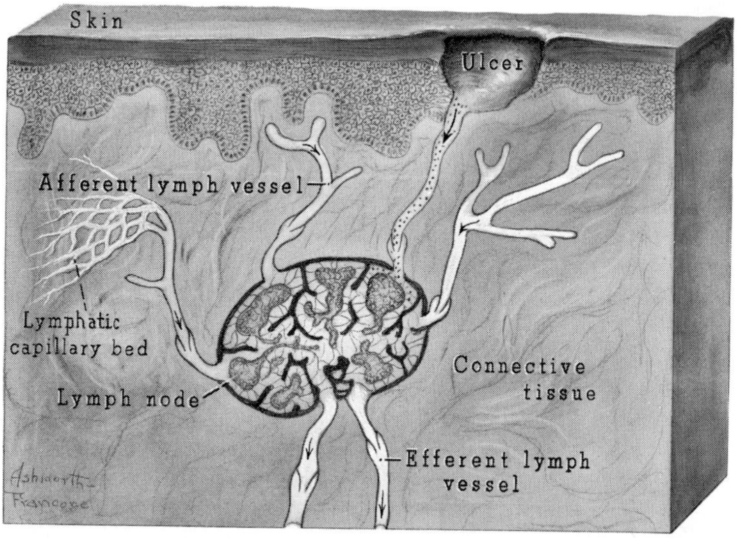

Figure 397. Diagrammatic drawing of a lymph node in the area of an infected ulcer.

teric (attachment of the mesentery of the small intestine), and portal (portal fissure of the liver) nodes.

CLINICAL CONSIDERATIONS

Lymph nodes filter products resulting from bacterial and nonbacterial inflammation and prevent the products from entering the general circulation. This process often produces tenderness and swelling in nodes of an infected area. If bacteria in an area drained by a node become too numerous, they may attack the node itself, resulting in an abscess (a localized collection of pus in a cavity formed when tissue disintegrates).

Lymphangitis is an inflammation of a lymphatic vessel in which narrow red streaks may be seen in the skin extending from the infected area to the draining group of lymph nodes. These streaks represent inflamed subcutaneous lymph vessels.

Lymph node enlargement may be local or widespread and may be accompanied by signs of acute inflammation, including heat and tenderness. As a result of inflammation, nodes may fuse with one another instead of remaining discrete. Causes of lymph node enlargement include infection, allergy, primary disease of the node (such as Hodgkin's disease, a cancer of the lymph nodes), leukemia, and spread of malignant disease from elsewhere in the body.

One feature of the lymphatic system is its significance in the spread of tumors. Car-

cinoma, cancer arising in epithelial tissues, occasionally produces a secondary growth in regional lymph nodes. Many of these secondary growths (metastases) result from tumor emboli detaching from the point of origin and lodging in nodes of the lymphatic vessels. In general if the tumor has reached the lymph nodes at the time of surgery, the outlook for survival of the patient is less favorable.

RELATED ORGANS

Three organs closely related to the lymphatic system are the spleen, tonsils, and thymus. All of these organs are composed largely of lymphoid tissue, a specialized form of connective tissue characterized by a framework of reticular tissue (see Chapter 3, page 65) and the presence of lymphocytes.

Spleen

Location and Structure. The spleen is a soft, vascular, oval body, 5 inches long and 3 inches wide, weighing approximately 7 ounces. It lies in the left upper abdomen beneath the diaphragm and behind the lower ribs and costal cartilages (Fig. 398).

The splenic hilum is the site of entrance and exit of the vessels of the spleen. The body of the spleen has a covering of elastic tissue and smooth muscle. From this in-

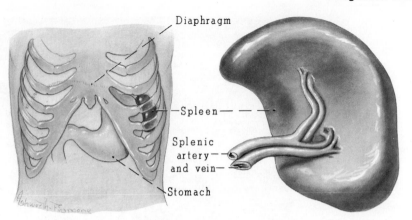

Figure 398. The spleen and its relation to the stomach and rib cage.

vestment partitions pass into the substance, reaching the hilum and dividing the organ into compartments. In these compartments one can see a spongelike network of cells separated by many blood channels called sinusoids. The elastic nature of the framework allows the spleen to vary its size considerably.

Functions. The spleen has four major functions.

1. *Blood destruction.* Old red blood cells, having reached their normal life span of approximately 120 days, are destroyed in all parts of the reticuloendothelial system, including the lymph nodes and spleen. The spleen, however, is the major site of erythrocyte destruction.

2. *Immunologic function.* The spleen, along with other lymphoid tissues, participates in the immune response (described in the following section).

3. *Blood storage.* The spleen serves as a reservoir for blood or, more specifically, for red blood cells, as most of the plasma is returned to the circulation whereas RBC are enmeshed in the splenic pulp. Marked contraction of the spleen occurs during muscular exercise, thereby releasing RBC to aid in oxygen transport to active muscles. The spleen undergoes rhythmic variations in size in response to physiologic demands, such as exercise and hemorrhage, and thus influences the volume of circulating blood. The volume of stored blood may vary from 1000 to as little as 50 ml.

4. *Blood filtration.* The spleen, serving as a part of the body's reticuloendothelial defense mechanism, filters microorganisms from the blood.

An individual can survive with no apparent disability if the spleen has been removed; however, diseases affecting the spleen may profoundly affect several important body functions.

Tonsils

Several groups of tonsils, forming a ring of lymphoid tissue, guard the entrance of the alimentary and respiratory tracts from bacterial invasion. The components of this ring are the palatine tonsils, nasopharyngeal tonsil (adenoids) and lingual tonsils (Figs. 399 and 400).

The **palatine tonsils,** known more commonly as the "tonsils," are two oval masses of lymphoid tissue attached to the side wall of the back of the mouth between the anterior pillar (palatoglossal arch) and posterior pillar (palatopharyngeal arch), constituting the opening between the oral cavity proper and the oropharynx (Fig. 399). The tonsils are larger in children than in adults.

The **nasopharyngeal tonsil, or adenoids,** is a mass of lymphoid tissue located in the nasal pharynx extending from the roof of the nasal pharynx to the free edge of the soft palate (Fig. 400).

The **lingual tonsils** are two masses of lymphoid tissue found on the dorsum of the tongue, extending from the vallate papillae of the tongue to the epiglottis (Fig. 400).

Chronic infection of the tonsils is not so common as was once suspected. The term "chronic tonsillitis" is frequently misused to indicate any type of sore throat occurring

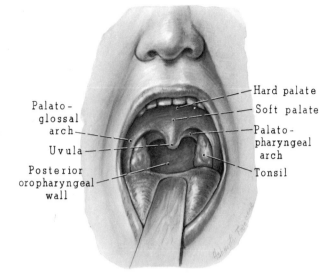

Figure 399. Relationship of tongue, uvula, and tonsils.

Palato-glossal arch

Uvula

Posterior oropharyngeal wall

Hard palate

Soft palate

Palato-pharyngeal arch

Tonsil

when the tonsils are still present. With tonsillitis, enlargement and tenderness of the anterior cervical lymph nodes are common. The tonsils may be enlarged and red or covered with pus. If both tonsils and adenoids are infected, the lymph nodes of the posterior triangle of the neck enlarge.

Fewer tonsillectomies and adenoidectomies are being performed today than were done 40 years ago. This is because recent knowledge indicates that removal of tonsils and adenoids may not significantly lower the incidence of upper respiratory infection unless the tonsils themselves have been infected. Tonsils may also be important in the development of immune bodies; however, true recurrent infection of the tonsils is still an indication for their removal by operation.

Thymus

The thymus is a flat, pinkish-gray, two-lobed organ lying high in the chest anterior to the aorta and posterior to the sternum (Fig. 401).

This gland is one of the central controls of

Figure 400. The nasopharyngeal tonsil extends from the roof of the nasal pharynx to the free edge of the soft palate; the palatine tonsils are attached to the side walls of the back of the mouth between the anterior and posterior pillars; the lingual tonsils are located on the dorsum of the tongue from the vallate papillae of the tongue to the epiglottis.

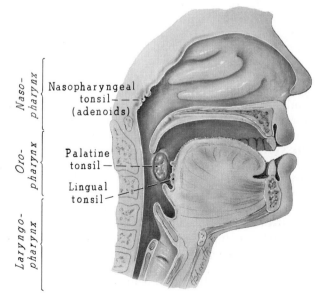

Naso-pharynx

Oro-pharynx

Laryngo-pharynx

Nasopharyngeal tonsil (adenoids)

Palatine tonsil

Lingual tonsil

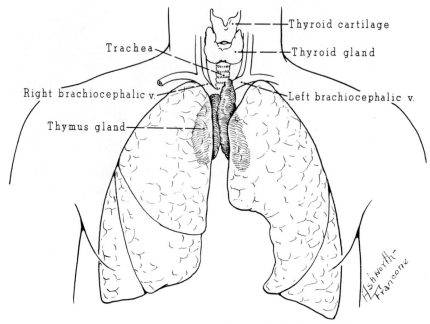

Figure 401. Location of thymus gland and relationship to lungs.

the development of the body's immunity system (described below). It is relatively large in relation to body size during fetal life and the first two years after birth. It increases in size until adolescence and then begins to atrophy.

THE IMMUNE RESPONSE

The immune response not only resists invasion by infectious microorganisms but also functions to identify and destroy whatever can be described as "nonself," including transplanted organs and malignant cells. Two immune systems can be distinguished; in each a different population of lymphocytes is activated and a different agent combats the invasion. In one, the **B cell system,** the response is mediated by proteins, called **antibodies;** in the other, the **T cell system,** the response is mediated by **specialized cells** sensitized to foreign substances. The former response is called *humoral immunity,* the latter *cellular,* or *cell-mediated, immunity.* The B cell system is most effective against acute bacterial infections, such as those caused by streptococci, pneumococci, some influenza bacilli and meningococci, and against viral reinfections. The T cell system is most active in

combating viruses, fungi and bacteria causing chronic infections, such as tuberculosis. Cell-mediated immunity is also especially active against malignant cells and the cells of transplanted organs.

B and T lymphocytes have a common parent cell; namely, the *stem cell* of the red bone marrow (see Chapter 10, page 335). However, T cell differentiation, that is, the transformation of precursor cells into mature T cells, takes place in the *thymus gland* (hence the name T cell). This occurs during embryological development and early childhood. The site of B cell differentiation in humans is unknown, but it is presumed to occur in the equivalent of the *bursa of Fabricius* (hence the name B cell) of birds, a lymphoid organ located at the posterior end of the gastrointestinal tract. In birds this organ is essential for the development of mature B cells. B and T cells are found in lymph, the blood stream, and lymphoid tissue, which constitutes the bulk of lymphoid organs and is found in various locations as diffuse lymphoid tissue, especially in the digestive and respiratory tracts. Lymphocytes are present in greatest number in lymph nodes. The role of the thymus gland in immunity ends when the maturation of T cells is completed.

The triggering agents of the immune

response are called **antigens.** These are large molecules, such as proteins or polysaccharides, and are generally surface components of foreign substances. Antigens provoke the same response in B and T cells: rapid cell division, with the formation of distinct *clones* (colonies of cells arising from a single parent cell) in lymphoid tissue. The cells produced by successive cell divisions become more and more specialized. The end result of B cell proliferation is the formation of cells, called **plasma cells,** that manufacture (at a rate of about 2000 per second) identical antibodies constructed to combine selectively with the triggering antigen. The specialized cells formed in T cell clones are sensitive to and capable of binding the triggering antigen. B cell response to many antigens requires assistance from T cells. In such cases antibodies will not be produced unless "helper" T cells are present.

At one time it was generally believed that antigens entered antibody-producing cells and acted as templates for molding antibodies into complementary shapes. This "instructive" theory has been discarded in favor of the "selection" theory first proposed by Sir Macfarlane Burnet in the 1950's. According to the **selection theory,** the antigen simply selects cells endowed with genes coded for the synthesis of matching antibodies. The selection is accomplished by a "fit" between patches on the antigens called *antigenic determinants* and binding sites on receptors (glycoproteins) on the surface of B cells. The receptors apparently are antibody molecules with antigen-combining sites identical to the combining sites of antibodies later synthesized by plasma cells.

Since antibodies are proteins classified as globulins (gamma group—see Chapter 10, page 334) and have immunological properties, they are called **immunoglobulins.** There are five classes of immunoglobulins, designated IgM, IgG, IgA, IgD and IgE. IgG is the most common, accounting for about 70 per cent of the circulating antibodies. IgG consists of four protein chains, two heavy and two light (Fig. 402). Each half, one heavy and one light chain, is identical to the other half. (This basic four-chain unit is common to all antibodies, but in some classes the units combine into multiunit forms.) At one end of each chain

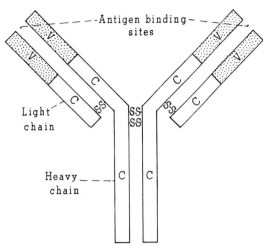

Figure 402. Schematic drawing of an IgG antibody showing the arrangement of two heavy and two light polypeptide chains. Chains are divided into a variable (V) portion, in which the amino acid sequence varies from one IgG antibody to another, and a constant (C) portion, in which the amino acid sequence is the same for all IgG antibodies.

the amino acid sequence varies from one IgG antibody to another. These *variable regions* provide two antigen-binding sites. The diversity of amino acid sequences in the variable regions makes possible the wide range of configurations necessary for binding a great variety of antigens. The variable regions then confer **antigen-binding specificity.** The amino acid sequence of the remaining portion of each chain is the same in all IgG antibodies. This *constant region* determines the class of the antibody and is responsible for functional properties of antibodies other than antigen binding. For example, a segment of the constant region of IgG binds a family of serum enzymes known as **complement,** thereby initiating a sequence of reactions capable of destroying cells.

The term complement was originally meant to indicate that these blood proteins helped antibodies defend against infectious organisms. As it turned out, the antibody's role is to identify the invading agent as foreign and activate and bind complement. The complement reaction sequence leads to the formation of surface lesions that can kill the invading cell. In addition, some complement products attract *phagocytes* (neutrophils and macrophages) to the scene. Others promote binding of these phagocytic cells to the invading cells. Still others stimulate the release of histamine by mast cells. Histamine increases the permeability of capillaries, facilitating penetration of phagocytes into the region where the immune response is in progress. These actions increase the susceptibility of invading microorganisms to phagocytosis (the process of facilitating phagocytosis is called *opsonization).*

Promoting phagocytosis seems to be the principal means by which sensitized cells derived from T cells combat invading agents. After binding to antigens they release substances that attract macrophages to the vicinity and increase their activity.

Immunological Memory. One of the distinctive features of the immune response is immunological memory—the ability of individuals who have recovered from an infection to respond more effectively and vigorously to reinfection. This is explained, in large part, by the formation (in clones of B and T cells during the first attack) of so-called *memory cells,* which give rise to clones of their own when the infectious agent reappears some time later. In effect, the first encounter with an antigen greatly expands cells to be selected during a subsequent invasion.

Immunological Tolerance and Autoimmune Diseases. The immune system, as we have seen, distinguishes between self and nonself. The lack of response by the immune system to self is referred to as *tolerance.* It is generally believed that tolerance develops in the fetus as a result of the destruction, following contact with native, potentially antigenic substances, of lymphocytes that would produce self-recognizing antibodies. Supporting this view is an observation made in an unusual pair of fraternal twins who shared a common placental circulation. (Such twins, a rarity, have two blood groups, their own and that of their twin.) These twins accepted skin cross-grafting as if they were identical, rather than fraternal, twins.

Occasionally the tolerance mechanism goes awry and the immune system attacks one's own tissues. When this happens, the resulting disorder is called an *autoimmune disease.* It has been suggested that in some cases the autoimmunity may arise because tolerance fails to develop in the first place. Isolation of some substances from the circulation, as in the interior of the thyroid

gland, may keep them from making contact with lymphocytes during the time the immune system is developing. If, for some reason, such a substance later gains access to the body fluids, it may act as an antigen and stimulate an immune response. A number of thyroid diseases do, in fact, appear to result from autoimmunity. Other autoimmune diseases include myasthenia gravis (see Chapter 7, page 155) and rheumatic fever, a condition in which the heart and joints are subject to autoimmune damage weeks following a specific type of acute streptococcal infection.

Allergen-Reagin Reactions. IgE, one of the classes of antibodies, is responsible for allergic reactions known as **anaphylaxis.** These include, among other reactions, hay fever, asthma, hives and reactions to bee stings or to the injection of certain drugs. IgE antibodies are called *reagins;* antigens that react with IgE are called *allergens.* Reagins have the property of adhering to **mast cells** and, when allergens enter the body and react with reagins affixed to mast cells, the mast cells rupture, releasing massive amounts of *histamine* and other substances. Histamine passing into the circulation can cause widespread vasodilation and increased capillary permeability. Excessive loss of fluid from the circulation following these events can cause sudden death from circulatory shock. Histamine is also responsible for the swellings in the nasal passages in hay fever and in the skin in hives. In asthma, the periodic attacks are precipitated by a substance released from mast cells that causes spasm of bronchiolar smooth muscle.

SUMMARY

THE LYMPHATIC SYSTEM

Components of Lymphatic System and Lymph Flow

1. Blind end lymph capillaries, into which interstitial fluid flows, branch throughout the intercellular space and converge to form larger and larger lymph vessels. Eventually two main trunks are formed, the thoracic duct, which empties into the left subclavian vein, and the right lymphatic duct, which empties into the right subclavian vein.

2. Valves in lymphatic vessels allow lymph to flow in only one direction—from the tissue spaces to the blood stream. Lymph is propelled largely by the massaging action of skeletal muscles, pressure changes accompanying breathing, and contraction of stretched smooth muscle of vessel walls.

3. Lymph is similar in composition to plasma except for the low concentration of proteins.

4. Lymph passes through groups of lymph nodes before reaching the blood stream.

Functions of Lymphatic System

1. Returns to the blood stream protein and fluid lost from the capillaries.
2. Defense against disease
   a. Phagocytic action of macrophages in lymph nodes
   b. Immune response by lymphocytes in lymph nodes.

3. Lipid absorption.

Immune Response

1. Function of lymphocytes in lymphoid tissue, especially the lymph nodes.

2. Two immune systems, the B cell system (humoral immunity) and the T cell system (cell-mediated immunity), can be distinguished. Both B and T cell lymphocytes respond to specific antigens by rapidly dividing to form clones. Plasma cells formed in B cell clones produce antibodies, which combine with the triggering antigens and initiate events that lead to the destruction of these antigens. Specialized antigen-sensitive cells produced in T cell clones bind to the invading antigens and initiate events that lead to their elimination.

3. Both B and T cells are derived from a common parent cell, the stem cell of the red bone marrow. T cell differentiation occurs in the thymus gland; B cell differentiation presumably occurs in the equivalent of the bursa of Fabricius of birds.

4. The B cell system is most effective against acute bacterial infections (including those caused by streptococci, pneumococci and meningococci) and viral reinfections. The T cell system is most active against viruses, fungi and chronic bacterial infections (such as tuberculosis). Cell-mediated immunity is also especially active against cancer and organ transplants.

chapter 12

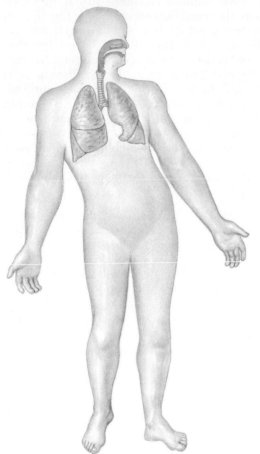

The Respiratory System

Objectives

The aim of this chapter is to enable the student to:

Describe the structures forming the upper respiratory tract and the divisions of the bronchial tree within the lungs.

Describe the structure and function of the alveoli of the lungs.

Explain the importance of the surfactant coating of the alveoli.

Explain the roles of the diaphragm and external intercostal muscles in breathing.

Outline the pressure changes in the thorax and lungs during inspiration and expiration.

Define the different types of abnormal breathing.

Discuss the factors influencing the efficiency of breathing.

Describe the mechanisms of oxygen and carbon dioxide transport in the blood.

Explain how a normal respiratory rhythm is maintained.

Discuss the regulation of pulmonary ventilation.

Describe the characteristics of several respiratory disorders.

HISTORY

The rising and falling of the chest proved mysterious to the Greeks and Romans as

they observed the changes in rate and rhythm during excitement and fear. To them, air was an intangible, divine spirit known as "pneuma," presumably entering the body at birth and leaving it at death. Aristotle actually believed that respiratory activity cooled the blood. Five hundred years later, in A.D. 170, Galen showed that the arteries were filled with blood and that the lungs added and removed something from the blood. In addition, Galen recognized several of the respiratory muscles and nerves. Circulation of the blood was traced through the lungs in the sixteenth century by Realdo Colombo. Scheele, a Swedish chemist, demonstrated in 1770 that air contained an invisible material essential to life and to the burning of a flame. In 1785, Priestley and Lavoisier showed that this substance was oxygen.

GENERAL FUNCTION AND ANATOMY

The term respiration is defined as the union of oxygen with food in the cells, with the subsequent release of energy for work, for heat, and for the release of carbon dioxide and water. The respiratory system functions to supply oxygen for the metabolic needs of the cells and to remove one of the waste materials of cellular metabolism, carbon dioxide. This involves the process of *external respiration*, absorption of O_2 and removal of CO_2 from lungs, and *internal respiration*, gaseous exchanges between the cells of the body and their fluid medium. The *nose, pharynx, larynx, trachea,* and *bronchi* are parts of an open passage leading from the exterior to the lungs comprising the upper respiratory tract. In the lungs, the successive divisions of the bronchial tree (the smaller bronchi, *bronchioles* and *alveolar ducts*) lead to the **alveoli**, the functional units of the lungs. Gaseous exchange between blood and air occurs only in the alveoli.

The Nose

The term nose includes the external nose, that part of the upper respiratory tract that protrudes from the face, and the nasal cavity; only a small part of the nasal cavity is in the external nose, most of it lying over the roof of the mouth. Figures 403 and 404 show the location of cartilage and bones in the nose. The septal cartilage forms the anterior part of the nasal septum, which divides the nasal cavity into two lateral halves. The lateral cartilages are winglike expansions of the septal cartilages. The alar cartilages are U-shaped and are located on the sides of the nose below the lateral cartilages. The external openings of the nasal cavities are called the anterior nares, or nostrils.

The bony roof of the nose consists of an anterior portion, the nasal and frontal bones; a middle portion, the cribriform plate of the ethmoid; and a posterior portion, parts of the sphenoid, vomer, and palatine bones. The floor of the nose is formed by the maxillary and palatine bones.

The nasal cavity, or internal nose, is composed of two wedge-shaped cavities separated by a septum formed largely by

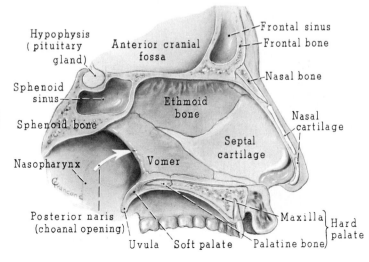

Figure 403. Sagittal section through nose showing components of nasal septum.

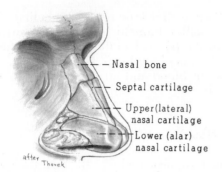

Figure 404. The lower portion of the external nose has a cartilaginous rather than a skeletal framework consisting of a septal cartilage, two lateral cartilages, and a series of smaller cartilages.

the perpendicular plate of the ethmoid bone, the vomer bone, and the septal cartilage (Fig. 403). The crests of the nasal bones form a small part of the superior aspect of the septum; the crests of the maxilla and palatine bones complete the inferior aspect. (See pages 97–100 for supplemental diagrams.)

The lateral wall of the nose has three bony projections, the superior, middle, and inferior conchae, or turbinates, beneath which lie the superior, middle, and inferior meatuses (air passages), respectively. Each concha is covered by a thick mucous membrane, functioning to warm and moisten air (Fig. 405).

The anterior portion of the nasal cavity is

lined with a thick layer of *stratified squamous epithelium* containing sebaceous glands. The spongy conchae increase the amount of tissue surface within the nose, and the respiratory epithelium of the conchae secretes mucus. Mucous membranes also filter out bacteria and dust particles. Air must be warmed; otherwise the tissue lining the respiratory tract functions poorly. Absence of moisture for even a few minutes destroys the cilia of the respiratory epithelium.

The nose filters substances in two ways. (1) Vibrissae (the hairs that can be seen in the nose) around the anterior nares filter out the coarsest bodies, such as insects. (2) Air currents passing over the moist mucosa in curved pathways deposit fine particles, such as dust, powder, and smoke, against the wall. These fine particles are subsequently conveyed to the pharynx and swallowed.

The mucous membrane of the nose continues anteriorly with the skin lining the vestibule and posteriorly with the mucous membrane of the nasopharynx. The posterior part of the nasal cavities and the nasopharynx is lined with *pseudostratified ciliated columnar epithelium.* The cilia wave back and forth about 12 times per second and help the mucus to clean the air. The superior portion of the nose is lined with neuroepithelial tissue containing olfactory cells which function in the sensation of smell.

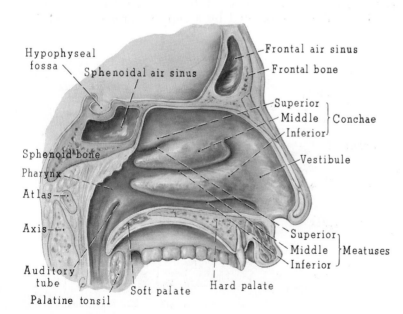

Figure 405. Nasal septum removed, showing lateral aspect of nasal cavity with conchae (turbinates).

The Paranasal Sinuses (Figs. 406 and 407)

Paranasal sinuses are air-containing spaces communicating with the nasal cavity and lined with a mucous membrane. Although they are paired, they are commonly asymmetrical. The paired sinuses include the *maxillary, frontal, ethmoid,* and *sphenoid sinuses.* The primary function of paranasal sinuses is to lighten the bones of the skull. Secondarily, they function to provide mucus for the nasal cavity and act as resonant chambers for the production of sound.

The maxillary sinuses are the largest of the paranasal sinuses. Each is located in the maxilla and opens into the middle meatus. The frontal sinuses, located in the frontal bone superior and medial to the orbit of the eye, empty into the middle meatus. The ethmoid air cells are numerous, irregularly shaped air spaces that open into the middle and superior meatuses.

The sphenoid sinus is in the sphenoid bone. It is located posterior to the eye, behind the upper portion of the nasal cavity. An infection of the sphenoid sinus can damage vision because of its proximity to the optic nerve. Drainage from the sphenoid sinus is into the superior meatus.

The nasolacrimal duct extends from the eye to the inferior meatus and drains the lacrimal secretions which constantly bathe the surface of the eye (see Chapter 9).

The Pharynx

The pharynx is a musculomembranous tube, 5 inches in length, extending from the base of the skull to the esophagus. The posterior aspect abuts against the cervical vertebrae. The pharynx is divided into three parts—nasal, oral, and laryngeal.

The *nasopharynx* lies behind the nose; the *oropharynx* lies behind the mouth. The nasopharynx and oropharynx are separated by the soft palate, a membranous sheet of muscle covered by mucous membrane. The

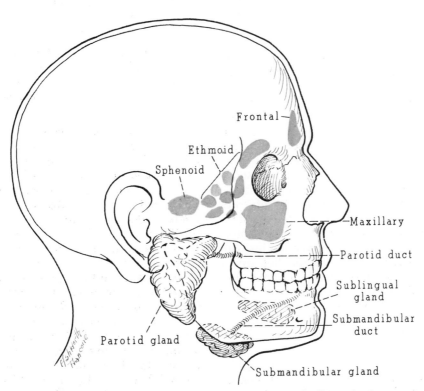

Figure 406.   Lateral view of head showing sinuses and salivary glands.

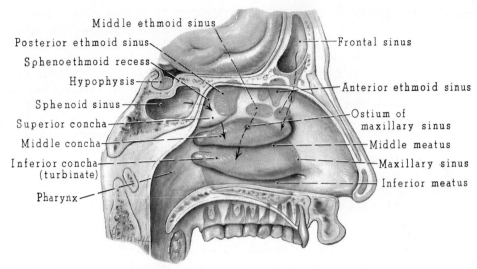

Middle ethmoid sinus

Posterior ethmoid sinus

Sphenoethmoid recess

Hypophysis

Sphenoid sinus

Superior concha

Middle concha

Inferior concha (turbinate)

Pharynx

Frontal sinus

Anterior ethmoid sinus

Ostium of maxillary sinus

Middle meatus

Maxillary sinus

Inferior meatus

Figure 407. Sagittal section of the nasal cavity showing anatomy of the sinuses and direction of normal drainage. Note that drainage from frontal, maxillary, and anterior sinuses is into the middle meatus, while the posterior ethmoid and sphenoid sinuses drain into the superior meatus.

laryngopharynx lies below the hyoid bone and behind the larynx.

There are four openings into the nasopharynx—two from the auditory (eustachian) tubes and two from the nose, the *posterior nares.* The oropharynx has a single opening, called the *fauces,* which communicates with the mouth. The laryngopharynx opens into the larynx and esophagus.

The *adenoids,* or pharyngeal tonsil, lie in the nasopharynx near the posterior nares. If it becomes enlarged, it can obstruct the posterior nares (see Figure 400, Chapter 11). When an individual has enlarged adenoids, mouth breathing and a nasal or plugged quality to the voice develop. The palatine tonsils at the lateral margins of the throat and the lingual tonsils at the base of the tongue are located in the oropharynx. The palatine tonsils are commonly referred to as "the tonsils" and are removed when the patient has a tonsillectomy (see Chapter 11). The pharynx serves as a passage for two systems—the respiratory and the digestive. It also assumes an important function in the formation of sound, particularly in the creation of vowel sounds.

The Larynx

The larynx, or "voice box" (Figs. 408 and 409) connects the pharynx with the trachea.

Its opening is at the base of the tongue. The larynx is broad superiorly and shaped like a triangular box. It joins the trachea inferiorly, where it is narrower and round. It consists of nine cartilages united by extrinsic and intrinsic muscles as well as by ligaments.

There are three paired and three unpaired cartilages of the larynx:

Unpaired	*Paired*
Thyroid	Arytenoid
Cricoid	Cuneiform
Epiglottic	Corniculate

The *thyroid* cartilage is the largest cartilage in the larynx. It gives the anterior aspect of the larynx its characteristic triangular shape and is sometimes called the "Adam's apple." In the male the thyroid cartilage increases in size at puberty.

The leaf-shaped *epiglottis* is attached to the superior border of the thyroid cartilage. It has a hinged, doorlike action at the entrance to the larynx. During swallowing, it acts as a lid to help prevent aspiration of food into the trachea. The *cricoid* cartilage is the most inferior of the nine layngeal cartilages; it is shaped like a signet ring with the signet facing posteriorly. The *arytenoid cartilages* are small and are attached to the superior portion of each cricoid lamina. The arytenoid cartilage is pyramidal in shape. The *corniculate car-*

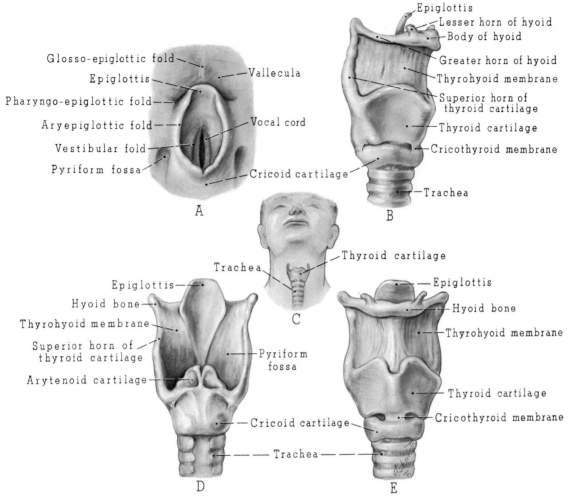

Figure 408. The larynx as viewed from above (*A*), from the side (*B*), in relation to the head and neck (*C*), from behind (*D*), and from the front (*E*).

tilages extend from the arytenoid cartilages medially and backward. Each corniculate cartilage is a small cone of elastic tissue articulating with an arytenoid cartilage. The *cuneiform cartilage* is a small elastic cartilage in the aryepiglottic fold in front of the corniculate cartilage. The vocal cords are attached to the vocal processes at the base of each arytenoid cartilage; their backward motions tense the cords.

Musculature of the Larynx. Two sets of muscles are found in the larynx, extrinsic and intrinsic. The extrinsic muscles take origin in structures surrounding the larynx and function to move the larynx. The intrinsic muscles are located within the larynx proper. These muscles open and close the glottis during inspiration and expiration. They close the laryngeal aperture and glottis during swallowing and regulate the tension of the vocal folds in the production of sound. Both the intrinsic and extrinsic muscles are composed of striated muscle fibers.

The cricothyroid joint is located on the medial and posterior surface of each plate of the thyroid cartilage. This joint permits the thyroid cartilage to swing up and down. When the thyroid cartilage swings superiorly, a higher note is produced; when it swings inferiorly, lower notes are produced.

The cricoarytenoid joint is important in movements of the vocal cords. The *rima glottidis* is a space between the cords. Pitch depends on the length and space between

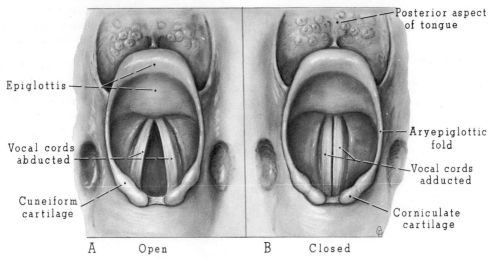

Epiglottis

Vocal cords
abducted

Cuneiform
cartilage

Posterior aspect
of tongue

Aryepiglottic
fold

Vocal cords
adducted

Corniculate
cartilage

A   Open   B   Closed

Figure 409.   Superior view of vocal cords.

the cords. In the female, the cords are shorter, more taut, and closer together, producing the characteristic high voice. In the male, the cords are longer, less taut, and farther apart, producing the characteristic low voice.

The larynx is supplied by branches of the vagus nerve, including the *recurrent laryngeal* and *superior laryngeal branches.* The recurrent laryngeal nerve enters the larynx from below and behind the cricothyroid joint. The superior nerve passes into the larynx by piercing the thyrohyoid membrane. The recurrent laryngeal nerve is mainly motor, supplying the muscles to the larynx, while the superior laryngeal nerve is chiefly sensory. If the recurrent laryngeal nerve is injured during surgery of the thyroid, hoarseness or an inability to speak may result.

Function of the Larynx.   The chief function of the larynx is *phonation.* The pitch of sound is determined by the shape and tension of the vocal cords. Long, lax cords produce low-pitched tones and short, tense cords give higher tones. The voice is refined by the nose, mouth, and pharynx, as well as by the sinuses, which act as sounding boards and resonating chambers. The organs of phonation in man are similar to those of many animals much lower in the animal hierarchy; however, man has a greater variety and control of his sounds because of greater development of the related association areas of the brain.

The Trachea

The trachea, or "windpipe," is a cylindrical tube about 4 to 5 inches in length. The trachea is flattened posteriorly where it comes into contact with the esophagus. It extends from the level of the sixth cervical vertebra to the fifth thoracic vertebra and divides into two primary bronchi. The inferior portion of the trachea is crossed by the arch of the aorta. The thyroid gland lies anterior to the second, third, and fourth tracheal rings.

The trachea consists of four layers: a mucous membrane (mucosa); submucosa; a layer containing cartilage, fibrous connective tissue, and smooth muscle; and an outer covering of connective tissue, the adventitia. The inner layer (mucous membrane) is composed of a *pseudostratified ciliated columnar epithelium* with mucus-secreting goblet cells, anchored by a basement membrane to an underlying connective tissue. These cilia sweep inhaled particles to the pharynx to be swallowed. The submucosa is loose connective tissue containing glands and fat cells. In the third layer, about 20 horseshoe-shaped hyaline cartilages form incomplete rings around the trachea, preventing its total collapse. The posterior gaps in the rings are bridged by interlacing bundles of smooth muscle. A dense connective tissue with elastic and collagenous fibers fills the spaces between the rings of cartilage. The adventitia is a loose connec-

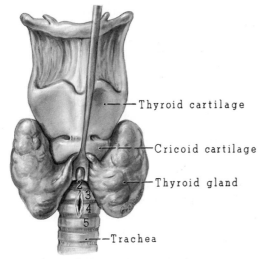

Figure 410.   Incision for a tracheotomy.

of the bronchial tree arising from the primary bronchi include: three right and two left **secondary,** or **lobar, bronchi;** 10 right and eight left **segmental bronchi;** 50 to 80 **terminal bronchioles** for each segmental bronchus; two or more **respiratory bronchioles** for each terminal bronchiole; and two or more **alveolar ducts** for each respiratory bronchiole.

Those portions of the primary bronchi external to the lungs have essentially the same structure as the trachea but are of smaller diameter. Within the lungs the bronchial cartilages assume a platelike shape, and some completely encircle the bronchi. Inferiorly, as the bronchi become narrower, the amount of cartilage decreases and no longer forms complete rings. The cartilage finally disappears at the bronchioles. With the decrease in cartilage there

tive tissue containing blood vessels and autonomic nerves.

Function of the Trachea. The trachea functions as a simple passageway for air to reach the lungs; occasionally it becomes occluded, either from swelling of the mucosal lining, accumulated secretions, or aspirations of material into it. Occlusion of the trachea necessitates either a tracheotomy or a tracheostomy (Fig. 410). The term *tracheotomy* means merely an opening into the trachea. *Tracheostomy* is a procedure in which the trachea is brought to the skin or a tube is placed into it to keep it open for a period of time. A tracheotomy or tracheostomy is performed for emergency release of obstructions at or above the level of the larynx. Symptoms of laryngeal obstruction are frightening and include difficult respiration (dyspnea) and inspiratory stridor (a harsh, high-pitched sound often heard in laryngeal obstructions).

The Bronchi and Branches

The two **primary bronchi** split from the trachea at the level of the superior border of the fifth thoracic vertebra. The right bronchus differs from the left in that it is shorter and wider and takes a more vertical course. Foreign bodies from the trachea usually enter the right bronchus because of these characteristics. The primary bronchi lie posterior to the pulmonary vessels with the left behind the aorta. Successive divisions

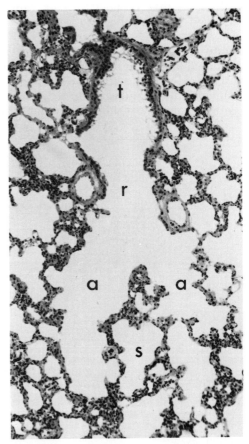

Figure 411.   Section of a lung showing a terminal bronchiole (t) leading into a respiratory bronchiole (r), which divides into two alveolar ducts (a). Alveolar sacs (s) and alveoli are also seen. (Magnified 75×.) (From Leeson, C. R., and Leeson, T. S.: Histology. 3rd ed., Philadelphia, W. B. Saunders Co., 1976.)

is a concomitant increase in smooth muscle, which is intermingled with numerous elastic fibers.

The pseudostratified ciliated columnar epithelium of the trachea continues into the bronchi, changing to simple ciliated columnar epithelium in the bronchioles and to cuboidal ciliated, without goblet cells, in the smaller terminal bronchioles. The epithelium becomes less ciliated as it approaches the alveolar ducts. Alveolar ducts are simply thin tubes composed of a single layer of squamous epithelium surrounded by fibroelastic tissue. The ducts open into **alveoli,** generally arranged in clusters forming **alveolar sacs** (see Fig. 411). Smooth muscle cells surround the openings. Three types of cells are found in alveoli: thin *squamous epithelial cells*, forming a continuous lining; larger *cuboidal epithelial cells* (known as *type II cells*) which secrete a substance that reduces surface tension (discussed in the following section); and *macrophages*, active phagocytic cells which migrate through the epithelium and are eliminated largely in the sputum. Underlying these cells is a basal lamina (filamentous collagenous fibers) adjacent to a framework of reticular and elastic fibers (alveolar septa)

housing the *alveolar capillary network,* embedded in a protein-polysaccharide ground substance.

The nerves supplying the trachea and bronchi are derived from the vagus by way of the recurrent laryngeal branch, and from the sympathetic division of the autonomic nervous system. The arterial supply to the trachea is from the inferior thyroid arteries; the arterial supply to the bronchioles comes from the bronchial arteries, which take origin from the aorta.

The Thoracic Cavity. The thoracic cavity is separated from the abdomen by the diaphragm, a large sheet of muscle. The center of the cavity contains other structures between the lungs which are enclosed in an oblong, wide area called the *mediastinum* (Fig. 412). The mediastinum, the middle compartment of the chest, is located between the two pleural cavities. It is bounded anteriorly by the sternum, posteriorly by the bodies of the 12 thoracic vertebrae, superiorly by the thoracic inlet, and inferiorly by the diaphragm. The sides of the mediastinum are formed by the mediastinal pleura. Contents of the mediastinal space include the pericardial cavity (enclosing the heart), aortic arch, thymus,

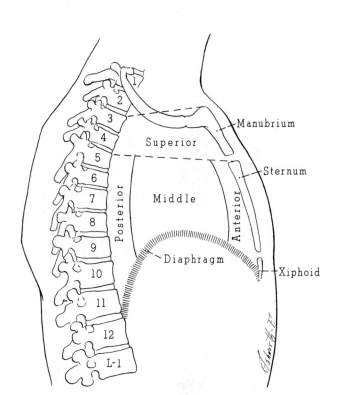

Figure 412. Subdivisions of the mediastinum.

vagus nerve, esophagus, trachea and numerous blood vessels. There are two pleural cavities lined with pleura on either side of the mediastinum in the thorax. Each lung is enclosed in *visceral pleura*. Another layer of serous membrane, the *parietal pleura*, is in close contact with the diaphragm and interior border of the chest. Between the visceral and parietal pleurae is a potential space containing a small amount of pleural fluid for lubrication. The normal pleural arrangement allows for respiration with minimal friction, but when the pleura is inflamed (pleurisy) breathing becomes painful.

The Lungs. The lungs (Figs. 413 and 414) are cone-shaped organs which completely fill the pleural spaces, extending from the diaphragm to about 1½ inches above the clavicle (Fig. 416). The part of the lung above the clavicle is called the *cupula*. The medial surface of each lung is concave around the mediastinum. The primary bronchi and pulmonary arteries enter a slit in each lung called the *hilum* via the root of the lungs—the only real connection of the lungs with the body itself.

The lungs are divided by fissures (Fig. 417). The *oblique* and *horizontal fissures* divide the right lung into superior, middle, and inferior lobes. On the left side, there is only an oblique fissure, dividing the left lung into superior and inferior lobes. Additional units of the lung are recognized, each supplied by a single segmental bronchus. There are ten bronchial segments in the right lung and eight in the left (Fig. 418).

The adult lung is a spongy mass, frequently blue-gray in color because of inhaled dust and soot in the respiratory lymphatics. In contrast, the lung of a baby is pink, since no foreign material has yet entered. Prior to the age of 3 weeks, some of the pulmonary tissue can be incompletely filled with air. At birth, the lungs are filled with fluid; when the first breath is taken, the lungs begin to become spongy, eventually filling with air to a degree similar to that found in the adult.

The interior of the lung is by far the most extensive body surface in contact with the environment. In the normal adult, this area is approximately the size of a tennis court. Normal life processes require about 1 square meter of lung surface for each kilogram of body weight.

The alveoli of the lungs (Fig. 419) are coated with a surface-active substance, or **surfactant** (a lipoprotein in which the active components are phospholipids), which lowers surface tension. *Surface tension* in the lungs (resulting from the contraction of

Text continued on page 434

Figure 413.   Lungs and associated visceral and parietal pleura.

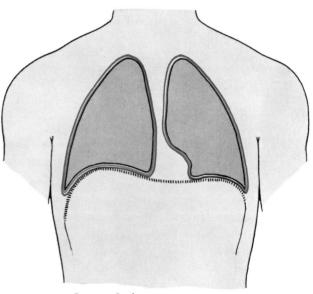

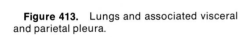

Parietal pleura ———
Visceral pleura ———

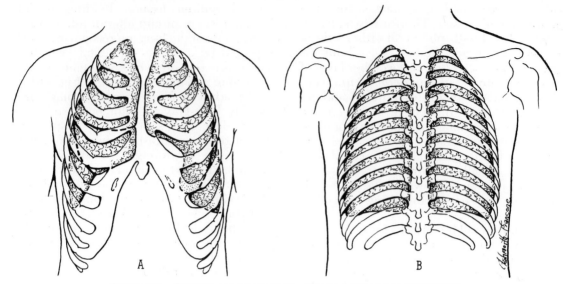

Figure 414.   Relation of lungs to thorax anteriorly (*A*) and posteriorly (*B*).

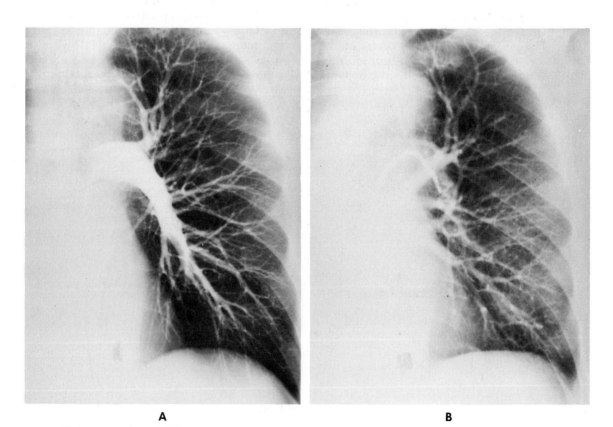

| A | B |

Figure 415.   *A*, Angiograph of pulmonary arterial system. *B*, Angiograph of pulmonary venous system.

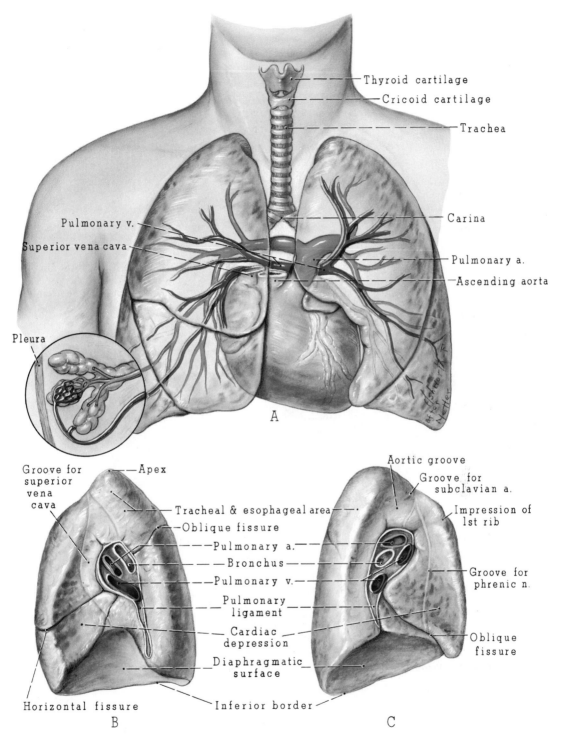

Thyroid cartilage

Cricoid cartilage

Trachea

Pulmonary v.

Superior vena cava

Carina

Pulmonary a.

Ascending aorta

Pleura

A

Groove for
superior
vena
cava

Apex

Aortic groove

Groove for
subclavian a.

Tracheal & esophageal area

Oblique fissure

Pulmonary a.

Bronchus

Pulmonary v.

Pulmonary
ligament

Cardiac
depression

Diaphragmatic
surface

Impression of
1st rib

Groove for
phrenic n.

Oblique
fissure

Horizontal fissure

Inferior border

B

C

Figure 416. *A*, Relationships of lungs to heart and pulmonary vessels. *B*, Medial aspect of right lung. *C*, Medial aspect of left lung.

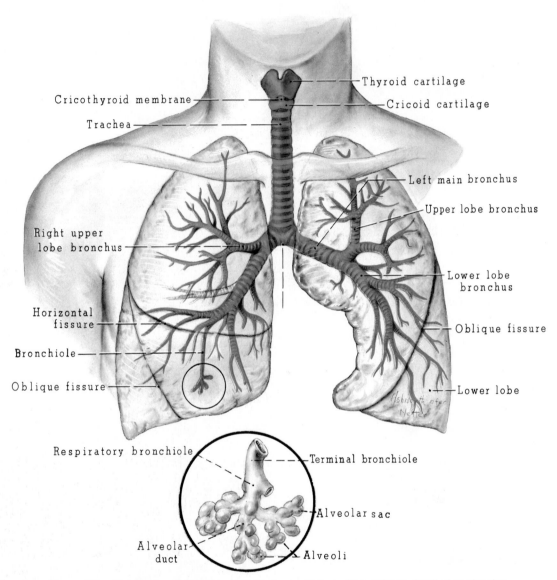

Figure 417. Distribution of bronchi within the lungs. Enlarged inset shows detail of an alveolus.

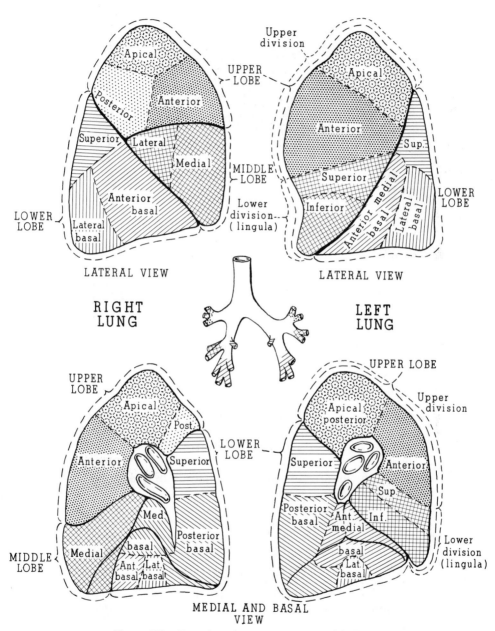

Figure 418. Bronchopulmonary segments of the lungs.

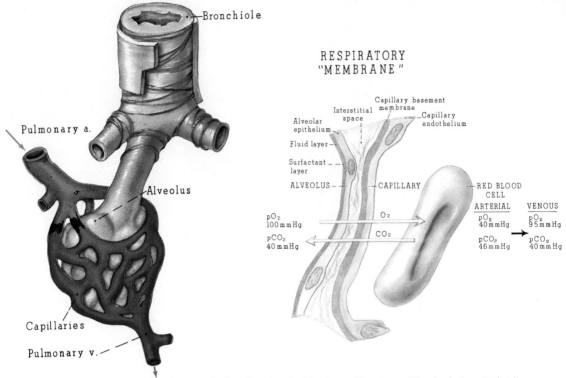

Bronchiole

Pulmonary a.

Alveolus

Capillaries

Pulmonary v.

RESPIRATORY
"MEMBRANE"

Capillary basement
Interstitial membrane
Alveolar space — Capillary
epithelium endothelium

Fluid layer

Surfactant
layer

ALVEOLUS — CAPILLARY — RED BLOOD
CELL

ARTERIAL VENOUS

pO_2 O_2 pO_2 pO_2
100 mm Hg   40 mm Hg   95 mm Hg

pCO_2 CO_2 pCO_2 pCO_2
40 mm Hg   46 mm Hg   40 mm Hg

Figure 419.   Basic microscopic functional unit of the lung. (Courtesy of Roche Laboratories.)

the thin layer of water moistening alveolar surfaces at the air-water interface) is a powerful force, accounting for about one-half to two-thirds of the lungs' elastic recoil. The surfactant prevents lung collapse from excessive surface tension. It also equalizes surface tension as the alveoli expand and contract—surface tension increases as the radii of the alveoli decrease, but this is counterbalanced by the thickening of the surfactant layer, which decreases surface tension. By the same token, differences between large and small alveoli in surfactant concentration bring about an even distribution of surface tension among alveoli of different sizes. Recent investigations have shown that fetal type II alveolar epithelial cells begin to manufacture surfactant about two months before birth. A deficiency in surfactant in premature infants can cause what is known as the **respiratory distress syndrome** (RDS)—extreme difficulty with inhalation because of the decrease in expandability of the lungs or, in serious cases, massive lung collapse. RDS is also called hyaline membrane disease because leakage of fluid in this condition gives

the alveoli a glassy, pink coating. Adrenal steroids and thyroid hormones appear to stimulate surfactant synthesis. These hormones may become useful in preventing RDS.

RESPIRATION

Mechanics of Breathing

Quiet breathing is accomplished by the alternate contraction and relaxation of the *diaphragm* and *external intercostal muscles*. Most of the air movement is accounted for by the action of the diaphragm.

Inspiration. When the diaphragm contracts, it descends and elongates the thoracic cavity (Fig. 420). The contraction of the external intercostal muscles raises the ribs at the sternal end. This action forces the sternum outward, increasing the anterior-posterior diameter of the thorax (Fig. 420). In addition, as the ribs swing upward (in a manner similar to the motion of a bucket handle), the lateral diameter of the thorax increases. As the thorax enlarges, cohesion

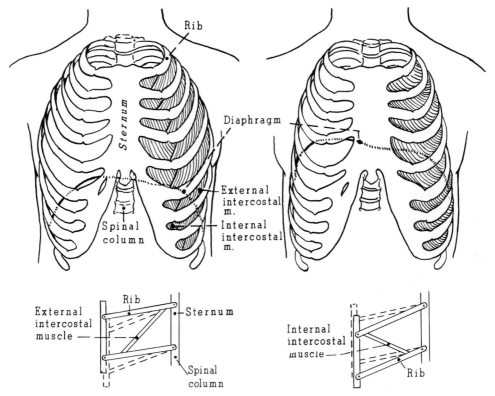

Figure 420. Thorax with associated actions during respiration.

between the visceral and parietal pleura causes both layers to expand, thereby enlarging the lungs. This reduces the pressure within the lungs (intrapulmonic pressure). *Intrapulmonic pressure* reaches a minimum at the midpoint of inspiration (approximately −2 mm Hg, that is, 2 mm Hg below atmospheric pressure — see Fig. 421). The reduction in intrapulmonic pressure causes air to rush into the lungs. At the end of inspiration the pressure between the lungs and atmosphere is equalized (Fig. 421).

Expiration. Expiration is a passive process, occurring as the diaphragm and external intercostal muscles relax. The thoracic cavity returns to its resting size and the lungs recoil. As mentioned, the surface tension of fluid lining the alveoli causes a continuous tending of the alveoli to contract, accounting for about one-half to two-thirds of the lungs' elastic recoil. Rebound of elastic fibers accounts for the remainder. Recoil contraction of the lungs increases intrapulmonic pressure (it reaches a maximum of about +4 mm Hg at the midpoint of expiration), forcing air out of the lungs. At

the end of expiration the pressure between the lungs and atmosphere is equalized (Fig. 421).

Forced Breathing. During quiet breathing, about 500 ml of air is inhaled and exhaled. At least 80 per cent of the air movement is brought about by the contraction and relaxation of the diaphragm. Forceful inspiration not only requires stronger contractions by the diaphragm and external intercostals but also calls forth the use of accessory muscles, principally the sternocleidomastoids, which lift the upper sternum, and the scalenes, which lift the first two ribs. Forced expiration, in distinction to quiet expiration, is an active process. Contraction of the muscles of the abdominal wall forces the abdominal contents against the diaphragm, raising it. Contraction of the internal intercostals reduces the diameter of the thorax by an action opposite to that of the external intercostals.

Intrapleural Pressure. At all times, the intrapleural, or intrathoracic, pressure is negative (Fig. 421). The negative pressure is maintained because the tendency of

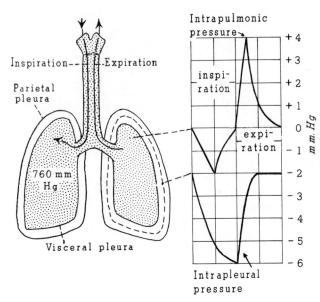

Intrapulmonic pressure

Intrapleural pressure

Figure 421. Changes in intrathoracic and intrapulmonic pressures during respiration.

elastic recoil to contract the lungs is opposed by the tendency of the chest wall to resist lung contraction. In effect, two coiled springs are pulling in opposite directions, thereby maintaining a negative pressure. When an opening is made in the chest wall, as frequently occurs in car accidents or in thoracic surgery, air enters the pleural space, a condition called **pneumothorax.** Separation of the visceral and parietal layers of the pleura eliminates the counterforce acting against the lungs' elastic recoil. Consequently, the lungs collapse. Since the two pleural cavities are not connected, the pneumothorax is usually unilateral; however, the increased pressure on the opened side pushes the mobile mediastinum toward the uninvolved side, exerting pressure on the normal lung and decreasing its ability to be expanded.

Types of Breathing

Normal, quiet breathing, is known as *eupnea. Apnea* is a temporary cessation of breathing. *Dyspnea* is difficult breathing. *Orthopnea* is the inability to breathe in a horizontal position. *Hyperpnea* is an increased depth of breathing. *Tachypnea* is excessively rapid and shallow breathing.

Lung Volumes

The normal resting lung volume in a man of average size is about 3 liters. Normal inspiration increases this volume by approximately 500 ml. Forced maximum inspiration raises this to about 6 liters. Forced maximum expiration lowers the lung volume to approximately 1 liter. The lung volumes are divided as follows (Fig. 422):

Vital capacity (VC)—the largest volume of air that can be expired after a maximal inspiration or the largest volume that can be inspired after maximal expiration.

Residual volume (RV)—the air remaining in the lungs even after maximal forced expiration.

Total lung capacity (TLC)—the total volume of air in the lungs upon maximal inhalation, including residual volume.

Tidal volume (TV)—the amount of air inspired or expired with each breath at rest or during any stated activity. The average figure at rest for an adult male is 500 ml. Of this, about 350 ml reaches the alveoli. The remaining 150 ml moves in and out of the so-called **dead space**—the nose, pharynx, larynx, trachea, and bronchial tree—and serves no useful purpose.

Inspiratory capacity (IC)—the volume capable of being inspired at the end of a quiet expiration.

Inspiratory reserve volume (IRV)—the volume capable of being inspired after quiet inspiration (inspiratory capacity less tidal volume).

Expiratory reserve volume (ERV)—the volume capable of being expired at the end of a quiet expiration.

Functional residual capacity (FRC)—expiratory reserve volume plus residual volume.

It will be noted that "capacities" consist always of two or more "volumes." The volumes and capacities are primarily dependent on the size and build of the individual. They change with body position, for the most part decreasing when the individual assumes a recumbent position and increasing when he stands. This is caused by abdominal pressure on the diaphragm during recumbency, along with a decrease in pulmonary volume in this position, thus decreasing the space available for air.

Ventilation

The volume of air exchanged in one minute (minute respiratory volume) is termed *ventilation.* Normal ventilation, representing a tidal volume of 500 ml and a respiratory rate of 12 breaths per minute, is approximately 6 liters per minute. *Maximum breathing capacity* is generally taken as the maximum ventilation during an

interval of 12 seconds. The maximum breathing capacity of a young male adult is about 125 to 170 liters per minute.

Clinical Spirometry

Clinically, respiratory volumes and capacities are recorded graphically by using a spirometer (Fig. 422 is actually such a record). The record is obtained by having the patient breathe in and out of the spirometer; movements are translated to the moving drum of a kymograph by means of a pen. Spirometry is an initial step in the physiologic evaluation of a patient with labored respiration. A reduction in vital capacity generally indicates a loss of functioning lung tissue or a decrease in *compliance* (expandability, defined specifically as the change in lung volume induced by unit change in distending pressure). In some diseases, such as pneumonia, cancer, and tuberculosis, both compliance and the amount of functioning tissue are reduced. If the impairment in maximum breathing capacity is greater than the impairment in

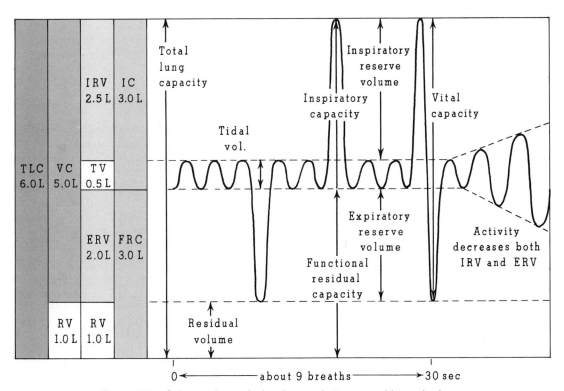

Figure 422. Spirometric graph showing respiratory capacities and volumes.

vital capacity, increased airway resistance, such as occurs in asthma, is indicated. Increased airway resistance can also be detected by measuring the *timed vital capacity*. A normal individual, when exhaling maximally, can expel at least 75 per cent of the vital capacity in one second, 85 per cent in two seconds and 95 per cent in three seconds. In patients with constricted airway passages, these percentages will be reduced.

The Economy of Energy Expenditure for Breathing

Normally, most of the work of breathing expands the lungs, overcoming elastic recoil (referred to as elastic work). Some work overcomes airway resistance, and a small amount overcomes tissue viscous resistance (resistance of nonelastic tissues to a change in shape). It has been calculated that providing adequate alveolar ventilation with a minimum expenditure of energy is accomplished by breathing at a rate of 15 breaths per minute, exchanging 500 ml of tidal air. Shallow, rapid breathing reduces elastic work, but this type of breathing is not maximally efficient because it increases the proportion of useless dead space ventilated. Breathing deeply and slowly fails to achieve maximum economy because, although it increases alveolar ventilation, it also increases elastic work considerably and, in addition, increases energy expenditure by using expiratory muscles to increase intrapulmonary pressure.

Normal, quiet breathing uses about 2 to 3 per cent of the body's total energy output. Heavy exercise increases the work of breathing about 25-fold but only approximately doubles the proportion of the total energy used. Diseases that reduce lung compliance or airway resistance, on the other hand, can increase the proportion of work used for breathing to about one-third or more of the total energy expended. A workload increase of this magnitude can be the cause of death in such diseases.

GAS TRANSPORT

In considering gas transport, Dalton's law of partial pressures must be understood.

This law states that the partial pressure of a gas in a mixture of gases is related directly to the concentration of that gas and the total pressure of the mixture. Alveolar air (dry) contains 14 per cent oxygen, 5.6 per cent carbon dioxide, and 80.4 per cent nitrogen. In order to calculate the partial pressure of each gas in this mixture, barometric pressure (760 mm Hg at sea level) must be corrected for the pressure exerted by water vapor (47 mm Hg) in alveolar air. Thus, the partial pressure (pO_2) of oxygen in alveolar air is equal to $.14 \times (760 - 47)$. This comes to almost 100 mm Hg. The partial pressure of carbon dioxide (pCO_2) in alveolar air, calculated in the same manner, is 40 mm Hg.

The partial pressure of a gas in a liquid is proportional to the amount of gas dissolved in the liquid. The amount dissolved is directly related to the partial pressure of the gas in the environment. A gas will diffuse into a liquid from a gaseous mixture over the liquid. For this reason, the blood flowing through the lungs tends to equilibrate its gaseous partial pressure with that of the alveolar air, that is, the pO_2 and pCO_2 of the blood leaving the lungs are nearly equal to the pO_2 and pCO_2 of the alveolar air.

The partial pressure principle would explain the transport of 0.3 ml of oxygen per 100 ml in arterial blood. This, however, is well below the level necessary to sustain life. There must be another method of oxygen transport in the blood. This other mechanism is the transport of oxygen as *oxyhemoglobin*. The chemical combination of oxygen with hemoglobin to form oxyhemoglobin accounts for 97 per cent of the oxygen delivered to the tissues. Hemoglobin consists of four polypeptide chains, each wrapped around a nonprotein, iron-containing group called *heme*. Each iron atom can loosely bind one oxygen molecule. The binding of oxygen by one iron atom causes structural changes in hemoglobin that increase the affinity of the remaining iron atoms for oxygen. This results in an S-shaped, or *sigmoid*, curve when the per cent saturation of blood with oxygen is plotted against the partial pressure of oxygen (such a plot is called the oxygen dissociation curve—see Fig. 423). Normal blood contains 15 grams of hemoglobin per 100 ml of blood, and each gram is capable of

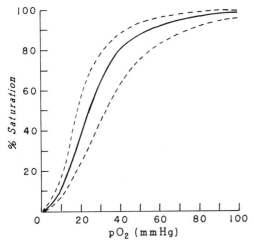

Figure 423. Oxygen dissociation curves of human blood. The solid line is the dissociation curve determined at a carbon dioxide partial pressure of 40 mm Hg. An increase in pCO₂ shifts the curve to the right, a decrease shifts it to the left. Curve to the right determined at pCO₂ of 90 mm Hg, curve to the left determined at pCO₂ of 20 mm Hg.

combining with 1.34 ml of oxygen. Thus, if hemoglobin in the blood stream were 100 per cent saturated, the total amount of oxygen bound to hemoglobin would be 1.34 × 15, or about 20 ml of oxygen per 100 ml of blood (commonly expressed as 20 volumes per cent). In arterial blood, hemoglobin is 97 per cent saturated and, therefore, contains 19.4 ml of oxygen bound to hemoglobin per 100 ml of blood (19.4 volumes per cent).

As blood passes through the tissue capillaries, oxygen leaves the blood and the pO₂ of blood drops on the average (varying from tissue to tissue) to 40 mm Hg. At this partial pressure, hemoglobin is 75 per cent saturated (Fig. 423) and the concentration of oxygen in blood is about 14.7 volumes per cent. In other words, the blood surrenders to the tissues about 5 ml of oxygen per 100 ml of blood. During strenuous exercise as much as 15 ml of oxygen per 100 ml of blood may be released from the blood to the tissues. Under these conditions, increased oxygen consumption by active skeletal muscles leads to a sharp drop in interstitial pO₂. This increases oxygen diffusion from the blood to the tissues, lowering blood pO₂ and increasing oxygen dissociation from hemoglobin.

One of the important properties of hemoglobin is its response to changes in carbon dioxide concentration of pH. Increases in carbon dioxide concentration or decreases in pH reduce the affinity of hemoglobin for oxygen. At any given partial pressure of oxygen, hemoglobin is combined with less oxygen. This shifts the hemoglobin oxygen dissociation curve to the right. Decreases in CO₂ concentration or increases in pH have the reverse effect. These phenomena (known as the *Bohr effect*) are especially important during strenuous exercise, when the rise in the production of carbon dioxide and metabolic acids by active muscles increases oxygen release by hemoglobin.

When carbon dioxide diffuses from the tissues to the blood (increasing the concentration of carbon dioxide in blood from about 48 to 52 volumes per cent, pCO₂ increasing from 40 to 46 mm Hg), about 70 per cent is transported as **bicarbonate ions,** about 20 per cent bound to the protein of hemoglobin (in combination with NH₂ groups, forming what is known as **carbaminohemoglobin**) and about 10 per cent in solution. The formation of bicarbonate ions occurs in the following manner. In the red blood cells, the enzyme **carbonic anhydrase** catalyzes the formation of carbonic acid:

$$H_2O + CO_2 \rightarrow H_2CO_3$$

Carbonic acid dissociates into hydrogen and bicarbonate ions:

$$H_2CO_3 \rightarrow H^+ + HCO_3^-$$

Without the help of carbonic anhydrase, little carbonic acid and bicarbonate would be formed (carbonic anhydrase increases the rate of carbonic acid formation 5000-fold). After the bicarbonate ions are formed inside the RBC most of them diffuse out of the red cell into the plasma and an equal number of chloride ions (Cl⁻) diffuse into the cells in exchange. This shifting of chloride ions into the cell to satisfy the ionic equilibrium is referred to as the *chloride shift.* Thus, as the bicarbonate content of the plasma increases, the chloride content decreases.

While these processes are occurring, oxygen is being released from oxyhemoglobin, resulting in the accumulation of *reduced hemoglobin* (a misnomer, since it suggests a gain of electrons by iron, which, in fact, remains in the divalent, or ferrous,

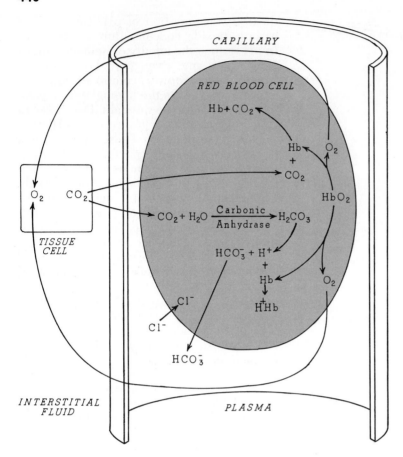

Figure 424. Exchange of respiratory gases in the tissues.

form). Reduced hemoglobin is a weaker acid than oxyhemoglobin and, therefore, can combine with more hydrogen ions than oxyhemoglobin. This prevents the accumulation of hydrogen ions in the blood (hemoglobin is a blood buffer). Some of the carbon dioxide combines with hemoglobin to form carbaminohemoglobin. This reaction is increased by the dissociation of oxygen from hemoglobin. The exchange of respiratory gases in the tissues is summarized in Figure 424.

When venous blood reaches the lungs, carbon dioxide diffuses out of the plasma into the alveoli, and the processes described above are reversed. About 4 ml of carbon dioxide per 100 ml of blood is released from the blood stream to the alveoli during the passage of blood through the respiratory surfaces of the lungs. Figure 425 summarizes the exchange of respiratory gases in the lungs.

CONTROL OF RESPIRATION

Maintaining the Normal Respiratory Rhythm: Brain Centers and the Hering-Breuer Reflex

The diaphragm and other muscles of respiration are voluntary and can be controlled at will. However, normal breathing continues involuntarily even in an unconscious state, and removal of all parts of the brain above the pons does not significantly alter the respiratory rhythm.

Neurogenic mechanisms controlling respiration are located in the reticular substance of the medulla oblongata and pons. The area in the medulla is generally referred to as the **respiratory center**. Respiratory control areas in the pons are known as the *pneumotaxic center* and the *apneustic center.* Of paramount importance is the medullary respiratory center, consisting of

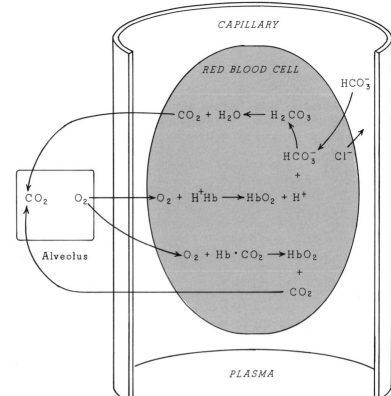

Figure 425. Exchange of respiratory gases in the lungs.

In the figure:

CAPILLARY

RED BLOOD CELL

$CO_2 + H_2O \longleftarrow H_2CO_3$

HCO_3^-

$HCO_3^- \quad Cl^-$

$+$

$O_2 + H^+Hb \longrightarrow HbO_2 + H^+$

$O_2 + Hb \cdot CO_2 \longrightarrow HbO_2$

$+$

CO_2

CO_2 O_2

Alveolus

PLASMA

bilateral, overlapping inspiratory and expiratory centers. If this center is destroyed, breathing ceases altogether.

The basic rhythm of respiration is established by the medullary respiratory center. However, the normal, automatic, alternating rhythm—on the average an inspiratory phase of two seconds and expiratory phase of three seconds—depends largely upon inhibitory inputs to the respiratory center from the lungs as they expand and from the pneumotaxic center. The regulation of the respiratory cycle by expansion of the lungs is known as the **Hering-Breuer reflex,** first described in 1868 by Hering and Breuer, who observed that inflation of the lungs arrested inspiration, expiration then following. The lungs contain stretch receptors which, when activated by expansion of the lungs, transmit impulses via the vagus nerve to the respiratory center that inhibit inspiration, thereby preventing further inflation.

Under normal conditions, the Hering-Breuer reflex plays the dominant role in maintaining the normal respiratory pattern. It is apparently supported by the *pneumo-taxic reflex,* which occurs as the pneumotaxic center receives discharges from the respiratory center during inspiration and returns impulses that inhibit inspiration. Section of the vagus nerve or removal of the pneumotaxic center in animals causes deep, slow breathing. The influence of the apneustic center on respiration can be demonstrated in some animals by eliminating both the vagus nerve and the pneumotaxic center. This elicits cramping of the inspiratory muscles (contractions lasting several seconds) caused by discharges from the apneustic center, no longer subject to inhibitory influences from the pneumotaxic center and vagus nerve. This type of response is often called apneusis. How important the apneustic center is in humans, however, is uncertain.

Regulation of Pulmonary Ventilation

A distinction can be made between maintaining a normal respiratory rhythm and adjusting ventilation to maintain normal concentrations of carbon dioxide, oxygen, and hydrogen ions in the blood or altering ventilation to meet the demands of changing conditions, such as exercising strenuously or living at high altitudes. Changes in blood levels of carbon dioxide, hydrogen ions, and oxygen induce changes in ventilation that tend to counter the changes in blood chemistry. Thus, a rise in carbon dioxide and hydrogen ion concentrations and a fall in oxygen concentration increase ventilation. The increase in ventilation restores the concentration of carbon dioxide, hydrogen ions, and oxygen to normal. Ordinarily, these interactions keep ventilation within narrow limits. Under some conditions, however, such as during heavy exercise or prolonged exposure to air with low oxygen concentration at high altitudes, additional mechanisms are called forth which cause substantial increases in ventilation.

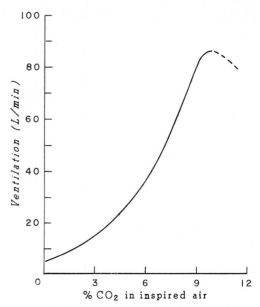

Figure 426.   Effect of carbon dioxide on ventilation. Carbon dioxide becomes intolerable when the percentage in inspired air exceeds 10 per cent.

Site of Action of Carbon Dioxide, Hydrogen Ions, and Oxygen on Ventilation

The primary site of action of carbon dioxide and hydrogen ions is the respiratory center of the medulla or the immediate vicinity. Reduced oxygen concentrations in the blood, on the other hand, act by stimulating chemoreceptors in the *carotid and aortic bodies* (located at the bifurcation of the common carotid arteries into the internal and external carotids and in the aortic arch). When these receptors are stimulated, impulses are transmitted to the respiratory center to increase ventilation. Although a reflexive increase in ventilation in response to increases in carbon dioxide concentrations in blood flowing to the carotid bodies can be demonstrated, it is generally believed that under normal conditions the increase in ventilation, induced by action on the respiratory center, prevents a rise in CO_2 to levels that would provoke a response from the peripheral chemoreceptors.

Quantitative Aspects of the Effects of Carbon Dioxide, Hydrogen Ions and Oxygen on Ventilation

Carbon Dioxide and Hydrogen Ions.   Inspired air normally contains about 0.04 per

cent carbon dioxide. Inhaling air with 4 per cent carbon dioxide, on the average, doubles ventilation (Fig. 426). Concentrations of up to 10 per cent CO_2 induce further increases in ventilation until a maximum of about 80 liters per minute is reached. Further increases in carbon dioxide concentration depress ventilation and cause considerable discomfort and dizziness. In terms of partial pressure, an increase in pCO_2 from 40 mm Hg (normal arterial level) to 42.5 mm Hg doubles ventilation. A rise to 60 mm Hg increases ventilation 10-fold. Lowering pCO_2 depresses respiration. The threshold value for pCO_2 is very close to 40 mm Hg. Lowering the carbon dioxide concentration below this causes apnea.

Since, as described earlier, carbon dioxide produces hydrogen ions by dissociation of carbonic acid, the question has been raised as to whether carbon dioxide itself stimulates respiration or whether it is the hydrogen ions that are responsible for this action. It is generally agreed that both influence the activity of the respiratory center. It has also been shown that an increase in the concentration of metabolic acids in the blood increases ventilation when carbon dioxide levels are not rising. The effects of carbon dioxide and acidity are additive; that is, the effects may summate or cancel one another.

Oxygen. Lowering the concentration of oxygen in the inspired air does not consistently increase ventilation until the levels are reduced to from 10 to 12 per cent. Ventilation does not increase until the pO_2 in blood falls below approximately 60 mm Hg. The response to a reduction in oxygen concentration is limited because the increase in ventilation induced by the lowering of pO_2 in blood blows off carbon dioxide. The reduction in carbon dioxide concentration in the blood decreases ventilation, braking the stimulatory effect of the reduced oxygen concentration on ventilation. When the blood pCO_2 is held constant by adding carbon dioxide to the inspired air, the stimulating effect of a lowering of blood pO_2 is more readily demonstrated. These observations indicate that under normal conditions changes in the carbon dioxide concentration in the blood is the primary regulator of pulmonary ventilation. However, when an individual breathes air low in oxygen concentration for an extended period of time after ascending to a high altitude, the reduction of blood pCO_2 no longer dampens the effect of low pO_2 on ventilation. Ventilation upon ascending to a high altitude promptly increases about 75 per cent. Over a period of a week it continues to increase up to about five- to seven-fold. The acclimatization is ascribed to an increase in the responsiveness of the respiratory center to carbon dioxide.

Effect of Exercise on Ventilation

During strenuous exercise, ventilation can increase as much as 15- to 20-fold. At one time, some respiratory physiologists believed that the increase in carbon dioxide production during exercise was responsible for the increase in ventilation. However, an increase of pCO_2 in arterial blood usually is not observed during exercise—the increase in ventilation prevents its accumulation in the blood. A number of observations indicate that the increase in ventilation results principally from stimulation of the respiratory center by reflexes originating in proprioceptors in the joints of the body and impulses transmitted from the cerebrum.

Other Factors Affecting Ventilation

Blood pressure also influences ventilation. A sudden drop of arterial pressure brings about an increase in ventilation, and a sudden rise in pressure brings about a decrease in ventilation. These effects are elicited from baroreceptors in the aortic arch and internal carotid artery that reflexly stimulate or inhibit the respiratory center. The increase in ventilation following the drop in blood pressure is of value because it increases the return of venous blood to the heart, thereby raising blood pressure. (Venous return increases because deeper inspirations increase the pressure gradient between the abdominal and thoracic cavities.) The effects of changes in blood pressure on ventilation, however, are observed only when the fall or rise in pressure is abrupt and pronounced.

Different sensory stimuli can also elicit reflex respiratory effects. For example, severe pain usually causes increased ventilation, and a sudden cold stimulus brings about temporary apnea. Another stimulus, that of stretching the anal sphincter, increases ventilation. Stretching the anal sphincter is sometimes employed to stimulate respiration during emergencies.

Age is another factor influencing ventilation. At birth, normal ventilation is about 500 ml per minute, with a respiratory rate of about 33 breaths per minute and a tidal volume of 15 ml. Ventilation increases to about 6 liters per minute in the adult (rate, 12 breaths per minute; tidal volume, 500 ml). This means that infants ventilate about 200 ml per minute per kilogram as compared to about half this amount per kilogram in adults.

RESPIRATORY PHENOMENA

Cough. A *cough* is a mechanism for clearing obstructions of the airway. During coughing, forcible expiratory effort against the closed glottis first raises the air pressure in the chest. The glottis then suddenly opens, reducing pressure in the trachea and large bronchioles to atmospheric level. The high pressure still remaining in the air spaces around the trachea collapses its posterior wall. As a result, air passes out through a much narrower trachea with a great force and velocity, blowing out foreign material and mucus with it.

Sneeze. A *sneeze* might be described as an upper respiratory cough. In the preparatory stages more and more air is inspired, and at the climax air is expelled with explosive force. During a sneeze the glottis is wide open and air meets its chief resistance in the mouth or nasal passages, so that the expiratory blast serves to clear the passages of the nose or mouth just as the cough clears the bronchi and trachea.

Yawn. *Yawning* aids respiration by more completely ventilating the lung. In ordinary breathing apparently not all of the alveoli of the lungs are equally ventilated; some actually periodically close. The blood passing through collapsed alveoli enters the arterial system without being oxygenated and dilutes the average oxygen content. Collapsed alveoli are opened by the long, deep inspiration of the yawn.

Hiccup. A *hiccup* is an abnormal response serving no known useful purpose. It is a spasmodic contraction of the diaphragm, resulting from stimulation either in the diaphragm itself or in the respiratory center of the brain, and caused by substances in the blood or by local circulatory abnormalities. The vocal cords usually open during inspiration (vocalization is produced normally only during expiration) and are apparently closed during the hiccup; the vibrations produce the characteristic sound. Persistent hiccups can generally be halted by inhalation of air containing 5 to 7 per cent carbon dioxide.

Cheyne-Stokes Breathing. *Cheyne-Stokes breathing* is a type of periodic breathing; that is, breathing characterized by alternating intervals of breathing and apnea. During the breathing period of Cheyne-Stokes breathing, the depth of respiration increases gradually to a maximum and then decreases rapidly. The use of narcotics, brain damage, and chronic heart failure are among the causes of Cheyne-Stokes breathing. Narcotics or brain damage apparently alter the sensitivity of the respiratory center. Higher than normal concentrations of carbon dioxide are needed to initiate respiration, but small increases in concentration provoke an excessive response. An episode of hyperventilation lowers the carbon dioxide concentration, reducing the activity of the respiratory center. Breathing becomes shallower and ceases because the center fails to respond rapidly enough to the rise in the concentration of carbon dioxide. Heart failure may cause Cheyne-Stokes breathing because of a delay in the flow of blood from the heart to the brain. Carbon dioxide fails to reach the respiratory center in time to prevent apnea. Cheyne-Stokes respiration often occurs as the respiratory pattern in premature infants. In normal adults, a few cycles of Cheyne-Stokes breathing may follow voluntary hyperventilation.

COMMON RESPIRATORY DISORDERS

The most important respiratory disorders are those in which the blood fails to become oxygenated (Fig. 427). Nearly all respiratory problems tend toward hypoxia. Hypoxia is sometimes manifested in *cyanosis*. This term refers to the fact that the skin, mucous membranes, and nail beds turn blue because of an increased presence of deoxygenated hemoglobin in the capillaries.

Emphysema. Emphysema is rapidly becoming one of the most common respiratory diseases, in part because aging is a factor and people live longer now than in the past, but primarily because it occurs more frequently in heavy smokers than in nonsmokers (smoking increases the susceptibility to any infectious disease). According to many clinicians, emphysema is initiated by a chronic infection causing bronchiolar inflammation *(bronchiolitis)*. Occluded bronchioles may trap air in alveoli and, if an individual happens to cough, the sudden rise in pressure may rupture alveolar walls (septa). The amount of functioning lung tissue may be greatly reduced. In cigarette smokers the bronchial walls are narrowed by hyperplasia (an increase in the number of cells), and mucous secretion is increased. Such conditions increase the vulnerability to infection and the likelihood of airway obstruction. The physiological effects of emphysema include increased airway resistance, with increased effort expended in breathing and greatly decreased diffusing capacity. The ability of the lungs to oxygenate the blood is decreased, and pulmo-

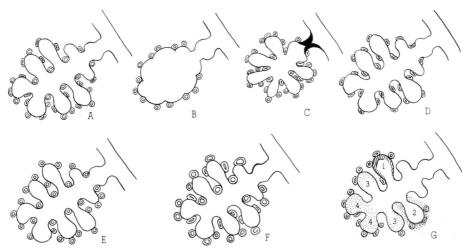

Figure 427. Area for gas exchange in the alveoli. *A*, Normal arrangement of alveoli clustered about an alveolar duct (about half the alveolar capillaries are open, and half are closed). *B*, Destruction of alveolar septa and about half the total available number of capillaries. *C*, Obstruction of bronchiole and decreased area for gas exchange with no decrease in potential alveolocapillary contact surface. *D*, Obstruction of the pulmonary circulation (no alveolocapillary blood flow). *E*, Increase in the number of open capillaries, as might occur in exercise. *F*, Capillary enlargement, as might occur in chronic mitral stenosis. *G*, Longer paths for diffusion due to (1) thickening of alveolar epithelium, (2) tissue separating alveolar capillary from alveolar epithelium, (3) beginning pulmonary edema and (4) nonventilated alveoli filled with edema fluid or exudate.

nary hypertension is induced, owing to the decrease in the number of pulmonary capillaries.

Atelectasis. Atelectasis (G. *ateles*, incomplete; G. *ektasis*, distention) is the term used to describe any condition that causes collapse of alveoli in a localized region, an entire lung, or both lungs. The respiratory distress syndrome (described on page 434) is one example of atelectasis. Common causes of atelectasis are a chest wound that permits air to leak into the pleural cavity and blockage of a primary bronchus or one of the smaller bronchial tubes following general anesthesia given for major surgery.

Bronchiectasis. Bronchiectasis is characterized by dilatation of the bronchi. It results from three factors: (1) flaccidity of the bronchial walls following chronic inflammation of the bronchial tree; (2) increase in the distending forces, as from long, continued cough; and (3) traction on the wall, as from fibrous tissue formation in the lung secondary to an inflammatory disease such as pneumonia. The symptoms of bronchiectasis are cough, voluminous sputum, and labored respiration on exertion. Pertussis immunization is helping to decrease the incidence of bronchiectasis.

Asthma. Substances in the air, such as pollen, may cause an allergic reaction when inspired, creating localized edema in the walls of the small bronchioles, secretion of thick mucus into their lumens, and spasm of their smooth muscular walls. Airway resistance is, therefore, greatly increased. Since during expiration the rise in intrathoracic pressure compresses smaller bronchi and bronchioles, airway resistance is greater during expiration than inspiration. Therefore, asthmatics may inspire adequately but expiration is difficult and prolonged. Over an extended period the lungs become increasingly distended; with long-standing asthma, the chest adopts a barrel-shaped appearance. In children asthma is commonly caused by sensitivities to food; in adults it is frequently caused by sensitivities to pollen. An asthmatic attack can be precipitated by an emotional crisis as well as by an allergen.

Pneumonia. The term pneumonia can be used to describe any lung condition in which alveoli become filled with fluid or blood cells, or both. The most common type is known as bacterial pneumonia and is usually caused by pneumococci.

The disease begins as an infection within the alveoli of one part of the lungs. The alveolar membrane becomes edematous and highly porous, to the point of allowing red blood cells and white blood cells to pass out of the blood into the alveoli. Therefore, the infected alveoli progressively fill with fluid and cells, and the infection spreads as bacteria extend to other alveoli.

Reduction in the total available surface area of respiratory membrane therefore occurs. As in many other pulmonary diseases, carbon dioxide is adequately excreted, but oxygenation of the blood is diminished. This is caused by the fact that carbon dioxide passes through the alveolar walls about 20 times as readily as does oxygen. Pneumonia occurs most frequently in young children and in the aged. In 95 per cent of the instances, the disease is due to an organism, the pneumococcus; the remainder of cases are caused by streptococci and the *Hemophilus influenzae* bacillus (Fig. 428).

Tuberculosis. In tuberculosis, the tubercle bacilli invade the lungs, producing a local tissue reaction. Initially, the area is invaded by macrophages and then becomes walled off by fibrous connective tissue. Thus, a characteristic "tubercle" is produced. In the late stages, secondary infection by other bacilli is present and more fibrosis results. The fibrosis reduces the lung compliance and lowers the vital capacity. Fibrosis also lowers the total pulmonary membrane area and increases the thickness of the membrane, thus decreasing the capacity for pulmonary diffusion.

Pulmonary Edema. Pulmonary edema influences respiration in much the same way as pneumonia. It is caused by an insufficiency of the left heart in pumping blood received from the lungs to the rest of the body, causing blood to back up into the pulmonary circulation. This is generally the result of cardiac insufficiency caused by poor blood supply to the muscles of the heart, but can also be caused by mitral or aortic valvular disease.

Infarction of the Lungs. The commonest source of pulmonary infarction is an embolus from the right atrium or from the lower extremities and pelvis which eventually obstructs a branch of the pulmonary artery. The symptoms of pulmonary infarction are a sudden onset of labored respiration, often with collapse of the lung and a bloody sputum. The acute onset is characteristic and can be followed rapidly by death.

Air Embolism. Air embolism is an unusual complication which occasionally follows the opening of a large vein in the neck during a surgical operation or the accidental injection of large volumes of air with blood transfusions. In the dog it is necessary to introduce 90 ml of air to produce death; however, the administration of even a small amount of air into the pulmonary vein—for example, as little as 1 ml—can cause death, since it frequently lodges in the brain.

Sinusitis. Sinusitis in the acute stage is manifested by pain referred to the maxillary and frontal sinuses. The nose is plugged, and nasal and postnasal mucus discharges occur. In the chronic form of sinusitis, the postnasal discharge becomes persistent.

General Signs and Symptoms

Signs and symptoms associated with respiratory disturbances include the following. A productive cough—or for that matter, a nonproductive cough—is a symptom common to disease of the trachea, bronchi, bronchioles, or pulmonary parenchyma, whether infectious or the result of tumor. *Hemoptysis*, or blood-streaked sputum, ac-

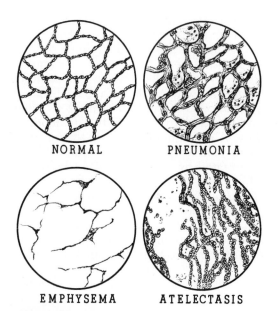

NORMAL   PNEUMONIA

EMPHYSEMA   ATELECTASIS

Figure 428. Histological sections of normal and diseased alveoli.

companies disease of the lung. Involvement of the pleura by infection or tumor is associated with pain intensified by respiration and coughing.

Spontaneous pneumothorax is characterized by pain and breathlessness. Breathlessness is a common symptom in pulmonary disease whenever there is decreased vital capacity below the normal minimum for the particular patient. This might be caused by pulmonary consolidation, emphysema, or disease of the heart.

ARTIFICIAL RESPIRATION

Mouth-to-Mouth Resuscitation

In 1958 the American Medical Association published a symposium concluding that mouth-to-mouth resuscitation was superior to all other means of artificial respiration. It is currently believed that mouth-to-mouth resuscitation is the only technique assuring adequate ventilation in all cases. The subject is placed in a supine position; the rescuer, behind the subject, grasps the subject's lower jaw and lifts it vertically upward. The rescuer then places his mouth over the subject's mouth and exhales. It is important that the subject's nostrils are either pinched shut or covered by the rescuer's mouth during resuscitation (Fig. 429).

There are many types of respirators for artificial respiration.

Iron Lung

The *tank respirator* (iron lung) is the apparatus that first made prolonged artificial respiration a practical matter. The patient is placed into a rigid tank from which only his head protrudes, and an airtight seal is made around his neck. To provide inspiration the bellows is expanded, so that the pressure in the tank becomes subatmospheric. Pressure in the patient's upper airway is atmospheric, so that the air flows along the trachea into the lungs. This flow of air continues until the lungs are sufficiently inflated for the elastic resistance of the lungs and the paralyzed chest wall to equalize the difference between atmo-

spheric pressure and the pressure within the tank. The intrathoracic pressure lies between the pressure in the trachea and that within the tank, its precise level depending on the elastic resistance of the lungs and chest wall. The principal use of the tank respirator is for patients with weakness of the respiratory muscles, such as sometimes occurs in poliomyelitis. The disadvantage of a tank respirator is that it is cumbersome and the patient is rather inaccessible to other forms of treatment and diagnosis. Iron lungs are infrequently used today.

Mechanical Respirator Therapy

Mechanical respirators are used intermittently or continuously for assisting or controlling breathing. Basically, there are two types. Pressure-cycle respirators inflate the lungs to a predetermined pressure; inspiration ceases and expiration begins when this pressure is reached. Acute respiratory distress is treated primarily with a volume-controlled respirator which delivers a predetermined volume of air with each inspiration. The Bennett respirator is shown in Figure 430.

Intermittent Positive Pressure Respiration

Most medical centers in the United States currently use different pieces of equipment for *intermittent positive pressure respiration* (Fig. 430). This is administered through an endotracheal tube passed into the nose or mouth. The larynx will not tolerate the presence of a tube for extended periods of time, and 24 hours is probably as long as it should be left in place. For long term intermittent positive pressure respiration, it is necessary to introduce gas into the lungs through a tracheostomy. When the patient is ill, a tracheostomy tube with an inflated cuff is usually employed to make an airtight seal with the walls of the trachea. This serves two purposes — prevention of saliva, vomit, or other foreign material from passing into the chest, and prevention of air which is blown into the chest from leaking through the nose and mouth. The tracheostomy tube is connected to the tubing from a respirator which, during inspiration, provides pressure above atmospheric pressure.

ARTIFICIAL RESPIRATION
MOUTH-TO-MOUTH (MOUTH-TO-NOSE) METHOD

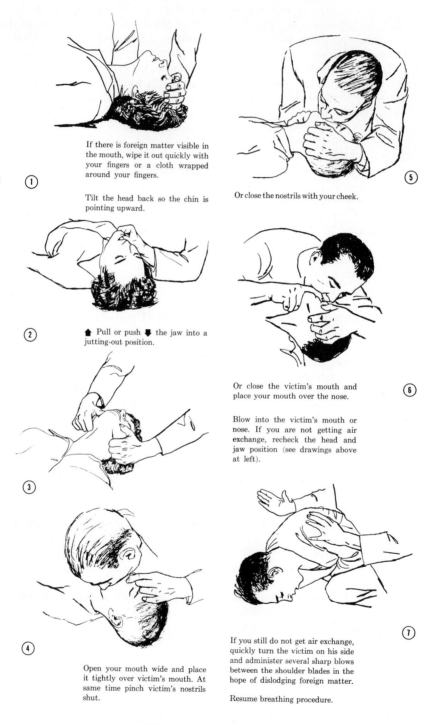

① If there is foreign matter visible in the mouth, wipe it out quickly with your fingers or a cloth wrapped around your fingers.

Tilt the head back so the chin is pointing upward.

② ⬆ Pull or push ⬇ the jaw into a jutting-out position.

③

④ Open your mouth wide and place it tightly over victim's mouth. At same time pinch victim's nostrils shut.

⑤ Or close the nostrils with your cheek.

⑥ Or close the victim's mouth and place your mouth over the nose.

Blow into the victim's mouth or nose. If you are not getting air exchange, recheck the head and jaw position (see drawings above at left).

⑦ If you still do not get air exchange, quickly turn the victim on his side and administer several sharp blows between the shoulder blades in the hope of dislodging foreign matter.

Resume breathing procedure.

THE AMERICAN NATIONAL RED CROSS

Figure 429. Mouth-to-mouth respiration. (Courtesy of the American National Red Cross.)

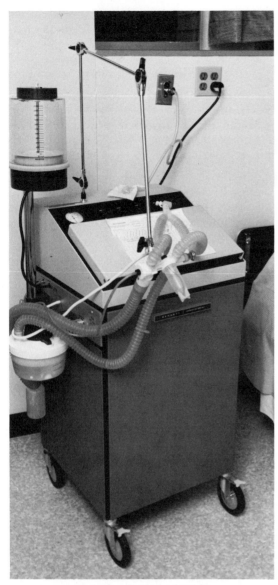

Figure 430. Artificial respirator.

Air passes into the chest until the pressure in the airway is balanced by the elastic resistance of the lungs and chest wall. The intrathoracic pressure is raised but remains less than the pressure in the airway. The intrathoracic pressure is, therefore, higher than atmospheric pressure applied to the trunk, limbs, and veins, so that intermittent positive pressure respiration impedes the venous return during inspiration in precisely the same way as the tank respirator. The principal use of intermittent positive pressure respiration is for the patient who

not only requires artificial respiration but also needs a tracheostomy.

SUMMARY

THE RESPIRATORY SYSTEM

Components and Function of the Respiratory System

1. Exchange of respiratory gases between the blood and air (uptake of oxygen, elimination of carbon dioxide) takes place in the alveoli of the lungs.

2. The nose, pharynx, larynx, trachea, and primary bronchi form an open passage, the upper respiratory tract, leading from the exterior to the lungs. In the lungs the primary bronchi subdivide into lobar and segmental bronchi, bronchioles, and alveolar ducts. The latter lead into the alveoli.

Nasal Cavity

1. Divided by a septum into right and left halves.

2. In each half superior, middle, and inferior meatuses lie below the superior, middle, and inferior conchae (turbinates).

3. Openings: anterior nares to outside; posterior nares to nasopharynx.

Pharynx

1. Musculomembranous tube lined with mucous membrane.

2. Nasopharynx (behind the nose) has four openings: two auditory (eustachian) tubes, two posterior nares.

3. Oropharynx (behind mouth) has one opening: the fauces.

4. Laryngopharynx (behind larynx) has two openings: into larynx and esophagus.

5. Contains pharyngeal tonsil (adenoids) in nasopharynx, palatine tonsils at junction of oral cavity and oropharynx, and lingual tonsils at base of tongue.

Larynx

1. Nine cartilages

a. Unpaired: thyroid (Adam's apple),

cricoid (signet ring), and epiglottis (lid to larynx).
b. Paired: arytenoid, cuneiform, and corniculate.

2. In phonation, long, lax cords give low-pitched voice; short, tense cords give high-pitched voice.

Trachea

1. Tube four to five inches long from larynx to bronchi containing 15 to 20 C-shaped cartilages. Openings of the "C's" face posteriorly and are bridged by smooth muscle; spaces between cartilages filled with elastic and collagenous fibers.

2. Tracheotomy: opening into trachea; tracheostomy: tube into trachea.

Bronchi and Branches

1. Primary bronchi formed by branching of trachea; right primary bronchi shorter, wider, more vertical.

2. Successive divisions: three right and two left secondary (lobar) bronchi; 10 right and eight left segmental bronchi; 50 to 80 terminal bronchioles; two or more respiratory bronchioles; two or more alveolar ducts.

Alveoli

1. Arranged in clusters called alveolar sacs.

2. Cells
   a. Thin squamous epithelial: single layer forms continuous lining.
   b. Type II epithelial (cuboidal): secrete surfactant that coats alveoli, lowering surface tension (deficiency in surfactant in premature infants can cause respiratory distress syndrome).
   c. Macrophages.

Mechanics of Breathing

1. Inspiration: accomplished actively — contractions of diaphragm and external intercostals enlarge thorax and expand lungs. Lowered intrapulmonic pressure causes air to move into the lungs (action of diaphragm accounting for most of air movement).

2. Expiration: accomplished passively — relaxation of diaphragm and external intercostals allows elastic recoil of lungs to force air out of the lungs.

Ventilation (Minute Respiratory Volume)

1. Normally, at rest, approximately 6 liters per minute, representing a tidal volume (volume of air inspired or expired with each breath) and a respiratory rate of 12 breaths per minute.

2. Shallow, rapid breathing decreases efficiency because it increases the proportion of air moving in and out of the dead space (nose, pharynx, larynx, trachea and bronchial tree).

3. Deep, slow breathing is not maximally effective because it increases the work required to expand the lungs (overcoming elastic recoil) and requires the use of expiratory muscles.

Oxygen Transport in Blood

1. Ninety-seven per cent of the oxygen delivered to the tissues is carried by hemoglobin.

2. As blood passes through tissue capillaries, the per cent saturation of hemoglobin with oxygen drops on the average from 97 to 75 and about 5 ml of oxygen per 100 ml of blood is released to the tissues.

3. An increase in carbon dioxide concentration or decrease in pH increases oxygen release by hemoglobin.

Carbon Dioxide Transport in Blood

1. When carbon dioxide passes from the tissues to the capillaries, the concentration of carbon dioxide in the blood increases on the average from 48 to 52 ml of carbon dioxide per 100 ml of blood.

2. About 70 per cent of the carbon dioxide is transported as bicarbonate ions (made possible by the enzymatic action of carbonic anhydrase in red blood cells), about 20 per cent is transported bound to hemoglobin, and the remainder is transported in solution.

Maintenance of Normal Respiratory Rhythm

1. Rhythmic breathing is dependent upon

the respiratory center in the medulla. Breathing ceases if this center is destroyed.

2. The depth and pattern of the breathing cycle is regulated by the Hering-Breuer reflex, which involves inhibition of inspiration by expansion of the lungs.

Regulation of Ventilation

1. Accumulation of carbon dioxide in the blood increases ventilation by directly stimulating the respiratory center. A reduction in carbon dioxide concentration has the reverse effect. Under normal conditions, change in the carbon dioxide concentration in the blood is the primary regulator of ventilation.

2. Reduced oxygen concentration in the blood increases ventilation by stimulating chemoreceptors in the carotid bodies, which in turn stimulate the respiratory center. This reflex is effective after breathing air with low oxygen concentrations for a prolonged period, as at a high altitude.

3. During exercise, ventilation is increased as a result of stimulation of the respiratory center by reflexes arising from proprioceptors in joints and impulses transmitted from the cerebrum.

chapter **13**

The Digestive System

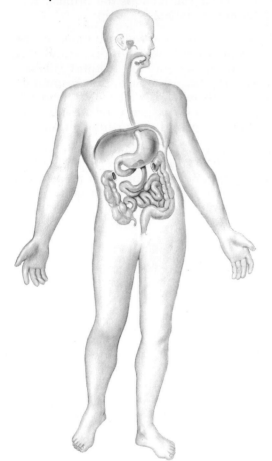

Objectives

The aim of this chapter is to enable the student to:

Describe the components of the digestive system and its associated structures.

Distinguish between the four layers of the digestive tract.

Identify the unique anatomical features of the small intestine.

List the sequence of events in swallowing.

Describe the motility of the separate parts of the gastrointestinal tract.

Outline the steps in the digestion of carbohydrate, protein and fat.

Discuss the regulation of the secretions of the digestive glands.

Describe the absorption of the products of digestion and identify their sites of absorption.

Explain the function of bile in absorption and digestion.

Summarize the functions of the liver.

Describe the disposition of the major foodstuffs following their absorption.

Briefly discuss the regulation of food intake.

Explain what is meant by the basal metabolic rate.

Describe the mechanisms of the regulation of body temperature.

HISTORY

The history of medicine gives an interesting account of the ideas and events leading to our present state of knowledge of the digestive system. In the early nineteenth century many physical and chemical theories of digestion were entertained but only meagerly substantiated or correlated. The detailed workings of the gastrointestinal system as a whole were largely a matter of dispute—even in the reliable textbooks of the period, one of which contained William Hunter's amusing remark that "Some physiologists will have it that the stomach is a mill, that it is a fermenting vat, and others, again, that it is a stew-pan; but, in my view of the matter, it is neither a mill, a fermenting vat, nor a stew-pan; but a stomach gentlemen, a stomach."

There was little factual knowledge concerning the relation between structure and function in the digestive system until 1833, when a significant advance was made with the publication of William Beaumont's "Experiments and Observations on the Gastric Juice and the Physiology of Digestion." The subject of this study was Alexis St. Martin, a Canadian voyageur who had been accidentally wounded by the discharge of a musket. The shot "entered posteriorly, and in an oblique direction, forward and inward, literally blowing off integuments and muscles the size of a man's hand, fracturing and carrying away the anterior half of the sixth rib, fracturing the fifth, lacerating the lower portion of the left lobe of the lungs, the diaphragm, and perforating the stomach."

After surgical repair and healing, there remained an aperture 2½ inches in circumference in both the wall of the stomach and the side of the patient. Beaumont attempted to close this wound but failed; subsequently, the natural protrusion of the layers of the stomach in a sort of fistula (an abnormal passage leading from the abdominal wall to one of the hollow abdominal organs) produced a permanent valve, which prevented the escape of gastric contents even when the stomach was full, but which could easily be depressed to permit the entrance of a tube or other instrument and the introduction of food substances. The interior of the stomach could be seen with the naked eye.

Realizing the unique opportunity presented, Beaumont conducted a series of experiments between 1825 and 1833, during which time St. Martin enjoyed normal, robust health. The most important of Beaumont's pioneering results contain concepts accepted as fundamental today.

ANATOMY

The digestive system (Figs. 431–433) consists of (1) a long, muscular tube beginning at the lips and ending at the anus, including the mouth, pharynx, esophagus,

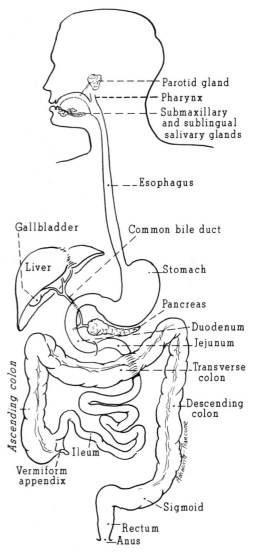

Figure 431.   The digestive system and its associated structures.

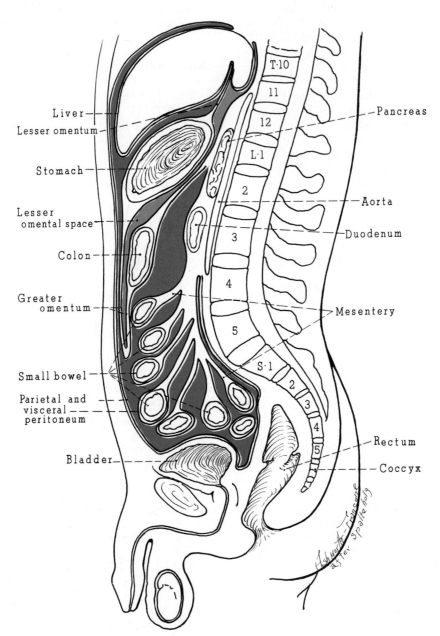

Figure 432. Mid-sagittal section through trunk, showing parietal and visceral peritoneum. (Note relationship between abdominal viscera and mesenteries.)

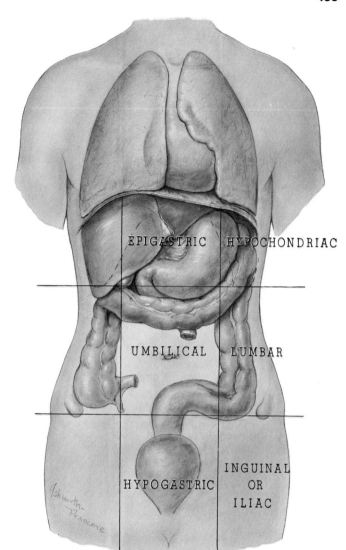

Figure 433. Regions of the abdomen and underlying viscera.

EPIGASTRIC HYPOCHONDRIAC

UMBILICAL LUMBAR

HYPOGASTRIC

INGUINAL OR ILIAC

stomach, and small and large intestine; and (2) certain large glands located outside the digestive tube, including the salivary glands, liver, gallbladder, and pancreas — all of which empty their secretions into the tube. The major functions of the digestive system are the digestion and absorption of ingested food and the elimination of solid wastes.

Lips

The lips have an outer surface covered by skin. The red, free margins represent a zone of transition from skin to mucous membrane. The epithelium of the inner surface of the lip is stratified squamous and is similar to the epithelium found on the inner surface of the cheek, pharynx, and esophagus. The substance of the lip consists of striated muscle fibers with fibroelastic connective tissue.

Cheeks

The cheeks, or side walls of the mouth, lined by *stratified squamous epithelium*, contain several accessory muscles of mastication, notably the buccinators, which prevent food from escaping the chewing actions of the teeth.

Teeth

Teeth (Fig. 434) develop in the seventh fetal week from ectodermal tissue and are all constructed on the following basic plan:

Each is divided into two principal parts: (1) the **crown**, projecting above the gum, or gingiva, and (2) the **root** (or roots), the portion embedded in the *alveolus* (bony socket) of the maxilla or mandible. The region of junction of the crown and root is called the *neck*. The central, hollow portion of the tooth, the *pulp cavity*, is filled with connective tissue (pulp). *Dentin*, a substance similar to bone in composition, but harder and more compact, surrounds the pulp cavity and forms the bulk of the tooth. The dentin of the crown is covered with *enamel*, the hardest substance in the body, composed mainly of calcium phosphate. *Cementum*, a bony tissue, covers the dentin of the root. Periosteal tissue (constituting the *periodontal membrane*), the tough fibrous membrane surrounding bones, lines the tooth socket, supplying nourishment. The cementum anchors the tooth to the periodontal membrane. Blood vessels and nerves pass through the apical foramen at the apex of the root and the root canal to reach the pulp cavity.

In the adult, each quadrant of the mouth has eight teeth: two *incisors*, one *canine* (cuspid), two *premolars* (bicuspids) and three *molars* (tricuspids). Solid food must be reduced to small particles before it can undergo chemical changes in the digestive tract. The teeth accomplish this function by the process of *mastication*. Each type of tooth is adapted to its function—incisors for cutting, canines for grasping, and molars for grinding. Faulty teeth cause indigestion or malnutrition.

Dental caries is a term applied to the disintegration of teeth by acids produced by bacterial fermentation of carbohydrates. It begins with the dissolving of enamel and results in the formation of cavities. Dental caries is at least partially preventable by ingesting fluoride. When optimal amounts of fluoride are ingested during dental development, a reduction in caries of about 60 per cent can be expected. Fluoridation of water is a widely accepted method of supplying dental fluoride. An alternative method, the oral fluoride supplement, is recommended for children in communities without natural or artificial fluoridation of water.

Pyorrhea is an inflammatory process of the gums in which the teeth become loose and fall out. Bacteria from dental infection

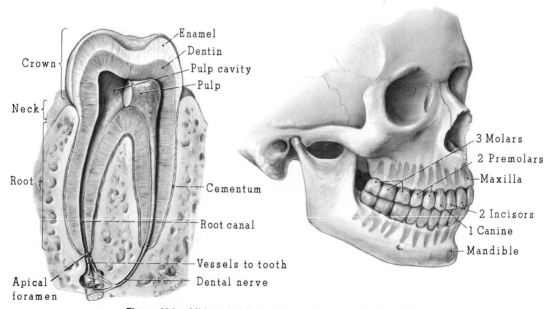

Figure 434. Mid-sagittal view of molar tooth, vertical position.

Tongue

The floor of the mouth contains the tongue, a highly movable structure composed of *extrinsic muscles* (with origins in the mandible, styloid process of the temporal bone, and hyoid bone) pulling in three directions and *intrinsic muscles* (superior and inferior longitudinal, transverse and vertical) lying entirely within the tongue. A fold of mucous membrane, the *frenulum,* attaches the tongue to the floor of the mouth. If the frenulum is too short, it may restrict the movements of the tongue (tongue-tie condition). The tongue functions to mix saliva with food and to keep the mass pressed between the teeth for chewing before it pushes the food backward for swallowing. Numerous taste buds are scattered over the surface of the tongue (Fig. 443).

The palate, or roof of the mouth, consists of two parts: an anterior portion, the hard palate, formed by the maxillary and palatine bones; and a posterior portion, the soft palate, composed of muscles ending in a free projection called the *uvula.* The opening of the pharynx lies behind the uvula (Fig. 435).

Pharynx

The pharynx is the portion of the digestive tract serving as a passageway for both the respiratory and digestive systems. It permits an individual to breathe through his mouth even if the nasal passages are obstructed. The pharynx has longitudinal and circular muscle layers of the striated type. The circular muscles are called constrictors.

Layers of the Wall of the Digestive Tract

A basic histologic plan is seen throughout the remainder of the digestive tract, although there are individual features peculiar to each region. In general the wall of the digestive tract is composed of the following layers:

Mucous Membrane, or Tunica Mucosa. This is the innermost layer of the digestive tract. It is composed of a superficial *epithelium* resting on a basement membrane and an underlying support of connective tissue, the *lamina propria,* with a thin arrangement of smooth muscle fibers, the *muscularis mucosae,* beneath the lamina propria. Glandular cells of the mucosa secrete digestive juices and mucus. Only mucus is secreted in the esophagus and colon. Accumulations of lymphoid tissue are often found in supporting connective tissue.

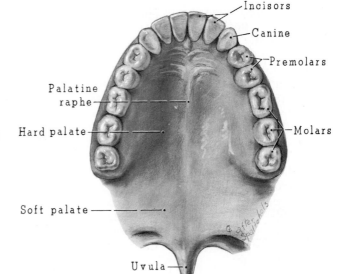

Figure 435. Roof of mouth with adult teeth.

Incisors
Canine
Premolars
Palatine raphe
Hard palate
Molars
Soft palate
Uvula

Submucous Layer, or Tela Submucosa. This layer is composed of areolar connective tissue with numerous lymphatics, blood vessels, and a nerve plexus known as *Meissner's plexus.* It is found between the mucous and muscular layers and acts to compensate for changes in size of the digestive tube during the passage of food.

Muscular Layer, or Muscularis Externa. This consists of smooth muscle fibers in two distinct sections. The inner circular layer, when contracted, narrows the lumen of the tube. The longitudinally arranged fibers of the outer layer serve to shorten the tube by their contraction. Between the two layers is a plexus of nerves called the *myenteric plexus* or *Auerbach's plexus.*

Serous Layer, or Adventitia. The outermost covering is the visceral layer of the peritoneum and is called the *visceral peritoneum* or *serosa.* The *parietal peritoneum* lines the abdominal wall. The peritoneal cavity exists in many areas of the abdomen between the visceral peritoneum and parietal peritoneum.

Esophagus

The esophagus is a long, straight tube communicating in a direct path with the stomach. Passage of food is facilitated by ordinary gravitational forces, as well as by the type and arrangement of muscles in the tube itself. The esophagus extends from the pharynx to the stomach for a distance of 10 inches. It is posterior to the trachea and anterior to the vertebral column; it passes through the diaphragm in front of the aorta to enter the stomach.

Although the esophagus is similar to the remaining portions of the digestive tract, there are a few differences. For instance, the epithelium of the esophagus is *stratified squamous,* whereas the epithelium of the stomach and intestine is columnar. The muscularis layer of the upper third of the esophagus is striated, and that of the lower third is smooth. A transitional zone exists in the middle and contains both striated and smooth muscle. The outer covering of the esophagus is not serous but thickened and fibrous in nature.

Stomach

The stomach, the most dilated portion of the digestive tract, lies under the diaphragm just below the costal margin in the upper abdomen. It serves mainly as a storage center for food prior to passage into the duodenum (the first part of the small intestine), but it permits some digestion.

The stomach consists of three parts: the *fundus,* an upper portion ballooning toward the left; a *body,* the central portion; and the *pyloric portion* (antrum), a relatively constricted portion at the terminal end just before the entrance into the duodenum (Fig. 436).

The wall of the stomach is composed of the same three layers found in other regions of the digestive tract, with certain modifications. The stomach, in addition to having an external longitudinal and an underlying circular layer of smooth muscle, has an oblique layer located inside the circular one. The musculature is heavier in the pyloric portion than in the rest of the stomach. The circular muscle layer is thickened in the pyloric region to form the *pyloric sphincter.*

The *cardia* is the opening between the esophagus and the stomach. It does not refer to any anatomical structure. The *pylorus* is the opening between the stomach and the duodenum. It too, strictly speaking, does not refer to an anatomical structure, although it is often used to designate the entire pyloric portion.

When the stomach is empty, the mucosa is thrown into prominent folds called *rugae,* which flatten out when the stomach is full. The epithelium is *simple columnar.* Densely packed gastric glands, numbering about 35 million, open at the surface via *gastric pits.* These glands are branched tubular and penetrate the lamina propria all the way to the muscularis mucosa.

Small Intestine

The small intestine extends from the distal end of the pyloric sphincter to the cecum, the first portion of the large intestine. It is approximately 18 feet in length and is divided into three portions: the *duodenum, jejunum,* and *ileum.* The duo-

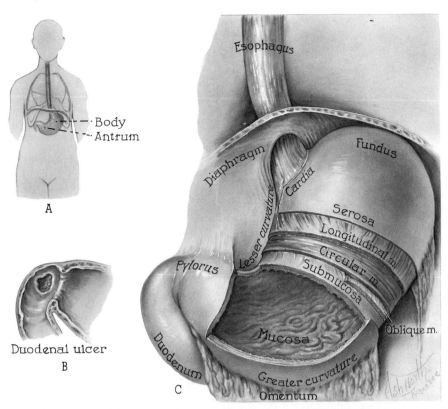

Figure 436. *A,* Anatomic position of esophagus and stomach. *B,* Duodenal ulcer. *C,* Anterior view of the stomach with portion of the anterior wall removed. (Note the various layers which make up the stomach wall.)

denum, named because it is about equal in length to the breadth of 12 fingers, is the shortest, widest, and most fixed portion of the small intestine. It receives secretions of the liver and pancreas. The junction between the duodenum and jejunum is demarcated by a ligamentous band known as the suspensory ligament to the duodenum (Treitz's ligament) (Fig. 437). The duodenum is supplied by branches of the celiac artery and the remainder of the small intestine by branches of the superior mesenteric artery. The mesentery consists of a double fold of serosa which anchors the small intestine to the posterior abdominal wall.

Histologically, the wall of the small intestine is typical of the digestive tract as a whole, but is distinguished by the following specializations of the mucosa which increase its surface area: (1) **Plicae circulares,** permanent transverse folds containing a core of submucosa that may extend two-thirds or more (but rarely completely)

around the circumference of the lumen (interior passageway). (2) **Villi,** fingerlike projections into the lumen. (3) **Microvilli,** numerous cylindrical processes on the free surface of the epithelial cells, which form the so-called *brush,* or *striated, border* (Fig. 438). Tubular glands, known as the *crypts of Lieberkühn,* are found between the bases of the villi. In the duodenum, *Brunner's glands* (which secrete a mucus high in bicarbonate content) are located in the submucosa. *Simple columnar epithelium* lines the small intestine (Fig. 439). The cells of the epithelium are interspersed with mucus-secreting *goblet cells.* The occurrence of these cells increases toward the caudal end of the digestive tube.

Large Intestine

The large intestine differs from the small intestine in several ways, including its

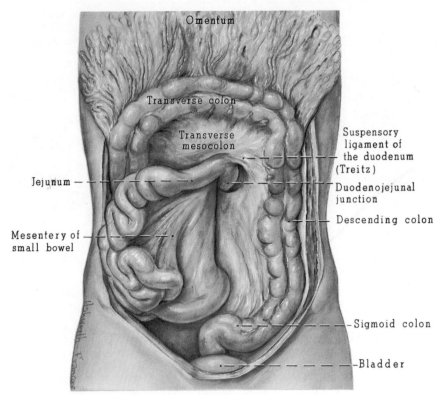

Figure 437.   Anterior view of the intestine with greater omentum raised. The small bowel has been retracted to show the junction of the duodenum and jejunum.

greater width and the following characteristics (Fig. 440):

1. There are no villi on the surface of the tunica mucosa.

2. The glands are of greater depth, are more closely packed, and contain many goblet cells.

3. The longitudinal muscle layer of the cecum and colon (see below) is limited to three bands, visible on the surface, called *teniae coli.*

4. Many appendices epiploicae, or extensions of fat-filled peritoneum, are apparent along the free border of the colon.

The cecum, or first portion of the large intestine, is an elongated pouch situated in the right lower portion of the abdomen. Attached to its base is a slender tube, the vermiform (wormlike) process, or appendix, which has a cavity communicating with the cecum. When infection occurs in the appendix, it is usually secondary to some obstruction of the appendix producing damage and inflammation. Appendicitis is treated by removing the appendix to prevent rupture and peritonitis (inflammation of the peritoneum).

The *ascending colon* extends upward from the cecum on the right posterior abdominal wall to the undersurface of the liver just anterior to the right kidney. The *transverse colon* overlies the coils of the small intestine and crosses the abdominal cavity from right to left below the stomach.

The *descending colon* begins near the spleen, passing downward on the left side of the abdomen to the iliac crest to become the pelvic colon. The descending colon is 6 inches in length and does not possess a mesentery. The pelvic, or sigmoid, colon is so called because of its S-shaped course within the pelvic cavity.

Rectum

The rectum (anatomically the lower end of the large intestine) lies on the anterior surface of the sacrum and coccyx and ter-

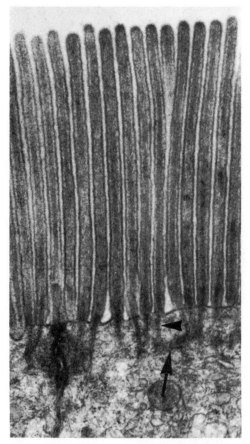

Figure 438. Electron micrograph of the microvilli of the brush border on the free surface of a duodenal columnar cell. Bundles of filaments in the core of the villi penetrate into the cytoplasm (arrow) and blend with the filamentous terminal web (arrow) of the apical cytoplasm. (From Leeson C. R., and Leeson, T. S.: Histology. 3rd ed., Philadelphia, W. B. Saunders Co., 1976.)

minates in the narrow *anal canal,* which opens to the exterior at the *anus* (Fig. 441). About 2.5 cm above the anus the epithelium changes from columnar to *stratified squamous.* At the anus the epithelium is keratinized. The circular smooth muscle of the anal canal is thickened to form the *internal sphincter.* Bundles of skeletal muscle surrounding the canal form the *external sphincter.* Vertical folds, called rectal columns, can be seen, each containing an artery and vein, the latter being subject to enlargements known as *hemorrhoids* (Fig. 442). Hemorrhoids are either internal or external and can cause bleeding and pain. An external hemorrhoid is covered by skin and an internal one by mucosa. Factors

predisposing to hemorrhoids include constipation, increased intra-abdominal pressure (as in pregnancy) and a general hereditary weakness of the vein wall.

ACCESSORY STRUCTURES

The pancreas, liver, and gallbladder, derivatives of that portion of the digestive tube which forms the small intestine, and the salivary glands, derivatives of the cranial portion of the foregut, are intimately associated with the physiology of digestion. The salivary glands secrete digestive enzymes into the mouth that initiate carbohydrate digestion. The pancreas secretes digestive enzymes that act on all three major foodstuffs—carbohydrates, fat and protein. Bile, secreted by the liver, is essential for the normal absorption of digested lipids. The gallbladder concentrates and stores bile. The duodenum receives pancreatic juice via the pancreatic duct, and bile via the common bile duct.

Salivary Glands. There are three pairs of salivary glands: parotid, submaxillary, and sublingual. The *parotid glands* are located in the subcutaneous regions of the cheek, anterior and inferior to the ears. The parotid duct opens just opposite the second upper molar. Each *submaxillary* gland is located in the floor of the mouth close to the angle of the jaw. The submaxillary duct opens laterally to the point at which the frenulum attaches to the tongue. The *sublingual* gland is located under the mucous membrane of the floor of the mouth, just lateral to the tongue. Several sublingual ducts open either near the tongue or into the submaxillary duct (Fig. 443).

Pancreas

The pancreas is a large, lobulated gland resembling the salivary glands in structure (Fig. 444). It has both exocrine and endocrine functions, secreting externally through a duct and internally into the blood or lymph, respectively. Pancreatic juice, a digestive juice, is the product of the exocrine pancreas. The secretions are collected by the major **pancreatic duct** and emptied into the duodenum.

Pancreatic secretion is under the control

Text continued on page 464

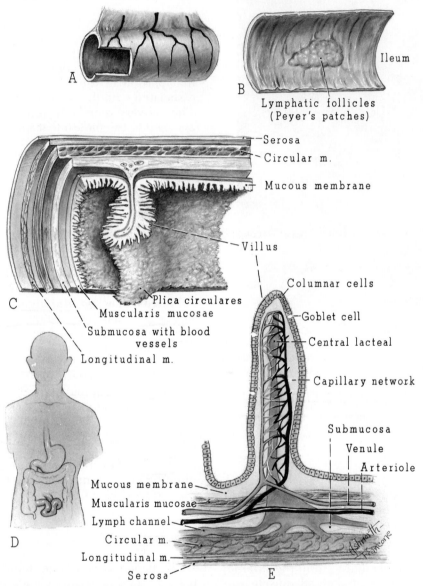

Figure 439. *A*, Segment of small intestine. *B*, Interior view of intestine with Peyer's patch. *C*, Layers composing intestinal wall. *D*, Anatomic position showing stomach and large and small intestines. *E*, Mid-sagittal section through villus.

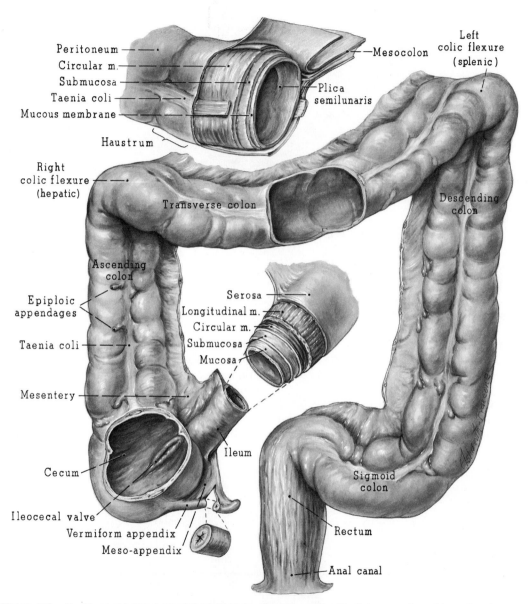

Peritoneum

Circular m.

Submucosa

Taenia coli

Mucous membrane

Haustrum

Mesocolon

Left colic flexure (splenic)

Plica semilunaris

Right colic flexure (hepatic)

Transverse colon

Descending colon

Ascending colon

Epiploic appendages

Taenia coli

Mesentery

Serosa

Longitudinal m.

Circular m.

Submucosa

Mucosa

Ileum

Cecum

Ileocecal valve

Vermiform appendix

Meso-appendix

Sigmoid colon

Rectum

Anal canal

Figure 440. Position and structure of the large intestine. The walls of both large and small intestines have been enlarged and dissected to show their various layers.

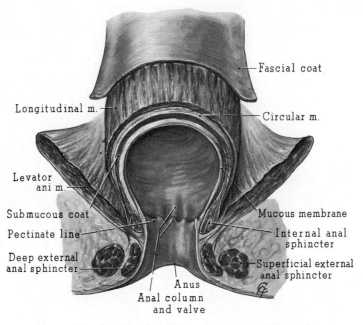

Figure 441.   Anal canal and the various layers of the rectum.

of the hormones *secretin* and *pancreozymin,* which are released from the duodenal mucosa and carried to the pancreas by the blood. They function in pH regulation and digestion, respectively.

Liver

The liver is the largest organ in the body and is located in the upper part of the abdominal cavity under the dome of the diaphragm (Fig. 445). Its superior surface,

in contact with the diaphragm, is smooth and convex. The inferior surface is concave and exhibits impressions marking the point at which the liver is in contact with the abdominal viscera. Blood is transported to the liver from the digestive tract, spleen and pancreas via the portal vein and from the aorta via the hepatic artery. The portal vein and hepatic artery enter the liver through a region called the porta hepatis; both the artery and vein are accompanied by bile ducts and lymphatic vessels (Fig. 446). The

Text continued on page 468

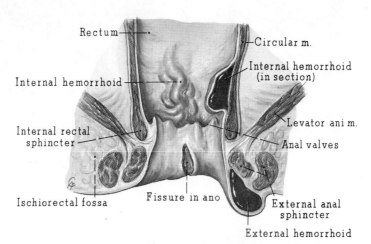

Figure 442.   Common disorders of the anal canal.

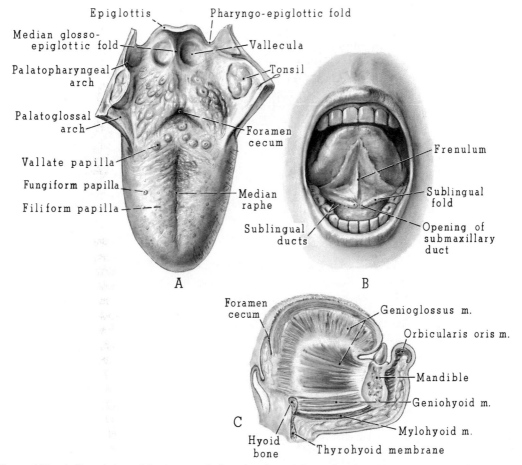

Figure 443. *A*, Dorsal view of the tongue. *B*, Anterior view of the oral cavity with tongue raised. *C*, Mid-sagittal section through the tongue.

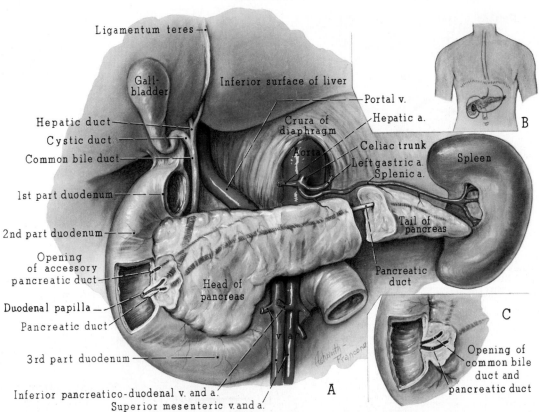

Ligamentum teres

Gall-
bladder

Inferior surface of liver

Portal v.

Hepatic duct

Cystic duct

Common bile duct

Crura of
diaphragm

Hepatic a.

Aorta

Celiac trunk

Left gastric a.
Splenic a.

Spleen

B

1st part duodenum

2nd part duodenum

Tail of
pancreas

Opening
of accessory
pancreatic duct

Pancreatic
duct

Head of
pancreas

Duodenal papilla

Pancreatic duct

C

3rd part duodenum

Opening of
common bile
duct and
pancreatic duct

Inferior pancreatico-duodenal v. and a.
Superior mesenteric v. and a.

A

Figure 444. *A,* Relationship of the pancreas to the duodenum, showing the pancreatic and bile ducts joining at the duodenal papilla. A section has been removed from the pancreas to expose the pancreatic duct. *B,* Anatomic position of the pancreas. *C,* Common variation.

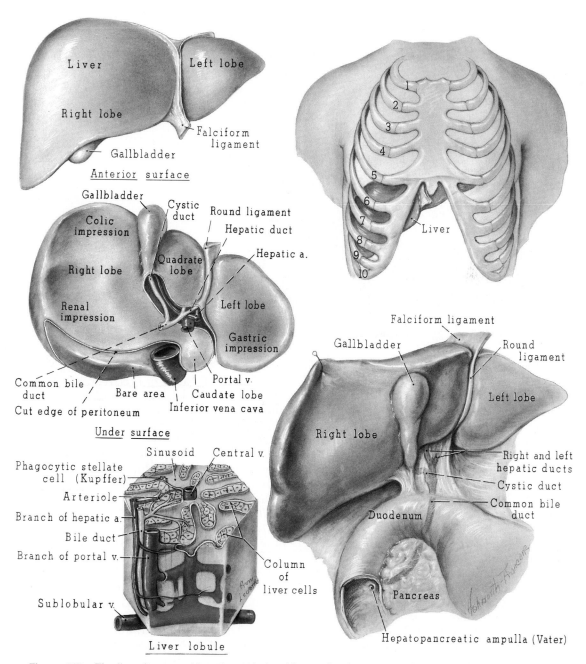

Figure 445. The liver, its normal location, relationships, and unit structure. (*Liver Lobule* section courtesy of Lederle Laboratories.)

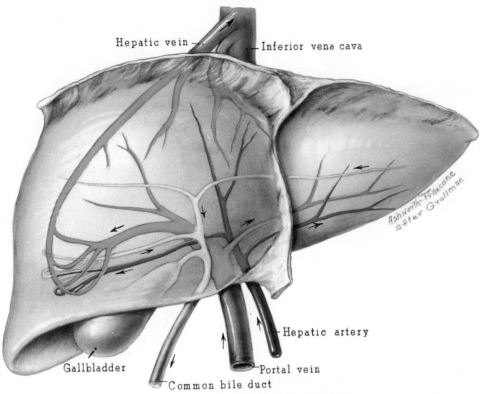

Hepatic vein — Inferior vena cava

Gallbladder

Common bile duct

Hepatic artery

Portal vein

Figure 446. Hepatic portal system of the liver.

portal vein and hepatic arteries repeatedly branch, making the liver a highly vascularized organ.

The liver is demarcated into four lobes. The two main lobes are the right and left, separated by the falciform ligament. The main right lobe is subdivided into a right lobe proper, the quadrate lobe, and the caudate lobe. Each lobe is divided into numerous *lobules,* which are the functional units of the liver. Each lobule is composed of branching plates of liver cells radiating from the center to its periphery (Fig. 445). Branches of the portal vein and hepatic arteries, accompanied by a bile duct, are situated adjacent to the liver lobule in the interlobular connective tissue. Liver sinusoids receive blood from the hepatic artery and portal vein. Phagocytic cells line the sinusoids. These engulf bacteria and other foreign particles in the blood. Blood flows from the sinusoids of the liver to the *central vein* of the lobule and continues to the hepatic veins via the intercalated (sublobular) and collecting veins.

The *bile ducts,* which drain the major right and left lobes of the liver, are formed by union of the bile capillaries, taking origin between the cords of liver cells. The bile ducts from the major lobes unite to form the *hepatic duct,* which is joined by the *cystic duct* from the gallbladder to form the **common bile duct,** which passes obliquely through the duodenal wall, joining the pancreatic duct to form the *duodenal papilla,* or *ampulla of Vater* (Fig. 444).

In relation to digestion and absorption, the major function of the liver is the production of *bile.* It is formed in a volume of 500 to 1000 ml daily, and is concentrated by the gallbladder. The *salts of bile acids* (which are synthesized in the liver from cholesterol) are the principal constituents of bile. These salts combine with the end products of lipid digestion to form water-soluble complexes, thereby greatly facilitating the absorption of these digestive products from the small intestine (for further details, see page 480). The bile pigment bilirubin (the waste product of red blood cell destruction) forms a substantial portion of bile. Inorganic salts and small amounts of cholesterol and phospholipid are other bile constituents. Control of bile secretion by the liver is due primarily to the hormone secretin, which can increase the output of bile some 10 to 20 per cent.

The liver, although considered a structural and functional part of the digestive system, functions in many activities not directly concerned with the process of digestion. Among these are hematopoiesis and coagulation, phagocytosis, and detoxification. The liver produces erythrocytes in the embryo—and in some abnormal states in the adult. It also synthesizes prothrombin and fibrinogen, both of which are necessary for coagulation of blood. The liver destroys old and worn-out erythrocytes and removes bacteria and foreign bodies from the blood via its Kupffer cells, which are a part of the reticuloendothelial system (see Chapter 3). It functions in detoxification by changing nitrogenous wastes, such as ammonia, into the less toxic urea. The mechanisms by which the liver detoxifies include oxidation (the principal mechanism), reduction, hydrolysis, and conjugation (chemical combination with some natural substance of the body such as the glucose derivative glucuronic acid).

The influences of the liver on nutrition include storage of glycogen; storage of vitamins A, D, E, and K, as well as B_{12} and certain other water-soluble vitamins; and metabolism of carbohydrates, fats, and proteins.

Cirrhosis is a disease of the liver representing a progressive degeneration of liver cells; it is characterized by an increase in connective tissue throughout the liver lobules.

Alcoholism is the most common cause of cirrhosis. Although malnutrition is common in alcoholics, and malnutrition does impair liver function, biopsy studies with human volunteers have demonstrated that the consumption of alcohol with nutritionally optimal diets causes the accumulation of fat in the liver (the characteristic "fatty liver," the first and reversible phase of the disease) and ultrastructural changes in the liver cell. Animal studies suggest that acetaldehyde, one of the metabolic products of alcohol, may have a direct, toxic effect on the liver cell and that hydrogen, another product of alcohol metabolism, may contribute to he-

patic fat accumulation. These observations raise doubts about a once widely held belief that malnutrition is the primary cause of alcoholic cirrhosis. In the usual sequence of events in the disease, the engorgement of the liver cells with fat interferes with their normal function and causes cell death. The necrosis triggers an inflammatory process (alcoholic hepatitis). In some cases death occurs at this stage. In the final stage fibrous scars, the hallmark of cirrhosis, disrupt the architecture of the liver cell and interfere with the flow of blood to and from the liver. Backup pressure in the portal system can lead to excessive fluid loss in the abdominal cavity (*ascites*). The accumulation of ammonia and other toxic substances in the blood as a result of decreased liver function can cause hepatic coma and death.

Gallbladder

The gallbladder is a saclike structure attached to the inferior surface of the liver and serving as a reservoir for bile. The cystic duct of the gallbladder joins the ductal system from the liver to form the common bile duct (Fig. 447).

Bile consists chiefly of water, salts of bile acids, pigments, inorganic salts, cholesterol, and phospholipids. Water, chloride, and bicarbonates are absorbed in the gallbladder, increasing the relative concentration of bile salts.

Contraction of the gallbladder with explusion of bile into the duodenum is stimulated by a hormonal mechanism. The presence of certain foodstuffs—particularly fat in the duodenum—causes release of a hormone, *cholecystokinin* (identical to pancreozymin), which then reaches the gallbladder via the blood and brings on contraction. Gallbladder contraction occurs within 30 minutes following a meal.

Gallstones (cholelithiasis). Gallstones are composed of the constituents of bile that have precipitated and formed into crystals. The incidence of gallstones increases with age and is twice as common among women as men. In about 90 per cent of the cases, cholesterol is the major or sole constituent of the stones. Calcium is sometimes an important component, and bilirubin predominates in some stones. Gallstone forma-

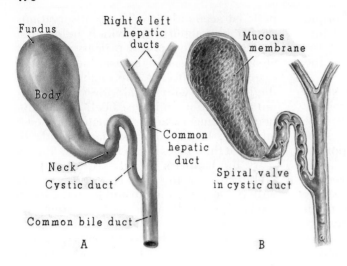

Figure 447. *A*, External view of the gall-bladder. *B*, Sagittal section through the gallbladder.

tion is associated, among other things, with a disturbance in gallbladder absorptive function due to injury or infection, stasis of bile, or abnormal cholesterol metabolism (which could mean some error in its absorption, utilization, excretion, or synthesis in the body from acetyl-CoA). The ratio of cholesterol and bile salts appears to be especially critical. It has been observed that most gallbladder patients have a smaller pool of bile acids in general and often much less *chenodeoxycholic acid* in particular. These findings have led to the introduction at the Mayo Clinic of so-called "cheno" therapy—ingestion of chenodeoxycholic acid. This treatment, which is quite successful, literally dissolves the gallstones.

Jaundice is a yellowish discoloration of the skin, mucous membrane, and body fluids because of an excess of biliary pigment. The most common type is *obstructive jaundice*, which is caused by internal occlusion of the bile duct by gallstones or by a growth such as a tumor. *Hemolytic jaundice* is a form of jaundice that results from an abnormally rapid formation of bile pigments following hemolysis (destruction of red blood cells). *Hepatic jaundice* is impaired excretion of bile due to damage to the hepatic cells.

Cholecystitis is an inflammation of the gallbladder. A patient with cholecystitis will experience intermittent attacks of severe pain, most often after heavy meals. Belching is a common finding with cholecystitis, as is intolerance to fats and leafy vegetables.

MOTOR ACTIVITIES OF THE DIGESTIVE TRACT

Swallowing. The process of swallowing (deglutition) is divided into three stages: buccal, pharyngeal, and esophageal. In the buccal phase the ground, rounded mass of food mixed with saliva, called the *bolus* (Latin for choice bit), passes through the oral cavity into the pharynx. In the pharyngeal phase the bolus passes through the pharynx into the esophagus, and in the esophageal phase it passes through the esophagus into the stomach. Only the buccal phase is under voluntary control. In this stage, the tongue is pulled backward and up against the hard and soft palates, forcing the bolus into the oral pharynx. As the bolus passes into the pharynx, it stimulates receptors surrounding the entrance to the oral pharynx which transmit impulses to the *swallowing center* located in the medulla near the respiratory center (Fig. 448). Signals from this center initiate a number of automatic responses including (1) raising the soft palate and pushing it against the posterior wall of the pharynx, thereby preventing regurgitation of food through the nose, and (2) pulling the larynx upward and forward under the tongue and drawing the vocal cords together. The upward motion of the larynx and backward movement of the tongue push the epiglottis into a horizontal position above the larynx. These actions, especially the approximation of the vocal cords, prevent food from passing through the larynx. During this time, discharges

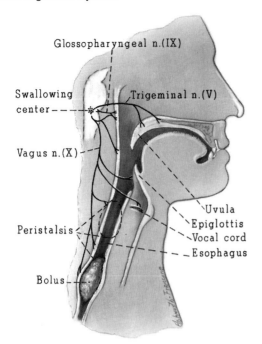

Glossopharyngeal n.(IX)

Swallowing
center

Trigeminal n.(V)

Vagus n.(X)

Peristalsis

Uvula
Epiglottis
Vocal cord
Esophagus

Bolus

Figure 448. Movement of bolus down esophagus.
The trigeminal nerve controls the muscles of mastication; the glossopharyngeal nerve, the stylopharyngeus
muscle; and the vagus nerve, esophageal peristalsis.

from the swallowing center inhibit respiration. Food, except for large quantities of
fluid, is deflected to one side or other of the
epiglottis rather than over its edge into the
pharynx.

When the bolus enters the pharynx, reflex
contraction of the superior constrictor muscle of the pharynx initiates a rapid **peristaltic** (G. *peristaltikos,* clasping and com-
pressing) **wave** propelling food down the
pharynx toward the esophagus. Relaxation
of the cricopharyngeus muscle and the
upper esophageal sphincter allows food to
enter the esophagus. The peristaltic wave
(comparable to constricting one's fingers
around a tube and sliding them toward one
end [see Fig. 449]) continues into the
esophagus and sweeps the bolus toward the
stomach. Before the wave reaches the
stomach, a slow wave of relaxation above
the stomach opens the lower esophageal, or
cardiac, sphincter. The cardiac sphincter is
anatomically indistinguishable from the rest
of the esophagus but physiologically represents a segment of the esophagus about 5
cm above the stomach that remains constricted until reflexively relaxed by an

approaching peristaltic wave. Its constriction prevents reflux of gastric contents into
the esophagus. A relaxed sphincter, a condition called *chalasia,* is sometimes seen in
infants but rarely in adults.

Peristalsis in the esophagus is largely a
vagal reflex; that is, fibers in the vagus nerve
conduct impulses from the esophagus to the
swallowing center and back again to initiate
peristalsis when food reaches the esophagus. Since the muscular layer of the
upper third of the esophagus is skeletal
muscle, severing branches of the vagus
nerve innervating the esophagus interferes
with swallowing. However, in time, the
intrinsic excitability of the smooth muscle
of the lower portion of the esophagus
becomes adequate, under these circumstances to trigger peristaltic waves when
gravity forces food into the lower regions of
the esophagus.

Peristalsis in the Stomach

Accumulation of food in the stomach
initiates peristaltic waves in the stomach
that serve to mix the contents and, as the
mixture becomes fluid, to gradually empty
the stomach by forcing fluid through the
pylorus into the duodenum. The murky,
semifluid mass of partially digested food
that passes along the digestive tract is called
chyme (G. *chymos,* juice).

Each peristaltic wave begins as a slight
constriction, usually near the midpoint of
the body of the stomach. The wave becomes
progressively deeper as it travels toward the
pylorus and ends with a contraction of the
pyloric sphincter. A new wave begins every
20 seconds, and each wave lasts about one
minute. Thus, three waves at a time travel
down the stomach. The rate of emptying is
determined largely by the strength of the
contractions. Relaxation of the sphincter, of
course, permits gastric contents to pass

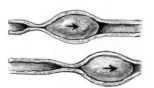

Figure 449. Peristalsis.

through the pylorus. But the narrow pylorus resists the passage of fluid, so that the strength of the peristaltic contraction determines the amount of chyme that is expelled into the duodenum in each cycle. Contraction of the sphincter at the end of each cycle prevents regurgitation of duodenal contents into the stomach.

Feedback from the duodenum is an important regulator of gastric emptying. Two control mechanisms are involved, one *neuronal*, the other *hormonal*. Both have **inhibitory** effects on gastric motility. The neuronal mechanism, known as the *enterogastric* (G. *enteron*, intestine; G. *gaster*, belly) *reflex* is mediated by the vagus nerve (through central connections in the medulla) and probably also by the myenteric nerve plexus. The reflex is activated, among other things, by acids, the products of protein digestion, hypo- or hypertonic fluids and a building up of pressure in the duodenum. Hormonal feedback inhibition of gastric motility is elicited largely by the accumulation of fat in the duodenum, as well as by acids and hypertonic solutions. These stimuli provoke the release of a hormone called *enterogastrone* from the mucosa of the duodenum which is transported by the blood stream to the stomach where it exerts an inhibitory effect on gastric contractions. The delay in stomach emptying induced by these feedback mechanisms protects the duodenum against overloading and excessive acidity and allows more time for the digestive processes in the duodenum to proceed.

Vagal reflexes are important for maintaining effective gastric peristalsis during digestion. Following section of the vagus nerve (vagotomy), peristaltic pressure may be insufficient for normal gastric emptying. Another cause of inadequate emptying of the stomach is *pylorospasm,* a congenital condition in infants but rarely seen in adults. Actually, the abnormality in congenital infant pylorospasm is not sustained contraction of the pyloric sphincter but rather hypertrophy of the pyloric muscle. Some clinicians, therefore, prefer to describe the condition as pyloric stenosis.

Hunger Contractions. When the stomach has been empty for a long time, so-called "hunger" contractions may occur. They are usually rhythmic, strong, peristaltic contractions lasting 20 seconds with no pause between successive contractions. Shorter, nonrhythmic contractions may also occur. Very strong contractions sometimes fuse to produce a sustained spasm lasting two to three minutes. At one time some physiologists believed that hunger pangs were the primary regulator of appetite. However, although some individuals describe hunger in terms of these localized contractions, others never experience them. Furthermore, surgical section of the vagus nerve, which eliminates hunger contractions, fails to diminish the sensation of hunger in patients who before surgery consistently felt these hunger pangs. Hunger, for these individuals, simply became the diffuse feeling it is with most people.

Vomiting

Vomiting is a reflex coordinated by a center in the medulla (called the *vomiting center*) which has the effect of emptying the upper gastrointestinal tract. Stimuli within the alimentary canal, especially the duodenum, may activate the vomiting center, as may stimuli from various other parts of the body. Nauseating odors or sights, seasickness, and emotional upset can trigger vomiting. Drugs such as apomorphine may induce vomiting by acting directly on the vomiting center. The sequence of events in vomiting is as follows: (1) Strong, sustained contractions occur in the upper small intestine; (2) the pyloric sphincter contracts; (3) the pyloric portion of the stomach contracts. These three responses fill the fundus and body of the stomach, which are relaxed and dilated. This is followed by (4) relaxation of the lower and upper esophageal sphincters and (5) inspiration and closure of the glottis. Contraction of the abdominal muscles and diaphragm then compresses the stomach, evacuating its contents.

Segmenting Contractions and Peristalsis in the Small Intestine

Contractions of the small intestine are of two types — peristalsis and those known as segmenting. The latter are rhythmic con-

Figure 450. Rhythmic segmenting contractions.

tractions occurring along a section of the intestine which divide it into small segments, giving it the appearance of a chain of sausages. When the rings of constriction relax, new contractions form rings in the middle of the previously formed segments, thereby forming new segments in different positions (Fig. 450). Intestinal contents are mixed by the repeated segmentations. In addition, the contractions travel toward the distal end of the intestine and help move the contents down the intestinal tract. The segmenting contractions occur at a rate of 11 per minute in the duodenum and eight to nine per minute in the ileum. In the regions between, the rates exhibit a gradient with highest activity toward the duodenum, lowest toward the ileum.

Peristaltic waves are usually superimposed upon the segmenting contractions and, as they travel along the intestine, sweep the contents toward the distal end. Ordinarily the waves occur at regular intervals and travel for varying distances.

Peristaltic contractions, characteristic of many tubular structures of the body, have one feature in common—the constricted ring moves in one direction only. These structures are intrinsically polarized. As mentioned, parasympathetic (vagal) stimulation increases the intensity of peristaltic contractions by smooth muscle of the alimentary canal, but surgical section does not abolish them. Paralysis of the myenteric nerve plexus, however, does eliminate peristalsis.

Ileocecal Valve and Movements of the Large Intestine

The lower end of the ileum projects as an invagination into the cecum, forming what is known as the ileocecal valve, which functions to permit gradual passage of small amounts of intestinal contents into the cecum while at the same time preventing regurgitation from the colon into the ileum. While digestion is in progress, the valve

opens rhythmically, each time allowing the injection of about 15 ml of fluid into the cecum. Ingestion of food intensifies ileal peristalsis and increases the frequency of opening of the ileocecal valve (so-called *gastroileal reflex*).

The principal type of colon contraction is similar to the segmenting contractions of the small intestine. A distinguishing feature of these contractions is the outward bulging of the relaxed segments between constricted rings into sacs called *haustra* as a result of the simultaneous contraction of longitudinal and circular muscle. This type of contraction serves primarily to *mix* colon contents, but may contribute to propulsive action by traveling in an analward direction. Of much less frequent occurrence than these mixing contractions are peristaltic contractions called *mass movements*. Mass movements generally occur no more than two or three times a day, most commonly shortly after or during a meal. This response to eating is referred to as the *gastrocolic reflex*. The mass movement wave is characteristically prolonged, lasting two to four minutes and has the effect of rapidly transferring the contents of the proximal colon to the distal colon. Since such movements are often followed by a desire to defecate, it is assumed they can be strong enough to move the colon contents into the rectum.

Defecation

The rectum is normally empty until just prior to defecation—the fecal mass is stored in the sigmoid (pelvic) colon. The desire to defecate arises when, usually as a result of mass movement, feces are forced into the rectum, raising rectal pressure. Rectal pressoreceptors can distinguish between increases in pressure resulting from feces, liquid or gas. Defecation is preceded by voluntary relaxation of the external sphincter and compression of the abdominal contents by straining efforts. These actions give rise to stimuli that support and augment the *defecation reflex,* which is responsible for evacuating the rectum. The defecation reflex is initiated by distention of the rectum. When this occurs, impulses are transmitted to the reflex centers in the spinal cord (sacral and lumbar segments) and brain (hypothalamus). Return signals to

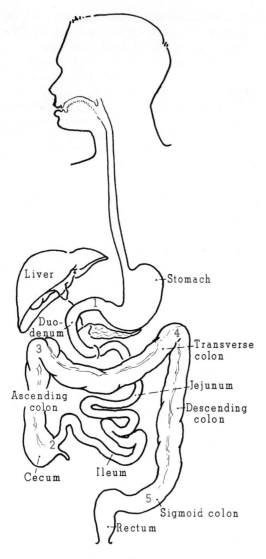

1– 1-5 min.
2– 4½ hrs.
3– 6½ hrs.
4– 9½ hrs.
5– 12–24 hrs.

Figure 451.   The time required for food substances to reach various portions of the digestive tract.

the colon, rectum, and anus trigger intense peristaltic contractions of the colon (the entire colon may be involved) and rectum, and relaxation of the internal anal sphincter. Voluntary control over the external anal sphincter either allows defecation to proceed or inhibits it. If an individual repeatedly ignores the defecation reflex, recondi-

tioning of the reflex occurs with the end result that rectal distention is no longer followed by an urge to defecate; consequently, feces are retained in the rectum and colonic stasis, or *constipation*, ensues.

DIGESTION

The process of digestion involves the enzymatic breakdown of food into products that can be absorbed from the intestinal tract into the blood stream. The major foods are **carbohydrates, fats,** and **proteins.** The principal carbohydrate in food is *starch*—plant polysaccharides constructed from glucose units. Among other dietary carbohydrates are *glycogen* (so-called "animal starch"), *sucrose* (table sugar), a disaccharide consisting of glucose and fructose, and *lactose* (milk sugar), a disaccharide composed of glucose and galactose.

Digestion begins in the mouth with the enzymatic action of **ptyalin,** salivary amylase (G. *amylon,* starch). Ptyalin hydrolyzes (splitting with the addition of water) starch (and glycogen) into the disaccharide *maltose.* However, food does not remain in the mouth long enough for more than a small percentage of dietary starch to be converted to maltose. The enzymatic action of ptyalin continues in the stomach for as long as several hours until the contents are mixed with gastric secretions. When this occurs, the acid mixture of the stomach inactivates ptyalin. About 30 to 60 per cent of the ingested starch is degraded to maltose before the action of ptyalin is halted.

In the stomach the only digestive process of any consequence initiated is the hydrolysis of proteins. The enzyme **pepsin** splits proteins into derivative proteins, known as *proteoses* and *peptones,* and into *large polypeptides.*

In the small intestine enzymes delivered to the duodenum in pancreatic juice continue the digestion of starch and protein. In addition, **pancreatic lipase** is responsible for the digestion of most of the dietary fat, splitting fat into *monoglycerides, fatty acids,* and *glycerol.* The pancreatic proteolytic enzymes, **trypsin, chymotrypsin,** and **carboxypeptidases,** degrade proteins and the products of pepsin digestion into smaller *polypeptides* and *dipeptides.* **Intes-**

Table 42. PRINCIPAL DIGESTIVE ENZYMES

ENZYME	SOURCE	SUBSTRATE	PRODUCTS	OPTIMAL pH
Ptyalin	Salivary glands	Starch	Maltose	6–7
Pepsin	Chief cells of stomach	Protein	Proteoses, peptones, polypeptides	1.6–2.4
Enterokinase	Duodenal mucosa	Trypsinogen	Trypsin	–
Trypsin	Exocrine pancreas	Proteins and polypeptides	Small polypeptides (also activates chymotrypsinogen and procarboxypeptidases)	8.0
Chymotrypsin		Proteins and polypeptides	Small polypeptides	8.0
Carboxypeptidases		Polypeptides	Smaller polypeptides,° amino acids	–
Pancreatic lipase		Fat	Monoglycerides, fatty acids, glycerol	8.0
Pancreatic amylase		Starch	Maltose units	6.7–7.0
Nucleases		Nucleic acids	Nucleotides	–
Aminopeptidases	Small intestine	Polypeptides	Smaller polypeptides,°° amino acids	8.0
Dipeptidase		Dipeptides	Amino acids	–
Maltase Lactase Sucrase		Maltose Lactose Sucrose	Hexoses (glucose, galactose and fructose)	5.0–7.0 5.8–6.2 5.0–7.0
Nucleotidase		Nucleotides	Nucleosides, phosphoric acid	–
Nucleosidase		Nucleosides	Purine or pyrimidine base, pentose	–
Interstinal lipase		Fat	Monoglycerides, fatty acids and glycerol	8.0

°Removal of C-terminal amino acid
°°Removal of N-terminal amino acid

tinal **aminopeptidases** and **dipeptidase** complete the degradation of poly- and dipeptides into *amino acids.* The end product of the digestive action of **pancreatic amylase** on starch is maltose, the same product formed by the action of ptyalin. **Intestinal maltase** splits maltose into two *glucose* molecules. Other intestinal enzymes digest sucrose and lactose. **Intestinal** **sucrase** splits sucrose into *glucose* and *fructose*; **intestinal lactase** degrades lactose into *glucose* and *galactose.* Table 42 lists the principal digestive enzymes. A description of the control of the secretion of digestive enzymes and further details of the digestive process in the mouth, stomach, and intestine appear in the following sections.

Table 43.   GASTROINTESTINAL HORMONES

HORMONE	SOURCE	AGENTS STIMULATING PRODUCTION	ACTION
Gastrin	Gastric mucosa of the pyloric antrum	Distention and protein derivatives in the region of the pyloric antrum	Stimulates the secretion of an acid-rich digestive juice by the gastric glands
Enterogastrone	Mucosa of the small intestine	Fats, hypertonic solutions and acid in the intestine	Inhibits gastric secretion and motility
Secretin	Duodenal mucosa	Principally acid in the duodenum	Stimulates secretion of watery pancreatic juice containing bicarbonate
Pancreozymin (cholecystokinin		Products of protein digestion (proteoses and peptones) and fat in the duodenum	Stimulates the production of an enzyme-rich pancreatic juice; stimulates contraction of the gallbladder
Villikinin	Mucosa of the small intestine	Chyme in the intestine	Stimulates movements of the intestinal villi

Salivary Secretions

Salivary secretions are of two types: (1) *serous secretion*, a clear solution containing the digestive enzyme ptyalin, and (2) *mucous secretion*, a thick, viscous solution containing mucus. The secretion of the parotid gland is serous. Submaxillary secretion is both serous and mucous, sublingual mucous only. The binding and lubricating properties of mucus facilitate mastication, the formation of the bolus and swallowing. Saliva is secreted continuously and is greatly increased by appetite-arousing stimuli. About 1 to 1.5 liters of saliva is secreted daily.

Salivary secretion is **exclusively under nervous control.** The control center for salivation, a group of nuclei between the medulla and pons, is stimulated by a variety of sensations. Thus, the taste, smell, or sight of food activates the center, and impulses conducted by parasympathetic nerve fibers (in the seventh and ninth cranial nerves) stimulate salivary secretion. Foods arousing pleasant sensations provoke a copious secretion. Those arousing unpleasant sensations cause far less secretion and may even inhibit salivation to the extent that swallowing is made difficult.

The characteristics and the actual volume of saliva are related to the type of food ingested. For example, acid substances and dry foods produce a large volume of thin, watery saliva; milk or cold water produces a smaller volume of viscous saliva. The enzymatic content of saliva varies with the stimulus. Meat and weak acids stimulate the production of similar volumes of saliva, but the enzyme content is greater with meat than with weak acids.

During periods of dehydration when the body has lost large quantities of fluid, salivary secretion is reduced or suppressed completely. This may also occur at times of emotional stress. Irritation of the esophageal, gastric, and duodenal mucous membranes reflexly stimulates salivary secretion. Thus, excessive salivation may be an early warning sign of disease of the upper digestive tract.

Gastric Secretion

Gastric glands are of two different types: *Pyloric glands,* as well as those surrounding the opening to the esophagus (cardiac glands), secrete mucus exclusively. The *fundic glands* secrete digestive juice which contains pepsinogen (the precursor of pepsin, the enzyme that digests protein to proteoses, peptones, and large polypeptides), hydrochloric acid, and some mucus. Mucus is also secreted by surface epithelial cells. The presence of a thick, tenacious layer of mucus protects the stomach lining from the acidity and the proteolytic action of gastric juice. Hydrochloric acid is secreted by the *parietal,* or *oxyntic* (G. *oxynein,* to make acid), cells located for the most part below the mucus-secreting cells, which are situated in the neck of the fundic glands. The *chief,* or *zymogenic,* cells, which secrete pepsinogen, are located at the base of the fundic glands.

A characteristic of proteolytic enzymes in the gastrointestinal tract is their synthesis as inactive precursors, called *zymogens,* which are stored in granules within the glandular cells. Synthesis in this form and storage in granules protect the cells from self-destruction. Pepsinogen, following its secretion, is transformed into pepsin upon contact with acid by a process known as *autoactivation.* In the initial step, a fragment is split off one end to produce active pepsin, which then catalyzes further activation at a rapidly accelerating rate.

Control of gastric secretion is **both nervous and hormonal.** In the first phase of gastric secretion, called the **cephalic phase,** sensations such as those caused by the sight, taste or smell of food stimulate gastric secretion. The nerve impulses eliciting secretion are conducted to the stomach by way of the vagus nerve. Gastric secretion is triggered (1) *directly* by stimulation of the gastric glands via the myenteric nerve plexus and (2) *indirectly* by stimulating, via the myenteric nerve plexus, pyloric mucosal cells that secrete the hormone *gastrin.* Gastrin is absorbed into the blood stream and transported to the gastric glands. The hormone causes considerably greater secretion by parietal cells than by chief cells. The cephalic phase of gastric secretion is abolished by section of the vagus nerve.

When food enters the stomach, pressure and chemical sensations stimulate gastric secretion by the same two mechanisms just described for the cephalic phase: (1) direct stimulation of the gastric glands and (2) indirect stimulation by activating the release of gastrin. Gastric secretion in response to food in the stomach is referred to as the **gastric phase** of secretion. The two phases overlap in time and interact so that the total effect of the two is greater than the sum of the individual phases. Interruption of the cephalic phase, for example, greatly reduces the response to the gastric phase.

The presence of certain digestive products in the upper part of the small intestine also stimulates secretion of gastric juice. This phase, of lesser importance than the first two, is called the **intestinal phase** of gastric secretion. The intestinal phase is mediated by a hormone (sometimes called "intestinal gastrin") released by the duodenum that acts on the stomach.

Inhibition of Gastric Secretion. The interplay between stimulation and inhibition of gastric secretion determines the activity of the gastric glands at any one time. Two inhibitory mechanisms have been well characterized; one operates through the stomach, the other through the duodenum.

The presence of a strong acid in the pyloric antrum results in a decrease in gastric secretion. It is believed that a pH of less than 2.5 inhibits the release of gastrin from the pyloric antrum and thereby decreases the secretion of an acid-rich gastric juice. The duodenal inhibitory mechanism is exerted largely by the hormone called enterogastrone, described earlier in connection with duodenal feedback inhibition of gastric motility. Fat, acid, or hypertonic solutions stimulate the release of enterogastrone, which inhibits gastric secretion. Another duodenal hormone, secretin, released when hydrochloric acid enters the duodenum, inhibits acid secretion by the stomach. (Secretin also stimulates bicarbonate secretion by the pancreas—see below.)

Despite all the mechanisms for inhibiting oversecretion of hydrochloric acid and damage to the mucosal wall of the stomach and duodenum from this acid, **peptic ulceration** frequently occurs. A peptic ulcer is an ulcer in either the stomach or the duodenum caused in part by the action of gastric juice. The major goal of both medical and surgical treatment of peptic ulcer is to reduce the production of hydrochloric acid by the parietal cells of the stomach. Medical reduction of parietal cell secretion involves neutralizing the acid after secretion by ingestion of antacids or by the use of anticholinergic drugs to block the stimuli for the secretion of acids.

Until a few years ago, the principal surgical means of reducing acidity was to remove the major portion of the stomach secreting hydrochloric acid. Now, the principal aim of surgical treatment is to reduce the stimuli for acid secretion. This is accomplished by cutting the vagus nerves and by removing the gastrin-producing pyloric gland area (antrum). Sectioning the vagus nerves, as mentioned, is associated with an impairment of gastric emptying; when this operation is employed, the surgeon must perform a concomitant drainage procedure, allowing the pylorus to drain freely into the duodenum, or must actually join the stomach to the jejunum to aid gastric emptying after surgery.

Pancreatic Secretion

As described above, enzymes in pancreatic juice continue the process of starch and protein digestion in the small intestine. Virtually all of the fat entering the duodenum is undigested. Only a small amount of butterfat is digested in the stomach by gastric lipase (a tributyrase). The bulk of the dietary fat is digested by pancreatic lipase. Intestinal lipase contributes to some extent to fat digestion. The importance of pancreatic lipase for normal fat digestion is made plain by the observation that the principal consequence of pancreatic exocrine insufficiency is excess fat excretion in feces (steatorrhea). Pancreatic juice also contains phospholipase, which digests phospholipids, and cholesterol esterase, which hydrolyzes cholesterol esters (splitting off the long-chain fatty acid portion).

The proteolytic enzymes, trypsin, chymotrypsin, and carboxypeptidases, are secreted as inactive precursors. *Trypsinogen* is converted to trypsin by the action of *enterokinase*, an enzyme secreted by the small intestine, and by an autoactivation process. Trypsin converts *chymotrypsinogen* and *procarboxypeptidases* to their active forms.

Pancreatic secretion is regulated by **both neuronal and hormonal** mechanisms. *Vagal stimulation* of the pancreas occurs at the same time as the cephalic phase of gastric secretion. Two hormones secreted by the duodenum, *secretin* and *pancreozymin*, act on the exocrine pancreas. The exocrine pancreas contains two types of secretory cells. One type (acinar cells) secretes *enzymes*. The other type (lobular duct cells) secretes *water and bicarbonate*. Secretin acts on duct cells to induce the secretion of water and bicarbonate. Vagal stimulation and pancreozymin induce the secretion of

enzymes by activating acinar cells. Hydrochloric acid is the most effective stimulus for the release of secretin. Induction of the release of bicarbonate by secretin protects the duodenum against peptic ulceration and creates a favorable pH for the activity of pancreatic enzymes. Certain products of digestion are the most effective stimuli for the release of pancreozymin.

Intestinal Enzymes

The small intestine furnishes enzymes that complete the digestion of protein and carbohydrate and contribute to some extent to the digestion of fat. There is no evidence supporting the secretion of enzymes by intestinal glands (crypts of Lieberkühn) other than enterokinase (the activator of trypsin) and amylase. The presence of other enzymes in the luminal contents can be accounted for by the dissolution of cells continuously shed at the tips of the intestinal villi. Cell division at the base of the crypts and migration of new cells up the villi continuously replace shed cells.

The duodenum contains special glands in the submucosa, called Brunner's glands, which secrete mucus. The ducts of these glands open into the crypts of Lieberkühn. Their secretion, as well as the secretion of mucus by mucosal goblet cells, is an important protective mechanism against ulceration.

ABSORPTION

The absorption of the end products of digestion occurs almost exclusively in the small intestine. Although some glucose, alcohol, and water are absorbed in the stomach, the amount so absorbed is negligible. Organic nutrients are not absorbed from the large intestine, but significant amounts of water and salts are.

The site of absorption in the small intestine is the columnar cells of the villi. Each villus contains a *rich capillary plexus* beneath the basement membrane and a large lymphatic vessel, called the *central lacteal*, in the core (Fig. 439). Thin smooth muscle fibers continuous with the muscularis mucosae are also present in the

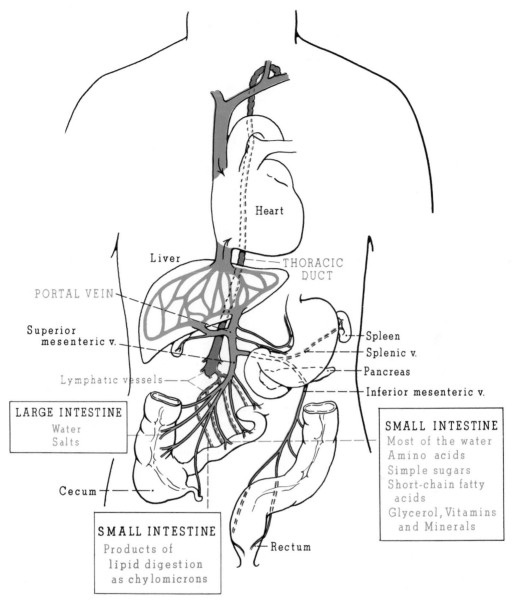

LARGE INTESTINE
Water
Salts

SMALL INTESTINE
Most of the water
Amino acids
Simple sugars
Short-chain fatty
 acids
Glycerol, Vitamins
 and Minerals

SMALL INTESTINE
Products of
lipid digestion
as chylomicrons

Figure 452.   Products of digestion are absorbed in the stomach and small and large intestines.

lamina propria of the villus. Their contraction is especially important for maintaining the flow of lymph. Simple sugars, amino acids, short-chain fatty acids (derived from butterfat), and glycerol are absorbed into the capillary network and transported to the liver via the *hepatic portal vein* (Fig. 452). The major products of lipid digestion are absorbed as chylomicrons (see below) into the central lacteal and carried via the intestinal lymphatics to the *thoracic duct,* which empties into the

left subclavian vein just above the heart (Fig. 452).

The simple sugars glucose, fructose, and galactose are absorbed by active transport processes. The active absorption of glucose and galactose is apparently coupled to the active transport of sodium. Inhibition of active sodium transport interferes with the absorption of these sugars. At one time it was generally believed that maltose, sucrose, and lactose were completely hydrolyzed to simple sugars in the intestinal lumen. A number of observations, however, indicate that some of these disaccharides are hydrolyzed within the microvilli of the brush border following their absorption. For example, it has been found that when preparations of hamster small intestine are incubated with sucrose solutions glucose accumulates within the epithelium to a concentration 20 times that of glucose in the incubation medium. In addition, the maltase, sucrase, and lactase activity of the mucosa is located primarily in the brush border.

In humans the activity of lactase is maximal immediately after birth. Thereafter it declines, reaching a minimum in most children after one and one-half to three years. High lactase activity in human adults is found only in dairying cultures, where milk consumption is traditionally high. Adults, other than those of milk-drinking populations, are intolerant to excessive amounts of dietary lactose. Apparently, lactose tolerance is transmitted genetically and as a dominant trait. **Lactose intolerance** in infants is of clinical importance. The consequences of intolerance are bloating, belching, flatulence, cramps, and explosive diarrhea. Two processes cause these symptoms: (1) the osmotic effect of lactose in the colon draws water into the lumen, and (2) fermentation of lactose by colon bacteria generates organic acids and carbon dioxide.

The absorption of amino acids also involves active transport mechanisms. The bulk of the ingested protein is hydrolyzed to amino acids, and the absorption of protein occurs essentially only as amino acids.

The efficient absorption of fat is made possible by the formation of a clear solution containing the digested products. This is accomplished by the formation of polymolecular aggregates called **micelles,** composed of monoglycerides, free fatty acids, cholesterol, phospholipids, and bile salts. The formation of micelles requires the presence of bile salts. In their absence the absorption of fat is greatly reduced and the absorption of cholesterol is completely abolished. When fat is undergoing digestion, pancreatic lipase acts at the interface of fat droplets and the water medium in which the droplets are suspended. As the digestion proceeds, two distinct phases can be distinguished—a clear phase containing micelles and an oily phase containing tri- and diglycerides. The formation of the clear phase not only provides a medium for absorption but also accelerates digestion by removing the end products of digestion from the site of enzyme action. When the micellar lipid products are absorbed, the bile salts return to the lumen for reuse in the formation of new micelles. At the lower end of the ileum, bile salts are absorbed into the blood stream, transported to the liver, and then resecreted into the bile duct. As a result of this so-called *enterohepatic circulation,* bile salts are used over and over again for micelle formation.

After entering the intestinal cell, much of the monoglyceride is hydrolyzed to fatty acids and glycerol. Triglycerides are then resynthesized (for the most part from fatty acids and glycerophosphate derived from the degradation of glucose). At the same time, two-thirds of the cholesterol is esterified with long-chain fatty acids. Following this, the lipids are packaged by the intestinal cell in the form of transport vehicles; namely, lipoproteins known as **chylomicrons** (a term coined in 1920 by Simon Gage to describe microscopic particles in chyle, the descriptive term for fat-laden intestinal lymph). Chylomicrons are spherical particles ranging from about 100 to 500 nanometers in diameter containing a core of neutral lipid (triglycerides and esterified cholesterol) surrounded by a membrane-like coat of protein and phospholipid (unesterified cholesterol is in both the core and the outer coat). Triglycerides account for more than 90 per cent of the weight of chylomicrons, protein less than 1 per cent. As mentioned, chylomicrons pass into the central lacteal of the villus and travel in intestinal lymph to the thoracic duct. Movement of lymph in lacteals is facilitated by the contraction of the muscularis mucosae and the smooth muscle fibers of the villi. Continuous lashing movements and rhythmic shortening and lengthening of the villi have the effect of "milking" the villi, propelling lymph toward the thoracic duct. Movement of the villi is triggered by a local reflex and a hormone called *villikinin* in response to chyme in the intestine. After chylomicrons enter the blood stream, they are taken up largely by adipose tissue fat depots, such as those in the subcutaneous layer of the skin and in the abdominal region.

Water and electrolytes are absorbed in both the small and large intestines. Electrolytes (salts) are absorbed most rapidly in the proximal portions of the small intestine because of the larger surface area and greater membrane permeability. It is also known that monovalent ions, such as sodium, potassium, chloride, and bicarbonate, are absorbed more readily than the polyvalent ions, such as calcium, magnesium, and sulfate. Sodium is absorbed by an active transport mechanism. Potassium and chloride ions are passively absorbed in response to concentration gradients. Calcium is absorbed by an active process requiring the presence of vitamin D (see Chapter 5, page 88). The parathyroid hormone plays a regulatory role in calcium absorption.

Iron is most readily absorbed if it is present in the intestine in its insoluble, inorganic, ferrous form. Most dietary iron is organic and ferric in form but is usually changed in the stomach to the ferrous component. It is now apparent that the acceptor mechanism for ferrous iron exists in the duodenal mucosa and is in equilibrium with plasma iron. The acceptor is a protein called *apoferritin*. Iron crosses the intestinal epithelium in the ferrous state, is oxidized to the ferric form, and then combines with apoferritin to yield ferritin. Prior to entering the blood, it is reduced and picked up by a globulin (transferrin) and transported in the ferric state.

In view of the slow equilibrium between mucosal and plasma iron, rapid relief of anemia is best achieved by the intramuscular administration of iron. Iron is most readily absorbed from the proximal portion of the small intestine. Absorption is favored when the mucosal iron content is low, since the mucosal iron content reflects the iron concentration in the plasma.

The absorption of water occurs by the simple physical process of osmosis.

Malabsorption Syndromes

General consequences of malabsorption syndromes include weight loss, disturbances of acid-base balance, impaired calcium absorption, and vitamin deficiencies. Patients with a malabsorption syndrome show diarrhea, weight loss, and weakness. Among the underlying mechanisms producing abnormal absorption can be included insufficient intestinal surface area, alteration in bowel motility, alterations in the autonomic nervous system, deficiencies in digestive enzymes, and diseases of the bowel lining.

Intravenous Hyperalimentation (Parenteral Alimentation)

There are periods of time during patient care when the gut cannot and should not be used for feeding purposes, and nutrition supplied via the veins becomes necessary. Intravenous hyperalimentation is employed in an attempt to meet the patient's nutritional requirements by concentrating nutrients as much as possible in order to stay within a daily fluid limit of about 2000 ml and to develop a delivery system that will avoid injury to the vascular system by a hypertonic solution. The most appropriate solution contains 20 per cent dextrose, 5 per cent protein and 5 per cent minerals and vitamins. This solution is delivered into a relatively large, high flow vessel such as the superior vena cava.

REGULATION OF FOOD INTAKE

It has been observed that individuals with tumors of the hypophysis that are encroaching upon the hypothalamus tend to become obese. In addition, destructive lesions in the hypothalamus, generally caused by vascular thrombosis, often result in severe inanition (L. *inanis*, empty), a pathological state due to lack of food. In animals two centers in the hypothalamus involved in controlling food intake have been identified. Destruction of the ventromedial hypothalamic nucleus (the so-called "satiety center") in rats, cats, and monkeys causes hyperphagia (G. *hyper*, over; G. *phagein*, to eat) and obesity. Destruction of the lateral hypothalamus nuclei (called the "feeding center") results in a cessation of feeding (aphagia). It has been suggested that when the desire for food is satisfied the satiety center inhibits the feeding center; if the satiety center is destroyed control over feeding is lost. The satiety center concentrates glucose and responds to increases in blood glucose levels with increased electrical activity. Drugs that reduce appetite, such as amphetamines, also increase the electrical activity of the satiety center. It is generally believed that the activity of the satiety center is also influenced by input from peripheral receptors. There is some reason to believe that feedback mechanisms developed early in life may permanently affect feeding habits. It has been found, for example, that overfed infants develop a greater number of fat cells in fat depots than normally fed infants. The number remains constant—weight-reducing regimens reduce the amount of fat in the cells but not the number of cells. This might explain why overfed infants tend to be overweight all their lives.

NUTRITIONAL REQUIREMENTS AND THE DISPOSITION OF MAJOR FOODSTUFFS

Organic Nutrients

Food supplies fuel for the cells' energy needs and the ingredients for manufacturing essential cell constituents. The body requires not only food in bulk but also specific food substances it cannot make. For example, the cells of the body lack the ability to manufacture a number of amino acids needed for protein synthesis and therefore must obtain them preformed in ingested food. Such amino acids are called *essential amino acids*. The adult human probably requires eight essential amino acids. These are tryptophan, lysine, methionine, threonine, phenylalanine, leucine, isoleucine, and valine.

Histidine and arginine, called essential amino acids by some authors, are actually synthesized in the body, but only in amounts sufficient to meet the demands of maintenance, not growth and repair. Other amino acids are known as nonessential amino acids. In fact, nonessential ones are just as important as the essential ones, since

both types are required for protein synthesis.

The body is also unable to synthesize two polyunsaturated fatty acids, linoleic and linolenic acid. These *essential fatty acids* must be obtained from plant foods. Immature rats deprived of these two fatty acids display severe pathological signs, grow poorly, and die prematurely. Humans with a congenital inability to absorb dietary fat as chylomicrons (due to a failure to synthesize the protein portion of chylomicrons) develop neurological symptoms, possess crenated red blood cells and have a limited life span. It is believed that these conditions are accounted for by the failure of cell membranes to function normally because of a deficiency of polyunsaturated fatty acids.

Vitamins, by definition, are essential organic nutrients required in trace amounts to maintain good health. Their usual source is food, but some can be synthesized in the body. Vitamins have widely divergent properties and many function as components of co-enzymes. They can be separated into two groups by virtue of their solubility characteristics. The fat-soluble vitamins are A, D, E, and K; the water-soluble vitamins include the B-complex, C, and compounds with related activity (see Table 44).

Metabolism of Foodstuffs

The chemical processing of foodstuffs is called *metabolism*. The term metabolism includes *anabolism* and *catabolism*. Anabolism is the process of building complex molecules from simpler ones. Catabolism is the reverse process. Catabolism is accompanied by the release of energy and its storage as adenosine triphosphate (ATP). In Chapter 2 (page 40) we described the production of ATP by the oxidative degradation of fatty acids and glucose to carbon dioxide and water via the citric acid (Krebs) cycle and by the anaerobic breakdown of glucose to lactic acid. ATP is also produced by the oxidative breakdown of amino acids via the Krebs cycle. In the initial steps of the breakdown of amino acids, the amino groups are removed. The biochemical pathways for the keto acids formed by the

Table 44. VITAMINS

VITAMIN	SOURCE	FUNCTION	DEFICIENCY
Fat Soluble			
A	Yellow vegetables, fish liver oils, milk, butter, eggs	Essential for maintenance of normal epithelium; synthesis of visual purple for night vision	Faulty keratinization of epithelium; susceptibility to night blindness
D	Egg yolk, fish liver oils, whole milk, butter	Facilitates absorption of calcium and phosphorus from the intestine; utilization of calcium and phosphorus in bone development	Rickets in children; osteomalacia in adults
E	Lettuce, whole wheat, spinach	Essential for reproduction in rats; no definite function has been determined in humans	Sterility in rats; no known effects on humans
K	Liver, cabbage, spinach, tomatoes	Synthesis by the liver of prothrombin; necessary for coagulation	Impaired mechanism of blood coagulation
Water Soluble			
B-Complex:			
B_1 (thiamine)	Whole grain cereals, eggs, bananas, apples, pork	Coenzyme in metabolism of carbohydrate as thiamine pyrophosphate (cocarboxylase); maintains normal appetite and normal absorption	Beriberi, polyneuritis
B_2 (riboflavin)	Liver, meat, milk, eggs, fruit	Coenzyme in metabolism (as flavoprotein)	Glossitis, dermatitis
B_6 (pyridoxine)	Whole grain cereal, yeast, milk, eggs, fish, liver	Coenzyme (as pyridoxal phosphate) in amino acid metabolism	Dermatitis
Niacin	Liver, milk, tomatoes, leafy vegetables, peanut butter	Niacinamide in metabolic processes, especially energy release	Pellagra
B_{12}	Liver, kidney, milk, egg, cheese	Maturation of erythrocytes	Pernicious anemia
Pantothenic acid	Egg yolk, lean meat, skim milk	Necessary for synthesis of acetyl coenzyme A, metabolism of fats, synthesis of cholesterol, and antibody formation	Neurologic defects
Folic acid	Fresh, leafy green vegetables, liver	Production of mature erythrocytes	Macrocytic anemia
Biotin	Liver, egg, milk; synthesized by bacteria in the intestinal tract	Coenzyme in amino acid and lipid metabolism	Not defined in man, since a large excess is produced by intestinal flora
C (ascorbic acid)	Citrus fruits, tomatoes, green vegetables, potatoes	Production of collagen and formation of cartilage	Scurvy; susceptibility to infection; retardation of growth, tender, swollen gums, pyorrhea, poor wound healing

deamination of amino acids converge upon terminal sequences leading to the formation of acetyl-CoA or compounds of the Krebs cycle. In some cases the acetyl-CoA is formed directly, in others indirectly via pyruvic or acetoacetic acid. Amino acids that give rise to pyruvic acid or compounds of the Krebs cycle are called *glucogenic* because pyruvic acid and Krebs cycle compounds are intermediates in the pathway leading to the synthesis of glucose. (In mammals, acetyl-CoA and acetoacetic acid are not converted to glucose.) Amino acids that give rise to acetoacetic acid are called *ketogenic* (acetoacetic acid is one of the so-called ketone bodies formed in especially large quantities when fatty acid breakdown is excessive, as in diabetes or fasting). Amino acids that give rise to acetoacetic acid are also ketogenic since acetoacetic acid can be formed from acetyl-CoA (the only pathway for its formation from fatty acids).

Disposition of the Major Foodstuffs Following Their Absorption

During the time a meal is being absorbed, essentially all of the body's energy needs are supplied by the breakdown of glucose. As mentioned, the greater part of the dietary fat is transported by chylomicrons to the fat depots. This stored fat remains untapped during the first few hours after eating. Glucose and amino acids are transported to the liver in the hepatic portal vein. A large proportion of the glucose is taken up by the liver and either utilized or converted to glycogen for storage. Glucose passing out of the liver is taken up by the working tissues, especially the brain and skeletal muscles. Amino acids taken up by the liver are used to manufacture proteins, especially the many blood proteins. Some are converted to glucose and glycogen. All of the dietary glucose and amino acids in excess of the body's needs and the liver's capacity to store glycogen (which is limited) are converted to fat (fatty acids are synthesized via acetyl-CoA) and transported (in the form of lipoproteins known as the very low density lipoproteins) to the fat depots.

About three or four hours after eating a meal, two events take place: (1) the concentration of fatty acids in the blood stream rises, and (2) the concentration of amino acids in the blood stream rises. The increase in blood levels of fatty acids is caused by the hydrolysis of triglycerides in the fat depots and the release of fatty acids into the blood stream. These fatty acids are transported (bound to plasma albumin) principally to skeletal muscle, the heart, and the liver (Fig. 453). In the postabsorptive period, working tissues, except the brain, rely to a great extent upon fatty acids for their energy needs. The liver receives considerably more fatty acids than it can use and returns the excess to the fat depots in the form of *very low density lipoproteins.* Some of the excess fatty acids transported by very low density lipoproteins are also taken up by skeletal muscle and the heart.

The rise in amino acid concentration in the blood is accounted for by the breakdown of protein in skeletal muscle and the transport of the released amino acids to the liver, where they are deaminated and converted to glucose. The conversion of amino acids to glucose, a process known as *gluconeogenesis,* is essential for maintaining normal blood glucose levels in the postabsorptive period because the demands of the brain for glucose exceed the ability of the liver to maintain blood sugar levels by degrading stored glycogen. Normally, glucose is the brain's exclusive fuel; it requires between 100 to 150 grams per day. The liver stores less than 100 grams of glycogen. Since part of this store is held in reserve for emergency needs and about a third of the glucose released by the liver in the postabsorptive period is consumed by organs other than the brain, the liver's supply of glycogen is insufficient for an overnight fast. Gluconeogenesis becomes an important source of blood glucose a few hours after a meal. Recent studies have shown that alanine is the major amino acid released by skeletal muscle into the blood stream. This is explained by the transfer of amino groups from other amino acids to pyruvic acid (by a process known as transamination), forming alanine.

If a fast is prolonged for a week or more, a number of adjustments are made to conserve body protein. The most important change is a shift by the brain from the

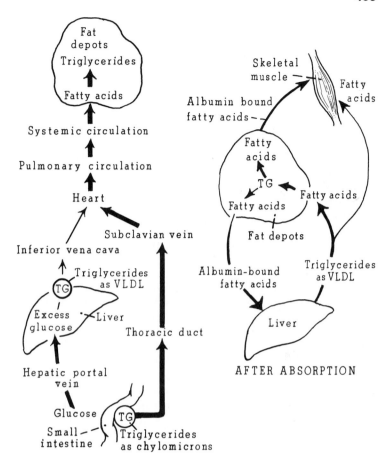

Figure 453. Transport of tri-glycerides (fat) and fatty acids during and after the absorption of a meal. During absorption, chylomicrons transport triglycerides from the small intestine to the fat depots, and very low density lipoproteins (VLDL) transport trigly-cerides synthesized from excess glucose (and amino acids) to the fat depots. Following hydrolysis of these triglycerides (by lipoprotein lipase) the released fatty acids are taken up by adipose tissue cells and new triglycerides are synthe-sized. About four hours after eating a meal, triglycerides are hydrolyzed in the fat depots and the fatty acids are transported, bound to albumin, principally to the liver and skeletal muscle (and the heart). Excess fatty acids received by the liver are returned to the depots as very low density lipoproteins. Some trigly-ceride fatty acids of very low density lipoproteins are also taken up by skeletal muscle (and the heart).

exclusive use of glucose for fuel to the consumption of *ketone bodies* (beta-hydroxybutyric acid and acetoacetic acid) as a primary source of energy. Ketone bodies accumulate in the circulation during fasting as a result of the excessive breakdown of fatty acids in the liver. After prolonged fasting ketone bodies provide about 50 per cent of the brain's energy needs, amino acids about 20 per cent, and glucose about 30 per cent. Another adaptive response is the use by other working tissues of proportionately more fatty acids and less glucose to supply their energy requirements.

Reference was made in the foregoing discussion to the very low density lipoproteins functioning as vehicles for transporting fat from the liver to the depots. This fat is synthesized from glucose and amino acids during the absorption of a meal and from excess fatty acids transported to the liver in the postabsorptive period. Very low density lipoproteins and chylomicrons

are two of four classes of lipoproteins found in plasma. The other two are known as *low density lipoproteins* and *high density lipoproteins*. Very low density lipoproteins contain on the average about 10 per cent protein, low density lipoproteins about 25 per cent protein, and high density lipoproteins about 50 per cent protein. The principal lipid component of low density lipoproteins is esterified cholesterol; phospholipid is the major lipid constituent of high density lipoproteins. Both of these groups of plasma lipoproteins apparently are vehicles for transporting cholesterol. High density lipoproteins perform another, rather curious function—carrying a protein that activates an enzyme, known as *lipoprotein lipase,* that is essential for the tissue uptake of the triglycerides of chylomicrons and very low density lipoproteins. This protein is transferred to chylomicrons and very low density lipoproteins after their entry into the blood stream. (Chylomicrons actually triple their protein content upon passing from the lymph into the blood.) Lipoprotein lipase, the enzyme responsible for triglyceride uptake from chylomicrons and very low density lipoproteins, is released from tissue cells and hydrolyzes triglycerides at the surface of the capillary endothelium. This is followed by cellular uptake of the released fatty acids and resynthesis of triglycerides (by combination of the fatty acids with α-glycerophosphate derived from glucose). An extremely high concentration of chylomicrons in plasma is found in individuals with an inherited deficiency of lipoprotein lipase. The blood of some of these patients has been described as resembling cream of tomato soup.

The action of lipoprotein lipase upon chylomicrons and low density lipoproteins leads to a loss of about 95 per cent of the triglycerides of these lipoproteins. The disposition of the remaining constituents results in the formation of the plasma low density lipoproteins. This transformation involves (1) loss of about 80 per cent of the cholesterol and phospholipid (some cholesterol is taken up by tissues along with fatty acids, but the bulk is delivered to the liver, as is part of the phospholipid); (2) transfer of some cholesterol and phospholipid, along with a portion of the protein, to high density lipoproteins; (3) esterification with long-chain fatty acids of a part of the cholesterol (individuals with an inherited deficiency in the plasma cholesterol-esterifying enzyme fail to form normal low density lipoproteins because a minimum amount of esterified cholesterol, a neutral lipid, is necessary for the rounded shape and stability of these lipoproteins). It has been estimated that the formation of low density lipoproteins following the disruption of chylomicrons and very low density lipoproteins accounts for about three-fourths of the plasma low density lipoproteins. The remainder are synthesized by the liver. The liver is the exclusive source of high density lipoproteins.

HEAT PRODUCTION AND BASAL METABOLIC WORK

Chemical energy is used to perform work. The categories of work energy are mechanical, electrical, and chemical. Chemical energy is transformed to work in the form of mechanical energy when a muscle shortens. It is transformed in the form of electrical energy when a nerve impulse is transmitted, and provides chemical energy during synthetic reactions. During the buildup of complex molecules, chemical energy is stored at the expense of energy supplied by the breakdown of other molecules. The body is only 20 per cent efficient in converting chemical energy to work energy. The remainder appears as thermal energy, or heat. Much work energy is ultimately converted to heat. Thus, a considerable amount of mechanical work of the heart is converted to heat in overcoming friction as blood passes through the circulatory system. When a muscle shortens, much of the energy overcomes viscosity, and friction again generates heat.

Thus, it is apparent that most of the chemical energy of the body is ultimately converted to heat, either directly from chemical reactions or indirectly from work energy. When no external work, such as lifting a load or exercising, is being done, essentially all metabolic energy ultimately appears as heat. With strenuous physical exertion about three-fourths of the increase in metabolic energy above the resting level appears as heat, the remainder as work.

Basal Metabolic Rate. Basal metabolism or basal metabolic rate (BMR) is the term applied to the utilization of energy occurring in a fasting and resting individual. Basal metabolic rate is determined clinically 12 to 18 hours after the last meal, usually in the morning following a normal period of sleep. During the test period, no voluntary muscle movement should occur. The room temperature is comfortable and the patient is physically and mentally at rest. The energy exchange so determined is that required to maintain the vital activities of the body. The units of BMR are usually given in Calories per square meter of body surface per hour. A calorie (spelled with a small c) is the amount of heat required to raise 1 gram of water 1° C. A Calorie (large C), the unit used for expressing basal metabolism, is equal to 1000 calories. Surface area is taken into consideration because tall, slender individuals have a higher surface-to-volume ratio than short, stocky individuals and, therefore, generally have a higher metabolic rate to compensate for the greater heat loss from the body surface. Determinations of BMR most commonly are based on oxygen consumption. For each liter of oxygen consumed an average of 4.825 Calories of heat are produced under basal conditions. Thus, if an individual consumes 12.5 liters of oxygen per hour (corrected to standard conditions), this would be 12.5 × 4.825, or about 60 Calories per hour. If this individual is five feet (152.4 cm) tall and weighs 120 pounds (54.5 Kg), there would be a surface area of 1.5 square meters (Fig. 454). The BMR of this individual would be 60/1.5, or 40 Calories per square meter per hour.

FACTORS INFLUENCING BMR. When a resting individual ingests food, heat production is increased above the basal level. This increased heat production produced simply from eating is known as the *specific dynamic action* of foods and varies with the type of food ingested. Protein has a greater specific dynamic action than either fat or carbohydrate. For example, if proteins are fed to an animal in an amount possessing a heat value equivalent to the basal metabolism, heat production will be raised by 30 per cent. Thus, feeding 100 Calories to an animal with a basal metabolism of 100 Calories per day will increase the heat production to 130 Calories per day. The extra heat is generated by the combustion of body constituents. The specific dynamic action of fats and carbohydrate amounts to 4 and 6 per cent, respectively. The higher specific dynamic action of protein is believed to be associated with deamination and urea formation.

Other factors influencing the total exchange of energy in the living organism include age and sex (Table 45), temperature and muscular exercise. Thyroid hormone exerts a considerable influence on the rate at which cellular oxidation occurs, and excesses and deficits of circulating thyroid hormone modify the metabolic rate. Certain other substances, such as male sex hormones, growth hormone, epinephrine, and norepinephrine, increase the metabolic rate because of their stimulating effect on cellular activity.

Temperature Regulations

Mammals and birds are *homeothermic*, or warm-blooded, animals, which means that they are capable of maintaining a

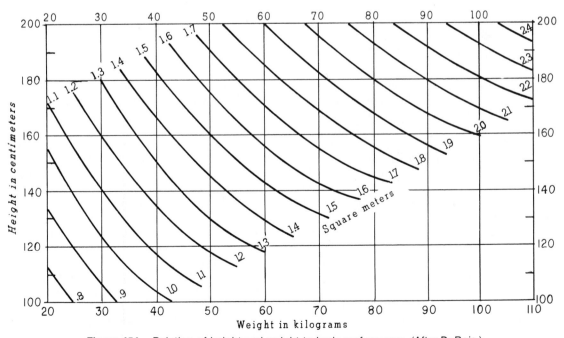

Figure 454. Relation of height and weight to body surface area. (After DuBois.)

Table 45. BASAL METABOLIC RATE
(calories/sq. meter/hr.)

AGE (Years)	MALES	FEMALES
10–12	49.5	45.8
12–14	47.8	43.4
14–16	46.0	41.0
16–18	43.0	38.5
18–20	41.0	37.6
20–30	40.5	36.8
30–40	39.5	36.5
40–50	38.0	35.3
50–60	36.9	34.4
60–70	35.8	33.6
70–80	34.5	32.6

nearly constant internal body temperature. If the body temperature varies with environmental changes, the term *poikilothermic*, or cold-blooded, is employed.

Body temperature is controlled by the activity of a *temperature regulating center* in the hypothalamus that is sensitive to changes in temperature in the blood and that receives input from peripheral receptors, especially receptors for warmth and cold in the skin.

Regulation of body temperature includes both heat production and heat dissipation. Metabolism constantly supplies heat and is considered a major heat source. Metabolic activity can be increased to provide more heat, but it cannot be effectively lowered in the temperature-regulating process. Heat production can be markedly increased by shivering in response to extreme cold. Input from temperature receptors in the skin to the hypothalamus is of primary importance in this response.

Evaporation of water is a mechanism for heat loss. Evaporation does not necessarily necessitate sweating, since there is a continuous diffusion of water molecules through the skin. Water evaporation also occurs through the lungs. Approximately 20 to 25 per cent of the basal heat production is lost by evaporation. This can be markedly increased in man during sweating and in animals by panting and salivation. Radiation, convection, and conduction are terms used to describe other mechanisms by which heat exchange can take place between the body and environment. Heat loss from the skin can be modified by controlling the conduction of heat

to the skin through the blood. Vasodilation increases and vasoconstriction decreases heat loss.

Temperature is a valuable barometer of disease. The figure 98.6° F. is usually quoted as the normal mouth temperature; however, in the normal individual there is some fluctuation. Upon awakening in the morning, the basal temperature can be as low as 97° F. This temperature usually rises during the day to reach 99° F. in the latter part of the afternoon. The temperature of the environment, unless extreme, does not greatly influence body temperature, since regulating mechanisms for heat maintain a homeothermic state. The body temperature is lowest in the female at the time of menstruation. In the aged, the temperature is usually lower than during the younger years.

Temperature can be determined most accurately rectally. The rectal temperature is approximately 0.9° F. higher than oral temperature. With a fever the difference is reduced between rectal and oral temperatures. Use of the axillary thermometer is reliable only if the axilla is sufficiently moist to exclude air and permit the skin to closely surround the bulb of the thermometer. The temperature in the axilla is usually 1 or 2 degrees lower than in the mouth. In taking an oral or rectal temperature, the thermometer should be allowed to remain in place for at least 5 minutes. The drinking of hot or cold fluids prior to taking the temperature will cause erroneous results. When taking an axillary temperature, the thermometer must be held with the upper arm closely pressed against the chest wall for at least 5 minutes.

HEAT EXHAUSTION. Heat exhaustion, or heat collapse, is characterized by sweating, weakness, reduced blood pressure, rapid pulse, normal or slightly elevated temperature, and the general findings of circulatory collapse. Heat exhaustion is associated with prolonged periods of hot weather and is precipitated by excessive exposure to sun or physical exertion. The onset of heat exhaustion is often preceded by a prolonged period of physical exertion in a hot and humid environment. Large, unreplaced losses of salt and water are the most important factors in the development of heat exhaustion. Treatment should be directed toward restoring the body fluid and temperature to normal and to re-establishing vasomotor tone. It is important to remove the patient to a cool environment. Administration of salt water solutions is beneficial.

HEATSTROKE. Heatstroke, or sunstroke, is characterized by high fever and profound coma and occurs primarily in individuals over the age of 60. As in heat cramp and heat exhaustion, when environmental temperature exceeds body temperature, heat must be lost by evaporation of sweat. A high relative humidity impedes the evaporation of sweat, and body temperature rises with an increase in the rate of sweating. Somewhere in this vicious cycle, sweat glands cease to function and body temperature rises to alarming levels because of absorption of heat from the environment. The patient lapses into coma. The reason for this sudden failure of thermal regulation is unknown. Heatstroke is a medical emergency, since the disease results from a breakdown of the thermoregulartory mechanisms. Treatment is directed primarily toward reducing body temperature.

DIFFERENTIAL CHARACTERISTICS OF HEAT CRAMP, HEAT EXHAUSTION, AND HEATSTROKE. *Heat cramp* is the mildest of the syndromes associated with excessive exposure to hot and humid environments. Cardiovascular and thermoregulatory mechanisms are intact. The patient has an essentially normal blood pressure but sweats profusely; his skin is moist and warm. The body temperature is normal or only slightly elevated. In *heat exhaustion* a loss of vasomotor control of the blood vessels occurs, along with circulatory shock. The skin is pale and cold, since the patient sweats, the skin is moist, and clammy. The pulse is rapid and the blood pressure low. In *heatstroke* a loss of thermoregulatory control occurs and sweating stops. The skin is flushed, hot, and dry, the pulse bounding and full, and the blood pressure elevated. Fever, delirium, and coma are present.

SUMMARY

THE DIGESTIVE SYSTEM

Anatomy

Consists of (1) an alimentary canal — a long, muscular tube beginning at the lips and ending at the anus, including the mouth, pharynx (oral and laryngeal portions), esophagus, stomach, and small and large intestine, and (2) accessory glands that empty secretions into the tube — salivary glands, pancreas, liver, and gallbladder.

1. **Teeth**

   a. Crown projects above the gum, root below. Dentin (bulk of tooth) surrounds pulp cavity. Enamel covers dentin of crown; cementum covers dentin of root and anchors tooth to periodontal membrane.
   b. Each quadrant of mouth has eight teeth — two incisors, one canine, two premolars and three molars.

2. **Esophagus**

   a. Mucous membrane lined with stratified squamous epithelium rather than simple columnar epithelium, as in stomach and intestine.
   b. Muscularis of upper third, striated; lower third, smooth; middle, both striated and smooth.
   c. Segment above stomach (indistinguishable anatomically from remainder of esophagus) functions as sphincter (cardiac sphincter), remaining closed until reflexively relaxed by approaching peristaltic wave.

3. **Stomach**

   a. Consists of upper fundus, central body, and constricted lower pyloric portion (antrum).
   b. Muscularis contains an oblique inner layer of smooth muscle in addition to external longitudinal and underlying circular smooth muscle layers found elsewhere in digestive tract.
   c. Thick circular muscle in pyloric portion forms pyloric sphincter.
   d. Openings: cardia between esophagus and stomach; pylorus between stomach and duodenum.

4. **Small Intestine**

   a. Divided into duodenum, jejunum, and ileum.
   b. Surface area, serving absorptive function, increased by
      (1) Plicae circulares (permanent transverse folds)
      (2) Villi (fingerlike projections)

(3) Microvilli (processes on free surface of epithelial cells that form the brush border).

c. Invagination of ileum into cecum forms ileocecal valve, which opens rhythmically during digestion, permitting gradual emptying of ileum and preventing regurgitation.

5. Large Intestine

a. Colon (consisting of ascending, transverse, descending and sigmoid portions), situated between cecum and rectum, forms major part of large intestine. Longitudinal muscle of colon composed of three bands (teniae coli).

b. The rectum, the lower end of the large intestine, terminates in the anal canal.

c. Thickened circular smooth muscle of anal canal forms the internal anal sphincter. Surrounding skeletal muscle forms the external sphincter.

6. Salivary Glands

a. Three pairs (parotid, submaxillary, and sublingual) with ducts opening into the mouth.

b. Two types of secretions
  (1) Serous, containing ptyalin (enzyme initiating digestion of starch)
  (2) Mucous, viscous, containing mucus, which facilitates mastication

7. Pancreas

a. Two types of secretory cells in exocrine pancreas:
  (1) Enzyme-secreting (acinar cells)
  (2) Bicarbonate-and-water-secreting (lobular duct cells)
  Enzymes digest all major foodstuffs.

b. Pancreatic duct empties pancreatic juice into duodenum.

8. Liver and Gallbladder

a. Bile secreted by liver is essential for normal absorption of digested lipids. Bile salts combine with products of lipid digestion to form water-soluble complexes (micelles) which are absorbed by intestinal cells.

b. Gallbladder concentrates and stores bile.

c. Hepatic duct, formed from bile duct system of liver, joins cystic duct of gallbladder to form common bile duct, which empties into duodenum.

Motility of Digestive Tract

1. Swallowing

a. In buccal stage (voluntary) bolus pushed toward pharynx

b. In pharyngeal and esophageal stages (involuntary) bolus passes through pharynx into esophagus and through esophagus into stomach

c. Reflexes raise soft palate, raise larynx and draw vocal cords together, inhibit respiration, initiate peristalsis in pharynx and esophagus, and relax upper esophageal and cardiac sphincters.

2. Peristalsis in Stomach

a. Mixes contents and forces chyme through pylorus.

b. Three waves (each beginning every 20 seconds near midpoint of stomach, lasting about one minute, and ending with contraction of pyloric sphincter) travel down stomach at one time.

c. Rate of emptying determined largely by strength of contractions.

d. Feedback from duodenum regulates gastric emptying. Two control mechanisms, one neuronal (enterogastric reflex), the other hormonal (mediated by enterogastrone), inhibit gastric motility.

3. Contractions of the Small Intestine

a. Segmenting: Rhythmic contractions along a section dividing it into segments; primarily mixing action.

b. Peristaltic waves superimposed upon segmenting contractions.

c. Ingestion of food increases ileal peristalsis and frequency of opening of ileocecal valve (gastroileal reflex).

4. Contractions of Large Intestine

a. Simultaneous contraction of circular and longitudinal muscle, forming haustra.

b. Infrequent (usually two or three times daily at most) mass movements transferring contents from proximal to distal colon and into rectum. Most commonly occur shortly after a meal (gastrocolic reflex).

5. Defecation Reflex

a. Distention of rectum triggers intense peristaltic contractions of colon and rectum and relaxation of internal anal sphincter.

b. Reflex preceded by voluntary relaxation of external sphincter and compression of abdominal contents.

Digestion

1. Mouth

a. **Enzymatic action:** Initiation of the digestion of carbohydrate by ptyalin, which splits starch into the disaccharide maltose. Action in mouth slight, but continues in stomach until acid medium inactivates ptyalin.

b. **Regulation:** Exclusively nervous — impulses transmitted from center in medulla (activated principally by taste, smell, or sight of food) to salivary glands by parasympathetic nerve fibers.

2. Stomach

a. **Enzymatic action:** Initiation of protein digestion by pepsin, producing proteoses, peptones and large polypeptides. Pepsinogen (secreted by chief cells) converted to pepsin by autoactivation process in presence of acid (secreted by parietal cells).

b. **Regulation**

(1) *Cephalic phase* (abolished by sectioning vagus verve): Initiated by taste, sight or smell of food; secretion stimulated via nerve plexus directly or indirectly by the hormone gastrin.

(2) *Gastric phase:* Initiated by food in stomach; secretion triggered directly or indirectly, as in cephalic phase.

(3) *Intestinal phase:* Initiated by digestive products in upper small intestine; mediated by hormone released by duodenum acting on stomach.

(4) *Inhibition:* Strong acid in antrum inhibits gastrin release. Acid or food products (especially fat) in duodenum stimulate release of hormones (enterogastrone, secretin) which inhibit gastric secretion.

3. Intestine

a. **Enzymatic action:** Fat digestion and continuation of carbohydrate and protein digestion.

(1) *Pancreatic enzymes:* Lipase splits fat into monoglycerides, fatty acids, and glycerol. Trypsin, chymotrypsin, and carboxypeptidases degrade proteins and product of pepsin digestion to smaller polypeptides and dipeptides. Amylase converts starch into maltose.

(2) *Intestinal enzymes:* Actions of aminopeptidases and dipeptidases yield amino acids; actions of maltase, sucrase, and lactase yield glucose, fructose, and galactose.

b. **Regulation of pancreatic secretion:** Parasympathetic (via vagus nerve), concurrent with cephalic phase of gastric secretion and two duodenal hormones — pancreozymin and secretin. Vagus stimulation and pancreozymin stimulate enzyme secretion; secretin stimulates bicarbonate secretion.

Absorption

1. Occurs almost exclusively in the small intestine.

2. Simple sugars, amino acids, short-chain fatty acids, and glycerol are absorbed into blood stream via capillary network of villi. Products of lipid digestion are absorbed as chylomicrons into intestinal lymphatics via central lacteal of villi.

Disposition of Major Foodstuffs

Absorbed fat, carried by chylomicrons, passes from thoracic duct into venous system; greater part taken up by fat depots and stored. Glucose and amino acids are transported to liver via hepatic portal vein; a portion is utilized and a portion passes to other tissues. Any excess that cannot be stored in liver as glycogen is converted to fat and transported as very low density lipoproteins to fat depots. During absorption of meal, glucose provides essentially all of body's energy needs. In postabsorptive period, fatty acids supply most of body's energy requirements; blood glucose (normally exclusive source of energy for brain) is maintained by conversion of amino acids

(derived from muscle protein) into glucose in liver.

Basal Metabolic Rate

Basal metabolic rate refers to energy production under basal conditions (resting in a comfortably warm environment 12 to 18 hours after a meal), usually expressed as Calories per square meter of body surface per hour. It is most commonly measured by rate of oxygen consumption (for every liter of oxygen consumed, an average of 4.825

Calories of heat are produced under basal conditions).

Temperature Regulation

Hypothalamus contains center for regulating body temperature which is sensitive to changes in blood temperature and which receives input from peripheral receptors. This center mediates homeostatic adjustments—sweating, changes in blood flow through skin, and shivering.

The Urinary System

chapter 14

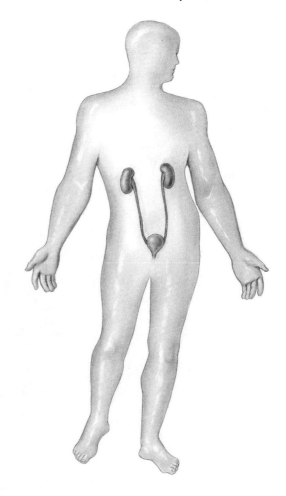

Objectives

The aim of this chapter is to enable the student to:

Describe the gross external and internal structure of the kidney.

Describe the microanatomy of the kidney and the nephron.

Distinguish between the two principal stages of urine formation.

Explain how a hypertonic urine is formed.

Discuss the role of aldosterone in regulating blood and urine volume.

Explain how the kidney helps maintain the buffering capacity of the body fluids.

Describe the structure and function of the ureters, urinary bladder, and urethra.

During the Egyptian era, 5000 years ago, the diagnosis of diabetes was actually made when the physician tasted the urine for sweetness. Later, during the Middle Ages, disease in general was evaluated by visually examining the urine. Medical reports during this time frequently stated that "the pulse was normal, the urine normal, yet the patient died." Urine became an accurate clue to body function only after the perfection of the microscope.

The urinary system is one of the four excretory pathways of the body; the others are the large bowel, the skin, and the lungs. It consists of two kidneys, which produce urine; two ureters, which convey urine to the bladder; and the urethra, which discharges urine from the bladder. Regulation of the concentration of substances excreted in the urine enables the body to control the concentration of substances in the blood so as to maintain homeostasis of the body fluids.

KIDNEYS

Gross Anatomy (Figs 455 and 456)

In the newborn the kidney is about three times as large in proportion to body weight as in the adult. The weight of the kidney ranges from 125 to 170 grams in the adult male, and from 115 to 155 grams in the adult female.

The kidneys are bean-shaped organs lying behind the parietal peritoneum against the muscles of the posterior abdominal wall, just above the waistline (Figs. 455 and 456).

Since the kidneys are in contact with the diaphragm above, they move slightly with this structure during respiration.

The upper poles of the kidneys are on a level with the upper border of the twelfth

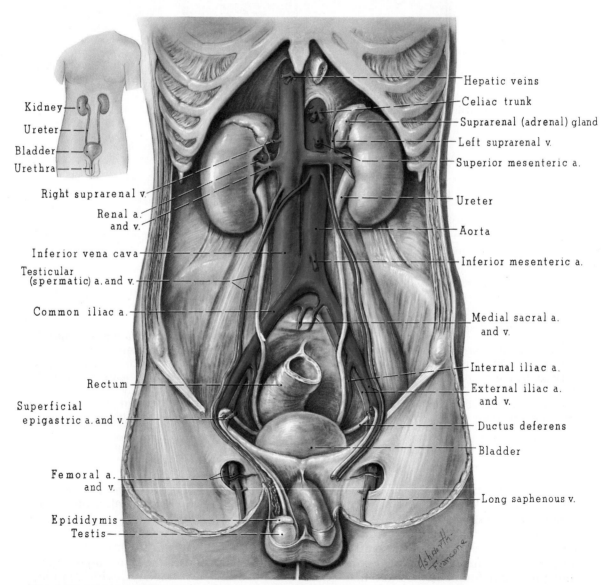

Figure 455. Posterior abdominal wall, showing relationship of urinary system, genital system, and great vessels.

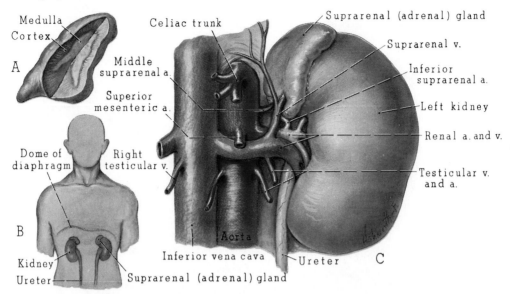

Figure 456. *A,* Suprarenal gland sectioned to show the medulla. *B,* Anatomic position of kidney and suprarenal glands. *C,* Anterior aspect of left kidney, showing adrenal gland and vascular supply.

thoracic vertebra; their lower poles extend to the level of the third lumbar vertebra. The right kidney is usually slightly lower than the left, possibly because of its close relationship to the liver. Anteriorly, the right kidney is covered by the suprarenal gland, the hepatic flexure of the colon, the descending portion of the duodenum, and the liver. The suprarenal gland, splenic flexure of the colon, stomach, pancreas, jejunum, and spleen are related to the anterior surface of the left kidney.

There are three capsules surrounding each kidney: the true capsule, the surrounding perirenal fat, and the renal fascia. The *true capsule* of the kidney, the capsule proper, is a smooth, transparent fibrous membrane closely applied to the surface. Normally it can be readily stripped from the organ. Adipose tissue, *perirenal fat,* surrounds the capsule proper and is in turn enclosed by the renal fascia, a thin fibrous layer which anchors the kidney to the surrounding structures and helps maintain the normal position of the organ.

When the kidney is inflamed, the renal tissue becomes adherent to the true capsule and cannot be removed without tearing the organ. If the adipose capsule or the renal fascia is deficient, ptosis (dropping) of one or both kidneys can occur.

External Structure. Each kidney presents an anterior and posterior surface and a convex lateral border. Medially the renal artery, vein, and nerves, as well as lymphatic vessels, enter and leave the concave surface through a notch called the *hilum.* The cavity located at the hilum is a saclike collecting portion called the *pelvis,* representing the upper expanded portion of the ureter.

Internal Structure (Fig. 457). In cross section, the kidney exhibits an inner darkened area, the *medulla,* and an outer pale area, the *cortex.* The medulla consists of from eight to 12 *renal pyramids,* with apices converging into projections known as papillae, which in turn are received by cavities (*calyces*) of the pelvis. The cortex consists of the peripheral layer extending from the capsule to the bases of the pyramids, and the *renal columns* traversing the area between the pyramids. It is divided into lobules composed of convoluted and radiant portions.

VASCULAR SUPPLY. Arteries from the aorta enter the hilum, on the medial surface of each kidney. After entering the hilum, the arteries divide into several branches called *interlobar arteries.* These extend to the boundary of the cortex and medulla of the kidney, where they branch as the

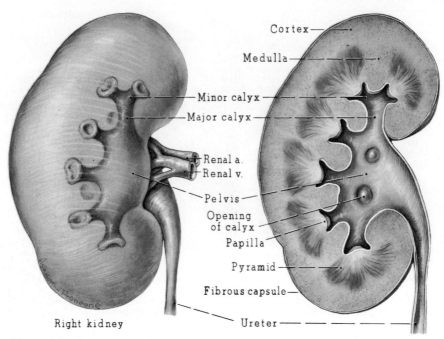

Cortex

Medulla

Minor calyx

Major calyx

Renal a.
Renal v.

Pelvis

Opening
of calyx

Papilla

Pyramid

Fibrous capsule

Right kidney   Ureter

Figure 457. Entire and sagittal views showing relation of calyces to kidney as a whole.

arcuate arteries which form arches across the bases of the pyramids. *Interlobular* arteries extend from the arcuate arteries into the convoluted portion of the cortex. Fine branches, the afferent arterioles, enter the glomerular capillary networks of the renal corpuscles (see below). An efferent arteriole leaves each glomerulus. Most efferent arterioles are short and branch to form capillary networks around the cortical tubules of the cortex and medulla. (Efferent arterioles that follow a different course will be described later in connection with the process of concentrating urine.) The capillary networks converge and lead into the interlobular and medullary veins which, in turn, empty their contents into the arcuate veins between the cortex and the medulla. The arcuate veins converge to form interlobar veins joining to empty into the renal veins. The *renal vein* leaves the kidney at the hilum, draining into the inferior vena cava.

INNERVATION OF THE KIDNEYS. The kidneys receive a rich supply of sympathetic, vasoconstrictor fibers extending from the fourth thoracic to the fourth lumbar segment of the spinal cord. Afferent fibers from the renal pelvis and ureters assume an important role in pain of renal origin.

Microscopic Anatomy

The functioning renal unit is called the **nephron** (Figs. 458 and 459). Each kidney contains about one million nephrons, each consisting of a renal corpuscle and tubular system. The blood supply initially comes into close relationship with the nephron by a tuft of capillaries derived from the afferent arteriole called the **glomerulus** resting in a cuplike depression of the tubular system called the *glomerular capsule*, or **Bowman's capsule.** Together these structures make up the *renal corpuscle*, or malpighian body. The capillaries of the glomerulus unite to form the outgoing efferent arteriole (of considerably smaller diameter than the afferent arteriole). The glomerular capillaries are thus uniquely situated between two arterioles. A long tubule consisting of three segments, a **proximal convoluted tubule,** a **loop of Henle,** and a **distal convoluted tubule,** extends from the glomerular capsule. The tubule unwinds from the cortical area and ends by joining other nephrons in a larger **collecting duct.** The tubules give a striated appearance to the medulla, and the renal corpuscles give a fine granular appearance to the cortex.

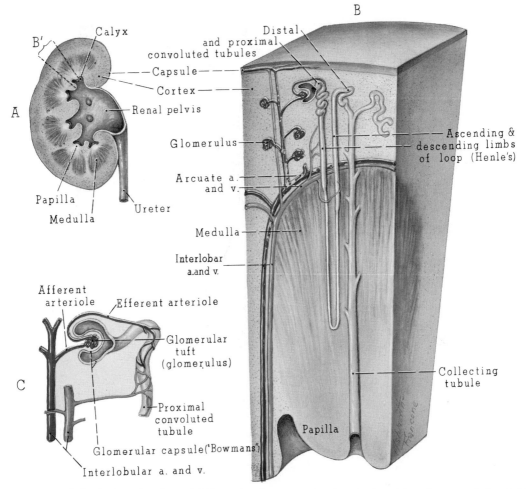

Figure 458. *A*, Sagittal section through kidney showing gross structure (note pelvis, calyces, medulla, cortex). *B*, Nephron and its relationship to medulla and cortex. The dotted lines in *A* show the area of the kidney from which this section was taken. *C*, Magnified view of nephron.

Urine is discharged at the apex of the medullary pyramid into the calyces of the pelvis and then flows down the ureter.

The point at which a portion of the distal convoluted tubule comes in contact with the afferent arteriole is called the *juxtaglomerular apparatus*, secreting renin, an enzyme of importance in regulating sodium and water retention and blood pressure.

The epithelium of Bowman's capsule is of the squamous type and consists of an outer (parietal) layer lining the capsule and an inner (visceral) layer covering the glomerulus. The cells of the visceral layer have interdigitating processes (pedicels). The proximal convoluted tubule is lined with cuboidal epithelium. This changes to squamous epithelium as the loop of Henle dips down into the medulla (portion with a small diameter known as the thin segment). A transition from squamous to cuboidal epithelium occurs in the straight, ascending, thick limb. The cuboidal epithelium continues into the distal convoluted tubule and the proximal portion of the collecting duct. Columnar epithelium lines the distal part of the collecting duct.

Kidney Regeneration

Renal reserve is dependent on the regenerative capacity of the kidney. When one kidney is removed, the opposite organ

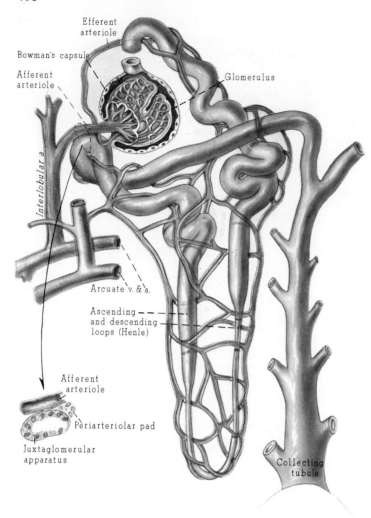

Efferent
arteriole

Bowman's capsule

Glomerulus

Afferent
arteriole

Interlobular a

Arcuate v. & a.

Ascending
and descending
loops (Henle)

Afferent
arteriole

Periarteriolar pad

Juxtaglomerular
apparatus

Collecting
tubule

Figure 459. Detail of nephron showing vascular supply, juxtaglomerular apparatus, and tubule.

undergoes an enlargement because of an increase in size of the contained nephrons rather than an increase in total number of nephrons. Only 25 per cent of the total renal mass is necessary for survival of the individual. The epithelium of the renal tubules can regenerate after injury—for example, in poisoning due to mercury; however, the entire nephron does not regenerate.

Kidney Transplantation (Fig. 460)

During the last 15 years almost 10,000 homologous kidney transplants have been done on patients dying of renal failure. The use of immunosuppressive drugs has allowed excellent long-term function in a majority of these patients. The best results in homotransplantation occur when the donor is closely related to the recipient; 90 per cent survive for two years or longer. Kidney transplants between *identical twins* may function for years.

It should be noted, however, that even in transplants between identical twins, the cause of damage to the original kidney may subsequently affect the transplanted kidney; despite acceptance of the transplant, the patient dies due to recurrence of the disease.

Another problem in transplantation of the kidney is one of logistics, particularly of preservation of the kidney prior to transplantation. In general, sub-zero preservation is probably superior to preservation above zero, but no organ can be successfully frozen and remain alive. The freezing point of an entire kidney has been depressed to 6 degrees below zero C without the kidney actually freezing (soft state), and the kidney has been retransplanted as an autologous

RECIPIENT   DONOR

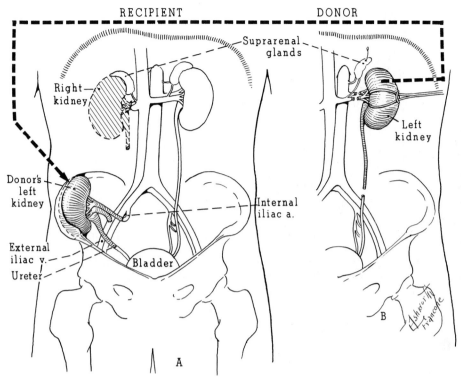

Figure 460. *A* illustrates kidney transplanted to right pelvis. *B* shows kidney of donor.

kidney (from the same animal to the same animal). When the opposite kidney is removed, the stored kidney sustains life as the only remaining kidney.

Physiology of Urine Formation

Urine Composition (Table 46). Urine is 96 per cent water, in which salts, toxins, pigments, hormones, and wastes from protein metabolism are dissolved. It is a complex, aqueous solution of inorganic and organic substances. The urinary output is approximately 1500 ml daily, 60 gm of which are solutes.

Mechanism of Urine Formation and Excretion. There are primarily two stages in the elaboration of urine by the kidney, the glomerular stage (formation of primitive urine by filtration) and the tubular stage, with the successive or simultaneous processes of reabsorption (from the tubular lumen to the blood) and secretion (from the blood to the tubular lumen). Except for its absence of proteins, the glomerular filtrate is almost identical in composition to plasma. Reabsorption and secretion markedly

Table 46. **COMPOSITION OF URINE**

Solutes 60 gm. daily	Organic wastes 35 gm.	Urea	30 gm.
		Creatinine	1–2 gm.
		Ammonia	1–2 gm.
		Uric acid	1 gm.
		Others	1 gm.
	Inorganic salts° 25 gm.	Chloride	Sodium
		Sulfate	Potassium
		Phosphorus	Magnesium

° Sodium chloride is the chief inorganic salt in urine.

change the composition of the filtrate. These two processes provide mechanisms for eliminating or conserving substances in accordance with the body's requirements. Thus, nutritionally valuable substances are completely or almost completely reabsorbed, and waste products are not absorbed, poorly absorbed, or secreted. In addition, the reabsorption and secretion of a number of substances are continuously regulated in order to maintain their normal concentrations in the body fluids.

GLOMERULAR FILTRATION. The glomerulus acts as a semipermeable membrane permitting a protein-free filtrate of plasma to pass through to Bowman's capsule. The glomerular filtrate has a pH of approximately 7.4 with a specific gravity of 1.010. Normal levels of various substances exist in the following concentrations:

glucose	80 mg/100 ml
urea nitrogen	15 mg/100 ml
sodium	140 mEq/l
chloride	100 mEq/l
bicarbonate	27 mEq/l
potassium	4.5 mEq/l

As we can see, the filtrate produced is similar to plasma without plasma proteins. The process of glomerular filtration is essentially a passive one, similar to the diffusion of substances from the vascular capillary to the interstitial spaces.

As mentioned, blood is supplied to the glomerulus by an afferent arteriole. The glomerular capillaries unite to form an outgoing efferent arteriole, which gives rise to the peritubular capillary network. The resistance of the narrow efferent arteriole to the flow of blood is an important factor in maintaining a high glomerular pressure (while at the same time creating a low pressure in peritubular capillaries, a condition favorable for tubular reabsorption). The filtration pressure represents the glomerular blood (hydrostatic) pressure less the glomerular osmotic pressure and capsular hydrostatic pressure. According to recent estimates, the glomerular filtration pressure is approximately 10 mm Hg (Fig. 461).

The principal barrier in the wall of the glomerular capsule is the basement membrane. The basement membrane is situated between a fenestrated capillary endothelium (cells perforated with pores—see Chapter 10, page 361) and the epithelial lining of the glomerulus, which contains clefts called "slit pores" (each bridged by a thin membrane), formed by the interdigitating projections of starfish-shaped epithelial cells.

Approximately 1200 ml of blood (containing 650 ml of plasma), or 24 per cent of the total cardiac output, passes through the kidney per minute. Of this, the fluid filtered from all glomeruli of both kidneys into Bowman's capsules amounts to about 125 ml per minute. This *glomerular filtration rate* varies directly with the filtration pressure.

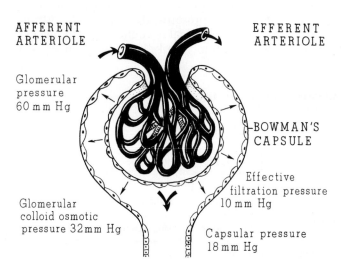

AFFERENT ARTERIOLE

EFFERENT ARTERIOLE

Glomerular pressure 60 mm Hg

BOWMAN'S CAPSULE

Effective filtration pressure 10 mm Hg

Glomerular colloid osmotic pressure 32 mm Hg

Capsular pressure 18 mm Hg

Figure 461. The normal filtration pressure is about 10 mm. of mercury. Glomerular hydrostatic pressure (60 mm. Hg) minus glomerular colloid osmotic pressure (32 mm. Hg) minus capsular pressure (18 mm. Hg) equals filtration pressure, 10 mm. Hg. The passage of substances in and out of the tubule varies in different portions of the tubule and collecting duct.

Tubular Reabsorption and Secretion. The final composition of urine is determined to a much greater extent by tubular reabsorption than by tubular secretion. Secretion is, however, the principal determinant of the concentration of potassium ions in the urine, and the synthesis and secretion of hydrogen ions by tubular cells play an important role in regulating acid-base balance in the body fluids (described later). Reabsorption and secretion can occur by both active and passive processes.

Substances actively reabsorbed include sodium ions, glucose, amino acids, uric acid, beta-hydroxybutyric acid, acetoacetic acid, calcium ions, phosphate ions, and sulfate ions. Most of the reabsorption occurs in the proximal tubules, in which the absorptive surface is greatly increased by the presence of numerous microvilli (see Chapter 13, page 459, and Fig. 438) on the free surface of the cuboidal epithelial cells. The active transport of *sodium ions* accounts for the greater part of the oxygen consumption of the kidney. This process not only restores most of the sodium temporarily lost in the glomerular filtrate but, by its electrical effect, also leads to the reabsorption of *chloride ions* accompanying the sodium ions. In addition, the active transport of sodium provides the principal driving force for the passive reabsorption of *water* by osmosis. Since sodium salts make up 90 per cent of the solute in the body fluids, under normal conditions the amount of sodium reabsorbed determines the amount of water reabsorbed. Usually about 99 per cent of the fluid is reabsorbed and about 1 ml of urine is formed per minute. *Glucose* and *amino acids* are normally completely reabsorbed from the proximal tubule. However, *glycosuria* (glucose in the urine) will occur if the concentration of the glucose in the plasma exceeds about 300 mg per 100 ml. At this concentration, the carrier system for tubular glucose transport is apparently saturated, and all of the filtered glucose in excess of this concentration appears in the urine.

Urea, the most abundant substance in the urine, is passively reabsorbed in consequence of the concentration gradient created by the reabsorption of water. However, since a much smaller proportion of urea than water is reabsorbed, the concentration of urea in urine is 60 to 70 times greater than in plasma.

Potassium is about 12 times more concentrated in urine than in plasma. It is both reabsorbed and secreted. The secretory process accounts for the elevated urine concentration. Most of the reabsorption of potassium occurs in the proximal tubules, apparently passively. Secretion takes place in the distal tubules and collecting ducts by a passive process involving an exchange of potassium for sodium ions. The active reabsorption of sodium provides the driving force, with potassium ions diffusing into the lumen in response to the electrical gradient created by the outflow of sodium. This exchange process is opposed by the reabsorption of small amounts of potassium by active transport.

The proximal tubule actively secretes certain waste products such as *para-aminohippuric acid*, drugs such as *penicillin*, and a number of substances administered for diagnostic purposes, such as *Diodrast* (iodopyracet — used for x-ray of the kidney).

Clearance. The efficiency with which the kidney excretes any substance is often expressed as its clearance. Clearance represents the volume of plasma that is cleared of a given substance each minute. In the case of a substance such as *inulin* (a polymer of fructose), which is neither reabsorbed nor secreted by the tubules, the volume of plasma cleared of it per minute is the same as the volume of plasma filtered per minute (glomerular filtration rate). If 125 ml of plasma per minute is filtered and 1 ml of urine per minute is excreted, inulin would be 125 times more concentrated in urine than in plasma, and inulin clearance could be calculated as $125/1 \times 1$, or 125 ml per minute. In general terms, the ratio of urine to plasma concentration multiplied by the volume of urine per minute represents the clearance of any substance (usually expressed as follows: $C_x = U_x/P_x \times V$). By comparing the clearance of a substance with inulin clearance, it can be determined whether the particular substance undergoes a net reabsorption or a net secretion. A clearance lower than inulin's means that a net reabsorption of the substance has occurred; a higher value means a net secretion has occurred. The clearance of a substance, such as glucose, that is completely reabsorbed by the tubules is zero. The clearance of a substance that is completely secreted by the tubules is equal to the total plasma flow through the kidney.

Alteration of Urine
Concentration and Volume

The ability of the kidney to form urine either much more concentrated (hypertonic) or much more dilute (hypotonic) than plasma has intrigued physiologists for many years. There are two aspects to this function. One is the *regulatory mechanism*, the other is the *concentrating mechanism*. Regulation of the concentration of urine is accomplished by the *antidiuretic hormone* (ADH), secreted by the neurohypophysis (posterior pituitary gland). This hormone is synthesized in the hypothalamus and stored in the neurohypophysis. When fluid loss exceeds fluid intake, osmoreceptors in the hypothalamus respond to the rise in the osmotic pressure of the plasma by stimulating the release of ADH by the neurohypophysis. ADH makes the distal convoluted tubule and collecting duct permeable to water. Normally, about 80 per cent of the water is reabsorbed before the urine reaches the distal tubule, and the fluid entering it is hypotonic. Hypertonic urine can be formed by reabsorption of water from the distal convoluted tubule and collecting duct only if ADH is present. When the body fluids become diluted following the intake of a large volume of water, ADH is not secreted and a dilute, voluminous urine is secreted.

The steps in the formation of a concentrated urine are illustrated in Figure 462. As mentioned, most of the tubular reabsorption occurs in the proximal tubule. As the filtrate passes through this segment, it is reduced to about one-third of its original volume, remaining essentially isotonic. Since this reduction in volume occurs whether the urine formed is concentrated or dilute, the term *obligatory water reabsorption* is applied to the reabsorption of water in this portion of the kidney in distinction to the variable water reabsorption in the distal segments, generally referred to as *facultative water reabsorption*.

The concentration of the medullary interstitial fluid increases from the cortical to the papillary end, where the concentration is up to eight times greater than plasma. This condition arises because the ascending loop of Henle is impermeable to water, and, as fluid ascends, sodium salts are removed while water remains behind. The descending loop of Henle is highly permeable to water; therefore, fluid leaving the proximal tubule becomes progressively more concentrated as it descends the loop of Henle, acquiring the same osmotic pressure as the surrounding fluid, and then becoming progressively more dilute as it ascends, entering the distal convoluted tubule as a hypotonic solution. If ADH is absent, the active reabsorption of sodium salts from the distal tubule further dilutes the fluid and a large

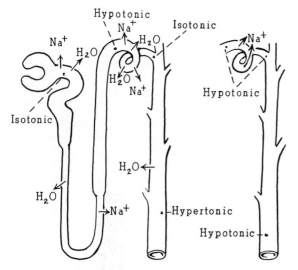

Figure 462. Schematic representation of the formation of concentrated and dilute urine, showing the transfer of sodium (Na^+) and water (H_2O) from the tubules to the interstitial fluid and the changes in tonicity of tubular fluid.

Formation of concentrated urine (in presence of ADH)

Formation of dilute urine (in absence of ADH)

volume of hypotonic urine is excreted. If ADH is present, water is removed from the distal convoluted tubule, and the fluid entering the collecting duct is isotonic. Then, as the fluid flows down the collecting duct, it becomes progressively more concentrated.

It is perhaps apparent that the formation of a hypertonic urine depends upon the maintenance of a hypertonic medullary interstitial fluid. This means that the sodium salts transferred from the ascending limb of the loop of Henle to the interstitial fluid of the medulla must not be immediately carried away by the blood stream. This does not happen, because of the countercurrent flow of blood through the medulla. Each efferent arteriole arising from a glomerulus near the junction of the cortex and medulla (juxtamedullary glomeruli) divides into a group of descending, straight vessels (**descending vasa recta**). These vessels supply a capillary network which then gives rise to ascending, straight vessels (**ascending vasa recta**) that enter the venous system. As blood flows down the vasa recta, the plasma becomes progressively more concentrated. In the ascending vasa recta, salts pass from the plasma to the interstitial fluid. In effect, the vasa recta functions as a **countercurrent exchanger** as salts are transferred from the ascending to the descending vessels (Fig. 463). The important point is that the recirculation of salts through the interstitial fluid of the medulla maintains the high osmotic pressure of this fluid.

Effect of Aldosterone on Sodium and Water Retention. Adrenal steroid hormones, particularly aldosterone, are important regulators of blood and urine volumes. Aldosterone increases tubular sodium reabsorption (by increasing the synthesis of a protein involved in active sodium transport), which in turn leads to an increase in water reabsorption. The release of aldosterone is triggered by *angiotensin II,* an octapeptide produced in blood in two stages. In the first stage, angiotensin I, a decapeptide, is formed from a precursor circulating globulin by the action of *renin,* an enzyme secreted by the juxtaglomerular apparatus of the kidney (page 497); in the second, angiotensin I is split upon passage through the lungs into angiotensin II. (A subsequent reaction produces angiotensin

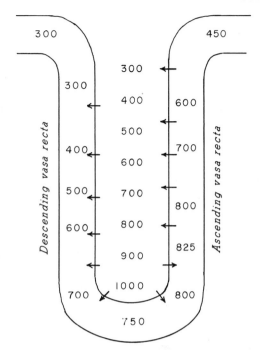

Figure 463. Diagrammatic representation of the recirculation of sodium salts (arrows) through the medullary interstitial fluid via the countercurrent exchanger mechanism of the loop of the vasa recta. Sodium salts passing into the blood of the descending vasa recta are partially returned to the interstitial fluid from the ascending vasa recta. The values for the concentrations of the tubular and interstitial fluid are in milliosmols. (A 1-osmolal solution contains 1 mole of a solute per kilogram of water, which depresses the freezing point 1.86° C. A milliosmol is 1/1000 of an osmol. The milliosmolality of a given solution is defined as the freezing point depression divided by 0.00186.) The concentration of the medullary interstitial fluid can be seen to increase from 300 milliosmols at the cortical end to 1000 milliosmols at the papillary end.

III, a heptapeptide. Although it now appears that angiotensins I and III are not simply inactive precursors and breakdown products, angiotensin II is the major active substance.) Low blood volume stimulates the release of renin. This leads to the formation of angiotensin II and the release of aldosterone, which increases the reabsorption of sodium and water by the kidney, restoring blood volume. Many useful diuretics function by blocking the action of aldosterone in the kidney. Angiotensin II also causes widespread vasoconstriction. This action and the expansion of the blood volume by angiotensin II raise blood pressure.

Renal Regulation of Acid-Base Balance

Hydrogen ions are synthesized and secreted by the cells of the proximal and distal convoluted tubules, the collecting ducts, and the thick portion of the loop of Henle. The **secretion of hydrogen** is accompanied by the **restoration of bicarbonate** to the blood. This helps maintain the buffering capacity of the body fluids. The most abundant buffer in the extracellular fluids is the sodium bicarbonate-carbonic acid system. Strong acids derived from dietary sources and metabolic processes react with bicarbonate (using hydrochloric acid as an example) as follows:

$$HCl + NaHCO_3 \rightarrow NaCl + H_2CO_3$$
$$H_2CO_3 \rightarrow H_2O + CO_2$$

These reactions result in the conversion of a strong acid to a weak one, namely, carbonic acid, and the dissociation of carbonic acid into carbon dioxide, which is expired, and water. At the same time, however, one mole of bicarbonate is lost from the extracellular fluid for each mole of acid reacting with the buffer system. The bicarbonate must be replaced in order to maintain the buffering capacity of the body fluids.

Renal cells produce bicarbonate and hydrogen ions by a reversal of the above reaction sequence. Carbon dioxide, derived from the blood or metabolic reactions in the tubular cell, combines with water in the presence of the enzyme carbonic anhydrase to form carbonic acid, which ionizes to form bicarbonate and hydrogen ions. Following this, the hydrogen ions are secreted into the tubular lumen in exchange for sodium ions. The sodium and bicarbonate ions are transferred to the blood, thereby replenishing the depleted bicarbonate. (This sequence is shown in Figure 464.) The secreted hydrogen ions react with constituents of the tubular fluid as follows:

1. With bicarbonate ions (usually combined with sodium) to form carbonic acid, which in turn dissociates into carbon dioxide and water. The water becomes part of the tubular fluid; the carbon dioxide diffuses out of the tubular lumen and may be utilized to regenerate bicarbonate. The net result is the removal of sodium bicarbonate from the tubular fluid.

2. With dibasic phosphate (Na_2HPO_4), forming monobasic phosphate (NaH_2PO_4), which is excreted in the urine. The released sodium is exchanged for the secreted hydrogen that reacted with the dibasic phosphate.

3. With ammonia (which is continuously formed in the tubular cell, for the most part from the amino acid glutamine) to form ammonium ions (NH_4^+). The ammonium ions are excreted in the urine, largely in combination with chloride ions.

It should be apparent that, when hydrogen ions react with bicarbonate ions, the carbonic acid formed disappears from the tubular fluid as carbon dioxide, and hydrogen ions do not accumulate. Hydrogen reacting with dibasic phosphate and other weak acids, however, will appear in the excreted urine as what is called the *titrat-*

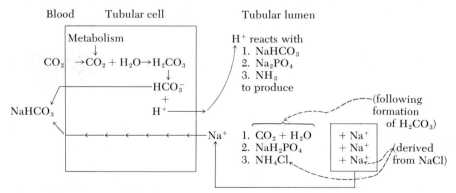

Figure 464. Chemical reaction sequences leading to the secretion of hydrogen ions in exchange for sodium ions, the replenishment of blood sodium bicarbonate, and the formation of titratable acid (NaH_2PO_4) and ammonium ions.

able acid (determined by the amount of alkali required to titrate the urine to the pH of plasma). When the concentration of bicarbonate in the plasma and glomerular filtrate is high (above about 28 mEq per liter), bicarbonate, but not titratable acid, will appear in the excreted urine. When the plasma concentration of bicarbonate is low, the secreted hydrogen ions will neutralize all of the available bicarbonate in the tubular fluid, and the urine will contain titratable acids or ammonium ions but no bicarbonate. The urine normally is slightly acid (pH approximately 6.0).

URINALYSIS

The normal volume of urine voided in one day is between 1000 and 1500 ml, being less in summer and more in winter. An adult voids on the average of five to nine times daily, the volume each time being between 100 and 300 ml.

A urinalysis properly done will reveal the presence of renal disease, give clues as to the nature of the disease if present, provide a valuable tool in following the progression of disease, and give an immediate assessment of renal function.

Freshly voided urine is usually transparent and the color varies from a pale to dark yellow. Upon inspection, color variations may exist which indicate the following:

a) yellow-brown to deep olive green produced by increased bilirubin content;

b) red hues produced by blood, foods such as beets, and some drugs such as phenolphthalein found in some laxatives;

c) brown-black produced by old blood.

Upon shaking, white foam indicates the presence of bile salts and pigment, a small amount of which is normal. An increased amount of foam will, however, be indicative of excess amounts of protein in the urine.

Fresh urine normally has a characteristic aromatic odor which develops into the pungent odor of ammonia upon standing. Certain ingested substances, such as asparagus, create characteristic odors while the sweet smell of acetone or acetoacetic acid is recognized in diabetic ketosis. Heavily infected kidneys may produce urine which has a particularly unpleasant odor.

The concentration of urine (or the number of particles of solute dissolved in a unit of urine water) is usually determined by testing for specific gravity, the normal range of which is from 1.003 to 1.030. In an individual with healthy kidneys, this test will provide information about the state of hydration of the patient (if the urine is highly concentrated, the patient is dehydrated). Specific gravity tests will also determine the presence of parenchymatous renal disease, and will help distinguish between acute renal failure and dehydration.

Testing the urine for pH, which is normally very close to 6.0, can reveal such problems as infection with urea-splitting organisms, with the liberation of ammonia causing the urine to be more alkaline.

Glucose, protein, or sediment (cellular elements such as RBC, WBC, yeast, epithelial cells, and casts, crystals and bacteria) in the urine are all indicative of particular disease states or problems. Testing for these substances involves microscopic examination of stained material.

Congenital Malformations

Polycystic Kidneys. Polycystic kidneys are caused by a failure of the tubules of the collecting system to fuse with the mesodermal-derived tubules of the functioning nephron, resulting in many cystlike structures. This is an hereditary abnormality which, in its more severe form, is not compatible with life. A patient with this abnormality usually dies before the age of 1 year. In milder cases sufficient kidney tissue is present to maintain life up to the fiftieth year.

Horseshoe Kidney. From the initial position in the pelvis, the kidney normally ascends to the lumbar region. On occasion the kidneys join each other at their lower poles during the ascent. This fused kidney is known as a "horseshoe kidney" and occurs about once in every 1000 births. In most instances, the kidney is fused at its lower pole. These fused kidneys are capable of normal function, but stones are slightly more common because of the angulation of the ureter, which results in stasis of the urinary flow.

Diseases Associated With the Kidney

Hypertension. Kidney damage and a diminished blood supply to the kidney as a result of narrowing of one or more renal arteries are known causes of hypertension. The release of renin and the production of angiotensins are responsible for the elevated blood pressure. Angiotensins, as we have seen, increase blood volume and cause widespread vasoconstriction. Angiotensins also raise blood pressure by increasing the activity of the sympathetic nervous system. Most hypertensive individuals have what is called "essential" hypertension ("essential" means the cause is unknown). It has been observed, however, that some individuals with essential hypertension have elevated concentrations of renin in the blood with no apparent kidney damage. Thus, some forms of essential hypertension may be due to subtle alterations in kidney function.

Nephritis.   Acute glomerulonephritis (inflammation of the kidney) generally develops during the first two decades of life, 10 to 20 days after an acute infection, as a result of an antigen-antibody reaction. Most patients recover spontaneously; in only 2 per cent does the disease become chronic. Chronic glomerulonephritis can result in hypertension and eventually uremia. *Pyelonephritis,* on the other hand, is caused by actual invasion of renal tissue by bacteria and in its advanced stages can also cause uremia.

Uremia.   Uremia, literally meaning "urea in the blood," is a symptom complex which follows renal insufficiency and involves other systems. One of the characteristic signs of uremia is a "uremic" odor to the breath caused by NH_3 produced by bacterial decomposition of large amounts of urea in the saliva. Most patients with uremia are anemic. Many patients are lethargic and have an elevated blood pressure.

Dialysis

Hemodialysis (Fig. 465) exploits the simple principle of diffusion. A semipermeable membrane is interposed between the blood of the patient and a wash solution. The changes that follow depend on the characteristics of the membrane and the molecular composition of the solution as compared to that of the blood. If there is a relatively high level of any substance in the blood of a

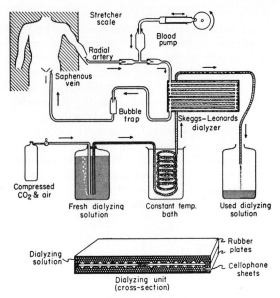

Figure 465. Schematic diagram of the Skeggs-Leonards artificial kidney.

patient and none in the wash solution, that substance will diffuse from the patient into the solution. Urea, potassium, phosphate, and other molecules present in toxic quantities in the uremic patient can thus be removed by hemodialysis.

A model of an artificial kidney shown in Figure 465 includes a steel tub 2 feet deep and 2 feet in diameter. In the center is a spiral of cellophane tubing connected to plastic tubes which carry the blood from the patient to be purified in the wash solution and then back again to the patient. Microscopic pores are present in the cellophane tubing. Elements with a molecular weight of less than 5000 can pass through these pores.

At the beginning of treatment, the artificial kidney is primed with blood matching that of the recipient, insuring a continuous flow of blood. The tub is filled with 25 gallons of ordinary tap water, heated to body temperature by coils at the base of the machine. Chemicals including salt, sugar, sodium bicarbonate, and other components of the blood in normal concentrations are dissolved in the water. This solution bathes the outside of the cellophane spiral, which is about 20 yards long when extended. Excess substances pass from the blood through the porous walls of the tubing into the bath solution, where they are retained.

It is now possible by hemodialysis to keep patients alive without any functioning kidney tissue for as long as 10 years or more.

URETERS

The ureters are two tubes which function to convey urine from the kidneys to the bladder. Each begins as a number of cup-like divisions of the renal pelvis known as *calyces*, joining to form two or three short tubes which unite into the funnel-shaped, dilated renal pelvis. The ureter proper passes from the pelvis to the posterior aspect of the urinary bladder. Each is 25 to 30 cm in length, 4 to 5 mm in diameter, and consists of outer fibrous, middle muscular, and inner mucous layers. Contraction of the muscular layer produces characteristic peristaltic waves beginning at the renal pelvis and ending at the bladder.

Narrowed areas along the course of the ureter are of practical importance, since stones are likely to lodge at these narrowed points. The first narrowed area or constriction is at the junction of the ureter and renal pelvis; the next is at the point at which the ureter crosses the iliac artery; the third is at the position of entrance of the ureter into the bladder wall. At all three of these regions the lumen is sufficiently narrowed so that stones frequently become lodged.

The location of the ureter in the female is of particular interest, since its proximity to the uterus and cervix predisposes it to injury during surgery of the uterus. The female ureter lies close to the unattached border of the ovary on the lateral wall of the pelvis and enters the base of the broad ligament crossed by the uterine artery. As it approaches the bladder it lies adjacent to the cervix, where it can be injured in removal of the uterus (hysterectomy).

A double ureter is not an uncommon abnormality; it can be either partial or complete. If two completely separate ureters exist on one side, the two ureteral orifices are usually present on the same ureteric ridge. Occasionally the ureter is ectopic; that is, opening into an abnormal location such as the urethra itself or the vagina. An ectopic ureter can cause incontinence (continuous dripping), especially when its opening into the urogenital tract occurs below the sphincter of the bladder. Ectopic ureter should be considered in the young female child with enuresis (page 509).

URINARY BLADDER

The urinary bladder (Figs. 466 and 467) lies posterior to the symphysis pubis; it is separated from the rectum by the seminal vesicles in the male and by the vagina and uterus in the female. The superior surface of the bladder is covered by peritoneum. Laterally the bladder is supported by the levator ani musculature, and posteriorly it rests on the obturator internus muscle.

Basically, the bladder consists of two parts—a small triangular area near the mouth of the bladder called the *trigone*, on which both the ureters and urethra open; and the *detrusor muscle* (smooth muscle of bladder wall), forming the principal portion of the body.

The trigonal muscle extends inferiorly on the floor of the proximal urethra and anchors the ureters as the bladder fills. The detrusor muscle encircles the vesical neck and also extends inferiorly adjacent to the proximal urethra.

The wall of the bladder is composed of four layers (from within outward): *mucosal, submucosal, muscular,* and *serosal.* Transitional epithelium lines the mucosal layer.

Urinary bladder activity is controlled by the parasympathetic nervous system with centers in the spinal cord. There is no evidence that sympathetic fibers are concerned with micturition other than that they constrict the blood vessels of the bladder.

Micturition

The bladder, serving as a reservoir for urine, gradually fills and becomes distended. In the distended state, the muscular wall contracts and the pressure within the bladder increases. The normal capacity of the bladder is from 300 to 350 ml. As the volume increases, the tension rises. When the pressure within the bladder reaches 18 cm of H_2O, stretch and tension receptors are stimulated producing the desire to urinate. Voluntary control can be exerted until the bladder pressure increases to 100 cm of

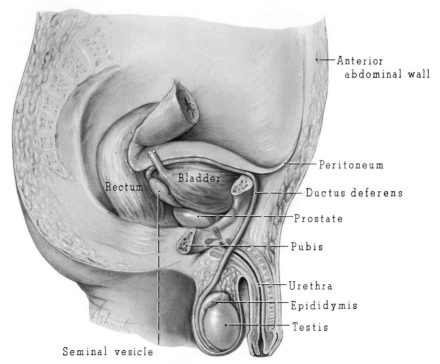

Figure 466. Sagittal section through the male pelvis.

H_2O, at which point involuntary micturition begins. It is currently believed that the entire urethra in the female and the prostate and the membranous urethra in the male function as the internal sphincter of the bladder. Circular skeletal muscle of the urogenital diaphragm, located a few centimeters below the bladder and through which the urethra passes, forms an external sphincter. When the fluid volume reaches about 150 ml, impulses are transmitted via the pelvic nerves to the micturition spinal reflex center in the sacral region of the spinal cord, but the return of impulses to the bladder (via parasympathetic fibers in the pelvic nerves) is blocked by inhibitory signals

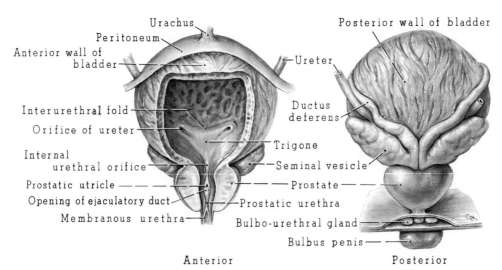

Figure 467. Internal and external aspects of the urinary bladder and related structures.

from the brain. When the inhibition is voluntarily lifted, the sphincters relax, and contraction of the detrusor muscle empties the bladder. Voiding is accelerated by contraction of the diaphragm and abdominal wall.

Enuresis. Enuresis (involuntary bed-wetting during sleep by a child over 3 years of age) can be caused by many factors, including local irritation of the bladder and urethra and emotional instability. When the child possesses a normal mental capacity and does not have actual disease, the outlook is favorable. The habit of voiding voluntarily should be established in children by the third year.

URETHRA

The male urethra is a narrow musculo-membranous tube extending from the bladder to the external urethral meatus (Figs. 466 and 467). It follows a tortuous course for a distance of approximately 8 inches and is divided into three portions: prostatic, membranous, and cavernous.

The first part, the *prostatic urethra*, about 3 cm in length, commences at the bladder neck (outlet of the bladder) and traverses the prostate to the two-layered triangular ligament. The *membranous urethra*, about 1 cm in length, lies between the two layers of the triangular ligament, connecting the penile and prostatic urethrae. The *cavernous urethra* (penile portion), about 15 cm long, extends from the triangular ligament to the urethral orifice (see Chapter 17, pages 567 and 569, for supplemental diagrams).

The urethral wall consists of three layers: mucosal, submucosal, and muscular. The prostatic urethra is lined with transitional epithelium. Pseudostratified columnar epithelium lines the remaining portions, except for the terminal dilation of the penile urethra (fossa navicularis), which is lined with stratified squamous epithelium.

The urethra serves as the distal portion of the urinary tract for eliminating urine from the body; additionally, the male urethra is the terminal portion of the reproductive tract, serving as a passageway for semen.

The female urethra, which serves only a urinary function, is about 4 cm in length and is supported by the anterior wall of the vagina. The urethra adjacent to the bladder is lined with transitional epithelium, the remainder largely with stratified squamous epithelium. Skene's glands open into the urethra just within the external urinary meatus. The female urethra is generally recognized as being surrounded by a complex network of glands and ducts that form ideal foci for chronic infection. The epithelial lining of the female urethra is subject to hormonal influence and takes part in the general atrophy of the adjacent vaginal mucosa in the postmenopausal period. The urethral meatus is bathed by vaginal, uterine, and rectal discharges throughout life, exposing the delicate urethral structures to irritation and bacterial invasion.

SUMMARY

THE URINARY SYSTEM

Gross Anatomy

1. The kidneys are two bean-shaped organs, retroperitoneal in position, situated on the musculature of the posterior abdominal wall at the level of the twelfth thoracic and first three lumbar vertebrae. The right kidney is slightly lower than the left.

2. Three renal capsules surround the kidney: the capsule proper, perirenal fat, and the renal fascia.

3. External Structure

The hilum is a notch on the concave surface of the kidney where the renal vessels and nerves enter and leave the kidney substance.

4. Internal Structure

    a. Inner layer called the medulla.
    b. Outer layer called the cortex.
    c. The renal pyramids are triangle-shaped wedges of medulla with apices projecting as papillae and ending in calyces of the pelvis of each ureter.
    d. Renal columns are inward extensions of cortex between the pyramids.

5. Vascular Supply

    a. Renal vessels enter the hilum and divide into interlobar vessels that

travel to the cortex and break up into
arcuate vessels.

b. Interlobular vessels extend from the
arcuate vessels into the cortex.

Microscopic Anatomy

1. Arterial blood enters Bowman's capsule
via an afferent arteriole to form a capillary
tuft called the glomerulus. Bowman's capsule, together with the glomerulus, forms
the renal corpuscle.

2. The complete functional unit of the kidney is the nephron, composed of the renal
corpuscle and its tubular extensions — proximal convoluted tubule, loop of Henle,
distal convoluted tubule, and collecting
duct.

3. Blood leaves the glomerulus via an efferent arteriole that gives rise to the peritubular capillaries.

Urine Formation

1. Urine Formed in Two Stages

a. Glomerular filtration
b. Tubular reabsorption and secretion.

2. About 125 ml per minute of the approximately 650 ml per minute of plasma flowing through the glomeruli is filtered into
Bowman's capsules. The filtrate is almost
identical to plasma in composition except
for the absence of plasma proteins.

3. Tubular reabsorption and secretion, in
accordance with the body's needs, markedly change the composition of the filtrate; reabsorption to a greater extent than
secretion determines the final composition
of urine.

4. Reabsorption of sodium by active transport is followed by the passive reabsorption of water. Glucose and amino acids are
normally completely reabsorbed by active
processes. Urea is passively reabsorbed
but is 60 to 70 times more concentrated in
urine than in plasma.

5. Potassium, about 12 times more concentrated in urine than in plasma, is both
reabsorbed and secreted, secretion (by a
process involving sodium-potassium exchange) accounting for the high urine concentration. Certain waste products and
drugs are eliminated by active secretion.

Formation of Concentrated Urine

1. Dependence on ADH

a. ADH makes the distal convoluted tubule and collecting duct permeable
to water.
b. When fluid loss causes concentration
of the plasma, hypothalamic osmoreceptors stimulate the release of ADH
from the neurohypophysis.

2. Impermeability of ascending loop of
Henle to water concentrates medullary interstitial fluid. Countercurrent exchange
system of descending and ascending vasa
recta maintains hypertonicity of medullary
fluid, permitting urine to become concentrated.

Regulatory Action of Aldosterone

Aldosterone, a hormone secreted by the
adrenal cortex, increases reabsorption of
sodium, and consequently of water. Its release occurs as follows:

a. Low blood volume stimulates the release of renin, an enzyme, from the
juxtaglomerular apparatus of the kidney.
b. Renin initiates the formation in the
blood of angiotensin II, which triggers aldosterone secretion.

Renal Regulation of Acid-Base Balance

The action of carbonic anhydrase in tubular cells results in the formation of hydrogen and bicarbonate ions. Hydrogen is secreted in exchange for sodium, and
bicarbonate replenishes blood bicarbonate.
Secreted hydrogen ions react with

a. Bicarbonate, forming carbon dioxide
and water
b. Dibasic phosphate, forming monobasic phosphate
c. Ammonia, forming ammonium ions.

Ureters

1. Location and Structure

a. Retroperitoneal, extending from the
kidneys to the posterior part of the
bladder.
b. Ureters begin in the kidney as several calyces, which unite to form a
pelvis.

c. The walls are of smooth muscle with a mucous lining and a fibrous outer layer.

2. Function

Collect urine and convey it to the bladder.

Urinary Bladder

1. Location and Structure

a. Posterior to symphysis pubis.
b. Bladder consists of trigone, with three openings (one urethral, two for ureters), and detrusor musculature.

2. Function

a. Storage of urine.
b. Reservoir that expels urine from the body. Process of urination is called voiding or micturition. This occurs as follows:
    (1) When the fluid volume in the bladder reaches about 150 ml, signals are transmitted to micturition reflex center in sacral region of spinal cord.
    (2) When inhibition from brain is lifted, return impulses trigger relaxation of urethral sphincters and contraction of detrusor muscle.

Urethra

1. Location and Structure

a. Musculomembranous tube lying behind symphysis pubis and extending through prostate gland, triangular ligament and penis in male.
b. Lies anterior to vagina in female.

2. Function

a. Male: passageway for expulsion of urine and semen.
b. Female: passageway for expulsion of urine from the body.

chapter 15

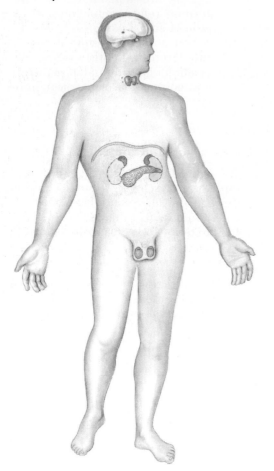

The Endocrine System

Objectives

The aim of this chapter is to enable the student to:

Define the term hormone and discuss the origin of the modern concept of endocrine function.

Distinguish between the mechanisms of action of the two major classes of hormones.

Describe the anatomical relationship between the hypothalamus and hypophysis.

Discuss the interrelation between the hypothalamus and the endocrine system.

Locate and describe each endocrine gland.

Summarize the actions of the hormones secreted by each endocrine gland.

Describe the disorders of endocrine glands.

TERMINOLOGY AND GENERAL FUNCTIONS

Introduction

The endocrine system is composed of a diverse group of tissues which function to produce and release into the blood stream substances known as **hormones**, a term derived from the Greek word hormaein—to set in motion. The hormones are usually released in very low concentrations and transported to their sites of action elsewhere in the body, where they exert regulatory effects on cellular processes. Hormones may act upon the cells of specific

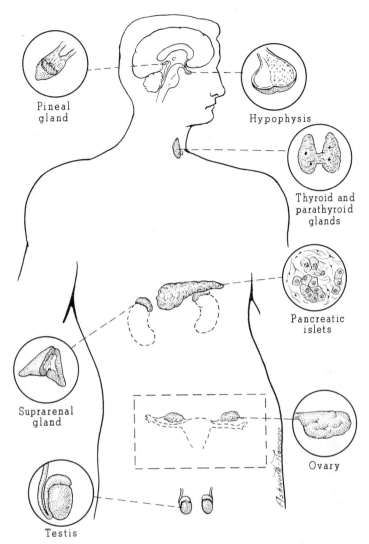

Figure 468. Location of eight glands of internal secretion.

organs, referred to as *target organs*, or upon cells widely distributed throughout the body. Cellular processes regulated by hormones include the permeability of cell membranes, the activity of specific enzyme systems, and gene transcription, leading to the synthesis of enzymes and other proteins.

The first experiment demonstrating an endocrine function was performed in 1849

Table 47. **GLANDS OF INTERNAL SECRETION**

GLANDS	LOCATION
1. Hypophysis (pituitary)	Sella turcica of the sphenoid bone
2. Thyroid	Neck, with one lobe on each side of the trachea
3. Parathyroids (four)	Posterior aspect of the thyroid gland
4. Pancreatic islets	Scattered throughout the pancreas
5. Suprarenal glands (two)	Superior to each kidney
6. Ovaries (two)	In pelvis, one on each side of the uterus
7. Testes (two)	One in each side of the scrotal sac
8. Pineal	Above the superior colliculi of the midbrain

by A. A. Bertold at the University of Göttingen. Bertold observed that the atrophy of the comb and loss of male behavior in cockerels following castration could be prevented by grafting a testis into the abdominal cavity. He concluded that the testis released something into the circulation that maintained male secondary sexual characteristics and behavior. However, these observations went unnoticed for many years and about 40 years elapsed before it became generally understood that the ductless glands functioned by releasing "chemical messengers" into the blood.

The origin of the modern concept of endocrine function can be traced to events that led to an understanding of the function of the thyroid gland. In 1883 three Swiss surgeons surgically removed enlarged thyroids (goiters) from 46 patients to relieve pressure on the trachea. The operation relieved the mechanical stress but caused the most extreme form of symptoms frequently seen in endemic goiter (especially prevalent in certain mountainous regions, such as the Alps, and now known to be due to a deficiency in dietary iodine). These symptoms included a low basal metabolic rate and a lethargic state of mind. This observation, and the duplication in thyroidectomized animals of certain signs (such as stunted growth) of infant endemic goiter (cretinism), suggested that the thyroid gland produces a substance necessary for normal development and health. By 1890, hypothyroid patients were being treated successfully by adding sheep's thyroid to their diet. The success of the substitution therapy refuted the view that the function of the thyroid and other ductless glands was to remove hypothetical noxious substances from the blood. This "detoxification theory" had been widely accepted as an explanation for syndromes described for diseased states of the adrenals, pancreas, and parathyroids, as well as the thyroid.

The view that endocrine glands regularly released into the blood stream substances necessary for the normal development and function of other parts of the body was clearly stated in 1891 by Brown-Séquard and D'Arsonval. At the beginning of the 20th century the understanding of endocrine function was further advanced by the discovery that a hormone may be secreted in response to a specific stimulus and be the mediator of a specific response. Such was the case with the intestinal hormone secretin which, as we have seen (Chapter 13), is secreted in response to acid in the duodenum and stimulates the exocrine pancreas. In 1902 Bayliss and Starling prepared an extract of the intestinal mucosa which, when injected into an animal, caused the secretion of pancreatic juice. Bayliss and Starling proposed the term *hormone* to identify this and similar substances.

The release of a hormone is frequently triggered by a change in the concentration of some substance in the body fluids. The effect of the hormone is corrective, eliminating the stimulus and reducing the secretion. Such a sequence is characteristic of a negative feedback homeostatic control system. Hormones, then, perform a number of functions—they coordinate body activities, control growth and development, and maintain homeostasis. In addition, the endocrine system interacts with the nervous system to bring about various responses to changes in the external and internal environment.

Listed below are the endocrine glands that will be discussed in this chapter and their secretions:

1. **Hypothalamus:** Thyrotropin-releasing factor (TRF), corticotropin-releasing factor (CRF), follicle-stimulating-hormone-releasing factor (FRF), luteinizing-hormone-releasing factor (LRF), growth-hormone-releasing factor (GRF), growth-hormone inhibitory factor (GIF), prolactin inhibitory factor (PIF), prolactin-releasing factor (PRF), melanocyte-stimulating-hormone-releasing factor (MRF), and melanocyte-stimulating hormone inhibitory factor (MIF).

2. **Hypophysis** (pituitary gland)
   a. Neurohypophysis (posterior pituitary gland): Antidiuretic hormone (ADH) and oxytocin. These hormones are synthesized in the hypothalamus and transported to the neurohypophysis via nerve fibers.
   b. Adenohypophysis (anterior pituitary gland): Thyroid-stimulating hormone (TSH), adrenocorticotropic hormone (ACTH), follicle-stimulating hormone (FSH), luteinizing hormone (LH), prolactin, growth hormone (GH), and melanocyte-stimulating hormone (MSH).

3. **Thyroid:** Thyroxine, triiodothyronine, and calcitonin.
4. **Parathyroid:** Parathyroid hormone.
5. **Adrenal**
   a. Adrenal cortex: Cortisol and aldosterone.
   b. Adrenal medulla: Epinephrine and norepinephrine. The adrenal medulla, innervated by preganglionic sympathetic nerve fibers, functions as a component of the sympathetic nervous system.
6. **Isles of Langerhans of the pancreas:** Insulin and glucagon.
7. **Ovary:** Estrogens and progesterone.
8. **Testis:** Testosterone.
9. **Pineal gland:** Melatonin.
10. **Placenta:** Chorionic gonadotropin, estrogens, and progesterone.

Mechanism of Hormone Action

Hormones can be divided into two major classes: (1) *proteins, peptides, and derivatives of amino acids,* and (2) *steroids,* all synthesized from cholesterol. Steroid hormones are the hormones of the adrenal cortex, the female sex hormones (estrogens and progesterone), and the male sex hormones (androgens, principally testosterone). All other hormones listed in the preceding paragraph belong to the first-mentioned class. The two classes of hormones operate through distinctly different mechanisms as follows:

Protein, Peptide and Amino Acid Derivative Hormones. Many hormones of this class have been found to exert their actions via a "second messenger," **cyclic AMP** (cyclic 3′, 5′-adenosine monophosphate). In the first step the hormone binds to a receptor protein on the surface of the cell membrane. This binding increases the activity of an enzyme in the membrane called *adenyl cyclase,* which converts the abundant ATP in the cytoplasm in contact with the inner side of the membrane to cyclic AMP. Cyclic AMP then induces a change in some cellular process. This may involve changing the rate of enzymatic reactions, altering membrane permeability, or stimulating the release of stored hormones. The first cellular process shown to be mediated by cyclic AMP (by Earl Sutherland and colleagues in the late 1950's) was the

acceleration of the breakdown of glycogen to glucose in the liver cell by epinephrine and glucagon (Fig. 469). Since then, cyclic AMP has been shown to be the mediator of the actions of a considerable number of other hormones, including the hypothalamic releasing factors, thyroid-stimulating hormone, adrenocorticotropic hormone, follicle-stimulating hormone, luteinizing hormone, antidiuretic hormone, parathyroid hormone, and secretin.

Steroid Hormones. Steroid hormones function by entering target cells and activating specific genes. This occurs as follows: The hormone, after entering the cell, *binds to a receptor protein in the cytoplasm.* Receptor proteins consist of two subunits, each of which binds one hormone molecule. The binding alters the receptor protein in some way, enabling the complex to *migrate into the nucleus,* where one of the receptor subunits binds to a chromosomal protein. The receptor protein dissociates, and the liberated, unbound subunit interacts with DNA. The result is an increase in gene transcription, producing messenger RNA, which serves as a template for the synthesis of proteins. The activity of these proteins, most of which apparently function as enzymes, is responsible for the effect of the hormone on the target cell. Receptor proteins have been identified in target tissues of all the known steroid hormones.

Hypothalamus

Hormones of the Hypothalamus Acting on the Adenohypophysis. In the 1940's it was discovered that the hypothalamus synthesizes and secretes hormones (called *releasing and inhibitory factors*) that control the secretion of the hormones of the adenohypophysis (anterior pituitary gland). These factors are transported to the adenohypophysis by a portal system which forms a direct vascular link between the hypothalamus and the adenohypophysis. The hypophysis is connected to the hypothalamus by a stalk. *Portal vessels* arising from capillaries in the *median eminence* of the hypothalamus, adjacent to the pituitary stalk, pass down the stalk into the adenohypophysis (Fig. 470). Specialized neurosecretory cells in various parts of the hypothal-

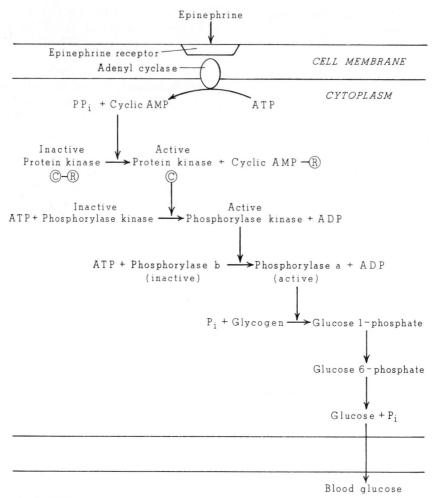

Figure 469. Cyclic AMP acting as a "second messenger" in the stimulation by epinephrine of glycogen break-down in the liver cell to yield blood glucose. Binding of epinephrine to a receptor on the outer surface of the membrane in some way activates adenyl cyclase, an enzyme located on the inner surface of the membrane that converts ATP into cyclic AMP. Cyclic AMP activates protein kinase, an enzyme consisting of two subunits, one regulatory, to which cyclic AMP binds, the other catalytic, inhibited by the regulatory subunit. The regulatory subunit dissociates from the catalytic subunit when cyclic AMP binds to it. The active subunit catalyzes the phosphorylation of inactive phosphorylase kinase to form active phosphorylase kinase. This enzyme, in turn, catalyzes the phosphorylation of phosphorylase b (inactive form) to phosphorylase a (active form), which then catalyzes the breakdown of glycogen to glucose 1-phosphate, from which glucose 6-phosphate and finally free blood glucose are formed. Stimulation of glycogen breakdown in the liver by epinephrine or glucagon was the first hormonal action found to be mediated by cyclic AMP.

amus synthesize the releasing and inhibitory factors. The nerve endings of these cells terminate in the median eminence, and the factors liberated by these endings are absorbed by the capillaries of the median eminence and then carried to the adenohypophysis. The most important factors are those stimulating the secretion by the adenohypophysis of the thyroid-stimulating hormone, adrenocorticotropic hormone, follicle-stimulating hormone, luteinizing hormone and growth hormone, and decreasing the secretion of prolactin.

(The names and abbreviations of all releasing and inhibitory factors have been listed on page 514.) Four of the hormones of the adenohypophysis control the functions of other endocrine glands; namely, the thyroid, adrenal cortex, ovary, and testis. Prolactin governs milk production, and growth hormone causes general body growth, among other things. It should be apparent, then, that the hypothalamus, by regulating the secretion of the hormones of the adenohypophysis, exerts considerable influence over a large part of the endocrine system.

Figure 470. Diagrammatic representation of the vascular and neural connections between the hypothalamus and hypophysis. Hypothalamic hormones (releasing and inhibitory factors) liberated at nerve endings in the median eminence of the hypothalamus and transported via portal vessels to the adenohypophysis control the secretion of adenohypophyseal hormones. ADH and oxytocin, synthesized in hypothalamic nuclei, pass down axons in the hypothalamic–hypophyseal tract to nerve endings in the neurohypophysis, where they are stored. Their release is governed by nerve impulses from the hypothalamic nuclei.

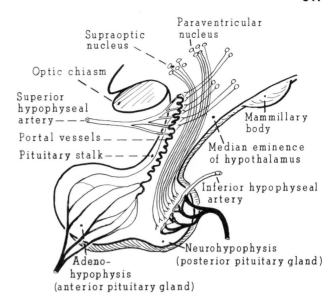

Neural Control of the Neurohypophysis and Adrenal Medulla by the Hypothalamus.

Long before it was discovered that the hypothalamus secretes releasing and inhibitory factors it was known that the *supraoptic* and *paraventricular nuclei* of the hypothalamus manufacture two hormones (**ADH** and **oxytocin**) that pass down axons of the hypothalamic-hypophyseal tract in the pituitary stalk to nerve endings in the neurohypophysis, where they are stored (Fig. 470). These hormones are released upon stimulation by impulses arising in the hypothalamic nuclei and transmitted in the hypothalamic-hypophyseal tract.

The hypothalamus controls the secretion of epinephrine and norepinephrine by the adrenal medulla by a direct nerve pathway: Fibers passing down the spinal cord synapse with preganglionic neurons whose fibers lead to the adrenal medulla.

The hypothalamus, then, exerts direct nervous control over the secretions of the neurohypophysis and adrenal medulla and, via portal blood vessels, hormonal control over the secretions of the adenohypophysis. In earlier chapters it has been noted that the hypothalamus contains centers for regulating body temperature and the volume of body fluids, among others, and is linked by nerve circuits to almost all parts of the brain. Utilizing input from other parts of the brain and information received from the blood passing through it, the hypothalamus continuously regulates almost the entire endo-

crine system. Ordinarily, these interactions contribute to normal development and health. Disturbed emotional states, however, may have the opposite effect. For example, poor growth in children deprived of normal parental affection (a condition called deprivation dwarfism) is apparently

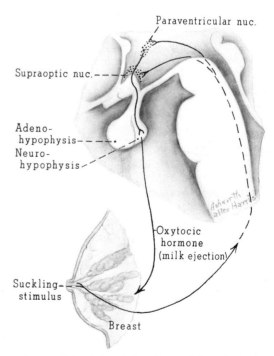

Figure 471. Interrelationships of hypothalamus, neurohypophysis, and breast.

in large measure a consequence of a deficiency in the secretion of hypothalamic releasing factors, including the growth-hormone-releasing factor.

HYPOPHYSIS (PITUITARY GLAND)

The hypophysis is a mass of tissue about 1 cm in diameter, weighing approximately 0.8 gm in the adult. It consists of two completely separate divisions: the *adenohypophysis,* or *anterior pituitary gland,* and the *neurohypophysis,* or *posterior pituitary gland,* and, as mentioned, is connected by a stalk with the hypothalamus of the brain. The adenohypophysis is embryologically derived from the endoderm of the developing pharynx, whereas the neurohypophysis is a neural ectoderm derivative.

Neurohypophysis

The neurohypophysis, as described above, does not actually produce any hormones, but functions in storing two hormones which are secreted by the hypothalamus and transported via nerve fibers to the neurohypophysis. The two hormones, oxytocin and ADH, are secreted from the neurohypophysis upon nervous stimulation by the hypothalamus. Both hormones are octapeptides. Six of the eight amino acids in the two molecules are identical, which explains why each exhibits to some extent the major actions of the other.

Antidiuretic Hormone (ADH). The major action of ADH (also known as *vasopressin*) is to increase the permeability of the distal convoluted tubules and collecting ducts of the kidney to water, thereby allowing greater amounts of water to be reabsorbed (see Chapter 14, page 502). In high concentration, ADH constricts arterioles, raising arterial blood pressure. This response may have physiological significance during severe hemorrhage. The rate of release of ADH from the neurohypophysis is governed by the concentration of the plasma and blood volume. According to some studies, cells in the supraoptic nuclei of the hypothalamus (the principal source of ADH) function as osmoreceptors, increasing or decreasing in size in response to changes in the concentration of the extra-

cellular fluid. In any case, when excess water loss increases the concentration of the plasma, the supraoptic nuclei are stimulated, and impulses transmitted to the neurohypophysis increase ADH release. Hemorrhage resulting in a loss of 10 per cent of the blood volume will also stimulate the release of ADH. A 25 per cent reduction in blood volume causes up to a 50-fold increase in the secretion of ADH. Low-pressure receptors in the left atrium appear to be the principal receptors in this response.

The most important disorder associated with deficiency of the neurohypophysis is **diabetes insipidus,** a disease caused by a diminished production of antidiuretic hormone. Deficiency of ADH prevents the reabsorption of water by the distal renal tubules and collecting ducts and leads to the excretion of large volumes of urine — up to 20 liters a day.

Oxytocin (pitocin). The primary function of oxytocin is to influence the lactating breast to release milk from the glandular cells into the ducts. This is brought about by contraction of the myoepithelial cells in the alveoli of the mammary glands. Suckling by the infant is the stimulus for the release of oxytocin. Impulses from the breast are transmitted to the hypothalamic nuclei, which trigger oxytocin release from the neurohypophysis (Fig. 471).

Oxytocin also stimulates the uterus to contract at the time of childbirth. It acts on the smooth muscle of the pregnant uterus to maintain labor. Commercial forms of oxytocin are sometimes employed to increase uterine contraction and decrease hemorrhage following delivery. Although the sequence of events during parturition is uncertain, it is known that stimulation of the pregnant uterus initiates nerve impulses that pass to the hypothalamus and induce an increase in the secretion of oxytocin, and that during labor the concentration of oxytocin in the blood increases.

Adenohypophysis (Fig. 472)

There are two major cell types composing the anterior lobe of the hypophysis which can be easily recognized by simple staining techniques. These are chromophils, which accept stains, and chromophobes, which do

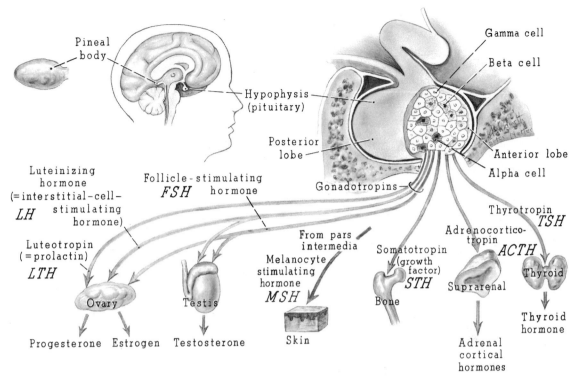

Figure 472. The adenohypophysis produces several hormones controlling the activity of a number of endocrine glands.

not accept stains. Chromophobes constitute 20 to 28 per cent of the cells of the adenohypophysis. Chromophils are subdivided into basophils, accepting basic dyes, and acidophils, accepting acid dyes. The *basophils* produce thyroid-stimulating hormone, follicle-stimulating hormone and luteinizing hormone; the *acidophils* produce growth hormone and prolactin; the *chromophobes* probably produce adrenocorticotropic hormone.

The major hormones of the adenohypophysis, with the exception of growth hormone, control the activities of specific target glands—the thyroid, adrenal cortex, ovary, testis, and mammary gland. All adenohypophyseal hormones are proteins.

Thyroid-Stimulating Hormone (TSH). The thyroid-stimulating hormone (also called *thyrotropin*) regulates the size and function of the thyroid gland, promoting tissue growth and the production and secretion of thyroid hormones (thyroxine and triiodothyronine). Removal of the hypophysis (hypophysectomy) causes degenerative changes in the thyroid gland and considerable, but not complete, loss of function. Severing the connection between the adenohypophysis and hypothalamus has a similar, but less pronounced, effect on the thyroid. Secretion of the thyroid hormones and thyrotropin is reciprocally regulated by a *negative feedback* mechanism. High blood levels of thyrotropin stimulate the secretion of thyroid hormones. The subsequent elevated level of thyroid hormones reduces thyrotropin secretion directly by acting on the adenohypophysis and indirectly by acting on the hypothalamus (decreasing the secretion of thyrotropin-stimulating-releasing factor). The lowering of the concentrations of the thyroid hormones increases thyrotropin secretion.

Adrenocorticotropic Hormone (ACTH). The adrenocorticotropic hormone, also called *adrenocorticotropin*, regulates the growth and function of the middle (*zona fasciculata*) and inner (*zona reticularis*) zones of the adrenal cortex, the regions that synthesize and secrete cortisol and similar steroid hormones (and small amounts of androgens). ACTH exerts almost no control over the thin outer region (*zona glomerulosa*) of the adrenal cortex, where aldosterone is synthesized. A hypophysectomized animal will show degenerative changes in the middle and inner zones but not in the zona glomerulosa. Secretion of ACTH and cortisol is regulated by essentially the same negative feedback mechanism described for the thyroid hormones and thyrotropin. ACTH has no effect on the adrenal medulla.

Gonadotropic Hormones. *Follicle-stimulating hormone* (FSH) stimulates the development of the ovarian follicle in females and spermatogenesis in males.

Luteinizing hormone (LH) is also called *interstitial cell-stimulating hormone* (ICSH) in the male. It controls the testicular production of testosterone. In the female, LH stimulates ovulation.

The feedback mechanism controlling the secretion of estrogens, progesterone, and the gonadotropins during the menstrual cycle is described in Chapter 17.

Prolactin. Prolactin stimulates the development of mammary gland alveoli, the secretory units, and the synthesis of milk. Its release from the adenohypophysis is controlled principally by prolactin-inhibitory factor (PIF). The secretion of prolactin is normally kept at a very low level by PIF. During lactation the production of PIF is suppressed. A prolactin-releasing factor has also been identified. It has been observed, however, that section of the pituitary stalk in animals results in a several-fold increase in prolactin secretion (the secretion of all other hormones of the adenohypophysis is greatly decreased or completely suppressed by this procedure).

Growth Hormone. Growth hormone, also called *somatotropin,* accelerates growth, increasing the size of all organs and promoting the growth of bone before closure of the epiphysis. It increases protein formation, decreases carbohydrate utilization, and increases the mobilization of fat for energy use. Some of the specific actions of growth hormone follow:

1. Growth hormone increases the length of bones by increasing the formation and release by the liver of the substance known as *somatomedin,* which stimulates the proliferation of cartilage cells at the epiphyseal disc, or growth plate. This widens the disc, and growth is proportional to the widening.

2. Growth hormone enhances protein

synthesis by increasing the uptake of amino acids by cells and by increasing the incorporation of amino acids into protein. Insulin has similar effects on protein formation, and the presence of insulin is necessary for the expression of the anabolic action of growth hormone, and for its growth-promoting activity in general.

3. Growth hormone treatment increases blood sugar. Injection of the hormone into animals decreases glucose uptake by cells (particularly skeletal and heart muscle) and the oxidation of glucose by these cells. These actions are opposite and antagonistic to the actions of insulin.

4. Growth hormone increases the transport of fatty acids from fat depots, principally to skeletal muscle, the heart, and the liver, by accelerating the hydrolysis of triglycerides in the depots. (It has been suggested, that, since fatty acids interfere with the uptake and oxidation of glucose, growth hormone impairment of glucose utilization is in part the result of its lipid mobilizing action.)

Low blood sugar levels stimulate the release of growth hormone. Thus the hormone may help to augment the use of fat for energy during fasting.

An underproduction of growth hormone in childhood results in **dwarfism.** The pituitary dwarf is generally a well-proportioned but small person. If there is an overproduction of growth hormone in children before the epiphyses of the long bones close, **gigantism** results (Fig. 473).

In the adult, overproduction of growth hormone results in **acromegaly.** Since bones cannot increase in length after the closure of the epiphyses in the adult, cancellous bones increase in thickness. As a result of acromegaly, the feet and hands become large and spadelike, while the bones of the face and skull become thicker. Hyperglycemia and glycosuria frequently occur. An acidophilic tumor is usually responsible for the condition.

Melanocyte-Stimulating Hormone (MSH). The melanocyte-stimulating hormone stimulates the epidermal melanocytes. Normally, small amounts of the hormone are secreted, but in Addison's disease (adrenal cortical hypofunction) hypersecretion causes darkening of the skin. This occurs because the low blood levels of adrenal cortical hormones cause an increase in the

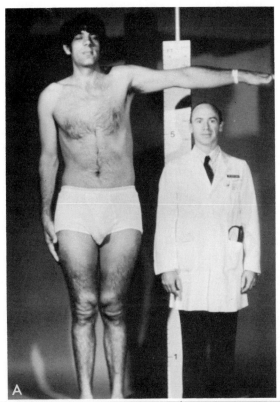

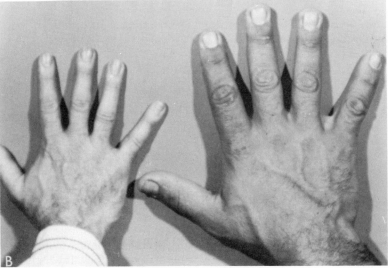

Figure 473. Gigantism with acromegaly in a male aged 28. *A*, Height approximately 7 feet, 6 inches. *B*, Hands of same individual as compared to normal sized hand.

Table 48. HYPOPHYSEAL HORMONES

NAME AND SOURCE	SYNONYMS	FUNCTION
Adenohypophysis (anterior lobe)		
TSH	Thyroid-stimulating hormone; thyrotropin	Stimulates thyroid growth and secretion.
ACTH	Adrenocorticotropic hormone; corticotropin	Stimulates adrenocortical growth and secretion
Growth Hormone	Somatotropin	Accelerates body growth
FSH	Follicle-stimulating hormone	Stimulates growth of ovarian follicle and estrogen secretion in the female and spermatogenesis in the male
LH	Luteinizing hormone (in the female); interstitial cell-stimulating hormone, ICSH (in the male)	Stimulates ovulation and luteinization of ovarian follicles in the female and production of testosterone in the male
Prolactin	Mammotropin, lactogenic hormone	Stimulates synthesis of milk
MSH	Melanocyte-stimulating hormone	Stimulates melanocytes causing pigmentation
Neurohypophysis (posterior lobe)		
Antidiuretic Hormone (ADH)	Vasopressin	Promotes water retention by way of the renal tubules and stimulates smooth muscle of blood vessels and digestive tract
Oxytocin		Stimulates release of milk and contraction of smooth muscle in the uterus

secretion of not only ACTH but also melanocyte-stimulating hormone.

A summary of hypophyseal hormones is included in Table 48.

THE THYROID GLAND

The human thyroid (Fig. 474) is composed of two lobes lying on either side of the trachea and connected in the midline by a thin isthmus extending over the anterior surface of the trachea. In the adult, the thyroid weighs from 20 to 30 grams. It is encapsulated by two layers of connective tissue—the outer one continuous with the cervical fascia and the inner one intimately adherent to the surface of the gland itself.

The ancients assigned the thyroid gland such functions as serving as a vascular shunt for cerebral circulation and beautifying the neck, especially when it enlarged into a "goiter."

Microscopic Anatomy of the Thyroid

The thyroid has a remarkable capacity to store secretions, as is reflected in its histology (which differs from other endocrine glands, in which the cells are arranged in sheets between blood vessels). Normally, the thyroid is composed of *follicles* of uniform size, each, in effect, a separate gland, and each about the diameter of a pinhead (Fig. 475). The sacs do not have external openings, but are richly supplied with minute blood and lymph vessels bringing supplies of iodine and carrying away thyroid hormone. In the healthy gland the follicle consists of a single, approximately spherical layer of cuboidal cells surrounding the cavity or lumen filled with a substance known as *colloid*. Colloid itself is a homogenous substance giving the gland its most distinguishing histologic characteristic. It is the storage product of the secretory epithelium. In iodine deficiency

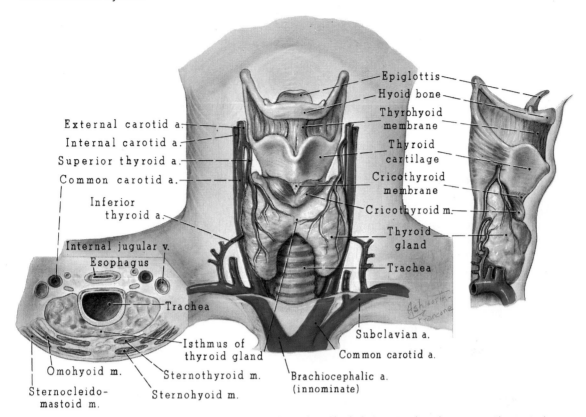

External carotid a.
Internal carotid a.
Superior thyroid a.
Common carotid a.
Inferior thyroid a.
Internal jugular v.
Esophagus
Trachea
Omohyoid m.
Sternocleido-mastoid m.
Isthmus of thyroid gland
Sternothyroid m.
Sternohyoid m.
Epiglottis
Hyoid bone
Thyrohyoid membrane
Thyroid cartilage
Cricothyroid membrane
Cricothyroid m.
Thyroid gland
Trachea
Subclavian a.
Common carotid a.
Brachiocephalic a. (innominate)

Figure 474. Plate of thyroid gland showing its blood supply and relations to trachea; in cross section, anterior, and right lateral views.

Figure 475. Photomicrograph of the thyroid gland showing normal follicles, each lined with simple cuboidal epithelium and filled with colloid. Magnification 50 ×. (From Leeson, C. R., and Leeson, T. S.: Histology. 3rd ed., Philadelphia, W. B. Saunders Co., 1976.)

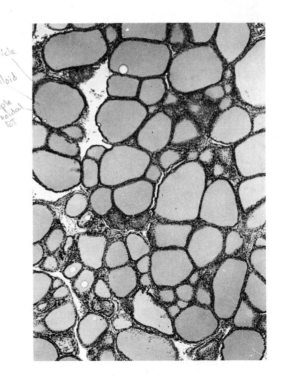

follicles become distended with colloid and the cells lining the follicles become flattened. When the thyroid overacts, colloid stores become depleted and the epithelium assumes a columnar shape. The stroma (delicate fibrous tissue), located between the follicles, is denser in some areas than in others, creating fibrous septa traversing the gland.

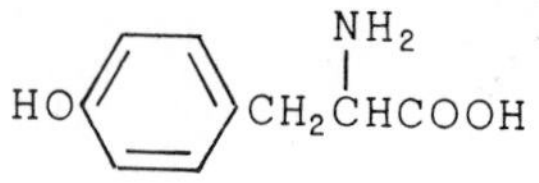

Tyrosine

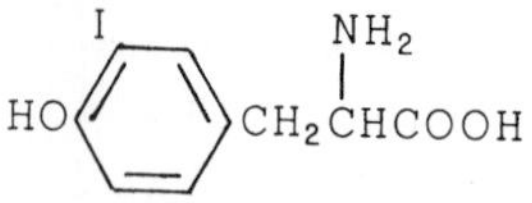

Monoiodotyrosine (MIT)

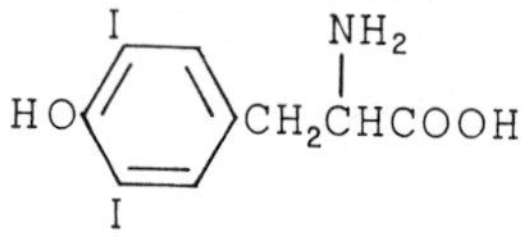

Diiodotyrosine (DIT)

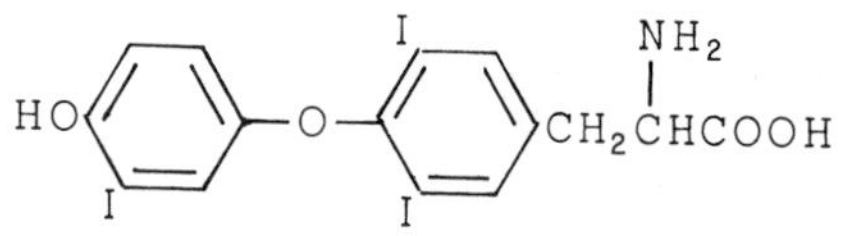

Triiodothyronine (T_3)

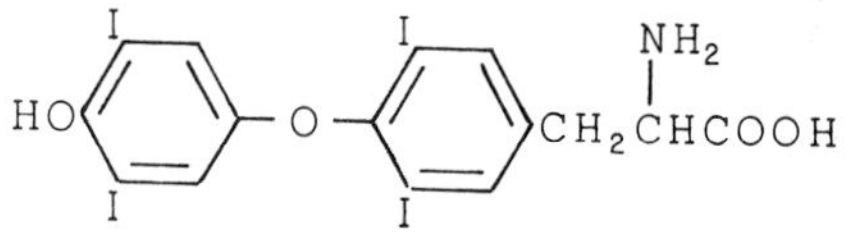

Thyroxine (T_4)

Figure 476. Tyrosine and compounds formed by its iodination in the thyroid gland, including the thyroid hormones T_3 and thyroxine.

Physiology of the Thyroid

The thyroid is one of the most sensitive organs of the body. During puberty, pregnancy, and physiologic stress it increases in size, becoming more active. Changes in activity and size normally occur during the menstrual cycle. Two hormones responsible for the major functions of the thyroid gland have been chemically defined. These are thyroxine (T_4 for the four iodine atoms attached to the thyronine nucleus) and triiodothyronine (T_3 for three iodine atoms). The thyroid secretes about 10 times as much thyroxine as T_3. However, since a fraction of the thyroxine is deiodinated as it circulates, about two or three times as much thyroxine as T_3 is available to the tissues. T_3 is three to five times more active than thyroxine, but the duration of the action of thyroxine is three to five times longer. The overall effect of the two hormones, therefore, is similar, and the functions they perform appear to be identical.

The synthesis of the thyroid hormones involves the following steps: (1) Uptake by thyroid cells of iodine as sodium or potassium iodide from the blood. This is an active transport process and is often called the "thyroid pump." (2) Oxidation of iodide (I^-) to form what is known as "active" iodine. (3) Combination of "active" iodine with the amino acid tyrosine (bound to the giant protein molecules thyroglobulin, the principal substance of colloid) to form monoiodotyrosine (MIT) and diiodotyrosine (DIT). This apparently occurs on the cell membrane at the cell-colloid interface. (4) T_3 is then formed by combination of MIT and DIT, thyroxine by combination of two molecules of DIT. (The structure of tyrosine and its iodinated derivatives are shown in Fig. 476.)

To be released from the gland, the hormones must be split from thyroglobulin by a proteolytic enzyme. This occurs in thyroid cells following pinocytosis of colloid and fusion of colloid-containing vesicles with lysosomes. MIT and DIT that do not combine to form T_3 and thyroxine are uncoupled from thyroglobulin at the same time the hormones are released and then enzymatically deiodinated. The deiodination serves the important function of conserving thyroidal iodine for recycling. A congenital absence of thyroid deiodinase causes iodine deficiency.

Thyroid-stimulating hormone promotes the uptake of iodide and all steps in the synthesis and release of the thyroid hormones. Following their secretion, thyroxine and T_3 are transported in the blood bound to proteins. Measurement of plasma-protein-bound iodine (PBI) is an index of thyroid function.

Actions of Thyroid Hormones

Although the thyroid hormones exert many effects on almost all tissues of the body, the basic cellular mechanism by which these hormones act is still poorly understood. In general, thyroid hormones promote growth and differentiation and increase oxidative metabolism. In 1895, Adolf Magnus-Levy demonstrated that the thyroid gland regulates the *basal metabolic rate* (BMR — defined in Chapter 13, page 486). He observed a low basal oxygen consumption in hypothyroid patients and was able to correct the deficiency by administering a thyroid extract. Hyperthyroid individuals have a high BMR.

Thyroid hormones have a "permissive action" on growth hormone secretion and function. In the absence of thyroid hormones, growth hormone is not secreted normally and does not have its normal growth-promoting actions. During growth, the action of thyroid hormones on protein metabolism is primarily anabolic. These hormones increase synthesis in almost all tissues of the body, and growth hormone cannot exert its normal effects on tissue and body growth unless they are present. In hyperthyroid adults, on the other hand, the catabolic effect of thyroid hormones on protein metabolism predominates.

The thyroid hormones are specifically required for the normal development of the central nervous system. This requirement, as well as the need for thyroid hormones for normal growth, is evident in children called cretins, who are hypothyroid from infancy. Such children are dwarfed and mentally retarded. (See Chapter 5, page 89, for a brief description of the action of thyroid hormones on bone.)

In the hyperthyroid condition, catabolic effects of thyroid hormones on carbohydrate and fat metabolism are apparent. The oxidation of glucose is increased, and fatty acids are mobilized from the fat depots and oxidized by active tissues at an increased rate. Thyroid hormones actually accelerate all aspects of carbohydrate metabolism, including absorption of glucose from the small intestine into the blood and its entry into tissue cells. Synthesis of glucose from noncarbohydrate precursors is also increased.

Thyroid hormones also augment the catabolism of cholesterol. In the hypothyroid state the reverse condition, a reduced catabolism of cholesterol and fat, is observed, and elevated blood lipids are a characteristic feature. The concentration of the cholesterol rich plasma low density lipoproteins is especially high in hypothyroid individuals. Since elevated levels of plasma low density lipoproteins, as has been noted (Chapter 10, page 369), accelerate the development of atherosclerosis, this disease is generally seen in prolonged hypothyroidism.

Goiter. Goiter (L. *guttur*, throat) is the descriptive term for any enlarged thyroid, whether it be secreting too little, too much, or normal amounts of thyroid hormones. At one time, in certain areas of the world where the iodide content of the soil was so low that the drinking water and locally grown food did not provide sufficient iodide for the synthesis of normal amounts of thyroid hormones, significant proportions of the populations had goiters. Goiters of this type, known as *endemic goiters,* developed because the low blood levels of iodine induced hypersecretion of TSH. The TSH-stimulated thyroids enlarged, the follicles becoming engorged with colloid. Many individuals with endemic goiters had sufficient amounts of circulating thyroid hormones for the maintenance of normal health; many others did not. *Toxic goiter* refers to a clinical hyperthyroid state. This type of goiter is often called *exophthalmic* (L. *ex-*, out of; G. *ophthalmos*, eye) *goiter* because most patients have prominent, protruding eyes.

Increased Secretion of Thyroxine. Hyperthyroidism was first described by the Irish physician Robert Graves in 1835, and is usually called *Graves disease*. In this condition the patient becomes excitable and nervous, exhibiting a moist skin, rapid pulse, elevated metabolic rate, intolerance to heat, weight loss, increased appetite, tremor of the hand, and exophthalmos (Fig. 477).

The treatment of hyperthyroidism is well established. A physician can choose among the alternatives of surgery, actually removing large segments of the thyroid, administration of radioactive iodine to destroy segments of the gland, or the use of antithyroid drugs to block the production of thyroid hormone.

Reduced Secretion of Thyroxine. The severe form of hypothyroidism in adults is known as *myxedema* because of the edematous, puffy thickening of the skin, especially below the eyes and of the lips, fingers, and legs (Fig. 478). Deposition of mucoprotein in the subcutaneous tissue, which absorbs fluid, is responsible for the thickening. The characteristic clinical signs of myxedema include a low basal metabolic rate, lethargy, slowing of the mental faculties, cool and dry skin, low heart rate and blood pressure, weight gain, and loss of hair. Adult hypothyroidism is most commonly seen in endemic goiter and an autoimmune disease known as *Hashimoto's disease.*

As mentioned, untreated thyroid deficiency in infancy results in *cretinism,* a condition characterized by stunted growth and mental retardation. Normal changes in body proportion fail to occur. Formation

Figure 478. Myxedema. Note thick lips, baggy eyes, loss of hair, and dry skin.

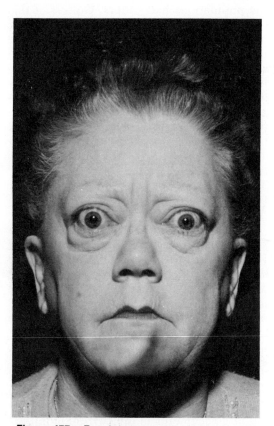

Figure 477. Exophthalmos. Note startled appearance and loss of eyebrows.

and eruption of teeth are delayed, and the child exhibits a broad face with large tongue and mouth. The condition may be caused by a congenital absence of the thyroid gland or failure to synthesize thyroid hormones because of a genetic enzymatic defect, or it may be the childhood form of endemic goiter. The diagnosis of hypothyroidism can be made by clinical findings, the thyroidal radioactive iodine (I^{131}) uptake, and measurement of serum protein-bound iodine. Hypothyroidism is treated by administration of thyroid hormone.

Cancer of the Thyroid. Cancer of the thyroid occurs in all age groups. Thirty years ago it was relatively common in infants following x-ray administration to the neck to combat an enlarged thymus. Treatment of thyroid carcinoma consists of surgical removal of the gland, or destruction by large doses of x-ray. Treatment with radioactive iodine holds hope for some patients in whom thyroid cancer has spread to other parts of the body.

Thyrocalcitonin. In the 1960's it was discovered that the thyroid produces another hormone, one that rapidly lowers blood calcium. The hormone, called thyrocalcitonin or calcitonin, is a polypeptide containing 32 amino acids and is synthesized by the parafollicular, or C, cells of the thyroid, located in the interstitial tissue between the follicles. Its action is opposite to that of the parathyroid hormone. High blood clacium stimulates its release, and it inhibits bone resorption and the liberation of calcium, thereby lowering blood calcium.

THE PARATHYROID GLANDS

The parathyroid glands were unknown to the medical profession until 1880 when they were described by a Swedish anatomist. Surgeons have learned that the accidental removal of these structures at the time of a thyroidectomy results in a serious condition known as tetany.

The parathyroid glands are yellowish or reddish-tan, flattened, oval bodies, 6 mm in length and 3 to 4 mm in breadth; usually four in number, they are located on the posterior aspect of the lobes of the thyroid

(Fig. 479). On histologic section, the parathyroid gland consists of two epithelial cell types: *chief* and *oxyphil*. The chief cell is the more numerous and has a large vesicular, centrally placed nucleus embedded in a faintly staining cytoplasm containing glycogen. The oxyphil cell, characterized by eosinophilic granulation, does not contain glycogen, and is slightly larger than the chief cell. Parathyroid hormone is produced by the chief cells. The function of the oxyphil cell, which appears after puberty, is unknown.

Physiology of the Parathyroids

The parathyroid gland secretes parathyroid hormone, a protein consisting of a single polypeptide chain composed of 83 amino acids with a molecular weight of 8000. Its function is closely linked with the homeostatic regulation of the calcium ion concentration of body fluids and secretion of the hormone is governed by a negative feedback system. The hormone raises blood calcium, principally by increasing bone resorption (Chapter 5, page 90). It also

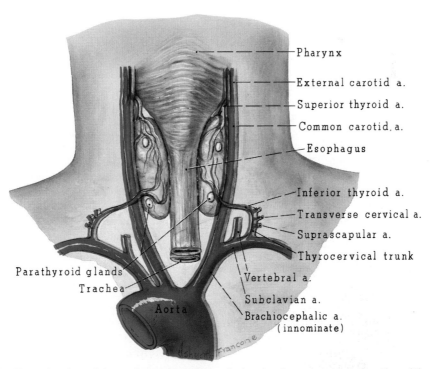

Pharynx

External carotid a.

Superior thyroid a.

Common carotid. a.

Esophagus

Inferior thyroid a.

Transverse cervical a.

Suprascapular a.

Thyrocervical trunk

Vertebral a.

Subclavian a.

Brachiocephalic a.
(innominate)

Parathyroid glands

Trachea

Aorta

Figure 479. Posterior view of the neck and thyroid gland, showing the approximate location of the parathyroid glands.

increases the reabsorption of calcium from the kidneys and, by stimulating the formation of 1,25-dihydroxyvitamin D_3 in the kidneys (Chapter 5, page 89), it increases the absorption of calcium from the small intestine. Elevated levels of blood calcium decrease the secretion of parathyroid hormone.

Calcium serves four major functions: bone formation, coagulation of blood, maintenance of normal cell permeability, and maintenance of normal neuromuscular irritability.

Although calcium is present in all body fluids, 99 per cent is contained in bone. The normal adult requirement is 1 gram per day. During periods of active growth, such as pregnancy, this requirement may increase to approximately 2 grams per day.

Diseases of the Parathyroid Glands

Hypoparathyroidism (Tetany). The findings associated with parathyroid underactivity include a drop in serum calcium and a rise in serum inorganic phosphorus. With parathyroid deficiency the urinary excretion of calcium diminishes. Common symptoms of parathyroid deficiency are increased excitability of the musculature to mechanical stimulation and fibrillary twitchings followed by jerky muscular contractions. The neuromuscular symptoms become more severe as the calcium level of the blood falls. Tetany is encountered following accidental removal or injury of the parathyroid glands when the thyroid has been surgically treated. One remaining parathyroid is thought to be sufficient to prevent the occurrence of tetany. Treatment of hypoparathyroidism must be considered from the point of view of acute and chronic phases. In the acute phase, which frequently occurs in the postoperative period following removal of the parathyroid with the thyroid, treatment is aimed at preventing muscle spasm and convulsions. This is accomplished by restoring the serum calcium level to normal by the intravenous injection of calcium salts.

During the chronic stage of hypoparathyroidism the major goal of treatment is to maintain the serum calcium level at normal, so as to prevent the symptoms and signs of tetany and to avoid future complications, including cataracts. Vitamin D is given to enhance the absorption of calcium by the small intestine. Oral calcium salts are also of value.

Hyperparathyroidism. The basic problem in hyperparathyroidism is excess circulating parathyroid hormone, leading to increased serum calcium levels (hypercalcemia). Calcium is precipitated in the urinary tract and results in the formation of stones in the kidney. These in turn may cause obstruction of the ureter with accompanying pain and infection. Excess parathyroid hormone causes excess resorption of bone, producing pain, tenderness, fracture, and deformity. X-ray evidence of demineralization of bones is present; if the disease is severe or of long standing, bone cysts can occur. The laboratory findings in hyperparathyroidism include an increase in serum calcium, a decrease in serum phosphorus, and an increase in excretion of body calcium and phosphorus in the urine. Hyperparathyroidism is usually caused by a parathyroid tumor. Treatment consists of surgical removal of the tumor.

SUPRARENAL GLANDS (ADRENAL GLANDS)

There are two suprarenal glands, one superior to each kidney. Each resembles an admiral's cocked hat in shape and each is about $1\frac{1}{2}$ inches in length and $\frac{1}{2}$ inch in diameter. The suprarenal gland varies in weight in different age groups, the average in the adult being about 4 grams. Each suprarenal gland has a cortex, or outer portion, and a medulla, or inner portion. The cortex and medulla are different in both origin and function: the cortex is derived from the mesoderm in close association with the developing gonads, whereas the medulla is neuroectodermal in origin.

Suprarenal Cortex

The cortex of the suprarenal gland is deep yellow in color and occupies three-quarters of the total width of the suprarenal gland in cross section. From the surface inward its component layers are the *zona glomerulosa,* the *zona fasciculata,* and the *zona reticularis.*

Three general types of substances are secreted by the cortex: mineralocorticoids, represented principally by *aldosterone;* glucocorticoids, represented chiefly by *cortisol (hydrocortisone);* and androgens, represented by *testosterone.* The mineralocorticoids and glucocorticoids are the major hormones. To some extent they share the same functions, but each has its own primary activity. The mineralocorticoids function primarily in influencing sodium and potassium excretion. The glucocorticoids, among other things, have important metabolic actions, are essential for a normal response to stress, and have anti-inflammatory and antiallergic activity.

In 1854 Brown-Séquard demonstrated that rabbits died if their adrenal glands were removed. Subsequently, it was found that high sodium and low potassium diets could prevent death.

Mineralocorticoids. Aldosterone (Fig. 480) is the principal natural mineralocorticoid and is the most active substance known to promote sodium retention. It is secreted by the outer zone, or zona glomerulosa, of the cortex.

The daily rate of aldosterone secretion in humans varies from 70 to 200 micrograms on a normal salt diet, compared with the secretion of 25 mg of cortisol daily. The secretion of aldosterone can increase up to 900 micrograms per day in the face of severe sodium restriction. Aldosterone is an important link in the regulation of water and electrolyte metabolism. It increases the renal tubular reabsorption of sodium and, consequently, the passive reabsorption of water (see Chapter 14, page 503). Deficiency in aldosterone secretion results in a marked reduction in plasma volume. Since tubular reabsorption of sodium in the kidneys is accompanied by the secretion of potassium, high potassium levels are a consequence of insufficient aldosterone secretion. This has a toxic effect on the heart, causing weak contractions and arrhythmia. Aldosterone also exerts extrarenal effects on electrolyte metabolism, decreasing sodium and increasing potassium concentration in saliva and sweat.

An understanding of the role of sodium in the cause of edema has led to the use of agents to block the renal tubular activity of aldosterone.

Glucocorticoids. Glucocorticoids influence the metabolism of glucose, protein, and fat. The term glucocorticoid refers to the action of these hormones in raising blood sugar. Cortisol is the principal glucocorticoid and is formed by the zona fasciculata and zona reticularis. Although there

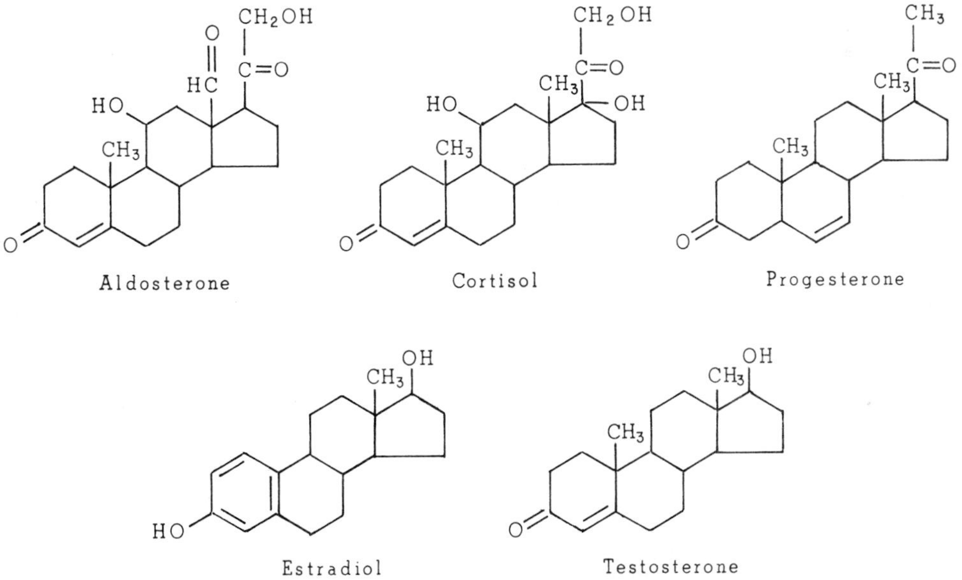

Figure 480. Major steroid hormones: aldosterone (mineralocorticoid) and cortisol (glucocorticoid), secreted by the adrenal cortex; progesterone, secreted by the corpus luteum and placenta; estradiol (estrogen), secreted by the ovarian follicle, corpus luteum, and placenta; testosterone (androgen), secreted principally by the testis. All are synthesized from cholesterol (see Chapter 2, page 26, Fig. 17).

are several glucocorticoids secreted by the cortex, 90 per cent of the total activity is represented by cortisol.

Metabolic Actions of Glucocorticoids. Glucocorticoids decrease the cellular uptake and incorporation of amino acids into proteins in skeletal muscle and increase the uptake and utilization of amino acids in the liver. Since the catabolism of protein and release of amino acids continue in skeletal muscle, the net effect is to increase the *mobilization of amino acids* from skeletal muscle to the liver. The most striking metabolic action of glucocorticoids in the liver is to increase *gluconeogenesis* (the formation of glucose from nonglucose precursors). Amino acids are the major source of metabolites for this process. Glucocorticoids apparently enhance gluconeogenesis by exerting a permissive action, as follows: Certain hormones, glucagon especially, epinephrine for another, bring about an increase in the concentration of cyclic AMP in liver cells. Cyclic AMP, acting as a second messenger, will stimulate gluconeogenesis, but only if glucocorticoids are present. (In adrenalectomized animals, cyclic AMP does not stimulate gluconeogenesis.) The effect of glucocorticoids on gluconeogenesis accounts, in part, for their tendency to raise the level of blood glucose. Glucocorticoids have another action that raises blood glucose—they decrease the uptake and oxidation of glucose by skeletal muscle cells.

Glucocorticoids increase the *mobilization of fatty acids* from the fat depots to active tissues. In this action, too, their role appears to be permissive. A number of hormones accelerate mobilization of fatty acids by increasing lipolysis (cleavage of triglycerides, forming fatty acids and glycerol) in adipose tissue. Cyclic AMP mediates this action, and glucocorticoids must be present for the response to occur.

Requirement of Glucocorticoids for a Normal Response to Stress. Stress of almost any kind, such as injury, burns, cold, pain, or fright, will cause an immediate, pronounced rise in ACTH blood levels, followed within minutes by an increase in the secretion of glucocorticoids. The ability of the body to cope normally with the stress depends upon glucocorticoid secretion. Why this is so is still not clear. It has been suggested that the requirement of glucocorticoids for the actions of norepinephrine and epinephrine on arterioles and the heart (page 531) is of importance in responding to stress. The muscular weakness and fatigue caused by glucocorticoid insufficiency may be partly accounted for by this action. Mobilization of fatty acids and amino acids may also have a role in dealing with stress. The amino acids can be utilized not only for gluconeogenesis but also for protein synthesis.

Anti-inflammatory and Antiallergic Effects of Glucocorticoids. Glucocorticoids in high concentrations have the following actions: (1) stabilization of lysosomal enzymes; (2) depression of the vasodilator action of histamine; (3) reduction of capillary permeability; (4) impairment of the migration of phagocytes; and (5) causing atrophy of all lymphoid tissue and, in consequence, a reduction in the number of circulation lymphocytes and antibodies. Because of these actions, glucocorticoids are used to treat a number of diseases, such as rheumatoid arthritis, in which the damage is caused by the inflammatory reaction, as well as allergic disorders, such as hay fever, allergic dermatitis, and asthma, in which inflammation or other consequences of anaphylaxis (see Chapter 11, page 418) have disturbing effects. In rheumatoid arthritis, stabilization of the lysosomal enzymes, thereby preventing the release of destructive enzymes, appears to be the major factor in alleviating the painful consequences of the disease. In some types of anaphylaxis, administration of cortisol has a life-saving effect by preventing death from shock. On the other hand, the anti-inflammatory and antiallergic actions of glucocorticoids can have harmful consequences in individuals with hypersecreting suprarenal glands. Patients with Cushing's syndrome (see below), for example, are abnormally susceptible to infectious diseases and suffer from poor wound healing because of a depressed inflammatory response.

Effect of Glucocorticoids on Blood Cells. Glucocorticoids apparently play a permissive role in the production of red blood cells. Deficiency in glucocorticoids often results in anemia; hypersecretion of glucocorticoids usually causes polycythemia. High concentrations of glucocorticoids also cause a rapid destruction of eosinophils. Eosinopenia is one of the diagnostic features of excessive secretion of glucocorticoids.

Androgens. Androgens, steroid hormones, produce masculinization. The most important androgen is testosterone, which is secreted by the testes. Suprarenal androgens are of minor importance, except when a suprarenal tumor develops, in which case excessive quantities of androgenic hormones are produced. This can cause a child or even an adult female to take on an adult masculine appearance, including growth of the clitoris to resemble a penis, growth of a beard, a change in the voice quality to bass, and increased muscular strength.

Abnormalities of Suprarenal Cortex Function. *Addison's disease* (described by Thomas Addison, 1855), a relatively rare disorder most common in middle life, occurs equally in both sexes. Addison's disease is a deficiency of function of the suprarenal cortex, with insufficient production of both glucocorticoids and mineralocorticoids, resulting in an incapacity of the renal tubules to adequately reabsorb sodium, accompanied by retention of potassium, and in metabolic defects. The loss of sodium, and chloride along with it, results in the excretion of large volumes of water. The plasma volume is reduced, followed by a drop in blood pressure. (If aldosterone secretion ceases altogether, the patient will die in shock within 4 days to 2 weeks unless treated with mineralocorticoids or given salt therapy.)

Other characteristic symptoms of Addison's disease include slow heart rate, abnormal electrocardiogram, muscular weakness, hypoglycemia, and gastrointestinal disturbances. Pigmentation of the skin and mucosa is another diagnostic feature. The excessive melanin deposition is caused by a lack of suprarenal feedback to the hypophysis, with a resultant increased secretion of ACTH and melanocyte-stimulating hormone. The outlook for patients with this disease is favorable with adequate substitution of suprarenal cortical hormones.

Cushing's disease (first described by Harvey Cushing in 1932), a primary disorder of the adenohypophysis, involves excess production of ACTH with resulting suprarenal hyperfunction (Fig. 481). The cortex can, however, be hyperfunctional without stimulation from the adenohypophysis (as in suprarenal tumors). The term Cushing's syndrome is generally applied to the clinical signs characterizing both types of adrenocortical hyperfunction. These include increased blood pressure (resulting from the sodium-retaining effects of aldosterone, augmented by the potentiation of the effects of norepinephrine and epinephrine on the cardiovascular system); nitrogen loss; hyperglycemia; decreased fat in the limbs; excess fat in the face ("moon face"), abdomen, buttocks, and shoulders ("buffalo torso"); and sometimes, in women, masculinization. As a result of the stimulatory effect of glucocorticoids on the brain, mental aberrations may also occur, ranging from euphoria to depression. If the cause of Cushing's syndrome is a pathological condition of the adenohypophysis, treatment is aimed at reducing the overproduction of ACTH. In many patients, irradiation of the adenohypophysis is successful in returning the secretion of ACTH to normal. When an adrenal tumor is responsible for the syndrome, the only satisfactory treatment is surgical removal.

Suprarenal Medulla

Whereas the hormones of the cortex are steroids, those of the medulla, epinephrine and norepinephrine, belong to a class of compounds called *catecholamines*. They are formed from the amino acid tyrosine (Fig. 482). The medulla is composed of irregular masses of cells separated by sinusoidal-type vessels. Adrenomedullary extracts are composed of both epinephrine and norepinephrine with constant proportions characteristic for a given species. The human medulla usually secretes four times as much epinephrine as norepinephrine.

The adrenal medulla is not essential for life, but functions in conjunction with the sympathetic nervous system to help the individual meet certain types of emergency situations. The hormones are released upon stimulation by preganglionic nerve endings, and their actions support and prolong what is known as the sympathoadrenal "fight or flight" response. The major effects are cardiovascular and metabolic. The overall effect of the two hormones on the cardiovascular system is to increase the

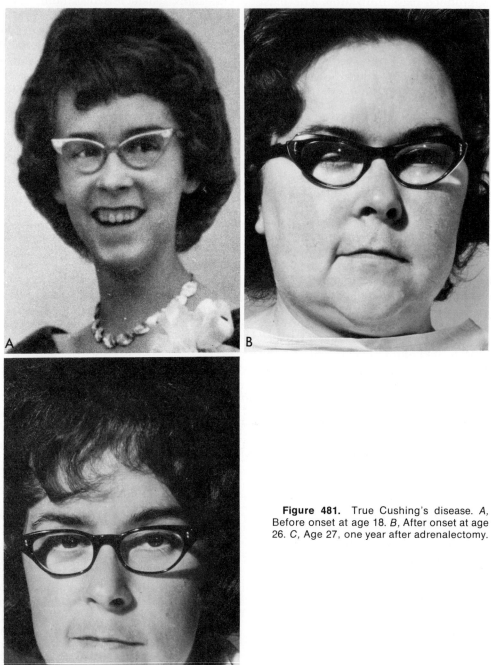

Figure 481. True Cushing's disease. *A*, Before onset at age 18. *B*, After onset at age 26. *C*, Age 27, one year after adrenalectomy.

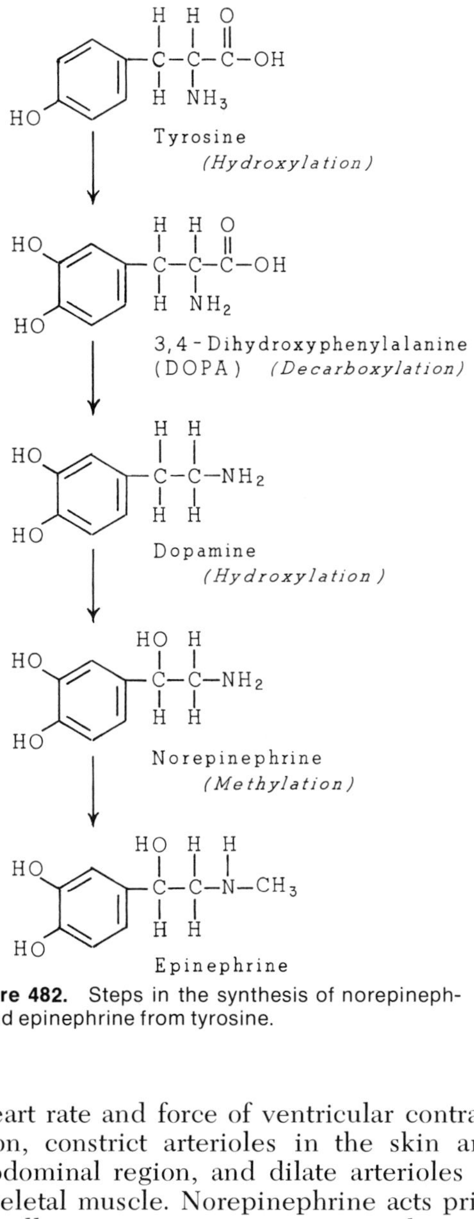

Tyrosine
(Hydroxylation)

3,4-Dihydroxyphenylalanine
(DOPA)   *(Decarboxylation)*

Dopamine
(Hydroxylation)

Norepinephrine
(Methylation)

Epinephrine

Figure 482. Steps in the synthesis of norepinephrine and epinephrine from tyrosine.

PANCREATIC ISLETS

The pancreatic islets of Langerhans, constituting about 2 per cent of the glandular tissue, are scattered throughout the pancreas (Fig. 483). The islets produce two polypeptide hormones, *insulin* and *glucagon*.

Structure of the Islets. The pancreatic islets of the human contain at least three cell types, *alpha, beta,* and *delta,* distinguished on the basis of histologic characteristics. Insulin is formed by the beta cells of the islets, and glucagon by the alpha cells. The function of the delta cells is unknown.

Insulin

In 1889, von Mering and Minkowski removed the pancreas from a dog to see whether it would survive without pancreatic digestive juice. The dog developed glycosuria and other symptoms strikingly similar to human diabetes. Thus it was discovered that the pancreas has other than digestive functions. Sometime later it was observed that, when a dog's pancreatic duct was ligated, the pancreas shriveled but the animal did not develop diabetes. Examination of the atrophied pancreas revealed that the acinar (exocrine) tissue degenerated but the islets, for the most part, remained normal in appearance. Apparently the islet

heart rate and force of ventricular contraction, constrict arterioles in the skin and abdominal region, and dilate arterioles in skeletal muscle. Norepinephrine acts principally as a vasoconstrictor; epinephrine is more potent as a stimualtor of the heart. The metabolic effects of the hormones include stimulating the breakdown of glycogen in the liver and skeletal muscle and gluconeogenesis in the liver (actions of epinephrine principally), and mobilizing fatty acids from the fat depots. The release of glucose from the liver into the circulation causes a rise in blood sugar. Table 35, page 278, in Chapter 8 lists the actions of the sympathetic nervous system. Essentially the same responses are brought about by the release of epinephrine and norepinephrine from the adrenal medulla.

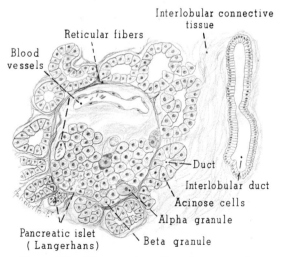

Figure 483. Microscopic section of pancreas showing pancreatic islets (of Langerhans).

tissue secreted some substance that prevented diabetes. In 1921, Frederick Banting, a Canadian surgeon, reasoned that the many attempts to extract an antidiabetic hormone from fresh pancreas failed because the digestive enzymes destroyed it. He, therefore, in collaboration with a young graduate student named Charles Best, tied off the pancreatic ducts of a number of dogs and waited for the acinar tissue to atrophy. Best prepared an extract of the pancreas tissue, which they injected into depancreatized dogs. The extract lowered blood sugar and brought about recovery from the diabetic state. In January of 1922 they successfully treated a 14-year-old boy who was terminally ill with diabetes with a pancreatic hormonal preparation given the name insulin.

Insulin, it is now known, consists of 51 amino acids arranged in two polypeptide chains connected by two disulphide bridges. In the 1950's Sanger and colleagues determined the complete amino acid sequence of bovine insulin (Fig. 484).

The overall effect of insulin on intermediary metabolism is to (1) increase the utilization and decrease the production of glucose, (2) increase the storage and decrease the mobilization and oxidation of fatty acids, and (3) increase the formation of protein (increasing cellular uptake of amino acids and the synthesis of protein from amino acids).

One of the earliest observed actions of insulin was its enhancement of the uptake of glucose in many nonhepatic tissues, especially skeletal muscle and adipose tissue. In skeletal muscle, when high levels of insulin and glucose promote the rapid influx of glucose into the cells, increased amounts of glucose are utilized for glycogen synthesis and oxidation to carbon dioxide and water. (Growth hormone and glucocorticoids inhibit the uptake and oxidation of glucose in skeletal muscle, thus opposing the effect of insulin.)

In adipose tissue the excess glucose taken into the cell is converted to fat. Insulin and glucose levels are high during the absorption of a meal, a period when uptake of fatty acids derived from chylomicron triglycerides by fat cells is also high (Chapter 13, page 484). This creates optimal conditions for triglyceride synthesis—an abundance of α-glycerophosphate derived from glucose

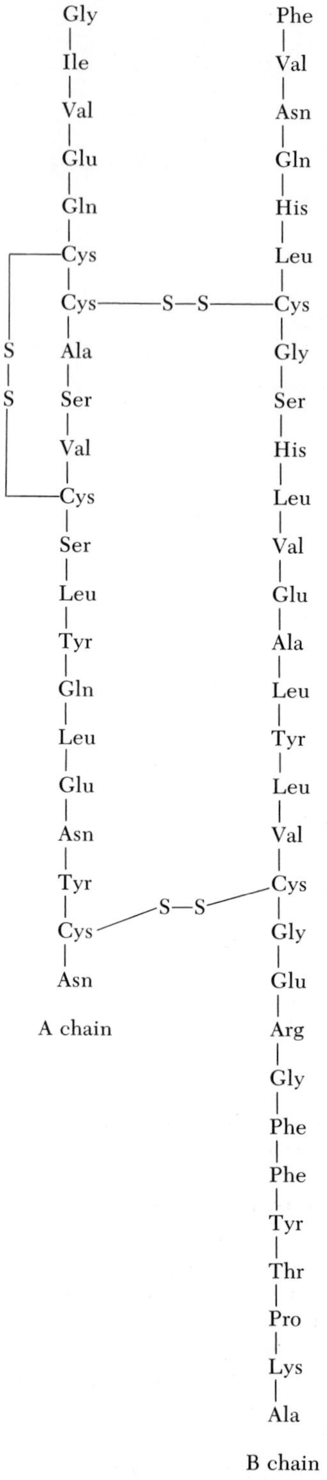

Figure 484. The amino acid sequence of bovine insulin. It consists of two polypeptide chains—the A chain, with 21 amino acids, and the B chain, with 30—crosslinked by two disulphide bridges. This was the first protein to have its amino acid sequence determined.

(glucose is the only source of α-glycerophosphate in adipose tissue, since the cells cannot phosphorylate glycerol), which will combine with fatty acids released from the dietary triglycerides or synthesized from glucose (via acetyl-CoA).

Insulin promotes fat storage in adipose tissue in another way—it inhibits the cleavage of triglycerides (lipolysis) by antagonizing the lipolytic action of several other hormones, including epinephrine, ACTH, TSH, growth hormone, and thyroxine. These hormones increase, whereas insulin decreases, the levels of cyclic AMP, the mediator of the lipolytic action. The effect of insulin on lipolysis is also opposite to that of glucocorticoids which, as we have noted, appear to play a permissive role in the lipolytic action of other hormones.

The production of glucose in the liver by the breakdown of glycogen (glycogenolysis) and synthesis from nonglucose sources (gluconeogenesis), principally certain amino acids, is inhibited by insulin in the same way it inhibits lipolysis in adipose tissue. The level of cyclic AMP, the second messenger in activating glycogenolysis and gluconeogenesis, is raised by glucagon and epinephrine and lowered by insulin. The permissive action of glucocorticoids in the stimulation by glucagon and epinephrine of gluconeogenesis has been mentioned. Thus, here again, the actions of insulin and glucocorticoids are opposite.

Since cyclic AMP inhibits glycogen synthesis, insulin, by lowering the concentration of cyclic AMP, increases glycogen synthesis. Other actions of insulin in the liver include increasing the oxidation of glucose and its conversion to fatty acids.

The primary regulator of insulin secretion is the level of blood glucose. At the fasting level, secretion is at a minimum, and secretion increases in response to a rise in blood sugar. Amino acids and three gastrointestinal hormones, gastrin, secretin, and cholecystokinin, also increase insulin secretion. After eating a meal, the blood level of insulin is high as a result of the release of the gastrointestinal hormones into the blood and the absorption of glucose and amino acids. As a consequence of the elevated levels of insulin, glucose, and amino acids, the depleted stores of glycogen (in the liver especially) and protein (principally in skeletal muscle) are replaced. In addition, adipose tissue fat stores are replenished.

The production of glucose in the liver and lipolysis in adipose tissue are inhibited. The oxidation of glucose is stimulated, and during this period glucose is utilized almost exclusively for energy.

In the postabsorptive period the blood level of insulin drops. In the liver, as a result of the loss of the restraining influence of insulin, the stimulating effect of glucagon and epinephrine on glycogenolysis and (with the permissive action of glucocorticoids) on gluconeogenesis predominates, and the production of glucose rises. The greater part of the glucose produced is derived from gluconeogensis, with amino acids from the breakdown of skeletal muscle providing the chief source of precursors for glucose synthesis. Glucose uptake by muscle and adipose tissue is inhibited. The brain, which does not require insulin for any of its metabolic functions, consumes the bulk of the blood glucose. Lipolysis in adipose tissue is unrestrained, and fatty acids are mobilized from fat depots. With the exception of the brain, the active tissues utilize fatty acids almost exclusively for energy in the postabsorptive period.

When insulin is lacking, as in severe **diabetes mellitus,** the shift from fatty acid to glucose utilization in response to a rise in blood sugar cannot take place. Glucose is not taken up by muscle and adipose tissue, and glucose production by the liver continues unabated. Fatty acids are rapidly mobilized from the depots. The liver, incapable of oxidizing to carbon dioxide the enormous amount of fatty acids it receives, and returning all of the surplus to the fat depots in very low density lipoproteins (Chapter 13, page 484), produces acetoacetic acid and other ketone bodies (β-hydroxybutyric acid and acetone), which are released into the blood. Since acetoacetic acid and β-hydroxybutyric acid are moderately strong acids, a state of *acidosis* develops. Diabetics also have elevated levels of plasma very low density lipoproteins.

If the condition is untreated, glucose levels will rise to values as high as 400 to 800 mg per 100 ml of blood. The extreme *hyperglycemia* leads to pronounced *glycosuria* and excretion of large volumes of water accompanying the glucose (osmotic diuresis). The patient, then, exhibits hyperglycemia, glycosuria, polyuria, dehydration, polydipsia (excessive thirst), polyphagia (increased eating), ketosis, weight loss, and wasting of muscles. The acidosis stimulates deep, rapid breathing (Kussmaul breathing). The usual terminal sequence is severe dehydration, decreased plasma volume, peripheral circulatory failure, coma, and death (see description of hypertonic dehydration in Chapter 16, page 545).

It should be apparent that the symptoms expressed by a lack of insulin are a consequence of an imbalance between the metabolic actions of insulin and the opposing actions of several other hormones. In 1931, long before the hormonal interrelations described above were recognized, Houssay and Biasotti demonstrated that removal of the hypophysis from a depancreatized dog (so-called *Houssay animal*) caused a marked amelioration of the symptoms of diabetes, a phenomenon that can be accounted for in large part by a loss of growth hormone and ACTH and a greatly reduced secretion of glucocorticoids. This discovery stimulated the worldwide investigations that led to an appreciation of the integrated action of insulin and antagonistic hormones in metabolic regulation.

Distinction Between Juvenile-Onset and Maturity-Onset Diabetes. Diabetes resulting from an insufficient secretion of insulin, known as juvenile-onset diabetes, can be distinguished from another form of the disease called maturity-onset diabetes. In maturity-onset diabetes the blood levels of insulin are generally normal or above normal. Juvenile-onset diabetes begins abruptly (hence also called acute-onset diabetes), and the entire range of symptoms usually appears immediately. Insulin treatment is essential. Maturity-onset diabetes, on the other hand, starts slowly and the symptoms are milder. This form can usually be treated by dietary regulation.

The defect in maturity-onset diabetes has been described as a reduced sensitivity to the effects of insulin, a phenomenon generally called *insulin resistance*. Recently it has been observed that monocytes from individuals with maturity-onset diabetes bind about 50 per cent as much insulin as monocytes from healthy individuals and that these cells have a lower than normal number of *insulin-binding receptors*. Since the effects of insulin are mediated from receptor sites on the cell surface, a deficiency in insulin binding could be responsible for the diabetic condition.

In both forms of diabetes, individuals have an inherited predisposition to the development of the disease. Recent findings support the view that the juvenile-onset form is initiated by certain types of viral infections (including mumps and German measles) and that the development of the disease is dependent upon a genetic susceptibility to pancreatic damage resulting from the infection.

Complications of Long-Standing Diabetes. Although successful treatment of the primary metabolic derangements of diabetes has greatly prolonged the life of diabetics, major complications arise in individuals who have had the disease for a long period of time. For example, *diabetic retinopathy* is the second major cause of blindness in this country. This condition results from the deterioration of tiny blood vessels in the eye and the growth of new vessels on the surface of the retina which tend to rupture and bleed into the vitreous humor. A new treatment called photocoagulation now holds promise for checking this disorder. In this procedure intense bursts of light from a green argon laser or white xenon arc fuse and destroy the new blood vessels.

Cataract formation in the lens of the eye occurs with much greater frequency in diabetic individuals than in normal ones. It has been demonstrated that cataract formation in rats is accelerated by the accumulation of sorbitol in the lens. Elevations of glucose levels in the eye stimulate the enzymatic conversion of glucose to sorbitol. The accumulation of sorbitol, which is removed very slowly by metabolism, increases the osmotic pressure of the lens. This draws in water, which causes swelling and disruption of the fibers of the lens.

It has been suggested that sorbitol accumulation contributes to the deterioration of blood vessels in retinopathy, but experimental proof for this contention is lacking.

Glucagon

Glucagon, the specific hormone produced by the pancreatic islets in the alpha cells, is a straight-chain polypeptide consisting of 29 amino acids. Recent studies have shown that measurable amounts of glucagon are present in circulating blood. The blood level of glucagon rises in response to *hypoglycemia*. The actions of glucagon have been described in the foregoing discussion of insulin. Glucagon, it has been noted, increases gluconeogenesis and glycogenolysis in the liver and lipolysis in adipose tissue.

OVARIES

The ovaries are two small glands located in the pelvic portion of the female abdomen and attached to the broad ligament. The outer layer of the ovary consists of a specialized epithelium which produces the ova. Two types of hormones are secreted by the ovary, estrogen and progesterone (see Chapter 17, page 587, for a description of their actions).

TESTES

The testes are small, ovoid glands suspended from the inguinal region by the spermatic cord and surrounded and supported by the scrotum. Two major types of specialized tissue are found in testicular substance—tubules containing germinal epithelium functioning in the formation of spermatozoa and interstitial Leydig's cells producing testosterone. (The functions of testosterone are described in Chapter 17, page 586.)

PINEAL GLAND

The human pineal gland is a small, conical organ, gray in color, lying at about the middle of the brain. It is attached anteriorly to the posterior wall of the third ventricle by the pineal stalk, located above the superior colliculi of the midbrain. The pineal is less than 1 cm in its longest diameter and weighs approximately 0.1 to 0.2 gram. It is not a functionless vestige, as had been previously believed. It synthesizes melatonin, a hormone that exerts inhibitory effects on the gonads. Prepubertal tumors associated with increased pineal secretion delay sexual development. Reduced pineal function causes precocious puberty. Recent evidence suggests that melatonin may act on the hypothalamus and adenohypophysis to modify the synthesis of gonadotropins and other adenohypophyseal hormones.

In animals melatonin appears to be involved in modulating biological (circadian) rhythms. In rats, for example, light accelerates the estrus cycle by inhibiting the formation of melatonin (blocking the release of norepinephrine from sympathetic nerves innervating the pineal gland).

PLACENTA

The placenta has been recognized as an endocrine organ since the earliest days of this century when it was noted that the ovaries of pregnant women could be removed after 3 or 4 months of gestation without terminating pregnancy. Chorionic gonadotropin, estrogen, and progesterone are produced by the placenta. There is some evidence that the placenta secretes relaxin and aldosterone.

Chorionic gonadotropin functions to keep the corpus luteum of the ovary intact and secreting estrogen and progesterone which, if stopped, would cause cessation of development of the fetus, with its subsequent expulsion. Production of chorionic gonadotropin begins when implantation occurs, and reaches a peak at about the eighth week of gestation.

Estrogen is produced by the placenta in progressively increasing amounts, reaching a peak just before birth. It functions during pregnancy to cause proliferation of the muscles of the uterus, increased vascular supply to the uterus, enlargement of the external sex organs and vaginal opening (in preparation for birth).

Moderate quantities of progesterone are produced during early pregnancy, reaching a peak toward termination. Its presence functions to increase the supply of nutrients to the developing ovum and to inhibit uterine musculature, allowing expansion for growth of the fetus.

Hormone-Producing Tumors of Nonendocrine Origin. Since all cells are capable of synthesizing proteins, it is not surprising that cancers have recently been found which secrete hormones indistinguishable from pituitary hormones. For example, oat cell carcinomas of the lung frequently produce ACTH. In turn, Cushing's syndrome results from ACTH stimulation of the suprarenal glands. Nearly all of the hormones of the pituitary gland have now been linked with cancers of various organs.

SUMMARY

THE ENDOCRINE SYSTEM

General Functions

Endocrine glands directly release into the blood stream substances called hormones that have a regulatory effect on cellular processes in other parts of the body. Hormones may act upon the cells of specific organs, called target organs, or upon cells widely distributed throughout the body.

Mechanisms of Hormone Action

1. *Via "second messenger":* Hormones classified as proteins, peptides, or amino acid derivatives activate an enzyme (adenyl cyclase) in the cell membrane that converts cytoplasmic ATP to cyclic AMP. Cyclic AMP, acting as a second messenger, induces a change in some cellular process.

2. *Gene activation:* Steroid hormones (adrenal cortical hormones and male and female sex hormones) bind a cytoplasmic receptor protein, which migrates into the nucleus and induces gene transcription, leading to the synthesis of proteins, most of which function as enzymes.

Hypothalamus

1. Secretes hormones, known as releasing or inhibitory factors, which control the secretion of the hormones of the adenohypophysis.

2. Synthesizes ADH and oxytocin, which pass down axons to nerve endings in the neurohypophysis, where they are stored. Release of these hormones from the neurohypophysis is governed by nerve impulses from the hypothalamus.

3. Controls the secretion of epinephrine and norepinephrine by the adrenal medulla via direct nerve pathways.

Hormones of the Neurohypophysis

1. ADH: Increases the permeability of the distal convoluted tubules and collecting ducts of the kidney to water. In high concentration, constricts arterioles.

2. Oxytocin: Stimulates the release of milk from the mammary glands. Stimulates contraction of the uterus at the time of childbirth.

Hormones of the Adenohypophysis

1. *Thyroid-stimulating hormone:* Stimulates thyroid growth and synthesis and secretion of thyroxine and T_3.

2. *Adrenocorticotropic hormone:* Stimulates growth of middle and inner layers of adrenal cortex and hormonal production and secretion by these layers (cortisol chiefly).

3. *Follicle-stimulating hormone:* Stimulates development of ovarian follicles in females and spermatogenesis in males.

4. *Luteinizing hormone:* Triggers ovulation. In males (called interstitial cell-stimulating hormone) stimulates production and secretion of testosterone.

5. *Prolactin:* Stimulates the development of mammary gland alveoli and milk synthesis.

6. Growth hormone

   a. Accelerates growth, increasing the size of all organs.
   b. Increases proliferation of cartilage cells at the growth plate of long bones.
   c. Increases amino acid uptake and protein synthesis by body cells generally.
   d. Increases blood glucose by decreasing glucose uptake and oxidation in skeletal and heart muscle particularly.
   e. Increases mobilization of fatty acids from the fat depots.

Hormones of the Thyroid Gland

1. *Thyroxine* (T_4) and *triiodothyronine* (T_3)

   a. Raises BMR.
   b. Exerts anabolic action on protein metabolism during growth and a permissive action on the effects of growth

hormone on tissue growth. Catabolic effect on protein metabolism predominates in hyperthyroid adults.

c. Required for normal development of the central nervous system.

d. Accelerates all phases of glucose metabolism, including absorption from the small intestine, uptake by tissue cells, and gluconeogenesis.

e. Increases mobilization and oxidation of fatty acids and the catabolism of cholesterol.

f. Abnormalities
   (1) Hypothyroidism: myxedema (adults), cretinism (infants).
   (2) Hyperthyroidism: Graves' disease (exophthalmic goiter).

2. *Thyrocalcitonin*: Lowers blood calcium by inhibiting bone resorption; secreted in response to high blood calcium.

Parathyroid Hormone

1. Raises blood calcium principally by increasing bone resorption; secreted in response to low blood calcium.

2. Deficiency of hormone causes tetany.

Major Hormones of the Adrenal Cortex

1. *Aldosterone* (principal mineralocorticoid): Regulates fluid and electrolyte balance by increasing the reabsorption of sodium by the kidney tubules.

2. *Cortisol* (principal glucocorticoid)

a. Increases mobilization of amino acids from skeletal muscle to the liver.

b. Increases gluconeogenesis (principally from amino acids) in the liver (permissive action).

c. Decreases uptake and oxidation of glucose by skeletal muscle.

d. Increases mobilization of fatty acids from fat depots (permissive action).

e. Required for a normal response to stress.

f. Exerts anti-inflammatory and antiallergic actions.

g. Abnormalities
   (1) Hyposecretion: Addison's disease.
   (2) Hypersecretion: Cushing's syndrome.

Hormones of the Adrenal Medulla

***Epinephrine and norepinephrine*: Function in conjunction with sympathetic nervous system (preganglionic sympathetic nerve fibers innervate adrenal medulla) in certain types of emergency situations. Actions prolong so-called sympathoadrenal "fight or flight" response.**

Hormones of Pancreatic Islets

1. *Insulin*

a. Increases glucose uptake by skeletal muscle, promoting increased utilization for oxidation and glycogen synthesis.

b. Increases glucose uptake by adipose tissue, promoting triglyceride synthesis.

c. Inhibits lipolysis of triglycerides in adipose tissue.

d. Increases utilization of glucose in the liver for oxidation, glycogen synthesis, and conversion to fatty acids.

e. Reduces production of glucose in the liver by inhibiting gluconeogenesis and glycogenolysis.

f. Increases cellular uptake of amino acids and protein synthesis.

g. Diabetes
   (1) Juvenile onset—insulin insufficiency.
   (2) Maturity onset—insulin resistance (possibly result of reduced number of insulin-binding receptors).

2. *Glucagon*

a. Increases gluconeogenesis and glycogenolysis in the liver.

b. Increases lipolysis in adipose tissue.

Hormone of Pineal Gland

***Melatonin*: Exerts inhibitory effect on endocrine functions of gonads.**

Hormones of the Placenta

1. *Chorionic gonadotropin*: Maintains corpus luteum of the ovary.

2. *Estrogens* and *progesterone* (see Chapter 17).

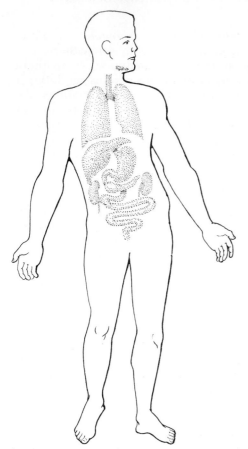

chapter 16

Fluids and Electrolytes

Objectives

The aim of this chapter is to enable the student to:

Identify the two major factors controlling distribution of water between the vascular and interstitial compartments of the extracellular fluid.

Describe the pathways of exchange of water between the body and the external environment, and the control mechanisms involved.

Differentiate and describe the three types of hypertonic dehydration.

Define the state of water excess, or intoxication, indicating its symptoms and possible etiology.

Distinguish between the various types of edema.

Discuss the treatment of burns in stages and relative to degree and scope.

Explain the mechanisms of potassium, magnesium, phosphate, and chloride balance.

Identify and explain the actions of the major buffer systems.

Differentiate between respiratory and metabolic acidosis and alkalosis in terms of etiology, symptoms, and treatment.

INTRODUCTION

The nineteenth century physiologist Claude Bernard first advanced the concept that there existed within higher organisms a purposeful tendency toward the constancy of the internal fluid environment of the body.

After Bernard, understanding of the role of body electrolytes increased only slowly. More recently practical methods for the exact analysis of electrolytes in body fluids and radioisotope techniques for determining the volume of the different types of body fluids have been associated with a markedly increased knowledge.

Body fluids have been "compartmentalized" by physiologists to help define their distribution. Fluids are in the *extracellular space* (outside cell membranes) or in the *intracellular space* (within cell membranes). The extracellular space is further divided into a *vascular*, or *plasma*, *compartment* (within blood vessels) and an *interstitial compartment* (between cells (Fig. 485).

What percentage, then, by weight of an animal is represented by water? An early human embryo is 97 per cent water; a newborn infant, 77 per cent water. Water constitutes 60 to 70 per cent of the weight of an adult male and slightly less of an adult female. Since fat is essentially free of water, the less fat present, the greater the percentage of body weight due to water.

Body water diffuses throughout the body without recognizing anatomic boundaries. For instance, water passes in a continuous manner across the connective tissue surface of the capillaries. If all the water molecules in the blood were suddenly labeled, perhaps only one-half of the labeled molecules would be present in the blood 1 minute later.

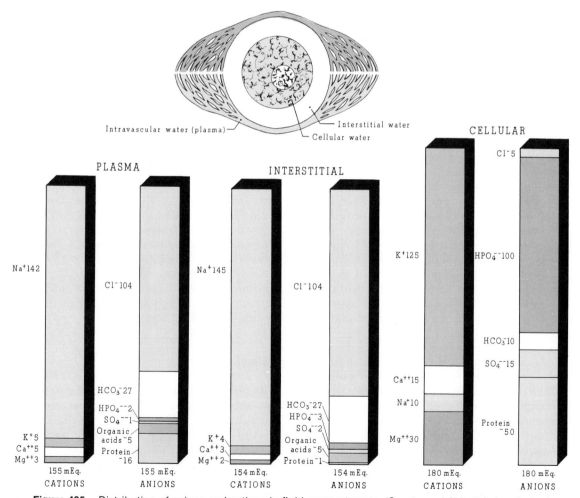

Figure 485. Distribution of anions and cations in fluid compartments. (Courtesy of Abbott Laboratories.)

Distribution and Movement of Water. In the human body about 60 to 70 per cent of the lean body weight is water; some two thirds of this is contained within the cells, while the remaining third is in the extracellular fluid. The extracellular fluid is divided into two compartments, the interstitial fluid lying between the cells and outside the vascular system, and the plasma and lymph water moving within the vascular and lymphatic systems.

The distribution of water between the cell and the internal environment of the body is controlled by the effective osmotic pressure across the cell membrane, which in turn depends primarily on the relative concentrations of sodium and potassium between the cell and the extracellular fluid. The cell membrane is relatively impermeable to sodium and the cell actively transports this cation out of the cell so as to maintain its internal concentration at a very low level. Potassium moves into the cell to maintain an electrochemical equilibrium, and as a result reaches a high concentration within the cell. Negatively charged ions (anions) balance these positively charged ions (cations) inside and outside the cell. The anions within the cell are primarily phosphate and protein; those outside are primarily chloride and bicarbonate.

If the concentration of water in the extracellular fluid increases, the concentration of sodium falls, and there is a net movement of water into the cells. If the concentration of water in the extracellular fluid decreases, the concentration of sodium increases and there is a net movement of water out of the cells. The effective osmotic pressure across the cell membrane can be temporarily altered or reversed in certain abnormal or disease situations that produce unusually high concentrations of glucose, urea, or other substances in the extracellular fluids.

Two main factors control the distribution of water between the vascular and interstitial compartments of the extracellular fluid — the effective osmotic pressure across the capillary membrane and the hydrostatic pressure of the blood in the capillary. Because of the different permeability characteristics of the capillary membrane, the solute that creates the effective osmotic pressure is the concentration of plasma proteins in the vascular fluid (plasma), a concentration which is much greater than that in the interstitial fluid (7 gm per 100 ml vs. 1 gm per 100 ml). In other words, the concentration of water is greater in the interstitial fluid than in the plasma, causing water to diffuse from the interstitial fluid into the vascular fluid of the capillary. This general osmotic tendency is opposed by the greater hydrostatic pressure in the capillary, which produces a net flow of water out of the capillary into the interstitial fluid. More specifically, there is an outflow of fluid from the arterial end of the capillary and an inflow in the venous end, so that there is a constant circulation of water and the substances dissolved in it between the fluids surrounding the cells and the blood. However, the system is not perfectly balanced — more fluid is filtered from the capillaries than is returned. Lost fluid, along with protein that leaks out of the capillaries, is returned to the blood stream by the lymphatic circulation.

Exchanges of Water with the External Environment

Water is taken into the body through the mouth and absorbed from the gastrointestinal tract. It is lost from the body to the external environment through the skin, respiratory tract, kidney, and, to a slight extent, the gastrointestinal tract. Generally speaking, the most important dependent variable controlling the total water content of the body is water intake, being adjusted or controlled to balance whatever is lost. The most important exception is a mechanism which permits the body to reduce the loss of water through the kidney to a minimum when a deficit occurs and environmental water is not readily available for ingestion (Fig. 486).

Water Loss

Water lost through the respiratory tract and skin is not under any direct control related to the content of water in the body. Loss of water from the respiratory tract is a consequence of the moist nature of the membranes of the tract. Water naturally evaporates from them to the inhaled dry (drier) air and is exhaled and lost to the

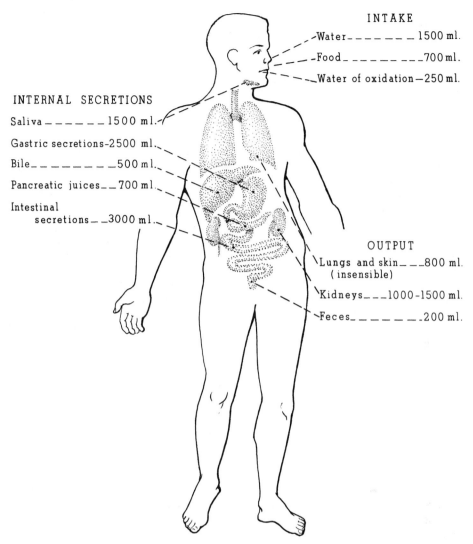

INTAKE
Water _ _ _ _ _ _ 1500 ml.
Food _ _ _ _ _ _ _ 700 ml.
Water of oxidation — 250 ml.

INTERNAL SECRETIONS

Saliva _ _ _ _ _ _ 1500 ml.

Gastric secretions-2500 ml.

Bile _ _ _ _ _ _ _ 500 ml.

Pancreatic juices _ _ 700 ml.

Intestinal
      secretions _ _ 3000 ml.

OUTPUT
Lungs and skin _ _ _ 800 ml.
   (insensible)
Kidneys _ _ _ 1000-1500 ml.
Feces _ _ _ _ _ _ 200 ml.

Figure 486. Balance between intake and output.

body. The rate of loss varies directly with the dryness and temperature of the inspired air and the depth and rate of ventilation. Rate of ventilation varies directly with the production of carbon dioxide and this, in turn, is proportional to the metabolic rate. Thus, an increased water loss from respiratory evaporation aids in the loss of heat produced by increased metabolism. It is important to note here that in this mechanism the control of water loss is sacrificed to the control of exchanges of carbon dioxide and heat, which have even greater priority in the homeothermic animal.

Likewise, no direct control system operates to govern loss of water from the skin. In humans, there is constant secretion from the sweat glands which, under normal conditions, immediately evaporates. In response to an increase in body temperature, central control mechanisms cause a marked increase in the secretion of sweat, enhancing the evaporative loss of heat. The loss of water by this route may reach dramatic proportions in humans (e.g., 2 liters per hour). This is another example of the priority of body temperature regulation over that of body water.

Sweat contains about one-half the concentration of sodium present in the extracellular fluid, so that a loss of sweat tends to increase the concentration of sodium in the internal environment. Loss of water from the respiratory tract has an even greater tendency, per volume of water lost, to increase internal sodium concentration, since pure water is lost by this route. However, because of the loss of sodium in sweating it is necessary to ingest salt (NaCl) when replacing this water; otherwise the extracellular fluid becomes hypotonic, which produces various uncomfortable and potentially dangerous effects. The student should note the overall priority of keeping the skin and respiratory tract functional, which entails keeping them moist, despite the consequence of continual water loss.

When solid foods or hypertonic solutions are ingested, water moves into the lumen of the upper gastrointestinal tract because of the effective osmotic gradient between the internal environment and the contents of the lumen. This movement continues until the contents of the lumen are isotonic with the fluids of the body and results in a temporary dehydration of the internal environment and the cells. This water is later reabsorbed from the lower tract through a reversal of the osmotic forces as the foodstuffs and salts are absorbed. Only a very small portion of this water is lost in the feces.

Some substances which cannot be absorbed (e.g., the osmotic cathartics such as magnesium sulfate) create a continuing osmotic pressure in the tract, leading to retention of water and its loss in the stool. Vomiting and diarrhea can result in sizable losses of fluid from the body. Even though this lost fluid is isotonic with the fluids of the body, it differs significantly in specific composition from the extracellular fluid owing to the selective secretion of ions in different parts of the tract. Vomiting results in a greater loss of hydrogen than sodium, whereas diarrhea usually results in a greater loss of potassium than sodium ions.

The kidney excretes water both as a vehicle for other materials and as "free" water. The excretion of free water is influenced by feedback mechanisms that can appreciate both the concentration and volume of water in the extracellular fluids. Aldosterone, the hormone of the adrenal cortex, causes the kidney to retain sodium in the body. The secretion of this hormone appears to be under the control of systems sensitive to decreases in sodium concentration and/or the extracellular fluid volume; that is, a decrease in either of these factors results in increased secretion of aldosterone and retention of sodium; conversely, an increase results in reduced secretion of the hormone. The resultant changes in the concentration of sodium and thus the effective osmotic pressure of the extracellular fluid will, in turn, affect the retention of water by influencing the secretion of antidiuretic hormone (ADH). Antidiuretic hormone causes the kidney to reabsorb free water that could otherwise be excreted. The ADH control system involves detection of salt concentration in the extracellular fluid by the osmoreceptor cells of the hypothalamus. These cells then send impulses to the neurohypophysis, causing secretion of ADH, which in turn promotes increased water reabsorption from the distal tubules and collecting ducts. This leads to a reduced extracellular fluid osmolality. ADH secretion is also secondarily stimulated by decreases in the volume of the extracellular fluid. Stretch, or distention, receptors in the walls of the atria and great veins activate vagal afferent nerves, and the information is relayed to the hypothalamus to inhibit ADH secretion, resulting in an increase in water loss.

It is important to remember that the movement of water in and out of the kidney tubules is always caused by osmotic forces. Thus, if there is a solute in the tubular urine that cannot be reabsorbed or if the quantity of solutes in the urine exceeds the maximum rate of reabsorption that the tubular cells can achieve for those solutes, the substances will remain in the lumen and create an effective osmotic pressure that will retain water and thus increase the urine flow and water loss to the body. An example of such an effect is the osmotic diuresis caused by intravenous infusion of mannitol or inulin, whose molecules are small enough to pass the glomerular filter but are too large to be reabsorbed from the tubule. As a result, these substances cause water retention in the tubule and marked diuresis.

The feedback control systems of the kidney can go only so far in maintaining homeostasis of the internal environment. The uncontrollable loss of water through the lungs and skin continues, and the kidney itself is always obliged to excrete sufficient water to meet the minimum osmotic requirements of the solutes that it excretes. Therefore, although these controls operate well in the immediate control of the water economy of the body, the long-term maintenance of this economy depends upon the intake of water.

Water Intake

Water intake is controlled by the central nervous system. Under normal circumstances, water enters the body only through the mouth and gastrointestinal tract. It may do so as water *per se,* as the vehicle in various fluid mixtures, and as the water contained in solid food. Another source of water to the body is metabolic water produced in the oxidation of foodstuffs. The specific sensory mechanisms of the feedback control of water content by water intake are rather complex and sophisticated, and their detailed description is beyond the scope of this discussion. Some general statements, however, may be valuable. The receptors that provide information to the central nervous system for water intake control include, on the positive side, those sensitive to changes in the effective osmotic pressure and to the volume of the internal environment or its vasclar component, and probably those sensitive to increases in peripheral and central temperature (in anticipation of water loss through perspiration) and to oral and pharyngeal hydration (dryness of the mouth and throat). On the negative side are those receptors sensitive to gastric distention and other learned gastrointestinal cues for metering intake. In addition to these, the control system for water intake behavior is influenced by information reflecting the priority of other demands on the animal's behavior.

Water Deficiency

The excessive loss of water from the body can cause electrolyte loss ranging from very light to very heavy. Dehydration is classified by the *resultant* concentration of electrolytes in the extracellular fluids. Accordingly, there is hypotonic, hypertonic, and isotonic dehydration of the extracellular space. The cellular space normally responds osmotically to the condition realized in the extracellular space. The clinical definition of dehydration is a water deficiency of 6 per cent or more of total body water. During the first few days of continuing dehydration the primary loss is of extracellular fluid. When 25 per cent or more of the volume of the extracellular fluid has been lost, the signs and symptoms of dehydration appear: (1) dry skin, parched tongue, and sunken eyeballs; (2) output of less than 500 ml of urine in 24 hours; (3) specific gravity of urine greater than 1.030; and (4) recent weight loss.

Hypertonic Dehydration (Table 49)

Three general conditions may lead to hypertonic dehydration:

First, hypertonic dehydration develops from water deprivation together with excessive water loss, typically through the lungs and skin, as on a hot day. This leads to a sharp rise in the hematocrit, with values as high as 65 per cent, and parallel increases in sodium ion concentration. These parallel increases in hematocrit and sodium concentrations reflect a loss of "pure" water and are sometimes referred to as desiccation or "true" dehydration; that is, the primary loss is water. Endogenous water diffuses out of the tissue cells but not in sufficient volume to offset the continuing loss from the skin and lungs. Urine becomes scanty and highly concentrated. Eventually, delirium, convulsions, and coma or shock develop. The net effect is cellular dehydration and hypertonic extracellular fluid.

Diabetic or uremic dehydration is distinct from the true desiccation and develops from the accumulation of an excessive amount of hypertonic nonelectrolytes in the extracellular fluid, such as glucose or urea. Water is

Table 49. CLINICAL SIGNS OF HYPERTONIC DEHYDRATION

	HEMATOCRIT	ELECTROLYTES
Desiccation ("true" dehydration)	Very high (parallel)	Very high
Diabetic and uremic dehydration	Very high ($>$)	High
Solute loading	Very high ($<$)	Extremely high

lost in the attempt to deal with this excess of nonelectrolyte solute; the water loss is in excess of salt loss, but the marked elevation of sodium concentration, as occurs in true desiccation, does not develop.

Despite the differences, both of these disorders should be treated similarly. Blood and interstitial fluid volumes and osmolarity must be restored. This is achieved by administering a sufficient volume of water by mouth or vein.

The third type of hypertonic dehydration occurs with the administration of excessive amounts of solute by mouth or vein. When the extracellular space is overloaded with more solute than the kidney can take care of, large amounts of water are excreted in an attempt to rid the body of excess solute. In true desiccation the concentrations of the various electrolytes parallel the rise in the hematocrit, but in "solute loading" the hematocrit lags behind the serum electrolyte values, which can become extreme. Cellular dehydration occurs from the osmotic pull of the hypertonic extracellular fluid, and large volumes of water are excreted into the urine, which has a fixed specific gravity. This solute diuresis persists despite intensive antidiuretic stimulation from the pituitary and adrenal glands.

Treatment consists in immediate cessation of the "solute loading" by mouth, tube, or vein and administration of generous volumes of water. Diabetics should be given supplements of insulin, and uremic patients should be allowed time for their kidneys to unload the excess solute.

Hypertonic dehydration may also develop in a number of other disorders: for instance, when swallowing is difficult or impossible as occurs in debilitated, comatose, or dysphagic patients; in patients whose kidneys are not able to concentrate water normally owing to a lack of ADH, as in diabetes insipidus; in diarrhea, when excessive water is lost with relatively small losses of electrolytes; and in burn cases, especially with open treatment.

Hypotonic Dehydration

Hypotonic dehydration is normally dealt with under the more general heading of *water intoxication*, which deals with all conditions leading to hypotonic extracellular fluid. It is worth mentioning here, however, that fasting with normal intake—the effect opposite to solute loading over time—will lead to a hypotonic extracellular fluid with normal water levels. Similarly, a loss of sweat, in which the water is replaced but not the salt, can lead to hypotonic extracellular fluid.

Water Excess or Intoxication

Water intoxication results from overloading the extracellular space with hypotonic fluid. The onset of water intoxication may be either acute or chronic but is usually preceded by a period of antidiuresis. The continued infusion of water eventually produces diuresis, but with excretion of larger quantities of sodium with the water. This compounds the problem, producing a very low serum sodium, even more so than was caused by the original dilution. Potassium levels usually remain around normal in such cases.

The development of symptoms of water intoxication actually depends upon the rate of infusion and the rate of renal excretion of hypotonic water. Symptoms appear when there is a rapid fall in serum sodium. Clinical features of water intoxication are weakness, lethargy, vomiting, drowsiness, edema, weight gain, coma, and convulsions.

All these signs and symptoms are readily reproduced by low serum sodium concentrations and cerebral edema. The brain is a unique organ in the body in that it is only slowly permeable to sodium ions. After an excess of hypotonic solution has been given to a patient, the brain becomes relatively hypertonic. Cerebral cells take up water but lose very few sodium ions. *Waterlogging of the neural cells* produces delirium, coma, and convulsions. Fundamentally, water intoxication is characterized by an excess of hypotonic extracellular fluid and a relative hypertonicity of the tissue cells, which subsequently produces cellular overhydration.

Treatment consists of withholding all fluid intake and allowing the body time to rid itself of excess extracellular water by way of the lungs, the skin, and the kidneys. When coma or convulsions are present, a hypertonic saline solution in small volumes may be given, such as 250 ml of a 3 per cent NaCl solution. Urea and mannitol infusions are also useful for dehydrating the brain.

Compulsive water drinking leads to water intoxication when the patient receives more water than his kidneys can excrete, which is about 13 ml per minute. Water intoxication may also occur when ADH secretion is excessive (this can occur as a result of fear, pain, or in acute infections such as pneumonia), as a result of most anesthetics or analgesics such as morphine and demerol, or as a result of acute stress, such as trauma or major surgery. The postoperative period of excessive ADH secretion is usually 12 to 36 hours.

It should always be kept in mind that an abnormal retention of water may serve a useful purpose, such as sustaining the plasma volume in adrenal insufficiency. In approaching treatment of fluid imbalances generally, the etiology of the disturbance should be determined as rapidly as possible, and it should be ascertained that the homeostatic mechanisms which regulate body fluid composition are normal. It is important in planning fluid therapy to know the sodium, potassium, calcium, CO_2, chloride, pH, nonprotein nitrogen, and glucose concentrations of the plasma and the hemoglobin concentration or hematocrit of whole blood. The lab data occasionally reveal the presence of markedly abnormal solute concentrations, which if not treated properly may lead to symptomatic solute defects and death.

Edema

When the volume of interstitial fluid has been increased to the point of being recognizable by clinical examination, edema is said to be present. This ranges from about 10 to 15 per cent increase in fluid content. Edema is of four fundamental types. The so-called *nephrotic type* is produced by a lowering of serum protein concentration due to protracted severe albuminuria or to low protein intake. If the level of serum protein falls below 4 grams per 100 ml, there is increased filtration into the interstitial space at the arterial end of the capillaries and diminished return into the capillaries at the venous end. This condition, leading to accumulation of fluid in the interstitial space, is seen most frequently in glomerulonephritis. It is also seen in protein starvation, although other factors found in this condition may be contributory.

A second type of edema, often called the *nephritic type*, is produced by damage to the capillary endothelium, allowing passage of excessive amounts of protein into the interstitial fluid. This sets up a new net osmotic pull toward the interstitial space, leading to the interstitial fluid buildup. Edema is believed to be produced by this mechanism in acute glomerulonephritis. This mechanism is more certainly involved in the production of blisters, hives, and localized inflammation, when local damage to capillaries is produced by toxins, trauma, histamine-like substances, or exposure to cold.

The third type, *cardiac edema*, is produced by increased venous pressure. This type of edema is seen with use of the tourniquet, in varicose veins, and, supposedly, in congestive heart failure. That increased venous pressure occurs in cardiac decompensation is generally recognized, but some doubt has been cast on the primary importance of this fact in the production of edema. Many believe that renal retention of sodium produced by forward failure of the heart is the primary phenomenon which leads to retention of water, then to increased venous pressure, then to edema. The increased venous pressure, in any case, acts to impede return of fluid to the vascular compartment from the interstitial spaces.

Obstruction of the lymphatics produces *lymphedema*, in which fluid and protein accumulate in the interstitial space as a result of insufficient lymph drainage. As in nephritic edema, interstitial protein accumulation draws large amounts of fluid from the capillaries.

Treatment of Burns

A burned area will exude large amounts of plasma. Thus, the individual with a severe burn presents a difficult problem in fluid and electrolyte therapy. Fluid requirements in burned patients are related to the degree of burn and to the total area of skin involved. This area must be carefully measured and is usually expressed as a percentage of total body surface, which can be conveniently expressed by the *rule of nines*. In this rule, the head equals 9 per cent of the surface area; each arm, 9 per cent; the anterior trunk, 18 per cent; the posterior trunk, 18 per cent; each lower extremity, 18 per cent; and the genitalia, 1 per cent (see Fig. 487).

Burns produce three characteristic features: (1) loss of plasma volume; (2) elevation of the hematocrit; and (3) oliguria (diminished quantity of urine). A basic feature is the loss of plasma to a third, or extracellular, space. This third space consists of the area of burned tissue into which water, electrolytes, and protein translocate.

Because of increased capillary permeability, water, electrolytes, and protein move from the vascular space into the third space of the burn. The protein loss is less than the water and electrolyte loss. Consequently, the plasma volume shrinks, the hematocrit rises, and the concentration of total protein increases. The net result is desalting, deproteinating, and dehydrating of the normal extracellular space owing to losses of water, electrolytes, and proteins into the burned tissues. The prerenal losses of water, especially into the burned tissues, evoke oliguria.

Endogenous water leaves the cells to replace the water lost from the extracellular space. Potassium moves along with this water into the interstitial space. Sodium then moves into the cells to maintain electrochemical balance. The net effect is a cellular K/Na exchange. In patients with oliguria, anuria, or adrenal insufficiency, the serum potassium level can increase to dangerous levels, leading to cardiac arrhythmias and diastolic arrest. More generally, the total body sodium and potassium concentrations drop because of extravasation of sodium and potassium ions into the third space, renal excretion, and cellular K/Na exchange.

Patients with less than 10 per cent of their body burned may only require fluid therapy for maintenance needs; whereas, if more than 20 per cent of the skin surface is involved, extensive fluid therapy may be required. In severe burns, in which the various volume control mechanisms fail to maintain blood pressure, shock will quickly ensue. The fluid treatment of burns, then, begins by combating shock with intravenous fluids, continually monitoring venous pressure to determine the proper infusion rate. One must also guard against administering an excessive amount of fluid, which can result in cardiac failure and pulmonary edema. Again, the most expedient method of avoiding hypervolemia is to determine the venous pressure repeatedly.

Combating shock also involves replacement of the proper amounts of colloids and salts as well as water. Dextran, albumin, plasma, saline, or blood also may be used for this purpose. A practical formula for fluid replacement consists of using 1 ml of

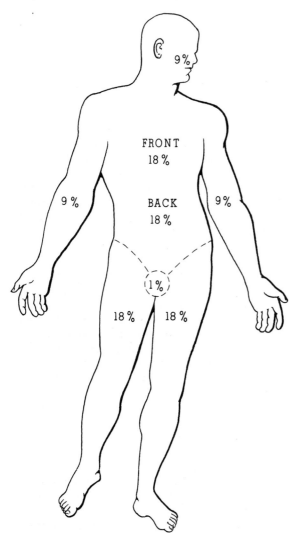

Figure 487. The *rule of nines* is a convenient method for rapidly estimating the percentage of surface area loss following a burn.

fluid for each percentage area of burn per pound of body weight. The total volume lost should be replaced within 24 hours after burning, and of this volume 40 per cent should be colloid and 60 per cent electrolyte solution.

Hyperkalemia sometimes develops in the early stages of burns when there is renal failure and an outflow of potassium from the destroyed cells. Hypokalemia may occur in the diuretic phase, when cells reaccumulate the potassium and sodium lost in the urine. Several days following a burn the fluid which accumulated in the interstitial phase may suddenly be reabsorbed, and acute overexpansion of the vascular system may occur. Sodium and water intake should be restricted during this period.

Regulation of Electrolyte Balance

Mechanisms regulating sodium and calcium balance have been described in the chapters on the urinary and endocrine systems. The following is a brief account of the mechanisms by which the concentrations and distribution of potassium, magnesium, phosphates, and chlorides are regulated.

Potassium Balance

Potassium is the major cation in the intracellular fluid and is important in regulation of intracellular fluid volume, neuromuscular irritability, and hydrogen ion concentration. When potassium moves out of the cell, sodium and hydrogen ions move into the cell. When extracellular concentrations of sodium and hydrogen become excessive, they are carried into the cells osmotically, and potassium moves out of the cells. Extracellular acidosis then causes potassium leakage from the cells and a high serum potassium; alkalosis has the opposite effect.

Normally, potassium is ingested in the diet and is excreted by the kidneys. But the body's mechanisms for conserving potassium are not as efficient as those for sodium. Some potassium is lost in the urine even when the intake of potassium is low. The rate of excretion of potassium is controlled by aldosterone, ADH, and the acid-base balance of the body. A high extracellular potassium concentration will increase aldosterone secretion, the feedback mechanism being just the opposite (complement) of that for sodium (a low extracellular sodium stimulates secretion of aldosterone). Thus, when the production of aldosterone is stimulated, sodium will be actively retained while potassium will be excreted. ADH increases the reabsorption of water by the kidneys and increases the excretion of potassium as it increases excretion of sodium. The renal tubules can excrete either potassium or hydrogen ions in exchange for the sodium they reabsorb. Therefore, if the kidneys excrete more hydrogen ions, fewer potassium ions will be excreted. Potassium may also be lost through gastrointestinal tract disturbances such as vomiting and diarrhea.

Magnesium Balance

The human body contains almost as much magnesium as it does calcium, sodium, or potassium. Most of the body's magnesium is intracellular, like potassium. Magnesium activates the enzyme systems needed to produce cellular energy by the breakdown of ATP to adenosine diphosphate (ADP). It also activates phosphatase, the enzyme that catalyzes essential chemical reactions of the liver and bone.

Most of the intracellular magnesium is bound to proteins and is not osmotically active (ionized), and each cell seems to have responsibility for the integrity of its internal magnesium concentration. Extracellular magnesium is only about one-tenth the intracellular content, and this concentration is maintained by the kidneys, apparently in direct relation to plasma concentration; that is, as plasma magnesium concentration increases, renal excretion of magnesium increases, and vice versa. Intestinal absorption of magnesium is rather poor, which serves to make various magnesium salts excellent laxatives; for instance, milk of magnesia, magnesium citrate, and magnesium sulfate. The lack of more precise controls over magnesium concentration seems apparent from the fact that in the presence of poor renal function, administration of magnesium compounds as laxatives leads to high blood concentration of magnesium.

There are similarities between the action of magnesium and calcium. There are also curious differences between these two ions. A low serum magnesium or calcium increases neuromuscular irritability, and a high concentration of these ions has a reverse effect. Magnesium narcosis, produced by injecting a magnesium preparation, can be promptly antagonized by the parenteral administration of calcium. However, the toxic effects of hypomagnesia can be aggravated by calcium or phosphorus in the diet. This latter effect may be due in part to the high magnesium content of bone tissue.

Phosphates

Intracellular phosphate concentration, which seems to be controlled by the individual cells, is many times the extracellular concentration. Within the cells phosphates are involved in high energy systems (e.g., ATP) and are necessary for the formation of nucleic acids.

The concentration of phosphate in the extracellular fluid is regulated by two related but partially independent mechanisms. Parathyroid hormone stimulates the osseous tissue to give up calcium phosphate to solution, but the feedback cutoff seems to be dependent on calcium concentration and not phosphate. The kidney is stimulated by parathyroid hormone to excrete phosphate so that the overall effect of its secretion is to increase calcium concentration, while phosphate concentration remains constant. The ultimate regulator of phosphate concentration in the extracellular fluid, then, is the kidney. Normally almost all ingested phosphate is excreted in the urine, only a small amount appearing in the stool.

Chloride Balance

Chloride is mainly an extracellular electrolyte; however, it diffuses readily between the intracellular and extracellular compartments. The ease with which chloride diffuses makes it particularly valuable in regulating osmotic pressure differences between fluid compartments and in the regulation of acid-base balance. A prime example of the role of chloride is seen in the *chloride-bicarbonate shift*. When bicarbonate ion is formed from carbonic acid, the concentration of bicarbonate ion increases in the red blood cells. Bicarbonate ions diffuse into the plasma. However, the potassium in the red blood cell, which electrically balances the bicarbonate ion in the cell, cannot pass as easily into the plasma. As a result, when bicarbonate ions diffuse out of the red blood cell, other negative ions must diffuse inward to take their place. The negative ion in greatest abundance in the plasma-chloride, therefore, enters the cell at the time the bicarbonate diffuses outward.

Consequently, as CO_2 leaves the tissues and enters the blood, bicarbonate ion shifts from the red blood cells into the plasma, and chloride ion shifts from the plasma into the red blood cells. As a result, the content of chloride in *venous* red blood cells is slightly higher than the content of chloride in *arterial* red blood cells, the opposite being true of the plasma.

Similarly, chloride responds to changes in protein concentrations of the various fluid compartments to maintain the electrical and osmotic gradients necessary for cellular functioning. Chloride also functions in compensating for other electrolyte imbalances. Because of its great osmotic ability it is in effect the first line of defense in the event of electrolyte imbalances.

Intake of chloride in the diet is usually in combination with sodium and, as a general rule, the regulation and behavior of chloride in the body is directly related to sodium regulation and behavior. Chloride may be lost from the kidneys, gastrointestinal tract, and skin. Chloride reabsorption by the kidneys is in direct proportion to sodium reabsorption and, in effect, the adrenocortical hormones, especially aldosterone, which increase reabsorption of sodium, also have the same consequence for chloride. Other factors affecting sodium concentration, like potassium increases, usually have a like effect on chloride concentrations. Gastrointestinal loss of chloride, on the other hand, is most severe in vomiting, where the concentrated HCl of the stomach is lost. Sodium chloride is lost through the skin in sweating.

Acid-Base Regulation

The problem of regulating acid-base balance is essentially one of preventing alterations in hydrogen ion concentration secondary to the continuous formation and expulsion of the acid end products of metabolism.

The acidity of a solution is determined by the concentration of hydrogen ions (H^+). Acidity is conveniently expressed by the symbol pH. Neutral solutions have a pH of 7. The pH of a strongly basic, or alkaline, solution may be as high as 14, while that of an acidic solution can be less than 1. The pH of extracellular fluid in health is maintained at a level between 7.35 and 7.45. To prevent acidosis or alkalosis, several special control systems are available in the body: (1) All the body fluids contain buffer systems which prevent excessive changes in hydrogen ion concentration. (2) The respiratory center is stimulated by changes in the carbon dioxide and hydrogen ion concentrations to alter pulmonary ventilation, which affects the rate of carbon dioxide removal from the body fluids. Since carbon dioxide forms a weak acid in solution, its removal lowers the hydrogen ion concentration. (3) The kidneys also respond to changes in hydrogen ion concentration by excreting either an acid or an alkaline urine.

These three control systems operate to-

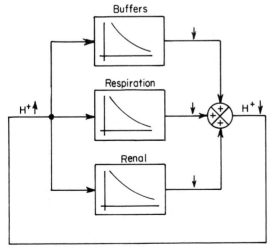

Figure 488. The regulation of acid-base balance. (From Milhorn, H. T., Jr.: The Application of Control Theory to Physiological Systems. Philadelphia, W. B. Saunders Co., 1966.)

gether in the maintenance of body fluid pH (Fig. 488). The buffer system can act within a fraction of a second, whereas the respiratory system takes 1 to 3 minutes to readjust the hydrogen ion concentration after a sudden change. The kidneys, although the most powerful of all acid-base regulatory systems, require from several hours to a day to readjust the hydrogen ion concentration.

Buffer Activity

A solution that has a tendency to resist changes in its pH when treated with strong acids or bases is called a *buffer*. A buffer solution contains weak acid or base and a salt of this acid or base. In biological fluids the bicarbonate-carbonic acid system, the phosphate system, the hemoglobin-oxyhemoglobin system, and the proteins act as the principal buffers in the regulation of pH.

The Bicarbonate-Carbonic Acid System

The sodium bicarbonate ($NaHCO_3$)-carbonic acid (H_2CO_3) buffer system is present in all body fluids (Fig. 489). It should be noted that carbonic acid is a weak acid; that is, it binds its hydrogen ions strongly. If a strong acid (one that is loosely attached to H) such as hydrochloric acid is added, it reacts almost immediately with the bicarbonate to form carbonic acid and sodium chloride. The system operates by changing the strong acid into a weak acid and successfully prevents a major change in pH. The fact that the carbonic acid can easily be reduced to carbon dioxide and water and removed from the body through respiration greatly enhances the combined efficiency of these mechanisms in responding to changes in hydrogen ion concentration.

Summary equations:

$$HCl + NaHCO_3 \rightarrow H_2CO_3 + NaCl$$

$$H_2CO_3 \rightarrow H_2O + CO_2$$

If a strong base such as sodium hydroxide is added, the carbonic acid reacts immediately with it to form sodium bicarbonate and water. Again the buffer mechanism has prevented a major change in pH by changing a strong base into the less alkaline sodium bicarbonate.

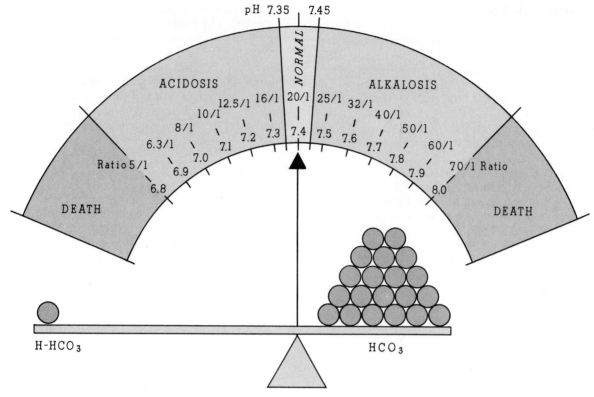

Carbonic acid in a ratio of 1:20 with bicarbonate salt
maintains a normal body pH

Figure 489. Acidosis and alkalosis showing ratio between carbonic acid and bicarbonate ion.

Summary equation:

$$NaOH + H_2CO_3 \rightarrow NaHCO_3 + H_2O$$

The Phosphate System

The phosphate buffer system is composed of NaH_2PO_4 and Na_2HPO_4 and functions very much like the bicarbonate buffer system.

Summary equations:

$$HCl + Na_2HPO_4 \rightarrow NaH_2PO_4 + NaCl$$

$$NaOH + NaH_2PO_4 \rightarrow Na_2HPO_4 + H_2O$$

In the first reaction the introduction of a strong acid leads to its conversion to a weak acid and NaCl. In the second reaction the strong base is converted to a less alkaline Na_2HPO_4 and water. The phosphate buffer system has a potential capacity and efficiency very much like that of the bicarbonate system. However, its concentration in the extracellular fluid is only one-sixth that of the bicarbonate buffer system; it should also be kept in mind that the actual capacity and efficiency of the bicarbonate system are greatly augmented by the respiratory expulsion of carbon dioxide. In urine and possibly in intracellular fluid, in which CO_2 concentration is higher, inorganic phosphate plays an important role as a buffer.

With the usual meat-containing diet, the urine is somewhat more acid than the blood. NaH_2PO_4 is formed when excess hydrogen ions combine in the kidney tubules with Na_2HPO_4. The NaH_2PO_4 then passes into the urine, and the sodium ion is absorbed from the tubules in place of the hydrogen ion, the result being to buffer the urine while allowing large quantities of hydrogen ion to be expelled.

The Protein Buffer System

The most abundant buffer of the body consists of proteins of the cells and plasma.

The protein buffer system operates in precisely the same manner as that of the bicarbonate system. However, unlike simpler buffers, the buffer effect of proteins is not concentrated at some specific pH, but rather exhibits some buffer action over nearly the entire pH scale. This is because proteins are composed of several different kinds of amino acids, each of which has its own specific acid-base properties. The two major groups that allow proteins to act as both acid and base buffers are first, the $-COOH$ group, which can dissociate into $-COO^-$ and H^+, and second, the common $-NH_3OH$ group, which can dissociate into $-NH_3^+$ and OH^-.

Summary equations:

$$^+NH_3-Pr-COOH+2OH^-\rightarrow$$
$$NH_2-Pr-COO^-+2H_2O$$

$$NH_2-Pr-COO^-+2H^+\rightarrow{}^+NH_3-Pr-COOH$$

Hemoglobin-Oxyhemoglobin System

Both hemoglobin and oxyhemoglobin are proteins and act as weak acids, with oxyhemoglobin being slightly more acidic. In the venous blood, where carbonic acid (dissolved CO_2) concentration is relatively high, the nonoxygenated hemoglobin — reduced hemoglobin — buffers the increase in hydrogen ion from carbonic acid formed in the red blood cell. The reduced hemoglobin is, of course, a weaker acid than carbonic acid or this would not occur. Reduced hemoglobin being partially in the form of a potassium salt, the reaction occurs as follows.

Summary equation:

$$K_2Hb + H_2CO_3 \rightarrow HKHb + KHCO_3$$

In the arterial blood, in which the carbonic acid concentration is significantly less than in the venous blood, oxyhemoglobin, which is more acidic than carbonic acid, operates to offset the loss of hydrogen ions from the loss of carbonic acid (CO_2) that occurs from respiratory ventilation.

Summary equations:

$$HKHb + O_2 \rightarrow KHbO_2 + H^+$$

$$H^+ + NaHCO_3 \rightarrow H_2CO_3 + Na^+$$

The hemoglobin-oxyhemoglobin system is perhaps best understood as a "second level" buffer system since it, in effect, buffers the bicarbonate-carbonic acid buffer system in the blood.

Respiratory Regulation of Acid-Base Balance

The carbon dioxide and hydrogen ion concentrations can affect the rate of alveolar ventilation by a direct stimulating action of both CO_2 and H^+ on the respiratory center in the medulla oblongata. The respiratory system operates as a feedback control for regulating carbon dioxide and hydrogen ion concentrations; that is, when such concentrations rise above normal, the respiratory system is stimulated to become more active and, as a result, carbon dioxide is removed at an increased rate and its concentration decreases in the extracellular fluids, thus reducing the hydrogen ion concentration back toward normal. Conversely, if a decrease in carbon dioxide and hydrogen ion concentrations occur, the respiratory center becomes depressed, alveolar ventilation decreases, and carbon dioxide and hydrogen ion concentrations build toward normal. This regulatory system is, of course, dependent on the fact that the carbon dioxide concentration in the atmosphere being breathed is much lower than that in body fluids. The overall "buffering power" of the respiratory system is approximately two times as great as that of all the chemical buffers combined; that is, about two times as much acid or base can normally be buffered by this mechanism as by the chemical buffers.

Renal Regulation of Acid-Base Balance

When the hydrogen ion concentration changes from normal, the kidneys tend to compensate for this excess by excreting hydrogen ion and returning bicarbonate to the plasma and extracellular fluid. The mechanisms by which the kidney accomplishes this are described in Chapter 14, page 504.

CLINICAL CONSIDERATIONS

Sodium Depletion and Imbalance

The effects of pure sodium depletion are strikingly different from those of pure water depletion. These two clinical states form the extremes of the range of fluid-electrolyte depletion in the body. Initially, water is lost in amounts comparable to sodium loss, thus maintaining a normal concentration of plasma sodium at the expense of extracellular fluid volume. With advancing sodium depletion, the relative water loss decreases and, consequently, the sodium concentration in the extracellular fluid (plasma) begins to decrease. Most patients with clinical sodium depletion (and hyponatremia) are first seen at this stage.

With the extracellular fluid gaining in hypotonicity, osmotic forces begin drawing water into the cells. The hematocrit rises, plasma-protein concentration rises; there is poor venous filling, diminished cardiac output, and a fall in systemic blood pressure. With severe sodium depletion, hypovolemia induces tachycardia; selective vasoconstriction may lead to diminished circulation through the skin and extremities, leading to cold limbs and dehydration fever, and also through the kidneys, leading to oliguria or anuria. These volume effects do not account for some of the changes observed in sodium depletion, such as muscle cramps, gastric atony with anorexia, and sometimes vomiting.

Clinical sodium depletion has been observed in numerous disease conditions. A low intake of sodium does not in itself lead to significant sodium depletion. The important causes are abnormal losses in gastrointestinal secretions, urine, and sweat. Losses of gastrointestinal secretions by diarrhea, vomiting, aspiration, or discharge from fistulae are the most common causes of severe sodium depletion, which is usually complicated by alkalosis or acidosis, depending on the relatively higher or lower losses of hydrogen ions.

Urinary losses are especially critical in that they are more likely to go unrecognized for a time than are gastrointestinal losses. Polyuria does not in itself lead to sodium depletion and, conversely, the absence of polyuria does not exclude the possibility of urinary loss of sodium. A common cause of sodium depletion through urinary loss is in solute loading—usually within glucose or urea. Lack of aldosterone to stimulate sodium reabsorption, as in Addison's disease, is another mechanism of loss.

The diagnosis of sodium depletion depends mainly on a knowledge of its causes and of the different clinical pictures which it may produce. Biochemical studies are of limited value in diagnosis, because the sodium concentration in the plasma *does not* reflect the true picture in many cases; the sodium balance may have been affected by changes in the water balance and by shifts of sodium into or out of cells and possibly bone.

Treatment of sodium depletion depends on its degree. For minor depletion, the addition of extra salt to the diet is effective both in treatment and in prevention. When sodium depletion is of moderate degree, as in diabetic coma, treatment with 0.9 per cent saline intravenously is satisfactory; the amount needed is commonly about 2 to 3 liters. When there is a complicating acidosis, part of the sodium should be given as bicarbonate or lactate. For severe sodium depletion, hypertonic 5 per cent saline produces a rapid restoration of plasma volume and renal circulation. Much of the dilution that occurs apparently comes from the excess intracellular water that builds up during depletion. Acidosis and alkalosis, which are common in severe cases stemming from gastric or intestinal losses, necessitate combining lactate with the hypertonic saline solution.

Two general thoughts should be kept in mind: (1) a low serum sodium is not in itself an indication for treatment with sodium salts; and (2) when diagnosis of sodium depletion is clear, the net treatment is to increase body sodium.

Acidosis

Acidosis may be defined as an excess of hydrogen ion within the body. The term is not synonymous with acidemia, which means an excessive concentration of hydrogen ion in the plasma. For instance, an increase in respiration may conserve a normal hydrogen ion concentration in the plasma even when excessive hydrogen ion is being produced in metabolism. The state of acidosis without acidemia has been referred to as *compensated* acidosis; this is not a stable situation and tends to break down into *uncompensated* acidosis if the cause of hydrogen ion excess persists. Since the buffers, the respiratory system, and the

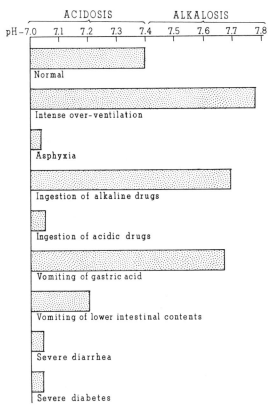

Figure 490. pH of the body fluids in various acid-base disorders.

Nonrespiratory compensation mechanisms operate primarily to increase the bicarbonate concentration in the extracellular fluid so as to reestablish the normal 20:1 bicarbonate to carbonic acid ratio. Carbon dioxide diffuses into the red blood cells, where it can be buffered. This will result in a chloride shift, liberating increased amounts of bicarbonate into the extracellular fluid. The kidney will increase its formation of ammonia, increase its excretion of hydrogen ion, and retain more bicarbonate. The increased pCO_2 will stimulate increased respiration, which will eliminate more of the carbon dioxide where this is possible. It is important to note that the nonrespiratory compensations are activated by the low pH of the blood, so that, as the blood pH increases, these mechanisms become less and less active, even though the pCO_2 may still remain high. Patients whose acidosis is relatively well compensated, as evidenced by a nearly normal pH, should not be treated overzealously. Lowering their pCO_2 too rapidly leaves them with a sizable bicarbonate excess, and shifts their acid-base balance into acute alkalosis.

Patients in acidosis usually complain of weakness and headache. CO_2 narcosis and CNS depression are marked by a decreased level of consciousness. In severe respiratory acidosis there may be cardiac arrhythmias and coma. Sodium lactate given intravenously may save the life of a patient with acute respiratory acidosis. However, more generally, establishing satisfactory ventilation and/or working to correct the basic disorder are first steps.

Metabolic Acidosis. Metabolic acidosis may occur from either abnormal metabolism, as in diabetic or lactic acidosis, or from impaired excretion, as in uremic acidosis. These conditions lead to an accumulation of acid metabolites in the bloodstream. Some conditions lead to excessive loss of bicarbonate, as in chronic renal disease, in which the kidney is unable to reabsorb tubular bicarbonate to the blood stream. Severe diarrhea or prolonged intestinal suction can also result in a loss of base and, consequently, metabolic acidosis. A third general cause of metabolic acidosis is the ingestion of acid or acid-producing substances. Ammonium chloride is an acid-producing salt, since the liver converts the ammonium to neutral urea, leaving chloride

kidneys all operate to maintain homeostasis of the pH of the various compartments, when one system malfunctions, leading to an imbalance somewhere, then compensation occurs in terms of the activity of the other systems. For instance, retention of CO_2 (potential hydrogen ion) in early respiratory failure can be compensated for by increased renal retention of bicarbonate, but with continued or increasing respiratory failure, acidemia is added to acidosis. There are many causes of acidosis, but they may be conveniently grouped under two major headings—respiratory acidosis and metabolic acidosis (Fig. 490).

Respiratory Acidosis. Respiratory acidosis is characterized by a primary rise in pCO_2, and invariably results from some form of respiratory failure. Acute respiratory acidosis usually stems from acute airway obstruction or central nervous system (CNS) depression, such as that from barbiturate poisoning. Chronic respiratory acidosis usually stems from chronic obstructive lung disease.

to circulate in the blood stream. Since chloride and bicarbonate are in relative balance in the blood, this increase in chloride causes a decrease in bicarbonate and results in acidosis. Ingestion of household metal polishes, laundry bleaches, or methyl alcohol, frequently used as a fuel for chafing dishes or fondue pots, will produce metabolic acidosis.

Respiratory compensation is produced by rapid breathing, which blows off CO_2 at an increased rate and results in a shift in the bicarbonate-carbonic acid ratio toward the alkaline. In severe cases this hyperventilation of metabolic acidosis is called Kussmaul breathing, although in extreme cases, when the pH has fallen to 7, these Kussmaul respirations may disappear. The kidney compensates for metabolic acidosis by retaining more bicarbonate, while increasing the formation of ammonia and elimination of hydrogen ion.

Patients with metabolic acidosis usually complain of general malaise, weakness, and headache. Nausea and vomiting may occur, as may hypotension, cardiac arrhythmias and, in severe cases, coma.

In the treatment of metabolic acidosis the goals are to halt the metabolic disturbance that produced the acidosis and to replace the electrolytes that have been lost. Alkalinizing salts such as sodium bicarbonate or sodium lactate are usually administered only to patients in severe metabolic acidosis (pH 7.2 or below). Alkalinizing solutions are dangerous because they may complicate matters by causing metabolic alkalosis. Ordinarily the acid-base balance will automatically return to normal when the metabolic disturbance has been corrected and the specific electrolytes have been replaced.

Alkalosis

The normal course of metabolism tends toward an excess of hydrogen ion, to be disposed of by the kidneys and, less directly, by the lungs. The more common metabolic disturbances tend to increase hydrogen ion production; and impaired renal and pulmonary function tends to produce acidosis by restricting the elimination of hydrogen ion. It is, therefore, not surprising to find that alkalosis is seldom a spontaneous state, but arises from the im-

position of alkali loads on the body or from the excessive activity of normal lungs. These two mechanisms correspond to metabolic and respiratory alkalosis (Fig. 490).

Respiratory Alkalosis. Respiratory alkalosis is characterized by a primary fall in pCO_2 caused by persistent hyperventilation. The cause of the hyperventilation may be anxiety, pulmonary emboli, congestive heart failure, cirrhosis of the liver, CNS injury to breathing centers, or severe infection.

The kidney compensates for the increased alkalinity by retaining hydrogen and chloride and by increasing its excretion of sodium, potassium, and bicarbonate. There may be a slowing of the rate of respiration, but this compensatory mechanism depends upon removal of the cause of hyperventilation.

The patient usually complains of dizziness and becomes apprehensive. There is numbness and tingling in the fingers and toes. There may be palpitations and tremors. In severe cases there may be signs of tetany. Only if the respiratory alkalosis is uncompensated should one undertake to restore the pCO_2 to normal. When the alkalosis is compensated, restoring carbon dioxide to normal without also giving sodium bicarbonate is almost certain to bring acidemia.

Metabolic Alkalosis. Administration of excessive amounts of sodium bicarbonate or sodium salts of other organic acids such as sodium lactate may produce metabolic alkalosis. The loss of chlorides as hyrochloric acid in persistent vomiting may result in high circulating levels of sodium bicarbonate, causing alkalosis. Another possible cause is excess excretion of acid or potassium into the urine, which may result from vigorous mercurial diuretic therapy, or from hyperadrenocorticism, such as occurs in Cushing's disease or steroid therapy.

The symptoms and signs of metabolic alkalosis are vague, but may include weakness, mental dullness, tetany, and paralytic ileus.

Treatment consists of restoration of volume and ionic depletions. It is particularly important to treat severe deficits of body potassium and chloride. Patients with severe losses of stomach contents (unless they have liver failure) may be saved by adding ammonium chloride to the IV solution to counteract the high bicarbonate levels. Electrolytes in urine or gastric fluid loss should be measured and total losses carefully estimated.

SUMMARY

FLUIDS AND ELECTROLYTES

Significance of Fluid and Electrolyte Balance

The maintenance of balance between the three major fluid compartments—the plasma, interstitial fluid, and intracellular fluid—in terms of the relative distribution of the total body water and electrolytes is involved in homeostasis.

Distribution and Movement of Water

1. Of the lean body weight 60 to 70 per cent is water, with about two-thirds contained in the cells and one-third in the extracellular fluid.

2. Distribution of water between the intracellular and extracellular spaces depends primarily on the effective osmotic gradients between these compartments. The regulation of sodium and potassium ions is most important in developing and maintaining these gradients.

3. The two main factors controlling distribution of water between the vascular and interstitial compartments of the extracellular fluid are: `

   a. The effective osmotic pressure across the capillary membrane, which depends primarily on the plasma protein concentration.
   b. Hydrostatic pressure of the blood in the capillary.

Exchanges of Water with the External Environment.

1. Water is taken into the body through the mouth and absorbed from the gastrointestinal tract.

2. Water is lost from the body through the skin, lungs, kidney, and gastrointestinal tract.

3. The most dependent variable controlling the total water content is water intake, being adjusted or controlled to balance whatever is lost.

Water Loss to the External Environment

1. Water loss from the skin and lungs is not under any direct control related to the content of body water.

   a. Loss from the lungs is due to their necessarily moist nature. Rate of loss varies with dryness of air and rate of ventilation.
   b. Loss from the skin is also due to its moist nature. Rate of loss depends upon regulation of body temperature.
   c. Loss from the lungs is pure water and loss from the skin is hypotonic, with sodium chloride concentration of about one-half that found in the extracellular fluid.

2. Water moves into the upper gastrointestinal tract in response to ingested solids and hypertonic solutions and is reabsorbed almost totally in the lower tract with absorbed nutrients. Only a very small portion of this water is lost in the feces.

3. The kidney excretes water both as a vehicle for other materials and as "free" water.

Water Intake

1. Water intake is controlled by the central nervous system.

2. The specific sensory mechanisms are complex and sophisticated.

Water Deficiency

1. There are three types of dehydration classified by the *resultant* concentration of electrolytes in the extracellular fluid: hypertonic, hypotonic, and, rarely, isotonic.

2. Hypertonic dehydration is distinguished into three types.

   a. First, hypertonic dehydration from water deprivation together with excessive water loss; typically through the lungs and skin as on a hot day.
   b. Second, diabetic or uremic dehydration, which develops from accumulation of glucose or urea.

c. Third, the type which occurs with the administration of excessive amounts of solute by mouth or vein.

3. Hypotonic dehydration is dealt with under the more general heading of water intoxication. It is the effective opposite of solute loading.

Water Excess or Intoxication

1. Water intoxication results from the overloading of the extracellular space with hypotonic fluid.

2. Symptoms of water intoxication appear with a rapid fall in serum sodium.

Edema

1. When the volume of interstitial fluid has been increased to the point of being recognizable by clinical examination (about 10 to 15 per cent), edema is said to be present.

2. Edema is of four fundamental types.

a. Nephrotic edema results from lowering the plasma protein concentration, which alters the effective osmotic gradient between the plasma and interstitial compartments.

b. Nephritic edema is produced by damage to the capillary endothelium, allowing passage of protein into the interstitial space, which sets up a new osmotic gradient, pulling water into the interstitial space. This mechanism is involved in blisters, hives, and localized inflammation.

c. Cardiac edema results from increased venous pressure, which opposes the reentry of water into the venous ends of the capillary.

d. Obstruction of the lymphatics produces lymphedema, in which fluid and protein accumulate in the interstitial space.

Treatment of Burns

1. Burns produce three characteristic features: loss of plasma, elevation of hematocrit, and oliguria.

2. Owing to increased capillary permeability, water, electrolytes, and protein move from the vascular space into the damaged third space of the burn.

a. The plasma volume shrinks, the hematocrit rises, and the concentration of total protein increases.

b. The net result is desalting, deproteination, and dehydration of the normal extracellular fluid.

3. A net K/Na exchange occurs as endogenous water leaves the intracellular space to replace water lost from the extracellular space and takes potassium with it; the potassium is replaced in the cells by sodium.

a. The potassium levels in the extracellular space can reach dangerous levels in this K/Na exchange, particularly in oliguria or anuria.

b. More generally, the body experiences a drop in total body sodium and potassium concentration, with renal excretion and extravasation of sodium and potassium into the third space of the burn.

4. In severe burn the volume control mechanisms fail to maintain blood pressure, and shock may quickly ensue.

a. Administration of intravenous fluid while monitoring venous pressure combats this problem.

b. Administering excess fluids can result in hypervolemia, cardiac failure, and pulmonary edema. Venous pressure must be continually monitored.

5. A practical formula for replacement of fluids consists of using 1 ml of fluid for each percentage area of burn per pound of body weight.

6. Hyperkalemia may develop in the early stages when there is renal failure and an outflow of potassium from destroyed cells.

a. Hypokalemia may occur in the diuretic phase, when cells reaccumulate the potassium lost with the endogenous water and excreted by the kidney.

b. Several days after the burn, the fluid of the third space may suddenly be reabsorbed and acute overexpansion of the vascular system may occur. Sodium and water intake should be restricted during this period.

Regulation of Electrolyte Balance

1. The regulation of electrolyte balance between the intracellular and extracellular compartments is best understood in two steps.

   a. The natural operation of each cell works to maintain certain concentrations within the cell, partially independent of the concentrations found in the extracellular fluid.
   b. The homeostatic organs and systems, the heart, lungs, skin, gastrointestinal tract, and various glands, especially the kidneys, operate to maintain homeostasis of fluid volume and composition of the extracellular fluid.

Potassium Balance

1. Potassium is the major cation of the intracellular fluid, and is important in regulation of intracellular fluid volume, neuromuscular irritability, and hydrogen ion concentration.

2. When potassium moves out of the cells, sodium (representing about 90 per cent of the cation concentration of extracellular fluid) and hydrogen move in. When sodium and hydrogen become excessive in the extracellular fluid and are osmotically forced into the cells, potassium moves out.

3. The feedback mechanism between potassium and aldosterone is just the opposite (reciprocal) of that of sodium.

4. Potassium may also be lost through gastrointestinal tract disturbances such as vomiting and diarrhea.

Magnesium Balance

1. Magnesium is primarily an intracellular cation.

   a. The body contains almost as much magnesium as it does calcium.
   b. Magnesium activates enzyme systems in the energy cycle and also activates phosphatase, the enzyme that catalyzes reactions in the liver and bone.
   c. Most intracellular magnesium is bound to protein and is not osmotically active (ionized).

2. Extracellular magnesium is only about one-tenth of the intracellular content.

   a. Extracellular magnesium concentration is maintained by the kidneys.
   b. The rate of renal excretion is directly related to extracellular fluid concentration.

3. Intestinal absorption of magnesium is rather poor, which serves to make magnesium salts excellent laxatives.

4. There are similarities between the actions of magnesium and calcium; also there are curious differences.

   a. A low serum magnesium or calcium increases neuromuscular irritability and a high concentration of either has the opposite effect.
   b. Magnesium narcosis is antagonized by parenteral administration of calcium.
   c. However, hypomagnesemia can be aggravated by calcium or phosphorus in the diet, being due in part to the high magnesium content of bone tissue.

Phosphate Balance

1. The regulation of phosphate concentrations is closely related to that of calcium.

2. Intracellular phosphate concentration is many times the extracellular concentration.

3. Phosphates within the cells are involved in high energy systems (e.g., ATP) and are necessary for formation of nucleic acids.

4. Two related, but partially independent, mechanisms regulate extracellular phosphate concentration.

   a. Parathyroid hormone stimulates osseous tissue to give up calcium phosphate to solution, but the feedback cutoff depends on calcium, not phosphate.
   b. The kidney is stimulated by parathyroid hormone to excrete phosphate.
   c. The kidney is the ultimate regulator of extracellular phosphate concentration.

5. Almost all phosphate is excreted in the urine, only a small amount appearing in the stool.

Chloride Balance

1. Chloride is mainly an extracellular anion; however, it diffuses readily between the intracellular and extracellular compartments.

2. Because it easily traverses the cell membrane, chloride is important in regulating both osmotic pressure and acid-base balance.

   a. The chloride-bicarbonate shift occurs when bicarbonate ion concentration increases in the red blood cells because of carbonic acid formation. Bicarbonate diffuses into the plasma, and chloride diffuses into the cell from the plasma.
   b. As a result, the content of chloride in *venous* red blood cells is slightly higher than that in *arterial* red blood cells.
   c. Chloride also responds to changes in protein concentration in various fluid compartments to maintain electrical and osmotic gradients.

3. Chloride may be lost from the kidneys, gastrointestinal tract, and skin.

   a. Chloride reabsorbed by the kidneys is in direct proportion to sodium reabsorption, so that chloride reabsorption is affected by the same factors controlling sodium reabsorption, especially aldosterone.
   b. Gastrointestinal loss is most severe in vomiting, when the concentrated HCl of the stomach is lost.
   c. Sodium chloride is lost through sweating.

Acid-Base Regulation

1. Regulation of acid-base balance is essentially a problem of preventing alterations in hydrogen ion concentration secondary to the continuous formation and expulsion of the acid end products of metabolism.

2. The acidity or alkalinity of a solution is determined by the concentration of hydrogen ions.

   a. Acidity is expressed as pH.
   b. The pH of normal extracellular fluid is between 7.35 and 7.45.

3. To prevent acidosis or alkalosis, several special control systems are available in the body.

   a. All body fluids contain buffer systems which prevent excessive changes in hydrogen ion concentration.
   b. The respiratory center is stimulated by changes in CO_2 and H^+ concentrations to alter the rate of pulmonary ventilation and thus CO_2 is removed from body fluids. About two times as much acid or base can be buffered by this mechanism as by all the chemical buffers combined.
   c. The kidneys excrete either acidic or alkaline urine in response to changes in hydrogen ion concentration of the filtrate.

4. The buffers act within a fraction of a second, the respiratory system takes 1 to 3 minutes, and the kidneys, although most powerful, require from several hours to a day to readjust the hydrogen ion concentration.

Buffer Activity

1. A buffer solution contains a weak acid or base and a salt of this acid or base.

2. The bicarbonate-carbonic acid buffer system is contained in all body fluids.

   a. When a strong acid (HCl) is added, it reacts with the bicarbonate to form weak carbonic acid and sodium chloride.
   b. When a strong base (NaOH) is added, it reacts with the carbonic acid to form sodium bicarbonate and water.
   c. The actual capacity and efficiency of this buffer system are greatly augmented by the respiratory expulsion of carbon dioxide.

3. The phosphate buffer system acts almost identically to the bicarbonate buffer system.

   a. A strong acid is converted into a weak acid and sodium chloride.
   b. A strong base is converted into the less alkaline Na_2HPO_4 and water.
   c. The potential capacity and efficiency of the phosphate and bicarbonate buffer systems are similar.
   d. The concentration of phosphate in the

extracellular fluid is only about one-sixth that of bicarbonate.

e. The phosphate system also plays an important role in aiding excretion of hydrogen ion in the urine.

4. The protein buffer system is the most abundant and operates the same as the bicarbonate system.

a. Unlike the other systems, the buffer effect of proteins covers the whole pH scale.

b. This breadth of action is due to the variety of amino acids composing the proteins, each of which has its own specific acid-base properties.

c. The two major groups involved in protein buffering are the $-COOH$ group, which dissociates to give off a hydrogen ion, and the common $-NH_3OH$, which dissociates to give off a hydroxyl ion.

Sodium Depletion and Imbalance

1. Pure sodium depletion is the extreme opposite of pure water depletion (desiccation).

2. With increasing sodium depletion (and hypotonicity), osmotic forces begin drawing water into the cells.

a. The hematocrit rises, plasma protein concentration rises, and there are poor venous filling, diminished cardiac output and a fall in systemic blood pressure.

b. With severe sodium depletion, hypovolemia induces tachycardia; selective vasoconstriction may lead to diminished circulation through the skin, extremities, and kidneys, leading to cold limbs and to oliguria or anuria.

3. Clinical sodium depletion has been observed in numerous disease conditions.

a. *Loss* of gastrointestinal secretion by diarrhea, vomiting, aspiration, or discharge from fistulae is common and is usually complicated by alkalosis or acidosis.

b. Urinary losses from polyuria are especially critical because they are easily overlooked. Solute loading with glucose or urea is a common cause of sodium depletion, as is lack of aldosterone, as found in Addison's disease.

Acidosis

1. Acidosis may be defined as an excess of hydrogen ion in the body. The term is *not* synonymous with acidemia, which means an excess of hydrogen ion in the plasma.

2. The state of acidosis without acidemia has been referred to as *compensated* acidosis; this not a stable situation and tends to break down into *uncompensated* acidosis if the cause of hydrogen ion excess persists.

Respiratory Acidosis

1. Respiratory acidosis is characterized by a primary rise in pCO_2, and invariably results from some form of respiratory failure.

Metabolic Acidosis

1. Metabolic acidosis may occur either from abnormal metabolism, as in diabetic or lactic acidosis, or from impaired excretion, as in uremic acidosis.

2. Respiratory compensation is produced by rapid breathing, which blows off CO_2 at increased rate.

Alkalosis

1. Alkalosis results either from the imposition of alkali loads on the body or from excessive activity of the lungs.

Respiratory Alkalosis

1. Respiratory alkalosis is characterized by a primary fall in pCO_2 due to persistent hyperventilation.

Metabolic Alkalosis

1. Administration of excessive amounts of sodium bicarbonate or sodium salts of other organic acids such as sodium lactate may produce metabolic alkalosis.

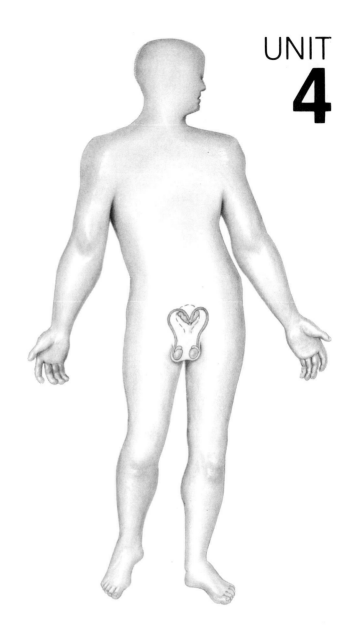

Reproduction

The Reproductive System

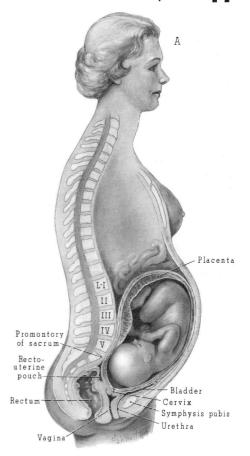

chapter 17

A

Placenta

L-I
II
III
IV
V

Promontory
of sacrum

Recto-
uterine
pouch

Rectum

Vagina

Bladder
Cervix
Symphysis pubis
Urethra

Objectives

The aim of this chapter is to enable the student to:

Describe the anatomy of the external and internal organs and associated structures of the male reproductive system and explain their functions.

Summarize the congenital abnormalities related to the development of the penis and descent of the testes.

Describe the anatomy of the external and internal organs and associated structures of the female reproductive system and explain their functions.

Describe the structure and functions of the mammary glands.

Describe the processes of spermatogenesis and oogenesis.

Outline and discuss in stages: ovulation, fertilization, and implantation.

Summarize the three stages of the menstrual cycle and discuss menstrual problems and menopause.

Describe the interrelations between estrogens, progesterone, and gonadotropins during the menstrual cycle.

Summarize the functions of androgens, estrogens, and progesterone.

Name and describe briefly the different layers of the placenta and discuss its overall functions.

Describe the stages of labor.

HISTORICAL DEVELOPMENT

Many early scientific explanations of reproduction were more mystical than scientific. Hippocrates believed that "seeds from all parts of the male and female bodies flowed together to unite and form the fruit." Aristotle opined that the male factors provided movement and the female factor provided substance, with the sex of the baby depending upon which factor predominated. In 1672 de Graaf observed the follicles of an ovary and mistakenly thought they were ova. The actual ovum was not seen until 1827, when von Baer traced its course along the uterine tube into the uterus. Spermatozoa were so named because they were originally thought to be "small parasitic animals." In 1853 fertilization was properly described as the entry of the spermatozoon into the ovum; however, the vast knowledge at our disposal today concerning reproduction came about largely as the product of investigation during the last five decades.

MALE REPRODUCTIVE SYSTEM

External Organs (Figs. 491 to 493)

Scrotum and Penis. The scrotum and penis are the external male organs of reproduction. The scrotum is a pouch which hangs behind the penis and is suspended from the pubis. It is a continuation of the abdominal wall and is divided by a septum into two sacs, each containing and supporting one of the testes with its *epididymis*, or connecting tube. After adolescence the skin of the scrotum is more heavily pigmented than the covering of the general body, and is covered with sparse hair. Scattered in the subcutaneous tissue of the scrotum are fibers of smooth muscle (the dartos layer). The fibers of the dartos layer contract in the presence of reduced ambient or body temperature, and give an increased wrinkled appearance to the scrotum. This contraction of the dartos causes the testes to be positioned close to the perineum (region between the thighs at the lower end of the trunk; see Fig. 493), where they can absorb body heat and maintain a temperature compatible with the viability of spermatozoa. Under conditions of normal temperature, muscle fibers are relaxed, the scrotum

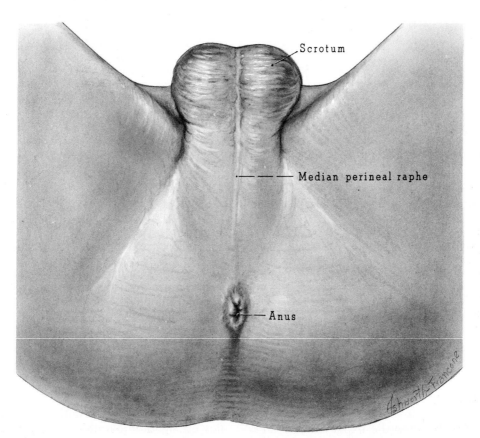

Figure 491. Superficial view of the male perineum (subject in supine position with thighs fully abducted).

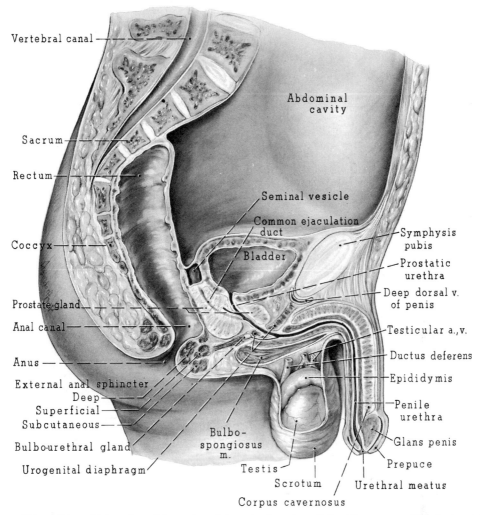

Figure 492.   Mid-sagittal section of the male pelvis and external genitalia. (The course of the ductus deferens is shown in Figure 466.)

is pendulous, and the walls are relatively free from wrinkles.

The penis, the male organ of copulation, is a flaccid structure when not stimulated. It is attached to the anterior and lateral walls of the pubic arch in front of the scrotum, and is composed of three longitudinal columns of erectile tissue bound together by fibrous bands and covered with skin. The skin of the penis, like that of the scrotum, is more highly pigmented than the skin of the remainder of the body, and is covered with hair only at its base. Two of the longitudinal columns are located laterally and are called the **corpora cavernosa** of the penis. They are spongelike in nature and contain large venous sinuses (Fig. 494).

The phenomenon of *erection* occurs with sexual stimulation. The arteries supplying the penis dilate, and a large quantity of blood under pressure enters the cavernous spaces of the erectile tissue. As these spaces expand, they compress the veins supplying the penis, thus retaining all the entering blood. This causes the penis to become firm and erect and facilitates its penetration into the female vagina during sexual intercourse. When the arteries constrict, more blood leaves the penis than enters, and the organ returns to its flaccid state.

The third longitudinal column of the penis is also erectile tissue and it too becomes engorged with blood during erection. This column, known as the **corpus**

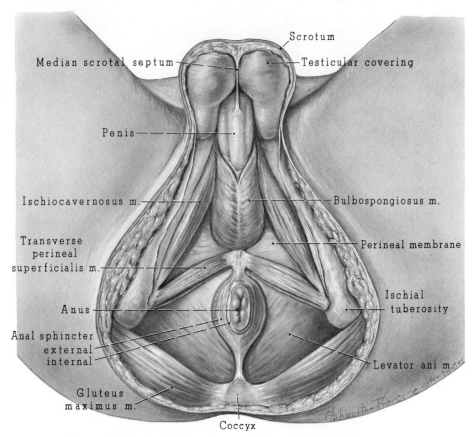

Median scrotal septum

Penis

Ischiocavernosus m.

Transverse
perineal
superficialis m.

Anus

Anal sphincter
external
internal

Gluteus
maximus m.

Scrotum

Testicular covering

Bulbospongiosus m.

Perineal membrane

Ischial
tuberosity

Levator ani m.

Coccyx

Figure 493. Male perineum with skin and superficial fascia removed.

spongiosum or **corpus cavernosum urethrae,** is the medial column, and it lies between the two corpora cavernosa. It contains the urethra, which transmits urine as well as semen, the male sexual secretion. At its distal end, the corpus cavernosum urethrae is larger, forming the *glans penis,* upon which the urethral orifice is located. Overhanging the glans is the *prepuce,* a loose skin folded inward and then backward upon itself. In current practice this foreskin is usually removed in newborn boys by the simple surgical procedure known as *circumcision* (Fig. 495).

The penis may be the site of several abnormalities noted at birth (Fig. 495). Two of these are *hypospadias* and *epispadias.* Malformations of the urethral groove and urethral canal sometimes create abnormal openings either on the ventral surface of the penis (hypospadias) or on the dorsal surface (epispadias). Such abnormalities are generally associated with a failure of normal descent of the testes and with malformations of the urinary bladder. Both hypospadias and epispadias should be surgically corrected.

PHIMOSIS. When the orifice of the prepuce is too narrow to permit retraction over the glans penis, the condition is known as phimosis. Phimosis prevents cleanliness and permits accumulation of secretions under the prepuce, favoring the development of secondary bacterial infection. Circumcision obviates phimosis and possibly protects against the development of tumors by lessening the accumulation of secretions, minimizing the tendency to irritation and infection.

Internal Organs

The internal organs of reproduction in the male can be divided into three groups. First there are the male gonads, or testes. The

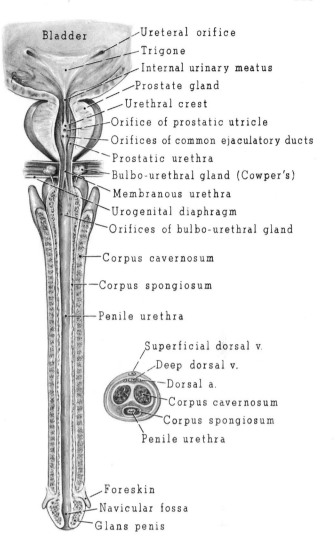

Figure 494. Section through the bladder, prostate gland, and penis.

Bladder
Ureteral orifice
Trigone
Internal urinary meatus
Prostate gland
Urethral crest
Orifice of prostatic utricle
Orifices of common ejaculatory ducts
Prostatic urethra
Bulbo-urethral gland (Cowper's)
Membranous urethra
Urogenital diaphragm
Orifices of bulbo-urethral gland
Corpus cavernosum
Corpus spongiosum
Penile urethra
Superficial dorsal v.
Deep dorsal v.
Dorsal a.
Corpus cavernosum
Corpus spongiosum
Penile urethra
Foreskin
Navicular fossa
Glans penis

Figure 495. In *circumcision* the prepuce is removed. *A* shows incision in the prepuce. Closure of the wound after removal of the prepuce is shown in *B*.

The penis may be the site of several abnormalities at birth. Among these are *hypospadias,* in which the urethral opening is on the ventral surface of the penis; *epispadias,* in which the urethral opening appears on the dorsal surface; and *phimosis,* in which the orifice of the prepuce is too narrow to permit retraction over the glans penis.

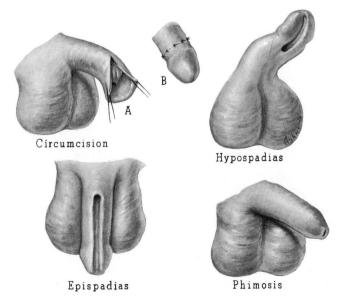

Circumcision

Hypospadias

Epispadias

Phimosis

second group consists of a series of ducts, including the epididymis, ductus deferens, and urethra. The third group of internal organs are the accessory glands: seminal vesicles, prostate, and bulbourethral (Cowper's) glands.

Testes. The testes correspond to the ovaries in the female. Each is an oval organ about 2 inches in length, lying within the abdominal cavity in early fetal life. About 2 months prior to birth the testes leave the abdomen and descend into the scrotum.

Occasionally the testes do not descend, but remain in the abdomen, giving rise to a condition known as *cryptorchism;* this can happen unilaterally or bilaterally. The cause of this condition is poorly understood. In a small percentage of cases it is believed to be an hereditary abnormality; but in most instances it is an isolated anatomic abnormality or mechanical obstruction to descent. When cryptorchism is discovered before the age of puberty, the testes are usually normal in size but in an abnormal location. When the condition is discovered at or after the age of puberty, the testes have already commenced to atrophy and decrease in size. A concomitant hernia in the inguinal area can accompany the abnormal position of the testes. Such a position in the inguinal canal is particularly susceptible to trauma by crushing against ligaments and bones.

The outer layer of the testis is known as the *tunica albuginea* (Fig. 496), a dense layer of fibroelastic connective tissue containing scattered smooth muscle cells, especially in the region adjacent to the epididymis. At its posterior border it is reflected into the testis, forming an in-

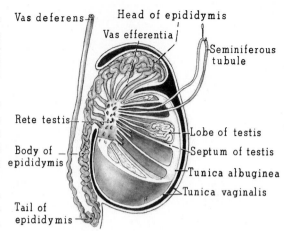

Figure 497. Diagram of a section of the male testis showing detail of a seminiferous tubule.

complete vertical septum known as the *mediastinum testis.* Fibrous septa extend into the substance of the testis, dividing it into about 250 wedge-shaped lobes. Each lobe contains from one to three narrow, coiled tubes known as **seminiferous tubules** (Fig. 497). If uncoiled, a tubule would measure about two feet in length. Male reproductive cells at different stages of development are found within these tubules. The maturing spermatozoa are usually seen in the center of the tubule and the premature spermatogonia and primary spermatocytes at the periphery of the tubule nearer the germinal epithelium.

In addition to reproductive cells, supportive and nutritive cells known as *Sertoli's cells* are found in the testis. These cells supply nutrients to the spermatozoa. *Interstitial cells of Leydig* are scattered among the tubules and are responsible for the production of male hormones.

The seminiferous tubules unite to form a series of larger, straight ducts, which in turn form a network known as the *rete testis.* About 20 small, coiled ductules, the *vasa efferentia,* leave the upper end of the rete testis, perforate the tunica albuginea, and open into the epididymis (Fig. 497).

Epididymis. The epididymis is the first part of the ductile system of the testis. It is a coiled tube lying on the posterior aspect of the testis and extending from the upper end downward for about 1½ inches. About 16 feet of tube are coiled within this short distance.

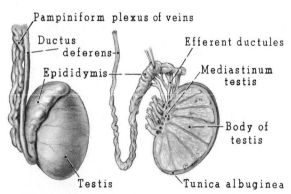

Figure 496. Male testis, entire and sectioned views.

Ductus Deferens. The ductus deferens is a straight tube leading from the lower portion of each epididymis. It ascends for about 18 inches along the posterior border of the testis through the inguinal canal to enter the abdomen. The ductus deferens consists of an inner mucous layer, a middle muscular layer, and an outer fibrous layer. It can be considered as a continuation of the epididymis and has been described as "the excretory duct of the testis." The ductus deferens, together with nerves, lymphatics, and blood vessels, forms the *spermatic cord* (Figure 466 shows the ductus deferens).

Seminal Vesicles. There are two seminal vesicles, membranous pouches lying posterior to the bladder near its base, each consisting of a single tube coiled upon itself. The seminal vesicles secrete a thick, nutrient-containing fluid. The tube of each seminal vesicle ends in a straight, narrow duct joining the ductus deferens to form the **ejaculatory duct.** The ejaculatory duct is a tube about 1 inch in length penetrating the base of the prostate gland and opening into the prostatic portion of the urethra. This duct actually ejects the spermatozoa and seminal vesicle fluid into the urethral lumen (Fig. 498).

Prostate. The prostate gland is a conical body about the size of a chestnut lying inferior to the bladder. It surrounds the first inch of the urethra and secretes a thin, milky, alkaline fluid which aids in maintaining the viability of sperm cells. In older men a progressive enlargement of the prostate commonly obstructs the urethra and interferes with the passage of urine. This condition calls for the surgical removal of a

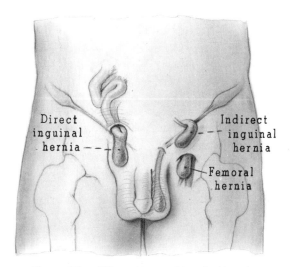

Figure 499.   Different types of inguinal hernias.

part of the prostate gland. The prostate is also a frequent site of cancer in elderly men.

Bulbo-Urethral   Glands.   The   bulbo-urethral glands (Cowper's) are two glands, each about the size of a pea, located inferior to the prostate on either side of the urethra. These discharge a lubricating mucous secretion prior to ejaculation which also becomes part of the semen.

The **male urethra** is a tubelike organ responsible for transmitting both semen and urine. It extends from the internal urethral orifice in the urinary bladder to the external urethral orifice at the distal end of the penis (see Chapter 14).

FEMALE REPRODUCTIVE SYSTEM

External Organs

Vulva.   The external female reproductive organs (Fig. 500) are collectively known as the vulva, which includes the mons pubis, labia majora, labia minora, clitoris, vestibular glands, and hymen (see Fig. 501).

MONS PUBIS AND LABIA MAJORA.   The most anterior of the anatomic structures of the vulva is the mons pubis (mons veneris), a firm, cushionlike elevation of adipose tissue over the symphysis pubis, covered by pubic hair. The labia majora are two rounded folds of adipose tissue with overlying skin; they extend from the mons pubis

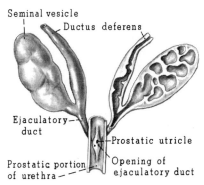

Figure 498.   Seminal vesicle and related parts. On the left the vesicle and duct are intact; the right side is sectioned to show internal detail.

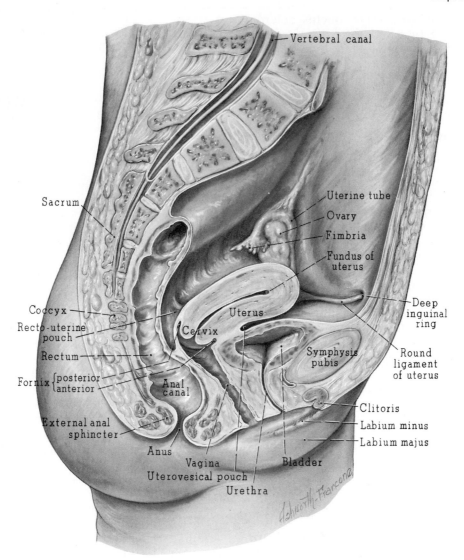

Figure 500. Mid-sagittal section of the female pelvis.

downward and backward to encircle the vestibule. The outer surfaces of these folds are covered with hair, whereas the inner surfaces containing sebaceous follicles are smooth and moist. The labia majora are united anteriorly by a fold of skin, the anterior commissure. They are not united posteriorly although a posterior commissure may be present anterior to the anus. The labia majora are homologues of the scrotum in the male.

LABIA MINORA. The labia minora are two folds of skin lying medial to the labia majora and enclosing the vestibule. Anteriorly, the labia minora divide into two layers. The upper folds join just in front of

the clitoris to form the prepuce, while the lower folds are attached to the inferior aspect of the glans of the clitoris to form its frenulum.

Posteriorly, the labia minora become less distinct and appear to join the labia majora in a transverse fold of skin, the posterior *fourchet*. A depression known as the fossa navicularis is located between the fourchet posteriorly and the posterior margin of the vaginal orifice.

Clitoris. The clitoris is a pea-shaped projection of erectile tissue, nerves, and blood vessels occupying the apex of the vestibule anterior to the vagina. It is partially covered by the anterior ends of the

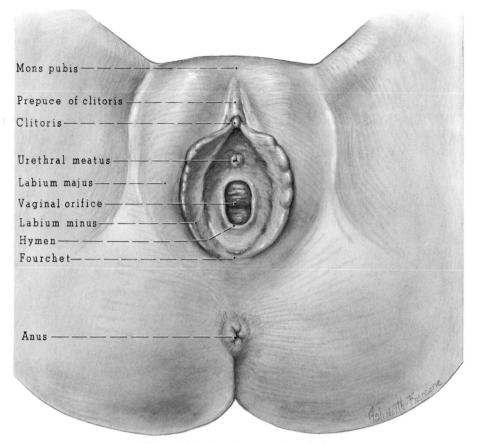

Mons pubis

Prepuce of clitoris

Clitoris

Urethral meatus

Labium majus

Vaginal orifice

Labium minus

Hymen

Fourchet

Anus

Figure 501.   Female external genitalia.

labia minora and is highly sensitive to tactile stimulation. The clitoris is important in the sexual excitation of the female and represents the homologue of the penis in the male, but it is not traversed by the urethra.

VESTIBULE.   The vestibule of the vagina is the cleft between the labia minora. Situated within the cleft of the vestibule are the hymen, the vaginal orifice, the urethral orifice and the openings of the vestibular glands. The urethral orifice is an opening 4 to 6 mm in diameter, located about 1 inch posterior to the clitoris. Multiple small *paraurethral glands* (Skene's) surround the orifice and are homologous to the prostate in the male. These glands open by way of a pair of ducts placed laterally in the submucous layer of the urethra at its orifice.

The vaginal orifice occupies the greater portion of the posterior two-thirds of the vestibule. On either side of the vaginal orifice, deep within the perineal tissues, are

the two *greater vestibular glands* (Bartholin's glands) (Fig. 502). Each opens by means of a duct placed laterally in a groove between the hymen and the labium minus. The greater vestibular glands, homologous to the bulbo-urethral glands in the male, elaborate a mucous secretion which acts as a lubricant during sexual intercourse.

HYMEN.   The hymen is a thin fold of vascularized mucous membrane separating the vagina from the vestibule. It can be entirely absent or can cover the vaginal orifice partly or completely. If the hymen completely covers the vaginal orifice, it is known as an imperforate hymen. Anatomically, neither its absence or presence can be considered a criterion for virginity (Fig. 503).

Perineum.   The perineum is the inferior outlet of the pelvis, bounded anteriorly by the symphysis pubis, anterolaterally by the inferior rami of the pubis and the ischial tuberosities, and posteriorly by the tip of

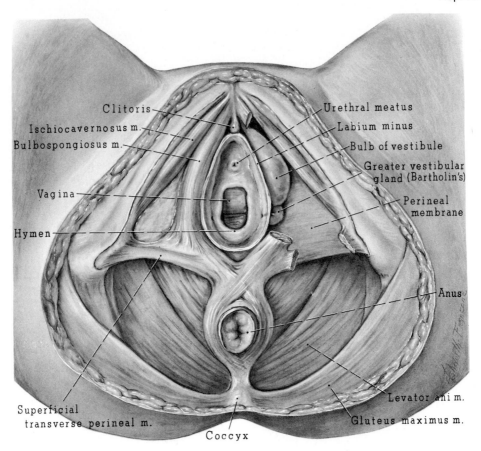

Figure 502.   Female perineum with skin and superficial fascia removed.

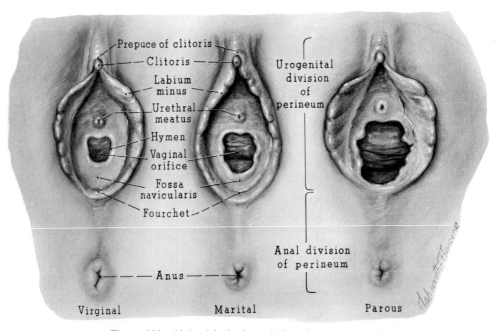

Figure 503.   Vulva (virginal, marital, and parous states).

the bony coccyx. When the thighs are fully abducted, the perineum assumes a diamond shape which is further divided into anterior and posterior regions by a line drawn between the two ischial tuberosities. The triangle anterior to the line is called the *urogenital triangle* and contains the external urogenital organs. The triangle posterior to the line is the rectal triangle, containing the anus.

The perineal structures are sometimes torn during childbirth. Tears can extend from the vaginal orifice posteriorly through the perineum and damage the anal sphincters. To avoid this danger an incision is deliberately made in the perineum just prior to the passage of the fetus through the vagina. This incision (episiotomy) allows enough room for the infant to pass and thus minimizes perineal damage.

Internal Organs

Vagina. The internal organs of reproduction (Fig. 504) include the vagina, uterus, uterine tubes, and ovaries. The vagina is a tubular canal 4 to 6 inches in length, directed upward and backward and extending from the vestibule to the uterus. It is situated between the bladder and the rectum. The vaginal wall consists of an internal membranous lining and a muscular layer capable of constriction and enormous dilatation, separated by a layer of erectile tissue. The mucous membrane, consisting of stratified squamous epithelium, forms thick transverse folds and is kept moist by cervical secretions (the cervix is the lower part of the uterus). The vaginal walls are normally folded in close apposition to each other, forming a collapsed tube. The vagina serves as part of the birth canal and represents the female organ of copulation.

Uterus. The uterus is a pear-shaped, thick-walled, muscular organ suspended in the anterior part of the pelvic cavity above the bladder and in front of the rectum. In its normal state it measures about 3 inches in length and 2 inches in width. The lower end of the uterus projects into the vagina; this portion, called the *cervix*, corresponds to the stem of an inverted pear. The *corpus,* or *body, of the uterus* is superior to the cervix. The uterine tubes enter into the upper end

of the uterus, one on each side. The *fundus* is the uppermost, rounded portion of the organ, lying between the two uterine tubes. The uterus, tilted forward and projecting above the bladder from behind, is freely movable; consequently, its position varies with the state of distention of the bladder and rectum (Fig. 500). The uterine cavity is normally triangular and flattened anteroposteriorly, making the cavity appear as a mere slit when it is observed from the side.

The uterus is covered with a layer of peritoneum and is attached to both sides of the pelvic cavity by means of a double sheet of peritoneum, or *broad ligaments,* through which the uterine arteries course (Fig. 506). The principal supports of the uterus, the *cardinal ligaments,* lie in the base of the broad ligaments. There are also two *round ligaments,* attached on either side and near the uterine tubes, which hold the uterus in its anterior position. The two *uterosacral ligaments* are fibrous bands curved along the floor of the pelvis from the junction of the cervix and corpus to the sacrum. The uterosacral ligaments aid in supporting the uterus and maintaining its position.

The wall of the uterus consists of three layers. The outer layer is a peritoneal investment of the organ, continuous on each side with the peritoneum of the broad ligament. The middle layer, **myometrium,** a thick, muscular layer, consists of bundles of interlaced, smooth muscle fibers embedded in connective tissue. The myometrium in turn is subdivided into three ill-defined but intertwining muscular layers, the middle of which contains many large blood vessels of the uterine wall. It is this intertwining arrangement of muscles that presses against the blood vessels and stops them from bleeding after delivery.

During pregnancy, there is a marked increase in the thickness of the myometrium. This occurs not only because of hypertrophy (actual enlargement of existing fibers) but also because of the addition of new fibers derived from transformation and division of mesenchymal cells. The inner coat of the uterine wall is the mucous membrane, or **endometrium.** It consists of an epithelial lining and connective tissue called the endometrial stroma. The stroma supports the tubular epithelial glands

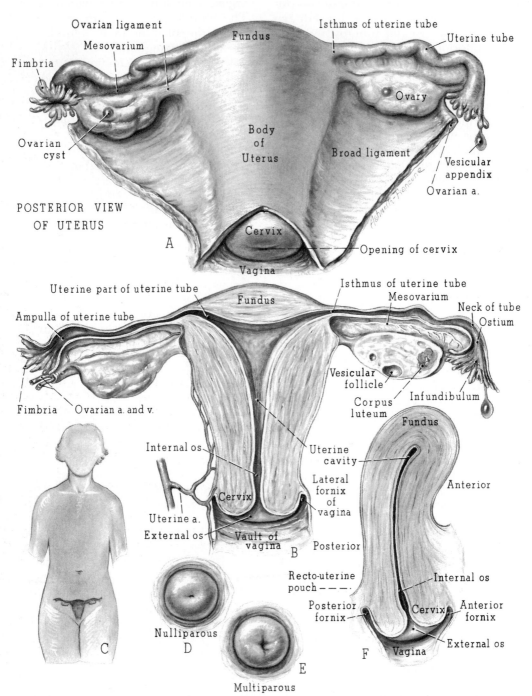

Figure 504. Female organs of reproduction. *A*, Uterus, posterior view. *B*, Uterus sectioned to show internal structure. *C*, Position in body. *D* and *E*, Shape of cervix before and after childbirth. *F*, Right lateral sagittal view.

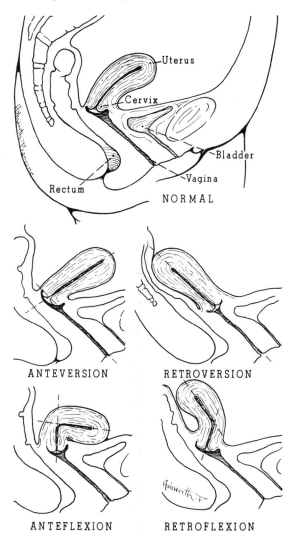

Figure 505. Normal and abnormal positions of the uterus.

opening into the uterine lumen. Two types of arteries supply blood to the endometrium. The straight arteries supply the deeper layer and the coiled type supplies the superficial layer. The coiled arteries undergo progressive changes during the menstrual cycle and are sloughed during menstruation.

Uterine Tubes. The uterine tubes (fallopian tubes) are two flexible, trumpet-shaped, muscular tubes approximately 4½ inches in length, extending from the fundus of the uterus on either side toward the pelvic brim. The uterine tubes are suspended by a fold of the broad ligament called the *mesosalpinx*. The wall of the tube

is composed of the same three layers as the uterus—mucous, smooth muscle, and serous layers. The mucous, or internal, layer is lined with ciliated columnar epithelium and is continuous with the epithelium of the uterus as well as with the peritoneum in the abdominal cavity. The muscular coat consists of a circular inner layer and a discontinuous longitudinal outer layer. One end of the tube, the *isthmus*, opens into the uterine cavity and is continuous with the *ampulla*. The ampulla is the dilated, central part of the tube curving over the ovary, and is in turn continuous with the *infundibulum*, which opens into the abdominal cavity (Fig. 504).

The infundibulum is surrounded by finger-like projections, or *fimbriae*. The fimbriated portion of the uterine tube curves about the ovary and is adjacent to but not necessarily in direct contact with it. When an ovum is expelled from the ovary, the fimbriae work like tentacles to draw the ovum into the tube, where fertilization may occur. Then, by muscular peristaltic contractions and ciliary activity, the tube conducts the ovum to the uterine cavity.

Ovaries. The ovaries, often referred to as the primary reproductive organs of the female, are two oval-shaped structures about 1½ inches in length; they are located in the upper part of the pelvic cavity, one on each side of the uterus. The ovaries are suspended from the broad ligament of the uterus by the *mesovarium*, a fold of peritoneum, and are anchored to the uterus by the ovarian ligament. The infundibulopelvic, or suspensory, ligament of the ovary extends from its upper pole to the pelvic wall.

A thin layer of cuboidal cells, the germinal epithelium, covers each ovary. The inner structure, or stroma, of the ovary consists of a meshwork of spindle-shaped cells, connective tissue, and blood vessels. Minute follicles at various stages of development are present within each ovary. The ova develop within these follicles. The two major functions of ovaries are development and expulsion of the female ova and elaboration of female sex hormones.

Mammary Glands

The two mammary glands, or breasts, are accessory reproductive organs. The breasts

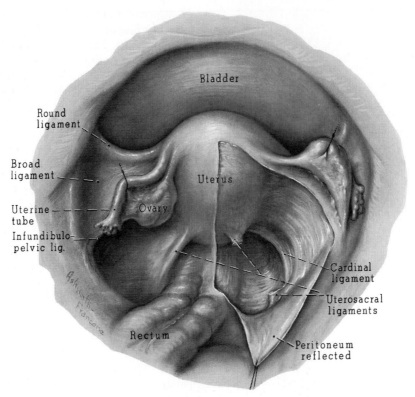

Figure 506.   View from above and behind of uterine structures as they are seen in the pelvic cavity. The peritoneum has been reflected on the right side, and the uterosacral ligament has been cut to expose the cardinal ligament found in the base of the broad ligament.

of postpartum women secrete milk available for nourishment of the newborn. Each breast is located anterior to the pectoral muscles and extends as a convex structure from the lateral margin of the sternum to the anterior border of the axilla (Fig. 507).

The nipples, containing the openings of the milk ducts, are located near the center of the breasts. A wider circular area of pigmented skin, known as the *areola*, surrounds each nipple. There are from 15 to 20 lobes of glandular tissue arranged radially within the breast. Each is embedded in fat and connective tissue and each has its own excretory duct, the lactiferous or milk producing duct. The lobes converge toward the areola, beneath which they form the ampulla, which serves as a reservoir for milk.

Further Development. Increasing amounts of ovarian hormones and a conspicuous growth and branching of the ductal system, along with an extensive deposition of fat, occur at puberty. In the postpubertal female, slight fluctuations in breast size may be correlated with changes in the reproductive cycle. A characteristic differentiation of glands of the breast occurs during pregnancy. The duct system branches extensively, and the terminal branches end in secretory alveoli. The alveolar lining constitutes the secretory surface from which milk arises. After parturition (childbirth) the secretion of milk begins; the gland then gradually involutes until lactation ceases. Breast tissue atrophies, becoming less prominent at the time of menopause.

Physiology of the Mammary Gland. Two components of mammary gland physiology will be described—development of the glands and the formation and evacuation of milk.

DEVELOPMENT TO A FUNCTIONAL STATE. Experimental studies in animals have shown that prolactin from the hypophysis, as well as the ovarian hormones estrogen and progesterone, are all essential for normal growth and development of the breast. Ovarian hormones exert specific control over growth of the breast and its

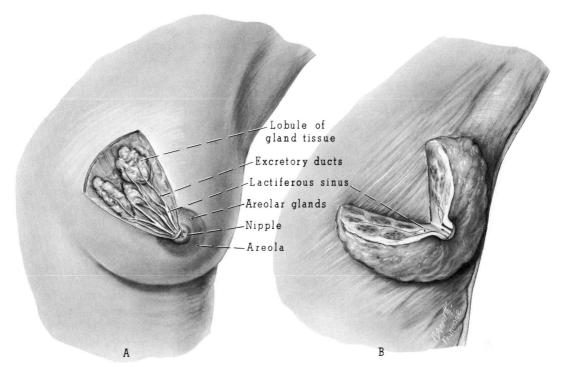

Lobule of
gland tissue

Excretory ducts

Lactiferous sinus

Areolar glands

Nipple

Areola

A   B

Figure 507. The female breast. *A,* The skin has been partly removed to show the underlying structures. *B,* A section has been removed to show the internal structures in relation to the muscles.

development. Estrogen stimulates the development of the ducts, progesterone influences the growth of the alveoli.

There are cycle changes in the mammary glands associated with a rise and fall of hormonal secretions during the menstrual cycle. Many women notice fullness, tightness, heaviness, and, occasionally, pain in the breast just before the time of menstruation. This correlates with the observed limited growth of ducts and alveoli and also with swelling in the connective tissues of the breast just prior to the time of menstruation. Regression occurs after menstruation, and the connective tissue becomes more fibrous.

During pregnancy, the rapid increase of estrogen and progesterone produced by the ovary and later by the placenta causes alterations in the mammary glands more marked than the premenstrual changes. Each breast becomes larger with an increase in the number of ducts and the complexity of the alveoli. The color of the areola darkens.

FACTORS CONTROLLING LACTATION. Lactation is a complex process requiring the interplay of various hormonal and nervous factors. The exact mechanisms underlying the sudden onset of lactation after childbirth have not been fully explained. It is apparent, however, that the hypothalamus, hypophysis, suprarenal cortex, and thyroid are important control centers for initiation and maintenance of secretion of milk. Prolactin elaborated by the adenohypophysis appears to be the prime factor.

After parturition, there is a fall in the circulating estrogen and progesterone levels and a rise in the level of prolactin.

SUCKLING STIMULUS. There is a well-recognized nervous factor in the maintenance of normal milk secretion—that is, the suckling stimulant to the mother's breast by the infant. Suckling by the newborn stimulates nerve endings at the nipple, and impulses are carried through the hypothalamic region to the neurohypophysis. There, oxytocin is released and taken by the blood to the mammary glands. Oxytocin causes contraction of the myoepithelial cells surrounding the alveoli, forcing the contents into the lactiferous ducts to be made available to the infant. It has been shown that failure of the ejection reflex eventually leads to a failure of lactation.

PHYSIOLOGIC PROCESSES RELATED TO REPRODUCTION

Spermatogenesis

Spermatogenesis is the production of spermatozoa. It takes place in the seminiferous tubules of the testis when sexual maturity is reached.

In the embryo original, or *primordial,* germ cells differentiate and appear in the region in which the reproductive organs form. As the primordial germ cells multiply by mitotic cell division, some differentiate and form the youngest male gametes, or spermatogonia. Others are organized to form the seminiferous tubules, in which young germ cells grow and develop. The designated spermatogonia then multiply several times and enter a growth period. After birth, through infancy and childhood, these remain in a relatively inactive state. At the time of sexual maturity they again become active when spermatogenesis — the formation of spermatozoa from spermatogonia — is initiated. This usually occurs at the age of 12 to 15 in the adolescent male.

Spermatogenesis may be divided into three major phases: (1) formation of primary spermatocytes from spermatogonia; (2) meiotic division of spermatocytes, producing haploid spermatids; and (3) differentiation of spermatids into spermatozoa.

In the first phase, **spermatogonia** (often referred to as stem cells) undergo mitotic division to give rise to two populations of cells. One represents a reservoir of spermatogonia. The other continues to divide, the last generation of cells becoming transformed into **primary spermatocytes** by enlarging and undergoing other morphological changes in preparation for meiosis. In the first meiotic division (reduction division), each primary spermatocyte produces two cells, called **secondary spermatocytes,** each containing one set of double-stranded chromosomes. Each of these, in turn, undergoes a second meiotic division, forming two **spermatids,** each of which contains a single set of chromosomes. Thus, four

haploid spermatids arise from each primary spermatocyte (see Chapter 2, page 47, for a more complete description of meiosis). The spermatids gradually become transformed into **spermatozoa.** During this transformation the spermatids remain attached to Sertoli's cells, which presumably supply nutrients and other substances necessary for bringing about the differentiation of the spermatids into spermatozoa.

About 10 to 11 weeks are required for the formation of the highly specialized spermatozoa from the primitive spermatogonia. The spermatozoon is often described as being tadpole shaped. It consists of an oval head, containing a nucleus; a middle piece, or body, of cytoplasm (separated from the head by a narrow neck); and a long tail, which aids in motility by its lashing movement (Fig. 508). The head is capped by a structure called the **acrosome,** derived from the Golgi apparatus, which contains digestive enzymes used, among other things, to aid in penetrating the surrounding investments of the ovum. The midsection contains numerous mitochondria.

Spermatozoa released from Sertoli's cells in the seminiferous tubules are still functionally immature; that is, they are immotile and lack the ability to effect fertilization. They acquire motility and the ability to fertilize during passage (about two weeks) through the epididymis, in a process called *maturation.* The final phase of maturation, called *capacitation,* is a period of conditioning believed to involve activation of

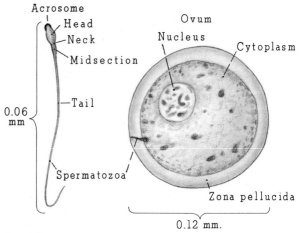

Figure 508. Size relations of sperm and ovum.

acrosomal enzymes. In a number of lower animals, capacitation has been shown to occur in the female reproductive tract. Whether or not some degree of capacitation also occurs in the human female reproductive tract is uncertain.

During ejaculation, the spermatozoa and seminal and prostatic secretions are transported in the ductus deferens to the ejaculatory duct through the urethra and are deposited in the vagina close to the cervix.

SEMEN. During transit the fluid receives ingredients from the secretion of seminal vesicles and prostate and bulbo-urethral glands, forming the final product called semen. These secretions provide nutrients and buffer the acidity encountered in the female genital tract. Normally the volume of semen in a single discharge is about 2 to 3 ml, and the number of spermatozoa is between 200 to 300 million.

The most important factors influencing the fertility of male spermatozoa are the actual number of spermatozoa (sperm count), the percentage of abnormal forms, and the motility. The actual number is the most important. A sperm count of less than 60,000,000 per ml results in decreased fertility.

Oogenesis. Oogenesis is the development of the ovum, which takes place within the ovary. As in the male, the female primordial germ cells are derived from the germinal epithelium in the embryo. These multiply and form primitive ova, or **oogonia.** As in spermatogenesis, the mitotic division of the oogonia results in daughter cells with a diploid (46) number of chromosomes. The cells formed in the final mitotic division enter a period of growth and are transformed into **primary oocytes** with the diploid number of chromosomes. All ova produced by the female during reproductive life are derived from primary oocytes already present in the ovaries at birth.

When sexual maturity is reached, meiotic division of the primary oocytes occurs, with the production in the first, or reduction, division of cells containing one set (23) of double-stranded chromosomes. Here, unlike the corresponding stage of spermatogenesis, the division of the cytoplasm is unequal, producing the large and functional **secondary oocyte** and the small, nonfunctional first polar body, which usually undergoes rapid degeneration but which can occasionally undergo meiotic division, forming two functionless cells. During the second, or mitotic, division of meiosis the secondary oocyte divides, again unequally, to produce a **mature ovum** and a second *polar body.* Thus, from each primary oocyte only one mature haploid ovum is produced (while each primary spermatocyte gives rise to four mature spermatozoa) (see Fig. 509).

The mature ovum is large in comparison with the spermatozoon (Fig. 508). It is nonmotile and barely visible to the naked eye. The nucleus of the ovum is surrounded by cytoplasm containing a small quantity of nutritive material in the form of yolk granules.

FOLLICLE MATURATION AND OVULATION. When the primary oocytes are formed, each is surrounded by a single layer of cells derived from the germinal epithelium. A primary oocyte (in prophase I of meiosis) and its surrounding layer of cells (called granulosa cells) are known as a **primary follicle** (see Fig. 510). About 400,000 primary follicles are present in the ovaries when the reproductive period of the female begins. At the onset of puberty, when the secretion of large amounts of follicle-stimulating hormone (FSH) commences, a mature ovum develops from a primary oocyte approximately once every 28 days. Changes in the ovary associated with the regular development of ova are referred to as the *ovarian cycle.* (Changes taking place in the uterine endometrium at the same time are known as the menstrual cycle.) During an ovarian cycle a group of follicles undergo growth and development, but only one reaches maturity and ovulates; all others degenerate (a process called *atresia,* forming what are called *atretic follicles*). Maturation of a follicle is characterized by (1) proliferation of granulosa cells; (2) formation of a capsule of connective tissue from the ovarian stroma around the follicle (consisting of an inner vascular layer, the theca interna, and an outer fibrous layer, the theca externa); (3) completion of the first meiotic division with the formation of a secondary oocyte, the second meiotic division of which is arrested at metaphase (the condition at ovulation and fertilization); and (4) expulsion of the first polar body.

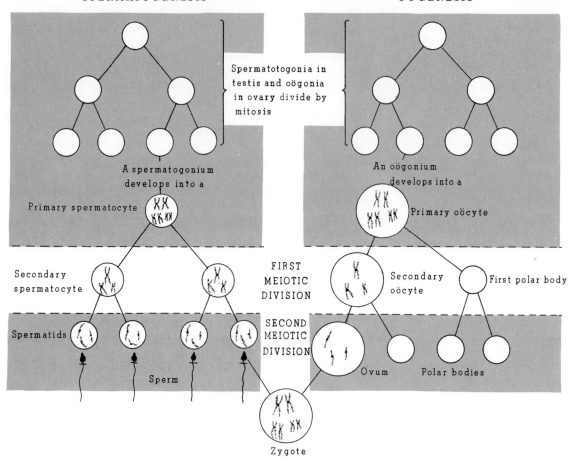

Figure 509. Gametogenesis.

As the follicle develops, a cavity soon appears, separating the mass of proliferating granulosa cells into two parts. The cavity, or antrum, is filled with fluid (liquor folliculi) believed to be secreted by the cells of the follicle. The oocyte becomes pressed to one side of what at this stage is called the *vesicular follicle* and is separated from the surrounding layer of cells by a transparent membrane known as the *zona pellucida.* A mound of cells surrounding the oocyte, known as the *cumulus oophorus,* projects into the antrum. The follicle becomes distended by an accumulation of contained fluid and moves outward to the surface of the ovary. Once a month, usually about the middle of a 28-day menstural cycle, the process of ovulation occurs. A mature follicle ruptures and the ovum (more precisely,

the secondary oocyte), surrounded by a ring of granulosa cells called the **corona radiata,** slowly oozes out of the ovarian surface in a stream of follicular fluid. *Ovulation is initiated by a steep rise in the release of luteinizing hormone (LH) from the adenohypophysis.* Rupture of the follicle is *not* caused by an increase in intrafollicular pressure arising from the accumulation of fluid within the antrum. On the contrary, ovulation is preceded by a slight fall in intrafollicular pressure. The cause of rupture is an increase in distensibility and reduction in breaking strength of the follicular wall (theca externa). This appears to occur as follows: LH (with cyclic AMP acting as a second messenger) stimulates the secretion of progesterone by follicular tissue. Progesterone, in turn, induces the

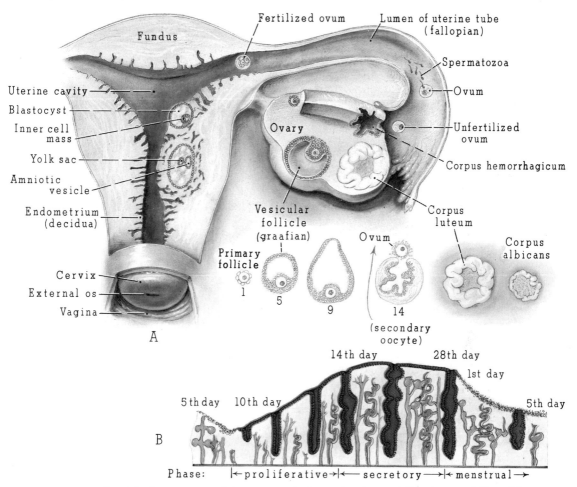

Figure 510. *A*, Physiologic processes of the ovary and uterus, showing ovulation, transportation of the ovum, and implantation. *B*, Cyclic menstrual changes in the uterine endometrium.

production of an enzyme (collagenase) that weakens the framework of the theca externa.

Once ovulation has occurred, definite changes take place within the ovary. First there is minimal hemorrhage into the ruptured follicle, forming a blood clot, the *corpus hemorrhagicum*. Then the cells of the ruptured follicle undergo alteration and create a mass known as the **corpus luteum** (yellow body), which absorbs the corpus hemorrhagicum. The corpus luteum secretes large amounts of progesterone and lesser amounts of estrogens. If fertilization occurs, the corpus luteum continues to function until about the third month of pregnancy, when the placenta takes over its function and it begins to slowly degenerate.

It is still present in the ovary at the time of birth. If fertilization does not occur, the corpus luteum degenerates and menstruation follows (described later). The location of the old corpus luteum is marked by an area of white scar tissue in the ovary known as the *corpus albicans*.

Fertilization

After its discharge from the ovary, the ovum (secondary oocyte, actually) begins a 6- to 8-day journey, with its destination, the uterus, more than 3 inches away. It does not have any means of locomotion and must be transported through the uterine tube by peristaltic contractions of smooth muscles and by the activity of cilia present in the tube.

Fertilization normally occurs when the ovum is about one-third of the way down the tube. Spermatozoa reach this point 5 minutes after coitus. The mechanism by which the spermatozoon travels from the cervix to the uterine tube so rapidly is still uncertain. Some believe it is caused largely by muscular contractions of the uterus and fallopian tube.

When the sperm reaches the ovum, it releases acrosomal enzymes, including hyaluronidase, which aid in dispersal of the corona radiata, and a proteolytic enzyme utilized in penetrating the zona pellucida. Normally only one sperm enters the ovum. As soon as penetration has occurred, the sperm sheds its tail and the chromosomal material forms the male *pronucleus*. Simultaneously, the ovum becomes impenetrable to other spermatozoa and prevents fertilization by several sperm.

The presence of the male pronucleus induces the secondary oocyte to proceed with the second meiotic division, and it casts off the second polar body. The male and female pronuclei approach each other and join into one. The union of the two gametes restores the chromosome number to 46, and the fertilized ovum (also known as the *zygote*) begins its first cleavage in the process of development.

Menstrual Cycle and the Menopause

The Menstrual Cycle. Menstruation commences at the age of puberty (menarche) and continues until the menopause, approximately 40 years later. The day of onset of the menstrual flow is considered the first day of the cycle. The cycle ends on the last day prior to the next menstrual flow. Normally the cycle is 28 days in duration, but it can vary from 22 to 35 days. Three phases of the menstrual cycle are distinguished—menstrual, proliferative, and secretory (see Fig. 510).

MENSTRUAL PHASE. The menstrual phase lasts from the first day to the fifth day of the cycle. Menstruation occurs when the expectation of implantation of the fertilized ovum is not fulfilled. The endometrial lining is destroyed and is rebuilt for the next possible implantation. When the ovum is

not fertilized, the corpus luteum regresses; the subsequent deficiency of progesterone and estrogens leads to disintegration of the uterine endometrium. This is preceded by intermittent constriction of the coiled arteries, which causes anoxia and results in shriveling of the superficial (functional) layer of the endometrium. Necrotic tissue is shed, and this is followed by rupture of surface vessels. The entire functional layer is eventually sloughed, leaving only the deep (basal) layer intact (Fig. 510).

PROLIFERATIVE PHASE. The proliferative phase, characterized by estrogen stimulation, begins at about the fifth day of the cycle and extends through ovulation, which usually occurs near the midpoint of the cycle (14 days *before* the onset of menstruation). The endothelium thickens as estrogen secretion rises. There is rapid proliferation of both glands and stroma. Coiled arteries grow into all but the superficial third of the regenerating tissue (supplied by capillaries only).

The ovulatory process is initiated by a sharp rise in the secretion of luteinizing hormone. Conspicuous changes do not occur in the endometrium at this point. A distinct rise in basal body temperature occurs a day or so after ovulation and remains high until the onset of the next menstrual period. The presence of progesterone accounts for this temperature rise.

SECRETORY PHASE. During the secretory (progestational) phase, progesterone levels gradually rise; there is a concomitant but lesser rise in estrogens. The endometrium differentiates into a secretory type of tissue capable of fulfilling the requirements for implantation of the embryo. The glands hypertrophy and take on a coiled and tortuous appearance, and the stroma becomes edematous. This further thickens the endometrium. Coiled arteries grow almost to the surface of the endometrium. If implantation does not occur, the corpus luteum decreases in functional activity, degenerative changes are observed in the uterine endometrium, and the menstrual phase starts again.

Menstrual Problems. Delay of the menarche, infrequent or irregular menstruation, prolonged menstruation, and menstrual pain are among the most frequent menstrual problems.

Absence of menstruation after the age of

16 is rarely normal. On the other hand, menstrual irregularity, characterized by scanty or heavy flow at intervals of several months or even less than 28 days, is quite common during adolescence. It is usually associated with failure of ovulation. Dysmenorrhea, or menstrual pain, is sometimes experienced by apparently healthy women, although their periods tend to be regular and normal in amount and duration. No specific causes are known.

Menopause. The menopause marks the cessation of menstrual activity. It occurs generally between the ages of 45 and 55, often gradually, but sometimes with a sudden change in body physiology. The two major symptoms are (1) *flushes,* sometimes lasting for hours, involving the head, neck, and upper part of the thorax (these may appear years prior to the actual cessation of menstruation) and (2) brief, intense suffusions of heat over the entire body, called *flashes,* accompanied by reddening of the face and sweating. Several years before menopause, the menstrual cycles may become irregular, both shortening and lengthening, and the menstrual flow may vary from very light to very heavy.

Menopausal symptoms occur when almost all of the primary follicles have either matured or degenerated. Unlike other endocrine glands, the ovary has a limited span of functional life, lasting about 40 years. In the majority of women, an increase in hypophyseal gonadotropins occurs coincidentally with ovarian failure. The normal reciprocal relationship between the ovary and the adenohypophysis is interrupted. Since the atrophic ovary is unable to produce enough estrogens to inhibit the production of FSH, a high excretion of hypophyseal gonadotropins results.

Gradual rise in FSH following
fall in estrogens and progesterone
↓
FSH stimulates follicle development
↓
Follicle secretes estrogens
↓
Estrogen peak causes surge in
release of FSH and LH
↓
LH surge triggers ovulation
↓
Corpus luteum develops and secretes
progesterone and estrogens
↓
Rise in estrogens and progesterone
inhibits LH and FSH secretion

Fertilization ⊖   Fertilization ⊕
↓   ↓
Fall in LH causes   Implantation
regression of corpus luteum   ↓
↓   Chorionic gonadotropin
Sharp fall in   prevents regression
progesterone and estrogens   of corpus luteum
↓   ↓
MENSTRUATION   Placenta secretes
                                           estrogens and progesterone
                                           ↓
                                           PREGNANCY continues

Figure 511.   Hormonal interrelations during the menstrual cycle and hormonal changes following interruption of the cycle by fertilization.

Hormonal Interrelations During the Menstrual Cycle

The interrelation between the secretion of estrogens and progesterone and the secretion of gonadotropins during the menstrual cycle is complex (Figs. 511 and 512). Negative feedback can only partially account for the changes in gonadotropin levels. The fall in plasma levels of FSH and LH in the postovulatory phase of the cycle is a result of negative feedback inhibition caused by rising concentrations of estrogens and progesterone. Gonadotropin secretion is regulated by hypothalamic releasing factors (Chapter 15, page 515), and inhibition of the secretion of these factors plays a role in the negative feedback response. Release

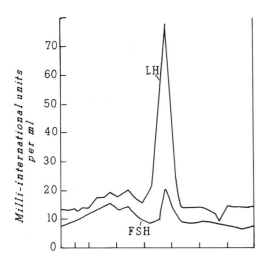

from this inhibition causes the gradual rise in FSH and LH at the end of the cycle, when estrogen and progesterone levels decline following regression of the corpus luteum (as a result of the fall in blood levels of LH). Clearly inconsistent with negative feedback control, however, is the preovulatory surge in gonadotropins, particularly LH, immediately following the steep rise in the secretion of estrogens by the maturing follicle (Fig. 512). Recent studies suggest that this paradox may be explained, in part, by a change in the sensitivity of the adenohypophysis to hypothalalmic releasing factors in response to changes in estrogen levels. The peak in estrogen concentration in the plasma apparently augments the responsiveness of the adenohypophysis to gonadrotropin releasing factors. An increase in the secretion of the hypothalamic releasing factors may also occur at that time. A converse response seems to be involved in the postovulatory period. The high concentration of progesterone and estrogens, it is believed, reduces the sensitivity of the adenohypophysis to gonadotropin releasing factors.

The pronounced inhibitory effect of progesterone on the secretion of LH is utilized in **birth control pills** to prevent ovulation. The most commonly used pills contain a synthetic progesterone and a very small amount of synthetic estrogen. Taking the pill for 21 consecutive days, beginning with the fifth day of the cycle, effectively inhibits the preovulatory surge in LH, thereby preventing ovulation.

Functions of Androgens

Testosterone, the principal and most potent androgen, is formed by the interstitial cells of Leydig within the seminiferous tubules of the testes. (The structure of testosterone and of other major steroid hormones is shown in Fig. 480, Chapter 15, page 529.) During embryological development, testosterone is responsible for **sexual differentiation.** Whether or not testes or ovaries develop is determined by the X and Y sex chromosomes. If a sperm bearing an X chromosome fertilizes an ovum (producing a zygote with two X chromosomes), ovaries will develop; if a sperm bearing a Y

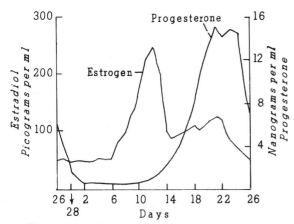

Figure 512. Typical changes in plasma concentrations of follicle-stimulating hormone (FSH), luteinizing hormone (LH), estradiol and progesterone during a 28-day menstrual cycle.

chromosome fertilizes an ovum (producing a zygote with one X and one Y chromosome), testes will form. (For a description of human chromosomes, see Chapter 2, page 46.) Secretion of testosterone by the embryonic testicular Leydig cells leads to the formation of the male ductile system, accessory organs, and external genitalia. In the absence of testosterone, the female reproductive organs and genitalia develop. In other words, male sexual differentiation is imposed upon the natural inclination of the embryo (without hormonal stimulation from either gonad) toward female development. Recent findings suggest that in target areas which give rise to the external genitalia (urogenital sinus, tubercle, and swellings) testosterone functions as a prehormone and is enzymatically converted to 5α-dihydrotestosterone, the active hormone in these regions.

Testosterone also brings about *sexual differentiation of the brain.* If the fetal brain is not exposed to testosterone, a cycling regulatory center for gonadotropin secretion develops in the hypothalamus. If it is exposed to testosterone, a noncycling center develops and, at the onset of puberty, when the hypothalamus secretes large amounts of gonadotropin releasing factors (see Chapter 15, page 515), the secretion of these releasing factors, gonadotropins, and testosterone is reciprocally controlled by negative feedback so as to maintain relatively constant blood levels of testosterone and gonadotropins.

The increase in testosterone secretion at the time of puberty is responsible for the pronounced growth of the penis, prostate, scrotum, testes, and seminal vesicles, and for the appearance of the **secondary male characteristics,** including deepening of the voice (as a result of enlargement of the larynx and thickening of the vocal cords), male hair pattern, and greatly increased muscular development. Testosterone also promotes protein anabolism, increases the formation of red blood cells, accelerates the deposition of bone matrix, and, to a slight extent, increases sodium and water retention in the kidney.

Functions of Estrogens

Estrogens are secreted by the developing ovarian follicle and later by the corpus luteum. During pregnancy they are secreted by the placenta. *Estradiol* (see Fig. 480, Chapter 15, page 529) is the major estrogen; significant amounts of estrone are also secreted.

Estrogens are responsible for the increased growth of the uterus and vagina at puberty; development of secondary sex characteristics, such as the female figure; and repair of the endometrium following menstruation.

Estrogens exercise partial control over breast development and function. In pregnancy and puberty, estrogens stimulate the formation of ducts in the mammary glands. Estrogens also tend to increase the motility of the uterus and its sensitivity to oxytocin. In this respect its action is opposite to that of progesterone. Toward the end of pregnancy the ratio of estrogens to progesterone increases. This change is believed to be partly responsible for the increased contractility of the uterus at that time. Other actions of estrogens include slightly increasing sodium and water reabsorption by the renal tubules and increasing matrix formation in bone. Diminished secretion of estrogens produces irregularity of the menses and underdevelopment or atrophy of the breast and uterus.

Functions of Progesterone. Progesterone is secreted by the corpus luteum and placenta. It converts the already partially thickened uterine endometrium into a secretory structure specialized for the process of implantation, it is responsible for development of the milk-secreting cells of the mammary glands, and it decreases the motility of the uterus. Diminished secretion of progesterone leads to menstrual irregularities in nonpregnant women and spontaneous abortion in pregnant women.

Clinical Considerations of Abnormalities of Sex

As mentioned, development of the male ductile system, accessory organs, and external genitalia occurs normally in genetic males in response to secretion of testosterone by the embryonic testes. However, male genital development may also occur in genetic females exposed to androgens from some other source, such as overactive suprarenal glands, drugs, or tumors. The resulting individual is known as a female pseudohermaphrodite. A *pseudohermaphrodite* is an individual with the genetic constitution and gonads of one sex and the external genitalia of the other (a *true hermaphrodite* has the gonads of both sexes). On the other hand, there is a condition known as male pseudohermaphrodism, in which female external (and even internal) genital development occurs in genetic males. In this condition the embryonic testes are defective and deficient in androgens.

Chromosomal Abnormalities. Abnormalities in the number of human sex chromosomes can arise as a result of a phenomenon called *nondysjunction* — failure during meiosis of a pair of chromosomes to separate in the first division or failure of two strands of an individual chromosome to separate in the second division. As a result, gametes with an excess or absence of X or Y chromosomes can be produced. Chromosomal abnormalities resulting from fertilization with such gametes are likely to have adverse effects on development. Individuals with the following chromosomal patterns have been described: XO, XXX, XXY, XXXY, XXXXY and XYY. The YO genotype is apparently lethal.

In individuals with the XO pattern, ovaries are absent and female genitalia are present. Stature is short, and maturation does not occur at puberty. This symptom complex is referred to as ovarian agenesis (absence of the ovaries), or Turner's syndrome.

Individuals with the XXY pattern have the genitalia of the normal male, and testosterone production at puberty is often sufficient for the development of male characteristics; however, seminiferous tubules are abnormal. Individuals with this genotype tend to be tall, and frequently suffer from speech and language difficulties. A number of individuals with XXX patterns have been reported; this is associated with oligomenorrhea (diminished menstruation), sometimes sterility, and a higher than normal incidence of mental deficiency. The rare individuals with XXXY and XXXXY chromosomal patterns have testes and masculine characteristics.

The XYY genotype has received considerable public attention because of its association with an elevated crime rate and the suggestion that the extra Y chromosome contributes to "aggressive tendencies." In one recent study, however, it was concluded, on the basis of a careful analysis of the records, that, although XYY males do have a higher rate of criminal convictions, the crimes generally are not acts of aggression against other individuals. Males with an XYY genotype are usually tall and score lower than average on intelligence tests.

Embryology (Fig. 513)

In its broadest terms, the science of embryology deals with the study of the embryo (a term denoting the juvenile stage of an animal while it is contained within the maternal body). However, in humans many call the developing young an embryo until organogenesis is completed at 12 to 14 weeks; others call it an embryo until 20 weeks or 1000 gm weight is reached. After that time and until birth it is referred to as the fetus.

Cleavage. Immediately following fertilization, the zygote begins to undergo rapid cell division, or mitosis. First two, four, then eight cells and so forth are formed, each containing 46 chromosomes. The 16-cell stage is reached about 96 hours after ovulation. This process of cell division is called cleavage.

At first the cells, called **blastomeres,** form a solid sphere; the cell mass is known as the **morula.** Successive cleavages produce cells of smaller size, so that the developing morula is only a little larger than the original zygote. As the cells of the morula continue to multiply, they form a hollow ball of cells known as the **blastocyst.** Differentiation of these cells continues to take place, forming one group of cells lying externally, known as the *trophoderm,* and the others internally, forming the *ectoderm* and *endoderm.* Hollow spheres begin to appear on either side of the ectoderm and endoderm which remain in contact with each other; it is in the region of attachment of these two layers, now called the *embryonic disc,* that the future embryo will develop. A third layer of cells, the *mesoderm*, begins to develop and spread out between the ectoderm and endoderm. Specific tissues will be derived from these three primary germ layers. The ectoderm devel-

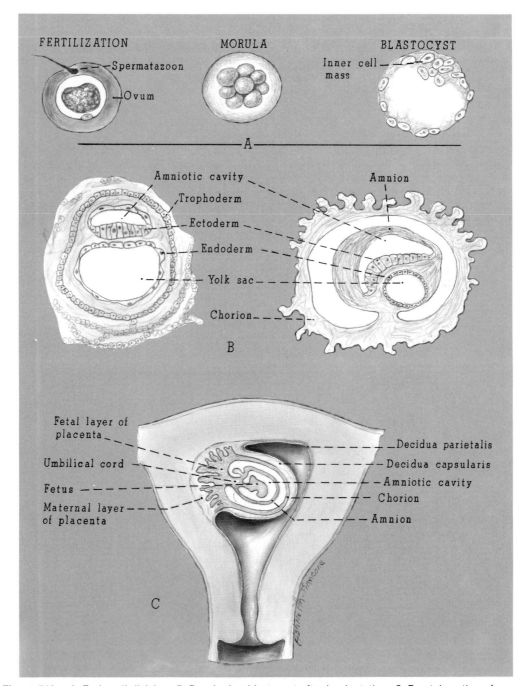

Figure 513.   *A*, Early cell division, *B*, Developing blastocyst after implantation. *C*, Frontal section of pregnant uterus showing fetal membranes.

ops into the epidermis and its appendages (nails, hair, etc.) and the tissues of the nervous system. The connective tissues, muscle tissues, bone tissues and tissues of the vascular and lymphatic systems are derived from the mesoderm. The epithelial lining of the digestive tract and its derivatives develop from the endoderm. Further details of the embryology of the various systems of the body are beyond the scope of this book.

Twinning.   Identical twins are the result of a division of a single fertilized ovum into two masses, each becoming a separate embryo. If the division occurs at the two-celled stage, each embryo can have separate membranes. If division does not occur until the formation of the inner cell mass, then both embryos usually have a single placenta. This is known as *monovular twinning. Binovular twinning* follows fertilization of two separate ova, resulting in fraternal twins. Both shed at approximately the same time, and each developing individual has his own membranes and placenta.

Implantation.   Six to eight days after fertilization, the *blastocyst,* having traveled down the uterine tube, enters the uterus and becomes embedded in the endometrium on the posterior wall of the fundus. This process is called *implantation.* The

lining of the uterus has been thickened in preparation for about 3 weeks. The trophoderm burrows into the endometrial lining and carves out a nest for the blastocyst, which then sinks into the underlying connective tissue. The uterine vessels and glands in the penetrated area disrupt; the fluid thus formed furnishes nourishment for the implanted blastocyst. The epithelium heals over, and the embryo develops within the tissues of the uterine wall — not in the cavity, as occurs in most lower animals. This connective tissue in which the embryo rests is called the *decidua basalis,* and the mucosa covering it, the *decidua capsularis.* These tissues will be described subsequently in relation to the formation of the placenta.

PREGNANCY

Fetal Membranes and the Placenta of Pregnancy

Immediately following implantation, the embryo with its fetal membranes, together with the well-prepared uterine endometrial lining, begins formation of the placenta, which functions in the exchange of gaseous, nutritive, and excretory products between fetal and maternal systems. The definitive

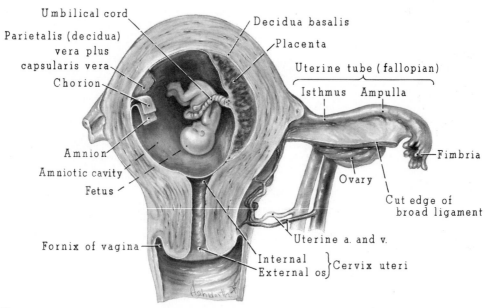

Figure 514.   Frontal section of pregnant uterus showing associated structures and fetal membranes.

placenta consists of two layers of fetal membranes, the amnion and chorion. The endometrial lining of the mother has been modified by continued progesterone production and is now called the decidua (Fig. 514).

Amnion. The amnion is derived from the inner layer of the trophoderm reinforced by mesodermal cells. It appears at an early stage as a small sac with an amniotic cavity covering the dorsal surface of the embryo. The amnion gradually enlarges to completely surround the embryo, coming into apposition with the inner surface of the chorion. The amniotic cavity is filled with amniotic fluid bathing the embryo. This serves to cushion the fetus against possible injury, to maintain the constancy of its temperature, and to furnish a medium in which the developing individual can readily move.

Chorion. The chorion is the outermost covering of the growing embryo, which provides nourishment and protection. The embryo is connected with the connective tissue layer of the chorion by the forerunner of the umbilical cord, and in it the fetal blood vessels develop.

The Decidua. The decidua is the mucous membrane of the uterus that has undergone certain changes under the influence of progesterone to prepare it for implantation and nutrition of the ovum. It is usually divided into three parts: the *decidua basalis,* that portion beneath the embryo between the chorionic vesicle and the myometrium of the uterus; the *decidua capsularis,* a thin layer of endometrium covering the embryo, which expands as the embryo grows, obliterating the uterine lumen; and the *decidua parietalis,* the remaining part of the uterine endometrium.

By the third month of pregnancy, the placenta is completely formed by the infiltration of the villi of the chorion into the decidua basalis. These villi enlarge, multiply, and branch to the point that each is bathed in a pool of maternal blood.

Actually, there is no exchange of blood between the fetal and maternal portions of the placenta. The maternal placenta receives its blood from the uterine arteries, and blood is returned by way of the uterine veins. The fetal placenta is bathed in maternal blood and receives nutrients ingested by the mother by diffusion through the villi. Oxygen from the mother's blood also diffuses into the blood of the fetus. The waste products diffuse from the fetal blood and are eliminated by the excretory organs of the mother. Thus, the placenta forms the only means by which the nutritional, respiratory, and excretory functions of the fetus are possible.

Functions of Placenta. The placenta also serves as an effective barrier against diseases of bacterial origin; however, viruses and some blood-borne diseases such as syphilis affect the fetus. Antibodies are transmitted by the mother to the developing embryo and fetus to build up immunity

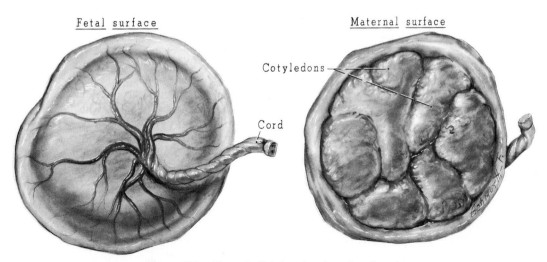

Fetal surface   Maternal surface

Cotyledons

Cord

Figure 515. Placenta (fetal and maternal surfaces).

against various diseases. (For discussion of the Rh factor, see Chapter 10.) This immunity is necessary during the first few months of life before the time when the infant can produce its own antibodies.

The mature placenta is a circular disc 8 inches in diameter and nearly 1 inch in thickness, weighing approximately 1 pound. The fetal surface is smooth and glistening, beneath which can be seen many large vessels. The maternal surface is red and fleshlike. At delivery, after the fetus is born, the placenta becomes detached from the uterus and is the "afterbirth" (Fig. 515).

Disorders of Pregnancy

Abortion is any interruption of pregnancy prior to the period when the fetus is viable. Abortion can be either spontaneous or induced. The fetus is considered viable when it weighs 500 grams or more and the pregnancy is over 20 weeks in duration. When infection occurs, the process is known as a septic abortion. Women who abort repeatedly are said to be habitual abortors. To the laity the term *miscarriage* merely means a spontaneous interruption of pregnancy — as distinguished from *abortion*, which the lay individual infers as a deliberate emptying of the uterus. This is a misconception; miscarriage is not a correct medical term. Abortion is, as we have seen, any interruption of pregnancy prior to the period when the fetus is viable.

Ectopic Pregnancy. Occasionally the fertilized ovum becomes implanted in the uterine tube, a serious condition known as an *ectopic pregnancy.* Ectopic pregnancy includes all cases in which the fertilized ovum becomes implanted at a site other than the decidua of the normal uterine cavity. The most common site for this to occur is the uterine tube, but there are also other regions, such as the ovary, cervix, broad ligament, and peritoneal cavity. The uterine tube must either expel the ovum from its implantation cavity in the tubal mucosa into its lumen (tubal abortion), or the tube must give way (tubal rupture). This mishap frequently occurs before the embryo reaches the age of 6 weeks; it endangers the life of the mother.

Laboratory Diagnosis of Pregnancy

Early diagnosis of pregnancy has recently concentrated on tests based on the presence or absence of a substance peculiar to the pregnant state, human chorionic gonadotrophic hormone, HCG.

To date, one of the most widely used tests has been to inject mice subcutaneously with acidified urine from the patient and on the fifth day examine the ovaries of the mouse for the presence of corpora hemorrhagica or corpora lutea, a positive sign that HCG is present and the patient is pregnant. The accuracy of this test has been relatively good, although it is time consuming and expensive.

Pregna-test involves gently heating a piece of pregna-test paper with acidified urine in a test tube and observing any color change.

Other tests that have been devised recently are based on the immunological response of blood cells or latex particles coated with HCG. In the *Ortho* test latex particles sensitized with HCG are added to a sample of urine. If the mixture remains cloudy the particles are still in suspension, i.e., no reaction has occurred between the HCG in the urine and the HCG-sensitized particles, the test is positive. If, however, visible agglutination with settling of the particles occurs in the test tube, this is an indication that there is no HCG present in the urine and antibodies remain free to bind with the HCG-sensitized particles.

Another simpler test based on this theory is the "Gravindex." For this test antiserum is mixed on a glass slide with urine. If visible agglutination occurs within a few minutes, the results are interpreted as negative. The absence of agglutination indicates a positive test.

All of these tests are used with varying degrees of accuracy and, although none are completely dependable, they promise to be more efficient and less expensive than previous tests, such as those dependent on the mouse.

Calculation of Term

On the assumption that the gestation period totals 280 days from the beginning of

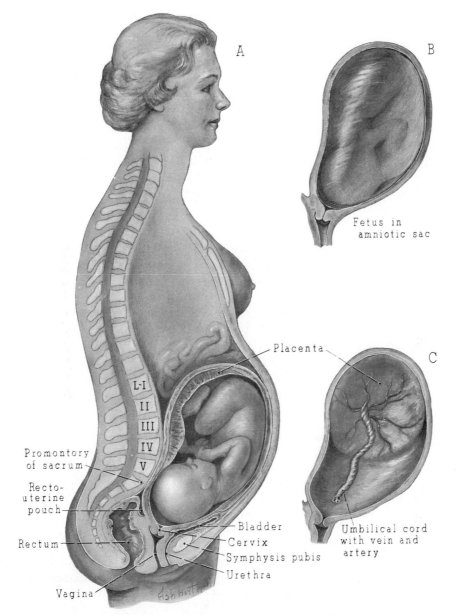

Figure 516. *A*, Mid-sagittal section of a pregnant woman showing fetal position. *B*, Amniotic sac with fetus. *C*, Placenta in uterus with fetus removed.

the last menstrual period, the date of confinement is estimated by adding one year and 7 days to the date of the last menstrual period and subtracting 3 months (Fig. 516).

Labor

The mechanisms involved in the onset of labor are complex and poorly understood. It is certain that labor is not initiated by a single event; it must be regarded as a consequence of many developments occurring during the course of gestation. The uterus is relatively quiescent during gestation, but, as labor approaches, there are signs of increasing myometrial irritability. There is also increased sensitivity of the uterine musculature to oxytocin, in preparation for the forceful muscular contractions required to expel the fetus.

The hormones generated from the placenta and ovaries are known to play key roles in determining the onset of labor. Progesterone exerts a pregnancy-stabilizing effect. Labor cannot occur until its influence is effectively diminished. Estrogens promote rhythmic contractility of the uterus. It is probably significant that estrogen increases in amount until the end of gestation, when secretion diminishes.

Oxytocin from the neurohypophysis is known to exert a powerful effect on uterine contractility. Relaxin acts to relax the liga-mentous structures. Without proper hormonal balance and timing, labor would not occur, or the fetus and mother would be injured. For example, it is well known that labor may be precipitated by administering large doses of oxytocin; however, if the cervical canal is not softened and the pubic ligaments not relaxed by the action of relaxin, violent uterine contractions would kill the fetus and rupture the uterus instead of expelling it through the vagina.

The stages of labor are conveniently described in three phases (Fig. 517). In the

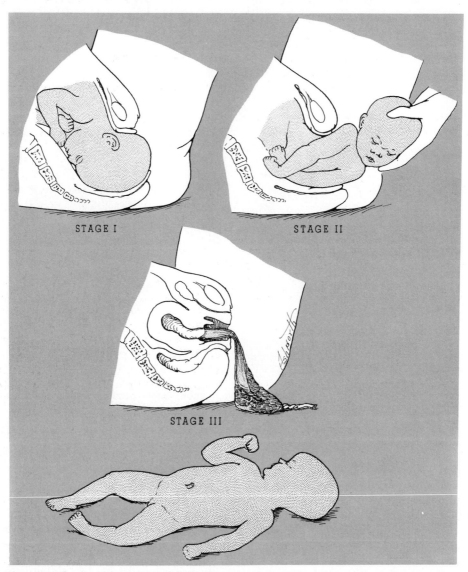

STAGE I

STAGE II

STAGE III

Figure 517.   The stages of labor can be described as follows. The first stage is characterized by regular contractions, rupture of the membranes and complete dilatation; the second stage extends from the time of complete cervical dilatation to delivery; during the third stage the "afterbirth" is delivered.

first stage, there are regular contractions, rupture of the membranes, and complete dilatation. The obstetrician follows the course of labor by frequent rectal examinations. Complete dilatation of the cervix is synonymous with the cervical dilatation of 10 cm. The second stage extends from the time of complete cervical dilatation to delivery. In the third stage, the "afterbirth" is delivered.

A dependable sign of impending labor is the so-called "show." This is the vaginal discharge of a small amount of blood-tinged mucus representing the extrusion of mucous blood which has filled the cervical canal during pregnancy. It is a late sign, and labor usually ensues within 24 hours. The quantity of blood escaping with the mucus (show) amounts to only a few milliliters. Any substantial loss of blood at this time should be regarded as suggestive of an abnormal condition.

True labor must be distinguished from false labor. In true labor the pains occur at regular intervals; the intervals gradually shorten, and the intensity of pain increases. The pain is located in the back and is intensified by walking. "Show" has occurred and the cervix dilates.

In false labor, pains occur at irregular intervals, the intervals remain long, intensity remains unaltered, pain is located in the abdomen, and walking either has no effect or can relieve the pain. In false labor there is no show, and the cervix remains closed.

Contraception

There are many and varied methods utilized in the prevention of pregnancy. Mechanical means by which contraception is achieved with varying degrees of success include the use of the condom, diaphragm, and, more recently, the intrauterine device (IUD). This latter device is simply a coil or loop placed within the uterus, the function of which is believed to prevent implantation of the fertilized ovum.

Physiologic or chemical means of contraception include the rhythm method, douching, suppositories, foams, and the contraceptive pill.

Oral contraceptives, as mentioned in the discussion of the hormonal interrelations during the menstural cycle, block ovulation and are usually taken for 21 consecutive days of each cycle. The rhythm method is useful only for women with regular periods, whose day of ovulation can be predicted with reasonable confidence. As a rule, ovulation occurs 14 days before the onset of menstruation. Thus, women with 22-, 28- and 34-day cycles will ovulate on the eighth, fourteenth and twentieth day, respectively. An ovum may be fertilized within 24 hours after ovulation, but spermatozoa retain their motility for up to five days; therefore, it is advisable to refrain from intercourse for 6 days before and 3 days after the day of ovulation.

VENEREAL DISEASE

When penicillin was introduced during World War II, it was predicted that the two major venereal diseases, syphilis and gonorrhea, would ultimately be eradicated. This has not occurred. In fact, there has been a worldwide resurgence of venereal disease which can be attributed to ignorance, false confidence, and reticence. Those most likely to be exposed, aged 17 to 35, are either uninformed or misinformed about cause, spread, and detection.

Gonorrhea is an infectious disease chiefly involving the mucous membranes of the genitourinary tract, the rectum, and the cervix. In the male, the typical onset consists of acute anterior urethritis (burning on urination). In the adult female, primary infection of the urethra, the cervix, or Bartholin's glands is usual. In many women, purulent discharge is present at the urethral meatus. Penicillin is the preferred drug.

Syphilis is a disease with an early infectious phase and a late chronic tendency. It is caused by a motile spirochete and is acquired through sexual contact. Syphilis is divided into three stages: primary, secondary, and tertiary. Primary syphilis is diagnosed by finding the primary chancre at the inoculation site. Primary lesions generally develop within 3 weeks after infection; the incubation period varies from 10 to 90 days. Chancres occur most commonly in the genital area, but extragenital involvement, such as of the rectum or lips, has been reported.

In secondary syphilis the manifestations appear 6 to 8 weeks after the chancre and remain for 2 to 6 weeks. Secondary syphilis is characterized by a generalized papulosquamous eruption including the palms and soles. Penicillin is considered the treatment of choice.

Tertiary syphilis is involvement found after the secondary phase. Many internal organs, including the brain and spinal cord, are involved. Treatment is not satisfactory, pointing up the importance of early therapy.

Herpes progenitalis is manifested by "cold sore"-like lesions around the male and female genital organs. It is caused by a virus and spread by sexual contact. Treatment, to date, has not been effective.

SUMMARY

THE REPRODUCTIVE SYSTEM

Male Reproductive System

1. **External Organs**
   a. Scrotum: pouch supporting testes.
   b. Penis: male organ of copulation; it contains three columns of erectile tissue—two lateral (corpora cavernosa penis), one medial (corpus cavernosum urethrae, or corpus spongiosum).
   c. Congenital abnormalities of penis: hypospadias and epispadias.
   d. Clinical consideration of penis: circumcision and phimosis.

2. **Internal Organs of the Male Reproductive Tract**
   a. Male gonads: testes
      (1) Structure and location: 250 wedge-shaped lobes containing coiled seminiferous tubules.
      (2) Contains reproductive cells and supportive (Sertoli's) cells inside tubules, as well as interstitial cells between tubules.
      (3) Congenital defect: cryptorchism.
   b. Series of ducts
      (1) Epididymis: a coiled tube lying on posterior aspect of testis.
      (2) Ductus deferens: continuous with epididymis and joins duct of seminal vesicle to form ejaculatory duct.
      (3) Ejaculatory duct: tube for depositing semen into urethra.
      (4) Urethra: transmits semen and urine.
   c. Accessory glands adding secretions to semen
      (1) Seminal vesicles: membranous pouches lying posterior to the bladder; secretes thick, nutrient-containing fluid.
      (2) Prostate gland: surrounds first part of urethra; secretes a thin, milky, alkaline fluid.
      (3) Bulbo-urethral glands: located below prostate; discharge lubricating mucous secretion prior to ejaculation.

Female Reproductive System

1. **External Organs: Vulva**
   a. Mons pubis: adipose tissue over symphysis pubis.
   b. Labia majora: rounded folds of adipose tissue extending downward from mons pubis to encircle vestibule; homologous to scrotum.
   c. Labia minora: two smaller, medial folds surrounding vestibule.
   d. Clitoris: a small projection of erectile tissue anterior to vagina; homologous to penis.
   e. Vestibule: region between labia minora containing the vaginal orifice and urethral orifice. Greater vestibular glands are adjacent to vaginal orifice.
   f. Hymen: mucous membrane separating vagina from vestibule; can be present or absent in virginity.

2. **Internal Organs**
   a. Vagina: tubular canal
      (1) Structure: three layers.
      (2) Location: between bladder and rectum.
      (3) Function: forms part of birth canal and represents female organ of copulation; capable of constriction and enormous dilatation.
   b. Uterus
      (1) Location: between bladder and rectum.

(2) Consists of three parts: cervix, corpus and fundus.

(3) Supporting ligaments

(a) *Cardinal ligaments: principal support of uterus.*

(b) *Broad ligaments: to both sides of pelvic cavity.*

(c) *Round ligaments: hold uterus in forward, tilted position.*

(d) *Uterosacral ligaments: help support and maintain position of uterus.*

(4) Wall of uterus: divided into three layers

(a) *Outer serous layer of peritoneum.*

(b) *Middle muscular layer, myometrium, divided into three ill-defined, intertwining layers, the middle of which is thickened and contains large blood vessels.*

(c) *Inner mucous layer, endometrium, subject to regulation by ovarian hormones and responsible for menstruation and implantation; superficial layer sloughs during menstruation.*

c. Uterine tubes: pair of flexible muscular tubes

(1) Location: extend from upper angle of uterus on either side toward sides of pelvis.

(2) Attachment: suspended by peritoneal fold, the mesosalpinx.

(3) Structure: three layers, mucous, smooth muscle, and serous; mucous layer is lined with ciliated epithelium.

(4) Infundibula with fimbriae open into abdominal cavity.

(5) Function: to convey ovum to uterus by muscular contraction and ciliary action. Fertilization takes place in uterine tube.

d. Ovaries: primary reproductive organs of female

(1) Location: in upper part of pelvic cavity.

(2) Attachment: each suspended from broad ligament by peritoneal fold, mesovarium; anchored to uterus by ovarian ligament.

3. Mammary Glands

a. Location: anterior to pectoral muscles of chest.

b. Structure: convex structure of adipose tissue and ducts

(1) Nipple surrounded by circular area of pigmented skin (areola).

(2) Fifteen to 20 lobes arranged radially within breasts, embedded in fat and connective tissue.

(3) Each lobe has its alveoli and own excretory duct (lactiferous duct).

c. Further development after puberty

(1) Growth and branching of duct system.

(2) Intensive deposition of fat.

(3) Fluctuation of breast size correlates with reproductive cycle.

(4) After menopause breast tissue atrophies and becomes less prominent.

d. Physiology of mammary glands

(1) In development to functional state prolactin, estrogens, and progesterone are important.

(a) *Estrogens stimulate development of ducts.*

(b) *Progesterone influences growth of alveoli.*

(c) *Cyclic changes during menstrual cycle are associated with rise and fall of hormones.*

(d) *During pregnancy alterations more marked than premenstrual changes.*

(2) Factors controlling lactation and milk secretion

(a) *Lactation initiated by prolactin from adenohypophysis.*

(b) *Suckling stimulus responsible for milk secretion. Stimulus is carried through hypothalamus and neurohypophysis to release oxytocin. Failure of ejection reflex leads to failure in lactation.*

Spermatogenesis: Production of Spermatozoa

1. Formation of primary spermatocyte from spermatogonia.

2. Formation from each spermatocyte of two secondary spermatocytes in first meiotic division and four haploid spermatids in second meiotic division.

3. Differentiation of spermatids into spermatozoa.

Oogenesis and Ovulation

1. Ova produced during reproductive life of female derived from primary oocytes present at birth.

2. About 400,000 primary follicles (each a primary oocyte surrounded by a layer of granulosa cells) are present in ovaries at the onset of the reproductive life of the female.

3. Meiotic divisions occur with unequal distribution of cytoplasm, forming one large, mature ovum and nonfunctional polar bodies.

4. FSH initiates follicle maturation; first meiotic division occurs prior to ovulation.

5. Ovulation triggered by sharp rise in LH blood levels.

Fertilization

1. Transportation of ovum: peristalsis and ciliary flagellation.

2. Site of fertilization: one-third of the way down uterine tube.

3. Penetration of ovum (actually secondary oocyte) by spermatozoon initiates second meiotic division.

4. Union of male and female pronuclei forms diploid zygote.

Menstrual Cycle and Menopause

1. Menstrual cycle normally requires 28 days, and three phases are distinguished:

    a. Menstrual—day 1 to 5: sloughing of superficial endometrium.
    b. Proliferative (characterized by estrogen stimulation)—day 5 to 14: rebuilding of endometrium.
    c. Secretory (characterized by progesterone stimulation)—day 14 to 28: preparation for implantation.

2. Menstrual problems

    a. Amenorrhea: absence of menses.
    b. Dysmenorrhea: menstrual pain.

3. Menopause, permanent cessation of menstrual activity, usually occurs between ages 45 and 55, when almost all primary follicles have matured or degenerated. Its chief symptoms are:

    a. Flushes over head, neck, and upper thorax, usually lasting hours.
    b. Flashes—brief suffusions of heat over entire body, accompanied by sweating.

Hormonal Interrelations During Menstrual Cycle

1. Rise in FSH and LH at end of cycle follows decline in estrogen and progesterone blood levels (release from negative feedback inhibition).

2. Steep rise in estrogen secretion by maturing follicle causes surge in gonadotropin secretion, especially LH (in part due to increased sensitivity of adenohypophysis to gonadotropin-releasing factors).

3. LH induces ovulation.

4. Corpus luteum secretes progesterone and estrogens.

5. Rise in concentration of progesterone and estrogens causes fall in LH and FSH secretion (negative feedback inhibition).

6. Fall in LH causes regression of corpus luteum and decline in progesterone and estrogen blood levels.

7. Pronounced inhibition of LH secretion by progesterone utilized in birth control pills to block ovulation.

Functions of Testosterone (Principal Androgen, Secreted by Interstitial Cells of Leydig)

1. Induces sexual differentiation during embryological development.

2. Stimulates growth of genitalia and appearance of secondary sex characteristics at puberty.

3. Promotes protein anabolism.

4. Accelerates deposition of bone matrix.

Functions of Estrogens (Secreted by Ovarian Follicle, Corpus Luteum and, During Pregnancy, Placenta)

1. Stimulate growth of uterus and vagina and development of secondary sex characteristics at puberty.

2. Induce repair of endometrium following menstruation.

3. Promote growth of duct system of mammary glands.

4. Increase motility of uterus and its sensitivity to oxytocin.

5. Accelerate matrix formation in bone.

Functions of Progesterone (Secreted by Corpus Luteum and, During Pregnancy, by Placenta)

1. During the postovulatory period converts partially thickened uterine endometrium to a secretory structure suitable for implantation.

2. Promotes growth of mammary gland alveoli.

3. Decreases motility of the uterus.

Cleavage: Cell Division of an Embryo

1. Morula stage with blastomeres.

2. Blastocyst: a hollow ball of cells with a thin layer of trophoderm.

3. Implantation at blastocyst stage.

4. Twinning

    a. Monovular twinning: identical twins — division of a single fertilized ovum into two masses.

    b. Binovular twinning: fertilization of two separate ova, giving rise to fraternal twins.

Embryology: Science Dealing with the Developing Embryo

Three germ layers develop in the embryo, from which specific tissues are eventually derived:

1. Ectoderm: epidermis and tissues of the nervous system

2. Mesoderm: connective and muscular tissue.

3. Endoderm: lining of the digestive tract and its derivatives.

Placenta

1. Formed about the third month of pregnancy by infiltration of villi of chorion into the decidua basalis of the uterus.

2. Functions

    a. Exchange of food, gas, and waste products without actual exchange of blood.

    b. Effective barrier against bacteria.

    c. Transmission of antibodies.

    d. Production of estrogens and progesterone.

Labor

1. Increased sensitivity of uterine musculature.

2. Progesterone exerts a stabilizing effect.

3. Estrogens and oxytocin increase uterine contraction.

4. Balance of the above factors brings about labor and parturition.

5. Three stages of labor: period of dilatation, complete cervical dilatation to delivery, and delivery of "afterbirth."

6. Show: vaginal discharge of blood-tinged mucus.

7. True labor: pains at regular intervals, intervals shorten, pain increases, pain in back, and show.

8. False labor: no show, pains at irregular intervals, pain located in abdomen, and cervix closed.

appendix A

Basic Chemistry

ATOMIC STRUCTURE OF THE ELEMENTS

All matter is composed of entities called **elements**. There are 92 naturally occurring elements, and each is designated by one or two letters of its name. Thus, the symbols for carbon, oxygen, hydrogen, and nitrogen are C, O, H, and N, respectively. The symbol for chlorine is Cl; for sodium, Na (*natrium* is the Latin word for sodium); and for potassium, K (*kalium* is the Latin word for potassium).

Each element is composed of individual units of matter called **atoms**. Any quantity of an element contains identical atoms, and one element is distinguished from another by the nature of its atoms. All atoms consist of a dense inner core, or **nucleus**, containing positively charged particles called **protons** and neutral particles called **neutrons**, surrounded by orbiting negatively charged particles called **electrons**. Electrons occupy most of the space of an atom, but essentially all of the atom's mass is concentrated in the nucleus. Both protons and neutrons have masses of approximately 1 (a relative unit based on a scale in which carbon is assigned a value of 12), and the sum of the number of protons and neutrons of an atom is its mass number, or **atomic weight**.

Protons bear a charge of $+1$, electrons of -1. The number of protons in an atom, called the **atomic number**, is its unique identifying characteristic. It determines the number of planetary electrons (equal to the number of protons) and the chemical properties of the element. The atomic weight of an element, on the other hand, may vary. Most oxygen atoms, for example, contain 8 protons and 8 neutrons, and have an atomic weight of 16. A small proportion, however, have 9 or 10 neutrons and atomic weights of 17 and 18, respectively. Such different forms of an element are called **isotopes**. The isotopes of oxygen may be written $_8O^{16}$, $_8O^{17}$ and $_8O^{18}$ (or, more simply, without the subscript). One of the isotopes of carbon, $_6C^{14}$, is *radioactive*; that is, it is unstable and the nucleus emits radiations that result in the transformation of carbon 14 into the stable configuration of nitrogen ($_7N^{14}$).

The motions of electrons do not follow fixed paths, but can be described in terms of probable positions called **orbitals**. Each orbital represents not only spatial orientations of electrons but also a unique energy state. Orbitals are, in turn, subdivisions of what are known as *energy levels,* formed by groups of orbitals.

The atoms of each element have specific *electron configurations* representing the number of electrons in specific orbitals (each designated by a specific letter) in each energy level. For our purposes, the important consideration is the number of electrons in orbitals designated by the letters s and p, because the number of electrons in these two orbitals of the outermost energy level determines the combining property of an element. This is so because *atoms tend to form combinations that fill the outer s and p orbitals* to their capacities (the s and p orbitals, filled to capacity, contain 2 and 6 electrons, respectively).

THE COVALENT BOND

Tabulated below are the electron configurations of hydrogen, carbon, nitrogen, and oxygen, the most abundant elements in living matter.

Energy level	1	2	
Orbital	s	s	p
Hydrogen	1		
Carbon	2	2	2
Nitrogen	2	2	3
Oxygen	2	2	4

Note that carbon, nitrogen, and oxygen need 4, 3, and 2 electrons, respectively, to fill their outer s and p orbitals with a total of 8 electrons and that hydrogen lacks one electron in its s orbital. These orbitals can be filled by *electron sharing*. For example, in the methane molecule (CH_4) a carbon atom shares each of its outer s and p orbital electrons with a different hydrogen atom, completing the s orbitals of the four hydrogen atoms and in turn filling its own s and p orbitals by sharing their electrons. In a molecule of ammonia (NH_3), a nitrogen atom shares each of its outer p orbital electrons with a hydrogen atom. In the oxygen molecule (O_2), each oxygen atom shares two of its four outer p orbital electrons with the other. A hydrogen molecule consists of two hydrogen atoms sharing a pair of s orbital electrons.

The joining of two atoms by sharing electrons is known as a **covalent bond.** Sharing one pair of electrons is called a *single bond,* and is generally represented by a dash drawn between the two atoms. Two dashes drawn between two atoms signify a *double bond,* or two pairs of shared electrons; three dashes indicate a *triple bond,* or three pairs of shared electrons. In the illustrations below, on the left ammonia, acetaldehyde, and ethyl alcohol are drawn with dashes to show the bonding arrangements. To the right of each, all of the outer s and p orbital electrons, shared and unshared, are represented by dots.

$$
\begin{array}{cc}
\begin{array}{c} H \\ | \\ H{-}N \\ | \\ H \end{array}
&
\begin{array}{c} H \\ H:N: \\ \;\; \cdot\cdot \\ H \end{array}
\end{array}
$$

Ammonia

$$
\begin{array}{cc}
\begin{array}{c} H\;\;O \\ |\;\;\| \\ H{-}C{-}C{-}H \\ | \\ H \end{array}
&
\begin{array}{c} H:O: \\ \;\;\cdot\cdot\;\cdot\cdot \\ H:C:C:H \\ \;\;\cdot\cdot \\ H \end{array}
\end{array}
$$

Acetaldehyde

$$
\begin{array}{cc}
\begin{array}{c} H\;\;H \\ |\;\;| \\ H{-}C{-}C{-}O{-}H \\ |\;\;| \\ H\;\;H \end{array}
&
\begin{array}{c} H\;\;H \\ \cdot\cdot\;\;\cdot\cdot\;\;\cdot\cdot \\ H:C:C:O:H \\ \cdot\cdot\;\;\cdot\cdot\;\;\cdot\cdot \\ H\;\;H \end{array}
\end{array}
$$

Ethyl alcohol

It should be apparent that hydrogen, oxygen, nitrogen, and carbon form 1, 2, 3, and 4 covalent bonds, respectively, and that, when these bonds are formed, the outer s and p orbitals of the carbon, nitrogen, and oxygen atoms are filled with 8 electrons and the s orbital of each hydrogen atom is completed with 2 electrons. The term used to indicate the bonding capacity of any element is **valence.** Hence, the valence of hydrogen is 1, oxygen 2, nitrogen 3, and carbon 4.

Another way atoms achieve the state of completed outer s and p orbitals is by *giving up or accepting electrons.* Tabulated below are the electron configurations of the sodium and chlorine atoms.

Energy level	1	2		3		
Orbital	s	s	p	s	p	d
Sodium	2	2	6	1		
Chlorine	2	2	6	2	5	

When sodium combines with chlorine to form sodium chloride, the single electron in sodium's third energy level is transferred to chlorine. As a result, both atoms have 8 electrons in their outermost s and p orbitals. Such a union between atoms involving electron transfer is called an **ionic bond.** When sodium chloride is dissolved in water, it dissociates, but the transferred electron remains with chlorine. As a result, *sodium ions*, bearing a charge of $+1$, and *chloride ions*, bearing a charge of -1, are released into the solution.

MOLECULES AND MOLES

In the foregoing discussion we have used the term molecule for the stable combination of 2 atoms of hydrogen, 2 atoms of oxygen, and the combinations of atoms in methane, acetaldehyde, and ethyl alcohol. Any stable combination of atoms, then, is a *molecule*. When we wrote ammonia as NH_3 and methane as CH_4, these were their *molecular formulas*. The molecular formula of glucose is $C_6H_{12}O_6$. If we add up the weight in grams of all of the atoms in glucose, we have its *molecular weight*: $6(12) + 12(1) + 6(16)$, or 180, grams. The number of grams equal to the molecular weight of a molecule represents 1 **mole** of that molecule. Thus, 1 mole of glucose contains 180 grams of glucose.

CONDENSATION REACTIONS AND HYDROLYSIS

In many of the synthetic reactions carried out by the body's cells, the joining together of two molecules involves the removal of a molecule of water (H_2O) between them. Such a reaction is called a **condensation reaction.** Some examples are (1) linking glucose molecules to form the polysaccharide glycogen by splitting out a water molecule between the hydroxyl (OH) groups of two glucose molecules, (2) combining long-chain fatty acids with glycerol (to form fat) or with cholesterol with the removal of a water molecule between the carboxyl (COOH) groups of the fatty acids and the hydroxyl groups of glycerol or cholesterol (bonds formed by this type of reaction are called **ester bonds**), and (3) synthesis of proteins by the formation of **peptide bonds** between amino acids, in which a water molecule is eliminated between the amine group (NH_2) of one amino acid and the carboxyl group of another. The formation of peptide and ester bonds is illustrated in Figure 518.

When proteins, lipids, and glycogen are degraded into their constituents, linked together by condensation reactions, water is added in a reverse reaction called **hydrolysis.**

pH

pH is a convenient expression of the hydrogen ion concentration of a solution. Pure water dissociates very slightly, releasing hydrogen (H^+) and hydroxyl (OH^-) ions. The concentration of each of these ions in pure water is 10^{-7} (.0000001) mole per liter. If an *acid,* a substance that dissociates to form hydrogen ions, is added to water, the concentration of hydrogen ions increases and the concentration of hydroxyl ions decreases (the product of the two remains 10^{-14}). If a *base,* a substance that combines with hydrogen ions, is added to water, the reverse occurs.

pH is defined as the *negative logarithm of the hydrogen ion concentration.* The logarithm of 10^{-7} is -7; the negative logarithm is 7. Hence, the pH of pure water is 7. This is the neutral condition. If, by the addition of acid to water, the hydrogen ion concentration is increased from 10^{-7} to 10^{-4} mole per liter, the pH of the solution will be reduced to 4. If, by the addition of a base, the hydrogen ion concentration is lowered to 10^{-10}, the pH of the solution will be raised to 10. The pH of an acidic solution, then, is less than 7, of a basic solution, greater than 7.

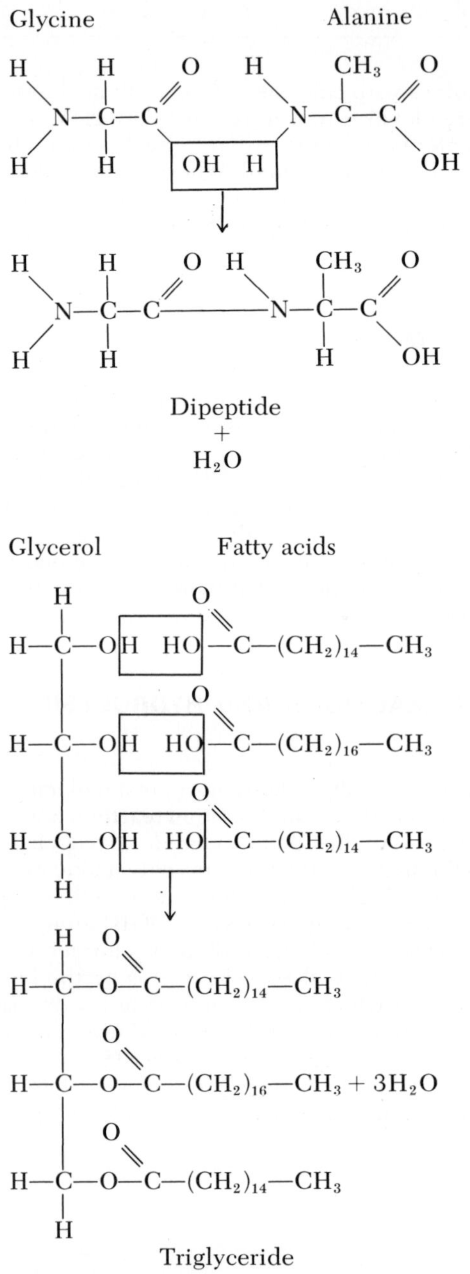

Figure 518. Condensation reactions. *Top,* Peptide bond formation between two amino acids. *Bottom,* Formation of ester bonds between glycerol and three fatty acids.

appendix **B**

Prefixes, Suffixes, and Combining Forms

a-, ab-	away from, away	chromo-	color
a-, an-	without, lack, not	circum-	around
ad-	to, toward	-cle	small
adeno-	gland	con-	with, together
adip-	fat	contra-	opposed, against
af-	to	cortic-	rind, bark
-algia	pain	costo-	rib
alve-	trough, channel, cavity	cuti-	skin
amyl-	starch	cyst-	bladder
angi-	vessel	cyt-	cell
ante-	before		
anti-	against	de-	remove, decrease
apo-	away from, detached	derm-	skin
arach-	spider	di-	two
arthro-	joint	dia-	through, between
-ase	enzyme	dis-	denoting separation
auto-	self	dys-	bad, difficult
bi-	two	ecto-	on outside
blast-	bud, germ	ef-	out of
brachi-	arm	-emia	blood
brachy-	short	endo-	within
brady-	slow	entero-	intestine
		epi-	upon, above
calc-	heel, limestone	erythro-	red
carbo-	coal, charcoal	eu-	good, well
cardi-	heart	ex-	out, away from
cephal-	head		
cerebro-	brain	fasc-	band
chole-	bile	-ferent	bear, carry
chondr-	cartilage		

605

galact-	milk	-oid	resembling
gastr-	stomach	-ole	small
-genesis	origination, production	olfact-	to smell
glome-	ball	oligo-	scant, sparse
glosso-	tongue	-oma	tumor, swelling
glyc-	sweet	ophthalmo-	eye
-gnosis	knowledge	-opia	vision
gusta-	to taste	-osis	a condition, a process
gyn-	woman	oss-, ost-	bone
gyr-	ring, circle	ot-, oto-	ear
		ov-	egg
hem-	blood		
hemi-	half	para-	beside, near, beyond
hepat-	liver	patho-	disease
hetero-	varied, unlike, different	peri-	around
homeo-	alike	pes-, ped-, pod-	foot
homo-	same	phago-	eat
hydro-	water	phlebo-	vein
hyper-	above, excess	-pnea	breathing
hypo-	below, deficient	pneum-	air
hystero-	uterus	poly-	many
		post-	behind, after
in-	into, not	pre-	before, in front of
infra-	below, under	pro-	before, giving rise to
insul-	island	psycho-	mind
inter-	between	pulmo-	lung
intra-	within		
iso-	equal, like	reti-	network
-itis	inflammation	retro-	backward, behind
		rhin-	nose
juxta-	next to	-rrhea	flow
kerat-	horn	sarc-	flesh
		scler-	hard
labi-	lip	semi-	half
leuk-	white	sept-	fence, wall off
lip-	fat	soma-, -some	body
-lysis	dissolving, destruction, separation	sperma-	seed
		sub-	below
macro-	large	super-	above, upon, excessive
mal-	bad	supra-	above, upon
mega- megalo-	large, great	syn-	with, together
melan-	black	tachy-	swift
mening-	membrane	thrombo-	clot, lump
mens-	month	trans-	across
meso-	middle	tri-	three
mono-	one, single	-trophe	nourishment
morpho-	shape, form		
myo-	muscle	-ule	small
		ultra-	beyond, excess
necro-	dead	uni-	one
nephr-	kidney		
neuro-	nerve	vas-, vaso-	vessel

appendix **C**

Metric Units and U.S. Equivalents

Nomenclature for Metric Units

m = *milli* = 0.001 = 10^{-3} meter or gram or liter (thousandth)
μ = *micro* = 0.000,001 = 10^{-6} meter or gram or liter (millionth)
n = *nano* = 0.000,000,001 = 10^{-9} meter or gram or liter (billionth)
p = *pico* = 0.000,000,000,001 = 10^{-12} meter or gram or liter (trillionth)
For example:
mm = millimeter = 10^{-3} meter (=10^7 Å)
μm = micrometer = 10^{-6} meter (also, μ = micron)
nm = nanometer = 10^{-9} meter (also, millimicron = mμ)
Å = angstrom = 10^{-10} meter (= 0.1 nm; 10 Å = 1 nm)
pm = picometer = 10^{-12} meter
pg = picogram = 10^{-12} g
ppm = μg/cc (ml); μg/g

Linear Measure

1 centimeter (cm) = 0.3937 inch
1 inch = 2.54 cm
1 meter (m) = 39.37 inches

Weights

1 gram (g) = 0.03527 ounce
1 ounce = 28.3495 grams
1 kilogram (kg) = 2.2046 pounds
1 pound = 0.4536 kilogram

Liquid Measure

1 liter (l) = 1.0567 quarts
1 quart = 0.9464 liter
1 gallon = 3.7856 liters

Temperature

Degrees Celsius (°C) (Centigrade)	Degrees Fahrenheit (°F)
100	212
90	194
80	176
70	158
60	140
50	122
40	104
37	98.6
30	86
20	68
10	50
0	32

$$°C = 5/9 \ (°F - 32)$$
$$°F = (9/5 \ °C) + 32$$

Suggested Additional Reading

THE CELL

Bretscher, M. S.: Membrane structure: Some general principles. Science 181:622–629, 1973.
Buffaloe, N. D., and Throneberry, J. D.: Concepts of Biology. Englewood Cliffs, N.J., Prentice-Hall, Inc., 1973.
deDuve, C.: The lysosome. Scientific American, May, 1963.
DeRobertis, E. D. P., Saez, F. A., and DeRoberts, E. M. F., Jr.: Cell Biology. 6th Ed., Philadelphia, W. B. Saunders Co., 1975.
Fox, F. C.: The structure of cell membranes. Scientific American, February, 1972.
Kornberg, A.: The synthesis of DNA. Scientific American, October, 1968.
Palade, G.: Intracellular aspects of the process of protein synthesis (Nobel lecture). Science 189:347–357, 1975.
Readings from Scientific American/Facets of Genetics. San Francisco, W. H. Freeman and Company, 1970.
Rothfield, L. I. (Ed.): Structure and Function of Biological Membranes. New York, Academic Press, 1971.
Toner, P. G., and Carr, K. E.: Cell Structure: An Introduction to Biological Electron Microscopy. 2nd Ed. Baltimore, Williams & Wilkins, 1971.

TISSUES

Arey, L. B.: Human Histology. 4th Ed., Philadelphia, W. B. Saunders Co., 1974.
Bloom, W., and Fawcett, D. W.: A Textbook of Histology. 10th Ed., Philadelphia, W. B. Saunders Co., 1975.
Lentz, T. L.: Cell Fine Structure. Philadelphia, W. B. Saunders Co., 1971.
Odland, G., et al.: Human wound repair. J. Cell Biol., 39:135–151, October, 1968.
Tanzer, M. L.: Cross-linking of collagen. Science 180:561–566, 1973.

SKIN

Braverman, I. M.: Skin Signs of Systemic Disease. Philadelphia, W. B. Saunders Co., 1970.
Epstein, E. (Ed.): Skin Surgery. 3rd Ed., Springfield, Charles C Thomas, 1970.
Montagna, W.: Advances in Biology of Skin. (Twelve Volumes.) New York, Appleton-Century Crofts, 1972.
Pillsbury, D. M.: Manual of Dermatology. Philadelphia, W. B. Saunders Co., 1971.
Scheuplein, R. J., et al.: Permeability of the skin. Physiol. Rev. 51:702–747, 1971.
Sundell, B.: Principles of skin grafting in burns, Ann. Chir. Gynaecol. Fenn. 60:5–8, 1971.
Tregear, R.: Physical Functions of Skin. New York, Academic Press, 1966.

THE SKELETAL SYSTEM

Bourne, G. W.: The Biochemistry and Physiology of Bone. 2nd Ed., New York, Academic Press, 1972.
Harris, W. H., and Heaney, R. P.: Skeletal Renewal and Metabolic Bone Disease. Boston, Little, Brown and Co., 1970.
Kolata, G. B.: Vitamin D: Investigations of a new steroid hormone. Science 187:635–636, 1975.
Napier, J.: The antiquity of human walking. Scientific American, April, 1967.
Trueta, J.: Studies of the Development and Decay of the Human Frame, Philadelphia, W. B. Saunders Co., 1968.
Vaughan, J. M.: The Physiology of Bone. Oxford, Clarendon Press, 1970.
Warren, R.: Surgery. Philadelphia, W. B. Saunders Co., 1963, Chapter 13.

THE ARTICULAR SYSTEM

Evans, F. G. (Ed.): Studies in the Anatomy and Function of Bone and Joints. New York, Springer-Verlag, 1966.
Herring, G. M.: The chemical structure of tendon, cartilage, dentin and bone matrix. Clin. Orthop. 60:261–299, 1968.
Larson, C. B., and Gould, M.: Orthopedic Nursing. 8th Ed., St. Louis, C. B. Mosby Co., 1974.

Rancho Los Amigos Hospital Staff Assn.; Bones, Joints and Muscle of the Human Body: A Programmed Text for Physical Therapy Aides. Riverside, N.J., Glencoe Press, 1970.
Ziff, M.: Pathophysiology of rheumatoid arthritis. Fed. Proc. 32:131–133, 1973.

THE MUSCULAR SYSTEM

Basmajian, J. F., and MacConall, M. A.: Muscles and Movements: A Basis for Human Kinesiology. Baltimore, Williams & Wilkins, 1969.
Bendall, J. R.: Muscles, Molecules and Movement. New York, American Elsevier, 1969.
Bethlem, J.: Muscle Pathology. New York, American Elsevier, 1970.
Close, R. I.: Dynamic properties of mammalian skeletal muscles, Physiol. Rev. 52:129–197, 1972.
Cohen, C.: The protein switch of muscle contraction. Scientific American, Nov., 1975.
Hoyle, G.: How is muscle turned on and off? Scientific American, April, 1970.
Huxley, H. E.: The mechanism of muscular contraction. Science 164:1356–1366, 1969.
Laki, K.: Contractible Muscle and Proteins. New York, Marcel Dekker, 1971.
Margaria, R.: The sources of muscular energy. Scientific American, March, 1972.
Podolsky, R. J.: Muscle activation: The current status. Fed. Proc. 34:1374–1378, 1975.

THE NERVOUS SYSTEM

Axelrod, J.: Neurotransmitters. Scientific American, June, 1974.
Barr, M. L.: The Human Nervous System. New York, Harper and Row, 1972.
Easton, T. A.: On the normal use of reflexes. American Scientist 60:591–599, 1972.
Edshage, S.: Peripheral nerve injuries – diagnosis and treatment. New Eng J. Med. 278:1431–1436, June, 1968.
Epstein, B. S.: The Spine, A Radiological Text and Atlas. Philadelphia, Lea and Febiger, 1969.
Geschwind, N.: The organization of language and the brain. Science 170:940–944, 1970.
Geschwind, N.: The apraxias: Neural mechanisms of disorders of learned movement. American Scientist 63:188–195, 1975.
Greenough, W. T.: Experimental modification of the developing brain. American Scientist 63:37–46, 1975.
Hornykiewicz, O.: Parkinson's disease: From brain homogenate to treatment. American Scientist 32:183–190, 1973.
Johnston, R., and Roots, B.: Nerve Membranes, New York, Pergamon Press, 1973.
Lasek, R.: Axonal transport and the use of intracellular markers in neuroanatomical investigations. Fed. Proc. 34:1603–1611, 1975.
Nachmansohn, D.: Proteins in excitable membranes. Science 168:1059–1066, 1970.
Noback, C. R., and Demarest, R. J.: The Nervous System: Introduction and Review. 2nd Ed., New York, McGraw-Hill Book Co., 1977.
Robertson, D. M., and Dinsdale, H. B.: The Nervous System: Structure and Function in Disease. Baltimore, Williams & Wilkins, 1972.
Wallace, P.: Neurochemistry: Unraveling the mechanism of memory. Science 190:1076–1078, 1975.
Wise, C. D., and Steen, L.: Dopamine-B-hydroxylase deficits in the brains of schizophrenic patients. Science 181:344–347, 1974.

SPECIAL SENSES

Barber, G. W.: Physiological chemistry of the eye. Arch. Ophthalmol. 87:72–106, 1972.
Cain, W. S.: Differential sensitivity for smell: "Noise" at the nose. Science 195:796–798, 1976.
Davis, H., and Silverman, S. R.: Hearing and Deafness. New York, Holt, Rinehart and Winston, 1970.
Fisher, K. D., Carr, C. J., Huff, J. E., and Huber, T. E.: Dark adaptation and night vision. Fed. Proc. 29:1605–1638, 1970.
Gordon, B.: The superior colliculus of the brain. Scientific American, Dec., 1972.
Harpen, R.: Human Senses in Action. Baltimore, Williams & Wilkins Co., 1972.
Pettigrew, J. D.: The neurophysiology of binocular vision. Scientific American, Aug., 1972.
Siegel, M.: Optics and visual physiology. Arch. Ophthalmol. 86:100–112, 1971.
Sinclair, J. G.: Reflections on the role of receptor systems for taste and smell. Int. Rev. Neurobiol. 14:159–171, 1971.
Somjen, G. G.: Sensory Coding in the Mammalian Nervous System. New York, Appleton-Century Crofts, 1972.
Wilentz, J. S.: Senses of Man. New York, Apollo Editions, 1971.

THE CIRCULATORY SYSTEM

Adolph, E. F.: The heart's pacemarker. Scientific American, 216:32–37, March, 1967.
Bain, W. H., and Harper, A. M.: Blood Flow Through Organs and Tissues. Baltimore, Williams & Wilkins Co., 1968.
Berne, R. M., and Levy, M. N.: Cardiovascular Physiology. 3rd Ed., St. Louis, C. V. Mosby Co., 1977.
Bocci, V.: Metabolism of plasma proteins. Arch. Fisiol. 67:314–444, 1970.

Henry, J. P., and Meehan, J. P.: Circulation: An Integrative Physiological Study. Chicago, Year Book Medical Publishers, 1971.

Holmes, W. L.: Blood Cells as a Tissue. New York, Plenum Press, 1971.

Kolata, G. B.: Atherosclerotic plaques: Competing theories guide research. Science 194:592–594, 1976.

Maugh, T. H.: Hemoglobin model systems shed light on oxygen binding. Science 187:154–156, 1975.

Mollison, P. L.: Blood Transfusion in Clinical Medicine. Philadelphia, F. A. Davis Co., 1972.

Ratnoff, O. D., and Bennett, B.: The genetics of hereditary disorders of blood coagulation. Science 179:1291–1298, 1973.

Ross, R., and Harker, L.: Hyperlipidemia and atherosclerosis. Science 193:1094–1100, 1976.

Rossi, E. C.: The function of platelets in hemostasis. Med. Clin. North Amer. 56:25–33, 1972.

THE LYMPHATIC SYSTEM

Cooper, M. D., and Lawton, A. R.: The development of the immune system. Scientific American, Nov., 1974.

Elues, M. W.: The Lymphocytes. Chicago, Year Book Medical Publishers, 1972.

Marx, J. L.: Antibody structure: Now in three dimensions. Science 189:1075–1076, 1114, 1975.

Mayer, M. M.: The complement system. Scientific American, Nov., 1973.

Mayerson, H. S. (Ed.): Lymph and the Lymphatic System: Proceedings Conference on Lymph and the Lymphatic System. Springfield, Charles C Thomas, 1968.

Paul, W. E., and Benacerraf, B.: Functional specificity of thymus-dependent lymphocytes. Science 195:1293–1300, 1976.

THE RESPIRATORY SYSTEM

Avery, M. E., Wang, N., and Taeusch, H. W., Jr.: The lung of the newborn infant. Scientific American, April, 1973.

Campbell, F. J., et al. (Eds.): The Respiratory Muscle: Mechanics and Neural Control. 2nd Ed., Philadelphia, W. B. Saunders Co., 1970.

Cherniack, R. et al.: Respiration in Health and Disease. 2nd Ed. Philadelphia, W. B. Saunders Co., 1972.

Comroe, J. H., Jr.: The lung. Scientific American, Feb., 1966.

Crofton, J., and Douglas, A.: Respiratory Diseases. 2nd Ed., Philadelphia, F. A. Davis Co., 1975.

Fraser, R. G., and Paré. J. A. P.: Organ Physiology: Structure and Function of the Lung, 2nd Ed., Philadelphia, W. B. Saunders Co., 1977.

Pace, N.: Respiration at high altitude. Fed. Proc. 33:2126–2132, 1974.

Safer, P.: Respiratory Therapy: Resuscitation and Intensive Care. Philadelphia, F. A. Davis Co., 1972.

Slonin, N. B., and Hamilton, L. H.: Respiratory Physiology. 3rd Ed., St. Louis, C. V. Mosby Co., 1976.

THE DIGESTIVE SYSTEM

Davenport, H. W.: Physiology of the Digestive Tract: An Introductory Text. 4th Ed., Chicago, Year Book Medical Publishers, 1977.

Davidson, C. S.: Liver Diseases. Philadelphia, Lippincott, 1971.

Fredrickson, D. S.: Plasma lipoproteins and apolipoproteins. Harvey Lectures, Series 68:185–237, 1973.

Goldsmith, G. A.: The new dietary allowances. Nutrition Today, December, 1968.

Kassel, B., and Kay, J.: Zymogens of proteolytic enzymes. Science 180:1022–1027, 1973.

Kretchner, N.: Lactose and lactase. Scientific American, Oct., 1972.

Lossow, W. J., Lindgren, F. T., Murchio, J. C., Stevens, G. R., and Jensen, L. C.: Particle size and protein content of six fractions of the Sf > 20 plasma lipoproteins isolated by density gradient centrifugation. J. Lipid Res. 10:68–76, 1969.

Mayer, J.: Why people get hungry. Nutrition Today, June, 1966.

Rubin, E., and Lieber, C. S.: Experimental alcoholic hepatitis: A new primate model. Science 182:712–713, 1973.

Young, V. R., and Scrimshaw, N. S.: The physiology of starvation. Scientific American, Oct., 1971.

THE URINARY SYSTEM

Atherton, J. C.: Renal Physiology. Br. J. Anaesth. 42:236–245, 1972.

Brenner, B. M.: Renal handling of sodium. Symp. Fed. Proc. 33:13–36, 1974.

Chapman, W. H.: Urinary System: An Integrated Approach. Philadelphia, W. B. Saunders Co., 1973.

Geschickter, C. V., and Autonougch, T. T. (Eds.): Kidney in Health and Disease. Philadelphia, Lippincott, 1971.

Hamburger, J., Richet, G., and Grunfeld, J. P.: Organ Physiology: Structure and Function of the Kidney. Philadelphia, W. B. Saunders Co., 1971.

Kaye, D. (Ed.): Urinary Tract Infection and Its Management. St. Louis, C. V. Mosby Co., 1972.

Mitchell, J. P.: Urology for Nurses. Baltimore, Williams & Wilkins Co., 1970.

Rouillen, C., and Mullen, A. (Eds.): Kidney: Morphology, Biochemistry, Physiology. Vols. 1 and 2. 1969; Kidney, Vols. 3 and 4. New York, Academic Press, 1971.

THE ENDOCRINE SYSTEM

Fawcett, D. W., et al.: The ultrastructure of endocrine glands. Recent Progr. Hormone Res. 25:315–380, 1969.
Field, J. (Ed.): Handbook of Physiology. Section 7: Endocrinology, Baltimore, Williams & Wilkins Co., 1972.
Hamwi, G. J.: Nutrition and diseases of the endocrine glands. Amer. J. Clin. Nutr. 23:311–329, 1970.
Locke, W., et al. (Eds.): Hypothalamus and Pituitary in Health and Disease. Springfield, Charles C Thomas, 1972.
Maugh, T. H.: Diabetes: Epidemiology suggests a viral connection. Science 188:347–351, 1975.
O'Malley, B. W., and Schrader, W. T.: The receptors of steroid hormones. Scientific American, Feb., 1976.
Schally, A. V., Arimura, A., and Kastin, A. J.: Hypothalamic regulatory hormones. Science 179: 341–350, 1973.
Sutherland, E. W.: Studies on the mechanism of hormone action (Nobel lecture). Science 177: 401–408, 1972.

FLUIDS AND ELECTROLYTES

Goldberger, F.: Primer of Water, Electrolyte and Acid-Base Syndromes. Philadelphia, Lea and Febiger, 1970.
Maxwell, M. H., and Kleeman, C. R.: Clinical Disorders of Fluid and Electrolyte Metabolism. 2nd Ed., New York, McGraw-Hill Book Co., 1972.
Mikal, S.: Homeostasis in Man. Boston, Little, Brown and Co., 1967.
Searcy, R. L.: Diagnostic Biochemistry. New York, McGraw-Hill Book Co., 1969.
Share, L., et al.: Regulation of body fluids. Ann. Rev. Physiol. 34:235–260, 1972.
Sundell, B.: Evaluation of fluid resuscitation in the burned patient. Ann. Chir. Gynaecol. Fenn. 60:192–195, 1971.
Wedeen, R. P., et al.: Mechanisms of edema and the use of diuretics. Pediat. Clin. North Amer. 18:561–576, 1971.

THE REPRODUCTIVE SYSTEM

Brackett, B. G.: Mammalian fertilization in vitro. Fed. Proc. 32:2065–2068, 1973.
Catt, K. J.: IV Reproductive Endocrinology. Lancet 1:1097–1104, 1970.
Colman, L., and Colman, A. D.: Pregnancy: The Physiological Experience. Henden and Henden, 1972.
Field, J. (Ed.): Handbook of Physiology. Sect. 7, vols. 2 and 3. Baltimore, Williams & Wilkins Co., 1972.
Imperato-McGinley, J., Guerrero, L., and Peterson, R. E.: Steroid 5 β-reductase deficiency in man; an inherited form of male pseudohermaphroditism. Science 186:1213–1215, 1974.
Newton, N., and Newton, M.: Psychologic aspects of lactation. New Engl. J. Med., 277:1179, November 30, 1967.
Page, E. W., Villee, C. A., and Villee, D. B.: Human Reproduction: the Core Content of Obstetrics, Gynecology and Prenatal Medicine. 2nd Ed., Philadelphia, W. B. Saunders Co., 1976.
Rhodes, P.: Reproductive Physiology for Medical Students. Baltimore, Williams & Wilkins Co., 1969.
Rondell, P.: Follicular processes in ovulation. Fed. Proc. 29:1875–1879, 1970.
Segal, S. J.: The physiology of human reproduction. Sci. Amer., Sept., 1974.
Shearman, R. P. (Ed.): Human Reproductive Physiology. Oxford, Blackwell Scientific Publications, 1972.

ADDITIONAL REFERENCES

Best and Taylor's Physiological Basis of Medical Practice. 9th Ed., Edited by J. R. Brobeck. Baltimore, Williams and Wilkins Co., 1973.
Crouch, J. E.: Functional Human Anatomy. Philadelphia, Lea and Febiger, 1972.
Cunningham, D. J.: Textbook of Anatomy. Edited by G. J. Romanes; 11th Ed., Oxford, Oxford University Press, 1972.
Downman, C. B. B. (Ed.): Modern Trends in Physiology. Appleton-Century Crofts, 1972.
Ganong, W. F.: Review of Medical Physiology. 7th Ed., Los Altos, California, Lange Medical Publications, 1975.
Guyton, A. C.: Textbook of Medical Physiology. 5th Ed., Philadelphia, W. B. Saunders Co., 1976.
Leeson, C. R., and Leeson, T. S.: Histology. 3rd Ed., Philadelphia, W. B. Saunders Co., 1976.
Lehninger, A. L.: Biochemistry. 2nd Ed., New York, Worth Publishers, Inc., 1975.

GLOSSARY

abdomen (ab-dō′men): the portion of the body lying between the diaphragm and the pelvis.

abduct (ab-dukt′): to draw away from the median line.

ablation (ab-lā′shun): removal of a part, especially by cutting.

absorption (ab-sorp′shun): the taking up of fluids or other substances by the skin, mucous surfaces, or vessels.

accommodation (ah-kom″o-da′shun): focusing of the image on the retina by the lens.

acetabulum (as′e-tab′u-lum): the large, cup-shaped cavity with which the head of the femur articulates.

acetylcholine (as″ĕ-til-ko′lēn): a neurotransmitter released at the neuromuscular junction, synapses, and parasympathetic postganglionic nerve endings.

Achilles tendon (ah-kil′ēz): the powerful tendon at the back of the heel which connects the triceps surae muscle with the tuberosity of the heel.

acid (as′id): sour, having properties opposed to those of the alkalis; characterized by excess hydrogen ions, giving it a pH less than seven.

acidophils (ah-sid′o-fils): acid-staining cells, especially those of the adenohypophysis, which produce growth hormone and prolactin.

acidosis (as″ĭ-do′sis): a pathologic condition resulting from accumulation of acid or loss of base in the body and characterized by increase in hydrogen ion concentration (decrease in pH).

acinus (ass′i-nus): a saccular terminal division of a compound gland.

acromegaly (ak″ro-meg′ah-le): overproduction of growth hormone in adults.

acromion (ah-krō′me-on): outward extension of the scapula forming the point of the shoulder.

acrosome (ak′ro-sōm): a cap on the sperm head with enzymatic function.

active transport: any movement of particles across a membrane against the concentration gradient, thus requiring an expenditure of energy.

Addison's disease (ad′ĭ-sonz): deficiency of suprarenal cortex functions.

adduct (ah-dukt′): to draw toward a center or toward a median line.

adenohypophysis (ad″ē-no-hi-pof′ĭ-sis): the anterior portion of the hypophysis.

adenoid (ad′ĕ-noid): generally, anything referring to glands; usually used in the plural for the nasopharyngeal tonsil.

adenosine triphosphate, ATP (ah-den′o-sin): a nucleotide with two additional phosphate groups found in all cells and serving as a direct source of energy for cellular processes.

adhesion (ad-hē′zhun): abnormal union of two surfaces.

adiadochokinesis (ah-di″ah-do″ko-ki-nē′sis): inability to perform rapidly alternating movements.

adipose (ad′ĭ-pos): of a fatty nature; fat.

ad libitum (ad-lib′i-tum): freely; as much as wanted.

adrenal (ad-rē′nal): suprarenal glands, located above the kidneys.

Adrenalin (ad-ren′ah-lin): trademark for a preparation of epinephrine.

adrenergic (ad″ren-er′jik):   activated or transmitted by norepinephrine; a term applied to those nerve fibers that liberate norepinephrine.

adventitia (ad′ven-tish′e-ah):   the outermost covering of a structure but not forming an integral part of it.

aerobic (ā-er-o′bik):   growing only in the presence of molecular oxygen.

afferent (af′er-ent):   conveying toward a center.

agglutination (ah-gloo″tĭ-nā′shun):   a joining together; an aggregation of suspended particles.

agglutinin (ah-gloo′tĭ-nin):   antibody which clumps a particular antigen.

agglutinogen (ag′loo-tin′o-jen):   antigen stimulating the production of an agglutinin.

agraphia (ah-graf′e-ah):   inability to write with meaningful content.

albumin (al-bū′min):   plasma protein largely responsible for the osmotic pressure of blood.

aldosterone (al″do-ster′ōn):   the principal mineralocorticoid secreted from the cortex of the adrenal glands.

alexia (ah-lek′se-ah):   inability to read with comprehension.

alimentary (al″e-men′tar-e):   pertaining to food or nutritive material.

alkaline (al′kah-līn):   basic, see **base.**

alkalosis (al″kah-lo′sis):   a condition in which there is an excessive proportion of alkali in the blood.

alveolus (al-ve′o-lus):   a small cavity; usually refers to the air sac in the lungs.

ameboid movement (ah-mē′boid):   movement of an ameba or leukocyte by a protrusion of a footlike structure, or movement similar to it.

amenorrhea (ah-men″o-rē′ah):   absence or abnormal stoppage of the menses.

amine (am′in):   any organic compound containing nitrogen.

amino acid (a-mē′nō):   an organic compound with an NH_2, and a COOH group in its molecule, and having both acid and basic properties. Amino acids are the structural units from which proteins are built.

amniocentesis (am″ne-o-sen-tē′sis):   transabdominal perforation of the uterus to obtain a sample of amniotic fluid.

amnion (am′ne-on):   the thin, transparent, silvery and tough inner membrane which protects the embryo in the uterus during pregnancy.

amorphous (ah-mor′fus):   having no definite form; shapeless.

amphiarthrosis (am″fe-ar-thro′sis):   form of articulation permitting little motion.

ampulla (am-pŭl′lah):   a saclike dilation of a tube or duct.

amylase (am′ĭ-lās):   an enzyme that hydrolyzes starch to maltose.

anabolism (ah-nab′o-lizm):   any constructive process in which simple substances are converted by living cells into more complex compounds, such as conversion of simple compounds into protoplasm.

anaerobic (an″ā-er-o′bik):   growing only in the absence of oxygen.

analgesia (an″al-jē′ze-ah):   loss of sensitivity to pain.

anaphylaxis (an″ah-fi-lak′sis):   an allergic response involving interaction between allergens and reagins (IgE antibodies).

anastomosis (ah-nas″to-mō′sis):   a surgical connection between vessels or between parts of a tube, such as the stomach to the small intestine.

androgen (an′dro-jen):   any substance that possesses masculinizing activities, specifically the testicular hormone.

anemia (ah-nē′me-ah):   condition in which oxygen transport by red blood cells is deficient.

anesthesia (an″es-thē′ze-ah):   loss of sensation.

aneurysm (an′u-rizm):   a sac formed by the dilatation of the wall of an artery or of a vein and filled with blood.

angina (an'jĭ-nah) or (an-jī'nah): any disease characterized by spasmodic choking, or suffocative pain.

angina pectoris (an'jĭ-nah pec'toris): periodic severe pain in the chest radiating to the left shoulder and down the inner side of the arm, usually precipitated by physical exertion or emotional stress.

angiocardiography (an″je-o-kar″di-og′rah-fe): roentgenography of the heart and great vessels after intravenous injection of opaque fluid.

annulus (an'u-lus): ring, or ringlike or circular structure.

anorexia (an″o-rek′se-ah): lack or loss of the appetite for food.

anosmia (an-oz′me-ah): absence of sense of smell.

anoxia (an-ok′se-ah): reduction of oxygen in body tissues below physiologic levels.

antagonistic muscle (an-tag′o-nist-ik): muscle which acts in opposition to the action of another muscle.

anterior: situated in front of, or in the forward part.

antibody (an′tĭ-bod″e): agglutinin; a protein (serum globulin) synthesized by an animal in response to an antigen which has entered the body.

antigen (an′tĭ-jen): agglutinogen; a substance which, on gaining access to the blood stream of an animal, stimulates the formation of specific antibodies.

antrum (an′trum): a cavity or chamber, especially one within a bone.

anuria (ah-nu′re-ah): absence of excretion of urine.

aorta (ā-or′tah): the main vessel rising from the left ventricle of the heart from which the systemic arterial circulation proceeds.

aperture (ap′er-chūr): an opening or orifice.

apex (ā′peks): the top, or the pointed extremity of a conical part.

aphagia (ah-fā′je-ah): nonfeeding.

aphasia (ah-fā′ze-ah): defect or loss of the power of expression by speech.

aplastic (hypoplastic) **anemia** (ah-plas′tik ah-ne′me-ah): reduced RBC formation caused by damage to the red bone marrow.

apnea (ap-ne′ah): the transient cessation of the breathing impulse that follows forced breathing.

apneusis (ap-nu′sis): breathing characterized by cramping of inspiratory muscles.

aponeurosis (ap″o-nu-ro′sis): a flattened tendinous expansion.

appendage (ah-pen′dij): a thing or part affixed or attached.

apraxia (ah-prak′se-ah): inability to carry out purposeful movements in the absence of paralysis or other motor sensory impairment.

aqueduct (ak′we-dukt″): a channel in a body structure or organ, especially a canal for the conduction of liquid.

aqueous humor (a′kwe-us hū′mor): fluid produced in the eye, occupying the anterior and posterior chambers of the anterior cavity.

arachnoid (ah-rak′noid): the middle of the three coverings (meninges) of the brain.

areola (ah-re′o-lah): minute space in a tissue; the pigmented ring around the nipple.

areolar (ah-re′o-lar): pertaining to or containing areolae; containing minute interspaces.

arrhythmia (ah-rith′me-ah): any variation from the normal rhythm of the heartbeat.

arteriole (ar-te′re-ōl): a minute arterial branch, especially one just proximal to the capillary.

artery (ar′ter-e): a vessel through which the blood passes away from the heart to the various parts of the body.

arthritis (ar-thrī′tis): inflammation of a joint.

arthrosis (ar-thro′sis): a joint or articulation.

articular (ar-tik′u-lar): of or pertaining to a joint.

articulation (ar-tik″u-lā′shun): the site of union or junction between two or more bones in the skeleton.

ascites (ah-sī′tez):   accumulation of serous fluid in the abdominal cavity.

asphyxia (as-fik′se-ah):   loss of consciousness because of deficient oxygen supply.

aspirate (as′pĭ-rāt):   to remove fluids or gases from a cavity by suction.

asthenia (as-thē′ne-ah):   bodily weakness.

asthma (az′mah):   an allergic reaction to inspired foreign substances that creates localized edema in the walls of the small bronchioles, secretion of thick mucus, and spasms of the bronchiole walls.

astigmatism (ah-stig′mah-tizm):   defective curvature of refractive surfaces of the eye; as a result a ray of light is not focused sharply on the retina, but is spread over a diffuse area.

astrocyte (as′trō-sīt):   star-shaped cell, especially of the neuroglia.

ataxia (ah-tak′se-ah):   loss of muscle coordination.

atelectasis (at″e-lek′tah-sis):   incomplete expansion of the lungs at birth; lung collapse.

athetosis (ath″e-to′sis):   slow, involuntary, writhing movements.

atony (at′o-ne):   lack of normal tone or strength.

atrium (ā′tre-um):   a chamber or cavity; usually the upper chambers of the heart.

atophy (at′ro-fe):   a wasting away or diminution in the size of a cell, tissue, organ, or part.

audiogram (aw′de-o-gram″):   the record of a test of pure sound tones used to determine the extent of hearing loss.

auricle (aw′re-kl):   the flap of the ear.

autoimmune disease (aw″to-im-mun′):   the attack by the immune system on one's own tissues.

autonomic (aw″to-nom′ik):   self-controlling; functionally independent.

autophagy (aw-tof′ah-je):   the eating of one's own flesh; nutrition of the body by the consumption of its own tissues.

axial (ak′se-al):   of, or pertaining to, the axis of a structure or part.

axilla (ak-sil′ah):   armpit.

axolemma (ak-so-lem′ah):   the surface membrane of an axon.

axon (ak′son):   neuronal process conducting impulses away from the cell body.

B cell system: immunity mediated by proteins (antibodies) to combat acute bacterial infections.

Babinski reflex (bah-bin′skē):   abnormal response to sole of foot stimulation after damage to motor tracts or spinal cord transection.

bacteriophage (bak-te′re-o-fāj″):   bacterial virus; an agent that parasitizes a bacteria.

baroreceptors (bar″o-re-sep′tors):   receptors responding to change in blood pressure, located in the aortic arch and internal carotid arteries.

Bartholin's glands (bar′to-linz) (greater vestibular glands):   between the labium minus and the hymen.

basal ganglia (ba′sal gang′ gle-ah):   4 paired masses of gray matter embedded in the white matter of the cerebral hemispheres and concerned with regulating motor activity.

base: nonacid; characterized by excess OH ion and a pH greater than seven.

bel: a unit for measuring loudness of sound.

benign (be-nīn′):   not malignant; not life-threatening.

biceps (bī′seps):   a muscle having two heads.

bifurcate (bī-fur′kāt):   forked; divided into two like a fork.

bilateral (bī-lat′eral):   pertaining to both sides of the body.

bile (bīl):   a fluid secreted by the liver and poured into the intestines. It aids in the absorption and digestion of fat.

bilirubin (bil″e-roo′bin):   red pigment in the bile.

biliverdin (bil″e-ver′din):   green pigment in the bile.

binocular (bin-ok′u-lar):   the visual field produced by two eyes.

binocular parallax (par′ah-laks):   the difference in the view of an object seen by each eye, making possible depth perception.

binovular (bin-ov′u-lar):   pertaining to or derived from two distinct ova.

bipennate (bi″pen′āt):   said of muscles whose fibers are arranged on each side of a tendon, like the barbs on the shaft of a feather.

blast: an immature stage in the formation of a blood cell before the development of the definitive characteristics of the cell.

blastocyst (blas′to-sist):   a modified blastula; that is, a stage in the development of the embryo when the cells are arranged in a single layer to form a hollow sphere.

BMR (basal metabolic rate):   the exchange of energy occurring in a fasting and resting individual.

bolus (bō′ lus):   a rounded food mass of soft consistency.

bone shaft: the body (diaphysis) of a long bone.

boutons (boo′tuns):   presynaptic terminals.

Bowman's capsule (**bo**′manz):   the glomerular capsule; the cuplike depression of the tubular system of a nephron that surrounds a tuft of capillaries.

brachial (brā′ke-al):   pertaining to the arm.

bradycardia (brād″e-kar′de-ah):   abnormal slowness of the heartbeat, as evidenced by slowing of the pulse rate to 60 per minute or less.

Broca's area (bro′kahz):   area of the brain for programming speech muscles.

bronchiole (brong′ke-ōl):   one of the finer subdivisions of the branched bronchial tree of the lungs.

bronchus (brong′kus):   either one of the two main branches of the trachea.

brownian movement (brow′ne-an):   the dancing motion of minute particles suspended in a liquid.

Brunner's glands (brun′erz):   glands of the duodenum which secrete a mucus high in bicarbonate content.

buccal (buk′al):   pertaining to the cheek.

buffer (buf′er):   a substance in a fluid medium which lessens the change in hydrogen or hydroxyl ion concentration when an acid or base is added.

bursa (bur′sah):   sac or saclike cavity filled with a viscid fluid situated at places in the tissue at which friction would otherwise develop.

calculus (kal′ku-lus):   stone formed in various parts of the body, principally in ducts, hollow organs, and cysts.

Calorie (kal′o-re):   equal to 1000 calories.

calorie: a unit of heat, being the amount of heat required to raise 1 gram of water from 15° to 16°C. The calorie used in the study of metabolism is the kilocalorie (kcal.), the amount of heat required to raise 1 kilogram of water from 15° to 16°C.

calyx (ka′liks):   a cup-shaped organ or cavity.

canaliculus (kan″ah-lik′u-lus):   a small canal or channel.

cancellous (kan′se-lus):   of a reticular, spongy, or latticelike structure.

capacitation (kah-pas′i-tā-tion):   the final stage of maturation of sperm cells.

capillary (kap′ĭ-lar″e):   any one of the minute vessels that connect the arterioles and the venules, forming a network in nearly all parts of the body.

carbohydrate (kar″bo-hī′drāt):   an organic compound containing carbon, hydrogen, and oxygen (the latter in the same proportions as in water); includes sugars and glycogen.

carcinoma (kar″si-nō′mah):   a malignant new growth made up of epithelial cells tending to infiltrate the surrounding tissues.

carotid (kah-rot′id):   principal artery of the neck.

carpal (kar′pal):   of or pertaining to the wrist.

casein (kā′se-in): principal protein of milk.

catabolism (kah-tab′o-lizm): any process by which complex substances are converted by living cells into simpler compounds.

catalyst (kat′ah-list): a substance which changes the velocity of a reaction but does not form part of the final product.

cataract (kat′ah-rakt): an opacity of the eye lens.

cation (kat′i-on): ion carrying a positive charge.

caudal (kaw′dal): denoting a position more toward the tail.

cecum (sē′kum): a dilated pouch that is the first portion of the large intestine.

celiac (sē′le-ak): pertaining to the abdomen.

cementum (sē-men′tum): a layer of bony tissue covering the root of a tooth.

centimeter (sen′ti-me″ter): a unit of linear measure of the metric system, being 1/100 meter or about 2/5 inch.

cephalic (sĕ-fal′ik): pertaining to the head or superior end of the body.

cerebellum (ser″e-bel′um): division of the brain concerned with coordination of movements, located behind the cerebrum and above the pons and fourth ventricle.

cerebral cortex (ser′e-bral): the gray matter covering the cerebrum.

cerebral dominance (dom′ĭ-nans): specialization of one side of the brain.

cerumen (sĕ-roo′men): waxlike secretion found within the external meatus of the ear.

cervix (ser′viks): the neck or any necklike part; usually, the lower end of the uterus.

chemoreceptor (kem′o-re-sep-tor): a receptor adapted for excitation by chemical substances.

Cheyne-Stokes breathing (chān′stōks): breathing characterized by alternating intervals of stertorous respiration and apnea.

chiasm (kī′azm): an X-shaped crossing.

cholelithiasis (kō″le-li-thi′ah-sis) (gallstones): crystals of bile in the gallbladder.

cholesterol (kō-les′ter-ol): the most common steroid; present in bile, blood, and various tissues and the precursor of steroid hormones, vitamin D, and bile acids.

cholesterol esterase (es′ter-ās): an enzyme which hydrolyzes cholesterol esters.

cholinergic (kō′lin-er′jik): a term applied to those nerve fibers which liberate acetylcholine.

cholinesterase (kō″lin-es′ter-ās): a substance which hydrolyzes acetylcholine.

chorea (ko-rē′ah): the ceaseless occurrence of a wide variety of rapid, jerky but well-coordinated movements, performed involuntarily.

chorion (kō′re-on): the outermost envelope of the fertilized ovum which serves a protective and nutritive function.

choroid plexuses (kō′roid plek′suses): pouchlike projections of pia mater into the ventricles which secrete cerebrospinal fluid.

chromatid (krō′mah-tid): one of the two spiral filaments making up a chromosome which separate in cell division, each going to a different pole of the dividing cell.

chronaxie (krō′nax-e): measure of nerve fiber excitability, specifically the time required for twice the minimum voltage (rheobase) to cause excitation.

chyle (kīl): the milky fluid taken up by the lacteals from the food in the intestine after digestion.

chylomicron (kī″lo-mi′kron): a lipid particle (largely triglyceride) with a protein-phospholipid coat absorbed into the intestinal lymphatics and found in the blood during the digestion of fat.

chyme (kīm): semifluid, homogeneous, creamy material produced by the gastric digestion of food.

chymotrypsin (kī″mo-trip′sin): a protein-degrading enzyme secreted by the pancreas as the inactive precursor chymotrypsinogen.

cilia (sil′e-ah): minute, hairlike processes attached to the free surface of a cell.

cirrhosis (sir-rō′sis):   a disease of the liver in which there is degeneration of the liver cells and increase of connective tissue.

cisterna (sis-ter′nah):   an enclosed space serving as a reservoir for lymph or other body fluid. The *cisterna chyli* is the elongated sac from which the thoracic duct arises.

cleavage (klēv′ij):   mitotic segmentation of the zygote into blastomeres.

clone (klōn):   a group of cells arising by cell division from a single parent cell.

coagulation (kō-ag″u-lā′shun):   process of changing into a clot, or being changed into a clot.

coarctation (ko″ark-tā′shun):   a straightening or pressing together; a condition of stricture or contraction.

cochlea (kŏk′le-ah):   anything having a spiral form; part of the inner ear.

coenzyme (kō-en′zīm):   a nonprotein substance actuating an enzyme.

collagen (kŏl′ah-jen):   the main supportive protein of connective tissue.

collateral (kŏ′lăt′er-al):   accompanying; running by the side of; accessory.

colloid (kŏl′oid):   a state of matter in which matter is dispersed throughout a medium called the dispersion medium; the matter dispersed is termed the disperse phase. The particles are larger than a crystalloid molecule, but are not large enough to precipitate under the influence of gravity. They range in size from 0.1 micrometer to 1 micrometer.

colostrum (ko-lŏs′trum):   first milk secreted after childbirth.

coma (kō′mah):   profound unconsciousness.

commissure (kŏm′ĭ-sūr):   the bond of fibers joining corresponding opposite parts, mainly in the brain and spinal cord.

concha (kong′kah):   a structure resembling a shell in shape.

condyle (kon′dīl):   a rounded projection on a bone, usually for articulation with another bone.

congenital (kon-jen′ĭ-tal):   existing at, and usually before, birth.

conjugation (kon″ju-gā′shun):   the act of joining together; in biology, the union of one organism with another for an exchange of nuclear material.

contraceptive (kon″trah-sep′tiv):   any device used to prevent conception.

contraction (kon-trak′shun):   a shortening, as of a muscle in the normal response to a nervous stimulus.

contralateral (kon″trah-lat′er-al):   situated on or pertaining to the opposite side.

convoluted (kon′vo-lūt-ed):   rolled together or coiled.

coracoid (kor′ah-koid):   like a raven's beak in form.

corium (kō′re-um):   the true skin, or the dermis.

coronary (kor′o-na-re):   encircling in the manner of a crown; a term applied to vessels, nerves, and ligaments.

corpus (kor′pus):   the body as a whole, or the main part of any organ.

corpus albicans (al′bĭ-kanz):   scar tissue in the ovary.

corpus callosum (kah-lo′sum):   largest of the commissural tracts which connect the two brain hemispheres.

corpus luteum (lū′te-um):   a yellow mass in the ovary formed by a graafian follicle which has matured and discharged its ovum.

corpuscle (kor′pus-l):   any small mass or body.

cortex (kor′teks):   the outer layer of an organ, as distinguished from its inner substance.

costal (kos′tal):   pertaining to a rib or ribs.

crenation (kre-nā′shun):   the passage of the fluid within a cell into the surrounding medium, causing the cell to shrivel.

cretinism (krē′tin-izm):   a chronic condition due to congenital lack of thyroid secretion.

cribriform (krib′ri-form):   perforated like a sieve with small apertures.

cricoid (krī′koid):   ring-shaped.

cruciate (kroo'she-āt):   shaped like a cross.

crypt (krĭpt):   a minute, tubelike depression opening on a free surface.

cryptorchism (krĭp-tor'kizm):   failure of the testes to descend into the scrotum.

crypts of Lieberkühn (le'ber-kĭn):   glands of the small intestine.

crystalloid (kris'tal-loid):   a noncolloid substance which in a solvent passes readily through animal membranes.

cubital (kū'bĭ-tal):   pertaining to the ulna or to the forearm.

cupula (ku'pu-lah):   the portion of the lung above the clavicle.

Cushing's disease (koosh'ingz):   an excess of ACTH, resulting in adrenal cortex hyperfunction.

cutaneous (kū-ta'ne-us):   pertaining to the skin.

cyanosis (si″ah-no'sis):   a bluish appearance of the skin or nails secondary to deficient oxygenation of blood.

cytology (sī-tol'o-je):   the study of cells.

cytoplasm (sī'to-plazm″):   the protoplasm of a cell exclusive of that of the nucleus.

dead space: the air contained within the nose, pharynx, larynx, trachea, and bronchial tree.

deamination (de-am″ĭ-nā'shun):   a chemical reaction in which the amino group is split from an amino acid.

decibel (des'ĭ-bel):   1/10 of a bel.

decidua (de-sid'u-ah):   the mucous membrane lining of the uterus preparatory to implantation of the zygote.

deciduous (de-sĭd'u-us):   not permanent; cast off at maturity.

decussation (dē″kus-sa'shun):   a crossing over, particularly a band of nerve fibers crossing the median plane of any part of the central nervous system.

deglutition (deg″loo-tish'un):   the act of swallowing.

deltoid (del'toid):   having a triangular outline.

dendrite (den'drĭt):   a branched and tree-shaped protoplasmic process from a nerve cell which conducts impulses toward the cell body.

dental caries (kar'ēz):   disintegration of teeth by acids produced by bacterial fermentation of carbohydrates.

dentate (den'tāte):   having teeth or projections like saw teeth on the edges.

dentin (den'tin):   the chief tissue of the teeth which surrounds the tooth pulp.

deoxyribonucleic acid, DNA (de-ok″sĭ-ri″bo-nu-klē'ic):   nucleic acid present in chromosomes of the nuclei of cells and the chemical basis of heredity and the carrier of genetic information.

dermatome (der'mah-tōm):   a strip of skin supplied by one pair of spinal nerves.

dermis (der'mis):   the true skin, or corium; the second, major layer, beneath the epidermis.

dextrose (deks'trōs):   glucose, a monosaccharide, the principal blood sugar.

diabetes (di″ah-bē'tĕz):   a condition marked by a habitual discharge of an excessive quantity of urine; two major types are diabetes insipidus and diabetes mellitus.

diabetic retinopathy (di″ah-bet'ik ret″ĭ-nop'ah-the):   deterioration of tiny blood vessels in the eye and growth of new vessels on the surface of the retina which rupture and bleed into the vitreous humor.

dialysis (dī-al'ĭ-sis):   the process of separating crystalloids and colloids in solution by the difference in their rates of diffusion through a semipermeable membrane; crystalloids pass through readily, colloids slowly or not at all.

diaphragm (di'ah-fram):   a membrane or partition separating one thing from another.

diaphysis (di-af'ĭ-sis):   the shaft of a long bone.

diarthrosis (di″ar-thrō'sis):   a freely movable articulation.

diastole (dī-as'tō-lē):   the relaxation and dilation of the heart, especially of the ventricles, during which time it fills with blood.

diencephalon (dī″en-sef′ah-lon): the posterior division of the prosencephalon of the brain.

diffusion (dĭ-fū′zhun): net transfer of a substance from a region of high to a region of low concentration as a result of random motion of particles.

diplopia (dĭ-plō′pe-ah): the seeing of single objects as double or two.

disaccharide (dī-sak′ah-rīd): any one of a class of sugars which yield two monosaccharides upon hydrolysis; includes sucrose, lactose, and maltose.

distal (dis′tal): remote, farther from any point of reference.

diuresis (di″u-rē′sis): increased excretion of urine.

diuretic (di″u-ret′ik): increasing the volume of urine; an agent that increases the volume of urine.

diverticulum (dī″ver-tik′u-lum): a pouch or pocket from a main cavity or tube.

dorsal (dor′sal): denoting a position toward the back or posterior.

dorsum (dor′sum): the back.

dropsy (drop′se): accumulation of serous fluid in a body cavity, in tissues; edema.

duct: a tube for the passage of excretions or secretions.

dura mater (du′rah mā′ter): the outermost, toughest, and most fibrous of the three meninges of the brain.

dwarfism (dwarf′izm): smallness due to underproduction of growth hormone.

dysfunction (dis-funk′shun): partial disturbance, impairment, or abnormality of the functioning of an organ.

dysmenorrhea (dis″men-o-re′ah): menstrual pain.

dysmetria (dis-me′tre-ah): inability to judge extent of self-movements.

dyspnea (disp′ne-ah): difficult or labored breathing.

dystrophy (dis′tro-fe): defective nutrition; defective development or degeneration.

"ear drum": the tympanic membrane.

ectoderm (ek′to-derm): the outermost of the three primary germ layers of an embryo.

ectopic (ek-top′ik): not in the normal place or position, as ectopic pregnancy—implantation of the fertilized ovum in a place other than the uterus.

edema (e-dē′mah): the presence of an abnormally large volume of fluid in the interstitial spaces of the body.

efferent (ef′er-ent): conveying away from the center.

electrocardiogram (e-lek″tro-kar′de-o-gram): a graphic record of the electric current produced by the excitation of heart muscle.

electroencephalogram (e-lek″tro-en-sef′ah-lo-gram): the graphic record of the electrical activity of the brain.

electrolyte (e-lek′tro-līt): any solution conducting electricity by means of its ions.

electrophoresis (e-lek″tro-fo-rē′sis): the movement of charged particles suspended in a liquid on various media (e.g., paper, starch, agar) under the influence of an applied electric field.

embolus (em′bo-lus): clot or other plug brought by the blood from another vessel and forced into a smaller one so as to obstruct circulation.

embryo (em′bre-o): the early or developing stage of any organism; in humans, the organism in its first two months of existence in the womb.

emesis (em′e-sis): vomiting.

emphysema (em″fi-sē′mah): respiratory disorder characterized by increased airway resistance and distention and rupture of the pulmonary alveoli.

empyema (em″pĭ-ē′mah): accumulation of pus in a cavity of the body, especially in the chest.

encephalon (en-sef′ah-lon): the brain.

endemic goiter (en-dem′ic goi′ter): goiter peculiar to certain regions produced by hypersecretion of TSH due to insufficient dietary iodine.

endocardium (en″do-kar′de-um):   inner heart layer (endothelium).

endocrine (en′do-krin):   secreting internally; applied to organs functioning to secrete substances into the blood or lymph, producing an effect on another organ or part.

endoderm (en′do-derm):   innermost of the three germ layers of an embryo.

endogenous (en-doj′e-nus):   developing or originating within the organism, or arising from causes within the organism.

endometrium (en″do-mē′tre-um):   mucous membrane that lines the cavity of the uterus.

endomysium (en″do-mis′e-um):   the delicate connective tissue sheath surrounding each muscle fiber.

endoneurium (en″do-nu′re-um):   connective tissue in a nerve surrounding the individual fibers of a bundle, binding them together.

endoplasmic reticulum (en-dō-plaz′mik re-tik′ū-lum):   network of tubules and vesicles in cytoplasm.

endosteum (en-dos′te-um):   lining inside bones — marrow cavities and spaces.

enuresis (en″u-rē′sis):   involuntary urination.

enzyme (en′zīm):   a protein capable of accelerating or producing by catalytic action some change in a specific substrate.

ependymal cells (e-pen′dĭ-mal):   cells that line the cavities of the brain and central canal of the spinal cord.

epicardium (ep″i-kar′de-um):   external heart layer (visceral layer of pericardium).

epidermis (ep″i-der′mis):   the outermost and nonvascular layer of the skin; it is composed of five distinct layers.

epigastrium (ep″ĭ-gas′tre-um):   the upper middle region of the abdomen, located within the sternal angle.

epimysium (ep″ĭ-mis′e-um):   the fibrous sheath about an entire muscle.

epineurium (ep″ĭ-nu′re-um):   the connective tissue covering of a nerve.

epiphysis (e-pif′ĭ-sis):   a segment of bone separated from the long bone early in life by a piece of cartilage, but later becoming part of the larger bone.

epithelium (ep″ĭ-thē′le-um):   one of the four major types of tissues; consisting of closely packed cells covering internal and external surfaces of the body, including the lining of the vessels, and forming glands.

erythrocyte (e-rith′ro-sīt):   red blood cell, shaped like a biconcave disc.

erythropoiesis (e-rith″ro-poi-ē′sis):   the production of red blood cells.

essential amino acids: tryptophan, lysine, methionine, threonine, phenylalanine, leucine, isoleucine, and valine, which cannot be synthesized in the body and must be obtained in the diet.

essential fatty acids: linoleic and linolenic acid (unsaturated fatty acids with two and three double bonds, respectively), which cannot be synthesized in the body.

esterification (es-ter″ĭ-fi-kā′shun):   the process of converting an acid into an ester.

ethmoid (eth′moid):   cribriform; sievelike.

etiology (ē″tĭ-ol′o-je):   the study of cause, especially of disease.

eupnea (ūp-nē′ah):   normal respiration.

evagination (ē-vaj″ĭ-nā′shun):   an outpouching of a layer or part.

eversion (ē-ver′zhun):   a turning inside out.

excoriation (eks-ko″re-ā′shun):   a superficial loss of substance, such as is produced on the skin by scratching.

exocrine (ek′so-krin):   applied to glands which deliver secretions to an epithelial surface, directly or through ducts.

excretory (eks′kre-to-re):   pertaining to discharge of waste products from the body.

expiration (eks″pĭ-ra′shun):   expelling air from the lungs.

extrapyramidal (eks″trah-pi-ram′ĭ′dal):   outside the pyramidal tracts.

extravasation (eks-trav″ah-sa′shun): escape of blood, lymph, or serum from a vessel into tissue spaces.

extrinsic (eks-trin′sik): originating outside.

facilitation (fah-sil″ĭ-ta′shun): augmented response at synapse due to simultaneous or prior stimulation.

fascia (fash′e-ah): a sheet or band of fibrous tissue covering the body under the skin and investing muscles and other organs.

fascicle (fas′ĭ-k'l): a small bundle or cluster, especially of nerve or muscle fibers.

febrile (feb′ril): pertaining to fever.

fenestrated (fen′es-trāt″ed): pierced with one or more openings.

fertilization (fer-ti-li-zā′shun): union of ovum and spermatozoon.

fetus (fē′tus): the developing young in the uterus after the end of the second month.

fiber (fi′ber): an elongated, threadlike structure of organic tissue.

fibrillation (fī-brĭ-lā′shun): spontaneous contraction of individual muscle fibers no longer under control of a motor neuron; usually refers to spasmodic contraction of the cardiac muscle.

fibrin (fī′brin): a whitish, insoluble protein formed from fibrinogen, important in the clotting of blood.

fibrinogen (fī-brin′o-jen): a soluble protein in the blood plasma which, by the action of thrombin, is converted into fibrin, thus producing clotting of the blood.

fibroblast (fī′bro-blast): connective tissue cell that synthesizes the matrix of connective tissue proper.

filiform (fil′ĭ-form): thread-shaped.

filtration (fil-trā′shun): the passage of liquid and solutes through a semipermeable membrane under pressure.

filum terminale (fi′lum ter′min-ah-le): the portion of pia mater extending below the spinal cord.

fimbria (fim′bre-ah): any fringelike structure.

fissure (fish′ūr): any cleft or groove, normal or otherwise.

fistula (fis′tu-lah): a deep tract, often leading to an internal hollow cavity.

follicle (fol′ĭ-kl): a small excretory or secretory sac or gland.

foramen (fo-rā′men): a natural hole or passage, especially one into or through bone.

fossa (fos′ah): a pit or depression.

fovea (fō′ve-ah): a fossa, or cup; applied to various depressions in the structure of the body, such as the fovea centralis.

frenulum (fren′u-lum): a small fold of the integument or of mucous membrane, especially one that limits the movements of an organ or part of an organ.

fundus (fun′dus): the base or part of a hollow organ most remote from the entrance.

funiculus (fu-nik′u-lus): one of the three main divisions of the white matter of the spinal cord.

fusiform (fū′sĭ-form): spindle-shaped.

galactose (gah-lak′tos): a monosaccharide obtained from lactose, or milk sugar.

gametes (gam′ēts): sex cells.

gamma efferents (gam′mah ef′er-ents): neurons which control the sensitivity of the muscle spindle.

gamma globulin (glob′u-lin): the fraction of plasma globulin (one of the major classes of proteins in plasma), separated by electrophoresis, containing antibodies.

ganglion (gang′gle-on): a collection or mass of nerve cells

gene (jēn): the biologic unit of heredity; self-reproducing and located in a definite position on a particular chromosome.

geniculate (je-nik′u-lāt): bent, like a knee.

genitalia (jen″ĭ-tā′le-ah):   the reproductive organs.

genu (jē′nu):   the knee, or any structure bent like a knee.

germ layers: three primary layers of cells in an embryo from which the organs and tissues develop. They are the ectoderm, the mesoderm, and the endoderm.

gestation (jes-tā-shun):   pregnancy.

gland: an organ that produces a specific product or secretion.

globin (glō′bin):   the protein constituent of hemoglobin.

glomerulus (glō-mer′u-lus):   a coil or cluster of blood vessels.

glossal (glos′al):   pertaining to the tongue.

glucagon (gloo′kah-gon):   a hormone produced by the pancreas in response to hypoglycemia or to stimulation by the growth hormone of the anterior hypophysis.

glucocorticoid (gloo″ko-kor′tĭ-koid):   a corticoid which increases gluconeogenesis, raising the concentration of liver glycogen and blood sugar.

gluconeogenesis (gloo″ko-ne″o-jen′e-sis):   the synthesis of "new" glucose from substrates such as amino acids and lactic acid.

glucose (gloo′kōs):   a monosaccharide, the principal blood sugar. The term is generally used as a synonym for dextrose, which more precisely is dextro- or d-glucose.

gluteal (gloo′te-al):   pertaining to the buttocks.

glycogen (gli′ko-jen):   a polysaccharide which is the chief carbohydrate storage material in animals.

glycosuria (gli″ko-su′re-ah):   glucose excreted in the urine.

goblet cell: a form of epithelial cell containing mucin and bulged out like a goblet.

goiter (goi′ter):   enlargement of the thyroid gland, causing a swelling in the front part of the neck.

gonad (gon′ad):   ovary or testis.

graafian follicle (graf′e-an):   small, spherical, vesicular sac embedded in the cortex of the ovary which contains a developing ovum.

granulocyte (gran′u-lo-sīt):   a granular leukocyte, either a neutrophil, basophil, or eosinophil.

Graves' disease (grāvz):   hyperthyroidism.

groin: the lowest part of the abdominal wall, near its junction with the thigh.

gustatory (gus′tah-to″re):   pertaining to the sense of taste.

gyrus (jī′rus):   a convoluted ridge.

haploid (hap′loid):   having single (not paired) chromosomes.

haustra (haws′trah):   sacculations in the colon.

helix (hē′liks):   anything having a spiral form.

hematocrit (he-mat′o-krit):   volume percentage of erythrocytes in whole blood.

hematopoiesis (hem″ah-to-poi-e′sis):   the formation and development of blood cells.

heme (hēm):   the oxygen-transporting complex of hemoglobin composed of iron and protoporphyrin.

hemiparesis (hem″e-par-e′sis):   muscular weakness of one side of the body.

hemocytoblast (hē″mo-sī′to-blast):   undifferentiated stem cell which gives rise to all blood cells.

hemoglobin (he″mo-glo′bin):   the oxygen-carrying red pigment of the red blood corpuscles.

hemolysis (he-mol′i-sis):   the destruction of red blood cells and the liberation of hemoglobin.

hemolytic anemia (hē″mo-lit′ik):   anemia due to shortened *in vivo* survival of the erythrocytes and inability of the bone marrow to compensate for their decreased life span.

hemophilia (he″mo-fil′e-ah):   a disorder in blood clotting, transmitted as a sex-linked recessive trait, caused by a defective clotting factor.

hemorrhage (hem′or-ij):   a copious escape of blood; bleeding.

hemostasis (he″mo-stā′sis):   the checking of the flow of blood through any part or vessel.

heparin (hep′ah-rin):   an anticoagulant found mainly in the liver.

hermaphrodite (her-maf′ro-dīt):   an individual containing gonads of both sexes.

hernia (her′ne-ah):   protrusion of a loop or knuckle of an organ or tissue through an abnormal opening.

hilus, hilum (hi′lus, hi′lum):   depression where vessels enter an organ.

histology (his-tol′o-je):   that part of anatomy dealing with the minute structure, composition, and function of the tissues.

homeostasis (ho″me-o-stā′sis):   a tendency to uniformity or stability in an organism.

homogeneous (ho″mo-jē′ne-us):   having a similarity of structure.

homologous (ho-mol′o-gus):   corresponding in structure, position, and origin. In transplantation, tissues or organs are exchanged between two nonidentical individuals of the same species.

horizontal cell: neuron carrying signals across the retina.

hormone (hor′mōn):   a substance produced in one part of the body, most commonly an endocrine gland, that is transported in the blood to another part, often a specific target organ, where it exerts a regulatory action.

horn: any horn-shaped projection or extension.

Horner's syndrome: interruption of sympathetic nerve supply to the head, neck, and upper extremities.

hyaline (hī′ah-lĭn):   glassy; transparent or nearly so.

hydrocephalus (hi″dro-sef′ah-lus):   a condition characterized by abnormal accumulation of cerebrospinal fluid in the cranial vault.

hydrolysis (hī-drol′ĭ-sis):   decomposition due to the incorporation and splitting of water.

hydrostatic (hī″dro-stat′ik):   pertaining to a liquid in a state of equilibrium.

hyoid (hī′oid):   shaped like the letter U.

hypercapnia (hī″per-kap′ne-ah):   abnormally high blood CO_2 concentration.

hyperemia (hī″per-ē′me-ah):   increased blood in a part.

hyperglycemia (hī″per-gli-sē′me-ah):   concentration of glucose in the blood above the normal level.

hyperphagia (hī″per-fā′je-ah):   ingestion of a greater than optimal quantity of food.

hyperplasia (hī″per-plā′ze-ah):   abnormal multiplication or increase in the number of normal cells in a normal pattern.

hyperpnea (hī″perp-nē′ah):   abnormal increase in the depth and rate of the respiratory movements.

hypertension (hī″per-ten′shun):   abnormally high tension, especially high blood pressure.

hypertonic (hī″per-ton′ik):   having an osmotic pressure greater than that of a physiologic salt solution or other solution with which it is compared.

hypertrophy (hī-per′tro-fe):   the enlargement or overgrowth of an organ or part due to an increase in size of its constituent cells.

hypochondriac (hī″po-kon′dre-ak):   pertaining to the upper lateral region of the abdomen below the lowest ribs.

hypodermic (hī-po-der′mik):   applied beneath the skin.

hypoglycemia (hī″po-gli-se′me-ah):   concentration of glucose in the blood below the normal limit.

hypophysis (hī-pof′ĭ-sis):   any process or outgrowth, especially the hypophysis cerebri, or pituitary gland.

hypothalamus (hī″po-thal′ah-mus): the portion of the diencephalon which forms the floor and part of the lateral wall of the third ventricle; exerts control over visceral activities, water balance, temperature, sleep, etc.

hypotonic (hi-po-ton′ik): having an osmotic pressure lower than that of a physiologic salt solution or other solution with which it is compared.

hypoxia (hī-pox′se-ah): reduced oxygen level in the tissues.

impermeable (im-per′me-ah-b'l): not permitting a passage, as for fluid.

implantation (im″plan-tā′shun): attachment of the blastocyst to the epithelial lining of the uterus.

inanition (in″ah-nish′un): the physical condition which results from complete lack of food.

inclusion (in-klu′zhun): that which is enclosed, especially referring to any particle or foreign substance included within a cell.

incus (ing′kus): the anvil; the middle of the three ossicles of the ear.

infarction (in-fark′shun): process leading to the development of an infarct—an area of necrosis of tissue due to complete interference with blood flow.

inferior (in-fe′re-or): situated below or directed downward.

inflammation (in″flah-mā′shun): a series of reactions produced in the tissues by an irritant, marked by an erythema with exudation of serum and leukocytes.

infundibulum (in″fun-dib′u-lum): a funnel-shaped structure or passage.

ingestion (in-jes′chun): the act of taking food, medicine, etc., into the body by mouth.

inguinal (ing′gwĭ-nal): pertaining to the groin.

inhalation (in″hah-lā′shun): the drawing of air or other vapor into the lungs.

insertion: place of attachment of a muscle to the bone which it moves.

in situ (in sī′tu): in the normal place or confined to the site of origin without invasion of neighboring tissues.

inspiration (in″spĭ-ra′shun): breathing air into the lungs.

intercellular (in″ter-sel′u-lar): situated between the cells of any structure.

intercostal (in″ter-kos′tal): situated between the ribs.

interstitial (in″ter-stish′al): pertaining to or situated in the space or gaps of a tissue.

intima (in′tĭ-mah): innermost.

intravascular (in″trah-vas′ku-lar): within the blood vessels or the lymphatics.

intrinsic (in-trin′sik): situated within or pertaining exclusively to a part.

invaginate (in-vaj′ĭ-nāt): to infold one portion within another portion of the same thing.

inversion (in-ver′zhun): turning inward.

in vitro (in vī′tro): within a glass; observable in a test tube.

in vivo (in vī′vo): within the living body.

involution (in″vo-lu′shun): retrograde or degenerative change.

ion (ī′on): an atom or a group of atoms having a charge of positive or negative electricity.

ipsilateral (ip″sĭ-lat′er-al): pertaining to the same side.

irritability (ir″ĭ-tah-bil′ĭ-te): the quality of responding to stimuli.

ischemia (is-kē′me-ah): local and temporary deficiency of blood, chiefly due to contraction of a blood vessel.

isotonic (i″so-ton′ik): having the same osmotic pressure as a physiologic salt solution.

isthmus (is′mus): the neck or constricted part of an organ.

keratin (ker′ah-tin): an insoluble protein which is the principal constituent of hair and nails; contains large amounts of sulfur.

ketone (kē′tōn): any compound containing the carbonyl group CO.

kinesthesia (kin″es-the′ze-ah): "muscle sense"; i.e., sense of position and movements of body parts.

Kupffer's cells (koop'ferz): cells of the liver involved with destruction of erythrocytes and removal of bacteria and foreign bodies from the blood.

labium (lā'be-um): a lip or lip-shaped organ.

lacrimal (lak'rĭ-mal): pertaining to tears.

lactation (lak-tā'shun): secretion of milk, or the period of milk secretion; suckling.

lacteal (lak'te-al): pertaining to milk; any one of the intestinal lymphatics that take up chyle.

lactiferous (lak-tif'er-us): producing or conveying milk.

lactose (lak'tōs): a disaccharide obtained from cow's milk.

lacuna (lah-ku'nah): a small pit, hollow, or depression.

lamella (lah-mel'ah): a thin leaf or plate, as of bone.

lamina (lam'ĭ-nah): a thin, flat plate or layer.

larynx (lar'inks): the voice-box, located at the top of the trachea.

lateral: denoting a position toward the side and farther away from the median plane.

lemniscus (lem-nis'kus): a secondary pathway in the central nervous system which usually decussates and terminates in the thalamus.

lesion (le'zhun): any pathologic discontinuity of tissue or loss of function of a part.

leukocyte (lu'ko-sīt): a white blood cell, the two major types of which are granular and nongranular.

leukopenia (lū″ko-pē'ne-ah): a reduction of white cells.

ligament (lig'ah-ment): any tough, fibrous band connecting bone or supporting viscera.

limbic (lim'bik): pertaining to a border or margin.

lipid (lip'id): fat and fatlike compounds.

lipoprotein lipase (līp″o-prō'te-in līp'ās): an enzyme essential for the tissue uptake of the triglycerides of chylomicrons and very low density lipoproteins.

liter (lē'ter): the volume occupied by 1 kilogram of pure water at its temperature of maximum density and under standard atmospheric pressure. It is the equivalent of 1.0567 quarts liquid measure.

lobe: a well-defined portion of any organ.

lobotomy (lo-bot'o-me): incision into a lobe, e.g., a prefrontal lobotomy.

loin: the part of the back between the thorax and the pelvis.

lumbar (lum'bar): pertaining to the loins.

lumen (lu'men): the cavity or channel within a tube or tubular organ.

lymph: transparent liquid found in the lymphatic vessels.

lymphedema (lim″fe-dē'mah): edema resulting from deficient lymph drainage.

lymphocyte (lim'fo-sīt): one of the two kinds of nongranular leukocytes; two types, B cells and T cells, function in the immune response.

lysosome (lī'so-som): cytoplasmic particle containing hydrolyzing enzymes.

macrocyte (mak'ro-sīt): an abnormally large erythrocyte, i.e., one from 10 to 12 microns in diameter, found in the blood in certain anemias, especially pernicious anemia.

macrophage (mak'ro-fāj): a wandering phagocytic cell.

macroscopic (mak″ro-skop'ik): visible with the unaided eye or without the microscope.

macula (mak'u-lah): a spot.

malignant (mah-lig'nant): virulent; tending to go from bad to worse.

malleus (mal'e-us): the largest of the auditory ossicles; also called the hammer.

maltose (mawl'tōs): a disaccharide present in malt, malt products, and sprouting seeds; it is formed by the hydrolysis of starch and is converted into glucose by the enzyme maltase.

mammary (mam'er-e): pertaining to the breast.

mammillary (mam′ĭ-ler″e): like or pertaining to a nipple.

mandible (man′dĭ-bl): the horseshoe-shaped bone forming the lower jaw.

manometer (mah-nom′e-ter): an instrument for measuring the pressure or tension of liquids or gases.

manubrium (mah-nu′bre-um): uppermost portion of the sternum.

mastication (mas″tĭ-ka′shun): the chewing of food.

mastoid (mas″toid): breast-shaped, as the mastoid process of the temporal bone.

matrix (mā′triks): the ground substance in which cells are embedded.

meatus (me-ā′tus): a passage or channel, especially the external opening of a canal.

medial: pertaining to the middle; nearer the median plane.

mediastinum (mē″de-as-tī′num): partition separating adjacent parts; the space in the center of the chest between the two pleural cavities.

medulla (me-dul′ah): the central portion of an organ as contrasted with its cortex.

megakaryocyte (meg″ah-kar′e-o-sīt): the giant cell of bone marrow which gives rise to blood platelets.

meiosis (mī-ō′sis): a special type of cell division occurring during the maturation of sex cells by which the normal diploid number of chromosomes is reduced to a single (haploid) set.

melanocyte (mĕ-lan′o-sīt): the epidermal cell which synthesizes melanin.

membrane (mem′brān): a thin layer of tissue covering a surface or dividing a space or organ; the enclosure of a cell or cell organelle.

memory cells: those cells that give rise to clones of their own upon reappearance of the same infectious agent.

menarche (me-nar′ke): onset of menstruation.

meninges (me-nin′jēs): three membranes which cover and protect the brain and spinal cord. The innermost membrane is pia mater (pī-ah mā′ter); the middle membrane is arachnoid mater (ah-rak′noid); the outermost membrane is dura mater (du′rah).

menopause (men′o-pawz): cessation of menstruation in the human female, occurring usually between the ages of 45 and 55.

menstrual cycle (men′stroo-al): rhythmic hormonal stimulation of the female organs to prepare for pregnancy and withdrawal of hormones, with subsequent bleeding if the egg is not fertilized.

menstruation (men″stroo-ā′shun): cyclic physiologic uterine bleeding which normally recurs, usually at approximately 4-week intervals, in the absence of pregnancy during the reproductive period of the female of the human and a few other primates.

mesencephalon (mes″en-sef′ah-lon): the midbrain.

mesenchyme (mes′eng-kīm): the network of embryonic connective tissue in the mesoderm from which are formed the connective tissues of the body and also the blood vessels and lymphatic vessels.

mesentery (mes′en-ter″e): the peritoneal fold attaching the intestine to the posterior abdominal wall.

mesial (mē′ze-al): situated in the middle; nearer the middle of the body.

mesoderm (mes′o-derm): the middle layer of the three primary germ layers of the embryo, lying between the ectoderm and endoderm.

mesothelium (mes″o-thē′le-um): a layer of flat cells, which in the adult forms a squamous-celled layer of epithelium covering the surface of all serous membranes.

metabolism (mĕ-tab′o-lizm): the sum of all the physical and chemical processes by which living organized substance is produced and maintained, and also the transformation by which energy is made available for the use of the organism.

metachromatic (met″ah-krō-mat′ik): tissue in which different elements take on different colors with the same dye.

metastasis (mĕ-tas′tah-sis): the transfer of disease from one organ or part to another not directly connected to it.

meter (mē'ter): the basic unit of linear measure of the metric system, equivalent to 39.371 inches.

methylation (meth"ĭ-lā'shun): the process of substituting a methyl group for a hydrogen atom.

micelles (mī-sels'): polymolecular aggregates composed of monoglycerides, free fatty acids, cholesterol, phospholipids, and bile salts.

microglia (mī-krog'le-ah): a type of neuroglia with a phagocytic action.

microvilli (mī"kro-vil'ĭ): processes on the free surface of epithelial cells.

micturition (mik"tu-rish'un): the passage of urine.

mineralocorticoid (min"er-al-o-kor'ti-koid): a corticoid particularly effective in causing the retention of sodium and the loss of potassium.

mitochondria (mī"to-kon'dre-ah): cell organelles that produce most of the cell's ATP; known as the powerhouse of the cell.

mitosis (mī-to'sis): cell division producing two daughter cells with the same number of chromosomes as the parent cell.

mitral (mī'tral): shaped somewhat like a miter (a headdress worn by bishops); pertaining to the mitral, or bicuspid, valve—the AV valve on the left side of the heart.

monosaccharide (mon"o-sak'ah-rīd): a simple sugar which cannot be hydrolyzed into sugars of lower molecular weight; common examples are dextrose (glucose) and fructose.

monovular (mon-ov'u-lar): pertaining to or derived from a single ovum.

morbid (mor'bid): pertaining to disease.

morphology (mor-fol'o-je): a study of shape and structure of living organisms.

morula (mor'u-lah): the cleaving ovum during the stage in which it forms a solid mulberry-like mass of cells.

motile (mō'til): having a spontaneous but not conscious or volitional movement.

motor neuron: efferent neuron that carries impulses away from the brain and spinal cord to muscles and glands.

mucosa (mu-kō'sah): a mucous membrane, one which lines tracts and cavities opening to the exterior, consisting of a surface layer of epithelium and underlying connective tissue.

multiparous (mul-tip'ah-rus): having had two or more pregnancies resulting in viable offspring.

myelin sheath (mī'e-lin): lipoprotein sheath around nerve fibers; in peripheral nerves composed of the membrane of Schwann cells.

myocardium (mi"o-kar'de-um): the muscular substance of the heart muscle.

myoepithelial cells (mi"o-ep"ĭ-thē'le-al): epithelial cells with contractile properties found in the secretory units of the mammary, sweat, lacrimal, and salivary glands.

myopia (mi-o'pe-ah): nearsightedness; a defect in vision characterized by the focusing of parallel rays in front of the retina.

myosin (mi'o-sin): a protein forming the thick filaments of the myofibril of a muscle fiber.

myotactic reflex (mi"o-tak'tik): stretch reflex.

nares (na'rēz): the external openings into the nasal cavities; plural of naris.

navicular (nah-vik'u-lar): boat-shaped.

necrosis (ně-kro'sis): death of a cell or of a group of cells.

nephron (nef'ron): basic functional unit of the kidney; the tubular secretory portion of the kidney consisting of the renal corpuscle with its capsule of Bowman, the proximal convoluted tubule, the descending and ascending limbs of Henle's loop, and the distal convoluted tubule.

nerve: bundle of nerve fibers outside the brain or spinal cord.

neurilemma (nu"rĭ-lem'mah): the thin membranous outer covering surrounding the myelin sheath of a nerve fiber, consisting of flattened, living Schwann cells.

neuroglia (nu-rog′le-ah): supporting cells of nervous tissue; neuroglia and neurons are the two types of nerve cells.

neurohypophysis (nu″ro-hī-pof′ĭ-sis): the posterior portion of the hypophysis.

neuron (nu′ron): a nerve cell.

nodule (nod′ūl): a small node which is solid and can be detected by touch.

norepinephrine (nor″ep-ĭ-nef′rin): a neurotransmitter released at synapses and sympathetic postganglionic nerve endings; also a hormone secreted by the suprarenal medulla.

nuchal (nu′kal): pertaining to the back of the neck.

nucleotide (nu′kle-o-tīd): molecular unit from which nucleic acids are synthesized, consisting of a 5-carbon sugar, phosphate group, and nitrogenous base.

nucleus (nu′kle-us): a spheroid body within a cell, distinguished from the rest of the cell by its denser structure and by containing chromosomes; a collection of nerve cell bodies in the central nervous system.

nulliparous (nul-lip′ah-rus): having never given birth to a viable child.

occiput (ok′-sĭ-put): the back part of the head.

odontoid (o-don′toid): like a tooth.

olecranon (o-lek′rah-non): curved process of the ulna at the elbow.

olfactory (ol-fak′to-re): pertaining to the sense of smell.

oligodendroglia (ol″ĭ-go-den-drog′le-ah): type of neuroglia; gives rise to the myelin sheath of nerve fibers of the central nervous system.

oliguria (ol″i-gu′re-ah): diminished quantity of urine.

ophthalmic (of-thal′mik): pertaining to the eye.

organelle (or″gan-el′): one of the minute organs of cells concerned with the functions of metabolism, locomotion, etc.

orifice (or′ĭ-fis): the entrance or outlet of any body cavity.

orthopnea (or″thop-ne′ah): inability to breathe except in an upright position.

osmosis (os-mo′sis): the net transfer of water, when two solutions are separated by a membrane, from the more dilute solution (where the water molecules are in higher concentration) to the more concentrated solution.

osseous (os′e-us): of the nature or quality of bone; bony.

osteoblast (os′te-o-blast): a cell which arises from a fibroblast and which, as it matures, is associated with the production of bone.

ovulation (ov′u-lā′shun): rupture of an ovarian follicle with the release of a secondary oocyte (immature ovum).

oxygen debt (ok′sĭ-jen): following exercise, the amount of oxygen consumed above the basal oxygen consumption level.

oxyhemoglobin (ok″se-hē″mo-glo′bin): hemoglobin combined with oxygen.

oxyntic (oks-in′tik): secreting an acid substance.

pacinian corpuscles (pah-sin′e-an): receptors of deep pressure.

palate (pal′at): roof of the mouth.

palliative (pal′e-ā″tiv): affording relief, but not cure.

palpebrae (pal′pe-brē): eyelids.

papilla (pah-pil′ah): a small, nipple-shaped projection or elevation.

parasympathetic (par″ah-sim″pah-thet′ik): cranio-sacral division of the autonomic nervous system; in general, it is concerned with restorative processes, such as slowing the heart rate.

parenchyma (par-eng′kĭ-mah): the essential or functional elements of an organ.

paresthesia (par″es-thē′ze-ah): morbid or perverted sensation; an abnormal sensation, as burning, prickling, etc.

parietal (pah-rī′ĕ-tal): of or pertaining to the walls of a cavity.

Parkinson's disease: a disorder affecting the elderly, associated with degeneration of parts of the basal ganglion, characterized by tremor, rigidity, and hypokinesia.

parotid (pah-rot′id): situated near the ear.

paroxysm (par′ok-sizm): a sudden recurrence or intensification of symptoms.

parturition (par″tu-rish′un): labor; the act or process of giving birth to a child.

pathology (pah-thol′o-je): the study of disease, especially the structural and functional changes in tissues and organs of the body which are caused by disease.

pectineal (pek-tin′e-al): pertaining to the pubic bone.

pectoral (pek′to-ral): pertaining to the breast or chest.

peduncle (pe-dung′kl): a narrow part acting as a support; a large nerve fiber tract interconnecting parts of the brain, especially extending from the cerebellum.

pelvis (pel′vis): any basinlike structure, particularly the basin-shaped ring of bone at the posterior extremity of the trunk.

pendulous (pen′du-lus): hanging loosely; dependent.

pennate (pen′āt): shaped like a feather.

pepsin (pep′sin): a proteolytic enzyme of the stomach secreted as an inactive precursor, pepsinogen.

pericardium (per″ĭ-kar′de-um): the fibroserous sac that surrounds the heart.

perichondrium (per″ĭ-kon′dre-um): the connective tissue membrane covering the surface of a cartilage.

perikaryon (per″e-kar′e-on): the main protoplasmic mass of a cell; the cell body, as distinguished from the nucleus and the processes.

perimysium (per″ĭ-mis′e-um): the connective tissue enclosing a fascicle of skeletal muscle fibers.

perineurium (per″ĭ-nu′re-um): the connective tissue sheath surrounding each bundle of fibers in a peripheral nerve.

periosteum (per″e-os′te-um): the tough fibrous membrane surrounding the bone.

peripheral (pĕ-rif′ar-al): situated at or near the outward part or surface.

peristalsis (per″ĭ-stal′sis): the wormlike movement by which the alimentary canal or other tubular organs provided with both longitudinal and circular muscle fibers propel their contents. It consists of a wave of contraction passing along the tube.

pernicious anemia (per-nish′us): macrocytic anemia involving a pronounced reduction in red cell production due to vitamin B_{12} deficiency based on defect in gastric secretions.

peroneal (per″o-ne′al): pertaining to the fibula or to the outer side of the leg.

petechia (pe-te′ke-ah): a perfectly round, purplish spot caused by intradermal or submucous hemorrhage.

petrous (pet′rus): resembling a rock; hard; stony.

phagocyte (fag′o-sīt): any cell ingesting microorganisms, foreign particles, or other cells.

phagocytosis (fag″o-si-to′sis): the engulfing of microorganisms, other cells, and foreign particles by phagocytes.

phrenic (fren′ik): pertaining to the diaphragm.

pia mater (pī′ah-mā′ter): the innermost of the three meninges, or membranes, of the brain and spinal cord.

pilomotor (pi″lo-mo′tor): causing movement of hair.

pineal (pin″e-al): shaped like a pine cone.

pinocytosis (pi″no-si-to′sis): the engulfing of liquid globules by cells by a process in which minute incuppings or invaginations are formed in the surface of a cell and close to form vesicles containing extracellular material.

piriform (pir′ĭ-form): pear-shaped.

pisiform (pī′sĭ-form): like a pea in shape and size.

plantar (plan′tar): pertaining to the sole of the foot.

plantar reflex: flexion of toes.

plasma (plaz'mah):   the fluid portion of the blood in which the corpuscles are suspended.

plasmin (fibrinolysin) (plaz'min):   an enzyme capable of digesting fibrin clots. It is formed from plasminogen (a globulin) by enzyme action.

plasmolysis (plaz-mol'ĭ-sis):   contraction or shrinking of the protoplasm of a cell due to the loss of water by osmotic action.

platelet (plāt'let):   a circular or oval disc found in the blood of all mammals, concerned with the coagulation of blood.

pleura (ploor'ah):   membranous sac which encloses the lungs and lines the chest cavity. Parietal pleura lines the chest cavity, and visceral pleura adheres closely to the lungs.

plexus (plek'sus):   a network, especially of nerves, veins, or lymphatics.

plica (pli'kah):   a fold or ridge.

pneumothorax (nu"mo-tho'raks):   an accumulation of air or gas in the pleural cavity which may occur spontaneously or as a result of trauma or a pathological process, or be introduced deliberately.

polar body: a nonfunctional cell formed during oogenesis.

polycythemia (pol"e-si-the'me-ah):   excess in the number of red corpuscles in the blood.

polydipsia (pol"e-dip'se-ah):   excessive thirst.

polymer (pol'ĭ-mer):   a compound, usually of high molecular weight, formed by the combination of simpler molecules.

polymorphonuclear (pol"e-mor"fo-nu'kle-ar):   having a nucleus deeply lobed or so divided that it appears to be multiple.

polyphagia (pol"e-fā'je-ah):   increased eating.

polysaccharide (pol"e-sak'ah-rīd):   one of a group of carbohydrates which upon hydrolysis yields more than two molecules of simple sugar; e.g., glycogen, dextrin.

pons: a bridge connecting parts of an organ; the convex white eminence situated at the base of the brain.

popliteal (pop-lit'e-al):   pertaining to the posterior surface of the knee.

posterior: situated behind or toward the rear.

precursor (pre-kur'sor):   anything that precedes another, or from which another is derived.

presbyopia (pres"be-o'pe-ah):   oldsightedness; impairment of the ability to accommodate for near vision.

primordium (pri-mor'de-um):   the earliest discernible indication during embryonic development of an organ or part.

prolapse (pro-laps'):   the falling down of an organ or other part.

proliferation (pro-lif"er-a'shun):   the reproduction or multiplication of similar forms, especially of cells.

prone: lying with the face downward; of the hand, having the palm turned downward. Pronation is the act of making something prone.

protopathic (pro"to-path'ik):   primitive, nondiscriminatory sensibility.

protoplasm (pro'to-plazm):   the essential material of all plant and animal cells; the only known form of matter in which life is manifest.

protuberance (pro-tu'ber-ans):   a projecting part, process, or swelling.

proximal (prok'sĭ-mal):   nearest; closer to any point of reference.

pterygoid (ter'ĭ-goid):   shaped like a wing.

ptosis (tō'sis):   prolapse of an organ or part.

ptyalin (tī'ah-lin):   a salivary amylase which splits starch into maltose.

puberty (pu'ber-te):   the age at which the reproductive organs become functionally operative and secondary sex characteristics develop.

Purkinje system (pur-kin'je):   the fibers leaving the AV (atrioventricular) node.

pylorus (pi-lor'us):   the opening between the stomach and the duodenum.

racemose (ras'e-mōs):   resembling a bunch of grapes on its stalk.

ramus (rā'mus): a branch, as of an artery, bone, nerve, or vein.

receptor: a sensory nerve terminal or a specialized structure especially sensitive to a particular kind of stimulus to which it readily responds.

reduction: subtraction of oxygen from, or the addition of hydrogen to, a substance; more generally, the loss of positive charges and the gaining of electrons.

reflex (re'fleks): an involuntary response to a stimulus.

refraction (re-frak'shun): the bending of a ray of light as it passes from one medium into another of different density.

renal (rē'nal): pertaining to the kidney.

renin (rē'nin): an enzyme secreted by the kidney that initiates the formation of angiotensins in plasma.

resorption (re-sorp'shun): the loss of substance through physiologic or pathologic means.

respiration (res-pi-ra'shun): inspiration and expiration of air via the lungs.

reticuloendothelial (re-tik″u-lo-en″do-the'le-al): connective tissue cells carrying on the process of phagocytosis.

reticulum (re-tik'u-lum): a network, especially a protoplasmic network in cells.

retina (ret'ĭ-nah): the innermost, light-receptive layer of the eyeball.

Rh factor: a factor first isolated in rhesus monkey blood, consisting of 12 antigens; Rh positive refers to presence of antigen D.

rhinencephalon (rī″nen-sef'ah-lon): olfactory portions of the brain; prominent in lower animals, indistinct in humans, although designated as the hippocampus (an important center for emotions).

ribonucleic acid, RNA (ri″bo-nu-kle'ic): nucleic acid playing role in protein synthesis.

ribosome (rī'bo-som): dense aggregations of RNA and protein, usually attached to the endoplasmic reticulum; the site of protein synthesis.

rigor mortis (ri'gor mor'tis): stiffening of a dead body.

rostral (ros'tral): having to do with a beaklike appendage; toward the nose.

ruga (roo'gah): a ridge, wrinkle, or fold.

saccharide (sak'ah-rid): one of a series of carbohydrates, including the sugars.

saccule (sak'ūl): a little sac.

sagittal (saj'ĭ-tal): a plane or section parallel to the long axis of the body.

salpinx (sal'pinks): a tube.

saltatory conduction (sal'tah-to″re): conduction in nerve fiber in which an impulse jumps from one node to another.

sarcolemma (sar″ko-lem'ah): muscle fiber membrane.

sarcoma (sar-kō'mah): a tumor, often malignant, arising from connective or non-epithelial tissue.

Schwann cell (shvon): special cell forming the neurilemma of a nerve fiber; its membrane comprises the myelin sheath of peripheral nerve fibers.

sciatic (si-at'ik): pertaining to the ischium.

sclera (sklē'rah): the tough white outermost layer of the eyeball, covering approximately the posterior three-fourths of its surface.

sebum (sē'bum): the secretion of sebaceous glands.

semen (sē'men): thick, whitish secretion of the reproductive organs of the male; it consists of spermatozoa and secretions from several other accessory organs.

semilunar (sem″ĭ-lu'nar): resembling a crescent, or half-moon.

senescence (se-nes'ens): the process or condition of growing old.

sensory neuron (sen'so-re): afferent neuron that carries impulses from the skin to the brain and spinal cord.

septum (sep'tum): a dividing wall or partition.

serratus (ser-ra'tus): saw-toothed.

Sertoli's cells (ser-to'lēz): cells providing nutrients to spermatozoa.

serum (se'rum): plasma minus clotting substances.

sickle cell anemia: abnormality in the protein portion of hemoglobin causing misshaping of the RBC's and premature rupture.

sigmoid (sig'moid): shaped like a letter S.

sinoatrial node (si"no-a'tre-al) (pacemaker): neuromuscular tissue in the right atrium which generates electrical impulses that initiate the heartbeat.

sinus (si'nus): a recess, cavity, or hollow space.

skeleton (skel'ĕ-ton): the bony framework of the higher vertebrate animals.

Skene's glands (skēnz): small paraurethral glands.

soleus (so'le-us): pertaining to the bottom, the sole.

soma (sō'mah): the body as distinguished from the mind.

somatic (so-mat'ik): pertaining to the framework of the body, as distinguished from the viscera.

spasticity (spas-tis'ĭ-te): increased muscle tone producing stiffness.

spermatozoa (sper"mah-to-zo'ah): the mature male sex cells.

sphenoid (sfē'noid): wedge-shaped.

sphincter (sfingk'ter): a ringlike muscle enclosing a natural orifice; for example, the anal sphincter.

sphygmomanometer (sfig"mo-mah-nom'e-ter): instrument for measuring blood pressure in the arteries.

splanchnic (splangk'nik): pertaining to the viscera.

sputum (spu'tum): matter ejected from the mouth; saliva mixed with mucus and other substances from the respiratory tract.

squamous (skwā'mus): scaly or platelike.

stapes (stā'pēz): the innermost of the ossicles of the ear, shaped somewhat like a stirrup.

stasis (stā'sis): a stoppage of the blood or any other body fluid in any part.

stenosis (ste-no'sis): narrowing or stricture of a duct or canal.

stereognosis (ste"re-og-no'sis): ability to identify an object by means of tactile and kinesthetic sensations.

steroid (ste'roid): term applied to any one of a large group of substances chemically related to sterols; includes sterols, D vitamins, bile acids, certain hormones, etc.

stimulus (stim'u-lus): any agent, act, or influence producing a reaction in a receptor.

stratum (strā'tum): a layer.

striated (strī'āt-ed): striped; provided with streaks or lines.

stroma (stro'mah): the tissue which forms the ground substance, framework, or matrix of an organ.

subcutaneous (sub"ku-ta'ne-us): beneath the skin.

substrate (sub'strāt): a substance upon which an enzyme acts.

sulcus (sul'kus): a groove, trench, or furrow.

superior: situated above or directed upward.

supinate (su'pĭ-nāt): to turn the arm or hand so that the palm faces outward.

suprarenal (su"prah-re'nal): situated above the kidney; the suprarenal gland is the adrenal gland.

surfactant (sur-fak'tant): a lipoprotein which lowers surface tension in the lungs.

suture (su'tūr): a form of articulation characterized by the presence of a thin layer of fibrous tissue uniting the margins of the contiguous bones; found only in the skull.

sympathetic: thoracolumbar division of the autonomic nervous system; in general concerned with the expenditure of energy; for example, accelerating the heart rate.

symphysis (sim'fĭ-sis): the line of junction and fusion between bones originally distinct.

synapse (sin'aps): junctional region between two adjacent neurons, forming the place at which the nerve impulse is transmitted from one neuron to another.

synarthrosis (sin″ar-thro′sis): a form of articulation capable of no appreciable movement.

syncytium (sin-sit′e-um): a multinucleate mass of protoplasm produced by the merging of cells.

syndrome (sin′drōm): a group of symptoms and signs occurring together in such a way as to indicate the existence of a common cause.

synovial fluid (sĭ-no′ve-al): viscous fluid which is secreted by the synovial membrane to lubricate the joints.

synthesis (sin′thĕ-sis): putting together parts to form a more complex whole.

systemic (sis-tem′ik): pertaining to or affecting the body as a whole.

systole (sis′tō-lē): contraction of the heart; especially the contraction of the ventricles as distinguished from that of the atria.

T cell system: cell-mediated immune system that combats viruses, fungi, and chronic bacterial infections.

tachycardia (tak″e-kar′de-ah): excessive rapidity in the action of the heart.

tachypnea (tak″ip-ne′ah): excessively rapid and shallow breathing.

tegmentum (teg-men′tum): a covering.

tendon (ten′dun): the fibrous cord of connective tissue in which the fibers of a muscle end and by which a muscle is attached to a bone or other structure.

tension (ten′shun): the condition of being stretched.

thorax (tho′raks): the chest.

thrombin (throm′bin): the enzyme derived from prothrombin which converts fibrinogen to fibrin.

thrombocyte (throm′bo-sīt): a blood platelet.

thromboembolus (throm″bo-em′bo-lus): a dislodged blood clot that has resettled in an area different from that in which it was formed.

thrombus (throm′bus): a plug or clot in a blood vessel or in one of the cavities of the heart, formed by coagulation of the blood and remaining at the point of its formation.

tidal volume: the volume of air inspired or expired with each breath.

tonus (to′nus): the slight, continuous contraction of muscles, which in skeletal muscles aids in the maintenance of posture and the return of blood to the heart.

toxic (tok′sik): harmful to the body; poisonous.

toxic goiter: clinical hyperthyroidism (exophthalmic goiter).

trabecula (trah-bek′u-lah): a supporting or anchoring strand of connective tissue, as such a strand extending from a capsule into the substance of the enclosed organ; one of the plates, or spicules, of cancellous bone.

tracheostomy (trā″ke-os′to′me): a process in which a tracheal tube is placed to facilitate breathing in cases of obstruction.

tracheotomy (trā″ke-ot′o-me): an opening in the trachea.

tract: a region, principally one of some length; a collection or bundle of nerve fibers in the central nervous system having the same origin, function, and termination.

trauma (traw′mah): a wound or injury.

trigone (trī′gon): a small triangular area near the mouth of the bladder between the openings of the two ureters and the urethra.

trochlear (trok′le-ar): resembling a pulley.

trophic (trof′ik): of or pertaining to nutrition.

trypsin (trip′sin): a protein-degrading enzyme secreted by the pancreas as an inactive precursor, trypsinogen.

tubercle (tu′ber-kl): a nodule or small eminence.

tunica (tu′nĭ-kah): a membrane or other structure covering or lining a body part or organ.

tympanum (tim′pah-num): the cavity of the middle ear.

ulcer (ul'ser): a loss of substance on a cutaneous or mucous surface, causing gradual disintegration and necrosis of the tissues.

umbilicus (um"bĭ-lī'kus): the site of attachment of the umbilical cord in the fetus: the navel.

unilateral (u"nĭ-lat'er-al): pertaining to only one side of the body.

urea (u-re'ah): the chief nitrogenous constituent of the urine, produced in the liver from ammonia (derived chiefly from deamination of amino acids) and carbon dioxide.

uremia (u-rē'me-ah): urea in the blood.

utricle (u'tre-kl): a little sac.

vagina (vah-ji'nah): a sheathlike structure; usually the canal between the vulva and uterus of a female.

vagus (va'gus): "wandering"; designating the tenth cranial nerve.

vallate papilla (val'āt pah-pil'ah): largest papilla (nipple-like projection or elevation) of the tongue.

valve: a membranous fold in a canal or passage which prevents the reflux of its contents.

varicose (var'ĭ-kōs): vessels knotted and swollen with accumulated blood.

vas: a vessel or duct.

vascular (vas'ku-lar): pertaining to or full of vessels.

vasoconstriction (vas"o-kon-strik'shun): diminution of the diameter of vessels, especially constriction of arterioles, leading to decreased flow of blood to a part.

vasodilation (vas"o-di-la'shun): dilation of a vessel, especially dilation of arterioles, leading to increased supply of blood to a part.

vasomotor (vās"o-mo'tor): regulating the contraction (vasoconstriction) and expansion (vasodilation) of blood vessels.

vastus (vas'tus): wide; of great size.

vein: vessel which conveys blood to or toward the heart.

ventilation (ven"tĭ-lā'shun): the volume of air exchanged in one minute.

ventral (ven'tral): denoting a position more toward the belly surface than some other object of reference.

ventricle (ven'trĭ-kl): any small cavity.

venule (ven'ul): vessel of similar function to veins, but of smaller size.

vermiform (ver'mĭ-form): shaped like a worm.

vestibule (ves'tĭ-būl): a space or cavity at the entrance to a canal, especially that of the ear.

viable (vi'ah-bl): capable of living in the environment outside the mother's body.

villus (vil'us): a minute, elongated projection from the surface of a mucous membrane or other membrane.

viscera (vis'er-ah): the internal organs.

viscous (vis'kus): pertaining to sticky or gummy fluid which flows with difficulty.

vitamin (vi'tah-min): a general term for a number of unrelated organic substances that occur in many foods in small amounts and that are necessary for the normal metabolic functioning of the body.

vitreous humor (vit're-us hu'mor): transparent, gelatin-like substance filling the posterior cavity of the eye (behind the lens).

volar (vo'lar): pertaining to the palm or sole.

Wernicke's area (ver'ni-kez): area of the brain for language comprehension.

xiphoid (zif'oid): shaped like a sword.

zygot (zī'gōt): a fertilized egg.

zymogen (zi'mo-jen): the inactive precursor of an enzyme.

Index

Note: Page numbers in *italics* refer to illustrations. Page numbers followed by (t) refer to tables.